ARCO

Everything you need to score high on the

SSAT and ISEE

High School Entrance Exams

7th Edition

Margie Pascual

ARCO

Everything you need to score high on the

SSAT and ISEE

High School Entrance Exams

7th Edition

JACQUELINE ROBINSON, M.S.

formerly Director of Reading and
English and Reading Teacher
Lawrence Country Day School
Hewlett, New York

DENNIS M. ROBINSON, Ed.M.

formerly Mathematics and Science Teacher
Far Hills Country Day School Far Hills, New Jersey
Director of Science and Curriculum Coordinator
Lawrence Country Day School
Hewlett, New York

EVE P. STEINBERG, M.A.

Macmillan • USA

REFUND POLICY

ARCO agrees to refund the purchase price of your book if, after using it, your test score shows no increase compared to your test score prior to using the book. To claim your refund, submit a copy of the score confirmation you received before using this book and a copy of the score confirmation after use. Both score confirmation receipts must be issued by the authorised testing service for the exam. You must also enclose your dated sales receipt for the book which indicates purchase between the dates noted on your test score confirmations. Send these three documents along with this book to ARCO REFUND, Macmillan General Reference, 1633 Broadway, 7th Floor, New York, NY 10019. A check for the full purchase price of the book, as noted on the sales receipt, will be mailed to you. Please indicate the name that the check should be made payable to and mailing address.

Seventh Edition

Macmillan Reference USA
A Simon & Schuster Macmillan Company
1633 Broadway
New York, NY 10019-6785

Macmillan Publishing books may be purchased for business and sales promotional use. For information please write: Special Markets Department, Macmillan Publishing USA, 1633 Broadway, New York, NY 10019

An Arco Book

Manufactured in the United States of America

10 9 8 7 6 5 4 3 2 1

Library of Congress Number 97-81128

ISBN: 0-02-862405-X

The 10 Top Ways to Raise Your Score

Fine-tuning your verbal, math, and reading skills is surely a good way to prepare for any entrance exam (not to mention for your high school career!). However, when it comes to your test score, some skills will do you more good than others. There are concepts you can learn, techniques you can follow, and tricks you can use that will give you the biggest "bang for your buck." Here's our pick of the Top 10:

1. **Make a study plan and follow it.** The right study plan will help you get the most out of this book in whatever time you have. *See Chapter 1.*

2. **Learn the directions in advance.** If you already know what to do for each question type, you won't have to waste precious test time. You'll be able to jump right in and start answering questions as soon as the proctor says "Go!" *See Chapter 2.*

3. **Make educated guesses.** If you can eliminate one or more answer choices, you have everything to gain by guessing. *See Chapter 2.*

4. **Know what to expect.** Learn about question types in advance. Don't leave yourself open to surprises on test day. *See Chapters 3 and 4.*

5. **Word arithmetic can help you find the answer.** Words are the sum of their parts. Decipher synonyms, words, and answer choices and add them up to get their meanings. *See Chapter 6.*

6. **In SSAT analogy questions, a sentence can make the connection.** Analogies are about word relationships. The best way to figure out the relationship is to summarize it in a sentence. *See Chapter 8.*

7. **In ISEE sentence completions, look for clue words.** These words will reveal the meaning of the sentence and point you in the right direction. *See Chapter 9.*

8. **If a multiple-choice math question stumps you, work backwards from the answers.** The right answer has to be one of the choices. And since the choices are arranged in size order, start near the middle. That way you'll have to do the fewest calculations. *See Chapter 12.*

9. **In quantitative comparisons, consider all the possibilities.** Think what would happen if you plugged in 1, 0, a fraction, or a negative number for x in the expressions you're comparing. *See Chapter 13.*

10. **Neatness counts.** Fill in answer sheets carefully and watch your handwriting on the essay. If they can't read it, they won't use it. *See Chapter 15.*

HOW TO USE THIS BOOK

Congratulations! You've just picked up the best high school entrance examination preparation guide you can buy. This book has all the answers to your questions about the SSAT and the ISEE. It contains the most up-to-date information, more practice questions, and more solid test-taking advice than any other book of its kind. Here's how you can use it to get your best high school entrance exam score . . . and get into the secondary school of your choice.

- Start by reading Part One, "High School Entrance Exams Basics." It's full of answers to all your questions about the SSAT and the ISEE. You'll learn what kinds of questions to expect, how the tests are scored, what the questions look like, and how you can keep your cool on test day. And most important of all, you'll find out how you can create a study plan that lets you make the most of whatever time you have.
- Next, go on to Part Two, "Diagnosing Strengths and Weaknesses." Here's where you get your first chance to try your hand at sample questions from both exams. The Diagnostic Examination can show you where your skills are strong—and where they need some shoring up.
- The middle of the book—Parts Three, Four, Five, and Six—leads you through the subjects of the exams. Here you will review word analysis and basic mathematics. Skim, scan, or study these reviews depending on your own needs. You'll also learn about each question type you will see on your exam and you'll find the detailed, step-by-step methods that take the guesswork out of answering these questions. These chapters let you in on the secrets smart test-takers know—secrets that can add valuable points to your test score.
- Part Seven, "The Writing Sample," takes your hand as you face the part of the exam that most students find terrifying—The Essay. You'll learn how to organize and express your ideas under time pressure.
- When you come to Part Eight, "Four Practice Examinations," you've reached the heart of your preparation program. Each exam is as close as you can get to the real thing. Take at least one of your own exam. Take both if time allows. With more time, try the "other" exam as well. Remember: Practice makes perfect!
- Part Nine, "Other Exams," is for those of you who do not know what your exam will be. Here you'll get a glimpse of some totally different types of questions. If the high school you have chosen writes its own exam, you might see some of these question types.

ALL ABOUT ARCO

ARCO is America's leading publisher of test guides. Our 60 years of helping test-takers raise their scores makes us the longest-running and most reliable authority in the field. With a staff of test-smart coaches, writers, and editors, we track all the latest test developments, research the most effective test-prep techniques, and produce the best-selling study guides and software used successfully by more than 50 million test-takers.

Contents

PART TWO: Diagnosing Strengths and Weaknesses

PART THREE: Vocabulary

PART FOUR: Verbal Ability Questions

PART FIVE: Reading

PART SIX: Mathematics

PART SEVEN: The Writing Sample

17 Cooperative Entrance Exam (COOP): An Overview

PART

EVERYTHING YOU NEED!

High School Entrance Exams Basics

CHAPTER 1

Getting Started

You'll Find Answers to These Questions

Can you prepare for a high school entrance exam?
What is a high school entrance exam study plan?
How can you measure your progress?
How do you handle test anxiety?

CAN YOU PREPARE FOR A HIGH SCHOOL ENTRANCE EXAM?

This is the question of the day. Can you indeed prepare for a test that isn't like any of the ones you take in class and yet is so important to your future? Of course you can. Both the SSAT and the ISEE are long, and some of the questions can be tough, but the exams are *not* unconquerable.

There are many ways to prepare and many tricks and tips to learn. One of the most important things to learn is to think like the test-makers so you can find the answer they think is best. As you work through this book, you will see the difference between everyday thinking and standardized test thinking. Once you learn test thinking, you'll be more likely to pick the best test answer. And up go your scores.

WHAT IS A HIGH SCHOOL ENTRANCE EXAM STUDY PLAN?

As you can see, this book contains a lot of information about high school entrance exams, and you're going to need some help in getting through it. The right study plan will let you get the most out of this book in whatever time you have. It will help you work efficiently and keep you from getting stressed out.

PLAN A: ACCELERATED

Are you starting to prepare a little later than you had planned? Don't get upset; it happens. The Accelerated Course can get you through most of the material in 30 days. You'll probably have to sacrifice a bit on the practice, but you'll cover all of the chapters, learn about each question type, work plenty of sample questions, and take some practice exams. You'll find directions for Plan A at the beginning of each chapter.

PLAN B: TOP SPEED

If the calendar suddenly says that the exam is the week after next, Plan B is your best option. This superconcentrated study plan includes only the Diagnostic Examination and the critical parts of each chapter. Since you won't be taking any additional practice exams, try to complete the chapter exercises under test conditions. That is, follow the time limits and really stop when time is up. You'll find directions for following Plan B at the beginning of each chapter.

Choose the Plan That's Right for You

To decide on your study plan, first figure out how much time you have. That means answering two important questions: (1) How long do you have until your test date? (2) How much time can you devote to study for your high school entrance exam?

To make your job easier, we have a few suggestions. If you are starting early and your exam is still two or three months away, go for broke. Unless you are taking both exams, skip over the chapters that relate only to the exam you are not taking. (The chapters are keyed to the exams to which they apply.) Otherwise, do the book from beginning to end. However, if your exam is only a month or less away and you need a more concentrated test-prep course, go for one of our Timecruncher Study Plans. Plan A, the Accelerated Course, is your best bet if you have at least 30 days to prepare. But you'll need to shift into Plan B, the Top-Speed Course, if the exam is coming up in two weeks or less.

HERE'S THE ANSWER

How can I possibly wade through all this information in time for the test?

Choose a study plan. You can follow one of the three plans here or create your own. Either way, a plan will keep you on track.

Complete Course

You'll get the most out of your test preparation if you read this whole book from cover to cover except for the chapters that are irrelevant for your exam. No, you can't do that in a weekend! But if you have at least three months, you'll have enough time to read and reread at your own pace and to work through all of the examples, exercises, and practice exams without breaking a sweat.

Here's an important point: You don't have to go through the parts in order. You might want to start with the kind of question you find most difficult, perhaps reading comprehension or math. Then you can move to the next most difficult and so on down the line, saving your best stuff for last.

One more thing: Depending on your time frames and how many sections you want to cover, you can customize the plans to work best for you.

HOW CAN YOU MEASURE YOUR PROGRESS?

It does seem as if you're on a treadmill sometimes, doesn't it? Question after question after question; are you really getting anywhere? Is all of this studying really working?

The way to find out is to monitor your progress throughout the preparation period, whether it's three months, one month, or two weeks. The first thing to do is to take the Diagnostic Examination in Part Two of this book. After you score it, try to determine where you need to concentrate your efforts. Hang on to the scoring sheet so you know where you started.

Your next step is to see how you do at the end of each chapter. Complete the exercises according to the plan you've chosen. Take as many practice tests as you can. Count up your number of correct answers for however many practice tests you took and divide your number of correct answers by the number of questions in those practice tests. Multiply by 100 to convert your score to a percent. Now compare your score to your diagnostic score. How have you improved? Where do you still need work?

When you're ready, begin to take the full-length practice examinations. These are not real exams, but they are very similar to actual exams. You should try to simulate exam conditions as nearly as you can. After you score a practice exam, make another comparison to your chapter-by-chapter practice test scores and to the diagnostic exam. This will show you how your work is paying off and where you still need to spend more effort.

After your comparisons, go back and work again with any of the topics you still want to improve. When you take your second practice exam, make another set of comparisons. How much have you improved? Is there still more you would like to do? You should be pretty pleased with your progress—you've worked hard.

TESTSMARTS

Start with the tough stuff. To make the most of your study time, study the difficult sections first. If you run out of time later, you can just skim the sections that are easy for you.

HOW DO YOU HANDLE TEST ANXIETY?

Don't let anyone kid you—everyone is at least a little bit nervous on test day. And that's OK. But what you don't want is a full-blown case of the jitters, which can make you draw a blank and keep you from getting your best score. There are all kinds of myths and legends about how to calm the butterflies, stop your hands from shaking, and keep your cool at the test.

Do what's best for you. Some people will tell you to be sure to get at least eight hours of sleep the night before the test. Well, if you're used to getting only six hours, those extra two hours might make you groggy. Other people tell you to eat a big breakfast on the morning of the test. It's brain food, you know. But, if breakfast is not your thing, that won't help you on the test. Something you *can* do is make sure you have your sharpened pencils, your calculator, your admission ticket, and your picture ID ready the night before. You'll have that much less to worry about the next morning.

You've taken important tests before. You know the drill. Reassure yourself about the sections that you know you do well on. Remind yourself that you have given lots of attention to your weaker areas and that you have shown improvement. And remind yourself that you can get a very good score even if you don't answer all of the questions.

If you find yourself tensing up during the test, take a few seconds to close your eyes, think good thoughts (how about picturing yourself on a sunny beach?), and take some deep breaths. When you open your eyes, you'll feel refreshed and ready to get back on track.

HERE'S THE ANSWER

Can test anxiety ever help?

Yes, a little nervousness can be a good thing. It can pump you up and make you work harder.

CHAPTER 2

Check Out the Tests

You'll Find Answers to These Questions

What are the high school entrance exams?
How do I find out which exam I must take?
If I have a choice of exams, how do I choose?
What kinds of questions are asked on high school entrance exams?
How are the exams structured?
What do the answer sheets look like?
How are the exams scored?
What do smart test-takers know about pacing and guessing?

PLAN A: ACCELERATED

- ***Read*** "What Are the High School Entrance Exams?"
- ***Read*** "What Kinds of Questions Are Asked on High School Entrance Exams?"
- ***Read*** "How Are the Exams Structured?"
- ***Take*** a look at the scoring sheet sample
- ***Skim*** "If I Have a Choice of Exams, How Do I Choose?"
- ***Skim*** "How Are the Exams Scored?"
- ***Read*** "What Smart Test-Takers Know"

PLAN B: TOP SPEED

- ***Read*** "What Kinds of Questions Are Asked on High School Entrance Exams?"
- ***Read*** "How Are the Exams Structured?"
- ***Read*** "What Smart Test-Takers Know"

WHAT ARE THE HIGH SCHOOL ENTRANCE EXAMS?

The high school entrance exams are standardized exams. Independent, parochial, church-affiliated, and specialized public high schools use scores on these exams to help them make their admissions decisions.

There are a number of widely used standardized high school exams. The best known of these are:

- Secondary School Admission Test, **SSAT,** administered by the Secondary Schools Admissions Testing Bureau of Educational Testing Service of Princeton, New Jersey. Scores are accepted by over 600 schools, either exclusively or as an alternative to another exam, most often the ISEE. Schools that accept SSAT scores include independent unaffiliated private schools, nondiocesan Catholic schools or Catholic schools operated by religious orders, and non-Catholic religious-affiliated schools. Many boarding schools require the SSAT. The SSAT is offered at two levels—lower-level for students in grades 5,6, and 7 and upper-level for students in grade 8 and above. The upper-level exam is administered to high school applicants so this book concentrates on preparing you for the upper-level exam.
- Independent School Entrance Examination, **ISEE,** administered by Educational Records Bureau of New York City. The ISEE is accepted by 1,000 independent schools around the country, especially day schools. Many boarding

schools accept ISEE as an alternative to SSAT, though few mandate ISEE. The ISEE is accepted by all member schools of the Independent Schools Association of New York City and is the exam of choice at most of the independent schools in Philadelphia, San Diego, and Nashville. The ISEE is also the preferred exam of many non-Catholic religious-affiliated day schools. The ISEE is offered at two levels—middle-level for applicants for grades 6, 7, and 8 and upper-level for high school applicants. This book is limited to preparation for the upper-level exam.

- High School Placement Test, **HSPT,** administered by Scholastic Testing Service of Bensenville, Illinois. The HSPT is an examination specially designed for school systems with an 8/4 split. This means that the test measures aptitude and preparation for entrance to a four-year high school program. Because most Catholic high schools are organized in this manner, the HSPT is the exam of choice in more than 50 percent of Catholic schools nationwide. Some of the largest Catholic school systems in the country use the HSPT exclusively in selecting students for admission to their high schools. In Detroit, the HSPT is used for admission to public special academic high schools. Many independent Lutheran schools use the HSPT, as do a number of unaffiliated independent secondary schools. Because HSPT is used primarily by Catholic high schools, full preparation for this exam is offered in ARCO's *Catholic High School Entrance Examinations.* You will find a brief introduction to this exam in Chapter 16.
- Cooperative Entrance Exam, **COOP,** published by CTB/McGraw-Hill of Monterey, California. The COOP is administered only to students planning to enter ninth grade. It is the exclusive entrance examination of the Archdiocese of New York City, The Diocese of Brooklyn and Rockland County, the Diocese of Rockville Center, and the Archdiocese of Newark, NJ. Use in other systems or in independent schools is scattered. Because the COOP is used almost exclusively by Catholic high schools, full preparation is offered in ARCO's *Catholic High School Entrance Examinations.* Chapter 17 offers an overview of the COOP.
- New York City Specialized Science High Schools Admissions Test, **SSHSAT,** administered by the New York City Board of Education. This exam is only for eighth and ninth graders who live in New York City and who wish to attend Bronx High School of Science, Brooklyn Technical High School, or Stuyvesant High School. Because the use of SSHSAT is so limited, this book offers no preparation for it. If you will be taking the SSHSAT, purchase ARCO's *New York City Specialized Science High Schools Admissions Test.*
- Lesser-known or individually constructed exams. Some schools construct their own exams or purchase standardized exams from small companies. The subjects and question styles of these exams cover a wide range of possibilities, but verbal, reading, and mathematics skills are sure to be included. You should find this book helpful for any exam.

HOW DO I FIND OUT WHICH EXAM I MUST TAKE?

Call the admissions offices of all schools to which you are applying and ask which exam each school requires or which exam results the school will accept. Ask also for the cutoff dates by which your scores must be received by the school. Find out if the school has made special arrangements for testing its applicants on a specific date at a convenient location.

IF I HAVE A CHOICE OF EXAMS, HOW DO I CHOOSE?

If all your schools will accept scores from either the SSAT or the ISEE, you can choose on the basis of convenience of testing date and location. Or, if you began your preparations early enough and have tried a sample of each exam in this book, you can choose the exam with which you feel more comfortable.

You can get lists of testing locations, dates, registration deadlines, and fees along with official test descriptions, official sample questions, and registration forms by writing or calling or by visiting these Web sites:

SSATB
CN5339
Princeton, NJ 08543
(609) 683-4507
http://www.ssat.org/catalog

Educational Records Bureau
345 East 47th Street, 14th floor
New York, NY 10017
(800) 989-3721
(212) 705-8888
http://www.erb-test.com/isee

WHAT KINDS OF QUESTIONS ARE ASKED ON HIGH SCHOOL ENTRANCE EXAMS?

The field is pretty limited for both SSAT and ISEE. You will not find subject questions—no grammar or spelling, no geography or science. You will find questions testing your verbal, reading, and math skills—skills you've been working on since you were six years old.

Aside from the essay, which is not scored, all of the questions are multiple-choice questions. That's good; it means you have four (on the ISEE) or five (on the SSAT) answers to choose from. It means you always have the answer in front of you.

All right, so what exactly will you find in a "verbal ability" section? Well, this section has questions that test vocabulary and verbal reasoning. Both the SSAT and ISEE use synonym questions to test your vocabulary. The SSAT tests your verbal reasoning with analogy questions while the ISEE tests this same ability with sentence completions.

Synonyms

Synonym questions present a single word and ask you to choose the word with the same or most similar meaning. This is a pure test of vocabulary, though word-building skills may help you figure out meanings of some unfamiliar words.

HERE'S THE ANSWER

Do some question types count more than others?

No. On both the SSAT and the ISEE all question types count the same.

Analogies (SSAT only)

Analogies present a pair of words that have some logical relationship to one another. The correct answer consists of a pair of words with the same kind of relationship as the first pair.

Sentence Completions (ISEE only)

Sentence completion questions ask you to choose a word or words that fill in the blanks in a given sentence. They test how well you can use context clues and word meanings to complete a sentence.

Reading Comprehension

Reading comprehension questions relate to a passage that is provided for you to read. SSAT passages can be about almost anything. ISEE passages are based on social studies or science readings, but they do not test your knowledge in social studies or the sciences. Regardless of the subject matter of the reading passage, the questions after it test how well you understood the passage and the information in it.

Now let's talk a minute about math questions. The exams are structured somewhat differently, but both exams seek to measure your understanding and application of quantitative concepts—that is, arithmetic, algebraic, and geometric concepts. Both exams involve you in problem solving and calculations. Depending on the exam you are taking, you will see only standard multiple-choice questions or multiple-choice questions and quantitative comparisons.

Standard Multiple-Choice Questions

Standard multiple-choice questions give you a problem in arithmetic, algebra, or geometry. Then you choose the correct answer from the choices offered.

Quantitative Comparisons (ISEE only)

Quantitative comparison questions test your skills in comparing information and in estimating. You'll see two quantities, one in Column A and one in Column B. Your job is to compare the two quantities and decide if one is greater than the other, if they are equal, or if no comparison is possible.

HERE'S THE ANSWER

Are calculators allowed on either exam?

No. Leave calculators and scratch paper at home. Figure in your head or in test booklet margins.

HOW ARE THE EXAMS STRUCTURED?

SSAT

The SSAT is administered in six separately timed sections of 25 minutes each. The first section, Part I, is the writing sample. The other five sections, Part II, can appear in any order, since all are allotted the same 25 minutes for completion. Of the five sections, two always contain mathematics questions, one includes synonyms and analogies, and one tests reading comprehension. A fifth section is an additional section similar to any one of the other four sections in Part II. This "experimental section" does not count. It is included for purposes of testing out new questions. The experimental section looks so much like a section that counts that you will not be able to identify it, so you will have to do your best on all five sections. Every question on the multiple-choice part of the SSAT offers five answer choices lettered (A), (B), (C), (D), and (E).

Subject to the order of the sections, which may vary from booklet to booklet as a guard against cheating by looking at your neighbor's paper, here is a typical SSAT format and timetable.

Format of a Typical SSAT

Section		Number of Questions	Time Allowed
Part I:	Writing Sample		25 minutes
Part II:	Multiple-choice		
Section 1:	Quantitative Ability	25 questions	25 minutes
Section 2:	Verbal Ability	60 questions 30 Synonym questions 30 Verbal Analogy questions	25 minutes
Section 3:	Quantitative Ability	25 questions	25 minutes
Section 4:	Reading Comprehension	40 questions based on approximately 7 reading passages	25 minutes
Section 5:	Any one of the above		25 minutes

TESTSMARTS

Set your watch to exam time. At the beginning of each test section, set your watch to 12 o'clock. Then all you have to do is glance quickly at the hands (or the read-out of a digital watch) to see how much of the section has passed.

ISEE

The ISEE is administered in five separately-timed sections called "tests." The time limit for all tests is not identical, so all applicants at a given administration take the tests in the same order. However, your neighbor may get a booklet with different questions as a guard against cheating. The ISEE does not include an experimental section; every multiple-choice test counts, and every question counts. The essay, which is the final "test" of the ISEE, is not scored and does not count. A photocopy of your essay is provided to each school as a writing sample.

Each multiple-choice question on the ISEE offers four answer choices. These are lettered (A), (B), (C), and (D).

Here is a typical ISEE format and timetable:

Format of a Typical ISEE

Section		Number of Questions	Time Allowed
Test 1:	Verbal Ability	40 questions	20 minutes
	Synonyms		
	Sentence Completions		
Test 2:	Quantitative Ability	40 questions	35 minutes
	Concepts/Understanding and Application measured by Problem Solving and Quantitative Comparisons		
Test 3:	Reading Comprehension	40 questions based on approximately 9 reading passages	35 minutes
	Science Passages		
	Social Studies Passages		
Test 4:	Mathematics Achievement	50 questions	40 minutes
	Arithmetic Concepts		
	Algebraic Concepts		
	Geometric Concepts		
Essay			30 minutes

WHAT DO THE ANSWER SHEETS LOOK LIKE?

This is where we get to the bubbles. When you get the test booklet, you'll also get a separate sheet on which you'll mark your answers.

For each **multiple-choice** question, you'll see a corresponding set of answer ovals (these are the bubbles!). The ovals are labeled from A to D or E, depending on which exam you are taking: A to D for the ISEE; A to E for the SSAT. Here's the main point to remember: Answer sheets are read by machines—and machines can't think. That means it's up to you to make sure you're in the right place on the answer sheet every time you record an answer. The machine won't know if you really meant Question 25 when you marked the space for Question 26. Another thing to remember: Don't be a wimp with that pencil. Fill in your chosen answer ovals completely and boldly so there can be no mistake about which one you chose.

Take a look at this sample answer sheet. You can just imagine what the machine will do with it.

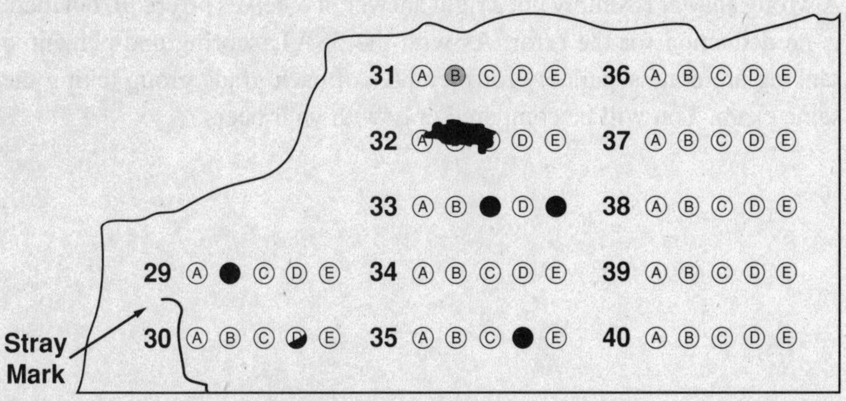

The only answers that will be registered correctly are 29 and 35. Question 30 isn't filled in completely, and Question 31 isn't dark enough, so the machine might miss them. Question 32 is a total mess—will the machine choose A, B, or C?

Since Question 33 has two ovals filled in, they cancel each other out, and this is registered as an omitted question. There's no penalty, but there's no credit either. The same will happen with Question 34; no answer, no credit.

AVOID THE TRAPS!

Make sure you're in the right place. Always check to see that the answer space you fill in corresponds to the question you are answering.

HOW ARE THE EXAMS SCORED?

OK, you've filled in all your bubbles, time is up (and not a moment too soon), and you turn in your answer sheet. What next? Off it goes to the machine at the central offices of the testing organization. The machine scans the sheet in seconds (aren't you glad you were careful with those bubbles?) and calculates a score. How it calculates your score depends on which exam you were taking.

SSAT

The scoring of the SSAT is as follows: You get one point for each correct answer, and you lose one-quarter of a point for each incorrect answer. Omitted answers have no effect on your score. Calculation of right answers minus one-fourth of wrong answers yields your raw score. Do not worry that your standing on the exam may suffer in comparison to students in other grades taking the same upper-level exam. SSAT scores are scaled and reported in percentiles comparing only students within the same age and grade group.

ISEE

Scoring of the ISEE is uncomplicated. You receive one point for every question that you answer correctly. There is no penalty for a wrong answer. A wrong answer is simply not a right answer; it receives no credit, but there is no deduction for the error. As with the SSAT, scoring and percentile ranking are done separately for members of each grade group taking the same exam. You will be compared only with your peers.

WHAT SMART TEST-TAKERS KNOW

What makes some people better test-takers than others? The secret isn't just knowing the subject, it's knowing specific test-taking strategies that can add up to extra points. This means psyching out the test, knowing how the test-makers think and what they're looking for, and using this knowledge to your advantage. Smart test-takers know how to use pacing and guessing to add points to their score.

Pacing

As any comedian will tell you, it's all in the timing. For example, an SSAT Quantitative Ability section contains 25 questions to be answered in 25 minutes. That means that you have a minute to answer each question. But smart test-takers know that that's not the best way to use their time. If you use less than a minute to answer the easier questions, you'll have extra time to help you answer the more difficult ones. That's why learning to pace yourself is so important.

TESTSMARTS

Move quickly on the easy ones. The questions in a set usually go from easiest to hardest. Try to go through the easy ones quickly.

QUESTION SETS USUALLY GO FROM EASIEST TO MOST DIFFICULT. YOU SHOULD, TOO.

Except for the reading comprehension questions, test questions follow this pattern. So work your way through the earlier, easier questions as quickly as you can. That way you'll have more time for the later, more difficult ones.

YOU CAN SET YOUR OWN SPEED LIMIT.

All right, how will you know what your speed limit is? Use the practice tests to check your timing and see how it affects your answers. If you've answered most of the questions in the time limit, but also have a lot of incorrect answers, better slow down. On the other hand, if you are very accurate in your answers but aren't answering every question in a section, you can probably pick up the pace a bit.

AVOID THE TRAPS!

Don't spin your wheels. Don't spend too much time on any one question. Give it some thought, take your best shot, and move along.

IT'S SMART TO KEEP MOVING.

It's hard to let go, but sometimes you have to. Don't spend too much time on any one question before you've tried all the questions in a section. There may be questions later on in the test that you can answer easily, and you don't want to lose points just because you didn't get to them.

THE EASY ANSWER ISN'T ALWAYS BEST.

Are you at the end of a section? Remember, that's where you'll find the hardest questions, which means that the answers are more complex. Look carefully at the choices and really think about what the question is asking.

YOU DON'T HAVE TO READ THE DIRECTIONS.

What? Yes, you read it correctly the first time—*you don't have to read the directions.* Look, by the time you actually sit down to take your exam, you've read this book, you've taken all the practice tests you could find, and you've read enough test directions to fill a library. So when the exam clock starts ticking, don't waste time rereading directions you already know. Instead, go directly to Question 1.

YOU'RE GOING TO NEED A WATCH.

If you're going to pace yourself, you need to keep track of the time—and what if there is no clock in your room or if the only clock is out of your line of vision? That's why it's a good idea to bring a watch to the test. A word of warning: Don't use a watch alarm or your watch will end up on the proctor's desk.

MARKING YOUR ANSWERS IN GROUPS SAVES TIME.

It's easy to lose your place when you move back and forth from the test booklet to the answer sheet after each question. Instead, try marking the answers in a group. Say, for example, that you're working with a set of six analogies. Read each one, and circle your answers right there in the test booklet. (It's OK, go ahead.) Then transfer them to the answer sheet in a group. This way you're making only one trip to fill in those bubbles.

Guessing

Guessing is always permissible, but is it always wise? That depends on whether or not you have a clue as to the possible answer, and it depends on which exam you are taking.

AN EDUCATED GUESS IS ALWAYS BEST.

Ah, yes, the process of elimination! This is the best way to improve your guessing odds. Check out the answer choices and try to knock out any that you definitely know are wrong. On an SSAT question, if you can knock out one choice out of five, you have a 25 percent chance of guessing correctly. If you can knock out two choices, the odds go up to $33\frac{1}{3}$ percent. If you can knock out three, you have a 50/50 chance of guessing the right answer. With odds like these, it makes sense to guess even on the SSAT where a wrong guess can count against you. And on the ISEE where a wrong guess doesn't hurt, an educated guess still will more likely add points to your score.

CONSIDER RANDOM GUESSING.
SSAT

If you are taking the SSAT, do not rush to make random guesses. The fractional deduction for wrong answers makes random guessing a wash—statistically speaking, you're unlikely to change your score. This means that if you come to a question that you have absolutely no idea how to answer, you're probably best off skipping it and going on. Just remember that if you skip a question, you must skip its answer space on the answer sheet. Mark your skips in the test booklet so that you can double check that your answers are in the right places.

ISEE

As for the ISEE, an educated guess is best, but a wild guess cannot hurt you. Try first to answer each question correctly. If you cannot figure out the best answer, eliminate those that are obviously wrong and make an educated guess. In your test booklet, mark the question "EG" for *educated guess.* Then, if you have time at the end of the section, you can return and try again. Since there is no subtraction for a wrong answer, there is no harm in a wild guess. By all means, guess; you might guess right. If you have no idea at all, do not skip the question. Leave no blanks. Mark one answer and code the question "WG" for *wild guess.* A second look later on, if you have time, may reveal the answer to you.

There is one more guessing strategy for the ISEE. Do not leave any blanks at the end of a test. Keep track of your time. If you still have questions remaining when time is almost up, pick a letter and mark all the remaining answer spaces with the same choice. Take advantage of the law of averages and give yourself a chance to pick up a free point or two.

CHAPTER 3

SSAT Questions: A First Look

PLAN A: ACCELERATED

- ***Read*** the chapter
- ***Study*** the answer explanations

PLAN B: TOP SPEED

- ***Read*** the chapter
- ***Skim*** the answer explanations

You'll Find Answers to These Questions

What can you expect on the test?
How does the SSAT test verbal ability?
What are synonym questions?
What are analogy questions?
How does the SSAT test quantitative ability?
How does the SSAT test reading ability?
What is the writing sample?
What is the experimental section?

WHAT CAN YOU EXPECT ON THE TEST?

The SSAT uses four question types to test your verbal and quantitative abilities and your reading comprehension. This chapter will describe each of them in turn and show you samples. Learning these question types in advance is the best way to prepare for the SSAT. They never change, so you'll know what to expect, and you won't have any unpleasant surprises when you show up to take the test. The SSAT also asks you to write a short essay on an assigned topic. This chapter will introduce you to the essay requirement.

HOW DOES THE SSAT TEST VERBAL ABILITY?

The SSAT tests your verbal ability with two question types:

- synonyms
- verbal analogies

A verbal ability section consists of 60 questions. 30 of these questions are synonyms and 30 are verbal analogies.

HERE'S THE ANSWER

What other kinds of questions will there be on the SSAT?

What you see is what you get—the questions on these pages show you what you'll find.

WHAT ARE SYNONYM QUESTIONS?

A synonym is a word with the same meaning or nearly the same meaning as another word. SSAT synonym questions ask you to choose the best synonym for a capitalized word.

The directions for SSAT synonyms questions look like this:

> **Directions:** Choose the word or phrase whose meaning is most similar to the meaning of the word in CAPITAL letters.

Here are two sample SSAT synonym questions. Try each one on your own; then read the explanation that accompanies it.

1. NOVICE

(A) competitive
(B) clumsy
(C) aged
(D) beginner
(E) impulsive

Choice (**D**) is correct. A NOVICE is a *beginner.* A novice may, of course, be competitive, clumsy, aged, or impulsive, but it is the aspect of being a beginner that makes a person a novice. You may; recognize the root of *novel,* meaning *new,* a clue to the definition.

2. CONVOY

(A) hearse
(B) thunderstorm
(C) group
(D) jeep
(E) journey

Choice (**C**) is correct. A CONVOY is a group traveling together for protection or convenience. You have probably seen convoys of military vehicles traveling single-file up the highway toward summer reserve camp. A jeep may be part of a convoy.

WHAT ARE ANALOGY QUESTIONS?

Analogy questions ask you to match up pairs of words that are related in the same way. Each question starts with a word pair. Your job is to find or create another pair of words that is related in the same way as the first pair.

SSAT analogy questions are presented in two different formats. In one format, you must choose a fourth word that relates to the third in the same way that the second word relates to the first. In the other format, you must choose a pair of words that is related in the same way as the first pair.

The directions are the same for both formats of analogy questions. They look like this:

> **Directions:** Find the relationship between the words. Read each question and then choose the answer that best completes the meaning of the sentence.

Here are two sample SSAT analogy questions, one of each type. Try each one on your own before reading the explanation that accompanies it.

3. Lid is to box as cork is to

(A) float

(B) bottle

(C) wine

(D) blacken

(E) stopper

Choice (**B**) is correct. The relationship is one of purpose. The purpose of a *lid* is to close a *box;* the purpose of a *cork* is to close a *bottle*. Cork is easily associated with all the choices, so you must recognize the purposeful relationship of the initial pair to choose the correct answer.

4. Poison is to death as

(A) book is to pages

(B) music is to violin

(C) kindness is to cooperation

(D) life is to famine

(E) nothing is to something

Ⓐ Ⓑ ● Ⓓ Ⓔ

Choice (**C**) is correct. This is a cause-and-effect relationship. *Poison* may cause *death; kindness* may lead to *cooperation.* Neither outcome is a foregone conclusion, but both are equally likely, so the parallel is maintained. Choice (B) offers a reversed relationship.

AVOID THE TRAPS!

Make the best of it. Note that the directions ask you to choose the *best* answer. That's why you should always read all the answer choices before you make your final selection.

HOW DOES THE SSAT TEST QUANTITATIVE ABILITY?

The SSAT tests your quantitative ability in two 25-question mathematics sections, that is, with 50 mathematics questions in all. The questions in each section measure your knowledge of algebra and quantitative concepts.

The directions are the same for both quantitative sections. Here's what they look like:

> **Directions:** Calculate each problem in your head or in the scratch area of the test booklet and choose the best answer.

Here are four sample SSAT quantitative ability questions showing the range of mathematical questions. Try each of these on your own before you read the explanation that accompanies it.

HERE'S THE ANSWER

May I use a calculator for quantitative ability questions?

No. Leave your calculator at home. Use the space provided in the test booklet for scratch work.

5. $\frac{1}{4}$% of 1,500 =

(A) 60.00

(B) 15.00

(C) 7.50

(D) 3.75

(E) 1.50

Choice (**D**) is correct. $\frac{1}{4}$% written as a decimal is .0025. (1,500)(.0025) = 3.75. You could have done this problem in your head by thinking: 1% of 1,500 is 15; $\frac{1}{4}$ of 1% = 15 ÷ 4 = 3.75.

6. If psychological studies of juvenile delinquents show *K* percent to be emotionally unstable, the number of juvenile delinquents not emotionally unstable per one-hundred juvenile delinquents is

(A) 100 minus *K*

(B) 1 minus *K*

(C) *K* minus 100

(D) 100 ÷ *K*

(E) *K* ÷ 100

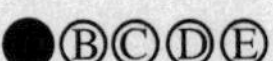

Choice (**A**) is correct. "Percent" means out of 100. If *K* percent are emotionally unstable, then *K* out of 100 are emotionally unstable. The remainder, 100 – *K*, are not unstable.

7. A piece of wood 35 feet, 6 inches long was used to make four shelves of equal length. The length of each shelf was

(A) 9 feet, $1\frac{1}{2}$ inches

(B) 8 feet, $10\frac{1}{2}$ inches

(C) 8 feet, $1\frac{1}{2}$ inches

(D) 7 feet, $10\frac{1}{2}$ inches

(E) 7 feet, $1\frac{1}{2}$ inches

Choice (**B**) is correct. First convert the feet to inches. 35 feet, 6 inches = 420 inches + 6 inches = 426 inches. 426 ÷ 4 = 106.5 inches per shelf = 8 feet, $10\frac{1}{2}$ inches per shelf.

8. Angle *ABD* is

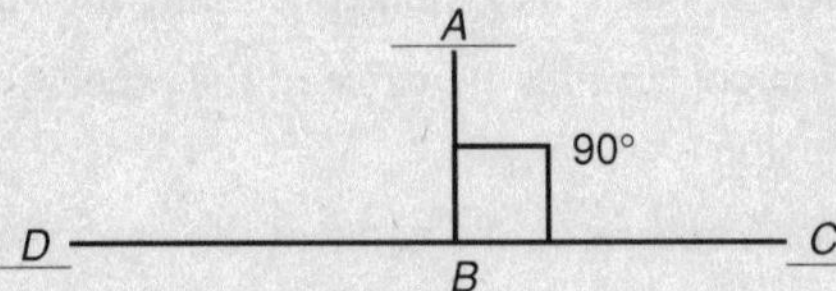

(A) a straight angle and contains 180°

(B) an acute angle and contains 35°

(C) an obtuse angle and contains 360°

(D) a right angle and contains 45°

(E) a right angle and contains 90° 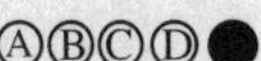

Choice (**E**) is correct. Angle *ABC* and angle *ABD* are supplementary angles. Since angle *ABC* = 90°, angle *ABD* must also equal 90° (180° – 90° = 90°). A right angle contains 90°.

HOW DOES THE SSAT TEST READING ABILITY?

TESTSMARTS

It's an open-book test. In SSAT reading comprehension questions, the answers will always be directly stated or implied in the passage.

The SSAT measures your ability to read quickly and to understand what you read by asking you questions about passages that you must read. The 40 questions in a reading comprehension section are based on about seven reading passages.

The directions for SSAT reading comprehension questions look like this:

> **Directions:** Carefully read each passage and the questions that follow it. Choose the best answer to each question on the basis of the information in the passage.

Here is a sample SSAT reading passage followed by four questions. Read the passage and try answering the questions on your own before reading the explanations.

Cotton fabrics treated with the XYZ Process have features that make them far superior to any previously known flame-retardant-treated cotton fabrics. XYZ Process-treated fabrics are durable to repeated laundering and dry cleaning; are glow resistant as well as flame resistant; when exposed to flames or intense heat form tough, pliable, and protective chars; are inert physiologically to persons handling or exposed to the fabric; are only slightly heavier than untreated fabrics; and are susceptible to further wet and dry finishing treatments. In addition, the treated fabrics exhibit little or no adverse change in feel, texture, and appearance, and are shrink-, rot-, and mildew-resistant. The treatment reduces strength only slightly. Finished fabrics have "easy care" properties in that they are wrinkle-resistant and dry rapidly.

9. It is most accurate to state that the author in the preceding selection presents

(A) facts but reaches no conclusion concerning the value of the process

(B) a conclusion concerning the value of the process and facts to support that conclusion

(C) a conclusion concerning the value of the process unsupported by facts

(D) neither facts nor conclusions, but merely describes the process

(E) the case for making all fabrics flame-retardant 

Choice (**B**) is correct. This is a combination main-idea and interpretation question. If you cannot answer this question readily, reread the selection. The author clearly thinks that the XYZ Process is terrific and says so in the first sentence. The rest of the selection presents a wealth of facts to support the initial claim.

10. For which one of the following articles would the XYZ Process be most suitable?

(A) nylon stockings

(B) woolen shirt

(C) silk tie

(D) cotton bedsheet

(E) polyester slacks 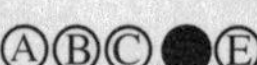

Choice (**D**) is correct. At first glance you might think that this is an inference question requiring you to make a judgment based upon the few drawbacks of the process. Closer reading, however, shows you that there is no contest for the correct answer here. This is a simple question of fact. The XYZ Process is a treatment for *cotton* fabrics.

11. The main reason for treating a fabric with the XYZ Process is to

(A) prepare the fabric for other wet and dry finishing treatment.

(B) render it shrink-, rot-, and mildew-resistant

(C) increase its weight and strength

(D) reduce the chance that it will catch fire

(E) justify a price increase 

Choice (**D**) is correct. This is a main-idea question. You must distinguish between the main idea and the supporting and incidental facts.

12. Which one of the following would be considered a minor drawback of the XYZ Process?

(A) forms chars when exposed to flame

(B) makes fabrics mildew-resistant

(C) adds to the weight of fabrics

(D) is compatible with other finishing treatments

(E) does not wash out of the fabric 

Choice (**C**) is correct. Obviously a drawback is a negative feature. The selection mentions only two negative features. The treatment reduces strength slightly, and it makes fabrics slightly heavier than untreated fabrics. Only one of these negative features is offered among the answer choices.

WHAT IS THE WRITING SAMPLE?

At the beginning of each SSAT testing session, you must write a 25-minute essay on an assigned subject. This essay is not scored. It is duplicated and sent to each school as a sample of your ability to express yourself in writing under the same conditions as all other candidates for admission to the school.

The directions for the SSAT writing sample look like this:

> **Directions:** Read the topic, choose your position, and organize your essay before writing. Write a convincing, legible essay on the paper provided.

Here is a sample SSAT essay topic. Try to organize and write an essay on this topic.

Topic: Bad things always happen in threes.

Assignment: Do you agree or disagree? Support your position with examples from your own experience, the experience of others, current events, or your reading.

WHAT IS THE EXPERIMENTAL SECTION?

The experimental section may be an additional verbal ability, quantitative ability or reading comprehension section. The experimental section is used for trying out new questions for later use. How well you do on the experimental section has no effect on your score. It is not graded, and it does not count. However, you will not know which duplicated section is the experimental section. It will look just like one other verbal ability, quantitative ability, or reading comprehension section. Because you will not know which section does not count, you must do your best on all sections.

HERE'S THE ANSWER

How will I recognize the experimental section?

You won't be able to. You must do your best on all sections.

CHAPTER 4

ISEE Questions: A First Look

PLAN A: ACCELERATED

- ***Read*** the chapter
- ***Study*** the answer explanations

PLAN B: TOP SPEED

- ***Read*** the chapter
- ***Skim*** the answer explanations

You'll Find Answers to These Questions

What can you expect on the test?
How does the ISEE test verbal ability?
What are synonym questions?
What are sentence completion questions?
How does the ISEE test quantitative ability?
What are quantitative comparisons?
How does the ISEE test reading comprehension?
How does the ISEE test mathematical achievement?
What is the essay question?

WHAT CAN YOU EXPECT ON THE TEST?

The ISEE uses four question types to test your verbal and quantitative abilities and your achievement in mathematics and reading comprehension. This chapter will describe each of them in turn and show you samples. Learning these question types in advance is the best way to prepare for the ISEE. They never change, so you'll know what to expect, and you won't have any unpleasant surprises when you show up to take the test. The ISEE also asks you to write a short essay on an assigned topic. This chapter will introduce you to the essay requirement.

HOW DOES THE ISEE TEST VERBAL ABILITY?

The ISEE tests your verbal ability with two question types:

- synonyms
- sentence completions

The verbal ability test consists of 40 questions. 20 of these questions are synonyms and 20 are sentence completions.

WHAT ARE SYNONYM QUESTIONS?

A synonym is a word with the same meaning or nearly the same meaning as another word. ISEE synonym questions ask you to choose the best synonym for a capitalized word.

The directions for ISEE synonyms questions look like this:

> **Directions:** Choose the word that is most nearly the same in meaning as the word in CAPITAL letters.

Here are two sample ISEE synonym questions. Try each one on your own; then read the explanation that accompanies it.

1. TENANT

(A) occupant
(B) landlord
(C) owner
(D) farmer 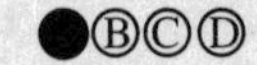

Choice (**A**) is correct. The most common sense of the word TENANT is *renter*. As such, the tenant is never the landlord. The owner may well be an occupant, but unless he or she occupies on a very temporary basis he or she is not considered a tenant. A tenant farmer lives on and cultivates the land of another.

2. CALCULATED

(A) multiplied
(B) added
(C) answered
(D) figured out 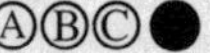

Choice (**D**) is correct. CALCULATING may well include multiplying or adding in order to arrive at the answer, but not all calculations need be mathematical. It is the *figuring out* that is the *calculating*.

WHAT ARE SENTENCE COMPLETION QUESTIONS?

Just as the name implies, sentence completions are "fill-in-the-blank" questions. ISEE sentence completion questions may have one or two blanks. Your job is to choose from among the answer choices the word or words that best fit each blank.

The directions for ISEE sentence completion questions look like this:

> **Directions:** The blanks in the following sentences indicate that words are missing. If there is one blank, only a single word is missing. If there are two blanks, a pair of words is missing. Choose the one word or pair of words that will best complete the meaning of the sentence as a whole.

Here are two sample ISEE sentence completion questions, a one-blank question and a two-blank question. Try each one on your own before reading the explanation that accompanies it.

3. Utility is not _____, for the usefulness of an object changes with time and place.

(A) planned

(B) practical

(C) permanent

(D) understandable 

Choice **(C)** is correct. If the usefulness of an object changes, then that usefulness is by definition *not permanent*.

4. A string of lies had landed her in such a hopeless _____ that she didn't know how to _____ herself.

(A) status … clear

(B) pinnacle … explain

(C) confusion … help

(D) predicament … extricate ⒶⒷⒸ●

Choice **(D)** is correct. "Hopeless predicament" is an idiomatic expression meaning "impossible situation." This is a reasonable position for one to be in after a string of lies. The second blank is correctly filled with a term that implies that she couldn't get out of the mess she had created.

AVOID THE TRAPS!

Make the best of it. Note that the directions ask you to choose the *best* answer. That's why you should always read all the answer choices before you make your final selection.

HOW DOES THE ISEE TEST QUANTITATIVE ABILITY?

The ISEE tests your understanding of quantitative concepts and your ability to apply those concepts with two question types:

- standard multiple-choice questions
- quantitative comparisons

The quantitative ability test consists of 40 questions. About half of these are standard multiple-choice questions, and the remainder are quantitative comparisons.

The directions for the standard multiple-choice questions look like this:

Directions: Work each problem in your head or on the space available on the pages of the test booklet and choose the correct answer. All figures are accurately drawn unless otherwise noted. All letters stand for real numbers.

Here are two sample ISEE standard multiple-choice quantitative ability questions. Try each of these on your own before you read the explanation that accompanies it.

5. If $A^2 + B^2 = A^2 + X^2$, then B equals

(A) X

(B) $X^2 - 2A^2$

(C) A

(D) $A^2 + X^2$

Choice (**A**) is correct. Subtract A^2 from both sides of the equation: $B^2 = X^2$, therefore $B = X$.

6. How much time is there between 8:30 AM today and 3:15 AM tomorrow?

(A) $17\frac{3}{4}$ hrs.

(B) $18\frac{1}{2}$ hrs.

(C) $18\frac{2}{3}$ hrs.

(D) $18\frac{3}{4}$ hrs.

Choice (**D**) is correct. 12:00 = 11:60
From 8:30 AM until noon today: 8:30 = – 8:30
3 hrs. 30 min.
From noon until midnight: 12 hrs.
From midnight until 3:15 AM: +3 hrs. 15 min.
18 hrs. 45 min. = $18\frac{3}{4}$ hours

WHAT ARE QUANTITATIVE COMPARISONS?

ISEE quantitative comparisons are probably not like any other math question you've ever seen. These questions present you with two quantities, one in Column A and one in Column B. Your job is to decide which quantity is greater, whether the two quantities are equal, or whether no comparison is possible. There are always four answer choices for this question type, and they are always the same. Here is what the directions look like:

Directions: For each of the following questions, two quantities are given—one in Column A, the other in Column B. Compare the two quantities and choose:

(A) if the quantity in Column A is greater

(B) if the quantity in Column B is greater

(C) if the quantities are equal

(D) if the relationship cannot be determined from the information given.

Notes:

(1) For some questions, information concerning one or both of the quantities to be compared is centered above the entries in the two columns.

(2) Symbols that appear in both columns represent the same thing in Column A as in Column B.

(3) Letters such as x, n, and k are symbols for real numbers.

(4) All figures are accurately drawn unless otherwise noted.

Here are two sample ISEE quantitative comparison questions. Try each of these on your own before you read the explanation that accompanies it.

	Column A	Column B

7.

Note: Figure not drawn to scale.

$180 - a$	$d + c - b$

Choice **(D)** is correct.

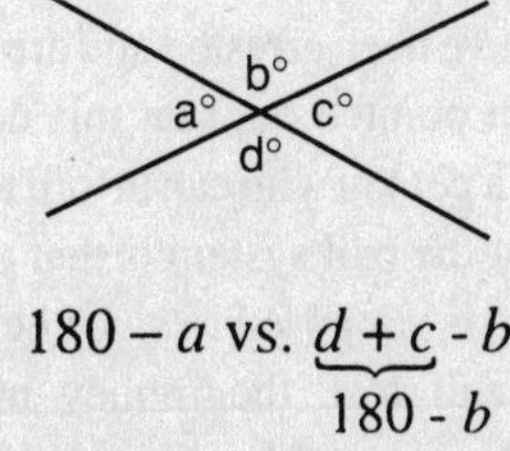

$$180 - a \text{ vs. } \underbrace{d + c}_{180\,-\,b} - b$$

Since we do not know if $a \gtrless b$, the relationship cannot be determined.

	Column A	Column B	
8.	$\frac{2}{\frac{3}{4}}$	$\frac{\frac{2}{3}}{4}$	●ⒷⒸⒹ

Choice (**A**) is correct.

$$\frac{2}{\frac{3}{4}} = \frac{2}{1} \bullet \frac{4}{3} = \frac{8}{3} \text{ vs. } \frac{\frac{2}{3}}{4} = \frac{2}{3} \bullet \frac{1}{4} = \frac{2}{12}$$

Column A > Column B

TESTSMARTS

It's an open-book test. In ISEE reading comprehension questions, the answers will always be directly stated or implied in the passage.

HOW DOES THE ISEE TEST READING COMPREHENSION?

The ISEE measures your ability to read quickly and to understand what you read by asking you questions about passages that you must read. The 40 questions in the reading comprehension section are based on about nine reading passages. Because the ISEE is interested in both your level of reading and your ability to comprehend material from the sciences and from social studies, the content of the reading passages is based on social studies and science.

The directions for the ISEE test of reading comprehension look like this:

> **Directions:** Each passage is followed by questions based on its content. Answer the questions following each passage on the basis of what is stated or implied in the passage.

Here are samples of two ISEE reading passages each followed by two questions. The first passage is a social studies passage and the second a science-based passage. Read each passage and try to answer the questions on your own before you read the explanations.

A large proportion of the people who are behind bars are not convicted criminals, but people who have been arrested and are being held until their trial in court. Experts have often pointed out that this detention system does not operate fairly. For instance, a person who can afford to pay bail usually will not get locked up. The theory of the bail system is that the person will make sure to show up in court when he is supposed to since he knows that otherwise he will forfeit his bail—he will lose the money he put up. Sometimes a person who can show that he is a stable citizen with a job and a family will be released on "personal recognizance" (without bail). The result is that the well-to-do, the employed, and the family men can often avoid the detention system. The people who do wind up in detention tend to be the poor, the unemployed, the single, and the young.

9. According to the preceding passage, people who are put behind bars

(A) are almost always dangerous criminals

(B) include many innocent people who have been arrested by mistake

(C) are often people who have been arrested but have not yet come to trial

(D) are all poor people who tend to be young and single 

Choice (**C**) is correct. The answer to this question is directly stated in the first sentence. (B) might be possible, but it is neither stated nor implied by the passage. The word *all* in choice (D) makes it an incorrect statement.

10. Suppose that two men were booked on the same charge at the same time and that the same bail was set for both of them. One man was able to put up bail, and he was released. The second man was not able to put up bail, and he was held in detention. The writer of the passage would most likely feel that this result is

(A) unfair, because it does not have any relation to guilt or innocence

(B) unfair, because the first man deserves severe punishment

(C) fair, because the first man is obviously innocent

(D) fair, because the law should be tougher on the poor people than on the rich ●ⒷⒸⒹ

Choice (**A**) is correct. You should have no difficulty inferring this attitude from the tone of the passage.

Fire often travels inside the partitions of a burning building. Many partitions contain wooden studs that support the partitions, and the studs leave a space for the fire to travel through. Flames may spread from the bottom to the upper floors through the partitions. Sparks from a fire in the upper part of a partition may fall and start a fire at the bottom. Some signs that a fire is spreading inside a partition are: (1) blistering paint, (2) discolored paint or wallpaper, or (3) partitions that feel hot to the touch. If any of these signs is present, the partition must be opened up to look for the fire. Finding cobwebs inside the partition is one sign that fire has not spread through the partition.

11. Fires can spread inside partitions because

(A) there are spaces between studs inside of partitions

(B) fires can burn anywhere

(C) partitions are made out of materials that burn easily

(D) partitions are usually painted or wallpapered ●ⒷⒸⒹ

Choice (**A**) is correct. This statement of fact is made in the second sentence.

12. If a firefighter sees the paint on a partition beginning to blister, he should first

(A) wet down the partition

(B) check the partitions in other rooms

(C) chop a hole in the partition

(D) close windows and doors and leave the room 

Choice (**C**) is correct. Blistering paint (line 6) is a sign that fire is spreading inside a partition. If this sign is present, the firefighter must open the partition to look for the fire (line 7). The way to open the partition is to chop a hole in it.

HOW DOES THE ISEE TEST MATHEMATICAL ACHIEVEMENT?

The ISEE tests your mathematics achievement by asking you to answer math questions that relate to:

- arithmetic concepts
- algebraic concepts
- geometric concepts

HERE'S THE ANSWER

May I use a calculator for quantitative ability or mathematical achievement questions?

No. Leave your calculator and scratch paper at home. Use the space provided in the test booklet for scratch work.

The mathematics achievement test consists of 50 questions, all of them of the standard multiple-choice type.

The directions for the mathematics achievement test look like this:

Directions: Read each question and choose the best answer based on calculations in your head or in the margins of the test booklet.

Here are four sample ISEE mathematics achievement questions. Try each of these on your own before you read the explanation that accompanies it.

13. If $\frac{3}{4}$ of a class is absent and $\frac{2}{3}$ of those present leave the room, what fraction of the original class remains in the room?

(A) $\frac{1}{4}$

(B) $\frac{1}{8}$

(C) $\frac{1}{12}$

(D) $\frac{1}{24}$ 

Choice (**C**) is correct. If $\frac{3}{4}$ are absent, $\frac{1}{4}$ are present. If $\frac{2}{3}$ of the $\frac{1}{4}$ present leave, $\frac{1}{3}$ of the $\frac{1}{4}$ remain. $\frac{1}{3} \times \frac{1}{4} = \frac{1}{12}$ remain in the room.

14. A cog wheel having 8 cogs plays into another cog wheel having 24 cogs. When the small wheel has made 42 revolutions, how many has the larger wheel made?

(A) 10

(B) 14

(C) 16

(D) 20

Choice (**B**) is correct. The larger wheel is 3 times the size of the smaller wheel, so it makes $\frac{1}{3}$ the revolutions: $42 \div 3 = 14$.

15. 75% of 4 is the same as what percent of 9?

(A) 25

(B) $33\frac{1}{3}$

(C) 36

(D) 40

Choice (**B**) is correct: 75% of 4 = 3
$3 = 33\frac{1}{3}\%$ of 9.

16. If $\frac{1}{2}$ cup of spinach contains 80 calories and the same amount of peas contains 300 calories, how many cups of spinach have the same caloric content as $\frac{2}{3}$ cup of peas?

(A) $\frac{2}{5}$

(B) $1\frac{1}{3}$

(C) 2

(D) $2\frac{1}{2}$

Choice (**D**) is correct: $\frac{1}{2}$ cup spinach = 80 calories.

$\frac{1}{2}$ cup peas = 300 calories
1 cup peas = 600 calories
$\frac{2}{3}$ cup peas = 400 calories
$400 \div 80 = 5$ half cups of spinach
$= 2\frac{1}{2}$ cups of spinach

HERE'S THE ANSWER

What other kinds of questions will there be on the ISEE?

What you see is what you get—the questions on these pages show you what you'll find.

WHAT IS THE ESSAY QUESTION?

At the end of each ISEE testing session, you must write a 30-minute essay on an assigned subject. This essay is not scored. It is duplicated and sent to each school as a sample of your ability to express yourself in writing under the same conditions as all other candidates for admission to the school.

The directions for the ISEE essay question look like this:

> **Directions:** Read the essay topic and decide what you want to say. Organize your thoughts carefully, then write a legible, coherent, and correct essay on the topic.

Here is a sample ISEE essay topic, also called a "prompt." Try to organize and write an essay on this topic.

Topic: An exchange student from China has just entered your school. What will you tell this student about student life at your school?

What You Must Know About Your High School Entrance Examination

This information is the foundation that you're going to build on as you prepare for the High School Entrance Examination.

- The SSAT is a three-hour test of verbal, quantitative, and reading ability.
- The ISEE is a three-hour test of verbal and quantitative ability, reading comprehension, and mathematics achievement.
- The SSAT deducts one-fourth of a point from your score for each incorrect answer. Random guessing will do no good. A calculated guess is always worthwhile.
- The ISEE gives you one point for each correct answer. Wrong answers do not affect your score. Leave no blanks.
- All SSAT quantitative questions are standard multiple-choice questions.
- Some ISEE mathematical questions are standard multiple-choice; some are quantitative comparisons.
- Only the SSAT has an experimental section, but you won't know which it is so you must do your best on all sections of either exam.
- The essay is only a writing sample. It is not scored.
- On both exams all questions within each set, except reading comprehension, are arranged from easy to hard.
- Use a process of elimination to make educated guesses when you are not sure.
- Your percentile ranking is based on comparison of your score with students in your own grade only.
- You *can* get a very good score even if you don't answer every question.

PART

TWO

EVERYTHING YOU NEED!

Diagnosing Strengths and Weaknesses

PLAN A: ACCELERATED

- ***Take*** sections of the Diagnostic Examination that apply to your exam
- ***Check*** your answers
- ***Read*** answer explanations
- ***Read*** "Planning Your Study Time" and follow instructions

PLAN B: TOP SPEED

- ***Take*** sections of the Diagnostic Examination that apply to your exam
- ***Check*** your answers
- ***Skim*** answer explanations
- ***Skim*** "Planning Your Study Time" and follow instructions

Diagnostic Examination

Answer Sheet

SYNONYMS

1. Ⓐ Ⓑ Ⓒ Ⓓ	5. Ⓐ Ⓑ Ⓒ Ⓓ	9. Ⓐ Ⓑ Ⓒ Ⓓ	13. Ⓐ Ⓑ Ⓒ Ⓓ	17. Ⓐ Ⓑ Ⓒ Ⓓ
2. Ⓐ Ⓑ Ⓒ Ⓓ	6. Ⓐ Ⓑ Ⓒ Ⓓ	10. Ⓐ Ⓑ Ⓒ Ⓓ	14. Ⓐ Ⓑ Ⓒ Ⓓ	18. Ⓐ Ⓑ Ⓒ Ⓓ
3. Ⓐ Ⓑ Ⓒ Ⓓ	7. Ⓐ Ⓑ Ⓒ Ⓓ	11. Ⓐ Ⓑ Ⓒ Ⓓ	15. Ⓐ Ⓑ Ⓒ Ⓓ	19. Ⓐ Ⓑ Ⓒ Ⓓ
4. Ⓐ Ⓑ Ⓒ Ⓓ	8. Ⓐ Ⓑ Ⓒ Ⓓ	12. Ⓐ Ⓑ Ⓒ Ⓓ	16. Ⓐ Ⓑ Ⓒ Ⓓ	20. Ⓐ Ⓑ Ⓒ Ⓓ

VERBAL ANALOGIES

1. Ⓐ Ⓑ Ⓒ Ⓓ	5. Ⓐ Ⓑ Ⓒ Ⓓ	9. Ⓐ Ⓑ Ⓒ Ⓓ	13. Ⓐ Ⓑ Ⓒ Ⓓ	17. Ⓐ Ⓑ Ⓒ Ⓓ
2. Ⓐ Ⓑ Ⓒ Ⓓ	6. Ⓐ Ⓑ Ⓒ Ⓓ	10. Ⓐ Ⓑ Ⓒ Ⓓ	14. Ⓐ Ⓑ Ⓒ Ⓓ	18. Ⓐ Ⓑ Ⓒ Ⓓ
3. Ⓐ Ⓑ Ⓒ Ⓓ	7. Ⓐ Ⓑ Ⓒ Ⓓ	11. Ⓐ Ⓑ Ⓒ Ⓓ	15. Ⓐ Ⓑ Ⓒ Ⓓ	19. Ⓐ Ⓑ Ⓒ Ⓓ
4. Ⓐ Ⓑ Ⓒ Ⓓ	8. Ⓐ Ⓑ Ⓒ Ⓓ	12. Ⓐ Ⓑ Ⓒ Ⓓ	16. Ⓐ Ⓑ Ⓒ Ⓓ	20. Ⓐ Ⓑ Ⓒ Ⓓ

SENTENCE COMPLETIONS

1. Ⓐ Ⓑ Ⓒ Ⓓ	5. Ⓐ Ⓑ Ⓒ Ⓓ	9. Ⓐ Ⓑ Ⓒ Ⓓ	13. Ⓐ Ⓑ Ⓒ Ⓓ	17. Ⓐ Ⓑ Ⓒ Ⓓ
2. Ⓐ Ⓑ Ⓒ Ⓓ	6. Ⓐ Ⓑ Ⓒ Ⓓ	10. Ⓐ Ⓑ Ⓒ Ⓓ	14. Ⓐ Ⓑ Ⓒ Ⓓ	18. Ⓐ Ⓑ Ⓒ Ⓓ
3. Ⓐ Ⓑ Ⓒ Ⓓ	7. Ⓐ Ⓑ Ⓒ Ⓓ	11. Ⓐ Ⓑ Ⓒ Ⓓ	15. Ⓐ Ⓑ Ⓒ Ⓓ	19. Ⓐ Ⓑ Ⓒ Ⓓ
4. Ⓐ Ⓑ Ⓒ Ⓓ	8. Ⓐ Ⓑ Ⓒ Ⓓ	12. Ⓐ Ⓑ Ⓒ Ⓓ	16. Ⓐ Ⓑ Ⓒ Ⓓ	20. Ⓐ Ⓑ Ⓒ Ⓓ

READING COMPREHENSION

1. Ⓐ Ⓑ Ⓒ Ⓓ	6. Ⓐ Ⓑ Ⓒ Ⓓ	11. Ⓐ Ⓑ Ⓒ Ⓓ	16. Ⓐ Ⓑ Ⓒ Ⓓ	21. Ⓐ Ⓑ Ⓒ Ⓓ
2. Ⓐ Ⓑ Ⓒ Ⓓ	7. Ⓐ Ⓑ Ⓒ Ⓓ	12. Ⓐ Ⓑ Ⓒ Ⓓ	17. Ⓐ Ⓑ Ⓒ Ⓓ	22. Ⓐ Ⓑ Ⓒ Ⓓ
3. Ⓐ Ⓑ Ⓒ Ⓓ	8. Ⓐ Ⓑ Ⓒ Ⓓ	13. Ⓐ Ⓑ Ⓒ Ⓓ	18. Ⓐ Ⓑ Ⓒ Ⓓ	
4. Ⓐ Ⓑ Ⓒ Ⓓ	9. Ⓐ Ⓑ Ⓒ Ⓓ	14. Ⓐ Ⓑ Ⓒ Ⓓ	19. Ⓐ Ⓑ Ⓒ Ⓓ	
5. Ⓐ Ⓑ Ⓒ Ⓓ	10. Ⓐ Ⓑ Ⓒ Ⓓ	15. Ⓐ Ⓑ Ⓒ Ⓓ	20. Ⓐ Ⓑ Ⓒ Ⓓ	

QUANTITATIVE ABILITY

1. Ⓐ Ⓑ Ⓒ Ⓓ 7. Ⓐ Ⓑ Ⓒ Ⓓ 13. Ⓐ Ⓑ Ⓒ Ⓓ 19. Ⓐ Ⓑ Ⓒ Ⓓ 25. Ⓐ Ⓑ Ⓒ Ⓓ

2. Ⓐ Ⓑ Ⓒ Ⓓ 8. Ⓐ Ⓑ Ⓒ Ⓓ 14. Ⓐ Ⓑ Ⓒ Ⓓ 20. Ⓐ Ⓑ Ⓒ Ⓓ 26. Ⓐ Ⓑ Ⓒ Ⓓ

3. Ⓐ Ⓑ Ⓒ Ⓓ 9. Ⓐ Ⓑ Ⓒ Ⓓ 15. Ⓐ Ⓑ Ⓒ Ⓓ 21. Ⓐ Ⓑ Ⓒ Ⓓ 27. Ⓐ Ⓑ Ⓒ Ⓓ

4. Ⓐ Ⓑ Ⓒ Ⓓ 10. Ⓐ Ⓑ Ⓒ Ⓓ 16. Ⓐ Ⓑ Ⓒ Ⓓ 22. Ⓐ Ⓑ Ⓒ Ⓓ 28. Ⓐ Ⓑ Ⓒ Ⓓ

5. Ⓐ Ⓑ Ⓒ Ⓓ 11. Ⓐ Ⓑ Ⓒ Ⓓ 17. Ⓐ Ⓑ Ⓒ Ⓓ 23. Ⓐ Ⓑ Ⓒ Ⓓ 29. Ⓐ Ⓑ Ⓒ Ⓓ

6. Ⓐ Ⓑ Ⓒ Ⓓ 12. Ⓐ Ⓑ Ⓒ Ⓓ 18. Ⓐ Ⓑ Ⓒ Ⓓ 24. Ⓐ Ⓑ Ⓒ Ⓓ 30. Ⓐ Ⓑ Ⓒ Ⓓ

QUANTITATIVE COMPARISONS

1. Ⓐ Ⓑ Ⓒ Ⓓ 5. Ⓐ Ⓑ Ⓒ Ⓓ 9. Ⓐ Ⓑ Ⓒ Ⓓ 13. Ⓐ Ⓑ Ⓒ Ⓓ 17. Ⓐ Ⓑ Ⓒ Ⓓ

2. Ⓐ Ⓑ Ⓒ Ⓓ 6. Ⓐ Ⓑ Ⓒ Ⓓ 10. Ⓐ Ⓑ Ⓒ Ⓓ 14. Ⓐ Ⓑ Ⓒ Ⓓ 18. Ⓐ Ⓑ Ⓒ Ⓓ

3. Ⓐ Ⓑ Ⓒ Ⓓ 7. Ⓐ Ⓑ Ⓒ Ⓓ 11. Ⓐ Ⓑ Ⓒ Ⓓ 15. Ⓐ Ⓑ Ⓒ Ⓓ 19. Ⓐ Ⓑ Ⓒ Ⓓ

4. Ⓐ Ⓑ Ⓒ Ⓓ 8. Ⓐ Ⓑ Ⓒ Ⓓ 12. Ⓐ Ⓑ Ⓒ Ⓓ 16. Ⓐ Ⓑ Ⓒ Ⓓ 20. Ⓐ Ⓑ Ⓒ Ⓓ

CHAPTER 5

Diagnostic Examination

You'll Find Answers to These Questions

Can I answer high school entrance examination questions in the time allowed?
How well can I do on each kind of question?

CAN I ANSWER HIGH SCHOOL ENTRANCE EXAMINATION QUESTIONS IN THE TIME ALLOWED?

The way to find out is to try. The diagnostic examination offers a sampling of question styles and timing from both the SSAT and the ISEE. Follow the directions precisely and see how far you get. This will give you a feeling for the pacing you must aim for.

Synonyms

20 QUESTIONS • TIME—10 MINUTES

Directions: Choose the word or phrase closest in meaning to the CAPITALIZED word.

1. INTERMITTENTLY
   (A) constantly
   (B) annually
   (C) using intermediaries
   (D) at irregular intervals

2. DECEPTION
   (A) secrets
   (B) fraud
   (C) mistrust
   (D) hatred

3. ACCLAIM
   (A) amazement
   (B) laughter
   (C) booing
   (D) applause

4. ERECT
   (A) paint
   (B) design
   (C) destroy
   (D) construct

5. RELISH
   (A) care
   (B) speed
   (C) amusement
   (D) enjoy

6. FORTNIGHT
   (A) two weeks
   (B) one week
   (C) two months
   (D) one month

7. IMPOSE
   (A) disguise
   (B) escape
   (C) require
   (D) tax

8. ALIAS
   (A) enemy
   (B) sidekick
   (C) hero
   (D) other name

9. ITINERANT
   (A) traveling
   (B) shrewd
   (C) insurance
   (D) aggressive

10. AMPLE
    (A) plentiful
    (B) enthusiastic
    (C) well-shaped
    (D) fat

11. STENCH
    (A) puddle of slimy water
    (B) pile of debris
    (C) foul odor
    (D) dead animal

12. SULLEN
    (A) grayish yellow
    (B) soaking wet
    (C) very dirty
    (D) angrily silent

13. TERSE
(A) pointed
(B) trivial
(C) nervous
(D) lengthy

14. INCREMENT
(A) an improvisation
(B) an increase
(C) feces
(D) specification

15. MISCONSTRUED
(A) followed directions
(B) led astray
(C) acting to supervise
(D) interpreted erroneously

16. VESTIGE
(A) design
(B) trace
(C) strap
(D) robe

17. CAPITULATE
(A) surrender
(B) execute
(C) finance
(D) retreat

18. EXTENUATING
(A) mitigating
(B) opposing
(C) incriminating
(D) distressing

19. SUBSERVIENT
(A) underestimated
(B) underhanded
(C) subordinate
(D) evasive

20. COLLUSION
(A) decision
(B) insinuation
(C) connivance
(D) conflict

STOP

END OF SECTION. IF YOU HAVE ANY TIME LEFT, GO OVER YOUR WORK IN THIS SECTION ONLY. DO NOT WORK IN ANY OTHER SECTION OF THE TEST.

Verbal Analogies

20 QUESTIONS • TIME—10 MINUTES

Directions: Find the relationships among the words. Select the answer choice that best completes the meaning of the sentence.

1. red is to pink as black is to
   (A) beige
   (B) white
   (C) dark
   (D) gray

2. youth is to young as maturity is to
   (A) people
   (B) parents
   (C) grandmother
   (D) old

3. one is to two as three is to
   (A) two
   (B) five
   (C) six
   (D) thirty

4. light is to lamp as heat is to
   (A) furnace
   (B) light
   (C) sun
   (D) room

5. week is to month as season is to
   (A) year
   (B) spring
   (C) harvest
   (D) planting

6. square is to circle as rectangle is to
   (A) round
   (B) triangle
   (C) oval
   (D) cube

7. choir is to director as team is to
   (A) sport
   (B) coach
   (C) player
   (D) athlete

8. sand is to beach as black dirt is to
   (A) earth
   (B) plants
   (C) water
   (D) farm

9. table is to leg as automobile is to
   (A) wheel
   (B) axle
   (C) door
   (D) fuel

10. arouse is to pacify as agitate is to
    (A) smooth
    (B) ruffle
    (C) understand
    (D) ignore

11. margarine is to butter as
    (A) cream is to milk
    (B) lace is to cotton
    (C) nylon is to silk
    (D) egg is to chicken

12. woodsman is to axe as
    (A) carpenter is to saw
    (B) mechanic is to wrench
    (C) soldier is to gun
    (D) draftsman is to ruler

13. worried is to hysterical as
(A) hot is to cold
(B) happy is to ecstatic
(C) lonely is to crowded
(D) happy is to serious

14. control is to order as
(A) joke is to clown
(B) teacher is to pupil
(C) disorder is to climax
(D) anarchy is to chaos

15. horse is to foal as
(A) donkey is to ass
(B) cow is to calf
(C) bull is to steer
(D) whinny is to moo

16. sleep is to fatigue as
(A) water is to thirst
(B) rest is to weary
(C) pillow is to blanket
(D) fatigue is to run

17. island is to ocean as
(A) hill is to stream
(B) forest is to valley
(C) oasis is to desert
(D) tree is to field

18. drama is to director as
(A) class is to principal
(B) movie is to scenario
(C) actor is to playwright
(D) magazine is to editor

19. request is to demand as
(A) reply is to respond
(B) inquire is to ask
(C) wish is to crave
(D) seek is to hide

20. wood is to carve as
(A) tree is to sway
(B) paper is to burn
(C) clay is to mold
(D) pipe is to blow

STOP

END OF SECTION. IF YOU HAVE ANY TIME LEFT, GO OVER YOUR WORK IN THIS SECTION ONLY. DO NOT WORK IN ANY OTHER SECTION OF THE TEST.

19

Sentence Completions

20 QUESTIONS • TIME—10 MINUTES

Directions: Each question is made up of a sentence with one or two blanks. The sentences with one blank indicate that one word is missing. The sentences with two blanks indicate that two words are missing. Each sentence is followed by four choices. On the answer sheet, mark the letter of the choice that will best complete the meaning of the sentence as a whole.

1. Although fortunetellers claim to _____ future happenings, there is no scientific evidence of their _____.

(A) cloud ... ability
(B) effect ... knowledge
(C) foretell ... fees
(D) predict ... accuracy

2. Great ideas have _____ youth: they are _____.

(A) no ... petrified
(B) eternal ... immortal
(C) constant ... ephemeral
(D) little ... frivolous

3. Each human relationship is unique, and the lovers who think there never was a love like theirs are _____.

(A) foolish
(B) blind
(C) prejudiced
(D) right

4. Rats give some _____ as scavengers, but this is over-balanced by their _____ activities.

(A) help ... useful
(B) service ... harmful
(C) problems ... nocturnal
(D) trouble ... breeding

5. Ancient societies gave authority to those who knew and preserved _____, for the idea of what was right lay in the past.

(A) order
(B) law
(C) intelligence
(D) tradition

6. The rare desert rains often come in _____, causing loss of life and property; thus, people living in an oasis think of rain with _____.

(A) floods ... longing
(B) torrents ... terror
(C) sprinkles ... fear
(D) winter ... snow

7. His admirers were not _____, for his essays were not widely known.

(A) respected
(B) numerous
(C) ardent
(D) interested

8. Archeologists found ruins of temples and palaces, but no _____; it was as though these people never _____.

(A) food ... lived
(B) tombs ... died
(C) plans ... built
(D) monasteries ... worshipped

9. Safe driving prevents _____ and the endless _____ of knowing you have caused others pain.

(A) disease ... reminder
(B) tragedy ... remorse
(C) accidents ... hope
(D) lawsuits ... expense

10. A true amateur plays because he _____ the game and will not cheat because that would _____ the game.

(A) studies ... lose
(B) understands ... improve
(C) knows ... forfeit
(D) loves ... degrade

11. Companies have found it pays to have _____ handy when a meeting is likely to be _____.
(A) food … prolonged
(B) secretaries … enjoyable
(C) telephones … successful
(D) money … interesting

12. He _____ apart, for he prefers _____ to the company of others.
(A) lives … books
(B) stays … throngs
(C) remains … vivacity
(D) dwells … solitude

13. The Constitutional duty to "take care that the laws be faithfully executed" makes the President the head of law _____.
(A) development
(B) interpretation
(C) education
(D) enforcement

14. A reduction of the work week to four days would certainly _____ the _____ industry.
(A) destroy … automobile
(B) stimulate … steel
(C) improve … electrical
(D) benefit … leisure

15. History tells us it took Athens less than a generation to change from a champion of _____ into a ruthless _____.
(A) democracy … republic
(B) freedom … tyrant
(C) independence … commonwealth
(D) dictatorship … liberator

16. The society was not _____ and required much outside aid.
(A) philanthropic
(B) destitute
(C) democratic
(D) self-sufficient

17. The _____ climate of the country _____ the delicate electronic equipment.
(A) intolerable … restored
(B) dry … vaporized
(C) changeable … demoralized
(D) humid … corroded

18. The value of _____ science to modern progress is _____.
(A) research … unimportant
(B) physical … unquestionable
(C) medical … unlikely
(D) statistical … unreliable

19. The final end of a nonadapting society is the same as for a nonadapting animal: _____.
(A) admiration
(B) resignation
(C) extinction
(D) immortality

20. Some temperamental actresses fail to understand that a director's criticism is aimed at their _____ and not at their _____.
(A) weaknesses … conduct
(B) stupidity … graciousness
(C) performance … personality
(D) prosperity … inability

STOP

END OF SECTION. IF YOU HAVE ANY TIME LEFT, GO OVER YOUR WORK IN THIS SECTION ONLY. DO NOT WORK IN ANY OTHER SECTION OF THE TEST.

Reading Comprehension

22 QUESTIONS • TIME—15 MINUTES

Directions: Read each passage and answer the questions that follow it.

If you are asked the color of the sky on a fair day in summer, your answer will most probably be "blue." This answer is only partially correct. Blue sky near the horizon is not the same kind of blue as it is straight overhead. Look at the sky some fine day and you will find that the blue sky near the horizon is slightly greenish. As your eye moves upward toward the *zenith*, you will find that the blue changes into pure blue, and finally shades into a violet-blue overhead.

Have you heard the story of a farmer who objected to the color of the distant hills in the artist's picture? He said to the artist, "Why do you make those hills blue? They are green. I've been over there and I know!"

The artist asked him to do a little experiment. "Bend over and look at the hills between your legs." As the farmer did this, the artist asked, "Now what color are the hills?"

The farmer looked again, then he stood up and looked. "By gosh, they turned blue!" he said.

It is quite possible that you have looked at many colors that you did not really recognize. Sky is not just blue; it is many kinds of blue. Grass is not plain green; it may be one of several varieties of green. A red-brick wall frequently is not pure red. It may vary from yellow-orange to violet-red in color, but to the unseeing eye it is just red brick.

1. The title that best expresses the ideas of this passage is
   (A) The Summer Sky
   (B) Artists vs. Farmers
   (C) Recognizing Colors
   (D) Blue Hills

2. At the zenith, the sky is usually
   (A) violet-blue
   (B) violet-red
   (C) greenish-blue
   (D) yellow-orange

3. The author suggests that
   (A) farmers are colorblind
   (B) perceived color varies
   (C) brick walls should be painted pure red
   (D) some artists use poor color combinations

4. The word *zenith* in the first paragraph probably refers to
   (A) a color
   (B) a point directly overhead
   (C) a point on the horizon
   (D) the hills

While the Europeans were still creeping cautiously along their coasts, Polynesians were making trips between Hawaii and New Zealand, a distance of 3,800 miles, in frail canoes. These fearless sailors of the Pacific explored every island in their vast domain without even the simplest of navigational tools.

In the daytime, the Polynesians guided their craft by the position of the sun, the trend of the waves and wind, and the flight of seabirds.

Stars were used during long trips between island groups. Youths studying navigation were taught to view the heavens as a cylinder on which the highways of navigation were marked. An invisible line bisected the sky from the North Star to the Southern Cross.

In addition to single canoes, the Polynesians often used twin canoes for trans-Pacific voyages. The two boats were fastened together by canopied platforms that shielded passengers from sun and rain. Such crafts were remarkably seaworthy and could accommodate 60 to 80 people, in addition to water, food, and domestic animals. Some of these vessels had as many as three masts.

These Pacific *mariners* used paddles to propel and steer their canoes. The steering paddle was so important that it was always given a personal name. Polynesian legends not only recite the names of the canoe and the hero who discovered a new island but also the name of the steering paddle he used.

5. The best title for this selection is

(A) European Sailors

(B) The History of the Pacific Ocean

(C) The Study of Navigation

(D) Early Polynesian Navigation

6. The Polynesians made trips to

(A) New Zealand

(B) the Atlantic

(C) the Southern Cross

(D) Europe

7. The word *mariner* means

(A) propeller

(B) seaman

(C) paddle

(D) navigation

8. This passage suggests that the Polynesians

(A) trained seabirds to guide their canoes

(B) had seen a line in the sky that was invisible to others

(C) used a primitive telescope to view the heavens

(D) were astronomers as well as explorers

The seasonal comings and goings of birds have excited the attention and wonder of all sorts of people in all ages and places. The oracles of Greece and the augurs of Rome wove them into ancient mythology. They are spoken of in the Books of Job and Jeremiah.

Nevertheless, it has been difficult for many to believe that small birds, especially, are capable of migratory journeys. Aristotle was convinced that the birds that wintered in Greece were not new arrivals, but merely Greece's summer birds in winter dress. According to a belief persisting in some parts of the world to this day, swallows and swifts do not migrate, but spend the winter in hibernation. (Swifts and swallows *do* migrate, just as most other northern hemisphere birds do.) Another old and charming, but untrue, legend enlists the aid of the stork in getting small birds to and from winter quarters: Small birds are said to hitch rides on the European stork's back.

It is clear why northern-hemisphere birds fly south in the fall; they go to assure themselves of food and a more favorable climate for the winter months. It is also clear where most of the migrants come from and where they go. Years of bird-banding have disclosed the routes of the main migratory species.

But there are other aspects of migration that remain, for all our powers of scientific investigation, as puzzling and mysterious to modern man as to the ancients. Why do migrant birds come north each spring? Why don't they simply stay in the warm tropics the whole twelve months of the year? What determines the moment of departure for north or south? Above all, how do birds—especially species like the remarkable golden plover, which flies huge distances directly across trackless ocean wastes—find their way?

9. The best title for this selection would be

(A) The Solution of an Ancient Problem

(B) Mysterious Migrations

(C) The Secret of the Plover

(D) Aristotle's Theory

10. Bird-banding has revealed

(A) the kind of food birds eat

(B) why the birds prefer the tropics in the summer

(C) why birds leave at a certain time

(D) the routes taken by different types of birds

GO ON TO THE NEXT PAGE

11. Swallows and swifts

(A) remain in Greece all year

(B) change their plumage in winter

(C) hibernate during the winter

(D) fly south for the winter

12. The article proves that

(A) nature still has secrets that man has not fathomed

(B) the solutions of Aristotle are accepted by modern science

(C) we live in an age that has lost all interest in bird lore

(D) man has no means of solving the problems of bird migration

Using new tools and techniques, scientists, almost unnoticed, are remaking the world of plants. They have already remodeled 65 sorts of flowers, fruits, vegetables, and trees, giving us among other things tobacco that resists disease, cantaloupes that are immune to the blight, and lettuce with crisper leaves. The chief new tool they are using is colchicine, a poisonous drug, which has astounding effects upon growth and upon heredity. It creates new varieties with astonishing frequency, whereas such mutations occur but rarely in nature. Colchicine has thrown new light on the fascinating jobs of the plant hunters. The Department of Agriculture sends agents all over the world to find plants native to other lands that can be grown here and are superior to those already here. Scientists have crossed these foreign plants with those at home, thereby adding to our farm crops many desirable characteristics. The colchicine technique has enormously facilitated their work, because hybrids so often can be made fertile and because it takes so few generations of plants now to build a new variety with the qualities desired.

13. The title that best expresses the ideas of the paragraph is

(A) Plant Growth and Heredity

(B) New Plants for Old

(C) Remodeling Plant Life

(D) A More Abundant World

14. Mutation in plant life results in

(A) diseased plants

(B) hybrids

(C) new varieties

(D) fertility

15. Colchicine speeds the improvement of plant species because it

(A) makes possible the use of foreign plants

(B) makes use of natural mutations

(C) creates new varieties very quickly

(D) can be used with 65 different vegetables, fruits, and flowers

16. According to the passage, colchicine is

(A) a poisonous drug

(B) a blight

(C) a kind of plant hunter

(D) a hybrid plant

Italy is a relatively small country. Its entire land area could be tucked into the borders of California, with plenty of room to spare, but Italy has a population of more than 45,000,000 people. The country is 760 miles long and, at most points, only 100 to 150 miles wide.

Italy's southern, eastern, and western borders are surrounded by water, making it a peninsula. To the north it is separated from France, Switzerland, Germany, and Yugoslavia by the towering mountain chain known as the Alps.

About two thirds of the Italian peninsula is mountainous. In addition to the Alps, there are the Apennines, which run almost the entire length of the country. This mountain chain is marked by the highly fertile river valleys that run across it.

Italy's climate is similar to that of Florida or California, except that winters in the northern part of the country tend to be colder than in either of these states. The result is a long, productive growing season in much of the country.

Tourists are often surprised at the full use to which the Italians put their soil. Because they are crowded in a small area, they cannot afford to let any land go to waste, and the Italians are accomplished farmers. They have cultivated the fertile valleys and banks of the rivers as well as the northern plains regions. Mountainous areas have even been utilized by cutting terraces into the steep slopes. Nearly half the population of Italy lives off the soil.

17. Which statement can be supported by the information in this passage?

(A) Italy is separated from the rest of Europe by natural boundaries.

(B) All of the Italian peninsula is a mountainous region.

(C) Italy is a rather large country with a small population.

(D) Few Italians cultivate the soil.

18. The winter climate of northern Italy is

(A) similar to that of Texas

(B) comparable to that of Switzerland

(C) colder than winters in Florida

(D) similar to the winters in California

19. The Italian peninsula

(A) has a larger land area than California

(B) is 760 miles long and about 150 miles wide

(C) is longer than Florida

(D) has plenty of room to spare

20. The Apennines are

(A) river valleys

(B) plains

(C) mountains

(D) peninsulas

21. Italy's northern border is formed by

(A) rivers

(B) the Apennines

(C) water

(D) the Alps

22. The northern plains and other flat areas of Italy make up how much of its land area?

(A) about half

(B) two thirds

(C) one third

(D) most of it

STOP

END OF SECTION. IF YOU HAVE ANY TIME LEFT, GO OVER YOUR WORK IN THIS SECTION ONLY. DO NOT WORK IN ANY OTHER SECTION OF THE TEST.

Quantitative Ability

30 QUESTIONS • TIME—30 MINUTES

Directions: Choose the correct answer to each question.

1. Which square has half of its area shaded?

(A) 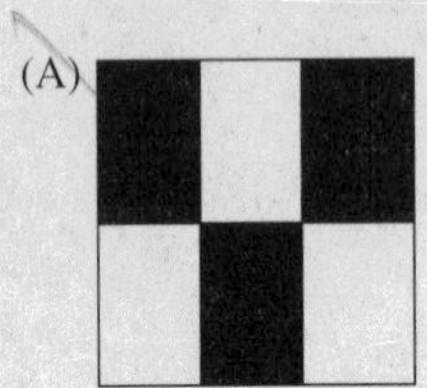

(B) 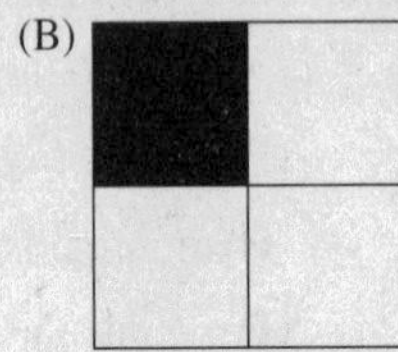

(C) 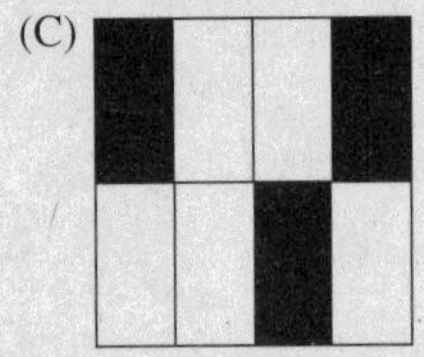

(D) 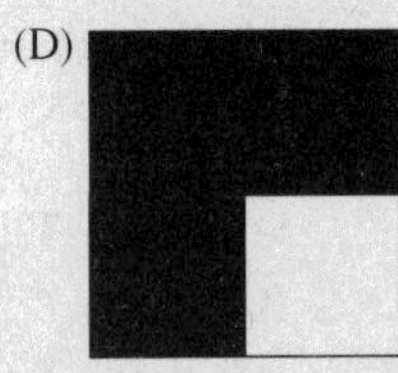

2. If 2 packages of cookies are enough for 10 children, how many will be needed for 15 children?
   (A) 6
   (B) 5
   (C) 4
   (D) 3

3. Which is equal to 9?
   (A) 4×5
   (B) 9×0
   (C) 9×1
   (D) 3×6

4. Jeff earns 12 dollars a week. Which of the following statements tells how many dollars he will earn in 5 weeks?
   (A) $12 - 5$
   (B) $12 \div 5$
   (C) $12 + 5$
   (D) 12×5

5. The distance from City X to San Francisco is 3 times the distance from City X to Chicago. How many miles away from City X is San Francisco? To solve this problem, what else do you need to know?
   (A) The distance from Chicago to San Francisco
   (B) The distance from City X to Chicago
   (C) The city of origination
   (D) Nothing else

6. If an odd number is subtracted from an odd number, which of the following could be the answer?
   (A) 1
   (B) 2
   (C) 7
   (D) 9

7. If $7 \times 6 = Y$, which is true?
   (A) $Y \div 7 = 6$
   (B) $Y \times 7 = 6$
   (C) $7 \div Y = 6$
   (D) $Y + 6 = 7$

8. $759 - 215 = \square$

   Which is closest to $\square$?
   (A) 200
   (B) 300
   (C) 400
   (D) 500

9. Edna bought 4 packages of balloons with 6 in each package, and 2 packages with 3 large balloons in each. How many balloons did Edna buy?
   (A) 10
   (B) 15
   (C) 26
   (D) 30

10. $a\overline{)4,028}$ with quotient 1

What number is *a*?

(A) 0

(B) 1

(C) 7

(D) 4,028

11. 7 + □ = 15

Which number is equal to □?

(A) 15 ÷ 7

(B) 15 − 7

(C) 15 × 7

(D) 15 + 7

12. Colleen is 14 years old. She babysits for $1.50 an hour. Yesterday she babysat for $3\frac{1}{2}$ hours. Which shows how much she earned?

(A) 14 × $1.50

(B) $2 \times 3\frac{1}{2}$

(C) $3\frac{1}{2}$ × $1.50

(D) $(3\frac{1}{2} \times 2)$ × $1.50

13.

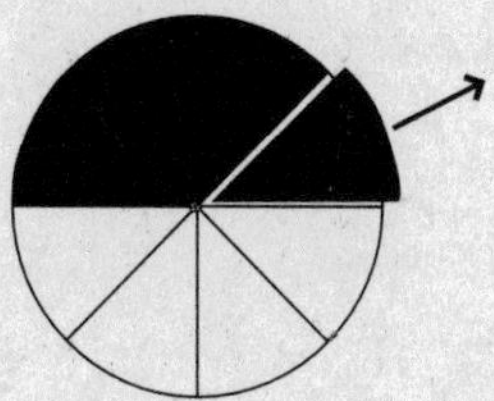

Which of the following describes the picture?

(A) $\frac{4}{8} - \frac{1}{8}$

(B) $\frac{4}{8} + \frac{1}{8}$

(C) $\frac{4}{12} - \frac{1}{12}$

(D) $\frac{4}{12} + \frac{1}{12}$

14. 8,862 < 8, ___62

What number should be inserted to make the above statement correct?

(A) 9

(B) 8

(C) 7

(D) Not enough information given

15. A fence is being installed around the 156-meter perimeter of a swimming pool. How many posts will be used if they are spaced 12 meters apart?

(A) 11

(B) 12

(C) 13

(D) 14

16. What is 28,973 rounded to the nearest thousand?

(A) 30,000

(B) 29,000

(C) 28,900

(D) 28,000

17. The bakery received a shipment of 170 cupcakes that will be sold by the box. If each box holds 12 cupcakes, approximately how many boxes will be needed?

(A) 8

(B) 14

(C) 20

(D) 25

GO ON TO THE NEXT PAGE

18.

What time will it be in $3\frac{1}{2}$ hours?

(A) 9:00

(B) 9:15

(C) 9:30

(D) 9:45

19. Which of these number sentences is not true?

(A) $\frac{3}{3} = \frac{5}{5}$

(B) $\frac{5}{5} = \frac{6}{6}$

(C) $\frac{8}{8} = 1$

(D) $\frac{7}{8} = \frac{8}{7}$

20.

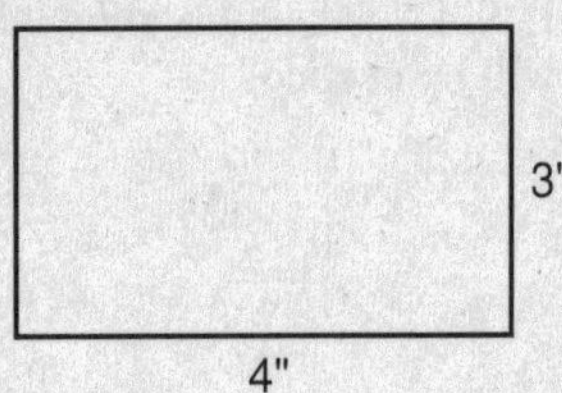

What is the area of this figure?

(A) 1 sq. inch

(B) 7 sq. inches

(C) 12 sq. inches

(D) 14 sq. inches

21. In order to make $\frac{7}{8}$ cup of salad dressing with our recipe, you add $\frac{1}{4}$ cup of vinegar to the oil. How much oil will you use?

(A) $\frac{3}{8}$ cup

(B) $\frac{5}{8}$ cup

(C) $\frac{6}{8}$ cup

(D) $\frac{3}{4}$ cup

22. Which digit is in the thousandths place?

A BC
↓ ↓↓
5,000.072

(A) only A

(B) only B

(C) only C

(D) B and C

23. Which is not true?

(A) $\frac{6}{8} = \frac{3}{4}$

(B) $\frac{2}{3} = \frac{6}{12}$

(C) $\frac{3}{4} = \frac{12}{16}$

(D) $\frac{3}{9} = \frac{6}{18}$

24. Which sequence of fractions is arranged in order of least to greatest?

(A) $\frac{1}{3}, \frac{1}{18}, \frac{1}{11}, \frac{1}{7}$

(B) $\frac{1}{18}, \frac{1}{11}, \frac{1}{7}, \frac{1}{3}$

(C) $\frac{1}{3}, \frac{1}{7}, \frac{1}{11}, \frac{1}{18}$

(D) $\frac{1}{18}, \frac{1}{7}, \frac{1}{11}, \frac{1}{3}$

25. In which of the following numbers does the digit 6 have a value 10 times greater than the value of the 6 in 603?

(A) 60

(B) 600

(C) 6,000

(D) 60,000

26. Which quotient would be approximately 5?

(A) $20\overline{)205}$

(B) $20\overline{)500}$

(C) $20\overline{)1000}$

(D) $200\overline{)1005}$

27.

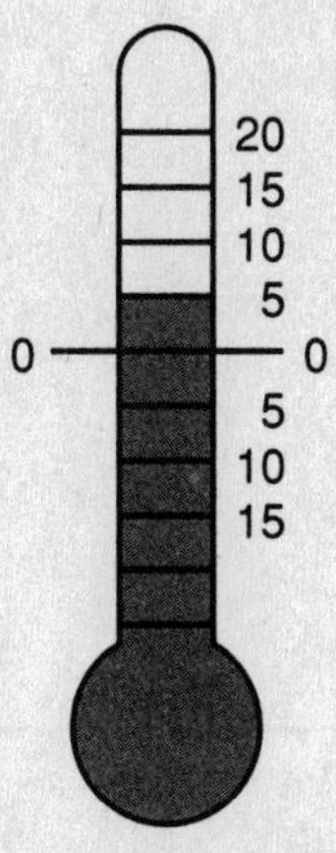

If the temperature decreases by 15 degrees below that shown on the thermometer, what will the new temperature be?

(A) 20°

(B) 10°

(C) –10°

(D) –20°

28. $5 \times (2 + x) = 15$

What number is x?

(A) 1

(B) 2

(C) 4

(D) 5

29. Which of the following has a quotient that is NOT smaller than the dividend?

(A) $0 \div 8$

(B) $1 \div 8$

(C) $2 \div 8$

(D) $8 \div 8$

30.

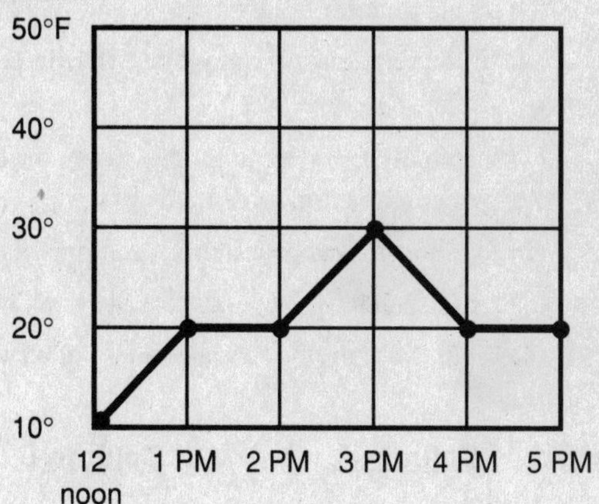

Which of the following is shown by the graph?

(A) There was no change in temperature between 1 and 2 PM.

(B) There was no change in temperature between 3 and 4 PM.

(C) The highest temperature occurred at 12 noon.

(D) The lowest temperature occurred at 5 PM.

STOP

END OF SECTION. IF YOU HAVE ANY TIME LEFT, GO OVER YOUR WORK IN THIS SECTION ONLY. DO NOT WORK IN ANY OTHER SECTION OF THE TEST.

Quantitative Comparisons

20 QUESTIONS • TIME—20 MINUTES

Directions: For each of the following questions, two quantities are given—one in Column A, the other in Column B. Compare the two quantities and mark your answer sheet as follows:

(A) if the quantity in Column A is greater

(B) if the quantity in Column B is greater

(C) if the quantities are equal

(D) if the relationship cannot be determined from the information given.

Notes:

(1) Information concerning one or both of the compared quantities will be centered above the two columns for some items.

(2) Symbols that appear in both columns represent the same thing in Column A as in Column B.

(3) Letters such as *x*, *n*, and *k* are symbols for real numbers.

(4) Figures are drawn to scale unless otherwise noted.

	Column A	Column B
1. $2x + 3 = 5$; $3y + 7 = 10$	x	y
2. $\frac{x}{36} = \frac{1}{3}$	$\frac{4}{x}$	$\frac{1}{3}$
3. x is an integer	x	$\frac{x}{-1}$
4.	Number of seconds in one day	Number of minutes in April
5. $9 < x < 10$; $9 < y < 11$	x	y
6.	Area of a triangle with base 5 and height 7	Twice the area of a rectangle with a base 5 and height 7
7. ABCD is a parallelogram	AB	DC
8. $4 \cdot a \cdot 4 \cdot 4 = 3 \cdot 3 \cdot 3 \cdot 3$	a	3

	Column A	Column B
9.	A single discount of 10%	Two successive discounts of 5% and 5%
10.	$\sqrt{49}+\sqrt{16}$	$\sqrt{65}$

11. The average age of Alan, Bob, and Carl is 17.

Column A	Column B
The sum of Alan's age and Bob's age	The sum of Alan's age and Carl's age

12.

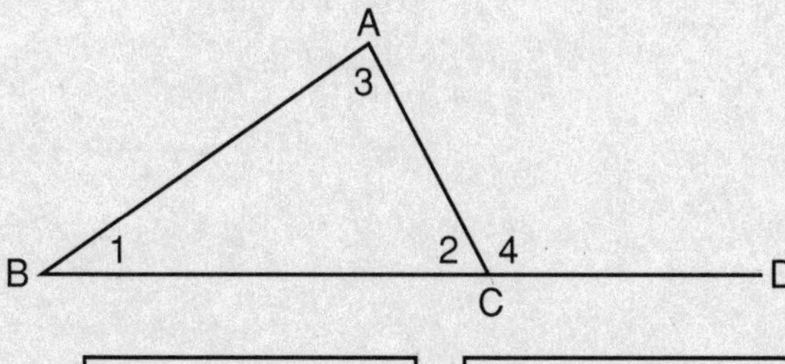

Column A	Column B
$\angle 1 + \angle 2 + \angle 3$	$\angle 2 + \angle 4$

13.

$$4 < a < b$$
$$4 \le b \le 6$$

Column A	Column B
a	b

14. Jack's salary is $\frac{3}{4}$ of Jim's salary and Joe's salary is $\frac{3}{2}$ of Jack's salary.

Column A	Column B
Jim's salary	Joe's salary

15.

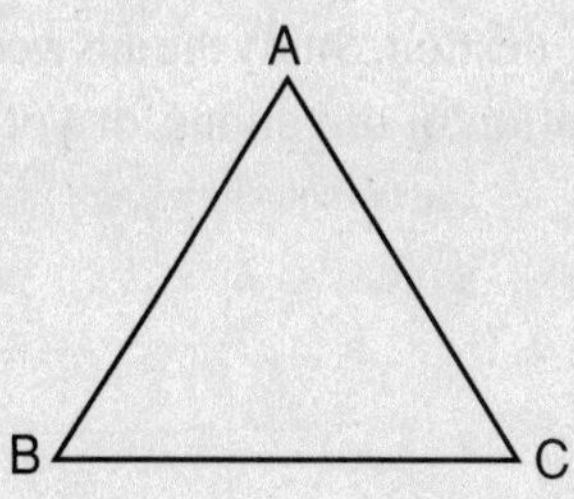

$AB = AC$

$\angle A = 60°$

Column A	Column B
AB	BC

16. $a > b > c > 0$

Column A	Column B
$\frac{a}{b}$	$\frac{a}{c}$

	Column A	Column B
17.	The total area of a cube with edge 6	6 times the total area of a cube with edge 2
18.	.5%	$\frac{1}{2}$
19.	18 • 563 • 10	12 • 563 • 16
20.	The number of posts needed for a fence 100 feet long if the posts are placed 10 feet apart	10 posts

STOP

END OF SECTION. IF YOU HAVE ANY TIME LEFT, GO OVER YOUR WORK IN THIS SECTION ONLY. DO NOT WORK IN ANY OTHER SECTION OF THE TEST.

HOW WELL CAN I DO ON EACH KIND OF QUESTION?

Check your answers against the correct answers on the answer key. Calculate your percentage score on each type of question. Study the answer explanations to see if your scores are influenced by carelessness, misinterpretation of directions, or your age and grade level.

DIAGNOSTIC EXAMINATION

Answer Key

SYNONYMS

1. D	5. D	9. A	13. A	17. A
2. B	6. A	10. A	14. B	18. A
3. D	7. C	11. C	15. D	19. C
4. D	8. D	12. D	16. B	20. C

VERBAL ANALOGIES

1. D	5. A	9. A	13. B	17. C
2. D	6. C	10. A	14. D	18. D
3. C	7. B	11. C	15. B	19. C
4. A	8. D	12. A	16. A	20. C

SENTENCE COMPLETIONS

1. D	5. D	9. B	13. D	17. D
2. B	6. B	10. D	14. D	18. B
3. D	7. B	11. A	15. B	19. C
4. B	8. B	12. D	16. D	20. C

READING COMPREHENSION

1. C	6. A	11. D	15. C	19. B
2. A	7. B	12. A	16. A	20. C
3. B	8. D	13. C	17. A	21. D
4. B	9. B	14. C	18. C	22. C
5. D	10. D			

QUANTITATIVE ABILITY

1. A	7. A	13. A	19. D	25. C
2. D	8. D	14. A	20. C	26. D
3. C	9. D	15. C	21. B	27. C
4. D	10. D	16. B	22. C	28. A
5. B	11. B	17. B	23. B	29. A
6. B	12. C	18. B	24. B	30. A

QUANTITATIVE COMPARISONS

1. C	5. D	9. A	13. D	17. A
2. C	6. B	10. A	14. B	18. B
3. D	7. C	11. D	15. C	19. B
4. A	8. B	12. C	16. B	20. A

Answer Explanations

SYNONYMS

1. **(D)** That which happens INTERMITTENTLY stops and starts again at intervals, or pauses from time to time. A pedestrian crossing light that is activated by a push button says "WALK" and "DON'T WALK" intermittently. You may see a relationship to *intermission,* which is a pause between parts of a performance.
2. **(B)** One who practices DECEPTION willfully tries to make another believe that which is not true to mislead or defraud. The verb on which this noun is based is *deceive.*
3. **(D)** To ACCLAIM is to greet with loud applause and approval. The winners of the World Series returned to the city to wild acclaim.
4. **(D)** To ERECT is to raise, construct, set up, or assemble. The adjective *erect* describes that which is vertical and straight up. You can see the relationship of verb and adjective.
5. **(D)** If you RELISH something, you enjoy it. You may be more familiar with the noun, with the relish that you put on your hot dog to make it more appetizing and to add to your enjoyment.
6. **(A)** A FORTNIGHT (fourteen nights) is a period of two weeks.
7. **(C)** To IMPOSE a tax is to place a tax upon the taxpayers and to require that it be paid. Be careful here. The *tax* (noun) is the object of to *impose* (verb), not the definition or a synonym.
8. **(D)** An ALIAS is an assumed name. The alias may be a pen name or a stage name, or may be a false name taken on for purposes of disguise.
9. **(A)** An ITINERANT peddler travels from place to place, selling his or her wares at each stop. The itinerant may follow an itinerary, a detailed outline for the proposed journey.
10. **(A)** That which is AMPLE is large, spacious, abundant, or plentiful. When referring to a figure, *ample* may imply *fat,* but the meaning of the word *ample* is simply *more than enough.*
11. **(C)** Stagnant water or a decaying dead animal may have a STENCH or foul odor. STENCH means *stink.*
12. **(D)** A SULLEN person is resentful, unsociable, and gloomy.
13. **(A)** TERSE means *concise* and *succinct.* It is the opposite of "lengthy" and has nothing at all to do with nerves or tension.
14. **(B)** An INCREMENT is a specified increase, usually a small one. Sometimes trying to figure out the meanings of words by looking at their roots just doesn't work. This word has nothing to do with "excrement" even though it looks like it.
15. **(D)** To MISCONSTRUE is to *misinterpret.* "Word arithmetic" works well with this synonym question. The prefix "mis" means *wrong;* the root is the same root as "construct," so to *misconstrue* is to *build up wrong* in one's mind.
16. **(B)** A VESTIGE is a *trace.* This is a difficult word, one that is picked up in the course of wide reading.
17. **(A)** To CAPITULATE is to *give in, give up,* or *surrender.* Capitulation is more a total act than a mere retreat.
18. **(A)** EXTENUATING is drawing out and thereby making thin or weaker. In sentencing a guilty party, the judge may consider extenuating circumstances, details that make the guilt thinner or weaker. If there are extenuating or mitigating circumstances, the sentence may be lighter. If you missed this question, do not be upset. Both the word and its definition are very high-level words.
19. **(C)** SUBSERVIENT—serving under—means *inferior, subordinate,* or *submissive.*
20. **(C)** COLLUSION is a *conspiracy,* a *secret agreement,* or a *connivance.* Use of this word implies an illegal goal.

VERBAL ANALOGIES

1. **(D)** The relationship is intensity or degree. PINK is a muted form of RED; GRAY is a muted form of BLACK. *White* is the opposite of *black,* while *dark* is one of *black's* characteristics.
2. **(D)** YOUTH is a noun form, YOUNG an adjective. Both refer to the early years. MATURITY is a noun form, OLD an adjective. *Maturity* and *old* refer to the later years of existence.
3. **(C)** The relationship between the first two terms cannot be determined until you look at the third term and the choices. At first you might think, "two follows one, so four should follow three." The problem is that "four" is not offered as an answer choice. Of the choices given, SIX is most related to THREE, since SIX is *twice* THREE. Looking back at the first pair, you can see that TWO is *twice* ONE. Since the "times two" relationship applies to both sides of the proportion, (C) is the correct answer.
4. **(A)** The relationship is effect/cause. LIGHT is produced by a LAMP: HEAT is produced by a FURNACE. The *sun* also produces heat, but the *sun* is a natural source. *Lamp* in the original pair is an artificial source of *light; furnace,* the *best* answer, is an artificial source of *heat.*
5. **(A)** The relationship is part to whole. WEEK is part of MONTH; SEASON is part of YEAR.
6. **(C)** A SQUARE is angular, a CIRCLE rounded; a RECTANGLE is angular, an OVAL rounded. You might say "angular is to rounded as angular is to rounded."
7. **(B)** The relationship is that of object to actor. The DIRECTOR leads the CHOIR; the COACH leads the TEAM.
8. **(D)** The relationship is one of characteristic. SAND is the soil that is characteristic of the BEACH; BLACK DIRT is the soil that is characteristic of a productive FARM.
9. **(A)** This is a true functional relationship. The TABLE is supported by LEGS; the AUTOMOBILE is supported by WHEELS. It is important to narrow to the functional relationship in order to eliminate (B) and (C). Use of the part/whole relationship would yield too many correct answers.
10. **(A)** AROUSE and PACIFY are antonyms; AGITATE and SMOOTH are antonyms. If you know the meanings of the words, this is an easy analogy question. *Ruffle* is a synonym for *agitate.*
11. **(C)** The relationship is that of artificial to real or substitute to the real thing. MARGARINE is imitation BUTTER; NYLON is imitation SILK. *Lace* is often made from *cotton* but does not substitute for it.
12. **(A)** The relationship is a very specific functional one. The WOODSMAN uses an AXE to cut; the CARPENTER uses a SAW to cut. In all the other choices we are offered a worker and a tool of his trade, but none of these tools is used specifically for cutting.
13. **(B)** The relationship is one of degree. One who is WORRIED may become HYSTERICAL (overwhelmed by fear); one who is HAPPY may become ECSTATIC (overwhelmed by joy).
14. **(D)** The relationship is one of cause and effect. CONTROL of a group results in ORDER; ANARCHY (lack of government or control) results in CHAOS (disorder).
15. **(B)** The relationship is one of degree (large/small) or, more specifically, that of parent to child. The HORSE is the parent of the FOAL; the COW is the parent of the CALF. *Donkey* and *ass* are synonyms. A *steer* is a *bull* raised for its meat.
16. **(A)** The best way to verbalize this relationship is to call it that of the cure to its ailment. SLEEP cures FATIGUE; WATER cures THIRST. Beware of the grammatical inconsistency in (B). *Rest* cures "weariness," not *weary.* The relationship of (D) is effect to cause.
17. **(C)** This is a variation of the part-to-whole relationship. An ISLAND is a small body of land within an OCEAN and wholly surrounded by it; an OASIS is a small, green, fertile spot within a large arid expanse of DESERT and wholly surrounded by it.
18. **(D)** The relationship is that of actor to object. The DIRECTOR is responsible for the production of a DRAMA; the EDITOR is responsible for the production of a MAGAZINE. The *principal* is responsible for an entire school, not just a *class.* Responsibility for a single class rests with a teacher.

19. **(C)** The relationship is one of degree. To DEMAND is to REQUEST very strongly; to CRAVE is to WISH for very strongly. The terms in (A) are synonyms, in (D) antonyms, and in (B) cause and effect.

20. **(C)** At first glance, the relationship is object to action. However, this definition is not specific enough to allow for a single answer choice. A careful look at the possible answers helps lead to a refinement of the relationship to "creative manual action upon an object or medium that is changed by that action." The only answer choice with this relationship is (C), CLAY is to MOLD.

SENTENCE COMPLETIONS

1. **(D)** The first blank must be filled with what it is that fortunetellers do. This narrows your choice to (C) or (D). There being no scientific evidence of their fees makes no sense, so the answer is (D).

2. **(B)** The sentence calls for synonyms, as the second clause merely expands upon the first. ETERNAL and IMMORTAL both mean everlasting.

3. **(D)** The second clause of the sentence is meant to corroborate the first. Since each human relationship is unique, the lovers who assume the uniqueness of their own relationship are RIGHT.

4. **(B)** The word "but" gives the clue that the blanks must be filled with contrasting terms. (B) best meets this condition.

5. **(D)** If the idea of what was right lay in the past, then authority would have to be given to those who knew and preserved ancient lore and habits, i.e., TRADITION.

6. **(B)** Since the desert rains cause loss of life and property, people in an oasis must think of rain with TERROR, (B), or fear, (C). The word that best fills the second blank will determine whether the correct answer is (B) or (C). Sprinkles, (C), would be unlikely to cause loss of life and property; TORRENTS, (B), is more appropriate.

7. **(B)** If the essayist's essays were not widely known, he would have few (not NUMEROUS) admirers.

8. **(B)** In light of the fact that archeologists found palaces, (A), (C), and (D) cannot be correct. The people clearly lived, thought, and built. (B) presents a mystery, but it does create a logically correct sentence.

9. **(B)** Safe driving prevents TRAGEDY, (B), accidents, (C), and lawsuits, (D). The second part of the sentence, however is reasonably completed only with (B).

10. **(D)** The purpose of amateur sports is recreation; the amateur participates for fun, for LOVE of the sport. (The word "amateur" is derived directly from Latin and means "lover.") Cheating is DEGRADING; it makes an activity less desirable.

11. **(A)** If there is to be a meeting, it might be well to have FOOD, (A), secretaries, (B), and telephones, (C), available. However, none of these is specifically needed at an enjoyable, (B), meeting or at a successful, (C), meeting. If the meeting is likely to be PROLONGED, (A), then it is worthwhile to provide FOOD.

12. **(D)** Both (A) and (D) form excellent completions for this sentence. (D) is the *best* answer because SOLITUDE is in direct contrast to the company of others.

13. **(D)** Executing the laws requires law ENFORCEMENT.

14. **(D)** A four-day work week would give workers much more LEISURE time, which would, in turn, greatly BENEFIT the LEISURE industry.

15. **(B)** The adjective "ruthless" (cruel) aptly describes a TYRANT. Since the sense of the sentence calls for contrast, a change from champion of DEMOCRACY to ruthless TYRANT fulfills the requirement.

16. **(D)** The reason that a society would need outside aid would be that the society was not SELF-SUFFICIENT.

17. **(D)** The sentence requires that there be a cause-and-effect relationship between the two words that fill the blanks. Only (D) meets this requirement.

18. **(B)** The meaning of any one of the choices would be equally appropriate for filling the first blank, though (A) would be grammatically incorrect. The words "value" and "progress" are positive words, suggesting the need for a positive completion for the second blank. The only positive second term is in choice (B).

19. **(C)** The final end is EXTINCTION.
20. **(C)** The role of a director is to perfect the PERFORMANCE through necessary criticism. A temperamental actress might misinterpret direction as PERSONAL criticism.

READING COMPREHENSION

1. **(C)** The main idea, the topic of this passage, is looking closely at colors in order to truly recognize them. The farmer is the vehicle for making the point, and the sky and hills are used as illustrations.
2. **(A)** The last sentence of the first paragraph gives you this detail.
3. **(B)** You should be able to infer this answer from the passage. If not, you can choose the correct answer by eliminating all the other choices as being ridiculous.
4. **(B)** Reread the first paragraph carefully if you got this wrong.
5. **(D)** You should have no trouble finding the main idea of this passage.
6. **(A)** The first sentence tells us that the Polynesians made trips to New Zealand.
7. **(B)** The first sentence of the last paragraph makes clear that mariners are people.
8. **(D)** The third paragraph tells us how the Polynesians used the stars for navigation. People who study and understand movements of the stars are astronomers. Although the Polynesians used movements of seabirds as a guide during the daytime, they had not trained the birds. There is no mention of telescopes.
9. **(B)** The topic of the passage is bird migration and the mystery it has presented throughout the ages.
10. **(D)** The last sentence of the third paragraph makes this statement.
11. **(D)** You will find this information within the parentheses in the second paragraph.
12. **(A)** This is the point of the last paragraph.
13. **(C)** Choosing the title for this paragraph takes more than one reading of the paragraph. This is not an easy question. After a couple of readings, however, you should be able to conclude that the all-inclusive subject of the paragraph is the remodeling of plants. An equally correct title, not offered here, might be "Uses and Effects of Colchicine."
14. **(C)** Buried in the middle of the paragraph is the sentence: "It creates new varieties with astonishing frequency, whereas such mutations occur but rarely in nature."
15. **(C)** This question becomes easy to answer after you have dealt with the previous question.
16. **(A)** The third sentence states that colchicine is a poisonous drug.
17. **(A)** The second paragraph gives this information. All the other choices are actually contradicted in the passage.
18. **(C)** See the fourth paragraph.
19. **(B)** This is stated in the first paragraph. The first paragraph also states that Italy is smaller than California. The length of Florida is not stated in the paragraph. (When answering questions based upon a reading passage, you must base your answer only on what is stated or implied in the passage, not upon your personal information or opinion.)
20. **(C)** If you missed this, reread the third paragraph.
21. **(D)** See the second paragraph.
22. **(C)** If two thirds of the peninsula is mountainous (third paragraph), then one third must be made up of northern plains and other flat areas.

QUANTITATIVE ABILITY

1. **(A)** This square is divided into six sections and three are shaded. Three is half of six.
2. **(D)** If 2 packages of cookies will serve 10 children, you may assume that 1 package will serve 5 children. Therefore, 3 packages will serve 15 children.
3. **(C)** $4 \times 5 = 20; 4 + 5 = 9$

   $9 \times 0 = 0$

   $3 \times 6 = 18; 3 + 6 = 9$
4. **(D)** $\$12.00 \times 5$ weeks $= 12 \times 5$
5. **(B)** If C represents the distance from City X to Chicago, and S represents the distance from City X to San Francisco, then $3 \times C = S$. You must know the value of C in order to find S.

6. **(B)** An odd number subtracted from an odd number will always result in an even number. Two is the only even number given.

7. **(A)** To check this problem, give Y the value of 42. Then, $7 \times 6 = 42$ and $42 \div 7 = 6$.

8. **(D)** $759 - 215 = 544$, which, when rounded to the nearest hundred, is 500.

9. **(D)** $4 \times 6 = 24$ and $2 \times 3 = 6$; $24 + 6 = 30$.

10. **(D)** Any number divided by itself equals one.

11. **(B)** $15 - 7 = 8$; $7 + 8 = 15$

12. **(C)** Three numbers are given in this problem, but only two are necessary to solve the problem: the charge per hour and the number of hours Colleen babysat. \$1.50 per hour $\times\ 3\frac{1}{2}$ hours = \$1.50 $\times\ 3\frac{1}{2}$.

13. **(A)** The pie has been divided into 8 pieces. One piece $= \frac{1}{8}$. Four pieces $= \frac{4}{8}$. Four pieces are left in this picture, and one is being taken away, therefore: $\frac{4}{8} - \frac{1}{8}$.

14. **(A)** The symbol $<$ means "is less than." Using response A, the statement reads: 8,862 is less than 8,962.

15. **(C)** 156 meters ÷ 12 meters = 13.

16. **(B)** In the number 28,973, the digit 8 is in the thousands place. The hundreds digit is greater than 5, so the next nearest thousand is 9; therefore, 29,000 is the answer.

17. **(B)** $170 \div 12 = 14$ with a remainder of 2. The closest number given is 14.

18. **(B)** The time is now 5:45. In three more hours it will be 8:45. Thirty minutes later the time will be 9:15.

19. **(D)** $\frac{3}{3} = \frac{5}{5} = 1$

$\frac{5}{5} = \frac{6}{6} = 1$

$\frac{8}{8} = 1$

$\frac{7}{8} \neq \frac{8}{7}$

20. **(C)** The area of a rectangle is found by multiplying the length by the width. 4" × 3" = 12 square inches.

21. **(B)** $\frac{1}{4} = \frac{2}{8}$, therefore, $\frac{7}{8} - \frac{2}{8} = \frac{5}{8}$.

22. **(C)** A is in the thousands place, and B is in the hundredths place.

23. **(B)** $\frac{2}{3} \neq \frac{6}{12}$; $\frac{2}{3} = \frac{8}{12}$; $\frac{6}{12} = \frac{1}{2}$.

24. **(B)** The denominator of a fraction shows how many parts the whole has been divided into. Therefore, $\frac{1}{18}$ is less than $\frac{1}{11}$, etc.

25. **(C)** The 6 in 603 represents 600. $600 \times 10 = 6000$.

26. **(D)** $1005 \div 200 = 5$, with a remainder of 5. The answer is *approximately* 5.

27. **(C)** $5° - 15° = -10°$

28. **(A)** $5 \times (2 + 1) = 5 \times 3 = 15$

29. **(A)** $0 \div 8 = 0$. The other responses work out this way: (B) $1 \div 8 = \frac{1}{8}$; (C) $2 \div 8 = \frac{2}{8}$; (D) $8 \div 8 = 1$. In $0 \div 8$, 0 is the dividend and 8 is the divisor. The quotient is the result obtained when the dividend is divided by the divisor.

30. **(A)** According to the graph, the temperature at 1 PM was 20°, and at 2 PM was *still* 20°.

QUANTITATIVE COMPARISONS

1. **(C)** Solving the equations, $x = 1$, $y = 1$.

2. **(C)** Solving for x, $x = 12$

$\frac{4}{12} = \frac{1}{3}$

3. **(D)** If $x > 0$, A is greater.

If $x < 0$, B is greater.

If $x = 0$, A and B are equal.

4. **(A)** 60 seconds = 1 minute

60 minutes = 1 hour

24 hours = 1 day

Seconds in 1 day = 60 • 60 • 24

There are 30 days in April.

Number of minutes in April = 60 • 24 • 30

Without any computation, A has the greater factors.

5. **(D)** x and y can take on values so that A is greater, B is greater, or they are both equal.

6. **(B)** Area of triangle $= \frac{1}{2} \cdot 5 \cdot 7$

Twice area of rectangle $= 2 \cdot 5 \cdot 7$

7. **(C)** Opposite sides of a parallelogram are congruent.

8. **(B)** If $64a = 81$, then a = a little more than 1.

9. **(A)** Column A represents a greater discount since the full 10% is taken from the original price.

10. **(A)** $\sqrt{49} + \sqrt{16} = 7 + 4 = 11$

    $\sqrt{65}$ is a little more than 8.

11. **(D)** There is no information about the age of any of these.

12. **(C)** Each of these is 180°.

13. **(D)** *a* and *b* can take on values to make either one greater or to make them equal.

14. **(B)** If Jim's salary = $8x$

    then Jack's salary = $6x$

    and Joe's salary = $9x$

15. **(C)** There are 120° left between angle B and angle C. Since they must be congruent, they are each 60° and the triangle is equilateral.

16. **(B)** Since the numerators are the same, the fraction with the smaller denominator will be larger.

17. **(A)** Area of a cube is the sum of 6 equal squares.

A	B
$6 \cdot 6^2$	$6 \cdot 6 \cdot 2^2$

    The factors are greater in *A*.

18. **(B)** $\frac{1}{2} = .5$

    $.5\% = .005$

19. **(B)** 18 times 10 = 180

    12 times 16 = 192

20. **(A)** Since a post is needed at the very beginning as well as at the end, *A* requires 11 posts.

PLANNING YOUR STUDY TIME

Begin by entering on the score sheet the number of questions you got correct in each section and calculate your percentage score. Your scores on the actual exam will not be reported in percentages. You will receive percentile scores that compare your performance with that of other students your age and in your grade. Your percentile standing is very useful information for the school that must base its admission decision on your preparedness. For your purposes, however, the percent of questions you got right can help you compare your own performance on each question type. Your percent score can point out to you your own strengths and weaknesses and help you to plan your study time.

Score Sheet

Section	No. correct	÷	No. of questions	=		×	100	=		%
Synonyms	____	÷	20	=		×	100	=		%
Verbal Analogies	____	÷	20	=		×	100	=		%
Sentence Completions	____	÷	20	=		×	100	=		%
Reading Comprehension	____	÷	22	=		×	100	=		%
Quantitative Ability	____	÷	30	=		×	100	=		%
Quantitative Comparisons	____	÷	20	=		×	100	=		%

As you look over your answer sheet, you may notice that you missed some of the earlier, "easier" questions and got some right near the end of a section. This should not surprise you. After all, you are an individual with your own interests, talents, and thought processes, and your current school may introduce some topics in a less usual order. If you were able to answer correctly many questions on the diagnostic exam, you are already ahead of the game. If you didn't get too far in the time limit or if you got many answers wrong, do not be discouraged. First consider your age and inexperience with some of the question styles. Then congratulate yourself that you had the foresight to plan a study program, and get to work.

Plot your standing on each section on the comparison chart below. Put a check mark into the boxes in which your scores fall. Now you can see at a glance exactly where you will have to concentrate your study.

Comparison Chart

	0–30	31–45	46–60	61–75	76–100
Synonyms					
Verbal Analogies					
Sentence Completions					
Reading Comprehension					
Quantitative Ability					
Quantitative Comparisons					

PART THREE

EVERYTHING YOU NEED!

Vocabulary

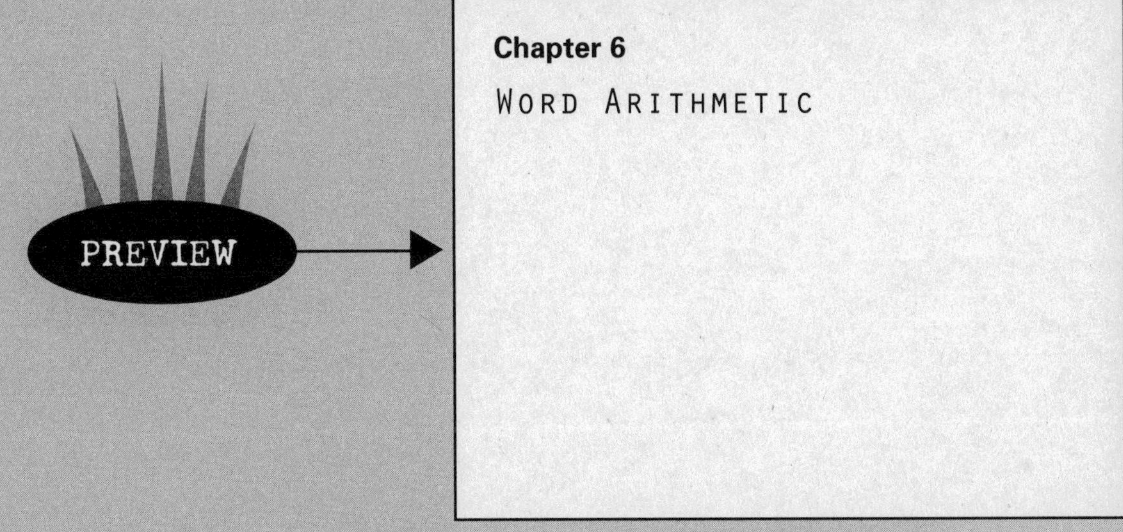

CHAPTER 6

Word Arithmetic

You'll Find Answers to These Questions

Why do they test my vocabulary?
How are words built?
How do word parts work?

PLAN A: ACCELERATED

- ***Read*** the sections "How Are Words Built?" and "How do Word Parts Work"
- ***Skim*** the "List of Common Word Parts" and the "Word List"

PLAN B: TOP SPEED

- ***Skip*** this chapter

WHY DO THEY TEST MY VOCABULARY?

Your ability to understand and to use words is essential to all your learning. If your test performance on verbal ability tests shows that you have a rich vocabulary, you are a good prospect for success at the schools to which you have applied.

HOW ARE WORDS BUILT?

The subject is not letters of the alphabet but rather the parts of words themselves. You can actually increase your vocabulary—and your test score—by learning about the structure of words. This will help you figure out the meanings of unfamiliar words you come across in the verbal ability section of your exam.

Knowing what the parts of words mean is the key to deciphering words you've never seen before. Let's take a look at the word *biography* and its parts. You know that a biography is something written about a person's life. How do the word parts tell you this? Well, the second part of the word, *graphy,* comes from a Greek word that means "writing." The first part of the word, *bio,* is also from Greek and it means "life." Put them both together and you get... *biography,* the story of a person's life. If you add the Latin word for "self"—*auto*—you get... *autobiography,* a story you write about your own life. Think about some other words that use one or more of these parts, like *automobile, biochemistry,* and *autograph.* Can you see how the meaning fits the word parts?

HOW DO WORD PARTS WORK?

Different kinds of word parts work together to make a fully functioning word. Think about it: If your car is going to do more than just sit there, it needs a collection of parts put together in the right way. Two steering wheels won't do you any good if you don't have a gas tank.

Each kind of word part has a specific purpose. There are three basic types of word parts:

Prefixes attach to the beginning of a root word to alter its meaning or to create a new word.

Roots or *stems* are the basic elements of a word that determine its meaning. Roots or stems are not words. They must be combined with prefixes, suffixes, or both. Groups of words from the same root word are called "word families."

Suffixes attach to the end of a root word to change its meaning, help make it grammatically correct in context, or form a new word. Suffixes often indicate whether a word is a noun, verb, adjective, or adverb.

A word can have a root, a prefix, and a suffix; it can have a root and two suffixes or a root and one prefix. The possibilities are endless (almost), but you must always have a root. Word analysis is a kind of arithmetic. Instead of adding numbers, we add the meanings contained in each part of an unfamiliar word. The sum of these parts is the definition of the whole word.

Use the word list that follows to expand your word horizons. Once you begin to learn the word parts on the list, you'll be able to take apart unfamiliar words like a master mechanic. As you make your way through the list, try to think of other words with the same parts. If you have time, check their meanings in a dictionary and take a look at the word origins in the entry.

List of Common Word Parts

PREFIX	MEANING	EXAMPLE
a	not	amoral
ab	away from	absent
ad, ac, ag, at	to, against	aggressive, attract
an	without	anarchy
ante	before	antedate
anti, ant	against	antipathy, antonym
bene	well	benefactor
bi	two	biannual
circum	around	circumvent
com, con, col	together	commit, collate
contra	against	contraband
de	from, down	descend
dis, di	apart, away	distract, divert
dom	home, rule	domicile, dominate
ex, e	out, from	exit, emit
extra	beyond, outside	extracurricular
in, im, ir, il, un	not	inept, irregular, illegal
in, im	in, into	interest, imbibe

PREFIX	MEANING	EXAMPLE
inter	between	interscholastic
intra, intro	within	intramural
mal	bad	malcontent
mis	wrong	misspell
non	not	nonentity
ob	against	obstacle
omni	all	omnivorous
per	through	permeate
peri	around, about	periscope
poly	many	polytheism
post	after	post-mortem
pre	before	premonition
pro	forward, for	propose
re	again, back	review, redeem
se	apart, away	seclude
semi	half	semicircle
sub	under	submarine
super	above	superimpose
sur	on, upon	surmount
syn, sym	together, with	sympathy
trans	across, beyond	transpose
un	not	unwelcome

SUFFIX	MEANING	EXAMPLE
able, ible	capable of, able	reversible (*adj.*)
age	place, thing, idea	storage (*n.*)
al	pertaining to	instructional (*adj.*)
ance	relating to	reliance (*n.*)
ary	relating to	dictionary (*n.*)
ate	an action of	confiscate (*v.*)
cy	the quality of	democracy (*n.*)
ed	past action	subsided (*v.*)
ence	relating to	confidence (*n.*)
er, or	one who	adviser, actor (*n.*)
ic	pertaining to	democratic (*adj.*)
ing	present action	surmising (*v.*)
ion	the act or state of	radiation (*n.*)
ious	full of	rebellious (*adj.*)

SUFFIX	MEANING	EXAMPLE
ive	having the quality of	creative (*adj.*)
ize	to make	harmonize (*v.*)
ly	to do with the quality of	carefully (*adv.*)
ment	the result of	amusement (*n.*)
ness	the quality of being	selfishness (*n.*)
ty	condition of being	sanity (*n.*)

STEM	MEANING	EXAMPLE
ag, ac	do	agenda, action
agri	farm	agriculture
aqua	water	aquatic
auto	self	automatic
biblio	book	bibliography
bio	life	biography
cad, cas	fall	cadence, casual
cap, cep, cept	take	captive, accept
capit	head	capital
ced, cede, ceed, cess	go	intercede
celer	speed	accelerate
chrom	color	monochromatic
chron	time	chronological
cide, cis	cut	incision
clude, clud, clus	close, close in	include, cluster
cog, cogn	knowledge of	recognize
cur, curs	run	incur, recur
ded	give	dedicate
dent, dont	tooth	dental
duce, duct	lead	induce, deduct
fact, feet, fict	make, do	perfect, fiction
fer, late	carry	refer, dilate
flect, flex	bend, turn	reflect
fring, fract	break	infringe, refract
graph, gram	picture, writing	graphic, telegram
greg	group, gather	gregarious
gress, grad	move	progress, degrade
hydr	water	hydrate
ject	throw	inject
jud	right	judicial

STEM	MEANING	EXAMPLE
junct	join	conjunction
juris	law, justice	jurist
lect, leg	read, choose	collect
logue	speech, speaking	dialogue
logy	study of	psychology
loq, loc	speak	elocution
lude, lus	play, perform	elude
manu	by hand	manuscript
mand	order	remand
mar	sea	maritime
med	middle	intermediate
ment, mem	mind, memory	mention
meter	measure	thermometer
micro	small	microscope
min	lessen	miniature
mis, miss, mit	send	remit, dismiss
mot, mov	move	remote, remove
mute	change	commute
naut	sailor, sail	nautical
nounce, nunci	declare, state	announce, enunciate
ped, pod	foot	pedal
pel, pulse	drive, push	dispel, impulse
pend, pense	hang, way	depend, dispense
plac	please	placate
plic	fold	implicate
port	carry	portable
pose, pone	put, place	depose, component
reg, rect	rule	regulate, direct
rupt	break	disruption
scend, scent	move	ascent
scribe, script	write	describe
sec, sect	cut	bisect
sed	remain	sedentary
sert	state, place	insert
serve	keep, save	preserve
sist	stand, set	insist
spect	look	inspect
spire, spirat	breath, breathe	perspire
strict	tighten	restrict

STEM	MEANING	EXAMPLE
tain	hold	detain
term	end	terminate
tort	twist	distort
tract	draw, drag	detract
vene, vent	come	intervene, invent
vict	overcome, conquer	evict
volve, volu	roll, turn	evolve, evolution

WORD LIST

The words in this list are grouped in "families," by their stems. The stems are arranged in alphabetical order. If you need help with words other than those listed here, check with your dictionary or thesaurus.

AQUA, AQUE: water

aquarium—a tank for fish and water plants

aquatic—having to do with water

aqueous—watery

subaqueous—under water

AUTO: self

autobiography—the story of one's life, written by oneself

autograph—a person's own signature

automatic—self-operating

automation—a system in which machinery does most of the work itself

BIBLIO: book

bibliography—a list of books used for reference

bibliolatry—worship of books

BIO: life

antibiotics—medicines that work against harmful life forms in the body

biography—the story of a person's life

biology—the study of various life forms

symbiosis—mutual interdependence of two different living organisms

CAP, CEP, CEPT: take

accept—to take in

capture—to take by force; to take prisoner

exception—something taken or left out

inception—the act of taking something in; a beginning

CED, CEDE, CEED, CESS; go, move

accede—to move toward; to grant

concede—to go with; admit

concession—an admission

exceed—to go over or outside of

excess—going over certain limits

intercede—to move between

precede—to go before or ahead of

proceed—to move forward

recede—to move back

secession—the act of moving apart; separation from the whole

CHRON: time

anachronism—something contrary to a particular era

chronometer—a tool that measures time

CIDE, CIS: cut

decide—to act; to cut off from further consideration

excise—to cut out or away

incision—a cut

CLUDE, CLUS: close, shut

exclude—to close or shut out

exclusive—having the quality of shutting out

include—to shut or close in

recluse—a person who shuts himself away from others

seclude—to shut apart from

COG, COGN: knowledge of

cognizant—the quality of being knowledgeable

incognito—unknown; disguised

recognition—the act of knowing again; recalling

CUR, CURS: run

concurrent—running with; at the same time

cursory—the quality of running through quickly

precursor—a forerunner

recurrent—running again

DUCE, DUCT: lead

abduct—to lead away; to kidnap

conducive—having the quality of leading together; persuasive

deduce—to lead from; to conclude

introduce—to lead into
reduction—the act of leading backward; a loss

FACT, FECT, FICT: make, do
affectation—something made up; a pretense
defect—something made apart from the ordinary
effect—something done outwardly; a change
fictitious—made up; not true

FER: carry, bring
conference—the state of bringing together; a meeting
differ—to carry apart; to disagree
infer—to bring in; to conclude
offer—to carry out
preference—the act of bringing first or before
reference—the act of carrying back
transfer—to carry across

FLECT, FLEX: bend, turn
circumflex—an accent mark that is bent over a letter
flexible—able to be bent or changed
genuflect—to bend the knees
reflect—to bend or turn something back
reflex—a return movement; a response

FRING, FRACT: break
fracture—a break in something hard
infraction—the breaking of a rule
infringe—to break into
refract—to break up

GRAPH, GRAM: picture, writing
diagram—information in picture form
epigram—a brief piece of writing
graph—information in picture form
seismograph—a picture record of earth movements
telegram—communication using sound and writing
telegraph—communication with sounds that are translated into writing

GREG: group, gather
aggregation—a group
congregate—to gather together

gregarious—having the characteristic of getting along well in a group; social
segregate—to group apart; to keep groups separate

GRESS, GRAD: move
aggressive—the characteristic of moving toward something
degrade—to move down
ingredient—something that is moved into something else
progress—to move forward
regress—to move backward
upgrade—to move up

HYDR: water
dehydrate—to remove water from
hydrant—something that gives out water
hydraulic—relating to water power
hydrogen—water gas
hydrology—the study of water
hydrophobia—fear of water
hydrotherapy—cure by water

JECT: throw
conjecture—something thrown together; a guess
dejected—thrown down
eject—to throw out
inject—to throw in
projectile—an object to throw forward
subjected—thrown under

JUNCT: join
conjunction—a word that joins parts of sentences together
enjoin—to join into; to enforce
injunction—an enjoining action
junction—a joining of two parts of something

JURIS: law, justice
jurisdiction—sphere of legal authority
jurisprudence—legal science
jurist—an expert in law

LOGUE: speaking, speech
dialogue—speech between two people
epilogue—a short ending speech
eulogy—a speech of praise

monologue—one person's speech
prologue—a speech given as a foreword

LOQ, LOC: talk, speak
colloquy—talking together
elocution—clear speech
interlocutors—speakers
loquacious—the quality of being talkative

LUDE, LUS: play
allude—to refer to casually or indirectly
allusion—a reference to
delude—to deceive; to mislead
elude—to escape through cleverness
prelude—an introductory period before a main event

MAND: order, command
countermand—an order placed against another order
mandate—a command
mandatory—ordered or required
remand—to order back

MANU: hand
manicure—care of the hands
manifest—as from an open hand; made obvious
manipulate—to handle
manual—a handbook
manuscript—a document written by hand

MEM, MENT: mind, memory
commemorate—to remember with
demented—out of one's mind
mention—a call to mind
reminisce—to call back memories

MIS, MISS, MIT: send
commit—to send together
dismiss—to send away
emit—to send out
remission—the state of being sent back
submit—to send under
transmit—to send across

PED, POD: foot
biped—an animal that walks on two feet
impede—to put a foot against; to obstruct
pedestrian—a person who is walking
podiatrist—a foot doctor
tripod—an object with three feet

PEL, PULSE: drive, push
dispel—to drive away
expel—to push out
impulse—to drive or push in
propel—to push forward
repel—to push back

PEND, PENSE: hang, weigh
appendix—part that hangs; a portion of a book usually found in the back
dispense—to apportion
expenditure—a sum paid out
impending—hanging over something
suspend—to hang from

PLAC: please
implacable—not able to be pleased or appeased
placate—to please
placebo—an inactive medicine designed to please or satisfy
placid—quiet, pleasing

PLI, PLIC: fold
implicate—to involve
pliable—easily folded or influenced

PONE, POSE, POSIT: place or put
components—units to be put together
depose—to put down
exponent—something or someone who puts something forth
oppose—to place against
proponent—a person who puts something forward; an advocate

PORT: carry, bring
deportation—the act of carrying out or away from
export—to carry trade out of a country
import—to carry trade into a country

report—to carry back
transport—to carry across

RECT, REG: to rule or lead, straight
erect—straightened upward
rectify—to straighten out; to correct
rectitude—moral uprightness
regulate—to rule

RUPT: break
disrupt—to break through or down
erupt—to break out
rupture—a break

SCEND, SCENT: climb
ascend—to climb up
condescend—to climb down with
descent—downward slope
transcend—to climb beyond

SCRIBE, SCRIPT: write
describe—to write about
inscription—something written in something else
prescription—written before receiving
proscribe—to write something out; to ban

SEC, SECT: cut
bisect—to cut in two
dissect—to cut apart
sector—a cutting or part of a whole

SERT: declare, state
assert—to state firmly
insert—to place within

SERVE: keep, save
conserve—to save (together)
preservation—the state of having kept before or first
reservation—something kept or saved aside

SIST: stand, set
desist—to stand away
inconsistent—not standing together; changing
insistent—having the quality of standing firmly

SPEC, SPECT: see, look

aspect—a way of looking at something

prospective—forward looking; future

spectrum—something seen broadly

speculate—to look at mentally

TAIN, TEN: hold

contain—to hold together

containment—the state of being held together

detain—to hold aside

retain—to hold back

tenacious—holding powerfully

TERM: end, limit

exterminate—to eliminate

interminable—not able to be ended; unending

terminate—to end

terminus—ending place

TORT: twist

contort—to twist together

distortion—something that twists away from the truth

extort—to twist away or out of

TRACT: draw, drag

attract—to draw toward

extract—to draw out

distraction—something that draws attention away from something else

intractable—not easily drawn or persuaded

protracted—drawn out

VENE, VENT: come

advent—a coming

circumvent—to avoid by going around

convene—to come together

intervene—to come between

VINCE, VICT: conquer, overcome

convince—to conquer

invincible—not able to be conquered

victor—conqueror

VOLVE, VOLU: roll, turn
convoluted—rolled or twisted together
evolution—the act of rolling forth; a gradual development
involve—to draw in
revolution—a rolling back; an overturning

WORD ARITHMETIC EXERCISE

To get yourself started, take a look at these examples of word analysis and arithmetic.

Example: PROCESSION
pro- is a prefix that means "forward."
cess is a stem that means "go" or "move."
ion is a noun suffix that means "the act of."
pro + cess + ion = *the act of going before*

Example: RECEDING
re- is a prefix that means "back."
cede is a stem that means "go."
ing is an active word suffix.
re + ced + ing = *going back*

Example: DISSECTED
dis- is a prefix that means "apart."
sect is a root meaning "cut."
ed is a verb suffix showing past action.
dis + sect + ed = *cut apart* or *took apart*

Practice word arithmetic with these words. The List of Common Word Parts and the Word List will help you. Write a definition for each word in the space. Correct answers follow.

1. revision ____________________
2. audible ____________________
3. adhere ____________________
4. retract ____________________
5. projection ____________________
6. preclude ____________________
7. recline ____________________
8. erupt ____________________
9. regression ____________________
10. revolution ____________________
11. retain ____________________

12. inscription ______________________________
13. divert ______________________________
14. conduct ______________________________
15. import ______________________________

WORD ARITHMETIC: ANSWERS

1. RE- *back, again* VIS *look, see* -ION *the act of*
   RE + VIS + ION = *the act of looking at or seeing again*
2. AUD *hear* -IBLE *able*
   AUD + IBLE = *able to be heard*
3. AD- *to* HERE *cling, stick*
   AD + HERE = *cling to*
4. RE- *back, again* TRACT *draw, pull*
   RE + TRACT = *to draw back*
5. PRO- *forward* JECT *throw* -ION *the act of*
   PRO + JECT + ION = *the act of throwing forward*
6. PRE- *before* CLUDE *close, close in*
   PRE + CLUDE = *to close in before*
7. RE- *back, again* CLINE *lean*
   RE + CLINE = *to lean back*
8. E- *out* RUPT *break*
   E + RUPT = *to break out*
9. RE- *back, again* GRESS *move* -ION *the act of*
   RE + GRESS + ION = *the act of moving backward*
10. RE- *back, again* VOLU *roll* -TION *the act of*
    RE + VOLU + TION = *the act of rolling again*
11. RE- *back, again* TAIN *to hold* -ED *indicates past action*
    RE + TAIN + ED = *held back*
12. IN- *in* SCRIPT *write* -ION *the act of*
    IN + SCRIPT + ION = *the act of writing in*
13. DI- *away, aside* VERT *turn*
    DI + VERT = *to turn away*
14. CON- *together* DUCT *lead*
    CON + DUCT = *to lead together*
15. IM- *in* PORT *to carry*
    IM + PORT = *to carry in*

TESTSMARTS

Practice word arithmetic. Words are the sum of their parts. If you come up against an unfamiliar word on your exam, decipher its parts and add them up to get the meaning.

PART

EVERYTHING YOU NEED!

Verbal Ability Questions

CHAPTER 7

Synonyms

PLAN A: ACCELERATED

- ***Read*** the chapter
- ***Skim*** the Learning Exercises
- ***Take*** the Practice Synonyms Tests

PLAN B: TOP SPEED

- ***Read*** the chapter
- ***Skim*** the Learning Exercises
- ***Read*** the Practice Synonyms Tests

You'll Find Answers to These Questions

How may synonym questions be presented?
What will my synonym questions look like?
How do you answer synonym questions?

HOW MAY SYNONYM QUESTIONS BE PRESENTED?

Synonyms are words with similar meanings, and synonym questions ask you to choose a word with a meaning similar to that of a given word. In real life situations, you will often find yourself looking for a synonym for a word within the context of a sentence. At other times, the synonym will appear in the form of a definition. Some standardized exams use these forms for testing. Answering synonym questions in these forms serves as an excellent way to learn.

Sentence Context

This type of question presents a word printed in either italics or boldfaced print and situated within a complete sentence. You are asked to choose a word that is closest in meaning to that word. The sentence context may give you clues to the meaning of the question word.

EXAMPLE:

Miss Payne was a *garrulous* old gossip. *Garrulous* means

(A) complaining
(B) overly friendly
(C) careless
(D) overly talkative

Garrulous is an adjective describing the noun "gossip" in this sentence. Since adjectives answer the question "What kind?", *garrulous* must be telling what kind of gossip Miss Payne is. *Garrulous* is therefore a word that must have something to do with gossipy conversation.

AVOID THE TRAPS!

Never choose an answer simply because it is the one word you don't recognize. The correct answer may be the easiest and most obvious word.

(A) "Complaining" may be a type of conversation, but gossips talk about other people, while complainers talk about themselves. Eliminate this choice.

(B) "Overly friendly" is a possible but unlikely choice, since it is related only indirectly to gossip.

(C) "Careless" is a word that usually describes physical actions. Eliminate this choice.

(D) "Overly talkative" is the best possibility. A gossip has earned that reputation by talking a great deal about others.

Using substitution, the sentence reads, "Miss Payne was an overly talkative old gossip." This new sentence makes sense. Therefore, **(D)** is the best answer choice.

Definition

This style of question presents an incomplete sentence with a word in italics. The sentence is to be completed by one of the choices.

EXAMPLE:

A *frugal* person is one who is

(A) cooperative

(B) thrifty

(C) proud

(D) sulky

Frugal means "economical" or "not wasteful." The advantage of the sentence here is that it gives you a clue that frugal is an adjective that may be applied to a person's behavior. A *thrifty* person is an economical one. Therefore (B) is the correct answer.

A variant of the definition style begins with one or two sentences that present a fact, a situation, or a description. You must draw a conclusion from the given information and choose the best word to complete the final sentence.

EXAMPLE:

Tommy disobeys school rules and rebels against his parents and teachers. Tommy is

(A) defiant

(B) independent

(C) determined

(D) vulnerable

This question asks you to interpret Tommy's actions, draw a conclusion about them, and choose an adjective to describe him. The key words in the question are *disobey* and *rebel*.

(A) "Defiant" is the adjective form of the verb defy. "Defy" means to "resist" or "oppose." Disobedience and rebellion are both ways of resisting authority. This is a good possible choice.

(B) "Independent" means "self-reliant," or "not needing the help of other people." An independent person may be rebellious, but a rebellious person is not necessarily independent. Eliminate this choice.

(C) "Determined" describes a person who means to achieve a goal no matter what. From the information given, there is no reason to believe that Tommy's actions are related to his desire to accomplish something. Eliminate this choice.

(D) "Vulnerable" means "open to hurt and disappointment." Although this may be true of Tommy, the word "vulnerable" is not directly related to rebellion and disobedience. Eliminate this choice too.

Choice (**A**) is the best answer: Tommy is *defiant*.

WHAT WILL MY SYNONYM QUESTIONS LOOK LIKE?

Both the SSAT and ISEE test you with straightforward synonym questions. They present a single word in capital letters and ask you to choose the word that is the best synonym for the question word.

Directions: Choose the word or phrase whose meaning is most similar to the word in CAPITAL letters.

Example:

PROFICIENT

(A) resentful
(B) amiable
(C) famous
(D) adept

Someone who is proficient is particularly good at doing a certain task or activity. *Adept* is a synonym for *proficient*. Thus, (**D**) is the best answer.

HERE'S THE ANSWER

What if no answer seems exactly right?

Remember: The directions tell you to choose the best answer. The correct answer won't necessarily be a perfect fit, but it will work better than the other choices.

HOW DO YOU ANSWER SYNONYM QUESTIONS?

To answer synonym questions, follow these steps:

Synonyms: Getting It Right

1. Read the question carefully. Consider *every* answer choice. One choice must always be the best response.
2. Eliminate obviously wrong responses immediately.
3. Use word-analysis techniques to help you with difficult words.
4. Try using the word in a sentence of your own; think about the meaning of the word as you have used it.

LEARNING EXERCISES: SYNONYMS

The questions in this section are arranged in boxes called "frames." The answer for each frame will be found in the box to the left of the question frame.

First, cover the answer boxes with a strip of paper. Circle your answer to the question. Then, move the paper down to expose the answer to that question.

Sentence Context Questions

ANSWER	QUESTION
1. (B) *Stimulate* comes from the word "stimulus." A stimulus is an incentive.	**1.** The change in procedure *stimulated* the men. *Stimulated* means (A) rewarded (B) gave an incentive to (C) antagonized (D) lowered the efficiency of
2. (C) "Impart gradually" is a synonym for the word *instill*.	**2.** Courage is difficult to *instill* in a person. *Instill* means (A) measure exactly (B) predict accurately (C) impart gradually (D) restrain effectively
3. (C) *Relevant* means "pertinent." The prefix *ir-* means "not." Therefore, the word *irrelevant* means "not pertinent."	**3.** His report contained many *irrelevant* statements. *Irrelevant* means (A) unproven (B) hard to understand (C) not pertinent (D) insincere
4. (D) A *prior* appointment is one that was made previously.	**4.** He had a *prior* appointment with the manager. *Prior* means (A) private (B) definite (C) later (D) previous
5. (A) "Used up," "consumed," and "exhausted" are all synonyms for the word *depleted*.	**5.** The supply of pamphlets has been *depleted*. *Depleted* means (A) exhausted (B) included (C) delivered (D) rejected

ANSWER	QUESTION
6. (C) A *candid* opinion is expressed freely and honestly. "Frank" is a synonym for *candid*.	**6.** Mr. Dorman asked for a *candid* opinion. *Candid* means (A) biased (B) written (C) frank (D) confidential
7. (A) "Sickness," "disease," and "illness" are all synonyms for the word *ailment*.	**7.** The patient had a serious *ailment*. *Ailment* means (A) illness (B) food allergy (C) operation (D) problem
8. (C) The stem *plac* means "pleased." The prefix com- means "with." The word *complacent* means "having the quality of being pleased with."	**8.** He was *complacent* in his new position. *Complacent* means (A) anxious (B) remorseful (C) satisfied (D) dejected
9. (D) "Apathy," "disinterest," and "indifference" are all synonyms for the word *nonchalance*.	**9.** His *nonchalance* was disturbing to the courtroom observers. *Nonchalance* means (A) interest (B) poverty (C) care (D) indifference
10. (C) "Essential" and "basic" are both synonyms for the word *fundamental*. "Basic" is the best choice in this sentence.	**10.** Our argument was based on *fundamental* economic principles. *Fundamental* means (A) adequate (B) essential (C) basic (D) truthful
11. (A) The stem *term* means "end." *Terminate* is a word that means to "bring to an end."	**11.** He wishes to *terminate* the conversation. *Terminate* means (A) end (B) ignore (C) postpone (D) continue

ANSWER	QUESTION
12. (D) *Reluctance* is a noun meaning "hesitation" or "unwillingness."	**12.** Miss Fulton showed her *reluctance* to serve as relief operator. *Reluctance* means (A) eagerness (B) ability (C) unreliability (D) unwillingness
13. (D) A *diligent* worker is one who works very hard. "Industrious" is a synonym for *diligent.*	**13.** His secretary was a *diligent* worker. *Diligent* means (A) incompetent (B) careless (C) cheerful (D) industrious
14. (D) The word *diversity* in this context means "differences that cover a broad range of possibilities."	**14.** There is considerable *diversity* in the submitted suggestions. *Diversity* means (A) similarity (B) triviality (C) value (D) variety
15. (A) Try substituting each of the four choices in the sentence. *Intact* means "together" or "in one piece" and is the best choice.	**15.** The vehicle was left *intact* after the accident. *Intact* means (A) undamaged (B) unattended (C) a total loss (D) repaired
16. (D) In this context, the word *resolve* means to "make up one's mind firmly." "Determined" is a synonym of *resolved.*	**16.** He *resolved* to act at once. *Resolved* means (A) offered (B) refused (C) hesitated (D) determined
17. (C) *Rigorously* or strictly enforced rules are kept without any exceptions.	**17.** The departmental rules were *rigorously* enforced. *Rigorously* means (A) usually (B) never (C) strictly (D) leniently

ANSWER	QUESTION
18. (A) The stem *ami* means "friend." "Friendly" is a synonym of *amicable*.	**18.** Relations between England and the United States are *amicable*. *Amicable* means (A) friendly (B) tender (C) accessible (D) inimical
19. (B) The words "plainly" and "crowd" are context clue words in this sentence. A *clamor* is an "uproar," a "great noise."	**19.** I could plainly hear the *clamor* of the crowd. *Clamor* means (A) murmur (B) noise (C) questions (D) singing
20. (D) *To decline* or refuse an offer is to "turn it down or away." The prefix *de-* means "down."	**20.** He *declined* our offers to help him. *Declined* means (A) suspected (B) misunderstood (C) consented to accept (D) refused
21. (B) Sometimes neither context nor etymology can help. Use a dictionary.	**21.** A person with a *sallow* complexion was seen near the car. *Sallow* means (A) ruddy (B) pale and yellowish (C) dark (D) highly freckled
22. (B) *Noxious* means "injurious" and "harmful to health."	**22.** It was reported that *noxious* fumes were escaping from the tanks. *Noxious* means (A) concentrated (B) harmful (C) gaseous (D) heavy
23. (D) *Trivial* means *insignificant*. Do you see *trivia* in this word?	**23.** They are discussing *trivial* matters. *Trivial* means (A) of a personal nature (B) very significant (C) interesting and educational (D) of little importance

ANSWER	QUESTION
24. (B) *Obsolete,* literally "grown out of use," means "out of date" or "passé."	**24.** This equipment is *obsolete.* *Obsolete* means (A) complicated (B) out of date (C) highly suitable (D) reliable
25. (A) *Dexterity* is "skill with the hands." The root is *dexter,* which refers to the right hand. (Bias: right is good.)	**25.** The operator was commended for her *dexterity.* *Dexterity* means (A) skill (B) punctuality (C) courtesy (D) cooperation
26. (D) *Recalcitrant,* literally "kicking back," means "disobedient" and "hard to handle."	**26.** The witness was *recalcitrant.* *Recalcitrant* means (A) cooperative (B) highly excited (C) accustomed to hard work (D) stubbornly resistant
27. (B) To *placate* is to "appease" or to "mollify."	**27.** He was asked to *placate* the visitor. *Placate* means (A) escort (B) appease (C) interview (D) detain
28. (D) *Latitude,* literally "breadth," can then be interpreted as "freedom from narrowness."	**28.** He was given considerable *latitude* in designing the program. *Latitude* means (A) advice and encouragement (B) assistance (C) cause for annoyance (D) freedom from restriction
29. (C) *Expedient,* related to *expedite,* refers to speed, efficiency, and practicality.	**29.** This is the most *expedient* method for achieving the desired results. *Expedient* means (A) inconvenient (B) expensive (C) efficient (D) time consuming

ANSWER	QUESTION
30. **(B)** *Prerogatives* are rights and privileges related to rank or position. The prefix *pre-* gives a clue.	**30.** The men refused to give up their *prerogatives* without a struggle. *Prerogatives* means (A) ideals (B) privileges (C) demands (D) weapons

Definition Questions

ANSWER	QUESTION
1. (B) The stem *cogn* means "knowledge of."	**1.** The word *cognizant* means (A) rare (C) reluctant (B) aware (D) haphazard
2. (D) The prefix *de-* means "down." The word *denote* means to "note down."	**2.** The word *denote* means (A) encumber (C) evade (B) furnish (D) indicate
3. (D) *Meager* means "scanty" or "very little."	**3.** To say that the information obtained was *meager* means it was (A) well received (C) valuable (B) long overdue (D) scanty
4. (A) For example: The infection had *impaired*, or weakened, his hearing.	**4.** To *impair* means to (A) weaken (C) conceal (B) improve (D) expose
5. (B) *Extensive* means "wide-ranging" or "broad."	**5.** To say that a man's knowledge of the law is *extensive* means it is (A) factual (C) sufficient (B) broad (D) hypothetical
6. (C) *Rigid* is synonymous with "stiff" and "inflexible." A *rigid* regulation is one that has no exceptions.	**6.** A regulation that is *rigid* is (A) precise (C) strict (B) clearly expressed (D) rarely applied
7. (C) The principal *commended* those students who had made the honor roll.	**7.** A *commendable* action is one that is (A) premeditated (C) praiseworthy (B) broad (D) hypothetical
8. (A) "Filled," "stuffed," and "packed" are synonyms for the word *replete*.	**8.** A pamphlet that is *replete* with charts and graphs (A) is full of charts and graphs (B) substitutes illustrations for information (C) deals with the construction of charts and graphs (D) is in need of charts and graphs

ANSWER	QUESTION
9. (D) *Authentic,* literally "itself," means "reliable" or "legitimate."	**9.** To say that a document is *authentic* means it is (A) fictitious (B) priceless (C) well written (D) genuine
10. **(B)** An *exacting* task must be done according to strict regulations.	**10.** An *exacting* task is one that is (A) brief (B) severe in its demands (C) arithmetical in nature (D) responsible
11. (C) More synonyms are "sloppy" and "untidy."	**11.** A person who is *slovenly* is (A) neat and well dressed (B) eager and ambitious (C) lazy and slipshod (D) aggressive and resentful
12. (B) *Vivacious* means "full of life."	**12.** A *vivacious* person is one who is (A) kind (B) lively (C) talkative (D) well dressed
13. (D) *Peremptory* commands also tend to be arbitrary and absolute.	**13.** *Peremptory* commands are those that are (A) unexpected (B) military (C) incomplete (D) dictatorial
14. (C) The prefix *re-* means "back." A *rescinded* order is one that has been taken back.	**14.** To say that the order was *rescinded* means it was (A) revised (B) misinterpreted (C) canceled (D) summarized
15. (B) Even beyond "praise," to *extol* is to "praise highly."	**15.** To *extol* is to (A) summon (B) praise (C) reject (D) withdraw
16. (C) To *appraise,* literally "to set a price," means "to judge value."	**16.** The word *appraise* means (A) consult (B) manage (C) judge (D) attribute
17. (C) A *diplomat* is skillful in dealing with people.	**17.** A *diplomatic* person is (A) domineering (B) verbose (C) tactful (D) deceitful
18. (C) Can you see the basis for "powerful" in *potent?*	**18.** A *potent* incentive is one that is (A) impossible (B) not practical (C) highly effective (D) a possibility
19. (A) The word *monomial* is used in algebra.	**19.** The word *monomial* refers to (A) one term (B) eyeglass (C) soliloquy (D) one tone

ANSWER	QUESTION
20. (C) *Toxin* means "poison." The prefix *anti-* means "against." An *antitoxin* is a substance used against a poison or disease in the body.	**20.** *Antitoxin* is used in cases of (A) corruption (B) sanitary inspections (C) disease (D) construction
21. (B) A *fulcrum* is the support for a lever when it is in operation.	**21.** A *fulcrum* is part of a (A) typewriter (B) lever (C) radio (D) lamp
22. (C) The *meticulous* person can even be finicky.	**22.** A person who is *meticulous* in his or her work is (A) alert to new techniques (B) likely to be erratic (C) excessively careful of small details (D) slovenly and inaccurate
23. (A) And a *prolific* tree bears much fruit.	**23.** A *prolific* writer is one who is (A) productive (B) talented (C) popular (D) forward looking
24. (C) *Oscillate* literally means "swing back and forth."	**24.** To *oscillate* means to (A) lubricate (B) decide (C) waver (D) investigate
25. (A) The prefix *homo-* means "same."	**25.** A *homogeneous* group of persons is (A) similar (B) discontented (C) teamwork (D) different
26. (D) A *vindictive* or vengeful person bears a grudge or seeks revenge.	**26.** A *vindictive* person is one who is (A) prejudiced (B) petty (C) unpopular (D) vengeful
27. (B) In fact, a *futile* effort is just about bound to fail.	**27.** A *futile* effort is one that is (A) strong (B) useless (C) clumsy (D) sincere
28. (C) Remarks might be *amplified,* or expanded, through the addition of more detail.	**28.** To say that the speaker *amplified* his remarks means the remarks were (A) shouted (B) analyzed (C) expanded (D) summarized
29. (C) *Innocuous* also means "noncontroversial" or "dull."	**29.** An *innocuous* statement is one that is (A) forceful (B) offensive (C) harmless (D) brief
30. (C) Word arithmetic leads you to "pulled together," or "convincing."	**30.** The word *cogent* means (A) confused (B) opposite (C) convincing (D) unintentional

Synonym Questions

ANSWER	QUESTION
1. (A) *Anticipate* your opponent's arguments and prepare your responses.	**1.** ANTICIPATE (A) foresee (B) annul (C) approve (D) conceal
2. (D) The frightened witness was a *reluctant* trial participant.	**2.** RELUCTANT (A) relaxed (B) drastic (C) constant (D) hesitant
3. (D) She has saved a great deal of money because she lives *frugally*.	**3.** FRUGAL (A) friendly (B) hostile (C) thoughtful (D) economical
4. (C) It is *imperative* that you see a doctor before the rash spreads.	**4.** IMPERATIVE (A) impending (B) impossible (C) compulsory (D) flawless
5. (B) Jim is the only person who has *access* to the safe.	**5.** ACCESS (A) too much (B) admittance (C) extra (D) arrival
6. (C) In *subsequent* meetings we will be discussing the progress of this project.	**6.** SUBSEQUENT (A) preceding (B) early (C) following (D) winning
7. (D) Americans were left a wonderful *heritage* by their ancestors.	**7.** HERITAGE (A) will (B) believer (C) legend (D) inheritance
8. (D) *Cultured* pearls are less expensive than natural ones.	**8.** CULTURED (A) malformed (B) decomposed (C) exiled (D) cultivated
9. (A) The prisoner wanted to *atone* for his past crimes.	**9.** ATONE (A) repent (B) rebel (C) sound (D) impotent
10. (D) Lions are *predatory* animals.	**10.** PREDATORY (A) introductory (B) intellectual (C) preaching (D) carnivorous
11. (A) Swords could not pierce a knight's suit of *mail*.	**11.** MAIL (A) armor (B) seaside (C) rapid travel (D) wool
12. (B) The salesman had a *florid* complexion.	**12.** FLORID (A) seedy (B) ruddy (C) hot (D) overflowing

ANSWER	QUESTION
13. (B) The engineers thought the bridge would be economically *feasible*.	**13.** FEASIBLE (A) simple (B) practical (C) visible (D) lenient
14. (B) In industry today, new ideas are constantly being *supplanted* by even newer ones.	**14.** SUPPLANT (A) approve (B) displace (C) widespread (D) appease
15. (C) A belief in the existence of witches was *prevalent* during the 17th century.	**15.** PREVALENT (A) current (B) permanent (C) widespread (D) temporary
16. (A) The defense attorney *contends* that his client was out of town when the crime was committed.	**16.** CONTEND (A) assert (B) agree (C) temper (D) appease
17. (A) The action showed her *flagrant* disregard for school rules.	**17.** FLAGRANT (A) glaring (B) hopeless (C) engrossing (D) motioning
18. (B) The storyteller *enthralled* his young audience.	**18.** ENTHRALL (A) throw in (B) captivate (C) support (D) deceive
19. (C) Vandals *desecrated* the flag by burning it.	**19.** DESECRATE (A) improve upon (B) occupy (C) profane (D) hide
20. (B) Children often *ostracize* classmates who seem different in any way.	**20.** OSTRACIZE (A) delight (B) exclude (C) include (D) hide
21. (D) Some tenants are charged *exorbitant* rents by greedy landlords.	**21.** EXORBITANT (A) priceless (B) worthless (C) extensive (D) excessive
22. (A) Civilization could be *obliterated* by an atomic war.	**22.** OBLITERATE (A) annihilate (B) review (C) demonstrate (D) detect
23. (C) Crude oil shortages make *austerity* a necessity.	**23.** AUSTERITY (A) priority (B) anxiety (C) self-discipline (D) solitude
24. (C) *Corroboration* of the defendant's alibi will be difficult to find.	**24.** CORROBORATION (A) expenditure (B) compilation (C) confirmation (D) reduction
25. (B) A decrease in contagious diseases shows the *salutary* effects of preventive medicine.	**25.** SALUTARY (A) popular (B) beneficial (C) urgent (D) forceful

ANSWER	QUESTION
26. (C) The police were forced to *acquiesce* to the kidnapper's demands.	**26.** ACQUIESCE (A) endeavor (C) agree (B) discharge (D) inquire
27. (A) Janet's *diffidence* kept her from participating in class discussions.	**27.** DIFFIDENCE (A) shyness (C) interval (B) distinction (D) discordance
28. (A) *Reprisals* were organized against the terrorists.	**28.** REPRISAL (A) retaliation (C) warning (B) advantage (D) denial
29. (B) Mr. Jones *capitulated* to his students' demands.	**29.** CAPITULATE (A) repeat (C) finance (B) surrender (D) retreat
30. (A) There were *extenuating* circumstances that caused the jury to vote for acquittal.	**30.** EXTENUATING (A) excusing (C) incriminating (B) opposing (D) additional

PRACTICE SYNONYMS TESTS

Directions: Select the word that is closest in meaning to the CAPITALIZED word and circle the letter that appears before your answer.

Consider the time limits as maximum time allowed. Your speed should improve with practice.

Mark every word you cannot define—capitalized word or answer choice. Look up these words in a dictionary and create your own personal vocabulary list for further study. Correct answers for all practice synonyms tests follow Test 10.

TEST 1 — 10 MINUTES

1. CHASSIS
(A) frame
(B) body
(C) form
(D) lubrication

2. ENLIGHTEN
(A) reduce
(B) bleach
(C) educate
(D) absorb

3. AFFIRM
(A) prove
(B) guarantee
(C) sign
(D) stick

4. FROCK
(A) dress
(B) coat
(C) hermit
(D) veil

5. KEG
(A) beer
(B) nails
(C) barrel
(D) understanding

6. LOGO
(A) symbol
(B) copyright
(C) gameplan
(D) magnet

7. MOUSY
(A) brown
(B) alcoholic
(C) gnawing
(D) timid

8. PARCH
(A) boil
(B) burn
(C) dry
(D) steam

9. REFUGE
(A) alibi
(B) shelter
(C) exile
(D) church

10. SKEPTIC
(A) doubter
(B) critic
(C) heretic
(D) opponent

11. TENUOUS
(A) boring
(B) impermanent
(C) nervous
(D) flimsy

12. VIE
(A) defeat
(B) hurry
(C) seek
(D) compete

13. ARMADA
(A) fleet
(B) battle
(C) defeat
(D) ship

14. DRIVEL
(A) saliva
(B) foam
(C) tension
(D) nonsense

15. BOOTY
(A) piracy
(B) riot
(C) plunder
(D) leather

16. PORTAL
(A) dockside
(B) carriage
(C) peephole
(D) gate

17. CAGEY
(A) imprisoned
(B) protected
(C) tricky
(D) wild

18. JUMBO
(A) egg
(B) elephant
(C) huge
(D) mixture

19. MYTHICAL
(A) ancient
(B) religious
(C) explanatory
(D) imaginary

20. NUGGET
(A) gold
(B) candy
(C) collision
(D) lump

TEST 2 — 7 MINUTES

Directions: Select the word that is closest in meaning to the CAPITALIZED word and circle the letter that appears before your answer.

1. ADULTERATE
   (A) cheat
   (B) age
   (C) shorten
   (D) idolize
   (E) dilute

2. BOARDER
   (A) carpenter
   (B) lumberman
   (C) edge
   (D) roomer
   (E) traveler

3. LEERY
   (A) obscene
   (B) uncontrolled
   (C) wicked
   (D) suspicious
   (E) sheltered

4. OVATION
   (A) speech
   (B) applause
   (C) egg dish
   (D) misjudgment
   (E) exaggeration

5. CORPULENT
   (A) ruddy
   (B) spiritual
   (C) bloody
   (D) fat
   (E) gluttonous

6. DIVERT
   (A) behave
   (B) amuse
   (C) annoy
   (D) arrange
   (E) disclose

7. CHATTEL
   (A) slaves
   (B) family
   (C) real estate
   (D) mortgage
   (E) movable property

8. RECTITUDE
   (A) honesty
   (B) posture
   (C) construction
   (D) correction
   (E) accusation

9. TRUCE
   (A) treaty
   (B) peace
   (C) pause
   (D) amnesty
   (E) silence

10. RAPACIOUS
   (A) hungry
   (B) jolly
   (C) dishonest
   (D) greedy
   (E) strict

11. SPECTRUM
   (A) rainbow
   (B) prism
   (C) range
   (D) magnifier
   (E) idea

12. IMPERIOUS
   (A) overbearing
   (B) waterproof
   (C) frightening
   (D) poor
   (E) perfect

13. LACONIC

(A) brief
(B) lacy
(C) easygoing
(D) servile
(E) sad

14. BENEFICENCE

(A) good fortune
(B) act of charity
(C) blessing
(D) thanks
(E) enlightenment

TEST 3 — 8 MINUTES

Directions: Select the word that is closest in meaning to the CAPITALIZED word and circle the letter that appears before your answer.

1. HUMUS
   (A) nerve
   (B) topsoil
   (C) modesty
   (D) tonnage

2. INVALUABLE
   (A) useless
   (B) untrue
   (C) uniform
   (D) priceless

3. BELLIGERENT
   (A) warlike
   (B) windy
   (C) noisy
   (D) overweight

4. ACRID
   (A) burnt
   (B) smoky
   (C) bitter
   (D) artificial

5. RIFE
   (A) widespread
   (B) mature
   (C) quarrelsome
   (D) broken

6. TACIT
   (A) understood
   (B) sensitive
   (C) sticky
   (D) skillful

7. SHROUD
   (A) cummerbund
   (B) coffin
   (C) veil
   (D) wake

8. WRIT
   (A) law
   (B) order
   (C) deed
   (D) prohibition

9. DOWDY
   (A) young
   (B) fluffy
   (C) widowed
   (D) shabby

10. MAUDLIN
   (A) spotted
   (B) sentimental
   (C) silent
   (D) juicy

11. ULCER
   (A) pain
   (B) stomach ache
   (C) sore
   (D) swelling

12. NIGGARDLY
   (A) haggling
   (B) stingy
   (C) quick
   (D) wormlike

13. SURLY
   (A) positively
   (B) confidently
   (C) unfriendly
   (D) overly

14. TOKEN
   (A) symbol
   (B) coin
   (C) omen
   (D) facsimile

15. ASYLUM

(A) madness
(B) illness
(C) prison
(D) sanctuary

16. PRUNE

(A) raisin
(B) fruit
(C) trim
(D) wrinkle

TEST 4 — 7 MINUTES

Directions: Select the word that is closest in meaning to the CAPITALIZED word and circle the letter that appears before your answer.

1. AMORPHOUS
(A) insomniac
(B) drug free
(C) shapeless
(D) headless
(E) unloved

2. PALTRY
(A) silo
(B) larder
(C) fowl
(D) foul
(E) meager

3. QUANDARY
(A) swamp
(B) prey
(C) argument
(D) nausea
(E) puzzlement

4. STERLING
(A) genuine
(B) plated
(C) excellent
(D) shiny
(E) heavy

5. TIC
(A) click
(B) twitch
(C) check mark
(D) insect
(E) game

6. VALET
(A) manservant
(B) bootblack
(C) chauffeur
(D) doorman
(E) rascal

7. BRUNT
(A) wide end
(B) heavy part
(C) sore spot
(D) harsh sound
(E) weakest member

8. LIMPID
(A) deep
(B) clear
(C) weak
(D) blue
(E) lame

9. NARRATE
(A) write
(B) dramatize
(C) tell
(D) summarize
(E) explain

10. ORGY
(A) drunken brawl
(B) dance festival
(C) triathlon event
(D) wild party
(E) long speech

11. MINCE
(A) chop
(B) meat
(C) fruit
(D) suet
(E) pie

12. DEPRAVE
(A) corrupt
(B) belittle
(C) remove
(D) portray
(E) destroy

13. GARBLE
   (A) build
   (B) overeat
   (C) dazzle
   (D) drool
   (E) confuse

14. EBB
   (A) flow
   (B) wax
   (C) tide
   (D) wane
   (E) ocean

TEST 5 — 8 MINUTES

Directions: Select the word that is closest in meaning to the CAPITALIZED word and circle the letter that appears before your answer.

1. FIAT
   - (A) decree
   - (B) failure
   - (C) quarrel
   - (D) story

2. EQUABLE
   - (A) hot
   - (B) fair
   - (C) measured
   - (D) calm

3. GUILELESS
   - (A) clumsy
   - (B) clever
   - (C) wistful
   - (D) frank

4. CURATOR
   - (A) doctor
   - (B) priest
   - (C) librarian
   - (D) pharmacist

5. DESPERADO
   - (A) cowboy
   - (B) hunter
   - (C) settler
   - (D) criminal

6. LASSITUDE
   - (A) femininity
   - (B) length
   - (C) weariness
   - (D) perseverance

7. OBVIATE
   - (A) prevent
   - (B) erase
   - (C) overeat
   - (D) clarify

8. HERMETIC
   - (A) airtight
   - (B) solitary
   - (C) contrary
   - (D) brave

9. KEEPER
   - (A) miser
   - (B) caretaker
   - (C) box
   - (D) jeweler

10. INIQUITY
    - (A) prejudice
    - (B) hatred
    - (C) forgery
    - (D) wickedness

11. ACCRUE
    - (A) blame
    - (B) accumulate
    - (C) authorize
    - (D) praise

12. ROUSE
    - (A) complain
    - (B) awake
    - (C) dig
    - (D) annoy

13. PROLETARIAT
    - (A) workers
    - (B) voters
    - (C) royalty
    - (D) judiciary

14. LIMBER
    - (A) nowhere
    - (B) tied
    - (C) loose
    - (D) happy

15. HIATUS

(A) mountain
(B) cymbals
(C) rumpus
(D) gap

16. UNBLUSHING

(A) pale
(B) shameless
(C) stoic
(D) bold

TEST 6 — 7 MINUTES

Directions: Select the word that is closest in meaning to the CAPITALIZED word and circle the letter that appears before your answer.

1. WHEEDLE
   (A) breathe loudly
   (B) give birth
   (C) coax
   (D) insinuate
   (E) squirm

2. UNLETTERED
   (A) pantomimed
   (B) illustrated
   (C) manuscript
   (D) numbered
   (E) illiterate

3. SOJOURN
   (A) trip
   (B) convent
   (C) pilgrimage
   (D) worry
   (E) visit

4. PENSIVE
   (A) sorrowful
   (B) hanging
   (C) thoughtful
   (D) poor
   (E) stingy

5. RADIATE
   (A) heat
   (B) expand
   (C) illumine
   (D) beam
   (E) energize

6. TRACERY
   (A) searching
   (B) design
   (C) copy
   (D) track
   (E) recording

7. AGOG
   (A) frightened
   (B) surprised
   (C) open
   (D) angry
   (E) upset

8. HIGHWAYMAN
   (A) truck driver
   (B) state trooper
   (C) mountain dweller
   (D) hermit
   (E) robber

9. BIBLIOGRAPHY
   (A) story of one's own life
   (B) story of another's life
   (C) list of books
   (D) footnote
   (E) card catalog

10. JOLLITY
    (A) piracy
    (B) peace
    (C) dessert
    (D) merriment
    (E) teasing

11. IGNOBLE
    (A) stupid
    (B) shameful
    (C) drunken
    (D) regal
    (E) erect

12. MUNIFICENT
    (A) lavish
    (B) urban
    (C) splendid
    (D) enormous
    (E) important

13. ODIOUS
(A) impossible
(B) perfumed
(C) bad smelling
(D) unpleasant
(E) strange

14. CRONE
(A) complainer
(B) bee
(C) hag
(D) singer
(E) friend

TEST 7 — 8 MINUTES

Directions: Select the word that is closest in meaning to the CAPITALIZED word and circle the letter that appears before your answer.

1. CUPIDITY
   (A) greed
   (B) love
   (C) archery
   (D) boldness

2. DELECTATION
   (A) hindrance
   (B) enjoyment
   (C) explanation
   (D) debate

3. GAINSAY
   (A) repeat
   (B) somersault
   (C) deny
   (D) enjoy

4. FOREGONE
   (A) previous
   (B) later
   (C) ended
   (D) preordained

5. OTTOMAN
   (A) foot stool
   (B) rug
   (C) sofa
   (D) blanket

6. GRATUITOUS
   (A) thankful
   (B) polite
   (C) unnecessary
   (D) annoying

7. OPULENT
   (A) busy
   (B) showy
   (C) abundant
   (D) enchanted

8. INTERMENT
   (A) apprenticeship
   (B) questioning
   (C) referral
   (D) burial

9. APOLOGIST
   (A) defender
   (B) petitioner
   (C) prisoner
   (D) repenter

10. SUNDER
    (A) separate
    (B) vary
    (C) darken
    (D) depress

11. QUADRANT
    (A) perpendicular
    (B) right angle
    (C) quarter
    (D) corner

12. PORTENTOUS
    (A) overweight
    (B) ominous
    (C) overbearing
    (D) ostentatious

13. VAULT
    (A) boast
    (B) display
    (C) jump
    (D) defy

14. PONDER
    (A) brag
    (B) consider
    (C) beat
    (D) mimic

15. ETIQUETTE

(A) manners
(B) dress code
(C) wedding
(D) aristocracy

16. GOUGE

(A) measure
(B) scoop
(C) stuff
(D) stab

TEST 8 — 7 MINUTES

Directions: Select the word that is closest in meaning to the CAPITALIZED word and circle the letter that appears before your answer.

1. CITADEL

(A) castle
(B) barricade
(C) mansion
(D) fort
(E) church

2. SMIRCH

(A) stain
(B) smile
(C) blow
(D) kiss
(E) particle

3. FURL

(A) wave
(B) flap
(C) roll up
(D) sail
(E) billow

4. MORTIFY

(A) change
(B) embed
(C) fasten
(D) embarrass
(E) piece together

5. FACILE

(A) lithe
(B) hairy
(C) copy
(D) partisan
(E) easy

6. NOSEGAY

(A) lunchbag
(B) gold ring
(C) bouquet
(D) wreath
(E) ribbon

7. GURNEY

(A) cow
(B) bubble
(C) body bag
(D) water spout
(E) stretcher

8. ETCH

(A) print
(B) engrave
(C) paint
(D) capture
(E) frame

9. HAMLET

(A) small pig
(B) glove
(C) basket
(D) village
(E) cabin

10. INSOLVENT

(A) solid
(B) liquid
(C) bankrupt
(D) suspended
(E) mixture

11. KNACK

(A) junk
(B) ability
(C) knowledge
(D) sausage
(E) noise

12. AVARICE

(A) gluttony
(B) starvation
(C) intelligence
(D) greed
(E) wealth

13. TOOTHSOME

(A) chewy
(B) causing cavities
(C) tasty
(D) menacing
(E) haggard

14. PEER

(A) equal
(B) juror
(C) legislator
(D) judge
(E) neighbor

TEST 9 — 8 MINUTES

Directions: Select the word that is closest in meaning to the CAPITALIZED word and circle the letter that appears before your answer.

1. CISTERN
(A) water tank
(B) sewage system
(C) stew pot
(D) drainage pipe

2. FORSWEAR
(A) curse
(B) repent
(C) empty
(D) give up

3. DOUSE
(A) soak
(B) divine
(C) conjure
(D) depress

4. LITIGANT
(A) reader
(B) cleric
(C) wrapper
(D) suer

5. ORDINANCE
(A) ammunition
(B) rule
(C) simplification
(D) suffering

6. MARQUEE
(A) nobleman
(B) billboard
(C) canopy
(D) gemstone

7. IMPASSIVE
(A) active
(B) obstructive
(C) calm
(D) fair

8. NEOPHYTE
(A) novice
(B) complainer
(C) baby
(D) wood nymph

9. HENCHMAN
(A) bartender
(B) gardener
(C) gangster
(D) follower

10. JUBILEE
(A) meeting
(B) year
(C) anniversary
(D) service

11. BAILIFF
(A) sailor
(B) moneylender
(C) dog
(D) court officer

12. TREMENDOUS
(A) frightening
(B) enormous
(C) shaking
(D) noisy

13. ROOT
(A) hurry
(B) hibernate
(C) dig
(D) perch

14. RAZE
(A) burn
(B) destroy
(C) loot
(D) obscure

15. REVULSION

(A) disgust
(B) insurgency
(C) twisting
(D) correction

16. GYRATE

(A) barbecue
(B) twist
(C) wobble
(D) spin

TEST 10 — 12 MINUTES

Directions: Select the word that is closest in meaning to the CAPITALIZED word and circle the letter that appears before your answer.

1. WREAK
   (A) smash
   (B) rage
   (C) poke
   (D) emanate
   (E) inflict

2. PHOBIA
   (A) attraction
   (B) love
   (C) fear
   (D) hatred
   (E) illness

3. STATIC
   (A) lively
   (B) electrical
   (C) unpleasant
   (D) shocking
   (E) inactive

4. AMULET
   (A) omen
   (B) necklace
   (C) charm
   (D) armband
   (E) flask

5. HAZY
   (A) polluted
   (B) indistinct
   (C) brown
   (D) annoyed
   (E) insane

6. KILN
   (A) skirt
   (B) plaid
   (C) oven
   (D) relative
   (E) weight

7. MIGRATE
   (A) go south
   (B) sleep
   (C) headache
   (D) travel
   (E) leave

8. OFFICIOUS
   (A) insulting
   (B) formal
   (C) meddling
   (D) distant
   (E) ceremonial

9. NIB
   (A) irritation
   (B) bite
   (C) bump
   (D) chill
   (E) point

10. GAINFUL
    (A) profitable
    (B) overflowing
    (C) enthusiastic
    (D) injurious
    (E) busy

11. FILAMENT
    (A) steak
    (B) thread
    (C) flavoring
    (D) decoration
    (E) failure

12. DELL
    (A) farm
    (B) barnyard
    (C) valley
    (D) bell
    (E) ring

13. COBBLE
(A) limp
(B) weave
(C) eat greedily
(D) repair shoes
(E) shoe horses

14. UNNUMBERED
(A) unclassified
(B) countless
(C) few
(D) lettered
(E) listed

15. IMPISH
(A) disrespectful
(B) mischievous
(C) rash
(D) unsaid
(E) relentless

16. BICEPS
(A) muscle
(B) tweezers
(C) dinosaur
(D) rowboat
(E) crossroads

17. THERAPEUTIC
(A) manipulative
(B) active
(C) athletic
(D) rigorous
(E) curative

18. STAID
(A) leftover
(B) guest
(C) sedate
(D) dirty
(E) immobile

19. PURIST
(A) perfectionist
(B) sanitarian
(C) laundress
(D) exorcist
(E) steward

20. FETISH
(A) charm
(B) foot
(C) dust ball
(D) gremlin
(E) hairdo

21. GOAD
(A) frog
(B) tadpole
(C) aspiration
(D) prod
(E) score

22. DISPENSARY
(A) military store
(B) infirmary
(C) confessional
(D) bus station
(E) court room

23. JOGGLE
(A) tinkle
(B) shake
(C) shove
(D) race
(E) surprise

24. VOUCH
(A) pay
(B) repeat
(C) agree
(D) comfort
(E) guarantee

Practice Synonyms Tests

Answer Key

TEST 1

1. **A**	5. **C**	9. **B**	13. **A**	17. **C**
2. **C**	6. **A**	10. **A**	14. **D**	18. **C**
3. **B**	7. **D**	11. **D**	15. **C**	19. **D**
4. **A**	8. **C**	12. **D**	16. **D**	20. **D**

TEST 2

1. **E**	4. **B**	7. **E**	10. **D**	13. **A**
2. **D**	5. **D**	8. **A**	11. **C**	14. **B**
3. **D**	6. **B**	9. **C**	12. **A**	

TEST 3

1. **B**	5. **A**	9. **D**	13. **C**
2. **D**	6. **A**	10. **B**	14. **A**
3. **A**	7. **C**	11. **C**	15. **D**
4. **C**	8. **B**	12. **B**	16. **C**

TEST 4

1. **C**	4. **C**	7. **B**	10. **D**	13. **E**
2. **E**	5. **B**	8. **B**	11. **A**	14. **D**
3. **E**	6. **A**	9. **C**	12. **A**	

TEST 5

1. **A**	5. **D**	9. **B**	13. **A**
2. **B**	6. **C**	10. **D**	14. **C**
3. **D**	7. **A**	11. **B**	15. **D**
4. **C**	8. **A**	12. **B**	16. **B**

TEST 6

1. **C**	4. **C**	7. **B**	10. **D**	13. **D**
2. **E**	5. **D**	8. **E**	11. **B**	14. **C**
3. **E**	6. **B**	9. **C**	12. **A**	

TEST 7

1. **A**
2. **B**
3. **C**
4. **D**
5. **A**
6. **C**
7. **C**
8. **D**
9. **A**
10. **A**
11. **C**
12. **B**
13. **C**
14. **B**
15. **A**
16. **B**

TEST 8

1. **D**
2. **A**
3. **C**
4. **D**
5. **E**
6. **C**
7. **E**
8. **B**
9. **D**
10. **C**
11. **B**
12. **D**
13. **C**
14. **A**

TEST 9

1. **A**
2. **D**
3. **A**
4. **D**
5. **B**
6. **C**
7. **C**
8. **A**
9. **D**
10. **C**
11. **D**
12. **B**
13. **C**
14. **B**
15. **A**
16. **D**

TEST 10

1. **E**
2. **C**
3. **E**
4. **C**
5. **B**
6. **C**
7. **D**
8. **C**
9. **E**
10. **A**
11. **B**
12. **C**
13. **D**
14. **B**
15. **B**
16. **A**
17. **E**
18. **C**
19. **A**
20. **A**
21. **D**
22. **B**
23. **B**
24. **E**

CHAPTER 8

Verbal Analogies

PLAN A: ACCELERATED

- ***Read*** the chapter
- ***Study*** "What Smart Test-Takers Know"
- ***Skim*** "Learning Exercises"
- ***Take*** "Practice Verbal Analogy Tests"

PLAN B: TOP SPEED

- ***Read*** the chapter
- ***Read*** "What Smart Test-Takers Know"
- ***Take*** "Practice Verbal Analogy Tests"

You'll Find Answers to These Questions

What makes a verbal analogy?
What do verbal analogy questions look like?
How do you solve verbal analogies?
What do smart test-takers know about analogies?

WHAT MAKES A VERBAL ANALOGY?

Verbal analogies are all about relationships. They test your ability to see a relationship between two words and to recognize a similar relationship between two other words. Verbal analogy tests measure not only your understanding of the words themselves but also your mental flexibility and ability to manipulate relationships. The key to analogy success is being able to express the relationship between the words in a pair—not what the words mean, but how they are related.

WHAT DO VERBAL ANALOGY QUESTIONS LOOK LIKE?

An analogy can be written in several different ways. It may be written as a sentence, using only words, or symbols may be substituted for the connecting words. SSAT analogy questions use only words.

EXAMPLE:

WINTER is to SUMMER as COLD is to

(A) wet
(B) future
(C) hot
(D) freezing

or

EXAMPLE:

WINTER:SUMMER::COLD:

(A) wet
(B) future
(C) hot
(D) freezing

The answer to this example is (**C**). WINTER and SUMMER are opposites, or antonyms. The antonym for COLD is HOT.

Some analogies supply three of the four necessary words. You must find the relationship between the first two words and then choose a word that is related to the third word in the same way.

EXAMPLE:

SPELLING is to PUNCTUATION as BIOLOGY is to

(A) science
(B) animals
(C) dissection
(D) chemistry

The answer to this example is (**D**). SPELLING and PUNCTUATION are two subjects studied in English. BIOLOGY and CHEMISTRY are two subjects studied in the field of science.

Other analogies begin with a pair of words. You must first decide how those words are related. Then, from a list of four or five pairs, you must choose the pair that illustrates the same relationship.

Example:

SPELLING is to PUNCTUATION as

(A) pajamas is to fatigue

(B) powder is to shaving

(C) bandage is to cut

(D) biology is to chemistry

SSAT verbal analogy questions appear in both formats. Some supply three words, requiring you to choose a fourth that is related to the third in the same way that the first two words are related. Other SSAT verbal analogy questions supply a pair of words and require you to choose another pair with the same relationship to one another.

HOW DO YOU SOLVE VERBAL ANALOGIES?

To solve verbal analogies, follow these five steps:

Analogies: Getting It Right

1. Figure out how the first two words are related.
2. Make up a sentence that expresses that relationship.
3. Try out your sentence on each answer choice and eliminate the ones that don't work.
4. If you're left with more than one answer—or no answer at all—go back and make your sentence fit better.
5. Choose the best answer. If none of the choices fits exactly, choose the one that works best.

HERE'S THE ANSWER

What if none of the answer pairs seems exactly right?

Remember: The directions tell you to choose the best answer. The correct answer won't necessarily be a perfect fit, but it will work better than the other choices.

WHAT SMART TEST-TAKERS KNOW

A SENTENCE CAN MAKE THE CONNECTION.

SCRIBBLE is to WRITE as

(A) inform is to supply

(B) mutter is to listen

(C) nuzzle is to feel

(D) ramble is to play

(E) stagger is to walk

Summarize each analogy relationship with a sentence. In this case, *scribbling is a bad kind of writing*. Use the same sentence to test connections between the words in the answer choices. When you find one that works, you've found your answer.

(A) *Informing* is a bad kind of *supplying*. (No.)

(B) *Muttering* is a bad kind of *listening*. (No.)

(C) *Nuzzling* is a bad kind *feeling*. (No.)

(D) *Rambling* is a bad kind of *playing*. (No.)

(E) *Staggering* is a bad kind of *walking*. (Yes!)

IT PAYS TO KNOW THE MOST COMMON VERBAL ANALOGY CATEGORIES

The same relationships appear over and over again in verbal analogy questions. Knowing what the categories are and looking for them as you tackle each problem will make your job easier. Some of the most commonly used with SSAT analogy questions are:

SYNONYM RELATIONSHIPS

Synonyms are words that have similar meanings.

EXAMPLE:

ENORMOUS is to HUGE as MUDDY is to

(A) unclear

(B) clean

(C) rocky

(D) roguish

The correct answer is (**A**). Something that is described as MUDDY is clouded, or UNCLEAR.

ANTONYM RELATIONSHIPS

Antonyms are words that have opposite meanings.

EXAMPLE:

GOOD is to EVIL as

(A) suave is to blunt

(B) north is to climate

(C) angel is to devil

(D) sorrow is to happiness

The correct answer is (**C**). ANGEL is the opposite of DEVIL.

NOTE: The words that have a positive association, GOOD and ANGEL, are the first words in each pair. The words with a negative association, EVIL and DEVIL, are the second words in each pair. "Sorrow is to happiness" also represents the antonym relationship, but it is an incorrect answer because the terms are in reversed order. A properly completed analogy consists of terms with the same relationship occurring in the same order.

PART-WHOLE RELATIONSHIPS

In this type of analogy, one of the words in each pair represents a single part of a whole person, place, thing, or idea.

EXAMPLE:

SNAKE is to REPTILE as

(A) patch is to thread

(B) hand is to clock

(C) hand is to finger

(D) struggle is to fight

The best answer here is (**B**). A SNAKE is part of the REPTILE family. A HAND is part of a CLOCK. Choice (C) also shows a similar relationship, but the words are given in the wrong order.

NOUN-VERB RELATIONSHIPS

In this type of analogy, one of the words in a pair names a person, place, thing, or idea. The other word represents an action that can be associated with that word.

EXAMPLE:

STEAK is to BROIL as

(A) food is to sell

(B) wine is to pour

(C) bread is to bake

(D) sugar is to spill

The best answer here is (**C**). One way to cook a STEAK is to BROIL it; similarly, we BAKE BREAD in order to cook it. Choices (B) and (D) both show noun-verb relationships, with the nouns and verbs in the correct sequence, but neither uses a verb that relates to cooking. Therefore, the best choice would be (C) because broiling and baking are both forms of cooking food.

CAUSE-AND-EFFECT RELATIONSHIPS

Two types of cause-and-effect relationships may be used in analogies. In the first type, one word in the pair will sometimes result in the second word.

EXAMPLE:

RACE is to FATIGUE as FAST is to

(A) track

(B) hunger

(C) run

(D) obesity

The correct answer is (**B**). Running a RACE may cause the runner FATIGUE. FASTING may cause HUNGER.

In the second type of cause-and-effect analogy, one word in a pair may produce the other.

EXAMPLE:

COW is to MILK as BEE is to

(A) honey

(B) drone

(C) nest

(D) wasp

The correct answer is (**A**). A COW produces MILK; a BEE produces HONEY.

AVOID THE TRAPS!

Don't confuse the order of the words. The relationship of the words in the answer must be in the same order as the relationship of the words in the first pair.

PURPOSE RELATIONSHIPS

In this type of analogy, one of the words in each pair is used in a task involving the other word in the pair.

EXAMPLE:

GLOVE is to BALL as

(A) hook is to fish

(B) winter is to weather

(C) game is to pennant

(D) stadium is to seats

The correct answer is (**A**). A GLOVE is used in baseball to catch a BALL. When fishing, a HOOK is used to catch a FISH.

ASSOCIATION RELATIONSHIPS

In this type of analogy, one word in a pair is commonly thought of in connection with the second word.

Example:

YOUNG is to LAMB as

(A) ram is to ewe

(B) old is to mutton

(C) lamb is to chop

(D) wool is to shear

The correct answer is (**B**). The meat of YOUNG sheep is called LAMB. The meat of OLD sheep is called MUTTON.

Other analogy categories with which you should also become familiar are:

- **"Type of" analogies**

  SWORD is to WEAPON A sword is a type of weapon.

  GRIMACE is to EXPRESSION A grimace is a type of expression.

  OAK is to TREE An oak is a type of tree.

  WATERCOLOR is to PAINTING A watercolor is a type of painting.

- **"Part of the definition of" analogies**

  GENEROSITY is to PHILANTHROPIST Generosity is part of the definition of a philanthropist.

  BRAVERY is to HERO Bravery is part of the definition of a hero.

  FALSE is to LIE It is part of the definition of a lie that it is false.

  INVENTION is to ORIGINAL It is part of the definition of an invention that it is original.

  FACULTY is to TEACH It is part of the definition of a faculty that it is supposed to teach.

- **"Lack of something is part of the definition" analogies**

  TRAITOR is to LOYALTY Lack of loyalty is part of the definition of a traitor.

  NEGLIGENT is to CARE It is part of the definition of being negligent that someone lacks care.

  ARID is to MOISTURE Lack of moisture is part of the definition of an arid region.

  IGNORANCE is to KNOWLEDGE Lack of knowledge is part of the definition of ignorance.

  POVERTY is to FUNDS Part of the definition of poverty is a lack of funds.

- **"Part to whole" analogies**

  MOVEMENT is to SONATA A movement is a part of a sonata.

  CHAPTER is to BOOK A chapter is a part of a book.

  ACTOR is to TROUPE An actor is a part of a troupe.

  LION is to PRIDE A lion is part of a pride.

  FINISH is to RACE The finish is part of a race.

- **"A place for" analogies**

  WITNESS is to COURTROOM A courtroom is the place for a witness.

  ACTOR is to STAGE A stage is the place for an actor.

  GRAIN is to SILO A silo is a place for storing grain.

  PILOT is to AIRPLANE An airplane is a place where you would find a pilot.

  ORE is to MINE A mine is the place where you would find ore.

- **"Degree" analogies**

  BREEZE is to GALE A gale is more powerful than a breeze.

  TRICKLE is to GUSH To gush is more forceful than to trickle.

  ANNOY is to ENRAGE To enrage is stronger than to annoy.

  MOUNTAIN is to HILL A mountain is a very large hill.

  WASH is to SCRUB To scrub is stronger than to wash.

TESTSMARTS

Make the sentence connection. Turn the analogy pairs into sentences to help you see the connection. Then fit the answer pairs into the same sentence until you find the one that works best.

THE MORE PRECISE YOUR SENTENCE, THE BETTER.

You cannot expect to solve every analogy by simply plugging in the list of common analogy types. Remember that the analogies get more difficult as you work your way through each group. Use the common categories as a starting point, but be prepared to refine the relationship by making your sentence more precise. Consider this example:

GRAIN is to SILO as

(A) pilot is to plane
(B) judge is to courtroom
(C) water is to reservoir
(D) clock is to time
(E) automobile is to highway

If you apply the "place where" idea without thinking, here is what happens:

A silo is a place where you would find grain.

(A) A plane is a place where you would find a pilot.
(B) A courtroom is a place where you would find a judge.
(C) A reservoir is a place where you would find water.
(D) A clock is a place where you would find time.
(E) A highway is a place where you would find automobiles.

You can eliminate (D), but that still leaves you with four possible answers. Now's the time to go back and make your original sentence fit better. How can you express the relationship between silo and grain more precisely?

A silo is a place where grain is stored.

(A) A plane is a place where a pilot is stored.
(B) A courtroom is a place where a judge is stored.
(C) A reservoir is a place where water is stored.
(E) A highway is a place where automobiles are stored.

Now it's easy to see that the correct answer is (C).

WORDS WITH SIMILAR MEANINGS CAN FOOL YOU.

In analogy questions, what counts is the relationship between the first two words. The words in the correct answer choice must have a similar relationship. There is no need for one or both to be related in meaning to the capitalized words. Consider this analogy:

TANGLED is to KNOT as

(A) snarled is to rope

(B) crumpled is to wrinkle

(C) mussed is to hair

(D) empty is to cup

(E) canned is to preserves

This is a "part of the definition of" analogy and the correct answer is **(B).** Part of the definition of a *knot* is that it is something *tangled.* Likewise, part of the definition of a *wrinkle* is that it is something *crumpled.* Don't be misled by (A). Although *snarled* is similar in meaning to *tangled,* a rope does not have to be snarled.

AVOID THE TRAPS!

Don't be fooled by similar words. In analogy questions, you're looking for similar relationships, not similar words.

SOME ANALOGIES WORK BETTER WHEN YOU TURN THEM AROUND.

Sometimes the first two words fall easily into a sentence that expresses their relationship—and sometimes they don't. If you're having trouble making up a sentence that relates the two words, be prepared to shift gears. Try reversing the order of the original word pair. Let's see how this technique works on the following analogy:

ICE is to GLACIER as

(A) train is to trestle

(B) sand is to dune

(C) path is to forest

(D) feather is to bird

(E) ocean is to ship

If you can't come up with a sentence relating ICE to GLACIER, try relating GLACIER to ICE:

A *glacier* is made up of *ice*.

Here's the only catch: If you reverse the order of the capitalized words, you must also reverse the order of the words in each answer choice. So when you apply your sentence to the answer choices this is how you'll have to do it:

(A) A *trestle* is made up of a *train.*

(B) A *dune* is made up of *sand.*

(C) A *forest* is made up of a *path.*

(D) A *bird* is made up of a *feather.*

(E) A *ship* is made up of an *ocean.*

Clearly **(B)** exhibits the same relationship as the original pair.

LEARNING EXERCISES: VERBAL ANALOGIES

The questions in this section are arranged in boxes called "frames." The answer for each frame will be found in the box to the left of the question frame.

First, cover the answer boxes with a strip of paper. Circle your answer to the question. Then, move the paper down to expose the answer to that question.

- The first pages organize the analogies according to specific types of relationships. This will help you recognize those relationships and concentrate on completing the analogy correctly.
- The second part contains a variety of analogy relationships in random order. This will give you practice in determining what the relationship is before you attempt to complete the analogy correctly.

Synonym Relationships

ANSWER	QUESTION
1. (D)	**1.** SMALL is to MINIATURE as LARGE is to (A) shark (C) minute (B) dwarf (D) giant
2. (A)	**2.** BOSS is to EMPLOYER as EMPLOYEE is to (A) worker (C) manager (B) president (D) director
3. (D)	**3.** DIG is to EXCAVATE as (A) attempt:prevent (C) try:convict (B) avenge:revenge (D) kill:slay
4. (B)	**4.** PLEASURE is to ENJOYMENT as (A) Satan:demon (C) fate:love (B) hate:abhorrence (D) hate:love
5. (B)	**5.** ORIGINATE is to INVENT as (A) song:score (C) study:work (B) copy:imitate (D) copy:work
6. (A)	**6.** LEXICON is to DICTIONARY as (A) officer:policeman (C) law:enforce (B) police:protection (D) law:crime
7. (D)	**7.** PERSISTENT:OBSTINATE:: (A) value:valiant (C) bravery:war (B) brutal:warfare (D) valiant:brave
8. (C)	**8.** DEVIOUS:CIRCUITOUS:: (A) yodel:yield (C) yield:submit (B) yield:wield (D) simmer:submit
9. (B)	**9.** FEDERAL:NATION:: (A) city:government (C) mayor:city (B) municipal:city (D) state:house
10. (B)	**10.** CONTEMPT:DISRESPECT:: (A) kempt:disarray (C) conceal:deter (B) hatred:dislike (D) cool:aloof

Antonym Relationships

ANSWER	QUESTION
1. (D)	**1.** LIGHT is to DARK as WET is to (A) snow (C) sand (B) rain (D) dry

ANSWER	QUESTION
2. (D)	2. SUMMER is to WINTER as EVENING is to (A) sunset (C) darkness (B) coolness (D) morning
3. (A)	3. RIGHT is to LEFT as LOW is to (A) high (C) sorrow (B) bottom (D) note
4. (C)	4. NOTHING is to EVERYTHING as WHISPER is to (A) mystery (C) shout (B) something (D) ghost
5. (D)	5. DAY:NIGHT::SUN: (A) solar (C) universe (B) heat (D) moon
6. (C)	6. WEAK:STRONG::INCAPABLE: (A) clumsy (C) adept (B) cowardly (D) failure
7. (C)	7. ADVANCE:HALT:: (A) stop:go (C) go:stop (B) return:change (D) conquer:take
8. (B)	8. SKILLFUL:CLUMSY:: (A) alert:sleepy (C) quick:swift (B) deft:awkward (D) smooth:slick
9. (D)	9. ENEMIES:FRIENDS:: (A) pacify:quiet (C) defeat:lose (B) hate:dislike (D) despise:esteem
10. (A)	10. BLAME:PRAISE:: (A) fail:succeed (C) succeed:defeat (B) defeat:condemn (D) emerge:emanate

Part-Whole Relationships

ANSWER	QUESTION
1. (A)	1. WINDOW:PANE::DOOR: (A) panel (C) jamb (B) knob (D) key
2. (B)	2. PARAGRAPH:SENTENCE::SENTENCE: (A) modifier (C) composition (B) word (D) grammar

ANSWER	QUESTION
3. (D)	3. NUT:SHELL::PEA: (A) shooter (C) green (B) soup (D) pod
4. (C)	4. ANTLER:DEER:: (A) tusk:husk (C) tusk:elephant (B) animal:elephant (D) horn:antler
5. (B)	5. JEWEL:RING:: (A) stone:ruby (C) precious:stone (B) locket:necklace (D) iron:chain
6. (A)	6. PIT is to PEACH as (A) sun:solar system (C) plane:Earth (B) moon:earth (D) noon:orbit
7. (C)	7. PAGE is to BOOK as (A) period:comma (C) word:page (B) novel:book (D) library:story
8. (A)	8. STATE is to COUNTRY as (A) continent:world (C) country:city (B) world:continent (D) ocean:shore
9. (B)	9. HAND is to BODY as STAR is to (A) sky (C) eye (B) universe (D) movie
10. (A)	10. PLAY is to PROLOGUE as CONSTITUTION is to (A) preamble (C) preview (B) Bill of Rights (D) Supreme Court

Noun-Verb Relationships

ANSWER	QUESTION
1. (C)	1. LETTER is to MAIL as MONEY is to (A) bank (C) invest (B) savings (D) account
2. (C)	2. SEAL is to FLOAT as BIRD is to (A) fly (C) soar (B) wing (D) nest
3. (A)	3. EGG is to SCRAMBLE as POTATO is to (A) mash (C) butter (B) skin (D) slice

ANSWER	QUESTION
4. (B)	**4.** ARTIST:PAINT::CONTRACTOR: (A) agreement (C) masonry (B) build (D) carpentry
5. (D)	**5.** SCISSORS:TRIM::SCALES: (A) fish (C) measure (B) weight (D) weigh
6. (B)	**6.** BED:SLEEP::CHAIR: (A) carry (C) stare (B) sit (D) recline
7. (A)	**7.** TASTE:TONGUE::TOUCH: (A) skin (C) feelings (B) arms (D) ears
8. (C)	**8.** BOX:COVER::BOTTLE: (A) glass (C) cork (B) contain (D) break
9. (D)	**9.** SHOE:LACE::DOOR: (A) hinge (C) swing (B) enter (D) lock
10. (B)	**10.** TYPEWRITER:WRITE::CALCULATOR: (A) add (C) percentage (B) compute (D) predict

Cause-and-Effect Relationships

ANSWER	QUESTION
1. (C)	**1.** SATISFACTION:GOOD DEED::IMPROVEMENT: (A) sin (C) criticism (B) fault (D) kindness
2. (C)	**2.** SEED:PLANT::EGG: (A) yolk (C) bird (B) crack (D) shell
3. (B)	**3.** WHEAT:FLOUR::GRAPE: (A) vintage (C) vine (B) wine (D) vineyard
4. (D)	**4.** HEAT:FIRE::CLOUD: (A) sky (C) sun (B) snow (D) moisture

ANSWER	QUESTION
5. (A)	**5.** THREAT:INSECURITY:: (A) challenge:fight (C) reason:anger (B) thunder:lightning (D) speed:brake
6. (D)	**6.** HEAT:RADIATOR:: (A) sea:wave (C) wind:trees (B) tree:breeze (D) breeze:fan
7. (A)	**7.** RETURN:REWARD:: (A) repent:forgiveness (C) listen:speak (B) sin:religion (D) try:attempt
8. (B)	**8.** WAR:GRIEF:: (A) joy:peace (C) peace:finish (B) peace:happiness (D) joy:happiness
9. (C)	**9.** MOON:LIGHT:: (A) sunset:sun (C) eclipse:dark (B) earth:orbit (D) gravity:earth
10. (A)	**10.** NOISE:DISTRACT:: (A) music:soothe (C) music:notes (B) violin:orchestra (D) loud:detract

Purpose Relationships

ANSWER	QUESTION
1. (D)	**1.** RING:FINGER::CUFF: (A) arm (C) hand (B) shoulder (D) wrist
2. (C)	**2.** GAS:VEHICLE::WOOD: (A) tree (C) stove (B) fire (D) heat
3. (D)	**3.** REFRIGERATOR:MEAT::BANK: (A) cashier (C) watchman (B) combination (D) money
4. (B)	**4.** WATCHMAN:PROTECT::NAVIGATOR: (A) navy (C) plan (B) guide (D) map
5. (A)	**5.** GYMNASIUM:GAME::AUDITORIUM: (A) production (C) cafeteria (B) script (D) actors

Association Relationships

ANSWER	QUESTION
1. (A)	**1.** PRESENT:BIRTHDAY::REWARD: (A) accomplishment (C) punishment (B) medal (D) money
2. (B)	**2.** GUEST:ACCEPTANCE::HOST: (A) party (C) hostess (B) invitation (D) refreshments
3. (B)	**3.** STICK:PUCK::BAT: (A) cricket (C) touchdown (B) ball (D) bowl
4. (C)	**4.** FEVER:SPRING::LEAVES: (A) October (C) autumn (B) season (D) sadness
5. (A)	**5.** HONOR:BRAVERY::GUILT: (A) crime (C) thief (B) jail (D) killer

Mixed Relationships

The analogies in this section are **not** arranged in any particular pattern. You must decide what type of relationship is being used in each item.

Directions: Find a relationship between the first two words in each question. To complete the analogy, choose the answer that shows a similar relationship. Answers and explanations can be found in the answer box.

ANSWER	QUESTION
1. (B) THANKSGIVING is in NOVEMBER; CHRISTMAS is in DECEMBER.	**1.** THANKSGIVING:NOVEMBER::CHRISTMAS: (A) Santa Claus (C) snow (B) December (D) Jingle Bells
2. (C) Antonym relationships	**2.** REMEMBER:FORGET::FIND: (A) locate (C) lose (B) keep (D) return
3. (A) ANCHORS stop SHIPS; BRAKES stop AUTOMOBILES. The second word in each pair is the part used to stop the first noun.	**3.** SHIP is to ANCHOR as AUTOMOBILE is to (A) brake (C) stop (B) wheel (D) accelerator
4. (A) The words in each pair are synonyms.	**4.** END is to ABOLISH as BEGIN is to (A) establish (C) tyranny (B) finish (D) crusade

DATE
NOTE

ANSWER	QUESTION
5. (B) WOOD DECAYS:IRON RUSTS. The first word in each pair is a noun. The second is a verb that relates to the first.	**5.** WOOD is to DECAY as IRON is to (A) dampness (B) rust (C) steel (D) ore
6. (D) A WEEK is part of a MONTH; a DAY is part of a WEEK.	**6.** MONTH:WEEK::WEEK: (A) month (B) hour (C) year (D) day
7. (B) FLOUR is ground WHEAT; GRAVEL is broken ROCK.	**7.** FLOUR:WHEAT::GRAVEL: (A) brick (B) rock (C) coal (D) bread
8. (B) The words in each pair are antonyms.	**8.** ATTACK:PROTECT::OFFENSE: (A) combat (B) defense (C) conceal (D) reconcile
9. (D) The words in each pair are antonyms.	**9.** DIVIDE:MULTIPLY::SUBTRACT: (A) plus (B) reduce (C) divide (D) add
10. (C) Each pair contains similar possessive pronouns.	**10.** MINE:MY::YOUR: (A) you (B) ours (C) yours (D) you're
11. (B) GLASSES and LIGHT enhance a person's VISION.	**11.** GLASSES:VISION:: (A) glass:mirror (B) light:vision (C) eating:fork (D) hand:object
12. (A) A FLAME may cause a BURN; an INSULT may cause ANGER.	**12.** FLAME:BURN:: (A) insult:anger (B) glass:crack (C) birth:life (D) sun:orbit
13. (C) SEEING is the result of LOOKING; HEARING is the result of LISTENING.	**13.** LOOK:SEE:: (A) illuminate:light (B) audition:speak (C) listen:hear (D) follow:lead
14. (A) WOLVES gather in PACKS; COWS gather in HERDS.	**14.** WOLF:PACK:: (A) cow:herd (B) cattle:farmer (C) cow:graze (D) farmer:farm
15. (D) The words in each pair are antonyms.	**15.** LEAVE:STAY::DEPART: (A) home (B) disembark (C) run (D) remain
16. (D) MECHANICS repair CARS; DOCTORS treat PEOPLE.	**16.** CAR:MECHANIC::PEOPLE: (A) butcher (B) lawyer (C) house (D) doctor

ANSWER	QUESTION
17. (A) A TREE is one part of a FOREST; a PERSON is one part of a CROWD.	**17.** FOREST:TREE::CROWD: (A) person (B) alone (C) men (D) many
18. (C) A NOVELIST writes FICTION; a HISTORIAN writes about FACTS.	**18.** FICTION:NOVELIST::FACTS: (A) legend (B) story (C) historian (D) research
19. (B) STRANGER is the noun form of the adjective STRANGE; ARTIST is the noun form of the adjective ARTISTIC.	**19.** STRANGER:STRANGE:: (A) oddest:odd (B) artist:artistic (C) art:artist (D) satirist:artist
20. (C) A LIBRARIAN works in a LIBRARY; a TEACHER works in a SCHOOL.	**20.** LIBRARIAN:LIBRARY:: (A) school:education (B) office:principal (C) teacher:school (D) gymnasium:workout
21. (C) The words in each pair are antonyms.	**21.** SICKNESS:HEALTH::DEATH (A) mortician (B) skull (C) life (D) pirate
22. (A) New MACHINES are created by INVENTORS; new BOOKS are created by AUTHORS.	**22.** INVENTOR:MACHINE::AUTHOR: (A) book (B) poet (C) creator (D) computer
23. (B) A POUND is a unit of WEIGHT; a MILE is a unit of DISTANCE.	**23.** WEIGHT:POUND::DISTANCE: (A) liter (B) mile (C) ruler (D) space
24. (B) The words in each pair are antonyms.	**24.** CONCEAL:REVEAL::ASCEND: (A) embark (B) descend (C) mount (D) leave
25. (D) A CAPE is a geographical part of a CONTINENT; a GULF is part of an OCEAN.	**25.** CAPE:CONTINENT:: (A) ocean:lake (B) lake:reservoir (C) reservoir:water (D) gulf:ocean
26. (A) A LENS is an aid to VISION; CRUTCHES aid MOBILITY.	**26.** VISION:LENS:: (A) mobility:crutches (B) crutches:legs (C) walking:paralysis (D) doctor:paralysis
27. (C) A BUS travels along a ROAD; a LOCOMOTIVE moves on a TRACK.	**27.** BUS:ROAD:: (A) wheels:street (B) steel:rails (C) locomotive:track (D) locomotive:steam
28. (B) YEAR is the whole; JULY is the part; METER the whole; CENTIMETER the part. All other part/whole relationships are reversed.	**28.** YEAR:JULY:: (A) week:month (B) meter:centimeter (C) month:century (D) millimeter:centimeter

ANSWER	QUESTION
29. (A) CLIMB a TREE; PADDLE a CANOE.	**29.** CLIMB:TREE:: (A) paddle:canoe (C) throw:balloon (B) horse:shoe (D) file:finger
30. (D) LINCOLN is a city in NEBRASKA; TRENTON is a city in NEW JERSEY.	**30.** LINCOLN:NEBRASKA:: (A) Washington:Oregon (B) New York:Kentucky (C) Chicago:New York (D) Trenton:New Jersey
31. (C) SHARPEN a PENCIL; SAW a piece of WOOD.	**31.** PENCIL:SHARPEN:: (A) knife:cut (C) wood:saw (B) carpenter:build (D) well:fill
32. (C) A FINGER is part of a HAND; a STRAND of hair is part of a head of HAIR.	**32.** FINGER:HAND:: (A) arm:sleeve (C) strand:hair (B) shoe:foot (D) blouse:skirt
33. (A) CONVEX, an outward curve, is the antonym of CONCAVE, an indented curve. Similarly, HILL and HOLE are antonyms.	**33.** CONVEX:CONCAVE:: (A) hill:hole (C) round:square (B) in:within (D) nose:mouth
34. (B) COWS produce MILK; BEES produce HONEY.	**34.** COW:MILK:: (A) rat:cheese (C) bird:wing (B) bee:honey (D) cat:dog
35. (D) EXERCISE aids weight REDUCTION; LUCK is an aid to WINNING.	**35.** EXERCISE:REDUCE:: (A) grumble:resign (C) spending:save (B) snow:freeze (D) luck:win
36. (A) A PEAK is the top part of a MOUNTAIN; a CREST is the top of a WAVE.	**36.** MOUNTAIN:PEAK:: (A) wave:crest (C) tide:ocean (B) storm:ocean (D) storm:hurricane
37. (A) FOOD enables a BODY to do work; FUEL, such as gasoline, enables an ENGINE to work in a similar way.	**37.** FOOD:BODY:: (A) fuel:engine (C) kite:tail (B) bat:ball (D) mechanic:engine
38. (A) A BAROMETER measures atmospheric PRESSURE; a THERMOMETER measures TEMPERATURE.	**38.** PRESSURE:BAROMETER:: (A) temperature:thermometer (B) speedometer:distance (C) meter:perimeter (D) comptometer:comptroller
39. (C) The words in each pair are antonyms.	**39.** FAMINE:ABUNDANCE:: (A) hunger:starvation (C) poverty:wealth (B) squalor:starvation (D) famine:hunger

ANSWER	QUESTION
40. (B) STUDIOUSLY is the adverb form of the verb STUDY; PLAYFULLY is the adverb form of the verb PLAY.	**40.** STUDY:STUDIOUSLY:: (A) work:learning (B) play:playfully (C) books:bookish (D) habit:habitual
41. (D) The words in each pair are synonyms.	**41.** DISCARD:DELETE:: (A) attach:detach (B) contagious:spread (C) further:far (D) alter:revise
42. (B) Having an AVERSION to something may cause one to REJECT it; a PREFERENCE causes one to CHOOSE it.	**42.** REJECT:AVERSION:: (A) think:consider (B) choose:preference (C) impose:act (D) content:change
43. (A) MEASLES is a kind of DISEASE; a FELONY is a kind of CRIME.	**43.** MEASLES:DISEASE:: (A) felony:crime (B) measles:mumps (C) felony:misdemeanor (D) crime:law
44. (A) The words in each pair are antonyms.	**44.** OCCASIONAL:CONSTANT:: (A) intermittent:incessant (B) intramural:inconsistent (C) frequent:incessant (D) inadvertent:accidental
45. (C) The word ACTIVE is associated with MOBILITY, or movement; SEDENTARY is associated with IMMOBILITY, or lack of movement.	**45.** ACTIVE:MOBILE:: (A) mobile:immobile (B) inflammable:extinguished (C) sedentary:immobile (D) sensational:movement
46. (B) An OPTIONAL item may be ELIMINATED; an ESSENTIAL one must be kept, or RETAINED.	**46.** ELIMINATE:OPTIONAL:: (A) maintain:option (B) retain:essential (C) option:opportunity (D) sequential:order
47. (D) The words in each pair have similar meanings.	**47.** ALLUDE:REFER:: (A) illusion:reality (B) similar:disparate (C) imply:state (D) conclude:infer
48. (C) Charter means to hire; CHARTER a PLANE, HIRE a PERSON.	**48.** PLANE:CHARTER:: (A) worker:use (B) assistant:appoint (C) person:hire (D) manager:salary
49. (A) The prefixes SUPER- and SUB- have opposite meanings; similarly, INTRO- and EXTRO- are antonyms.	**49.** SUPERSCRIPT:SUBSCRIPT:: (A) introvert:extrovert (B) introvert:convert (C) impede:intercede (D) subscription:prescription

ANSWER	QUESTION
50. (A) The words of each pair have related but different meanings; similar pronunciations but different spellings.	**50.** COMPLEMENT:COMPLIMENT:: (A) effect:affect (B) surfeit:surface (C) interface:surface (D) style:stile
51. (D) A PREMONITION is a feeling about the future; a PROPHESY is a statement about the future. HISTORY is what has happened in the past; ARCHIVES are the records of those happenings.	**51.** PREMONITION:PROPHESY:: (A) preface:prologue (B) predict:relate (C) prologue:epilogue (D) history:archives
52. (B) COLLABORATION requires COOPERATION; similarly, QUIET is necessary for CONCENTRATION	**52.** COLLABORATION:COOPERATION:: (A) collation:correction (B) concentration:quiet (C) coercion:submission (D) compromise:promise
53. (C) REVERSION is the noun form of the verb REVERT; SYMPATHY is the noun form of the verb SYMPATHIZE.	**53.** REVERT:REVERSION:: (A) interest:intercession (B) invert:overt (C) sympathize:sympathy (D) sympathy:sympathetic
54. (A) A COMMISSION is a percentage of sales paid to the SALESMAN; a ROYALTY is a percentage of book sales paid to the author.	**54.** SALESMAN:COMMISSION:: (A) author:royalty (B) agent:actor (C) tip:waiter (D) fee:charge
55. (A) HARASSMENT causes ANGER; DISAPPOINTMENT causes SORROW.	**55.** HARASSMENT:ANGER:: (A) disappointment:sorrow (B) height:weight (C) laughter:tears (D) marriage:love
56. (B) The words in each pair are synonyms.	**56.** DIVULGE:DISCLOSE:: (A) revise:create (B) appraise:estimate (C) dispel:collect (D) bulge:close
57. (C) SODIUM is an element of SALT; OXYGEN is an element of WATER.	**57.** SODIUM:SALT:: (A) torch:acetylene (B) ammonia:pneumonia (C) oxygen:water (D) balloon:helium
58. (A) The words in each pair are antonyms.	**58.** CAUTIOUS:IMPULSIVE:: (A) secretive:candid (B) caustic:biting (C) creative:work (D) punish:behavior

ANSWER	QUESTION
59. (A) The words in each pair are antonyms.	**59.** HIDDEN:OBVIOUS:: (A) reserved:rambunctious (B) emphatic:vehement (C) embezzle:steal (D) open:door
60. (D) A SWORD is the tool used for DUELING; a PEN is a tool used for WRITING.	**60.** SWORD is to DUELING as PEN is to (A) writer (C) ink (B) inkwell (D) writing
61. (B) A REPRIMAND is a verbal show of DISAPPROVAL; a COMPLIMENT is a verbal show of APPROVAL.	**61.** REPRIMAND is to DISAPPROVAL as COMPLIMENT is to (A) flatter (C) affirmation (B) approval (D) improvement
62. (C) GOLD is a deep shade of YELLOW; ROYAL is a deep shade of BLUE.	**62.** GOLD is to YELLOW as ROYAL is to (A) black (C) blue (B) purple (D) white
63. (D) A PERIODIC event RECURS; a DETERMINED person PERSEVERES.	**63.** RECURRENCE is to PERIODIC as DETERMINATION is to (A) cowardly (C) literary (B) hopeless (D) persevering
64. (B) ANARCHY occurs in the absence of LAW; DISCORD is the result of a lack of AGREEMENT.	**64.** ANARCHY is to LAW as DISCORD is to (A) difference (C) adaptation (B) agreement (D) confusion
65. (A) A CHANDELIER is attached to a CEILING; a PUPPET is held by a PUPPETEER.	**65.** CEILING is to CHANDELIER as PUPPETEER is to (A) puppet (C) stage (B) puppet show (D) ventriloquist
66. (C) An ACCIDENT may be the result of CARELESSNESS; a RESPONSE may be the result of a STIMULUS.	**66.** ACCIDENT is to CARELESSNESS as RESPONSE is to (A) answer (C) stimulus (B) correct (D) effect
67. (D) Something ERRONEOUS is in error and subject to CORRECTION; something AMBIGUOUS is confusing and subject to CLARIFICATION.	**67.** CORRECTION is to ERRONEOUS as CLARIFICATION is to (A) criticism (C) amend (B) failure (D) ambiguous
68. (B) HORSES were used for transportation before AUTOMOBILES; TELEGRAPHS were used for communication before TELEPHONES.	**68.** AUTOMOBILE is to HORSE as TELEPHONE is to (A) wagon (C) communication (B) telegraph (D) transportation

ANSWER	QUESTION
69. (A) The words in each pair are synonyms.	**69.** INTIMIDATE is to DAUNT as DISMAY is to (A) horrify (C) dismantle (B) destroy (D) forego
70. (B) The words in each pair are antonyms.	**70.** SPONTANEOUS is to CALCULATED as IMPROMPTU is to (A) ad lib (C) verbose (B) scheduled (D) prolific
71. (D) CRITICS criticize PLAYS; REVIEWERS criticize BOOKS.	**71.** CRITIC is to PLAY as REVIEWER is to (A) job (C) newspaper (B) work (D) book
72. (B) A SOLUTION follows MYSTERY; KNOWLEDGE follows STUDY.	**72.** SOLUTION is to MYSTERY as KNOWLEDGE is to (A) comics (C) school (B) study (D) detective
73. (A) A REFEREE enforces RULES; a CONSCIENCE enforces MORALITY.	**73.** REFEREE is to RULES as CONSCIENCE is to (A) morality (C) regulations (B) thoughts (D) behavior
74. (C) The second word in each pair refers to the theft of something represented by the first word in the pair.	**74.** MONEY is to STEAL as IDEA is to (A) lose (C) plagiarize (B) manuscript (D) thief
75. (D) BOOKS consist of PAPER pages; SCROLLS are pieces of PARCHMENT.	**75.** BOOK is to PAPER as SCROLL is to (A) cloth (C) roll (B) binding (D) parchment

PRACTICE VERBAL ANALOGY TESTS

TEST 1 — 5 MINUTES

Directions: Look at the first two words and decide how they are related to each other. Then decide which of the answer choices relates to the third word in the same way that the first two are related. Circle the letter that appears before your answer. Answer Keys for the Practice Analogy Tests begin after Test 12.

1. mow is to lawn as prune is to

(A) plum
(B) raisin
(C) tree
(D) hair
(E) meadow

2. antecedent is to precedent as consequent is to

(A) decadent
(B) subsequent
(C) ebullient
(D) transient
(E) penitent

3. bassinet is to crib as car is to

(A) bus
(B) airplane
(C) stroller
(D) bed
(E) taxicab

4. restaurant is to eating as barracks is to

(A) cleaning
(B) military
(C) inspection
(D) nutrition
(E) sleeping

5. flame is to fire as smoke is to

(A) heat
(B) ashes
(C) water
(D) fire
(E) flame

6. bludgeon is to spear as lathe is to

(A) vise
(B) carpenter
(C) battle
(D) curve
(E) construction

7. risk is to escapade as age is to

(A) hilarity
(B) intemperance
(C) luminosity
(D) mayhem
(E) heirloom

8. asset is to black as debit is to

(A) debt
(B) red
(C) blue
(D) left
(E) ledger

9. darkness is to eclipse as tidal wave is to

(A) tsunami
(B) eruption
(C) ocean
(D) moon
(E) earthquake

10. hen is to brood as mother is to

(A) family
(B) chickens
(C) children
(D) shoe
(E) mom

TEST 2 — 6 MINUTES

Directions: Decide how the words in the first pair are related. Choose a pair of words below that shows the same relationship. Circle the letter that appears before your answer.

1. flood is to drought as
- (A) rich is to poor
- (B) camel is to desert
- (C) drizzle is to downpour
- (D) evening is to night
- (E) gold is to silver

2. voracious is to gluttonous as
- (A) hungry is to thirsty
- (B) warm is to hot
- (C) potent is to strong
- (D) flight is to fight
- (E) yard is to meter

3. hurricane is to wind as
- (A) wind is to water
- (B) typhoon is to wind
- (C) tornado is to twister
- (D) tornado is to typhoon
- (E) hurricane is to typhoon

4. dung is to elephant as
- (A) horse is to manure
- (B) fish is to food
- (C) worm is to soil
- (D) oxygen is to tree
- (E) aquarium is to terrarium

5. centipede is to spider as
- (A) pentagon is to triangle
- (B) rowboat is to sailboat
- (C) BC is to AD
- (D) percussion is to string
- (E) duet is to trio

6. head is to hammer as
- (A) tooth is to saw
- (B) nail is to screw
- (C) awl is to punch
- (D) screw is to driver
- (E) beginning is to end

7. anthem is to inspire as
- (A) aspirin is to pain
- (B) light is to see
- (C) organ is to grind
- (D) ape is to copy
- (E) shuttle is to transport

8. hook is to eye as
- (A) sleeve is to coat
- (B) button is to hole
- (C) boot is to shoe
- (D) adhesive is to tape
- (E) honey is to bear

9. swing is to slide as
- (A) daisy is to poppy
- (B) up is to down
- (C) down is to up
- (D) push is to pull
- (E) infant is to child

10. goalie is to net as
- (A) hockey is to soccer
- (B) player is to game
- (C) sentry is to fort
- (D) bat is to ball
- (E) ice is to turf

11. topography is to geography as
- (A) water is to land
- (B) physics is to mathematics
- (C) geography is to history
- (D) mountain is to valley
- (E) biology is to science

12. rocket is to torpedo as
- (A) fire is to water
- (B) air is to water
- (C) explosion is to hole
- (D) up is to down
- (E) war is to peace

TEST 3 — 6 MINUTES

Directions: Look at the first two words and decide how they are related to each other. Then decide which of the answer choices relates to the third word in the same way that the first two are related. Circle the letter that appears before your answer.

1. vertical is to horizontal as erect is to

(A) honest
(B) construct
(C) prone
(D) lumber
(E) proper

2. oust is to overthrow as molt is to

(A) melt
(B) shed
(C) shape
(D) weaken
(E) spoil

3. inline skates is to motorcycle as skis is to

(A) snowmobile
(B) bicycle
(C) snow
(D) ice skates
(E) snowplow

4. scales is to fish as hide is to

(A) seek
(B) tan
(C) hole
(D) ride
(E) horse

5. wind is to seed as bee is to

(A) pollen
(B) honey
(C) hive
(D) bear
(E) flower

6. glove is to hand as hose is to

(A) garden
(B) water
(C) foot
(D) nozzle
(E) shoe

7. piglet is to pig as islet is to

(A) pond
(B) lace
(C) lake
(D) rivulet
(E) island

8. depressed is to mope as tired is to

(A) yawn
(B) cope
(C) car
(D) laugh
(E) suppressed

9. masticate is to chew as gesticulate is to

(A) vomit
(B) digest
(C) urbanize
(D) point
(E) offer

10. trees is to forest as sand is to

(A) dune
(B) details
(C) hours
(D) time
(E) sandwich

11. seemly is to behavior as gawky is to

(A) length
(B) teenager
(C) volume
(D) barnyard
(E) appearance

12. flit is to dart as foil is to

(A) fence
(B) thwart
(C) aluminum
(D) change
(E) surprise

TEST 4 — 6 MINUTES

Directions: Decide how the words in the first pair are related. Choose a pair of words below that shows the same relationship. Circle the letter that appears before your answer.

1. ravenous is to hungry as

(A) hungry is to thirsty
(B) stingy is to thrifty
(C) boil is to bake
(D) full is to empty
(E) small is to little

2. bonanza is to windfall as

(A) earn is to merit
(B) western is to eastern
(C) horse is to apple
(D) sun is to rain
(E) gift is to accident

3. cat is to dog as

(A) love is to hate
(B) warm is to cold
(C) in is to out
(D) vegetarian is to carnivore
(E) snake is to eel

4. dimple is to pimple as

(A) face is to back
(B) down is to up
(C) chin is to cheek
(D) baby is to adolescent
(E) love is to loathing

5. filch is to pilfer as

(A) steal is to squander
(B) squeal is to wriggle
(C) pinch is to puff
(D) fidget is to squirm
(E) rob is to fence

6. hindsight is to foresight as

(A) cure is to prevention
(B) then is to now
(C) later is to never
(D) prediction is to predilection
(E) vision is to perception

7. fodder is to cattle as

(A) water is to fish
(B) bird is to worm
(C) restaurant is to people
(D) silo is to corn
(E) fuel is to engine

8. affix is to stamp as

(A) letter is to postmark
(B) hammer is to nail
(C) run is to horse
(D) glue is to mucilage
(E) mail is to deliver

9. leeward is to windward as

(A) port is to starboard
(B) meadow is to ocean
(C) motor is to sail
(D) pirate is to privateer
(E) tugboat is to liner

10. punish is to berate as

(A) leafy is to green
(B) deep is to ocean
(C) jump is to leap
(D) soak is to dampen
(E) hike is to trek

11. tobacco is to cigarette as

(A) liquor is to drink
(B) cough is to cold
(C) wheat is to bread
(D) cow is to milk
(E) smoking is to cancer

12. shun is to embrace as

(A) shrink is to pounce
(B) slender is to sloping
(C) tousle is to muss
(D) show is to tell
(E) kiss is to hug

TEST 5 — 6 MINUTES

Directions: Look at the first two words and decide how they are related to each other. Then decide which of the answer choices relates to the third word in the same way that the first two are related. Circle the letter that appears before your answer.

1. comprehensive is to inclusive as apprehensive is to
(A) exclusive
(B) misunderstood
(C) caught
(D) uneasy
(E) understanding

2. chalk is to crayon as bed is to
(A) chair
(B) sleep
(C) bunk
(D) ladder
(E) seat

3. ceremonious is to informal as clerical is to
(A) typographical
(B) numerical
(C) religious
(D) retail
(E) secular

4. desist is to cease as resist is to
(A) oppose
(B) give up
(C) resolve
(D) remain
(E) presume

5. putrid is to garbage as aromatic is to
(A) smell
(B) pleasant
(C) spirits
(D) spray
(E) spice

6. harpoon is to whaling as buffoon is to
(A) sorcery
(B) clowning
(C) badminton
(D) spelunking
(E) ballooning

7. ingress is to entrance as inflation is to
(A) unemployment
(B) balloon
(C) recession
(D) increase
(E) depression

8. judgment is to decision as husbandry is to
(A) divorce
(B) commitment
(C) management
(D) marriage
(E) domestic violence

9. green is to youth as gray is to
(A) age
(B) hair
(C) gloom
(D) mare
(E) elderly

10. gridiron is to football as gridlock is to
(A) waffles
(B) chess
(C) prison
(D) wrestling
(E) traffic

11. sow is to reap as crawl is to
(A) sneak
(B) harvest
(C) walk
(D) cultivate
(E) wheat

12. horde is to throng as hurl is to
(A) thrust
(B) jump
(C) throw
(D) defeat
(E) smash

TEST 6 — 6 MINUTES

Directions: Decide how the words in the first pair are related. Choose a pair of words below that shows the same relationship. Circle the letter that appears before your answer.

1. salary is to income as
(A) income is to tax
(B) money is to evil
(C) spring is to water
(D) wages is to work
(E) dollars is to cents

2. tree is to climb as
(A) scale is to mountain
(B) horse is to ride
(C) garden is to eat
(D) gem is to die
(E) cat is to mouse

3. consider is to dismiss as
(A) reflect is to absorb
(B) wade is to swim
(C) current is to recent
(D) help is to assist
(E) decide is to determine

4. compost is to fertilizer as
(A) dentist is to teeth
(B) ball is to basket
(C) hole is to drill
(D) value is to price
(E) ice is to refrigerant

5. trance is to hypnosis as
(A) knowledge is to study
(B) poison is to ivy
(C) vaccination is to immunity
(D) banana is to plantain
(E) pie is to apple

6. pianist is to musician as
(A) organist is to pianist
(B) violinist is to fiddler
(C) musician is to writer
(D) mathematics is to mathematician
(E) psychiatrist is to physician

7. poetry is to prose as
(A) seeing is to hearing
(B) light is to heavy
(C) sonata is to étude
(D) opera is to book
(E) melody is to rhythm

8. hull is to strawberry as
(A) tree is to leaf
(B) hull is to ship
(C) puppy is to dog
(D) milk is to cow
(E) butter is to bread

9. poison is to skull and crossbones as
(A) rope is to gallows
(B) pirate is to gangplank
(C) antidote is to poison
(D) love is to heart
(E) bow is to arrow

10. trivial is to grievous as
(A) acid is to bitter
(B) light is to heavy
(C) boring is to sad
(D) oil is to water
(E) funny is to hilarious

11. ax is to hatchet as
(A) fish is to nursery
(B) chicken is to egg
(C) chop is to cut
(D) hammer is to sickle
(E) cello is to violin

12. fortuitous is to luck as
(A) chivalrous is to manners
(B) fossil is to fuel
(C) formula is to milk
(D) music is to dance
(E) pool is to swimming

TEST 7 — 6 MINUTES

Directions: Look at the first two words and decide how they are related to each other. Then decide which of the answer choices relates to the third word in the same way that the first two are related. Circle the letter that appears before your answer.

1. hassock is to feet as pillow is to
(A) cushion
(B) chair
(C) boots
(D) fight
(E) head

2. ghost is to haunt as guru is to
(A) frighten
(B) teach
(C) amuse
(D) adhere
(E) tempt

3. nail is to toe as lock is to
(A) key
(B) combination
(C) hair
(D) hammer
(E) barrel

4. sub is to under as super is to
(A) janitor
(B) chief
(C) terrific
(D) over
(E) better

5. deciduous is to leaves as evergreen is to
(A) needles
(B) tree
(C) Christmas
(D) conifer
(E) forest

6. flounder is to shark as tick is to
(A) clock
(B) deer
(C) flea
(D) insect
(E) woods

7. starch is to stiff as bleach is to
(A) smooth
(B) soft
(C) colorful
(D) dry
(E) white

8. shellfish is to lobster as poultry is to
(A) fowl
(B) spider
(C) chicken
(D) bird
(E) octopus

9. oval is to oblong as circle is to
(A) round
(B) square
(C) sphere
(D) cube
(E) rectangle

10. capacious is to cramped as agape is to
(A) ajar
(B) painful
(C) surprised
(D) empty
(E) sealed

11. brood is to litter as peon is to
(A) farmer
(B) slave
(C) migrant
(D) laborer
(E) scatter

12. anorexia is to bulimia as asthma is to
(A) eating
(B) breathing
(C) allergy
(D) emphysema
(E) headache

TEST 8 — 6 MINUTES

Directions: Decide how the words in the first pair are related. Choose a pair of words below that shows the same relationship. Circle the letter that appears before your answer.

1. felon is to crime as

(A) judge is to jury
(B) courtroom is to trial
(C) physician is to cure
(D) verdict is to sentence
(E) pharmacy is to pharmacist

2. odor is to stench as

(A) sad is to tragic
(B) rich is to poor
(C) green is to brown
(D) summer is to winter
(E) flower is to animal

3. suffix is to annex as

(A) before is to after
(B) subtraction is to addition
(C) reading is to writing
(D) more is to less
(E) word is to house

4. loom is to appear as

(A) weave is to wool
(B) root is to dig
(C) come is to go
(D) seem is to be
(E) warp is to woof

5. escape is to flee as

(A) run is to hide
(B) break is to enter
(C) hide is to seek
(D) captive is to captor
(E) dismount is to alight

6. assent is to dissent as

(A) assert is to desert
(B) compact is to expansive
(C) assist is to desist
(D) obtain is to retain
(E) future is to futility

7. nature is to nurture as

(A) father is to mother
(B) authentic is to artificial
(C) congenital is to acquired
(D) native is to alien
(E) home is to school

8. squat is to crouch as

(A) incise is to precise
(B) countenance is to face
(C) lax is to strict
(D) molten is to solid
(E) mongrel is to puppy

9. rudder is to steering as

(A) razor is to shaving
(B) wheel is to turning
(C) cow is to grazing
(D) cloud is to raining
(E) stapling is to stapler

10. standee is to seat as

(A) kitty is to litter
(B) apple is to pie
(C) salt is to ocean
(D) acorn is to oak
(E) nomad is to home

11. pauper is to poor as

(A) shoe is to pair
(B) book is to long
(C) skyscraper is to high
(D) bed is to make
(E) clever is to owl

12. snuff is to cigarette as

(A) illegal is to legal
(B) fire is to smoke
(C) spittoon is to ashtray
(D) nose is to mouth
(E) candle is to match

TEST 9 — 6 MINUTES

Directions: Look at the first two words and decide how they are related to each other. Then decide which of the answer choices relates to the third word in the same way that the first two are related. Circle the letter that appears before your answer.

1. prattle is to baby as discourse is to
(A) conversation
(B) scholar
(C) speech
(D) subject
(E) lecture

2. dose is to medicine as portion is to
(A) dessert
(B) serving
(C) potion
(D) food
(E) section

3. bowl is to soup as plate is to
(A) cup
(B) fork
(C) dinner
(D) china
(E) meat

4. gram is to ounce as meter is to
(A) mile
(B) pound
(C) yard
(D) weigh
(E) measure

5. flower is to seed as seed is to
(A) plant
(B) water
(C) grow
(D) food
(E) nut

6. oil is to earth as salt is to
(A) shaker
(B) pepper
(C) blood pressure
(D) lick
(E) sea

7. pest is to annoying as plateau is to
(A) level
(B) calming
(C) boring
(D) curved
(E) hilly

8. survive is to succumb as swim is to
(A) sail
(B) dive
(C) row
(D) sink
(E) float

9. taunt is to tease as voluble is to
(A) loud
(B) large
(C) talkative
(D) willing
(E) loyal

10. tiara is to wreath as jewel is to
(A) crown
(B) flower
(C) head
(D) woman
(E) door

11. torrid is to extreme as temperate is to
(A) warm
(B) hot
(C) climate
(D) moderate
(E) heat

12. axle is to wheels as chain is to
(A) necklace
(B) handcuffs
(C) door
(D) gang
(E) daisies

TEST 10 — 6 MINUTES

Directions: Decide how the words in the first pair are related. Choose a pair of words below that shows the same relationship. Circle the letter that appears before your answer.

1. peacock is to plumage as
(A) lion is to mane
(B) friend is to diamonds
(C) coat is to tails
(D) shine is to shoes
(E) dowager is to furs

2. quagmire is to quarry as
(A) hunter is to prey
(B) hide is to seek
(C) mud is to stone
(D) sink is to swim
(E) find is to keep

3. frog is to tadpole as
(A) toad is to tree
(B) mushroom is to toadstool
(C) moth is to polliwog
(D) butterfly is to caterpillar
(E) imago is to earthworm

4. cotton is to summer as
(A) rain is to snow
(B) wool is to winter
(C) boll is to weevil
(D) fur is to coat
(E) leaf is to tree

5. motion is to queasy as
(A) itchy is to rash
(B) unfamiliar is to strange
(C) round is to dizzy
(D) fever is to hot
(E) ocean is to wavy

6. nay is to yea as
(A) voices is to hands
(B) now is to later
(C) horse is to sleigh
(D) neither is to nor
(E) negate is to affirm

7. knocker is to doorbell as
(A) pen is to pencil
(B) sound is to alarm
(C) strike is to hours
(D) in is to out
(E) pleasant is to unpleasant

8. bullet is to gun as
(A) blade is to hatchet
(B) slingshot is to pebble
(C) arrow is to bow
(D) sword is to spear
(E) victim is to target

9. walrus is to seal as
(A) cow is to calf
(B) doe is to deer
(C) elephant is to lizard
(D) ram is to ewe
(E) goose is to duck

10. cassette is to tape as
(A) safe is to money
(B) record is to jacket
(C) turntable is to needle
(D) synthesizer is to compact disc
(E) video is to audio

11. hum is to sing as
(A) speak is to see
(B) deaf is to mute
(C) pantomime is to act
(D) play is to opera
(E) prose is to poetry

12. patriarch is to matriarch as
(A) church is to state
(B) leader is to follower
(C) noble is to common
(D) tailor is to seamstress
(E) ancient is to modern

TEST 11 — 6 MINUTES

Directions: Look at the first two words and decide how they are related to each other. Then decide which of the answer choices relates to the third word in the same way that the first two are related. Circle the letter that appears before your answer.

1. calligraphy is to precise as scrawl is to
- (A) handwriting
- (B) primitive
- (C) careless
- (D) illegible
- (E) scratchy

2. agitated is to stoic as sociable is to
- (A) hermit
- (B) socialite
- (C) cheerleader
- (D) friendly
- (E) acrobat

3. sweat is to perspire as swat is to
- (A) fly
- (B) destroy
- (C) exercise
- (D) kill
- (E) hit

4. nostalgia is to past as anticipation is to
- (A) excitement
- (B) future
- (C) present
- (D) apprehension
- (E) past

5. gleeful is to gloomy as organized is to
- (A) original
- (B) neat
- (C) unintellectual
- (D) disinterested
- (E) messy

6. spaghetti is to linguini as ziti is to
- (A) macaroni
- (B) pasta
- (C) sausage
- (D) sauce
- (E) parmesan

7. obedience is to obstinacy as peace is to
- (A) prosperity
- (B) patriotism
- (C) penury
- (D) war
- (E) tranquility

8. traitor is to treason as patriot is to
- (A) espionage
- (B) jingoism
- (C) loyalty
- (D) heritage
- (E) sacrifice

9. rink is to skate as sink is to
- (A) wash
- (B) swim
- (C) fish
- (D) soap
- (E) kitchen

10. gully is to water as furrow is to
- (A) brow
- (B) farm
- (C) erosion
- (D) rabbit
- (E) plow

11. desert is to jungle as dusty is to
- (A) damp
- (B) dirty
- (C) dry
- (D) hot
- (E) dark

12. steam is to boiling as smoke is to
- (A) heat
- (B) chimney
- (C) combustion
- (D) freezing
- (E) vapor

TEST 12 — 6 MINUTES

Directions: Decide how the words in the first pair are related. Choose a pair of words below that shows the same relationship. Circle the letter that appears before your answer.

1. till is to cultivate as
(A) plow is to horse
(B) tractor is to plow
(C) plant is to furrow
(D) farm is to soil
(E) toil is to work

2. tooth is to bone as
(A) tire is to fan belt
(B) pond is to forest
(C) fish is to bird
(D) star is to sun
(E) house is to home

3. fry is to stew as
(A) chicken is to beef
(B) heat is to fire
(C) pan is to pot
(D) dry is to wet
(E) meat is to potatoes

4. rustle is to roar as
(A) water is to wind
(B) walk is to run
(C) rain is to snow
(D) cattle is to coyote
(E) shout is to yell

5. fall is to leaf as
(A) melt is to snow
(B) build is to house
(C) shrub is to flower
(D) sneeze is to cough
(E) dig is to spade

6. spa is to health as
(A) museum is to pictures
(B) conservation is to zoo
(C) sport is to stadium
(D) library is to information
(E) quiet is to church

7. exacting is to demanding as
(A) burrowing is to building
(B) testing is to proving
(C) changing is to appearing
(D) thrilling is to boring
(E) extracting is to removing

8. labyrinth is to network as
(A) weather is to climate
(B) vein is to blood
(C) maze is to passages
(D) epic is to hero
(E) Greece is to myths

9. kiss is to cheek as
(A) cheek is to jowl
(B) shake is to hand
(C) hug is to bear
(D) nose is to rub
(E) milk is to cookies

10. ingest is to digest as
(A) sergeant is to captain
(B) eat is to drink
(C) drink is to drive
(D) spider is to fly
(E) understand is to study

11. imp is to horns as
(A) devil is to angel
(B) evil is to good
(C) halo is to wings
(D) mischief is to elf
(E) cherub is to wings

12. knead is to dough as
(A) rotted is to apple
(B) fallen is to arches
(C) soak is to beans
(D) drifted is to snow
(E) spent is to money

Practice Verbal Analogy Tests

Answer Key

TEST 1

1. **C**	3. **A**	5. **D**	7. **E**	9. **E**
2. **B**	4. **E**	6. **A**	8. **B**	10. **C**

TEST 2

1. **A**	4. **D**	7. **E**	10. **C**
2. **C**	5. **A**	8. **B**	11. **E**
3. **B**	6. **A**	9. **A**	12. **B**

TEST 3

1. **C**	4. **E**	7. **E**	10. **A**
2. **B**	5. **A**	8. **A**	11. **E**
3. **A**	6. **C**	9. **D**	12. **B**

TEST 4

1. **B**	4. **B**	7. **E**	10. **D**
2. **A**	5. **D**	8. **B**	11. **C**
3. **E**	6. **A**	9. **A**	12. **A**

TEST 5

1. **D**	4. **A**	7. **D**	10. **E**
2. **C**	5. **E**	8. **C**	11. **C**
3. **E**	6. **B**	9. **A**	12. **C**

TEST 6

1. **C**	4. **E**	7. **C**	10. **B**
2. **B**	5. **A**	8. **B**	11. **E**
3. **A**	6. **E**	9. **D**	12. **A**

TEST 7

1. **E**	4. **D**	7. **E**	10. **E**
2. **B**	5. **A**	8. **C**	11. **D**
3. **C**	6. **C**	9. **A**	12. **D**

TEST 8

1. **C**	4. **B**	7. **C**	10. **E**
2. **A**	5. **E**	8. **B**	11. **C**
3. **E**	6. **B**	9. **A**	12. **D**

TEST 9

1. **B**	4. **C**	7. **A**	10. **B**
2. **D**	5. **A**	8. **D**	11. **D**
3. **E**	6. **E**	9. **C**	12. **B**

TEST 10

1. **A**	4. **B**	7. **A**	10. **A**
2. **C**	5. **D**	8. **C**	11. **C**
3. **D**	6. **E**	9. **E**	12. **D**

TEST 11

1. **C**	4. **B**	7. **D**	10. **E**
2. **A**	5. **E**	8. **C**	11. **A**
3. **E**	6. **A**	9. **A**	12. **C**

TEST 12

1. **E**	4. **B**	7. **E**	10. **A**
2. **A**	5. **A**	8. **C**	11. **E**
3. **C**	6. **D**	9. **B**	12. **C**

CHAPTER 9

Sentence Completions

PLAN A: ACCELERATED

- ***Read*** the chapter
- ***Study*** "What Smart Test-Takers Know"
- ***Skim*** "Learning Exercises"
- ***Take*** "Sample Tests"

PLAN B: TOP SPEED

- ***Read*** "What Makes a Sentence Completion?"
- ***Study*** "What Smart Test-Takers Know"
- ***Take*** "Sample Tests"

You'll Find Answers to These Questions

What makes a sentence completion?
How do you answer sentence completion questions?
What do smart test-takers know about sentence completions?

WHAT MAKES A SENTENCE COMPLETION?

Are you drawing a blank? Get used to it, because you'll see a lot of them in the sentence completion questions on the ISEE. In this kind of question, you are given a sentence that has one or more blanks. A number of words or pairs of words are suggested to fill in the blank spaces. It's up to you to select the word or pair of words that will best complete the meaning of the sentence.

Why are there sentence completion questions on the ISEE? Sentence completion questions test your vocabulary as well as your ability to understand what you read. In a typical sentence completion question, several of the choices *could* be inserted into the blank spaces. However, only one answer will make sense and carry out the full meaning of the sentence.

HOW DO YOU ANSWER SENTENCE COMPLETION QUESTIONS?

Are you ready to start filling in some of those blanks? The following steps will help you answer sentence completion questions:

Sentence Completions: Getting It Right

1. Read the sentence carefully.
2. Guess at the answer.

3. Scan the answer choices for the word you guessed. If it's there, mark it and go on. If it's not, go on to step 4.
4. Examine the sentence for clues to the missing word.
5. Eliminate any answer choices that are ruled out by the clues.
6. Try the ones that are left and pick whichever is best.

Now let's try out these steps on a couple of sentence completion questions.

> Those who feel that war is stupid and unnecessary think that to die on the battlefield is ____.
>
> (A) courageous
>
> (B) pretentious
>
> (C) useless
>
> (D) illegal

1. Read the sentence.
2. Think of your own word to fill in the blank. You're looking for a word that completes the logic of the sentence. You might come up with something like *dumb.*
3. Look for *dumb* in the answer choices. It's not there, but *useless* is. That's pretty close, so mark it and go on.
4. If you couldn't guess the word, take your clue from the words *stupid* and *unnecessary* in the sentence. They definitely point toward some negative-sounding word.
5. The clues immediately eliminate (A) *courageous* which is a positive word.
6. Try the remaining choices in the sentence, and you'll see that *useless* fits best.

> Unruly people may well become ____ if they are treated with ____ by those around them.
>
> (A) angry . . . kindness
>
> (B) calm . . . respect
>
> (C) peaceful . . . abuse
>
> (D) interested . . . medicine

1. Read the sentence. This time there are two blanks, and the missing words need to have some logical connection.
2. Think of your own words to fill in the blanks. You might guess that the unruly people will become *well-behaved* if they are treated with *consideration.*
3. Now look for your guesses in the answer choices. They're not there, but there are some possibilities.
4. Go back to the sentence and look for clues. *Become* signals that the unruly people will change their behavior. How that behavior changes will depend on how they are treated.

5. You can eliminate choice (A) because a negative behavior change (*angry*) doesn't logically follow a positive treatment (*kindness*). Likewise, you can eliminate (C) because a *peaceful* behavior change is not likely to follow from *abuse*. Finally, you can eliminate (D) because *interested* and *medicine* have no logical connection.
6. The only remaining choice is (B), which fits the sentence and must be the correct answer.

What Smart Test-Takers Know

THINKING UP YOUR OWN ANSWER IS THE WAY TO START.

Robert was extremely ____ when he received a B on the exam, for he was almost certain he had gotten an A.

(A) elated

(B) dissatisfied

(C) fulfilled

(D) harmful

If you read this sentence carefully, you are likely to come up with the right answer, *dissatisfied,* on your own. But even if you didn't, you'd come up with something close, such as *upset* or *disappointed.* Then when you look at the answer choices, you will immediately see that the closest word is *dissatisfied.*

TOP 10 TIP

THE WORDS IN THE SURROUNDING SENTENCE OFFER CLUES TO THE MISSING WORD.

If you can't come up with the missing word immediately, look for clue words in the surrounding sentence. Clue words can tell you "where the sentence is going." Is it continuing along one line of thought? If it is, you're looking for a word that supports that thought. Is it changing direction in midstream? Then you're looking for a word that sets up a contrast between the thoughts in the sentence.

TESTSMARTS

Some words signal blanks that go with the flow:

- and
- also
- consequently
- as a result
- thus
- hence
- so
- for example

SOME BLANKS GO WITH THE FLOW.

The missing word may be one that supports another thought in the sentence, so you need to look for an answer that "goes with the flow."

The service at the restaurant was so slow that by the time the salad had arrived we were ____.

(A) ravenous

(B) excited

(C) incredible

(D) forlorn

Where is this sentence going? The restaurant service is very slow. That means you have to wait a long time for your food, and the longer you wait, the hungrier you'll get. So the word in the blank should be something that completes this train of thought. Answer choice (A), *ravenous,* which means very hungry, is the best answer. It works because it "goes with the flow."

As a teenager, John was withdrawn, preferring the company of books to that of people; consequently, as a young adult John was socially ____.

(A) successful

(B) uninhibited

(C) intoxicating

(D) inept

The word *consequently* signals that the second idea is an outcome of the first, so again, you are looking for a word that completes the train of thought. What might happen if you spent too much time with your nose stuck in a book (except for this one, of course)? Most likely you would be more comfortable with books than with people. Choice (D), *inept,* meaning awkward, is a good description of someone who lacks social graces, making this the right answer.

A decision that is made before all of the relevant data are collected can only be called ____.

(A) calculated

(B) laudable

(C) unbiased

(D) premature

The word *called* tells you that the blank is the word that the rest of the sentence describes. A decision that is made before all the facts are collected can only be described as *premature,* choice (D).

SOME BLANKS SHIFT GEARS.

The missing word may be one that reverses a thought in the sentence, so you need to look for an answer that "shifts gears."

The advance of science has demonstrated that a fact that appears to contradict a certain theory may actually be ____ a more advanced formulation of that theory.

(A) incompatible with

(B) in opposition to

(C) consistent with

(D) eliminated by

The correct answer is (C). Look at the logical structure of the sentence. The sentence has set up a contrast between what appears to be and what is actually true. This indicates that the correct answer will "shift gears" and be the opposite of *contradict*. The choice *consistent with* provides this meaning. The other choices do not.

TESTSMARTS

Some words signal blanks that shift gears:

- but
- yet
- although
- on the other hand
- in contrast
- however
- nevertheless

> Although she knew that the artist's work was considered by some critics to be ____, the curator of the museum was anxious to acquire several of the artist's paintings for the museum's collection.
>
> (A) insignificant
>
> (B) important
>
> (C) desirable
>
> (D) successful

The correct answer is **(A)**. The very first word of the sentence, *although,* signals that the sentence is setting up a contrast between the critics and the curator. The critics had one opinion, but the curator had a different one. Since the curator liked the artworks well enough to acquire them, you can anticipate that the critics disliked the artworks. So the blank requires a word with negative connotations, and choice **(A)**, *insignificant,* is the only one that works.

> After witnessing several violent interactions between the animals, the anthropologist was forced to revise her earlier opinion that the monkeys were ____.
>
> (A) peaceable
>
> (B) quarrelsome
>
> (C) insensitive
>
> (D) prosperous

Where do you begin? The words "forced to revise" clearly signal a shift in the anthropologist's ideas. Her discovery that the monkeys were violent made her abandon an earlier contrasting opinion. Among the answer choices, the only contrast to *violent* is choice **(A)**, *peaceable.*

HERE'S THE ANSWER

What if I think more than one answer seems to make sense?

Remember that there is only one correct answer. Make your best guess based on the full meaning of the sentence.

THE RIGHT ANSWER MUST BE BOTH LOGICAL AND GRAMMATICALLY CORRECT.

When answering sentence completion questions, you can always simply toss out any answer choices that do not make sense in the sentence or that would not be grammatically correct.

> An advocate of consumer rights, Nader has spent much of his professional career attempting to ____ the fraudulent claims of American business.
>
> (A) expose
>
> (B) immortalize
>
> (C) reprove
>
> (D) import

What would you do with a fraudulent claim? Immortalize it? Import it? Not likely. These choices are not logical. The only logical answer is **(A)**. You would *expose* a fraudulent claim.

Despite the harsh tone of her comments, she did not mean to _____ any criticism of you personally.

(A) infer

(B) aim

(C) comply

(D) imply

The correct answer is **(D)**, *imply,* which means "suggest indirectly." Choice **(A)**, *infer,* is a word often confused with *imply*. It means "conclude from reasoning or implication." A speaker implies; a listener infers. Choice **(C)**, *comply,* meaning "obey," makes no sense in this context. Choice **(B)**, *aim,* is more likely, but it doesn't work in the sentence as given. You might say, "she did not mean to *aim* any criticism *at* you," but you would not normally say, "she did not mean to *aim* any criticism *of* you."

TWO-BLANK QUESTIONS GIVE YOU TWO WAYS TO GET IT RIGHT. When there are two blanks in a sentence completion question, you have two ways to eliminate answer choices. You can start with either blank to eliminate choices that don't work. So pick the one that's easier for you. If you can eliminate just one of the words in a two-word answer choice, the whole choice won't work, so you can toss it out and go on.

LEARNING EXERCISES: SENTENCE COMPLETIONS

The questions in this section are arranged in boxes called "frames." The answer for each frame will be found in the box to the left of the question frame.

First, cover the answer boxes with a strip of paper. Circle your answer to the question. Then, move the paper down to expose the answer to that question.

ANSWER	QUESTION
1. (A) The first blank might be filled equally well by the first term of choice (A) or choice (D); however, the coordinating "and" implies that the second blank must be filled with something negative that he does to the facts. DISTORTS is the best word here.	**1.** His theory is not _____; it only sounds plausible to the uninformed because he _____ several facts and fails to mention the mountain of evidence that contradicts his ideas. (A) tenable . . . distorts (B) pliable . . . pursued (C) predominant . . . embellished (D) sufficient . . . invokes
2. (C) Choice (D) makes no sense. "Encouraging" is not a coercive type of activity, so (A) and (B) would be too forceful as completions in the first blank.	**2.** That organization _____ its concern for endangered species of wildlife by encouraging congressmen to pass laws that _____ these animals. (A) imposes . . . promote (B) manipulates . . . defend (C) manifests . . . protect (D) supplants . . . prohibit
3. (D) If no one else could locate the material, you may be pretty sure that his filing system was PECULIAR.	**3.** His filing system was so _____ that no one else in the department could locate material quickly. (A) specific (B) appropriate (C) intense (D) peculiar
4. (D) The list of items for consideration at a meeting is the AGENDA. When the business is completed, one might as well ADJOURN the meeting.	**4.** When the last item on the _____ had been taken care of, the meeting was _____. (A) roster . . . called to order (B) itinerary . . . finalized (C) table . . . sequestered (D) agenda . . . adjourned
5. (C) The barring of discrimination is an official act, so only (C) or (D) could fill the first blank. The second blank is best filled with the idiomatic "AFFECT hiring practices."	**5.** It has been predicted that the new _____ barring discrimination in employment on the basis of sexual orientation will dramatically _____ hiring practices. (A) morality . . . effect (B) permissiveness . . . reflect (C) legislation . . . affect (D) rulings . . . reset

ANSWER	QUESTION
6. (D) A search that lasts more than a month is most certainly a PAINSTAKING one.	**6.** The Navy scoured the area for over a month, but the _____ search turned up no clues. (A) cursory (B) fruitful (C) present (D) painstaking
7. (B) The first blank calls for a negative trait to contrast with her conscientiousness. (B) or (C) might both be correct, but ENTITLED TO better fits the informality of the sentence. "Eligible for" implies a legal requirement.	**7.** Although her personality is sometimes _____, she is a conscientious worker and is _____ better treatment than she has received. (A) pleasing . . . conscious of (B) abrasive . . . entitled to (C) gloomy . . . eligible for (D) cheerful . . . granted
8. (D) The coordinating "and" in the compound subject requires that both words have the same connotation. Since these acts led to the imposition of controls, we must assume that they were negative acts.	**8.** _____ manipulation of the stock market and other _____ practices in security sales resulted in the 1933 legislation for the control of security markets. (A) Degenerate . . . lucrative (B) Economic . . . useless (C) Continual . . . productive (D) Unscrupulous . . . unethical
9. (B) The style of a manual must be appropriate to the audience for which it is INTENDED.	**9.** The handbook _____ for beginners was written in an elementary style. (A) bound (B) intended (C) paged (D) authored
10. (C) The key here is that the workers' attention wanders. Attention wanders when one is BORED. One becomes BORED when the work is TEDIOUS.	**10.** When a job becomes too _____, workers get _____, their attention wanders, and they start to make careless errors. (A) diverse . . . busy (B) hectic . . . lazy (C) tedious . . . bored (D) fascinating . . . interested
11. (D) Only AMASS really makes sense in the first blank.	**11.** Because of her uncompromising stands on divisive issues, she was unable to _____ broad support among the voters; however, the minority who did support her were exceptionally _____. (A) alienate . . . many (B) survey . . . divided (C) cut across . . . quiet (D) amass . . . loyal

ANSWER	QUESTION
12. **(D)** Any remarks other than stupid or INSIPID ones should be taken seriously.	**12.** His remarks were too _____ to be taken seriously. (A) germane (B) crucial (C) pointed (D) insipid
13. **(B)** The second blank can be filled only by (B) or (D). (D) makes no sense in the first blank.	**13.** No training course can operate to full advantage without job descriptions which _____ those parts of the job that require the most training before the training course is _____. (A) list . . . improved (B) identify . . . implemented (C) teach . . . predicted (D) insulate . . . finished
14. **(D)** The "not only . . . but also" construction implies two complementary reasons why a classification of students might register for the course. Only (D) really fits this requirement. A course that is OPTIONAL and very difficult will draw FEW registrants.	**14.** Since the course was not only _____ but also had a reputation for being extremely difficult, _____ students registered for it. (A) enjoyable . . . many (B) required . . . some (C) useful . . . practical (D) optional . . . few
15. **(D)** The person who held this job before the current secretary was her PREDECESSOR.	**15.** The new secretary has a more businesslike manner than her _____ in the job. (A) precedent (B) ancestor (C) successor (D) predecessor
16. **(B)** Only (A) or (B) makes sense in the first blank. Synthetics are not in themselves a health hazard.	**16.** Because of the _____ hazard, regulations forbid the use of highly _____ materials in certain items such as children's pajamas. (A) health . . . synthetic (B) fire . . . flammable (C) drug . . . inflammatory (D) chemical . . . flame-retardant
17. **(A)** The report was submitted before the final draft. Only (A) or (D) can describe the report. A report is not made subject to references; it is made subject to REVISIONS before the final draft.	**17.** The _____ report was submitted, subject to such _____ as would be made before the final draft. (A) preliminary . . . revisions (B) ubiquitous . . . submissions (C) ultimate . . . editions (D) committee's . . . references

ANSWER	QUESTION
18. **(B)** Since the action was taken before brain damage could occur, the *best* completion implies speed.	**18.** _____ action on the part of a passerby revived the victim before brain damage could occur. (A) Physical (B) Prompt (C) Violent (D) Delayed
19. **(C)** The best thing to do with excess responsibility is to DELEGATE it.	**19.** As the workload _____, she _____ responsibility for many routine tasks to an assistant. (A) evolved . . . preserved (B) changed . . . handled (C) increased . . . delegated (D) steadied . . . abased
20. **(D)** The second blank must be filled by a negative word. This limits the answer to (B), (C) or (D). Of the three first-term choices, only SLUMS are recognized as the breeding grounds of disease, juvenile delinquency, and crime.	**20.** For many years _____ have been recognized as breeding disease, juvenile delinquency, and crime, which not only threaten the health and welfare of people who live there but also _____ the structure of society as a whole. (A) prisons . . . rebuild (B) schools . . . disengage (C) colonialization . . . alienate (D) slums . . . weaken
21. **(D)** The structure of the sentence leaves only (D) as a sensible completion.	**21.** As citizens we would be _____ if we did not make these facts public. (A) entitled (B) nominative (C) elective (D) derelict
22. **(D)** The words "not yet" imply that she was new to or a NOVICE in the diplomatic service. (B) is a possible answer as well, but (D) is better.	**22.** A _____ in the diplomatic service, she had not yet _____ such a question of protocol. (A) success . . . dispatched (B) volunteer . . . avoided (C) veteran . . . battered (D) novice . . . encountered
23. **(B)** Excessive fatigue can often be attributed to factors other than inhospitable working conditions, but OCCASIONALLY, INADEQUATE working conditions are its cause.	**23.** Excessive fatigue can _____ be attributed to _____ working conditions such as poor lighting. (A) inevitably . . . archaic (B) occasionally . . . inadequate (C) always . . . obsolete (D) never . . . demoralizing

ANSWER	QUESTION
24. **(D)** Money helps in the development of new processes and products. A SUBSIDY is money received in advance of the work. Rewards and honoraria follow a service.	**24.** The company received a _____ from the government to help develop new sources of energy. (A) reward (B) compendium (C) memorandum (D) subsidy
25. **(C)** The blanks could be filled with choices (A) or (C). However, frequent experience should lead to FACILITY in soothing INCONVENIENCED travelers, so (C) is the *best* answer.	**25.** The _____ with which the agent calmed the anxieties and soothed the tempers of the travelers _____ by the delay was a mark of frequent experience with similar crises. (A) evasiveness . . . angered (B) reverence . . . pleased (C) facility . . . inconvenienced (D) mannerism . . . destroyed
26. **(D)** It is reasonable to assume that a more CONCENTRATED ore would yield a greater quantity of the mineral and would thus be more cost efficient.	**26.** The greater the _____ of a mineral in an ore, the less it costs to refine it. (A) expense (B) weight (C) oxidation (D) concentration
27. **(D)** The word "and" connecting the two clauses implies that safety from prosecution applies to the church. A SANCTUARY is a place for refuge and protection, and all who ENTER it are safe.	**27.** The church had traditionally served as a _____ for debtors, and those _____ it were safe from prosecution. (A) prison . . . leaving (B) blessing . . . obeying (C) court . . . denying (D) sanctuary . . . entering
28. **(C)** Absorption of facts is PASSIVE, as opposed to the more active mode of education, the application of KNOWLEDGE.	**28.** Today's students are encouraged to absorb facts rather than to apply _____. Education is becoming _____. (A) understanding . . . regrettable (B) intelligence . . . invaluable (C) knowledge . . . passive (D) formulas . . . extensive
29. **(B)** The sentence, by the words "rather than," requires that the two words filling the blanks be opposites. Only (D) does not meet this requirement. However, mutual assistance implies COOPERATION, hence (B) is the correct answer.	**29.** Man's survival is a result of mutual assistance, since he is essentially _____ rather than _____. (A) superior . . . inferior (B) cooperative . . . competitive (C) individualistic . . . gregarious (D) selfish . . . stingy

ANSWER	QUESTION
30. **(C)** The sentence requires that the first blank be filled by a word that contrasts with body. Of the choices, MIND, (C), best meets this criterion.	**30.** Ancient Greeks were not only concerned with the development of the _____ but also felt training of the body was of _____ importance. (A) muscles . . . equal (B) psyche . . . little (C) mind . . . prime (D) physical . . . vital
31. **(C)** The construction of the sentence demands that the first blank be filled with a positive word while the second is filled with a less positive word. (C) best fits these requirements.	**31.** Although for years _____ resources had been devoted to alleviating the problem, a satisfactory solution remained _____. (A) natural . . . costly (B) adequate . . . probable (C) substantial . . . elusive (D) capital . . . decisive
32. **(D)** A missing-person report demands INVESTIGATION.	**32.** The police department will not accept for _____ a report of a person missing from his or her residence if such _____ is located outside of the city. (A) convenience . . . location (B) control . . . report (C) filing . . . department (D) investigation . . . residence
33. **(C)** All the consideration, amending, and debate will not put a treaty into effect until it is RATIFIED.	**33.** The treaty cannot go into effect until it has been _____ by the Senate. (A) considered (B) debated (C) ratified (D) shelved
34. **(D)** The words in the blanks should contrast with his lack of formal academic training.	**34.** His _____ of practical experience and his psychological acuity more than _____ his lack of formal academic training. (A) claims . . . comprise (B) background . . . educate for (C) brief . . . account for (D) wealth . . . compensate for
35. **(A)** The THESAURUS is a book of SYNONYMS.	**35.** Because I wanted to use a(n) _____, I looked the word up in the _____. (A) synonym . . . thesaurus (B) homonym . . . directory (C) antonym . . . encyclopedia (D) pseudonym . . . dictionary

ANSWER	QUESTION
36. **(B)** All choices except (C) might be correct, but the imperative of "you will *have* to" implies that I am not AUTHORIZED.	**36.** You will have to speak to the head of the department; I am not _____ to give out that information. (A) willing (B) authorized (C) programmed (D) happy
37. **(D)** No enmity is implied in this sentence, so (D) is a better answer than (C).	**37.** Research in that field has become so _____ that researchers on different aspects of the same problem may be _____ each other's work. (A) secure . . . bombarded with (B) partial . . . surprised at (C) departmental . . . inimical to (D) specialized . . . unfamiliar with
38. **(D)** One might break ground for (B), (C), or (D), but only INNOVATIONS for which one breaks ground are fully realized by others.	**38.** She _____ the way things were done, but many of the _____ for which she broke ground were left to be fully realized by others. (A) disliked . . . provocations (B) eliminated . . . foundations (C) implemented . . . buildings (D) revolutionized . . . innovations
39. **(D)** To EFFECT is to cause. *Inflict* has a negative connotation that is uncalled for in this sentence.	**39.** A change in environment is very likely to _____ a change in one's work habits. (A) affect (B) inflict (C) propose (D) effect
40. **(C)** Fuel materials that could be depleted are either (C) or (D). Only (C) fits into the first blank. The use of RENEWABLE resources would slow the depletion of IRREPLACEABLE fuel materials.	**40.** A shift to greater use of _____ or inexhaustible resources in the production of power would slow the depletion of _____ fuel materials. (A) synthetic . . . regional (B) natural . . . chemical (C) renewable . . . irreplaceable (D) unknown . . . fossil
41. **(D)** The type of advice must be appropriate to the giver. The advice of a CHARLATAN or imposter is likely to be UNRELIABLE.	**41.** A _____ is likely to give you _____ advice. (A) fool . . . useful (B) doctor . . . lethal (C) friend . . . harmful (D) charlatan . . . unreliable

ANSWER	QUESTION
42. (**C**) An accident report should be dependent only upon INFORMATION and not upon permission or certificates.	**42.** An accident report should be written as soon as possible after the necessary _____ has been obtained. (A) bystander (B) formulation (C) information (D) permission
43. (**B**) DELETION of identification insures PRIVACY.	**43.** To protect the respondents' _____, names and social security numbers are _____ the questionnaires before the results are tabulated. (A) privilege . . . referred to (B) privacy . . . deleted from (C) information . . . retained in (D) rights . . . appended to
44. (**D**) If fewer documents are being kept, we are probably discussing those that are RETAINED. Their usefulness is INSURED by an improved cataloguing system.	**44.** While fewer documents are being kept, the usefulness of those _____ is now _____ by an improved cataloguing system. (A) printed . . . documented (B) discarded . . . concurred (C) read . . . emblazoned (D) retained . . . insured
45. (**C**) The man would have interfered with the speaker even if he had shouted words of agreement. Since the point is made that the man shouted false accusations, the *best* answer is that he DISCONCERTED the speaker.	**45.** The man _____ the speaker at the meeting by shouting false accusations. (A) corrected (B) argued with (C) disconcerted (D) interfered with
46. (**A**) The second blank could be filled with (A) or (D); however, the first term of (D) makes no sense in the first blank.	**46.** For the sake of public _____, public officials should avoid even the _____ of a conflict of interest. (A) confidence . . . appearance (B) relations . . . actuality (C) appearances . . . apparition (D) commotion . . . hint
47. (**D**) VERIFICATION is at the heart of professionalism.	**47.** A professional journalist will attempt to _____ the facts learned in an interview by independent _____. (A) endorse . . . questions (B) query . . . situation (C) garnish . . . sources (D) verify . . . investigation

ANSWER	QUESTION
48. (**A**) Only the RECIPIENT would pick up the check.	**48.** The _____ of the award stopped by the financial aid office to pick up his check. (A) recipient (B) subject (C) donor (D) sponsor
49. (**C**) Modesty would lead one to BELITTLE his role. The connective HOWEVER makes the best transition between the two clauses.	**49.** He often, out of modesty, _____ his own contribution; without his efforts, _____, the program would still be in the planning stage. (A) affirms . . . therefore (B) represses . . . notwithstanding (C) belittles . . . however (D) rescinds . . . moreover
50. (**B**) The second blank might be filled by all choices except (C). However, the two terms of (D) make no sense in apposition. (A) is not the correct answer. The committee might have been incensed about the students' unrest but it would be unlikely to be incensed about the legitimate causes of that unrest. If it were UNINFORMED of the legitimate causes, its recommendations would be DEVOID OF value.	**50.** The committee was so _____ about the legitimate sources of the students' unrest that its recommendations were _____ value. (A) incensed . . . of moderate (B) uninformed . . . devoid of (C) uninterested . . . depreciating in (D) blasé . . . of incontestable

PRACTICE SENTENCE COMPLETION TESTS

TEST 1 — 5 MINUTES

Directions: Each of the following questions consists of an incomplete sentence followed by four words or pairs of words. Choose that word or pair of words which, when substituted for the blank space or spaces, *best* completes the meaning of the sentence, and circle the letter of your choice. Correct answers follow Test 5.

1. The Spanish dancer stamped her feet and _____ the rhythm with the click of _____.
(A) ignored . . . dice
(B) kept . . . cutlery
(C) accented . . . castanets
(D) diffused . . . a guitar

2. A bustling hospital floor is not _____ to a good night's sleep.
(A) related
(B) conducive
(C) necessary
(D) productive

3. The job applicant was so _____ as he approached the interview that his hands were _____ and his knees shook.
(A) confident . . . agitated
(B) impressed . . . clean
(C) unhappy . . . stiff
(D) nervous . . . clammy

4. A serious side effect of some drugs is recurrent _____.
(A) elucidations
(B) hallucinations
(C) formulations
(D) flagellations

5. Disgruntled _____ often become highly effective spies.
(A) defectors
(B) officers
(C) anarchists
(D) censors

6. I wish I could guarantee that the machine is _____ reliable, but in truth its performance is somewhat _____.
(A) invariably . . . sporadic
(B) often . . . skittish
(C) serially . . . erratic
(D) consistently . . . invincible

7. He extolled the juicy sweet fruit as being nothing less than _____.
(A) surreal
(B) saccharine
(C) cloying
(D) succulent

8. The military _____ of the burning buildings led the investigator to conclude that the fires had been set in an act of _____.
(A) location . . . arson
(B) significance . . . sabotage
(C) stance . . . sobriety
(D) discipline . . . treason

9. As the name of the prize winner was _____, the runner-up looked totally _____.
(A) extolled . . . exonerated
(B) awarded . . . devastated
(C) announced . . . crestfallen
(D) proclaimed . . . credulous

10. The unexploded device found rusting in the weeds must have been a _____.
(A) bomb
(B) decoy
(C) calamity
(D) dud

TEST 2 — 5 MINUTES

Directions: Each of the following questions consists of an incomplete sentence followed by four words or pairs of words. Choose that word or pair of words which, when substituted for the blank space or spaces, *best* completes the meaning of the sentence, and circle the letter of your choice.

1. The professor _____ had had a long and distinguished career and was held in high _____ by her peers.
   (A) eminent . . . stratosphere
   (B) emeritus . . . esteem
   (C) lecturing . . . tribute
   (D) triumphant . . . spirits

2. A famous person will sometimes prepare his own _____ to be engraved on his tombstone.
   (A) epitaph
   (B) elegy
   (C) epithet
   (D) eulogy

3. Common examples of verbal redundancies include expressions such as _____ poor and _____ natives.
   (A) indignant . . . indolent
   (B) indulgent . . . industrious
   (C) insolvent . . . iniquitous
   (D) indigent . . . indigenous

4. The stern teacher's _____ tone of voice _____ that the threat was not to be taken seriously.
   (A) gruff . . . belied
   (B) sprightly . . . inferred
   (C) jocular . . . implied
   (D) languid . . . asserted

5. Collecting cans and bottles and redeeming them for the deposit provides a meager _____.
   (A) squalor
   (B) subsistence
   (C) subsidy
   (D) supplement

6. Recent trials of serial murderers reveal _____ behavior including _____ and cannibalism.
   (A) lunatic . . . manipulation
   (B) lethargic . . . massacre
   (C) macabre . . . torture
   (D) mercurial . . . grimaces

7. As the bus rounded the curve, it _____ violently and caused some standees to lose their balance.
   (A) lunged
   (B) overturned
   (C) lurched
   (D) plummeted

8. The elderly gentleman was noticeably shaken when he read his own _____ in the local newspaper.
   (A) editorial
   (B) obituary
   (C) necromancy
   (D) necrology

9. We have narrowed our vacation options to two destinations, _____, the Florida Keys or a Caribbean island.
   (A) in fact
   (B) both
   (C) therefore
   (D) namely

10. The child appeared to be tall and _____, so his frequent absences for illness led the teacher to suspect that he was _____.
    (A) fat . . . faking
    (B) ruddy . . . sick
    (C) robust . . . malingering
    (D) lanky . . . truant

TEST 3 — 5 MINUTES

Directions: Each of the following questions consists of an incomplete sentence followed by four words or pairs of words. Choose that word or pair of words which, when substituted for the blank space or spaces, *best* completes the meaning of the sentence, and circle the letter of your choice.

1. The speaker rose from his seat, placed his notes on the _____, and began his address.
(A) podium
(B) dais
(C) rostrum
(D) lectern

2. The senator's attitude so _____ the community that the various groups came to _____ one another.
(A) energized . . . tolerate
(B) antagonized . . . respect
(C) polarized . . . despise
(D) divided . . . assist

3. It is _____ to tape record the testimony of a witness so as to have a (an) _____ record.
(A) advisable . . . verbatim
(B) illegal . . . accurate
(C) permissible . . . facsimile
(D) prudent . . . visible

4. The prodigy's grandmother felt _____ pleasure at her grandchild's piano success.
(A) violent
(B) vicarious
(C) virtuous
(D) vocal

5. Many people offered to adopt the _____ _____ who had been abandoned in the mall.
(A) rabid . . . mongrel
(B) crippled . . . cart
(C) winsome . . . waif
(D) fluffy . . . boa

6. The _____ costumes greatly increased the children's _____ as they witnessed their first ballet performance.
(A) elaborate . . . understanding
(B) grotesque . . . discomfort
(C) fanciful . . . delight
(D) comfortable . . . skill

7. The construction crew unexpectedly unearthed traces of a _____ unknown burial ground.
(A) historically
(B) hitherto
(C) fortunately
(D) persistently

8. I _____ my grandfather; to me he is the _____ of a gentleman.
(A) idolize . . . epitome
(B) despise . . . prototype
(C) adore . . . antithesis
(D) excuse . . . model

9. The young suspect was released on his own _____ with the _____ that he remain in school.
(A) volition . . . caveat
(B) recognition . . . promise
(C) signature . . . prerequisite
(D) recognizance . . . proviso

10. If a broken leg remains in a cast too long, the muscles may _____ from disuse.
(A) petrify
(B) exacerbate
(C) atrophy
(D) putrefy

TEST 4 — 5 MINUTES

Directions: Each of the following questions consists of an incomplete sentence followed by four words or pairs of words. Choose that word or pair of words which, when substituted for the blank space or spaces, *best* completes the meaning of the sentence, and circle the letter of your choice.

1. The judge _____ the physician to refrain from using too much medical _____ in his statement.
(A) admonished . . . jargon
(B) ordered . . . literature
(C) permitted . . . economics
(D) implored . . . jingoism

2. I am not _____ to walking in the rain, _____ if given the option I will ride.
(A) accustomed . . . however
(B) opposed . . . therefore
(C) averse . . . nonetheless
(D) agreeable . . . moreover

3. The psychiatrist feared that the suspect might commit suicide, so the suspect was kept under 24-hour _____.
(A) arrest
(B) constraints
(C) interrogation
(D) surveillance

4. The statement "You're only young once" is a (an) _____.
(A) spoof
(B) truism
(C) adage
(D) motto

5. That rice pudding is most _____; it looks like a (an) _____ mass.
(A) delicious . . . gargantuan
(B) unappetizing . . . glutinous
(C) cloying . . . quivering
(D) uninspiring . . . esoteric

6. With the current rise of _____ feeling, _____ are being kept busy delineating the shifting boundaries.
(A) entrepreneurial . . . artists
(B) antagonistic . . . governments
(C) cooperative . . . economists
(D) nationalistic . . . cartographers

7. I sat in the park and listened to the _____ from the nearby church tower.
(A) carillon
(B) harangue
(C) calliope
(D) sycophant

8. In the hot summer months, our city's air is often _____ with the _____ murk of pollution.
(A) endowed . . . luminous
(B) infused . . . negligible
(C) suffused . . . oppressive
(D) alleviated . . . aromatic

9. Could you supply some examples to _____ your argument?
(A) illustrate
(B) bolster
(C) destroy
(D) exaggerate

10. I fear the discipline in that household is so _____ that the children will grow up without character.
(A) rigid
(B) ludicrous
(C) attainable
(D) lax

TEST 5 — 5 MINUTES

Directions: Each of the following questions consists of an incomplete sentence followed by four words or pairs of words. Choose that word or pair of words which, when substituted for the blank space or spaces, *best* completes the meaning of the sentence, and circle the letter of your choice.

1. That strain of cancer is so _____ that no amount of treatment can _____ it.
(A) abundant . . . describe
(B) capricious . . . enhance
(C) virulent . . . destroy
(D) arcane . . . cure

2. He is a very _____ person, always carrying a rabbit's foot in his pocket as a (an) _____.
(A) timorous . . . omen
(B) superstitious . . . talisman
(C) gullible . . . charm
(D) conscientious . . . keyring

3. Sometimes the effect of a _____ meal is to make the diner very sleepy.
(A) hearty
(B) haughty
(C) healthy
(D) hasty

4. The _____ garden is _____ and fragrant.
(A) formal . . . overgrown
(B) artificial . . . infested
(C) public . . . forbidding
(D) vernal . . . verdant

5. The _____ vending machine spewed change all over the floor.
(A) recalcitrant
(B) zealous
(C) hulking
(D) rambunctious

6. The fire trucks arriving at the scene of the _____ created a massive traffic jam.
(A) convocation
(B) simulation
(C) conflagration
(D) mutiny

7. A _____ tends to rely on _____ evidence.
(A) visionary . . . prodigious
(B) pragmatist . . . empirical
(C) jury . . . spurious
(D) scientist . . . theoretical

8. I am pleased that I will be able to go swimming wearing my _____ watch.
(A) aquamarine
(B) digital
(C) liquefied
(D) submersible

9. Caring for younger siblings can be a (an) _____ responsibility for the child of a (an) _____.
(A) onerous . . . alcoholic
(B) preordained . . . acrobat
(C) negligible . . . supplicant
(D) appreciable . . . parent

10. The clergyman was so highly respected that no one could believe that he was a (an) _____.
(A) transgressor
(B) hemophiliac
(C) executor
(D) altruist

Practice Sentence Completion Tests

Answer Key

TEST 1

1. **C**	3. **D**	5. **A**	7. **D**	9. **C**
2. **B**	4. **B**	6. **A**	8. **B**	10. **D**

TEST 2

1. **B**	3. **D**	5. **B**	7. **C**	9. **D**
2. **A**	4. **C**	6. **C**	8. **B**	10. **C**

TEST 3

1. **D**	3. **A**	5. **C**	7. **B**	9. **D**
2. **C**	4. **B**	6. **C**	8. **A**	10. **C**

TEST 4

1. **A**	3. **D**	5. **B**	7. **A**	9. **B**
2. **C**	4. **B**	6. **D**	8. **C**	10. **D**

TEST 5

1. **C**	3. **A**	5. **D**	7. **B**	9. **A**
2. **B**	4. **D**	6. **C**	8. **D**	10. **A**

What You Must Know About Verbal Ability Questions

Review this page the night before you take your high school entrance exam. It will help you get the answers to verbal ability questions.

Synonyms

- These steps will help you answer synonym questions:
  1. Read the question carefully. Consider *every* answer choice.
  2. Eliminate obviously wrong responses immediately.
  3. Use word-analysis techniques to help you with difficult words.
  4. Try using the word in a sentence of your own; think about the meaning of the word as you have used it.
- The correct answer may not be a perfect synonym, but it will be the *best* choice.
- The correct choice might be the easiest word. Do *not* choose a word just because you do not know it.
- Synonym questions are arranged from easy to hard.

Verbal Analogies

- These steps will help you solve analogy questions:
  1. Figure out how the first two words are related.
  2. Make up a sentence that expresses that relationship.
  3. Try out your sentence on each answer choice and eliminate the ones that don't work.
  4. If you're left with more than one answer—or no answer at all—go back and make your sentence fit better.
  5. Choose the best answer.
- Remember the sentence connection. Create a sentence that summarizes the relationship between the original analogy words. Use the sentence to test the answer choices.
- The order of the relationship must be the same in both pairs.
- Some common verbal analogy categories are:

  SYNONYMS
  ANTONYMS
  PART-WHOLE

NOUN-VERB
CAUSE-AND-EFFECT
PURPOSE
ASSOCIATION
TYPE OF
PART OF THE DEFINITION OF
LACK OF SOMETHING IS PART OF THE DEFINITION
A PLACE FOR
DEGREE

- Analogies are arranged from easy to hard.

Sentence Completions

- These steps will help you as you work through this section:
  1. Read the sentence carefully.
  2. Guess at the answer.
  3. Scan the answer choices for the word you guessed. If it's there, mark it and go on. If it's not, go on to Step 4.
  4. Examine the sentence for clues to the missing word.
  5. Eliminate any answer choices that are ruled out by the clues.
  6. Try the ones that are left and pick whichever is best.
- Be alert for clues in the sentence. Look for negative words or positive words.
- Sentence completion questions go from easy to hard.

PART

EVERYTHING YOU NEED!

Reading

CHAPTER 10

Reading Comprehension

PLAN A: ACCELERATED

- ***Study*** "What Kinds of Questions Will I Be Asked?"
- ***Study*** "How Do You Answer Critical Reading Questions?"
- ***Study*** "What Smart Test-Takers Know"
- ***Skim*** "Learning Exercises"
- ***Take*** "Practice Reading Comprehension Tests"

PLAN B: TOP SPEED

- ***Read*** "What Kinds of Questions Will I Be Asked?"
- ***Study*** "How Do You Answer Critical Reading Questions?"
- ***Read*** "What Smart Test-Takers Know"
- ***Take*** "Practice Reading Comprehension Tests"

You'll Find Answers to These Questions

Why are they testing my reading ability?
What kinds of questions will I be asked?
How do you answer reading comprehension questions?
What do smart test-takers know about reading comprehension questions?

WHY ARE THEY TESTING MY READING ABILITY?

So now you're probably thinking, "Who *are* these people and why are they testing my reading? If I couldn't read, I couldn't take the test. Geez!" Well, they're not really testing your reading. They are testing how much you understand when you read, especially when you read something unfamiliar (and under incredibly torturous pressure, too).

WHAT KINDS OF QUESTIONS WILL I BE ASKED?

The questions that follow each passage are in the standard multiple-choice format with either four (ISEE) or five (SSAT) answer choices. On high school entrance exams, the questions tend to fall into four categories. These questions ask you to do one of the following:

- identify the main idea or the author's purpose
- locate details that support the main idea
- define a word based on its meaning in the passage
- draw inferences from ideas in the passage

Main Idea

This type of question presents several titles or phrases and asks you to choose the one that best expresses the main idea of the passage. Main ideas often can be found in a topic sentence. Topic sentences usually appear in the first paragraph, as part of the introduction, or in the last paragraph, as a summary.

EXAMPLE:

The social standing of a wife in colonial days was determined by the standing of her husband as well as by her own ability and resourcefulness. She married not only a husband but also a career. Her position in the community was established in part by the quality of the bread she baked, by the food she preserved for the winter's use, by the whiteness of her washing on the line, by the way her children were clothed, and by her skill in nursing. Doctors were scarce. In case of the illness or death of a neighbor, a woman would put aside her own work to help, and she was honored for what she could do.

TESTSMARTS

Answer the easier questions first. Start with the vocabulary questions. Then go on to details, main idea, and finally inferences.

The title that best expresses the main idea of this selection is

(A) Care of Children in Colonial Times
(B) Community Spirit
(C) Medical Care in Pre-Revolutionary Times
(D) The Colonial Housewife

This selection describes the various homemaking duties a colonial woman was expected to perform. Therefore, the correct response is **(D)**.

Details

Details are the facts and ideas in a selection that explain and support the main idea.

EXAMPLE:

There are many signs by which people predict the weather. Some of these have a true basis, but many have not. There is, for example, no evidence that it is more likely to storm during one phase of the moon than during another. If it happens to rain on Easter, there is no reason to think that it will rain for the next seven Sundays. The groundhog may or may not see his shadow on Groundhog Day, but it probably won't affect the weather anyway.

Which of the following is *not* listed as a predictive weather phenomenon?

(A) rain on Easter
(B) the phases of the moon
(C) pain in a person's joints
(D) the groundhog's shadow

The correct response is **(C)**. The other choices were mentioned in the passage.

Vocabulary

This type of question, sometimes called "words in context," asks you to choose a synonym for one of the words in the passage.

EXAMPLE:

The maritime and fishing industries find perhaps 250 *applications* for rope and cordage. There are hundreds of different sizes, constructions, tensile strengths, and weights in rope and twine. Rope is sold by the pound but ordered by length, and is measured by circumference rather than by diameter.

In this context, the word *application* means

(A) use
(B) description
(C) size
(D) type

The correct response is (**A**), "use." Try it in the sentence in place of the word *application:* "Use" makes sense in that context and keeps the meaning of the sentence intact.

TESTSMARTS

Don't go for the ordinary. Vocabulary-in-context questions seldom test the most common meaning of a word. Look for a meaning that is not the usual one.

Inference

An inference is a conclusion that is drawn from the details in a reading selection. The answer to an inferential question will not be found in the passage and is therefore the most difficult type of comprehension question to answer. You must read carefully and think logically in order to draw the correct conclusion from the information given.

EXAMPLE:

The facts, as we see them, on drug use and the dangerous behaviors caused by drugs are that some people do get into trouble while using drugs, and some of those drug users are dangerous to others. Sometimes a drug is a necessary element in order for a person to commit a crime, although it may not be the cause of his or her criminality. On the other hand, the use of a drug sometimes seems to be the only convenient explanation by means of which the observer can account for the undesirable behavior.

The author apparently feels that

(A) the use of drugs always results in crime
(B) drugs and crime are only sometimes related
(C) the relationship of drug use to crime is purely coincidental
(D) drugs are usually an element in accidents and suicides

The author states that drugs are sometimes a necessary element in a crime, but at other times are just an excuse for criminal behavior. Therefore, (**B**) is the correct response.

HERE'S THE ANSWER

Reading comprehension takes a lot of time. Is there a way to go faster?

Read the questions first so you know what to look for as you read the passage. Then you won't have to read things twice to find the information you need.

HOW DO YOU ANSWER READING COMPREHENSION QUESTIONS?

Success with reading comprehension questions requires both speed in reading and efficiency in answering questions. Two important techniques that you must master are:

- skimming
- scanning

Skimming

Skimming is a form of speed-reading that is useful for extracting the main idea and supporting details from a reading selection. As you skim a passage, pay special attention to the first and last sentences or paragraphs. The purpose of skimming is to locate the topic sentence, the main idea, and some of the major supporting details. This overview of the location of information within the passage will help you to answer the more difficult inference questions quickly.

Scanning

Scanning is a method of looking for specific information by looking for key words. Scanning is done without reading.

Reading Comprehension: Getting it Right

1. Read through the questions quickly. This will guide your reading by showing you what information you will be expected to find. Skip over the answer choices for now.
2. Read the passage.
3. Answer vocabulary questions first. Find the answers by scanning the passage.
4. Answer detail questions next. Pick a key word or two from the question itself and scan the passage until you find it. The sentence in which the word appears probably contains the answer to the question.
5. Answer main-idea questions by reading the first and last sentences of the passage.
6. Leave inference questions for last. Skim the passage. Eliminate choices that are obviously wrong. Take your best guess.

WHAT SMART TEST-TAKERS KNOW

Reading comprehension questions can eat up your time very quickly. Check out these tips for smarter solutions.

YOU ONLY HAVE TIME TO READ EACH PASSAGE ONCE.

Because there's only time to read each passage once, you'll want to answer every question that you can about the passage before moving on. If you skip a question and try to come back to it later, you might have to reread the whole passage to find the answer—and you'll be out of time. Guess if you have to, but finish all the questions that you can.

TESTSMARTS

Complete one passage at a time. Answer all the questions for the passage you have just read before moving to another passage. There is no time to go back and read again.

EVERYTHING YOU NEED TO KNOW IS RIGHT THERE IN FRONT OF YOU.

The introductory paragraph and the passage have all the information you'll need to answer the questions. Even if the passage is about the price of beans in Bulgaria or the genetic makeup of a wombat, don't worry. It's all right there on the page.

THE PASSAGES ARE SUPPOSED TO BE UNFAMILIAR.

In order to put all candidates on a level playing field, test-makers choose obscure reading passages. ISEE passages draw upon social studies and the sciences; SSAT passages cover more general topics or come from literature. Either way, you probably have not seen the reading material before, and it doesn't matter. Remember, you're not being tested on your knowledge of the topic, but on how well you:

- figure out the meaning of an unfamiliar word from its context
- determine what an author means by noting certain words and phrases
- understand the author's assumptions, point of view, and main idea

AVOID THE TRAPS!

Don't let unfamiliar topics throw you. There's no need to worry whether you know anything about a topic in a passage. The answers are based on the information in the passage, not on your knowledge or experience.

PASSAGES THAT INTEREST YOU ARE EASIER TO WORK ON.

If there's a choice, it's best to start with the passage that's more interesting to you, whether it's fiction, a science article, or whatever. If the style appeals to you, you will probably go through the passage more quickly and find the questions easier to deal with.

IT PAYS TO BE AN ACTIVE READER.

Since you've already scanned the questions, you know what to look for as you read. When you find these points, use your pencil to underline or circle them. You'll be able to find them easily when you need them to answer the questions.

DETAILS CAN BOG YOU DOWN.

Remember, you don't have to understand every bit of information. You just have to find the information you need to answer the questions. Don't waste your time on technical details or on information that the questions don't ask for.

AVOID THE TRAPS!

True doesn't mean correct! Be sure that the answer you mark is the answer to the question that is asked.

WHAT'S TRUE IS NOT NECESSARILY THE ANSWER.

What does that mean? It means that a certain answer choice may be perfectly true, but it might not be the correct answer to the question that's being asked. Read carefully—and don't be fooled!

YOU CAN SOLVE VOCABULARY-IN-CONTEXT QUESTIONS BY PLUGGING IN CHOICES.

For vocabulary-in-context questions, plug the choices into the original sentence and don't be fooled by the obvious synonym.

THE ANSWER TO A MAIN IDEA QUESTION IS NEITHER TOO GENERAL NOR TOO SPECIFIC.

For a question about the main idea or the author's purpose, look for an answer choice that states it. Don't be too general or too specific.

THE ANSWER TO A MAIN IDEA QUESTION IS OFTEN IN THE FIRST OR LAST PARAGRAPH.

Look in the first or last (or both) paragraph of the passage for answers to main idea/author's purpose questions.

YOU HAVE TO READ BETWEEN THE LINES.

When a reading comprehension question asks for something the author has suggested, implied, or not stated directly, you have to use the information in the passage and draw your own conclusions. Read between the lines to see if the author has given any hints that would lead you to the correct answer.

LEARNING EXERCISES: READING COMPREHENSION

The questions in this section are arranged in boxes called "frames." The answer for each frame will be found in the box to the left of the question frame.

First, cover the answer boxes with a strip of paper. Circle your answer to the question. Then, move the paper down to expose the answer to that question.

Main Idea

ANSWER	QUESTION
1. (A) Incorrect This answer suggests the discussion of more than one planet or celestial body. The selection talks only about the moon. (B) Incorrect This response implies a discussion of lifestyles. This is impossible as there is no life on the moon. (C) Incorrect The moon's atmosphere is only one of the subtopics—not the main idea—discussed in this selection. **(D)** Correct The word *conditions* covers all aspects of the moon discussed in this selection: the moon's size, its terrain, its atmosphere, temperature, etc.	At a distance of approximately 250,000 miles from Earth, the moon is our nearest celestial neighbor. A rugged terrain of mountains, cliffs, plains, and craters covers this globe of 2,000 miles in diameter, but this landscape contains no water. There is no precipitation of any kind on the moon because it lacks an atmosphere. For the same reason, a constant barrage of meteorites and other space debris reaches its surface without hindrance. The beautiful, silvery moon is, in actuality, a barren desert, suffering from great extremes of temperature and devoid of any life as we know it. **1.** The title that best expresses the main idea of this selection is (A) Landscapes in Space (B) Life on the Moon (C) The Moon's Atmosphere (D) Conditions on the Moon
2. (A) Incorrect Although all three of these are mentioned in this selection, they are not the *theme* of the selection. (B) Incorrect This topic is mentioned but not discussed. (C) Incorrect This subject is mentioned but not discussed. **(D)** Correct The selection discusses some of the reasons and remedies for the limitations of language.	The more complicated our thoughts and emotions, the less effective is language as a tool of expression. This is not a simple matter of style or eloquence, for even the finest speakers and writers, using the most sensitive language, would be incapable of putting certain thoughts into words. For this reason, many people use poetry and music instead of prose. These two forms of communication convey subtle yet powerful meanings that cannot be expressed with ordinary words. **2.** The title that best expresses the theme of this selection is (A) Words, Poetry, and Music (B) The Hidden Meanings of Words (C) The Eloquence of Fine Speakers (D) Limitations of Language

ANSWER	QUESTION
3. (A) Incorrect The selection does not compare the exports of these two areas. (B) Incorrect This subject is not mentioned in the selection. **(C)** Correct Both of these bodies of water serve the bordering land masses in similar ways. (D) Incorrect Living standards are not discussed in this selection.	The Caribbean Sea is to North and South America what the Mediterranean is to the European continent—a central sea. The American body of water is not landlocked. Double strings of islands—the Cuba group and the Bahamas—form an arc at the Atlantic entrance, and this arc is now firmly fortified. Since the Mediterranean of the West is the passage between the Americas, it must be controlled by these countries in order to carry on trade. This sea is as necessary to the Caribbean countries as the Mediterranean is to Italy. The countries of this area produce large quantities of oil, tropical fruits, and vegetables. They are also rich in minerals. This region is capable of supplying the United States with many goods formerly imported from Africa and Asia. In exchange, the countries of this region need the manufactured goods that can be provided only by an industrial nation. **3.** The Caribbean Sea and the Mediterranean are alike with respect to their (A) variety of exports (B) epidemics of serious diseases (C) geographical importance (D) living standards
4. (A) Incorrect The danger of storms is only one of the difficulties affecting migratory birds. **(B)** Correct Each sentence in this paragraph explains why migration is perilous. (C) Incorrect This topic is mentioned only in the first sentence. (D) Incorrect This subject is not discussed at all in this selection.	The dangers to which migratory birds are subjected during their journeys are but little less than those that would befall them if they remained in unsuitable zones. During long oversea passages, fatigue and hunger weed out the weaklings. Sudden storms and adverse winds strike migrating birds where no land is near, and they are often carried far from the goal they aimed at. Predatory birds accompany them, taking a toll en route, and predatory man waits for the tired wanderers with gun and net. **4.** The title that best expresses the main idea of this passage is (A) Dangers of Storms (B) Perils of Migration (C) Unsuitable Environment (D) How Birds Reach Goals
5. (A) Incorrect The selection does not describe the contents, appearance, or uses of the library. It is only mentioned in the first sentence.	In his library at Monticello, Jefferson made hundreds of architectural drawings, all of which have been preserved. He must have had a great gift of concentration and a real love for his subject to be able to work in a room with such an outlook. And what energy he had, to find time and will for this precise and exquisite work, at the same time riding over his estate, working in his garden, and carrying out correspondence with everyone from the Marquis de Lafayette to his youngest grandchild.

ANSWER	QUESTION
(B) Incorrect Only one aspect of this topic was mentioned—Jefferson working in his garden. (C) Correct The selection describes in detail Jefferson's "full life": his architectural drawings, his love of his estate and gardens, his correspondences, and his "prescription for life." (D) Incorrect This is only one aspect of Jefferson that is discussed in this article.	"Something pursued with ardor" was Jefferson's prescription for life, and he got the last ounce of excitement and interest out of everything that came to his notice. **5.** The main idea of this selection is expressed in the title (A) The Library at Monticello (B) The Care of the Estate (C) A Full Life (D) Jefferson, the Architect
6. (A) Incorrect Landing areas were referred to with regard to only one kind of lighting. (B) Incorrect Colored lights are just one type of lighting discussed in this selection. (C) Incorrect Just one type of lighting is related to airport identification. (D) Correct The selection describes several lighting requirements for airports.	Specific types of lighting are required at first-class airports by the Department of Commerce. To identify an airport, there must be a beacon light of not less than 100,000 candle power, with a beam that properly distributes light up in the air so that it can be seen all around the horizon from an altitude of 500 to 2,000 feet. All flashing beacons must have a definite Morse code characteristic to aid in identification. Colored lights are required to indicate where safe area for landing ends, red lights being used where landing is particularly dangerous. **6.** The best title for this selection is (A) Landing Areas (B) Colored Lights at Airports (C) Identification of Airports (D) Airport Lighting Requirements

Details

ANSWER	QUESTION
	Ants are very interesting insects. There are about 8,000 different kinds with various ways of finding food. There are hunter ants that capture other insects, shepherd ants that care for aphids from which they get sweet honeydew, thief ants that live by stealing, slave-making ants that kidnap the children of other ant nations, and mighty military ants that live by plundering and destroying, driving even men and elephants before them. A city of ants includes the queen, the workers, the baby ants, and their nurses. Ant babies change their form three times. First, they are small, white eggs. When they hatch, they are little, fat, white worms called larvae. The larvae change into pupae, and the

ANSWER	QUESTION
	pupae change into adults. The queen is the mother of all the ants in the community. The workers bring food to her and protect her from invaders.
7. (C) See paragraph one, sentence three.	**7.** Hunter ants (A) care for aphids (B) kidnap young ants from other colonies (C) capture other insects (D) plunder and destroy
8. (A) See paragraph two, sentence one.	**8.** A colony of ants (A) includes a queen, workers, babies, and their nurses (B) may have as many as 8,000 members (C) is built in a hill (D) protects its members
9. (D) See paragraph two, sentence five.	**9.** Adult ants (A) hatch from eggs (B) come from larvae (C) are all workers (D) come from pupae
	Commercial interests were quick to recognize the great possibilities of presenting by means of radio what is in effect a person-to-person appeal. At first the novelty made people listen to almost anything, but as the audiences became more accustomed to broadcasts, varied methods of capturing and holding the attention have developed. These vary from the frank interjection of advertising matter in a program of entertainment to the mere sponsoring of the program. Entertainment at first appeared to have the greatest appeal, and low comedy and jazz music filled the air. There has come, however, the realization that the radio audience is now as complex as the public and that programs must be set up to attract the attention of as many different types of hearers as possible.
10. (A) is the correct answer. See the second sentence.	**10.** When radio was new, (A) people would listen to almost anything (B) advertising was poor (C) advertising was interjected into the programming (D) entertainment was limited
	The part of the ear we see is only a cartilage and skin trumpet that catches sound waves. Buried in bone at the base of the skull is the delicate apparatus that makes hearing possible. A passage leads from the outer ear to a membrane called the eardrum. Sound waves striking the eardrum make it vibrate. On

ANSWER	QUESTION
	the other side of the eardrum lies a space called the middle ear. Across this a chain of three tiny bones carries sound vibrations to another space called the inner ear. Sound messages are conducted along the auditory nerve, located in the inner ear, to the brain for interpretation. The middle ear is connected to the throat by the Eustachian tube. This tube ends near the throat opening of the nose, close to the tonsils. The middle ear also communicates with the mastoid, or air cells in the bone behind the ear.
11. (C) See paragraph one, sentence one.	**11.** The outer ear is made of (A) a delicate apparatus (B) a membrane (C) cartilage and skin (D) three tiny bones
12. (A) See paragraph two, sentence one.	**12.** The eardrum is a(n) (A) membrane (B) piece of thin cartilage (C) air cell (D) short tube
13. (C) See paragraph two, sentence four. Sound messages are carried along the auditory nerve.	**13.** Sound vibrations are carried (A) along the auditory nerve (B) through the eardrum (C) to the inner ear across a chain of three tiny bones (D) to the base of the skull
	Track-and-field events are the only modern sports that would be recognizable in their original form. They can be traced back more than 2,500 years to the ancient civilization of Greece. The Greeks held their athletes in high esteem, and champions were looked upon as national heroes. The Greeks began the original Olympic games for the purpose of assembling the greatest athletes of their country. The games were religious pageants as well as peerless athletic events and were held every four years for more than eight centuries.
14. (D) See paragraph one, sentence three.	**14.** In ancient Greece, athletes were (A) trained as professionals (B) forced to participate in the games (C) usually defeated by the Romans (D) regarded very highly by the public

ANSWER	QUESTION
15. (A) See paragraph one, sentence two.	**15.** The present-day Olympics (A) have a 2,500-year-old history (B) are religious pageants (C) have been held every four years for eight centuries (D) are completely different from the Greek games
	Observe the people who make an abiding impression of strength and goodness, and you will see that their personal attractiveness and force are rooted in fundamentals of character. They have the physical vitality, endurance, and courage that come from good living. They have the mental stamina and penetration that come from facing up to one's problems, however difficult, and from keeping one's mind on things that really matter. They have the moral power that comes from an active sense of what is right, from doing their part to make truth, justice, and beauty prevail in the world. They have the inner peace and grace that are the basics of a truly charismatic personality. People trust them, like to be with them, and depend on them in emergencies. They are the salt of the earth.
16. (A) Incorrect See the second sentence. (B) Incorrect See the sixth sentence. (C) Correct (D) Incorrect See the fifth sentence.	**16.** A quality *not* mentioned by the author is (A) courage (B) dependability (C) tolerance (D) inner grace
	Although you may still enjoy fairy tales, they probably do not engross you to the degree that they might have a few years ago. Fairy tales belong primarily to a stage in our lives when we are most interested by the world of fantasy. Goblins, wizards, and dwarfs appeal to the young child's wandering imagination and contribute greatly to the development of creativity, but it is a temporary infatuation. As we grow older, real challenges begin to interest us more. The imaginary victories brought about by fairy godmothers lose their power of enchantment, and we become absorbed in the stories of real people, real success, and real accomplishment. The fascination of "Jack the Giant Killer" gives way to a keen interest in Commander Byrd's Antarctic exploration, Helen Keller's biography, or the harrowing adventures of spelunkers, deep-sea divers, and mountain climbers. This step marks one of the first great advances in the process of intellectual maturation.

ANSWER	QUESTION
17. (A) See the first paragraph.	**17.** Young children are primarily interested in (A) fantasy stories (B) horror stories (C) goblins and witches (D) adventure stories
18. (C) See paragraph two, sentences one and two.	**18.** People become interested in real-life stories when they (A) are young (B) are adults (C) begin to mature (D) are bored

Vocabulary

ANSWER	QUESTION
	In May of each year, the ghost of Mark Twain must hover over Angel's Camp, California, while all eyes in this colorful old mining town turn to the tailless, leaping *amphibians* of the genus Rana. It was just this sort of event that Twain made famous in his early humorous story, "The Celebrated Jumping Frog of Calaveras County." Thousands of spectators gather each year to watch the county's champions hop their way to fame and compete for a $500 first prize. Each frog must undergo a rigid inspection to insure against foul play, such as the loading of the competitor with buckshot, as happened in Twain's tall tale. Back in 1944, Alfred Jermy was the proud owner of Flash, a frog that held the world's championship with a fifteen-foot, ten-inch leap. In 1950, a seven-year-old boy's pet, X-100, stole top honors with three jumps averaging fourteen feet, nine inches. As amazing as these might seem to the *novice*, these are mere puddle jumps. Half the fun in visiting this Calaveras County contest is to be found in listening to the tales of 600-foot leaps in a favorable wind—well, why not?
19. (B) Frogs are a type of *amphibian*.	**19.** The *amphibians* mentioned in the first paragraph are the (A) storytellers (B) frogs (C) citizens of Calaveras County (D) human contestants
20. (D) The word *novice* means "inexperienced."	**20.** The word *novice* in the third paragraph means (A) the judges (B) the spectators (C) the owners of the frogs (D) inexperienced readers

ANSWER	QUESTION
	In the year 1799, an officer of the French Army was stationed in a small fortress on the Rosetta River, a mouth of the Nile, near Alexandria, Egypt. He was interested in the ruins of the ancient Egyptian civilization and had seen the Sphinx and the pyramids, those mysterious structures that were erected by men of another era. One day, as a trench was being dug, he found a piece of black slate on which letters had been carved. He had studied Greek in school and knew this was an *inscription* written in that language. There were two more lines carved into the stone: one in the Egyptian characters he had seen on other ruins, the other in completely unfamiliar characters. The officer realized the importance of such a find and *relinquished* it to scholars who had been puzzling over Egyptian inscriptions. In 1802, a French professor by the name of Champollion began studying the stone in an attempt to *decipher* the two unknown sets of characters using the Greek letters as a key. He worked with the stone for over 20 years and, in 1823, announced that he had discovered the meaning of the fourteen signs and in doing so had unlocked the secret of ancient Egyptian writing. Some 5,000 years after an unknown person had made those three inscriptions, the Rosetta Stone became a key, unlocking the written records of Egypt and sharing the history of that civilization with the rest of the world.
21. (A) *Decipher* means to break a code and translate the message.	**21.** The word *decipher* is synonymous with (A) translate (B) encode (C) transcribe (D) transmit
22. (C) Other examples of *inscriptions* are names carved into gravestones, and initials inscribed in jewelry. To inscribe is to write into.	**22.** The word *inscription* means (A) a picture carved in stone (B) a relief sculpture (C) letters carved into a hard substance (D) a written message
23. (A) The word *relinquish* means to "let go" or "give up."	**23.** The word *relinquish* means to (A) give up possession of something (B) lend to someone (C) sell an object (D) study an object

ANSWER	QUESTION
	The impressions that an individual gets from his environment are greatly influenced by his emotional state. When he is happy, objects and people present themselves to him in a favorable aspect; when he is depressed, he views the same things in an entirely different light. It has been said that a person's moods are the lenses that color life with many different hues. Not only does mood affect impression; impression also affects mood. The beauty of a spring morning may *dissipate* the gloom of a great sorrow; the good-natured chuckle of a fat man may turn anger into a smile; or a telegram may *transform* a house of mirth into a house of mourning.
24. (C) Other synonyms for the word *dissipate* are "scatter," "dissolve," and "evaporate."	**24.** The word *dissipate* means (A) condense (B) draw out (C) melt away (D) inflate
25. (A) When something is changed to something else, it is *transformed,* or converted.	**25.** The word *transform* is synonymous with (A) convert (B) conclude (C) interpret (D) convey

Inference

ANSWER	QUESTION
	Intuition is not a quality everyone can understand. As the unimaginative are miserable about a work of fiction until they discover what flesh-and-blood individual served as a model for the hero or heroine, so, too, many scientists scoff at the unscientific notion that intuition as a force exists. They cannot believe that a blind man can see something they cannot see. They rely utterly on the celebrated inductive method of reasoning: expose the facts and conclude from them only what can be proven. Generally speaking, this is a very sound rule, but can we be certain that the really great accomplishments are initiated in this plodding fashion? Dreams are made of quite different stuff, and if any are left in the world who do not know that dreams have remade the world, then perhaps there is little we can teach them.
26. (A) is the correct answer.	**26.** The author implies that intuition (A) is the product of imagination (B) relies on factual information (C) is an inductive reasoning process (D) is valueless

ANSWER	QUESTION
	It is exceedingly difficult to draw on a canvas the man whose nature is large and central, without cranks or oddities. The very simplicity of such souls defies an easy summary, for they are as spacious in their effect as daylight or summer. Often we remember friends by a gesture or a trick of expression, or by a favorite phrase. But with Nelson I do not find myself thinking of such idiosyncrasies. His presence warmed and lit up so big a region of life that in thinking of him one is overwhelmed by the multitude of things that he made better by simply existing among them. If you remove a fire from the hearth, you will remember the look, not so much of the blaze itself, as of the whole room in its pleasant glow.
27. (D)	**27.** The phrase "to draw on a canvas" is used in this context to mean (A) to paint a portrait (B) to summarize (C) to make a collage (D) to describe
28. (A)	**28.** The last sentence is a metaphor comparing Nelson to (A) the blaze in a fireplace (B) a hearth (C) fire (D) a pleasant glow
29. (B)	**29.** From the tone of this selection, you might draw the conclusion that the author (A) thinks of Nelson as a strange man (B) is describing a man who has died (C) is overwhelmed by Nelson (D) remembers Nelson only by his gestures
	A glass case in the British Museum houses the mummified remains of two Egyptian kings who lived beside the Nile. The exhibit includes a broken plow, a rusted sickle, and two sticks tied together with a leather strap. These were the "bread tools" of Egyptians who lived 4,000 years ago during the reigns of the two kings. They are not unlike the tools used by 18th century American farmers, and, in fact, similar sickles may be viewed at Mount Vernon, George Washington's Virginia home.
30. (C) is the correct answer.	**30.** We may conclude from this selection that the ancient Egyptians (A) had only two important kings (B) taught farming techniques to 18th century Americans (C) were relatively advanced in the use of agricultural tools (D) neglected their equipment

ANSWER	QUESTION
	The horn of an automobile is a valuable aid to good driving if properly used. When about to pass another car, it is advisable to notify the driver of the car ahead. Children or animals on the street should be given a warning note. Of course, a courteous driver would not blow his horn unnecessarily in the vicinity of a hospital or a place of worship. He should also be considerate of schools, where quiet is important. The way in which a driver uses his horn is a fairly accurate index to his character, for through the sound he expresses his impatience and his good manners, or the lack of them.
31. (C)	**31.** The place that a good driver would be least likely to use his horn is (A) St. James Theater (B) Riverdale Apartments (C) Memorial Convalescent Home (D) Yankee Stadium
32. (C)	**32.** The character of a driver who fails to sound his horn when a dog is crossing the street is (A) noble (B) impatient (C) selfish (D) bold
	According to early English history, a small group of people from northeastern Europe, called Easterlings, came by invitation to England to devise and develop a new system of coinage. These people lived in towns that were famous for the accuracy of their coins. The coins that they worked out for England were made of silver and came to be known as the Easterling coins. Later the word *Easterling* was shortened to sterling. The word *sterling* gradually came to be applied to all silver articles of very fine quality.
33. (A)	**33.** The passage implies that the Easterlings (A) had an excellent reputation (B) used silver exclusively (C) were silversmiths (D) coined the word *sterling*
34. (B)	**34.** The word *sterling* began to be used for high quality silver because (A) it was used to make English coins (B) the Easterlings were known for the quality of their work (C) silver is very expensive (D) the Easterlings were the only people who could make silver coins

PRACTICE READING COMPREHENSION TESTS

TEST 1 — 3 MINUTES

Directions: Read the following passage and then decide which of the responses is the best answer to each question. Circle the letter that appears before your answer. Correct answers follow Test 10.

Early in the 19th century, American youth was playing a game, somewhat like the English game of rounders, that contained all the elements of modern baseball. It was neither scientifically planned nor skillfully played, but it furnished considerable excitement for players and spectators alike. The playing field was a sixty-foot square with goals, or bases, at each of its four corners. A pitcher stationed himself at the center of the square, and a catcher and an indefinite number of fielders supported the pitcher and completed the team. None of these players, usually between eight and twenty on a side, covered the bases. The batter was out on balls caught on the fly or the first bound, and a base runner was out if he was hit by a thrown ball while off base. The bat was nothing more than a stout paddle with a two-inch-thick handle. The ball was apt to be an impromptu affair composed of a bullet, cork, or metal slug tightly wound with wool yarn and string. With its simple equipment and only a few rules, this game steadily increased in popularity during the first half of the century.

1. The title that best expresses the main idea of this selection is
(A) Baseball Rules
(B) An English Game
(C) Baseball's Predecessor
(D) American Pastimes

2. The rules of this game required
(A) eight fielders
(B) a pitcher, a catcher, and one fielder for each base
(C) twenty fielders
(D) no specific number of players

3. This selection suggests that
(A) the game of baseball has grown more complicated over the years
(B) the game described was very dangerous
(C) baseball originated in the United States
(D) the game described required skilled players

4. The word *impromptu* in line 19 means
(A) carefully planned
(B) careless
(C) informal
(D) skillful

TEST 2 — 3 MINUTES

Directions: Read the following passage and then decide which of the responses is the best answer to each question. Circle the letter that appears before your answer.

John J. Audubon, a bird watcher, once noticed that a pair of phoebes nested in the same place year after year, and he wondered if they might be the same birds. He put tiny silver bands on their legs, and the next spring the banded birds returned to the same nesting place.

This pair of phoebes were the first birds to be banded. Since that time, naturalists, with the aid of the federal government's Fish and Wildlife Department, band birds in an effort to study them. The bands, which are made of lightweight aluminum so as not to harm the birds, bear a message requesting finders to notify the department. Careful records of these notifications are kept and analyzed. In this way, naturalists have gained a great deal of knowledge about the nesting habits, migration patterns, and populations of a large variety of bird species. Most importantly, they are able to identify those species that are in danger of extinction.

1. The title below that best expresses the main idea of this passage is
(A) The Migration of Birds
(B) One Method of Studying Birds
(C) The Habits of Birds
(D) The Work of John Audubon

2. Audubon's purpose in banding the phoebes was to
(A) satisfy his own curiosity
(B) start a government study of birds
(C) gain fame as the first birdbander
(D) chart the phoebe's migration patterns

3. Audubon proved his theory that
(A) silver and aluminum are the best metals for birdbands
(B) the government should study birds
(C) phoebes are the most interesting birds to study
(D) birds return to the same nesting place each spring

4. The word *habits* in line 16 means
(A) naturalists
(B) living environments
(C) behaviors
(D) ecosystem

TEST 3 — 3 MINUTES

Directions: Read the following passage and then decide which of the responses is the best answer to each question. Circle the letter that appears before your answer.

A vast stretch of land lies untouched by civilization in the back country of the eastern portion of the African continent. With the occasional exception of a big-game hunter, foreigners never penetrate this area. Aside from the Wandorobo tribe, even the natives shun its confines because it harbors the deadly tsetse fly. The Wandorobo nomads depend on the forest for their lives, eating its roots and fruits and making their homes wherever they find themselves at the end of the day.

One of the staples of their primitive diet, and their only sweet, is honey. They obtain it through an ancient, symbiotic relationship with a bird known as the Indicator. The scientific community finally confirmed the report, at first discredited, that this bird purposefully led the natives to trees containing the honeycombs of wild bees. Other species of honey guides are also known to take advantage of the foraging efforts of some animals in much the same way that the Indicator uses men.

This amazing bird settles in a tree near a Wandorobo encampment and chatters incessantly until the men answer it with whistles. It then begins its leading flight. Chattering, it hops from tree to tree, while the men continue their musical answering call. When the bird reaches the tree, its chatter becomes shriller and its followers examine the tree carefully. The Indicator usually perches just over the honeycomb, and the men hear the humming of the bees in the hollow trunk. Using torches, they smoke most of the bees out of the tree, but those that escape the nullifying effects of the smoke sting the men viciously. Undaunted, the Wandorobos free the nest, gather the honey, and leave a small offering for their bird guide.

1. The word symbiotic is synonymous with
- (A) partnership
- (B) adversary
- (C) parasitic
- (D) opponent

2. According to the selection, one characteristic of the Wandorobo tribe is that its members
- (A) avoid the country of the tsetse fly
- (B) have no permanent homes
- (C) lack physical courage
- (D) live entirely on a diet of honey

3. The title that best expresses the topic of this selection is
- (A) Life in the African Backwoods
- (B) The Wandorobo Tribe
- (C) Locating a Honeycomb
- (D) Men and Birds Work Together

4. The word *incessantly* in line 23 means
- (A) intermittently
- (B) loudly
- (C) constantly
- (D) strangely

TEST 4 — 3 MINUTES

Directions: Read the following passage and then decide which of the responses is the best answer to each question. Circle the letter that appears before your answer.

The proud, noble American eagle appears on one side of the Great Seal of the United States, which is printed on every dollar bill. The same majestic bird can be seen on state seals, half dollars, and even in some commercial advertising. In fact, though we often encounter artistic representations of our national symbol, it is rarely seen alive in its native habitat. It is now all but extinct.

In the days of the founding fathers, the American eagle resided in nearly every corner of the territory now known as the continental United States. Today the eagle survives in what ornithologists call significant numbers only in two regions. An estimated 350 pairs inhabit Florida, and perhaps another 150 live in the Chesapeake Bay area of Delaware, Maryland, and Virginia. A few stragglers remain in other states, but in most, eagles have not been sighted for some time.

A federal law passed in 1940 protects these birds and their nesting areas, but it came too late to save more than a pitiful remnant of the species' original population.

1. An ornithologist is a person who studies
   (A) geographical regions
   (B) the history of extinct species
   (C) the populations of certain areas
   (D) the habits and habitats of birds

2. Today eagles are found in the greatest numbers in
   (A) Florida
   (B) Delaware
   (C) the Chesapeake Bay region
   (D) Virginia

3. The selection implies that
   (A) the number of eagles is likely to increase
   (B) the eagle population decreased because of a lack of protective game laws
   (C) there were only two localities where eagles could survive
   (D) the government knows very little about eagles

TEST 5 — 4 MINUTES

Directions: Read the following passage and then decide which of the responses is the best answer to each question. Circle the letter that appears before your answer.

The Alaska Highway, which runs 1,523 miles from Dawson Creek, British Columbia, to Fairbanks, Alaska, was built by U.S. Army Engineers to counter a threatened Japanese invasion of Alaska. It was rushed through in an incredibly short period of nine months and was therefore never properly surveyed. Some of the territory it passes through has not even been explored.

Although the story that the builders followed the trail of a wandering moose is probably not true, the effect is much the same. The leading bulldozer simply crashed through the brush wherever the going was easiest, avoiding the big trees, swampy hollows, and rocks. The project was made more complicated by the necessity of following not the shortest or easiest route but one that would serve the string of United States-Canadian airfields that stretch from Montana to Alaska. Even on flat land, the road twists into hairpin curves. In rough terrain it goes up and down like a roller coaster. In the mountains, sometimes clinging to the sides of cliffs 400 feet high, it turns sharply, without warning, and gives rear-seat passengers the stomach-gripping sensation of taking off into space. There is not a guardrail in its entire 1,500-mile length. Dust kicks up in giant plumes behind every car and on windless days hovers in the air like a thick fog.

Both the Canadian Army and the Alaskan Road Commission, which took over from the Army Engineers in 1946, do a commendable but nearly impossible job of maintaining the road. Where it is built on eternally frozen ground, it buckles and heaves; on the jellylike muskeg it is continually sinking, and must be graveled afresh every month. Bridges thrown across rivers are swept away in flash floods. Torrential thaws wash out miles of highway every spring. On mountainsides, you can tell the age of the road by counting the remains of earlier roads that have slipped down the slope.

1. The title that best expresses the main idea of this selection is
- (A) The Alaskan Road Commission
- (B) Building and Maintaining the Alaska Highway
- (C) Exploring Alaska
- (D) Driving Conditions in the Far North

2. The Alaska Highway was built to
- (A) make the route between Alaska and the States shorter
- (B) promote trade with Canada
- (C) meet a wartime emergency
- (D) aid exploration and surveying efforts

3. The job of maintaining the road is complicated by the
- (A) threat of invasion
- (B) forces of nature
- (C) lack of surveying
- (D) age of the road

4. The word *terrain* in line 20 refers to
- (A) geographical features of the land
- (B) mountains and valleys
- (C) a specific land area
- (D) swamps

TEST 6 — 3 MINUTES

Directions: Read the following passage and then decide which of the responses is the best answer to each question. Circle the letter that appears before your answer.

When the first white men came to North America, they found an abundance of valuable natural resources. Forests covered enormous areas; the soil was extremely fertile; and the forests, prairies, streams, and rivers abounded with wildlife. Later, huge quantities of gas, oil, and minerals were discovered.

These resources were so vast that it seemed they could never be exhausted. The forests were cleared for farmland. Grasslands and prairies were plowed and planted with crops. Mammals and birds were hunted for food and sport, and eventually factories, mills, and power companies were built on nearly every river. Minerals and oil were used to supply and power a young industrial nation.

The effects of these actions became apparent within a relatively short period of time. Timber shortages were predicted. The fertile soil was washed away by rain and blown about in great dust storms by the wind. Several species of birds began to disappear, and some of the great mammals became extinct. Many rivers were made unfit for fish by the pollution of factories. The seemingly inexhaustible stores of oil and minerals began to show signs of depletion.

Since that time, Americans have sponsored the creation of conservation programs in the hope that future generations may continue to share and enjoy the natural resources that are part of our heritage.

1. The title that best expresses the main idea of this selection is
- (A) The First White Men in America
- (B) The Loss of America's Natural Resources
- (C) Our American Heritage
- (D) The Cause of Our Timber Shortages

2. The word *depletion* in line 26 means
- (A) extinction
- (B) running out
- (C) having the quality of being inexhaustible
- (D) destruction

3. It seemed to the early settlers that
- (A) there was a shortage of minerals
- (B) there had been a great deal of soil erosion
- (C) the natural resources were inexhaustible
- (D) resources should be carefully used

TEST 7 — 4 MINUTES

Directions: Read the following passage and then decide which of the responses is the best answer to each question. Circle the letter that appears before your answer.

The peopling of the Northwest Territory by companies from the eastern states, such as the Ohio Company under the leadership of Reverend Manasseh Cutler of Ipswich, Massachusetts, furnishes us with many interesting historical tales.

The first towns to be established were Marietta, Zanesville, Chillicothe, and Cincinnati. After the Ohio Company came the Connecticut Company, which secured all the territory bordering Lake Erie, save a small portion known as fire lands and another portion known as Congress lands. The land taken up by the Connecticut people was called the Western Reserve and was settled almost entirely by New England people. The remainder of the state of Ohio was settled by Virginians and Pennsylvanians. Because the British controlled Lakes Ontario and Erie, the Massachusetts and Connecticut people made their journey into the Western Reserve through the southern part of the state. General Moses Cleaveland, the agent for the Connecticut Land Company, led a body of surveyors to the tract, proceeding by way of Lake Ontario. He quieted the Indian claims to the eastern portion of the reserve by giving them five hundred pounds, two heads of cattle, and one hundred gallons of whiskey. Landing at the mouth of the Conneaut River, General Moses Cleaveland and his party of fifty, including two women, celebrated Independence Day, 1796, with a feast of pork and beans with bread. A little later, a village was established at the mouth of the Cuyahoga River and was given the name of Cleaveland, in honor of the agent of the company. It is related that the name was afterward shortened to Cleveland by one of the early editors because he could not get so many letters into the heading of his newspaper.

1. Reverend Manasseh Cutler
- (A) led the Ohio Company
- (B) owned the Western Reserve
- (C) led the Connecticut Land Company
- (D) settled the Congress lands

2. The title that best expresses the main idea of this selection is
- (A) The Settling of the Northwest Territory
- (B) Control of the Great Lake Region
- (C) The Accomplishments of Reverend Manasseh Cutler
- (D) The Naming of Cleveland, Ohio

3. In the last sentence of the selection, the word *related* is used to mean
- (A) associated with
- (B) rumored
- (C) reported
- (D) thought

4. The selection suggests that General Cleaveland at first found the Indians to be
- (A) extremely noisy people
- (B) hostile to his party of strangers
- (C) starving
- (D) eager to work with him

TEST 8 — 3 MINUTES

Directions: Read the following passage and then decide which of the responses is the best answer to each question. Circle the letter that appears before your answer.

Along the shores of the Indian Ocean, from Africa around to the large islands southeast of Asia, is found a pretty little shellfish that is noted for furnishing what may have been the first money ever used. Its shell, called a cowrie, is white or light yellow, and is about one inch long. Millions of people around the ocean were using these cowries, separately or on strings, for money long before furs or cattle or other kinds of money were used anywhere, as far as is known. Cowries have been found in Assyria, many miles inland, and in China they were used with several other kinds of shells. Tortoise shells had the highest value there, so it might be said that the tortoise shells were the dollar bills while the cowries were the coins. Now, after thousands of years, there are still some tribes in Africa, India, and the South Seas that use cowries.

1. The author believes that the earliest money may have been in the form of
(A) cattle
(B) furs
(C) shells
(D) string

2. It is surprising to learn that cowries were used in Assyria because
(A) cowries are only one inch long
(B) cattle were plentiful in Assyria
(C) Assyria is away from the seacoast
(D) tortoise shells took the place of dollars

3. The Chinese used _____ for money.
(A) cattle
(B) tortoise shells
(C) shellfish
(D) whale's teeth

TEST 9 — 4 MINUTES

Directions: Read the following passage and then decide which of the responses is the best answer to each question. Circle the letter that appears before your answer.

From Gettysburg to the Battle of the Bulge, carrier pigeons have winged their way through skies fair and foul to deliver the vital messages of battle. Today, in spite of electronics and atomic weapons, these feathered heroes are still an important communication link in any army.

No one could be surer of this than the men at Fort Monmouth, New Jersey, the sole Army pigeon breeding and training center in this country. On the roosts at Fort Monmouth, perch many genuine battle heroes, among them veteran G.I. Joe.

In 1943, one-thousand British troops moved speedily ahead of the Allied advance in Italy to take the small town of Colvi Vecchia. Since communications could not be established in time to relay the victory to headquarters, the troops were due for a previously planned Allied bombing raid. Then, one of the men released carrier pigeon G.I. Joe. With a warning message on his back, he flew 20 miles in 20 minutes, arriving just as the bombers were warming up their motors. For saving the day for the British, the Lord Mayor of London later awarded G.I. Joe the Dickin Medal, England's highest award to an animal.

Even when regular message channels are set up, equipment can break or be overloaded or radio silence must be observed. Then, the carrier pigeon comes into his own. Ninety-nine times out of a hundred, he completes his mission. In Korea, Homer the homing pigeon was flying from the front to a rear command post when he developed wing trouble. Undaunted, Homer made a forced landing, hopped the last two miles and delivered his message. For initiative and loyalty, Homer was promoted to Pfc.—Pigeon First Class!

1. The writer of this passage evidently believes that carrier pigeons
- (A) have no usefulness in modern warfare
- (B) should be forced to fly only in emergencies
- (C) are remarkably reliable as message carriers
- (D) should receive regular promotions

2. G.I. Joe was rewarded for
- (A) preventing unnecessary loss of life
- (B) guiding a bomber's flight
- (C) returning in spite of an injured wing
- (D) bringing the news of an allied defeat

3. G.I. Joe's reward was a
- (A) promotion
- (B) reception given by the Lord Mayor
- (C) chance to retire to Fort Monmouth
- (D) medal

4. The word *vital* in line 3 means
- (A) extremely important
- (B) frequent
- (C) recent
- (D) written

TEST 10 — 3 MINUTES

Directions: Read the following passage and then decide which of the responses is the best answer to each question. Circle the letter that appears before your answer.

"Sophistication by the reel" is the motto of Peretz Johannes, who selects juvenile films for Saturday viewing at the Museum of the City of New York. Sampling the intellectual climate of the young fans in this city for the past two years has convinced him that many people underestimate the taste level of young New Yorkers. Consequently, a year ago he began to show films ordinarily restricted to art movie distribution. The series proved enormously successful, and in September, when the program commenced for this season, youngsters from the five boroughs filled the theater.

As a student of history, Mr. Johannes has not confined himself to productions given awards in recent years, but has spent many hours among dusty reels ferreting out such pre-war favorites as the silhouette films of Lotte Reiniger made in Germany. One program included two films based on children's stories, "The Little Red Lighthouse" and "Mike Mulligan and His Steam Shovel." The movies are shown at 11 AM and 3 PM, with a short program of stories and a demonstration of toys presented during the intermission.

1. Mr. Johannes found that the children's taste in motion pictures
- (A) was more varied than had been thought
- (B) ruled out pictures made before their own day
- (C) was limited to cartoons
- (D) was even poorer than adults had suspected

2. Admission to the program described is
- (A) limited to children in the neighborhood of the museum
- (B) for Manhattan only
- (C) available for all the city
- (D) for teenagers only

3. Mr. Johannes
- (A) followed an established policy in planning his programs
- (B) has failed so far to secure a good audience
- (C) limits his programs to the newest award winning pictures
- (D) evidently is a good judge of children's tastes

4. *Ferreting out* (line 17) a picture is
- (A) giving it a trial run
- (B) searching diligently for it
- (C) reviving it
- (D) banning it

Answer Key

TEST 1

1. **C** 2. **D** 3. **A** 4. **C**

TEST 2

1. **B** 2. **A** 3. **D** 4. **C**

TEST 3

1. **A** 2. **B** 3. **D** 4. **C**

TEST 4

1. **D** 2. **A** 3. **B**

TEST 5

1. **B** 2. **C** 3. **B** 4. **A**

TEST 6

1. **B** 2. **B** 3. **C**

TEST 7

1. **A** 2. **A** 3. **C** 4. **B**

TEST 8

1. **C** 2. **C** 3. **B**

TEST 9

1. **C** 2. **A** 3. **D** 4. **A**

TEST 10

1. **A** 2. **C** 3. **D** 4. **B**

SUMMING IT UP

What You Must Know About Reading Comprehension Questions

Review this page the night before you take your high school entrance exam. It will help you get the answers to reading comprehension questions.

- When you get to the reading comprehension section, take a deep breath and:
    1. Read through the questions quickly, noting what information you will have to find. Skip over the answer choices for now.
    2. Read the passage.
    3. Scan the passage and answer the vocabulary questions first.
    4. Tackle detail questions second. Pick a key word or two from the question and scan the passage for the location of the answer.
    5. Read the first and last sentences of the passage to answer main-idea questions.
    6. Skim for answers to inference questions. Eliminate wrong answers and make your best guess.
- All the information you need is right in the passage
- Reading comprehension questions are not arranged in order of difficulty.
- Don't get bogged down in details. Look for important ideas and mark them as you find them.
- Answer every question for a passage before starting the next passage.

PART

SIX

EVERYTHING YOU NEED!

Mathematics

CHAPTER 11

Mathematics Review

You'll Find Answers to These Questions

What mathematics must I know?
How do I estimate the answer?
When must I calculate?

WHAT MATHEMATICS MUST I KNOW?

The answer to this question is a question. What grade are you in? If you are in eighth grade, you must know basic arithmetic, fundamental operations using fractions and decimals, percents, and very basic algebra and geometry. If you are in twelfth grade seeking an extra year before college, you should be thoroughly familiar with complex algebra and geometry and with roots and exponents.

Remember that scoring of your high school entrance exam is based upon your grade. You do not need to know what you have not yet been taught. But you must have mastered all the mathematics appropriate to your grade level. Use your math textbook to help you limit the extent of your study in this chapter. Don't try to learn ahead. Concentrate on doing well on the math that a person your age must know.

THE FUNDAMENTAL OPERATIONS

Addition, subtraction, multiplication, and division are the basic operations upon which the structure of mathematics is based. *There is no substitute for having good skills in computation to achieve success on one of the high school entrance examinations.* Proceed through this section carefully, being honest with yourself about the accuracy and speed with which you solve these problems. Note problems that are difficult for you as well as those that are easy. Adjust your study plans accordingly.

PLAN A: ACCELERATED

- ***Read*** "What Mathematics Must I Know?"
- ***Study*** "How Do I Estimate?"
- ***Read*** "When Must I Calculate?"
- ***Read selectively*** "The Fundamental Operations," "Percentages," "Exponents," "Algebra," "Geometry," and "Word Problems"
- ***Do*** Short exercises appropriate to your grade level
- ***Skim*** "Learning Exercises"

PLAN B: TOP SPEED

- ***Read*** "What Mathematics Must I Know?"
- ***Read*** "How Do I Estimate?"
- ***Read*** "When Must I Calculate?"
- ***Skim*** "The Fundamental Operations," "Percentages," "Exponents," "Algebra," "Geometry," and "Word Problems"
- ***Do*** Short exercises appropriate to your grade level

The Number Line

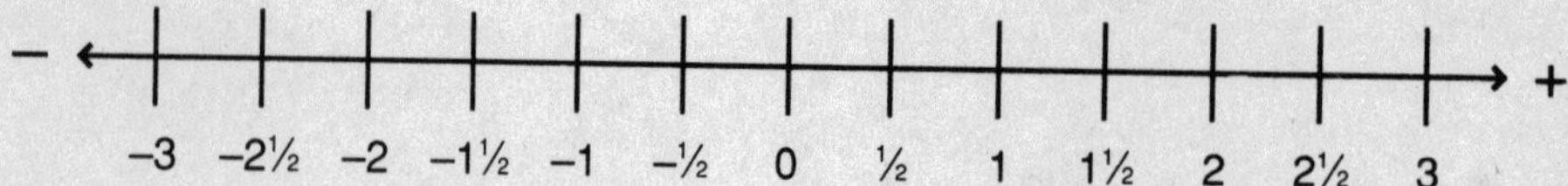

A number line is a convenient concept to use as a mental picture. The number line above shows whole numbers and fractions greater than zero and less than zero. Numbers increase in size as you move to the right and decrease in size as you move to the left. The number line above has an arrow at each end, meaning that the number line goes on infinitely in both positive and negative directions.

Number lines can be drawn to aid in basic mathematical calculations. Either fractions, whole numbers, or decimals can be used to name the intervals on the line. We suggest that you use number lines when dealing with signed (+, –) numbers and inequalities.

Addition

In the process of addition, we add together numbers, which we call *addends,* to result in a *sum.* Addends may be added in any order (commutative property).

EXAMPLE 1:

$$\underbrace{203 + 155 + 80}_{\text{addends}} = \underbrace{438}_{\text{sum}}$$

EXAMPLE 2:

$$\underbrace{17.4 + 6.2 + 2.2}_{\text{addends}} = \underbrace{25.8}_{\text{sum}}$$

EXAMPLE 3:

$$\underbrace{\frac{3}{4} + 1\frac{1}{2} + \frac{5}{8}}_{\text{addends}} = \underbrace{2\frac{7}{8}}_{\text{sum}}$$

EXAMPLE 4:

$$\underbrace{\frac{3}{5} + 1.25 + 2}_{\text{addends}} = 3.85 \text{ (decimal notation)}$$

$$3\frac{17}{20} \text{ (fractional notation)}$$

Simple addition problems may consist of only whole number addends (as in Example 1), of only decimal or fractional addends (as in Examples 2 and 3), or of a mixture of all three (as in Example 4).

Whole Number Addition

To add whole numbers as in Example 1, line up the addends in a column. Add each column of numbers carefully, making sure to carry tens to the next column:

$$\begin{array}{r} 203 \\ 155 \\ +\ 80 \\ \hline 438 \end{array}$$

Remember: Line the numbers up underneath each other carefully.

Try these problems. The answers are on page 285. Aim for 100% accuracy and note your errors.

EXERCISE 1

1. 463 + 729 + 36
2. 257 + 32
3. 174 + 20,962
4. 1,732 + 32,629
5. 33 + 472 + 8
6. 138 + 76 + 82 + 1,224
7. 59 + 732 + 111
8. 137,921 + 29 + 71
9. 393 + 462 + 1,701 + 733
10. 145 + 66 + 78

Decimal Addition

Decimals are a way of writing fractions using tenths, hundredths, thousandths, and so forth. If you can count money, make change, or understand a batting average, decimals should present no problem.

When writing decimals, the most important step is placing the decimal point. The whole system is based upon its location. Remember the decimal places?

EXAMPLE:

1, 2 3 6, 5 4 0 . 1 3 2 4 5 6

- 1 — MILLIONS
- 2 — HUNDRED THOUSANDS
- 3 — TEN THOUSANDS
- 6 — THOUSANDS
- 5 — HUNDREDS
- 4 — TENS
- 0 — ONES
- . — DECIMAL POINT
- 1 — TENTHS
- 3 — HUNDREDTHS
- 2 — THOUSANDTHS
- 4 — TEN THOUSANDTHS
- 5 — HUNDRED THOUSANDTHS
- 6 — MILLIONTHS

If you need practice reading decimals, try the exercises below. The answers are on page 285.

EXERCISE 2

1. .0076
2. 11.3
3. 1,402.639
4. $7,222.93
5. 0.50
6. 0.05
7. 16.2163
8. .00029
9. 3.0006
10. 62.391

If you did well on Exercise 2, try to determine which of these pairs of numbers is larger. The answers are on page 285.

EXERCISE 3

1. .5 or .05
2. 5.12 or 5.012
3. 0.007 or 0.07
4. 16.20 or 16.2
5. 10.7 or 1.70
6. 0.762 or 7.62
7. 3.009 or 3.0009
8. .143 or .1430

Adding decimals is no harder than adding whole numbers, as long as you pay attention to the decimal point. To add a group of decimals, place them in a column, *being certain* to line up the decimal points.

EXAMPLE: 17.4 + 6.2 + 2.2 = 25.8

SOLUTION:

$$\begin{array}{r} 17.4 \\ 6.2 \\ +\ 2.2 \\ \hline 25.8 \end{array}$$

Notice that the decimal point is brought straight down! Now, try the next example for practice. Where decimal places may be "missing," fill in with zeros if you need to.

EXAMPLE: Add 22.0061 + 7.003 + 2.1 + .001 + 100.01

SOLUTION:

$$\begin{array}{r} 22.0061 \\ \underline{0}7.003\underline{0} \\ \underline{0}2.1\underline{000} \\ \underline{00}.001\underline{0} \\ +\ 100.01\underline{00} \\ \hline 131.1201 \end{array}$$

The underlined numbers show where you may fill in with zeros if you want. Try these problems. The answers are on page 285.

EXERCISE 4

1. 7.223 + 60.1
2. .0792 + 5.06
3. 100.23 + 9.7962
4. 82.48 + 21.2417
5. .0323 + .06
6. 9623.2 + 43.788
7. 14.1414 + .044
8. .02 + 3.63 + 92.003
9. 720.72 + 69.58
10. 4.7 + 3.2 + .9 + 1.2

Fractions

Fractions are used when we want to indicate parts of things. A fraction consists of a numerator and a denominator.

$$\begin{array}{ccc} 3 & \leftarrow \text{ numerator } \rightarrow & 7 \\ \hline 4 & \leftarrow \text{denominator} \rightarrow & 8 \end{array}$$

The denominator tells you how many equal parts the object or number has been divided into, and the numerator tells how many of those parts we are concerned with.

EXAMPLES: Divide a baseball game, a football game, and a hockey game into convenient numbers of parts. Write a fraction to answer each question.

1. If a pitcher played two innings, how much of the whole baseball game did (s)he play?
2. If a quarterback played three parts of a football game, how much of the whole game did (s)he play?
3. If a goalie played two parts of a hockey game, how much of the whole game did (s)he play?

SOLUTIONS: 1. A baseball game is conveniently divided into nine parts (each an inning). The pitcher pitched two innings. Therefore, (s)he played $\frac{2}{9}$ of the game. The denominator represents the nine parts the game is divided into; the numerator, the two parts we are concerned with.

2. Similarly, there are four quarters in a football game, and a quarterback playing three of those quarters plays in $\frac{3}{4}$ of the game.

3. There are three periods in hockey, and the goalie played in two of them. Therefore, (s)he played in $\frac{2}{3}$ of the game.

Lowest Terms and Equivalence

Fractions having different denominators and numerators may actually represent the same amount. Such fractions are equivalent fractions.

For example, the circle below is divided into two equal parts. Write a fraction to indicate that half of the circle is shaded.

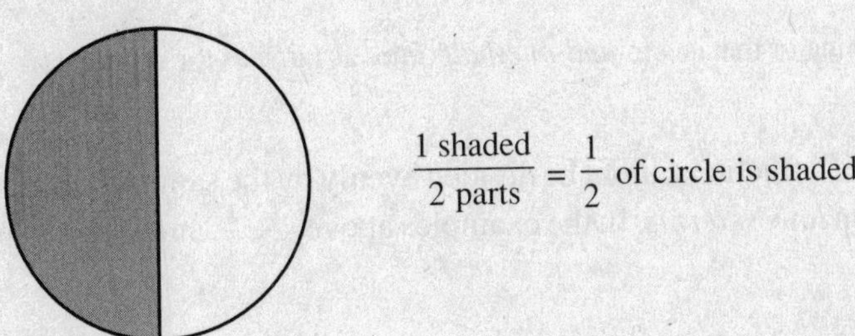

$$\frac{\text{1 shaded}}{\text{2 parts}} = \frac{1}{2} \text{ of circle is shaded}$$

The circle below is divided into four equal parts. Write a fraction to indicate how much of the circle is shaded.

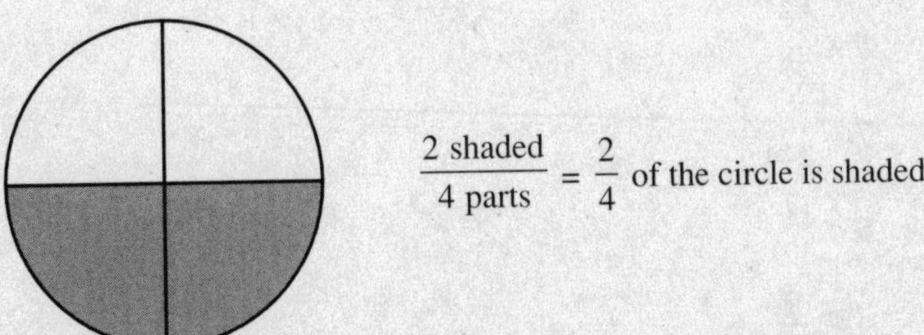

$$\frac{\text{2 shaded}}{\text{4 parts}} = \frac{2}{4} \text{ of the circle is shaded}$$

This circle is divided into eight equal parts. Write a fraction to indicate how much of the circle is shaded.

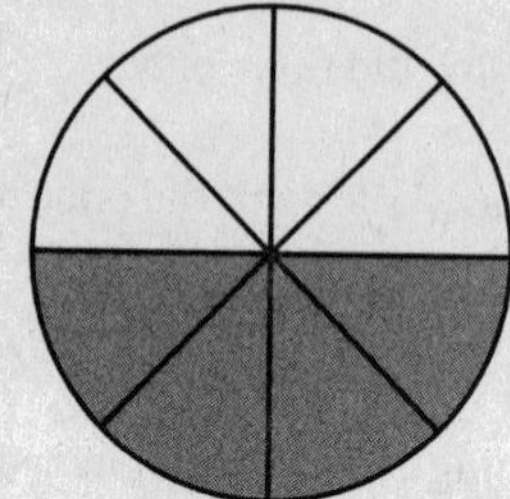

$\frac{\text{4 shaded}}{\text{8 parts}} = \frac{4}{8}$ of the circle is shaded

In each circle the same amount was shaded. This shows you that there is more than one way to indicate one half of something.

The fractions $\frac{1}{2}$, $\frac{2}{4}$, and $\frac{4}{8}$ that you wrote are *equivalent fractions* because they all represent the same amount. Notice that the denominator is twice as large as the numerator in *every* case. Any fraction you write that has a denominator that is exactly twice as large as the numerator will be equivalent to $\frac{1}{2}$.

EXAMPLE 1: Write other fractions equivalent to $\frac{1}{2}$.

EXAMPLE 2: Write other fractions equivalent to $\frac{1}{4}$.

EXAMPLE 3: Write other fractions equivalent to $\frac{2}{3}$.

SOLUTION 1: Any fraction that has a denominator that is *twice* as large as the numerator: $\frac{3}{6}$, $\frac{5}{10}$, $\frac{6}{12}$, $\frac{32}{64}$, etc.

SOLUTION 2: Any fraction that has a denominator that is *four* times as large as the numerator: $\frac{2}{8}$, $\frac{4}{16}$, $\frac{5}{20}$, $\frac{15}{60}$, etc.

SOLUTION 3: Any fraction that has a denominator that is *one-and-one-half* times as large as the numerator: $\frac{4}{6}$, $\frac{10}{15}$, $\frac{14}{21}$, $\frac{16}{24}$, etc.

When the numerator and denominator of a fraction cannot be divided evenly by the same whole number (other than 1), the fraction is said to be in *lowest terms*. In the examples above, $\frac{1}{2}$, $\frac{1}{4}$, and $\frac{2}{3}$ are in lowest terms.

Indicate which of the following fractions are in lowest terms. For those fractions that are not, try to reduce them. The answers are on page 285.

EXERCISE 5

1. $\frac{13}{42}$
2. $\frac{12}{18}$
3. $\frac{8}{48}$
4. $\frac{21}{26}$
5. $\frac{6}{9}$
6. $\frac{42}{48}$
7. $\frac{9}{24}$
8. $\frac{17}{32}$
9. $\frac{9}{108}$
10. $\frac{4}{24}$

To write equivalent fractions where the numerator is not 1 requires one more step.

EXAMPLE: What is the equivalent fraction for $\frac{4}{5}$ using 10 as a denominator?

SOLUTION: Each $\frac{1}{5}$ is equivalent to $\frac{2}{10}$; therefore, $\frac{4}{5}$ is equivalent to $\frac{8}{10}$.

The quickest way to find an equivalent fraction is to divide the denominator of the fraction you know *into* the denominator you want. Take the result and multiply it by the numerator of the fraction you know. This becomes the numerator of the equivalent fraction.

EXAMPLE: Change $\frac{3}{8}$ to an equivalent fraction having 16 as a denominator.

SOLUTION: $16 \div 8 = 2$. $2 \times 3 = 6$. Answer: $\frac{6}{16}$

EXAMPLE: Change $\frac{3}{4}$ into equivalent fractions having 8, 12, 24, and 32 as denominators.

SOLUTION: $\frac{3}{4} = \frac{6}{8}$ $(8 \div 4 = 2;\ 2 \times 3 = 6)$

$\frac{3}{4} = \frac{9}{12}$ $(12 \div 4 = 3;\ 3 \times 3 = 9)$

$\frac{3}{4} = \frac{18}{24}$ $(24 \div 4 = 6;\ 6 \times 3 = 18)$

$\frac{3}{4} = \frac{24}{32}$ $(32 \div 4 = 8;\ 8 \times 3 = 24)$

Try the problems below. The answers are on page 285.

EXERCISE 6

1. $\frac{5}{8} = \frac{?}{32}, \frac{?}{40}, \frac{?}{16}$
2. $\frac{7}{9} = \frac{?}{36}, \frac{?}{81}$
3. $\frac{4}{5} = \frac{?}{15}, \frac{?}{20}, \frac{?}{45}$
4. $\frac{2}{3} = \frac{?}{6}, \frac{?}{27}, \frac{?}{33}$
5. $\frac{1}{14} = \frac{?}{28}, \frac{?}{42}, \frac{?}{84}$
6. $\frac{5}{6} = \frac{?}{18}, \frac{?}{24}, \frac{?}{36}$
7. $\frac{1}{2} = \frac{?}{52}, \frac{?}{76}$
8. $\frac{4}{7} = \frac{?}{21}, \frac{?}{35}, \frac{?}{49}$
9. $\frac{3}{11} = \frac{?}{22}, \frac{?}{88}$
10. $\frac{2}{13} = \frac{?}{26}, \frac{?}{52}$

A fraction that has a numerator larger than the denominator is called an *improper fraction.* A number expressed as an integer together with a proper fraction is called a *mixed number*.

Examples of improper fractions include $\frac{3}{2}$, $\frac{12}{7}$, and $\frac{9}{5}$. Note that each is in lowest terms because the numerator and denominator cannot be divided evenly by a number other than 1.

Examples of mixed numbers include $1\frac{1}{2}$, $1\frac{5}{7}$, and $1\frac{4}{5}$. These are called mixed numbers because they have a whole number part and a fractional part. These mixed numbers are equivalent to the improper fractions given above.

To change a mixed number to an improper fraction is easy.

EXAMPLE: Change $2\frac{1}{4}$ to an improper fraction.

SOLUTION: The whole number 2 contains 8 fourths. Add to it the $\frac{1}{4}$ to create the equivalent fraction $\frac{9}{4}$.

An alternative way of figuring this is to multiply the denominator of the fraction by the whole number and add the numerator.

EXAMPLE: Change $2\frac{1}{4}$ to an improper fraction.

SOLUTION: $4 \times 2 = \frac{8}{4} + \frac{1}{4} = \frac{9}{4}$

To change an improper fraction to a mixed number, just proceed backwards.

EXAMPLE: Change $\frac{9}{4}$ to a mixed number.

SOLUTION: Divide the denominator into the numerator and use the remainder as the fraction:

$$9 \div 4 = 2 \quad \text{R1} = 2\frac{1}{4}$$

Try these, changing each to its equivalent form. The answers are on page 286.

EXERCISE 7

1. $3\frac{7}{8}$

2. $2\frac{9}{10}$

3. $11\frac{14}{15}$

4. $7\frac{2}{3}$

5. $1\frac{3}{4}$

6. $\frac{22}{7}$

7. $\frac{16}{3}$

8. $\frac{45}{8}$

9. $\frac{9}{2}$

10. $\frac{61}{12}$

Addition of Fractions

To add fractions you must first be sure that the addends have the same denominators.

EXAMPLE: Add: $\frac{1}{4} + \frac{3}{4} + \frac{3}{4}$

SOLUTION: The denominators are the same, so just add the numerators to arrive at the answer, $\frac{7}{4}$, or $1\frac{3}{4}$.

In most cases, denominators will be different and so you will have to find a *least common denominator*.

EXAMPLE: Add: $\frac{1}{4} + \frac{1}{2}$

SOLUTION: $\frac{1}{2}$ is equivalent to $\frac{2}{4}$, so $\frac{1}{4} + \frac{2}{4} = \frac{3}{4}$.

EXAMPLE: Add: $\frac{1}{4} + \frac{1}{3}$

SOLUTION: This problem is trickier. It requires the writing of *equivalent fractions* in a *common denominator* to which 4 and 3 can easily be connected.

$$\frac{1}{4} \text{ is equivalent to } \frac{3}{12}.$$

$$\frac{1}{3} \text{ is equivalent to } \frac{4}{12}.$$

We can now add the fractions because we have written equivalent fractions in a common denominator.

$$\frac{3}{12} + \frac{4}{12} = \frac{7}{12}$$

Therefore, $\frac{1}{4} + \frac{1}{3} = \frac{7}{12}$.

Seven-twelfths is in lowest terms, because 7 and 12 do not have a whole number (other than 1) that goes into both evenly.

How To Find a Common Denominator

You can *always* find a common denominator by multiplying the denominators together.

EXAMPLE: Find a common denominator for $\frac{3}{4}$ and $\frac{3}{8}$.

SOLUTION: Multiply 4×8: 32 is a common denominator. However, 16 and 24 are also common denominators for 4 and 8.

Don't worry about finding the *lowest* common denominator when you are adding fractions. When you see the sum, you will probably notice that the fraction can be reduced to lower terms. When you have reduced the fraction as far as you can, you have probably found the lowest common denominator.

Try the following problems. Find a common denominator, then reduce the answer to its lowest terms. The answers are on page 286.

EXERCISE 8

1. $\frac{3}{4} + \frac{9}{10} + \frac{1}{5}$
2. $\frac{3}{8} + \frac{1}{4}$
3. $5\frac{5}{7} + \frac{1}{3}$
4. $\frac{1}{9} + \frac{3}{4} + \frac{5}{6}$
5. $\frac{7}{9} + \frac{5}{8} + 1\frac{1}{12}$
6. $\frac{2}{3} + \frac{9}{13}$
7. $\frac{6}{7} + \frac{6}{9}$
8. $\frac{1}{2} + \frac{3}{4} + \frac{5}{8}$
9. $2\frac{2}{3} + 4\frac{5}{6}$
10. $\frac{3}{11} + \frac{2}{13}$

Subtraction

To subtract one number from another means to find the *difference* between them on the number line. The number being subtracted is called the *subtrahend;* the number being subtracted from is the *minuend.*

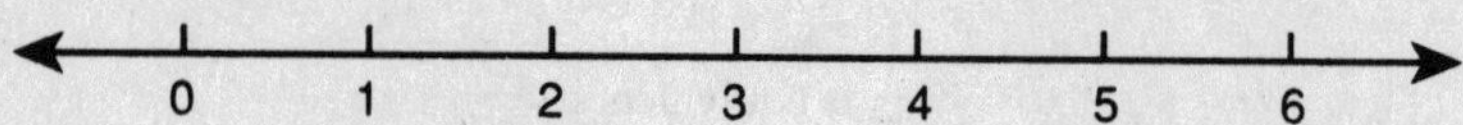

A number line such as the one above lets you *see* the difference between numbers before subtracting. For example, the difference between six and two is four units; therefore, 6 – 2 = 4. Or, the difference between six and zero is six units; therefore, 6 – 0 = 6. If you remember that when subtracting numbers you are interested in the *difference* between them on the number line, you will understand subtraction easily.

Subtraction *cannot* occur in *any* order, as can addition. For example, 6 – 3 is not the same as 3 – 6, nor is 100 – 1 the same as 1 – 100.

Subtracting Whole Numbers

To find the difference between a pair of whole numbers, write the smaller beneath the larger. Borrow a group from the next larger column when you are subtracting a larger numeral from a smaller one.

EXAMPLE: Find the difference between 6937 and 4178.

SOLUTION:

$$\begin{array}{r} 6937 \\ -\ 4178 \\ \hline 2759 \end{array}$$

Step 1. Begin by borrowing a group (leaving 2) to make 17. Eight from 17 is 9.

Step 2. Next, borrow a group from the 9 (leaving 8) to make 12. Seven from 12 is 5.

Step 3. Subtract 1 from 8, giving 7.

Step 4. Subtract 4 from 6, giving 2.

The correct difference, 2,759, can be checked by adding it to the number you first subtracted, 4,178. You should end with 6,937 again.

Practice subtraction with the problems below. The answers are on page 286.

EXERCISE 9

1. 703 – 98

2. 1,762 – 983

3. 429 – 108

4. 63,921 – 4,930

5. 278 – 88

6. 9,000 – 699

7. 13,706 – 4,838

8. 863 – 92

9. 7,333 – 6,444

10. 290,723 – 176,731

Subtracting Decimals

If necessary, review the basics of decimal notation that you studied earlier under decimal addition. Most of the same guidelines apply to the subtraction of decimals.

When finding the difference between two numbers written in decimal notation, be sure to arrange the smaller beneath the larger, keeping the decimal points in line. Then proceed just as if you were subtracting whole numbers.

As with addition, you may want to write in zeros to "fill in" those decimal places having no numerals in them.

EXAMPLE: Subtract 22.02 from 23.001.

SOLUTION:

$$\begin{array}{r} 23.001 \\ -\ 22.020 \\ \hline 00.981 \end{array}$$

Remember that the decimal point in the answer is placed directly below the decimal points of the subtrahend and minuend.

Try the following problems as practice. The answers are on page 286.

EXERCISE 10

1. 16.17 – .9902
2. .83 – .0624
3. .918 – .759
4. .360 – .204
5. 6.57 – 2.43
6. 28.47 – 3.622
7. 809.03 – 24.9
8. 37.94 – .4223
9. 38.83 – 9.003
10. 67.2115 – 3.79

Subtracting Fractions

To find the difference between two fractions having the same denominators, simply subtract the numerators, leaving the denominators alone.

EXAMPLE: Find the difference between $\frac{7}{8}$ and $\frac{3}{8}$.

SOLUTION: $\frac{7}{8} - \frac{3}{8} = \frac{4}{8}$. Reduced to lowest terms: $\frac{4}{8} = \frac{1}{2}$.

When subtracting mixed numbers having the same denominators, one more step is required.

EXAMPLE: Subtract $2\frac{3}{4}$ from $9\frac{1}{4}$.

SOLUTION: *Step 1.* Change the mixed numbers to improper form.

$$2\frac{3}{4} = \frac{11}{4} \quad (4 \times 2 + 3 = 11)$$

$$9\frac{1}{4} = \frac{37}{4} \quad (4 \times 9 + 1 = 37)$$

Step 2. Subtract the numerators, leaving the denominators alone.

$$\frac{37}{4} - \frac{11}{4} = \frac{26}{4} \quad \text{Reduced to lowest terms} = \frac{13}{2}$$

$$\text{Returned to mixed form} = 6\frac{1}{2}$$

Before trying to subtract mixed numbers having different denominators, review the procedure for writing equivalent fractions as it was explained earlier in the book. Finding the difference between two mixed numbers is easy after you find common denominators and equivalent fractions.

EXAMPLE: Subtract $3\frac{3}{4}$ from $6\frac{3}{8}$.

SOLUTION: *Step 1.* Change each mixed number to its improper form.

$$3\frac{3}{4} = \frac{15}{4} \quad (4 \times 3 + 3 = 15)$$

$$6\frac{3}{8} = \frac{51}{8} \quad (8 \times 6 + 3 = 51)$$

Step 2. Find a common denominator. For fourths and eighths, eighths are a good choice.

Step 3. Write the equivalent fractions.

$$\frac{15}{4} = \frac{30}{8} \quad (8 \div 4 = 2; 2 \times 15 = 30)$$

$$\frac{51}{8} = \frac{51}{8}$$

Step 4. $\frac{51}{8} - \frac{30}{8} = \frac{21}{8}$, or $2\frac{5}{8}$

Practice the following problems. The answers are on page 286.

EXERCISE 11

1. $\frac{15}{16} - \frac{2}{8}$
2. $\frac{7}{9} - \frac{2}{3}$
3. $1\frac{7}{10} - \frac{9}{16}$
4. $9\frac{5}{8} - \frac{6}{32}$
5. $3\frac{7}{12} - 1\frac{2}{3}$
6. $\frac{4}{7} - \frac{1}{4}$
7. $7\frac{9}{10} - \frac{19}{20}$
8. $\frac{3}{4} - \frac{2}{3}$
9. $2\frac{2}{3} - \frac{4}{5}$
10. $4\frac{2}{3} - \frac{3}{4}$

Multiplication

Multiplication is a shortcut for addition. For example, rather than add a number 12 times, we simply multiply it by 12. The result of multiplying two numbers is called the *product*. The numbers that are multiplied are called *factors*.

Most errors in multiplication result from not having memorized the multiplication tables. One of the best ways to improve your mathematics ability is to practice reciting the multiplication tables until you know them thoroughly. You can find these tables in any arithmetic textbook.

Multiplication of Whole Numbers

The following examples show the procedures used in multiplying whole numbers. Note the care with which the partial products are written in columns before being added. You should aim to be just as careful.

EXAMPLE: Multiply 435 by 253.

SOLUTION:

```
              435
           ×  253
             1305  ←
            2175   ←   Each line is a partial product.
            870
product → 110,055
```

Practice your multiplication using the following examples, and time yourself. The answers are on page 287. Then make up ten similar problems and try again, emphasizing speed and accuracy.

EXERCISE 12

1. 726 × 29
2. 33 × 14
3. 1,064 × 397
4. 512 × 136
5. 3112 × 223
6. 11,550 × 32
7. 4,619 × 550
8. 217 × 118
9. 1,214 × 104
10. 64,397 × 1,472

Multiplication of Decimals

Multiplication of decimals is no harder than multiplication of whole numbers. However, you must remember one more step: to count off the correct number of decimal places in the product.

The rule for counting off the correct number of decimal places is: *The number of decimal places in the product is equal to the total number of decimal places in both factors.*

The following three problems should make this rule clear.

EXAMPLE:

```
  3.11  ← 2 decimal places
×    2  ← 0 decimal places
  6.22  ← 2 decimal places
```

EXAMPLE:

$$\begin{array}{rl} 3.11 & \leftarrow \text{2 decimal places} \\ \times\ .2 & \leftarrow \text{1 decimal place} \\ \hline .622 & \leftarrow \text{3 decimal places} \end{array}$$

EXAMPLE:

$$\begin{array}{rl} .311 & \leftarrow \text{3 decimal places} \\ \times\ .2 & \leftarrow \text{1 decimal place} \\ \hline .0622 & \leftarrow \text{4 decimal places (A zero was added to make a fourth place.)} \end{array}$$

When multiplying larger decimals, line up the partial products carefully, count up the total number of decimal places in the factors, and place the decimal point in the product the same number of places from the last numeral.

EXAMPLE:

$$\begin{array}{rl} 2.301 & \leftarrow \text{3 decimal places} \\ \times\ 18.73 & \leftarrow \text{2 decimal places} \\ \hline 6903 & \\ 16107 & \\ 18408 & \\ 2301 & \\ \hline 43.09773 & \leftarrow \text{5 decimal places from right} \end{array}$$

Practice the following. The answers are on page 287.

EXERCISE 13

1. 7,209 × .3741
2. 103.2 × 97.1
3. 638.63 × 83.6
4. 29.10 × .04
5. 7.720 × .34
6. 8143.6 × 20.13
7. .0034 × .276
8. 93.2 × 1.26
9. 103.621 × .43
10. 72.7 × 63.8

Multiplication of Fractions

The multiplication of fractions is simple and straightforward. It consists of two steps:

- multiplying the numerator by the numerator and the denominator by the denominator
- reducing the product (answer) to the lowest terms

EXAMPLE: Multiply $\frac{3}{8}$ by $\frac{2}{3}$.

SOLUTION: We multiply straight across.

Step 1. $\frac{3}{8} \bullet \frac{2}{3} = \frac{6}{24}$

Step 2. Reduce $\frac{6}{24}$ to lowest terms.

$$\frac{6}{24} = \frac{1}{4}$$

There is no need to find common denominators when multiplying (or dividing) fractions. Simply remember to multiply straight across and reduce the product if necessary.

In some problems, one factor may be a mixed number and the other an improper fraction. In that case, proceed as follows:

EXAMPLE: Multiply $\frac{7}{8}$ by $2\frac{1}{2}$.

SOLUTION: Write the fractions as before, changing $2\frac{1}{2}$ to an improper fraction. Multiply straight across.

Step 1. $\frac{7}{8} \bullet \frac{5}{2} = \frac{35}{16}$

Step 2. Because the product is in lowest terms, leave it that way or rewrite it as the mixed number $2\frac{3}{16}$.

Practice on the following problems. The answers are on page 287.

EXERCISE 14

1. $\frac{3}{8} \bullet 3\frac{1}{6}$
2. $\frac{4}{7} \bullet \frac{9}{10}$
3. $\frac{2}{5} \bullet 60$
4. $1\frac{2}{11} \bullet 16\frac{1}{2}$
5. $2\frac{2}{3} \bullet \frac{9}{11}$
6. $100 \bullet \frac{3}{5}$
7. $\frac{6}{25} \bullet \frac{8}{45}$
8. $7\frac{7}{8} \bullet 6\frac{5}{9}$
9. $\frac{3}{4} \bullet \frac{1}{2} \bullet \frac{2}{3}$
10. $1\frac{1}{5} \bullet 5 \bullet \frac{3}{8}$

Squares and Square Roots

Squares

The product of a number times itself is called the *square* of that number. For example, 9 is the square of 3; 16 is the square of 4; and 25 is the square of 5. Any number we work with has a square; we simply multiply the number by itself to find it.

EXAMPLES: Find the squares of the following numbers:

(A) 15 (B) 3.22 (C) $\frac{3}{4}$ (D) .01 (E) 125 (F) $\frac{7}{6}$

SOLUTIONS:

(A) $15 \times 15 = 225$

(B) $3.22 \times 3.22 = 10.3684$

(C) $\frac{3}{4} \times \frac{3}{4} = \frac{9}{16}$

(D) $.01 \times .01 = .0001$

(E) $125 \times 125 = 15{,}625$

(F) $\frac{7}{6} \times \frac{7}{6} = \frac{49}{36}$ Or $1\frac{13}{36}$

The word *square* is also used as a verb to describe the process used to find the product of a number times itself. To *square a number* means to multiply it by itself. Special notation is used when working with squares. Rather than write $15 \times 15 = 225$, we use an exponent, $15^2 = 225$.

There is further discussion and practice in using exponents in the section "Exponents" on page 251.

You will find that test makers and mathematics textbook writers rely on easily recognized squares in many problems. For this reason, we think it is very important that you learn to recognize certain common numbers as squares of other numbers.

The table on pages 239 and 240 lists numbers and their squares. Note that once you learn the link between a number and its square, you can apply that knowledge regardless of where the decimal point is located. For example, if you know that $15^2 = 225$, you also know that $1.5^2 = 2.25$, and $.15^2 = .0225$, and $150^2 = 22{,}500$.

Study the table carefully. It is a good idea to memorize the squares of the numbers 1 through 25, 30, 40, 50, 60, 70, 80, 90, and 100, although you should not spend a great deal of time on it. The important thing is to understand the relationships in the table and to link in your mind a whole number with its square.

Square Roots

Every number that is a square has a *square root.* In the table on pages 239 and 240, for example, you can see that the number multiplied by itself to find the square is the *square root* of the square.

For example, 15 is the square root of 225, 1.5 is the square root of 2.25, and .15 is the square root of .0225.

Try these, using the table of squares. The answers are on page 287.

EXERCISE 15

Find the square root of:

1. 32,400

2. 1.96

3. 225

4. 441

5. 5.29

6. 625

7. 6.25

8. 900

A special notation called a *radical* ($\sqrt{\ }$) is used when working with square roots. For example, $\sqrt{9} = 3$ is read: "The square root of nine equals three." The radical over the number nine is read "square root of."

If you are asked to find the square root of a fraction, simply consider the numerator and denominator as separate numbers, and find the square root of each.

EXAMPLE: Find: $\sqrt{\dfrac{9}{16}}$

SOLUTION: $\dfrac{\sqrt{9}}{\sqrt{16}} = \dfrac{3}{4}$. The square root of $\dfrac{9}{16}$ is $\dfrac{3}{4}$.

Check: $\left(\dfrac{3}{4}\right)^2 = \dfrac{3}{4} \bullet \dfrac{3}{4} = \dfrac{9}{16}$

No doubt you have learned ways of finding square roots of numbers that don't fit so neatly into a table such as the one below. However, because such problems occur so rarely on high school entrance examinations, we will not review those methods in this book. In most cases, you will be able to estimate the square root of a number accurately enough to select the correct answer. That is why we suggest you study the table closely and learn to recognize those numbers and their squares and square roots.

Try the following problems without using the table. The answers are on page 287.

EXERCISE 16

1. $14^2 =$
2. $\sqrt{169} =$
3. $\sqrt{\frac{121}{81}} =$
4. $\sqrt{5.76} =$
5. $100^2 =$
6. $25^2 =$
7. $20^2 =$
8. $\sqrt{\frac{1}{4}} =$
9. $\sqrt{144} =$
10. $2.5^2 =$

You will find further work with exponents and other roots in the section entitled "Exponents."

Related Numbers and Their Squares

WHOLE NUMBER	SQUARE		
1	1	$.1^2 = .01$	$10^2 = 100$
2	4	$.2^2 = .04$	$20^2 = 400$
3	9	$.3^2 = .09$	$30^2 = 900$
4	16	$.4^2 = .16$	$40^2 = 1600$
5	25	$.5^2 = .25$	$50^2 = 2500$
6	36	$.6^2 = .36$	$60^2 = 3600$
7	49	$.7^2 = .49$	$70^2 = 4900$
8	64	$.8^2 = .64$	$80^2 = 6400$
9	81	$.9^2 = .81$	$90^2 = 8100$
10	100	$1.0^2 = 1$	$100^2 = 10{,}000$
11	121	$1.1^2 = 1.21$	$110^2 = 12{,}100$
12	144	$1.2^2 = 1.44$	$120^2 = 14{,}400$
13	169	$1.3^2 = 1.69$	$130^2 = 16{,}900$
14	196	$1.4^2 = 1.96$	$140^2 = 19{,}600$
15	225	$1.5^2 = 2.25$	$150^2 = 22{,}500$

WHOLE NUMBER	SQUARE		
16	256	$1.6^2 = 2.56$	$160^2 = 25{,}600$
17	289	$1.7^2 = 2.89$	$170^2 = 28{,}900$
18	324	$1.8^2 = 3.24$	$180^2 = 32{,}400$
19	361	$1.9^2 = 3.61$	$190^2 = 36{,}100$
20	400	$2.0^2 = 4$	$200^2 = 40{,}000$
21	441	$2.1^2 = 4.41$	$210^2 = 44{,}100$
22	484	$2.2^2 = 4.84$	$220^2 = 48{,}400$
23	529	$2.3^2 = 5.29$	$230^2 = 52{,}900$
24	576	$2.4^2 = 5.76$	$240^2 = 57{,}600$
25	625	$2.5^2 = 6.25$	$250^2 = 62{,}500$

You can refer to the table to find the square roots of some commonly used numbers.

Division

The process of division is used to determine the number of parts into which another number can be divided. A division problem is made up of the number that is being divided, called the *dividend;* the number that is doing the dividing, called the *divisor;* and the answer, called the *quotient*.

Division of Whole Numbers

The following examples show how long division is used when one whole number is divided into another. Note in two cases that the remainder is expressed as the numerator of a fraction having the divisor as the denominator. An alternative way to express the remainder is by continuing the long division and creating a quotient having a decimal remainder instead.

Study these examples carefully. Note that the decimal point in the quotient is located directly above the decimal point in the dividend. Note also that the first numeral of the quotient is placed very carefully in the correct decimal place.

EXAMPLE:

```
    15 5/8
8)125
  8
  45
  40
   5
```

or

```
            15.625  ←quotient
divisor → 8)125.000 ←dividend
            8
            45
            40
             50
             48
              20
              16
               40
               40
                0
```

EXAMPLE:

```
      20.571
35)720.000
   70
    200
    175
     250
     245
      50
      35
      15
     STOP
```

or

```
  20 20/35 = 20 4/7
35)720
   70
    20
```

EXAMPLE:

```
122)98
     98
  = ---
    122
     49
  = ---
     61
```

or

```
      .8032
122)98.0000
    976
      400
      366
       340
       244
        96
      STOP
```

When using decimal quotients and remainders, it is usually allowable to stop after three or four decimal places have been calculated. Note that you *can* continue to divide—in some cases, forever. Your goal should be to divide only as far as is necessary for you to come up with an answer that corresponds to the answer choices given in a particular question.

Try the following problems for practice. The answers are on page 287.

EXERCISE 17

1. 3867 ÷ 47

2. 935 ÷ 22

3. 103 ÷ 272

4. 5760 ÷ 139

5. 5015 ÷ 462

6. 4211 ÷ 104

7. 76 ÷ 93

8. 2200 ÷ 1113

9. 678 ÷ 803

10. 1930 ÷ 48

Division of Decimals

When the divisor is not a whole number but has tenths, hundredths, thousandths, and so forth as part of it, one additional step is required to solve the problem. For example:

$$12.5\overline{)250}$$

Here, we move the decimal point in the divisor as many places to the right as necessary to make the divisor a whole number. Then we add that same number of places to the dividend. In the example above:

$$12.5\overline{)2500.}$$

Now, the problem becomes one of simple whole number long division.

```
        20.
125 )2500.
      250
      ---
       00
```

Thus, 250 ÷ 12.5 = 20.

EXAMPLE: Divide .666 into .333.

SOLUTION: $.666\overline{).333}$ Move the decimal point, and add zeros.

```
       .50
666 )333.00
     333 0
     -----
         0
```

The answer is .5

or $666\overline{)333}$

$$= \frac{333}{666} = \frac{1}{2}$$

In those cases in which the divisor is not a whole number, be sure to move the decimal point the correct number of places in the divisor and dividend. Then, place the decimal point in the quotient directly above its new place.

Try the problems below for practice. The answers are on page 288.

EXERCISE 18

1. .396 ÷ 1.3

2. 493.2 ÷ 85.63

3. 1034.62 ÷ 7.88

4. 972.1 ÷ .0543

5. 42.678 ÷ 501.3

6. 45.776 ÷ 62.11

7. 9.1494 ÷ 933.06

8. 203.4 ÷ 38.32

9. 280.420 ÷ 1.980

10. .092 ÷ 47.4284

Division of Fractions

If you multiply fractions accurately, you can divide them just as easily. For example, to divide $\frac{3}{4}$ by $\frac{5}{8}$, invert the divisor and multiply. The problem $\frac{3}{4} \div \frac{5}{8}$ thus becomes $\frac{3}{4} \times \frac{8}{5}$.

Simply multiply straight across, and reduce the resulting fraction:

$$\frac{3}{4} \times \frac{8}{5} = \frac{24}{20} = \frac{6}{5} \text{ or } 1\frac{1}{5}$$

This procedure works whether both numbers are fractions or not. If a whole number is inverted, you should change it to a fraction first. For example, $\frac{3}{16} \div 2$ becomes $\frac{3}{16} \div \frac{2}{1}$. To divide, invert the divisor and multiply:

$$\frac{3}{16} \times \frac{1}{2} = \frac{3}{32}$$

Another example is $3\frac{1}{2} \div \frac{3}{8}$, which becomes $\frac{7}{2} \div \frac{3}{8}$. To divide, invert the divisor and multiply:

$$\frac{7}{2} \times \frac{8}{3} = \frac{56}{6} = 9\frac{2}{6} = 9\frac{1}{3}$$

When dividing fractions, estimating the quotient can be an important help. Try the following problems to practice dividing fractions. The answers are on page 288.

EXERCISE 19

1. $\frac{7}{8} \div \frac{2}{3} =$
2. $4\frac{3}{4} \div 2\frac{1}{2} =$
3. $\frac{6}{16} \div \frac{9}{13} =$
4. $\frac{9}{14} \div 9\frac{4}{8} =$
5. $\frac{3}{5} \div 6\frac{3}{8} =$
6. $20\frac{1}{3} \div \frac{1}{51} =$
7. $\frac{4}{5} \div 6 =$
8. $\frac{4}{21} \div \frac{3}{4} =$
9. $\frac{3}{8} \div 2 =$
10. $\frac{4}{15} \div \frac{2}{5} =$

Operations Using Fractions and Decimals

It is not uncommon to have fractions and decimals appear in the same problem. However, because they are different forms of notation, one must be changed to the other before you can perform any of the basic operations with them. *You may not add, subtract, multiply, or divide using both kinds of notation at once.*

For example, to add $3\frac{1}{2}$ and 1.35, you must convert either $3\frac{1}{2}$ to decimal notation or 1.35 to fractional notation. The examples below will show you both ways.

To change a fraction into its equivalent decimal, simply divide the denominator into the numerator.

EXAMPLE: Find the decimal equivalent of $\frac{3}{8}$.

SOLUTION:
$$\begin{array}{r} .375 \\ 8\overline{)3.000} \\ \underline{24} \\ 60 \\ \underline{56} \\ 40 \\ \underline{40} \\ 0 \end{array} \qquad \frac{3}{8} = .375$$

This process will always work, regardless of the fraction. It will be useful to memorize the decimal-fractional equivalents on page 249. Remember, though, that you can always find a decimal equivalent of a fraction by dividing its denominator into its numerator.

To change a decimal into a fraction requires a similar method. Simply write the decimal as a fraction, and reduce it as necessary.

EXAMPLE: Change .125 to a fraction.

SOLUTION: .125 is read "one hundred twenty-five thousandths."

Write it as $\frac{125}{1000}$, and reduce it by dividing the numerator and denominator by 125.

$$\frac{125}{1000} = \frac{1}{8} \qquad .125 = \frac{1}{8}$$

Practice the problems below. Convert fractions to decimals and decimals to fractions. The answers are on page 288.

EXERCISE 20

1. $\frac{4}{5}$

2. .75

3. $\frac{7}{25}$

4. $\frac{1}{3}$

5. .435

6. .18

7. $\frac{3}{10}$

8. .45

9. .125

10. $\frac{13}{50}$

It may be a good idea to review the fractional and decimal equivalents on page 249.

Combining Operations

Frequently, more than one operation must be used to arrive at an answer to a problem. That is, a series of calculations may have to be strung together to produce the correct answer. Problems of this type are no more complicated than the ones you have done already, but require one additional piece of knowledge.

For example, how would you approach this problem?

$$2\frac{1}{2} + 10 \div 1\frac{1}{4} - 3.125 \times .80$$

Which operations would you do first? Fortunately, the answer is clear, if you observe the following rules:

1. Do multiplication and division first, in order, from left to right.
2. Do addition and subtraction second, in order, from left to right.

Therefore, the first step is to put parentheses around the multiplication and division operations.

$$2\frac{1}{2} + (10 \div 1\frac{1}{4}) - (3.125 \times .80)$$

Then, do the operations inside the parentheses, and simplify.

$$2\frac{1}{2} + 8 - 2.5 = 8$$

Another example is a problem that looks simple but may be confusing, unless you understand the order of operations described above.

$$2 \div 3 + 1 \div 2 + 2 \times 3 + 1$$

To solve this problem, put parentheses around the multiplication and division operations. Then, perform the operations inside the parentheses, and simplify.

$$(2 \div 3) + (1 \div 2) + (2 \times 3) + 1 =$$

$$\frac{2}{3} + \frac{1}{2} + 6 + 1 = 8\frac{1}{6}$$

Solve the following problems, interchanging fractional and decimal notation when necessary. It is up to you to decide, based upon whichever is easier, whether to change the decimals to fractions or to change the fractions to decimals. For example, when adding $5\frac{3}{4}$ and .6157, it is easier to change $5\frac{3}{4}$ to 5.750 and add it to .6157 rather than the other way around. You must make the same choice when multiplying or dividing fractions with decimals.

Now, go on to the problems that follow. The answers are on page 288.

EXERCISE 21

1. $7\frac{1}{100} \times .467$

2. $-2\frac{1}{4} + 3.27$

3. $13\frac{2}{5} - 5.2$

4. $6\frac{3}{4} \div .375$

5. $9\frac{1}{8} \div 2.76$

6. $2\frac{3}{8} \times 10.65$

7. $-1\frac{1}{5} + .05$

8. $1\frac{1}{2} - .789$

9. $4\frac{1}{7} \times .9$

10. $6\frac{3}{10} + 15.65$

PERCENTAGE

Before starting this section, it is a good idea to have studied all of the previous sections about decimals in this book. If you can work easily with decimals, percentages should present no difficulty for you.

One percent is one one-hundredth of something. The last syllable of the word percent, *-cent,* is the name we give to one one-hundredth of a dollar.

One percent of $1.00, then, is one cent. Using decimal notation, we can write one cent as $.01, five cents as $.05, twenty-five cents as $.25, and so forth.

Twenty-five cents represents twenty-five one-hundredths of a dollar. Rather than say that something is so many one-hundredths of something else, we use the word *percent*. Twenty-five cents, then, is twenty-five *percent* of a dollar. We use the symbol % to stand for *percent*.

Percentage ("hundredths of") is a convenient and widely used way of measuring all sorts of things. By measuring in hundredths, we can be very precise and notice very small changes.

For example, suppose Jane drove a car 100 miles on Monday, and 101 miles on Tuesday. Notice that she drove *one percent farther* on Tuesday than on Monday. For the days listed below, by how much percent more, or less, did she drive compared to Monday, if she drove the following distances? The answers are on page 288.

EXERCISE 22

1. Wednesday 110 miles
2. Thursday 140 miles
3. Friday 100 miles
4. Saturday 99 miles
5. Sunday 90 miles

By what percent is the second number of each pair listed below larger or smaller than the first number? The answers are on page 289.

EXERCISE 23

1. 100, 150
2. 100, 73
3. 100, 80
4. 100, 1
5. 100, .5
6. 100, 200
7. 100, 450
8. 100, .01

Percentage is not limited to comparing other numbers to 100. You can divide *any* number into hundredths and talk about percentage.

EXAMPLE: Find 1% of 200.

SOLUTION: 1% of 200 is one one-hundredth of 200.

$200 \div 100 = 2$

Using decimal notation we can calculate one percent of 200 by:

$$200 \times .01 = 2$$

Similarly, we can find a percentage of any number we choose by multiplying it by the correct decimal notation. For example:

Five percent of fifty:	$.05 \times 50 = 2.5$
Three percent of 150:	$.03 \times 150 = 4.5$
Ten percent of 60:	$.10 \times 60 = 6.0$

Do the following problems for practice. The answers are on page 289.

EXERCISE 24

1. ten percent of eight
2. twenty-five percent of sixty
3. eleven percent of ten
4. one percent of three hundred fifty
5. ninety-nine percent of eighty
6. thirty-three percent of thirty-three
7. seventy-five percent of one hundred twelve
8. fifty percent of two hundred

All percentage measurements are not between one percent and one-hundred percent. We may want to consider less than one percent of something, especially if it is very large.

For example, if you were handed a book one thousand pages long and were told to read one percent of it in five minutes, how much would you have to read?

$$1000 \times .01 = 10 \text{ pages}$$

Quite an assignment! You might bargain to read one half of one percent, or one tenth of one percent, in the five minutes allotted to you.

Using decimal notation, we write one tenth of one percent as .001, the decimal number for one one-thousandth. If you remember that a percent is one one-hundredth of something, you can see that one tenth of that percent is equivalent to one one-thousandth of the whole.

In percent notation, one tenth of one percent is written as .1%. On high school entrance exams, students often mistakenly think that .1% is equal to .1. As you now know, .1% is really equal to .001.

For practice, change the following percents to decimal notation and vice versa. The answers are on page 289.

EXERCISE 25

1. 1%
2. 1.2%
3. .5%
4. .05
5. .001
6. .003
7. 1.5%
8. .015
9. 15%
10. .0001

Sometimes we are concerned with more than 100% of something. But, you may ask, if 100% constitutes all of something, how can we speak of *more* than all of it?

Where things are growing, or increasing in size or amount, we may want to compare their new size to the size they once were. For example, suppose we measured the heights of three plants to be 6 inches, 9 inches, and 12 inches one week, and discover a week later that the first plant is still 6 inches tall but the second and third ones are now 18 inches tall.

- The six-inch plant grew *zero percent,* because it didn't grow at all.
- The second plant *added 100%* to its size. It doubled in height.
- The third plant *added 50%* to its height.

We can also say:

- The first plant is 100% of its original height.
- The second plant grew to 200% of its original height.
- The third plant grew to 150% of its original height.

Practice the following problems. For each pair of numbers, tell (1) what percentage of the first number would have to be added to get the second number, and (2) what percentage of the first number is the second number.

EXAMPLE: 100, 150

SOLUTION: *Step 1.* Fifty percent of 100 would have to be added to 100 to get 150.

Step 2. 150 represents 150% of 100.

The answers are on page 289.

EXERCISE 26

1. 50, 75

2. 50, 100

3. 10, 15

4. 100, 132

5. 20, 24

6. 1, 1.5

7. .5, .75

8. 33, 44

9. 55, 55

10. 100, 1000

You may want to know a certain percentage of a fraction.

EXAMPLE: What is 50% of $\frac{2}{3}$? *or* What is 20% of $1\frac{1}{2}$?

SOLUTION: Change 50% to its equivalent fraction and multiply $\frac{1}{2} \bullet \frac{2}{3} = \frac{2}{6} = \frac{1}{3}$, or change $\frac{2}{3}$ and 50% to decimal notation and multiply:

$.50 \times .666 = .333.$

Similarly, the second example can be calculated as:

$\frac{1}{5} \times \frac{3}{2} = \frac{3}{10}$ *or* .20 × 1.5 = .30

Here are some common percentage and fractional equivalents you should remember:

- Ten percent (10%) = one tenth (.10), or $\left(\frac{1}{10}\right)$.
- Twelve and one-half percent (12.5%) = one eighth (.125), or $\left(\frac{1}{8}\right)$.
- Sixteen and two-thirds percent $\left(16\frac{2}{3}\%\right)$ = one sixth (16.666), or $\left(\frac{1}{6}\right)$.
- Twenty percent (20%) = one fifth (.20), or $\left(\frac{1}{5}\right)$.
- Twenty-five percent (25%) = one quarter or one fourth (.25), or $\left(\frac{1}{4}\right)$.
- Thirty-three and one-third percent = one third (.333), or $\left(\frac{1}{3}\right)$.
- Thirty-seven and one-half percent (37.5%) = three eighths (.375), or $\left(\frac{3}{8}\right)$.
- Fifty percent (50%) = one half (.50), or $\left(\frac{1}{2}\right)$.
- Sixty-two and one-half percent (62.5%) = five eighths (.625), or $\left(\frac{5}{8}\right)$.
- Sixty-six and two-thirds percent $\left(66\frac{2}{3}\%\right)$ = two thirds (.666), or $\left(\frac{2}{3}\right)$.
- Seventy-five percent (75%) = three quarters or three fourths (.75), or $\left(\frac{3}{4}\right)$.
- Eighty-three and one-third percent $\left(83\frac{1}{3}\right)$ = five sixths (.833), or $\left(\frac{5}{6}\right)$.
- Eighty-seven and one-half percent (87.5%) = seven eighths (.875), or $\left(\frac{7}{8}\right)$.

EXERCISE 27

Do the following for practice. The answers are on page 289.

1. What is 75% of $\frac{7}{8}$?
2. What is 10% of $3\frac{3}{4}$?
3. What is 40% of $\frac{2}{3}$?
4. What is 27% of $4\frac{1}{2}$?
5. What is $33\frac{1}{3}\%$ of $6\frac{2}{3}$?
6. What is 16% of $7\frac{5}{8}$?

Types of Percentage Problems

There are three types of percentage problems:

1. The problem asks you to find a percentage of a certain number.

   EXAMPLE: Find 22% of 50.

   SOLUTION: .22 × 50 = 11.0

2. The problem gives you a number and then asks you to find another number, of which the first is a certain percentage.

   EXAMPLE: 30 is 20% of what number?

   SOLUTION: If 30 is 20% of a number, it is one fifth of it. 30 is one fifth of 150. Or, 30 = .20 of the number.

Long division leads to the answer: 150.

$$\begin{array}{r} 150 \\ .20\overline{)30.00} \\ \underline{20} \\ 100 \\ \underline{100} \\ 0 \end{array}$$

Problems like this are easily solved using a short algebraic sentence. We know that 30 equals 20% of an unknown number. Thus, $30 = .20n$. Dividing both sides by .20, we get the answer, $n = 150$.

3. The problem asks you to find what percent one number is of another.

EXAMPLE: 15 is what percent of 60?

SOLUTION: This is a simple division problem in long division.

$$\frac{15}{60} = \begin{array}{r} 0.250 \\ 60\overline{)15.000} \\ \underline{120} \\ 300 \\ \underline{300} \\ 0 \end{array}$$

$.250 = 25\%$.

An alternative method is to reduce the fraction $\frac{15}{60}$ to its lowest term, $\frac{1}{4}$. The percentage equivalent of $\frac{1}{4}$ is 25%.

Final Words on Percentage

When solving problems involving percentages, be careful of common errors:

- **Read the notation carefully,** .50% is *not* fifty percent, but one half of one percent.
- When solving problems for percentage increases or decreases in size, **read the problem carefully.**
- **Use common sense.** If you want to find less than 100% of a number, your result will be smaller than the number you started with. For example, 43% of 50 is less than 50.
- **Using common sense works in the other direction as well.** For example, 70 is 40% of what number? The number you are looking for must be *larger* than 70, because 70 is only $\frac{40}{100}$ of it. Moreover, you can estimate that the number you are looking for will be a little more than twice as large as 70, because70 is almost half (50%) of that number.

Solve these problems. The answers are on page 289.

EXERCISE 28

1. 28% of 45 is _____.

2. $\frac{1}{4}$% of 75 is _____.

3. $2\frac{1}{2}$% of _____ is 75.

4. 35 is _____% of 70.

5. 50 is _____% of 12.5.

6. 1.5 is _____ % of 9.

7. 3% of 1.75 is _____.

8. 12 is 5% of _____.

9. 130% of 60 is _____.

10. 180 is 200% of _____.

11. 2.5% of 50 is _____.

12. 60 is _____% of 90.

13. 30 is 20% of _____.

14. $66\frac{2}{3}$% of _____ is 104.

EXPONENTS

It is frequently beneficial to use shorthand methods of writing numbers in mathematics. One of the most common is the use of *exponents*.

An exponent is a number that tells you how many times the number it refers to (called the *base*) is used as a factor in a given calculation.

For example,

$$10^3 \leftarrow \text{exponent}$$
$$\text{(10} \leftarrow \text{base)}$$

is a shorthand way of writing 10 • 10 • 10, or 1,000. Note that the exponent is written to the right and above the base, and, to avoid confusion, the numeral is smaller in size.

Take a minute to write out the following numbers as was done above. There is no need to calculate the actual product. For example: $5^4 = 5 \bullet 5 \bullet 5 \bullet 5$. The answers are on page 290.

EXERCISE 29

1. 10^7

2. 1^3

3. 3^2

4. $\left(\frac{1}{2}\right)^4$

5. $(.45)^5$

6. 11^2

7. 0^2

8. x^3

9. b^8

10. $(ab)^5$

Exponents are most useful in certain scientific realms in which very large or very small numbers are involved. For example, it is much easier to write 10^9 rather than 1,000,000,000.

Geometry is another subject that has frequent use for exponents. Area and surface area are measured in *square* units such as square feet, square inches, and so forth. Volume is measured in cubic feet, cubic inches, or in other *cubic* units.

For example, the area of a floor might be 200 square feet. Using an exponent, we can write 200 ft.^2. The volume of a cube might be 8 cubic feet. We can write this as 8 ft.^3.

The exponent "2" is read "square" or "squared." The exponent "3" is read "cube" or "cubed."

For exponents other than 2 and 3, we use the phrase "to the _____ power." For example, 5^6 would be read "five to the sixth power."

When the exponent is not written, as when we write most numbers, the exponent is understood to be equal to 1. Any number to the first power is equivalent to itself.

For example, $10 = 10^1$. We do not write 1 as an exponent.

There are two major rules to help you calculate numbers written in exponential form. Both require that the bases of the numbers be the same.

The *first rule* involves **multiplying numbers in exponential form having the same base.** In such instances, the product may be found by adding the exponents.

EXAMPLE: Multiply 10^3 by 10^5.

SOLUTION: $10^3 \bullet 10^5 = 10^{3+5} = 10^8$

EXAMPLE: Multiply 2^3 by 2^4.

SOLUTION: $2^3 \bullet 2^4 = 2^{3+4} = 2^7$

EXAMPLE: Multiply x^2 by x^3.

SOLUTION: $x^2 \bullet x^3 = x^{2+3} = x^5$

EXAMPLE: Multiply 3^3 by 3.

SOLUTION: $3^3 \bullet 3 = 3^{3+1} = 3^4$

It is very important to note that the bases were equal in each of the preceding problems. The exponents may be different.

The *second rule* involves **division of numbers in exponential form having the same base.** In finding the product of numbers in exponential form, we added the exponents. To find their quotient, we subtract the exponent of the divisor from that of the dividend.

EXAMPLE: Divide 10^3 by 10^2.

SOLUTION: $10^3 \div 10^2 = 10^{3-2} = 10^1 = 10$

EXAMPLE: Divide 5^6 by 5^3.

SOLUTION: $5^6 \div 5^3 = 5^{6-3} = 5^3$

EXAMPLE: Divide x^4 by x^2.

SOLUTION: $x^4 \div x^2 = x^{4-2} = x^2$

EXAMPLE: Divide a^3 by a.

SOLUTION: $\frac{a^3}{a} = a^{3-1} = a^2$

For each of the preceding examples, you may want to calculate the problem in standard fashion to prove to yourself that it works.

Practice the problems below. The answers are on page 290.

EXERCISE 30

1. $1^3 \div 1^2$
2. $6^{10} \div 6^8$
3. 15^5 times 15^3
4. M^3 times M^3
5. $10^{10} \div 10^8$
6. 3^6 times 3^2
7. a^2 times a^3
8. $100^{10} \div 100^9$
9. $\left(\frac{3}{4}\right)^3$ times $\left(\frac{3}{4}\right)^2$
10. $8^5 \div 8^4$
11. $a^5 \div a^3$
12. $\left(\frac{1}{2}\right)^5 \div \left(\frac{1}{2}\right)^4$
13. x^2 times x^2
14. $y^b \div y^c$

ZERO AND NEGATIVE EXPONENTS

You may have noticed while practicing that you can divide numbers written in exponential notation and end up with an exponent that is negative or equal to zero. Both results are perfectly acceptable; they will be mentioned only briefly because you will probably not encounter them on the high school entrance examination you take.

EXAMPLE: Divide 5^3 by 5^3.

SOLUTION: $5^3 \div 5^3 = 5^{3-3} = 5^0$

You may have realized that when we divide a number by itself, the result is 1. Therefore, any number (or variable representing a number) having zero as an exponent is equal to 1. For example:

$$10^6 \div 10^6 = 10^{6-6} = 10^0 = 1$$

$$x^3 \div x^3 = x^{3-3} = x^0 = 1$$

What happens if we divide 5^3 by 5^4?

$$5^3 \div 5^4 = 5^{3-4} = 5^{-1}$$

Notice that the exponent becomes negative. A negative exponent is the symbol for a reciprocal. For example:

$$\frac{5^3}{5^4} = \frac{5 \bullet 5 \bullet 5}{5 \bullet 5 \bullet 5 \bullet 5} = \frac{1}{5} = 5^{-1}$$

$$\frac{4^2}{4^5} = \frac{4 \bullet 4}{4 \bullet 4 \bullet 4 \bullet 4 \bullet 4} = \frac{1}{4^3} = 4^{-3}$$

$$\frac{10^3}{10^5} = \frac{10 \bullet 10 \bullet 10}{10 \bullet 10 \bullet 10 \bullet 10 \bullet 10} = \frac{1}{10^2} = 10^{-2}$$

You may want to multiply these examples out to convince yourself of their truth.

ALGEBRA

If you are finishing the eighth grade this year, you may not yet have had a formal algebra class. Nevertheless, you have probably used algebraic terms and expressions, and you have probably solved simple equations. This section reviews the skills you have acquired so far and shows you the kinds of questions you can expect to find on a high school entrance examination.

This section contains a review of:

- signed numbers
- operations with algebraic expressions
- evaluating formulas
- solving equations

Signed Numbers

The number line exists to both sides of zero. Each positive number on the right of zero has a negative counterpart to the left of zero. The number line below shows the location of some pairs of numbers (+4, –4; +2, –2; +1, –1).

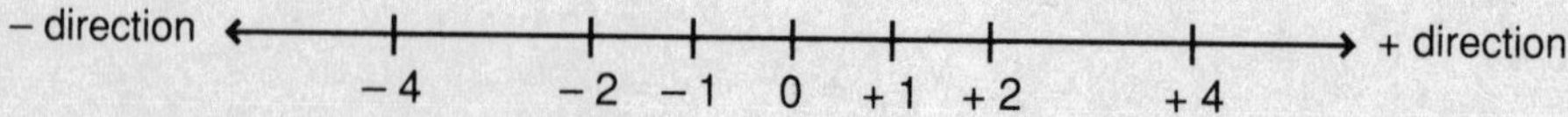

Because each number of a pair is located the same distance from zero (although in different directions), each has the same *absolute value*. Two vertical bars symbolize absolute value:

$$|+4| = |-4| = 4$$

The absolute value of +4 equals the absolute value of –4. Both are equivalent to 4. If you think of absolute value as distance from zero, regardless of direction, you will understand it more easily. The absolute value of any number, positive or negative, is always expressed as a positive number.

Addition of Signed Numbers

When two oppositely signed numbers having the same absolute value are added, the sum is zero.

EXAMPLE: $+10 + -10 = 0$ EXAMPLE: $-.010 + +.010 = 0$

EXAMPLE: $-1.5 + +1.5 = 0$ EXAMPLE: $+\frac{3}{4} + -\frac{3}{4} = 0$

If one of the two oppositely signed numbers is larger in absolute value, the sum is equal to the amount of that excess and carries the same sign as the number having the larger absolute value.

EXAMPLE: $+2 + -1 = +1$

EXAMPLE: $+8 + -9 = -1$

EXAMPLE: $-2.5 + +2.0 = -.5$

EXAMPLE: $-\frac{3}{4} + +\frac{1}{2} = -\frac{1}{4}$

Add the following groups of numbers. The answers are on page 290.

EXERCISE 31

1. -2, $+4$, -10, and -3
2. -1.2, 2.6, and $-.0005$
3. 9.001, -9.002, and 1.0
4. 125, -130, -27, and 63
5. $1\frac{3}{5}$, $6\frac{2}{3}$, -2, and -4
6. $-3\frac{1}{2}$, -1.25, and -6
7. $-\frac{5}{8}$, $1\frac{3}{4}$, and $-2\frac{1}{2}$
8. -100.1, -62.35, and 42.2
9. $.0002$, -3.6, and 1.85
10. 68.25, -74.35, and 6.10

Subtraction of Signed Numbers

Subtraction is the operation that finds the difference between two numbers, including the difference between signed numbers.

When subtracting signed numbers, it is helpful to refer to the number line.

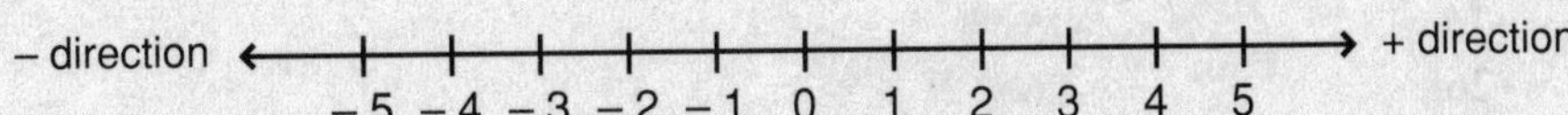

For example, if we want to subtract +2 from +5, we can use the number line to see that the difference is +3. We give the sign to the difference that represents the direction we are moving along the number line, from the number being subtracted to the number from which we are subtracting. In this case, because we are subtracting +2 from +5, we count three units in a positive direction from +2 to +5 on the number line.

When subtracting signed numbers:

- The distance between the two numbers gives you the absolute value of the difference.
- The direction you have to move from the number being subtracted to get to the number from which you are subtracting gives you the sign of the difference.

EXAMPLE: Subtract –3 from +5.

SOLUTION: Distance on number line between –3 and +5 is 8 units. Direction is from negative to positive—a positive direction. Answer is +8.

EXAMPLE: Subtract –6 from –8.

SOLUTION: Distance on number line between –6 and –8 is 2 units. Direction is from –6 to –8—a negative direction. Answer is –2.

EXAMPLE: Subtract +1.30 from –2.70.

SOLUTION: Distance between them on the number line is 4.0. Direction is from +1.30 to –2.70—a negative direction. Answer is –4.0.

Try these subtraction problems. Think before you answer! The answers are on page 290.

EXERCISE 32

1. –2 from –3
2. $-\frac{3}{5}$ from $1\frac{2}{5}$
3. 6.8 from 2.2
4. –3.6 from 5.5
5. –7.65 from .002
6. –1 from 1
7. .0019 from –.0010
8. 102 from 96.5
9. $-2\frac{1}{2}$ from $7\frac{2}{3}$
10. $-\frac{9}{10}$ from $-\frac{9}{10}$

A quick way to subtract signed numbers accurately involves placing the numbers in columns, reversing the sign of the number being subtracted, and then adding the two.

EXAMPLE: Subtract +26 from +15.

SOLUTION:

$$\begin{array}{r} +15 \\ -\ \ +26 \\ \hline \end{array} \quad = \quad \begin{array}{r} +15 \\ -26 \\ \hline -11 \end{array}$$

EXAMPLE: Subtract –35 from +10.

SOLUTION:

$$\begin{array}{r} +10 \\ -\ \ -35 \\ \hline \end{array} \quad = \quad \begin{array}{r} +10 \\ +35 \\ \hline +45 \end{array}$$

Notice that in each of the examples, the correct answer was found by reversing the sign of the number being subtracted and then adding.

Multiplication of Signed Numbers

Signed numbers are multiplied as any other numbers would be, with the following exceptions:

- The product of two negative numbers is positive.
- The product of two positive numbers is positive.
- The product of a negative number and a positive number is negative.

EXAMPLE: $-3 \times -6 = +18$

EXAMPLE: $-3.05 \times +6 = -18.30$

EXAMPLE: $+4\frac{1}{2} \times -3 = -13\frac{1}{2}$

EXAMPLE: $+1 \times -1 \times +1 = -1$

Practice with the following examples. Remember, the only way to get a negative product is with a pair of oppositely signed factors. The answers are on page 290.

EXERCISE 33

1. -5×-6
2. -2.5×-1.3
3. $-\frac{3}{4} \times 1\frac{1}{2}$
4. $+\frac{2}{7} \times -\frac{2}{3}$
5. $-1.2 \times -.75 \times -.1$
6. $-\frac{2}{3} \times -\frac{1}{2} \times -\frac{5}{4}$
7. $-10.6 \times 3.3 \times -1.01$
8. $-2\frac{1}{2} \times 5.5 \times 7\frac{3}{10}$
9. $+.001 \times -3.25 \times 10$
10. $\frac{5}{9} \times 3 \times -\frac{1}{3}$

Division of Signed Numbers

As with multiplication, the division of signed numbers requires you to observe three simple rules:

- When dividing a positive number by a negative number, the result is negative.
- When dividing a negative number by a positive number, the result is negative.
- When dividing a negative number by a negative number, or a positive number by a positive number, the result is positive.

EXAMPLE: $+6 \div -3 = -2$

EXAMPLE: $-6 \div +3 = -2$

EXAMPLE: $-6 \div -3 = +2$

EXAMPLE: $+6 \div +3 = +2$

Try the following problems. The answers are on page 291.

EXERCISE 34

1. $120 \div -8$
2. $-\frac{2}{3} \div +\frac{1}{3}$
3. $.43 \div -.2$
4. $-.063 \div +9$
5. $+122 \div -10$
6. $-1\frac{1}{2} \div -3$
7. $-\frac{7}{25} \div +\frac{1}{25}$
8. $-2.0002 \div -.01$
9. $\frac{1}{10} \div -.10$
10. $-100 \div -.25$

Variables and Coefficients

Algebra uses letters to stand for numbers. Letters of this kind having several possible values are called *variables*. The most commonly used variables are the letters x and y, although all other letters of the alphabet are also used.

The variable x looks very similar to the multiplication sign used in arithmetic. For this reason, it is a good idea to use a dot or parentheses to indicate multiplication, rather than the × symbol.

For example, if you want to write "six times five," write it like this 6 • 5 or 6(5), rather than 6 × 5.

Numbers used in front of variables to indicate how many of each variable you are working with are called *coefficients*. Coefficients may be whole numbers, decimals, fractions, or even Greek letters.

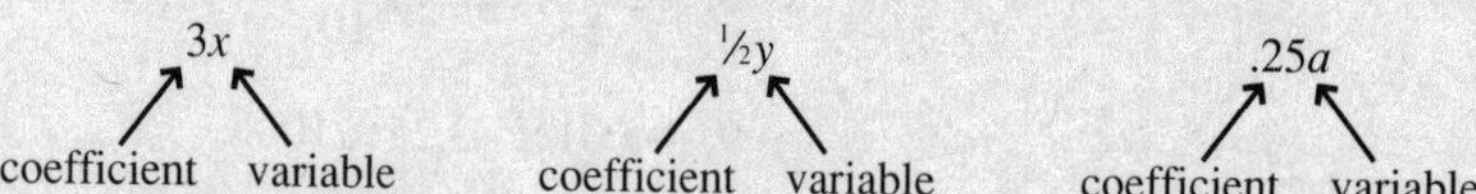

Example 1 indicates a number three times the size of x; Example 2, a number one half the size of y; and Example 3, a number one fourth the size of a.

Where you see no coefficient written, the coefficient is assumed to be 1.

Coefficients include negative numbers as well. For example, the examples below have coefficients of 1 or –1.

Adding and Subtracting Algebraic Expressions

Addition of algebraic expressions or terms such as the ones described above is quite easy. You can add expressions only if the variables are identical, and you do that by adding the coefficients together.

EXAMPLE: Add $2x$ and $3x$.

SOLUTION: $5x$

EXAMPLE: Add $\frac{1}{2}y$ and $2y$.

SOLUTION: $2\frac{1}{2}y$

EXAMPLE: Add $.50a$ and $.75a$.

SOLUTION: $1.25a$

EXAMPLE: Add b and b.

SOLUTION: $2b$

In the exercises below, add the expressions together to find an answer. Some cannot be combined because the variables are not identical. Others have negative coefficients, so be careful. The answers are on page 291.

EXERCISE 35

1. $a, 3a, 5a$
2. $10x, 4x, 20x$
3. $3m, 4r, 3s$
4. $-2b, -3b, 6b$
5. $-1.5r, 2r, 3s$, and $-2s$
6. $\frac{3}{4}t, \frac{2}{3}m, -1\frac{1}{4}t, \frac{2}{5}m$
7. $.001S, .210S, -1.25S$
8. $-20k, 2.5k, 1\frac{3}{4}k$
9. $-2x, -3y, 4x, -4z$
10. $1.02p, -.62p, -40r$

Subtracting algebraic expressions is accomplished by simply subtracting the coefficients. You must be careful if the coefficients are negative numbers, however. Use what you learned about signed numbers earlier in this book.

EXAMPLE: Subtract x from $4x$.

SOLUTION: $4x - x = 3x$

EXAMPLE: Subtract $-2x$ from $4x$.

SOLUTION: $4x - -2x = 6x$ (Remember the number line!)

Try the following problems. Some have fractional coefficients, some have decimal coefficients, and others cannot be subtracted because the variables are not identical. The answers are on page 291.

EXERCISE 36

1. $3d$ from $-4d$
2. $-1\frac{1}{2}x$ from $2x$
3. $6y$ from $-2b$
4. $-a$ from $-a$
5. $1.25m$ from $-2.25m$
6. $-.001x$ from $-.002x$
7. $2.483f$ from $-5.0f$
8. $-\frac{7}{16}r$ from $-\frac{9}{16}r$
9. $3p$ from $-2r$
10. $-16x$ from $-14x$

Multiplying Algebraic Expressions

First, review the section in this book about exponents. Pay particular attention to operations involving multiplication and division of numbers expressed with exponents.

When multiplying algebraic expressions, multiply the coefficients as you would any numbers and then add the exponents of the identical variables to find the product.

EXAMPLE: Multiply $2x \bullet 3x$.

SOLUTION: Multiply the coefficients and add the exponents of the identical variables: $2x \bullet 3x = 6x^2$.

Remember that where an exponent is not written, it is equivalent to 1.

EXAMPLE: $\frac{1}{2}x \bullet 3x = \frac{3}{2}x^2$

EXAMPLE: $-5y \bullet 2y = -10y^2$

EXAMPLE: $-2a^2 \bullet 2a = -4a^3$

EXAMPLE: $.25m^3 \bullet -.25m^3 = -.0625m^6$

Try the following problems. The answers are on page 291.

EXERCISE 37

1. $3x \bullet 2x$
2. $-\frac{2}{3}y \bullet -2y$
3. $-1.5a \bullet 3.2a$
4. $-2z^2 \bullet 3z$
5. $1.021r \bullet 1.010r^2$
6. $-3.65f \bullet 1.60f^3$
7. $\frac{5}{7}z \bullet \frac{1}{3}z$
8. $-\frac{5}{16}m \bullet \frac{1}{4}m^2$
9. $2.02x^2 \bullet -1.1x^2$
10. $-7.1b \bullet 10.1b^3$

Any two expressions can be multiplied together and rewritten as one expression. The same multiplication rules apply.

EXAMPLE: Multiply $2x \bullet 3y$.

SOLUTION: Multiply the coefficients and add the exponents of identical variables. Because the variables are not identical in this problem, we simply multiply them together. The product is thus $6xy$.

EXAMPLE: $-2a \bullet 3b = -6ab$

EXAMPLE: $.35m \bullet 2f = .70fm$

EXAMPLE: $-2x^2 \bullet -4y = 8x^2y$

EXAMPLE: $4\,a^2b \bullet -3ab^2 = -12a^3b^3$ (The exponents of the identical variables were added together.)

Try the following problems. The answers are on page 291.

EXERCISE 38

1. $7x \bullet 2y$
2. $\frac{3}{2}a^2 \bullet \frac{3}{2}b^2$
3. $1.2d \bullet 1.3f$
4. $-45x^2 \bullet .50y$
5. $-6.9a^2 \bullet 3.2b$
6. $100abc \bullet -a$
7. $-5q \bullet 1\frac{3}{10}r^2$
8. $-x^2 \bullet -y^2 \bullet -z^2$
9. $-2x^2 \bullet 4y^2 \bullet -3z$
10. $-3a \bullet 5b \bullet 2c$

Dividing Algebraic Expressions

Division is a process that reverses multiplication. When dividing algebraic expressions, divide the coefficients and subtract the exponents of the identical variables. You must also obey the rules governing division of signed numbers if the coefficients are signed.

Review the section on exponents if you cannot follow these examples.

EXAMPLE: Divide $6x$ by 2.

SOLUTION: $6x \div 2 = 3x$

EXAMPLE: Divide $4a^2$ by $2a$.

SOLUTION: $4a^2 \div 2a = 2a$

EXAMPLE: Divide $-3b^2$ by $.5b$.

SOLUTION: $-3b^2 \div .5b = -6b$

EXAMPLE: Divide $2x^2y^2$ by $.4xy$.

SOLUTION: $2x^2y^2 \div .4xy = 5xy$

EXAMPLE: Divide $-6x^3y^4$ by $-x^2y$.

SOLUTION: $-6x^3y^4 \div -x^2y = 6xy^3$

Try the following problems for practice. The answers are on page 291.

EXERCISE 39

1. $100c^2 \div 10c$
2. $-3.5x \div .7x$
3. $2.20y^2 \div -1.1y$
4. $-4a^2b \div 2a$
5. $22ab^2 \div -11b$
6. $-5.1abc \div 1.7bc$
7. $4\frac{1}{2}ax^2 \div -1\frac{1}{2}a$
8. $-.001y^3 \div .01y^2$
9. $-2.8r^2s \div -.7rs$
10. $70xy^2 \div -35xy^2$

Removing Grouping Symbols

Mathematics uses parentheses and brackets to group numbers for various reasons. When calculations have to be made, it is necessary to remove the grouping symbols and combine as many of the numbers as you can.

EXAMPLE 1: $6(3 + 5) = 6 \bullet 8 = 48$

EXAMPLE 2: $-6(1 + 2) = -6 \bullet 3 = -18$

EXAMPLE 3: $-2(a + b) = -2a + -2b = -2a - 2b$

In Examples 1 and 2, the operation inside the parentheses was carried out first, with the result then multiplied with the number outside the parentheses. In Example 3, the letters inside the parentheses could not be added, so –2 was multiplied by both a and b. In some cases, additional steps are required.

EXAMPLE: Simplify: $2 - [4 - (3 - 1) + 6]$

SOLUTION: Begin by working with the *innermost* parentheses, removing one set of grouping symbols at each step.

$2 - [4 - (3 - 1) + 6]$
$= 2 - [4 - 2 + 6]$
$= 2 - [8]$
$= 2 - 8$
$= -6$

This same procedure can be used with variables.

EXAMPLE: Simplify: $a - [b - (a - 2b) + 3a]$

SOLUTION: Begin with the innermost group and work outward.

$= a - [b - (a - 2b) + 3a]$
$= a - [b - a + 2b + 3a]$
$= a - [3b + 2a]$
$= a - 3b - 2a$
$= -a - 3b$

In the example above, it is important to note that the negative sign in front of the grouping symbol reverses the sign of the numbers within. A positive sign changes nothing.

Try the following problems. Remember to remove the grouping symbols in order, beginning with the innermost. The answers are on page 291.

EXERCISE 40

1. $2 + (3 - 2) - 2$

2. $-2 - [1 + (6 - 2)]$

3. $[a + (1 - 2) + b - 3]$

4. $-1 + 2 - (3 - 4)$

5. $-5 - [(6 - 3) - (1 - 2)]$

6. $a - [3 - (b - 2) - (a - 1)]$

Evaluating Algebraic Expressions

It is often necessary to determine the value of an algebraic expression if its variables are given precise numerical values. You have done this when finding the areas, perimeters, and volumes of geometric figures. When given a formula for the area of a triangle, for example, you can find the area if you know the base and the height. The same procedure is used in evaluating algebraic expressions.

EXAMPLE: Find the value of $10x$ if $x = 2$.

SOLUTION: Substitute 2 for x, and multiply $10 \bullet 2 = 20$.

EXAMPLE: Evaluate $3a^2$ if $a = 5$.

SOLUTION: Substitute 5 for a, and multiply $3 \bullet 5^2 = 3 \bullet 25 = 75$.

EXAMPLE: Evaluate $-2x^2y^2$ if $x = 2$ and $y = 3$.

SOLUTION: $-2 \bullet 2^2 \bullet 3^2 = -2 \bullet 4 \bullet 9 = -72$

EXAMPLE: Evaluate $\frac{2}{x^3}$ if $x = \frac{1}{2}$.

SOLUTION: $\frac{2}{\left(\frac{1}{2}\right)^3} = \frac{2}{\left(\frac{1}{8}\right)} = 16$

Try the following problems. The answers are on page 292.

EXERCISE 41

1. $3(x + y)$ $\quad x = 2, y = -1$

2. $a^2 - b^2$ $\quad a = 3, b = 4$

3. $4m^2n^2$ $\quad m = \frac{1}{2}, n = 1$

4. $\frac{1}{2}ax^2$ $\quad a = 32, x = 4$

5. $(b + c)(d + 2)$ $\quad b = \frac{3}{4}, c = 2, d = 0$

6. $\frac{1}{x^2}$ $\quad x = \frac{1}{a}$

7. $\frac{7y}{3}$ $\quad y = \frac{1}{3}$

8. $\frac{1}{2}(a + b)h$ $\quad a = 4, b = 3, h = 1.5$

9. $\frac{m_1m_2}{r^2}$ $\quad m_1 = 32, m_2 = 320, r = 10$

10. $\frac{by^2}{c}$ $\quad b = 4.8, c = 1.2, y = 1$

Solving Simple Equations

Much of the work in algebra consists of finding precise values for variables. To find these precise values, variables are set equal to known quantities in *equations*. For example, the simplest equation possible is $x = 2$. This equation says, "The variable x is equal to two."

One step further is: $2y = 2$. This says, "Two times y equals two."

In the equation $2y = 2$, let's find what y equals. If 2 times y equals 2, we know y equals 1.

EXAMPLE: $a + 1 = 3$

SOLUTION: Because the variable a plus 1 equals 3, 3 is 1 larger than a. $a = 2$.

EXAMPLE: $Z - 3 = 6$

SOLUTION: The variable Z minus 3 equals 6. Z is 3 larger than 6, so $Z = 9$.

Try the following examples. Solve the equation for the variable. The answers are on page 292.

EXERCISE 42

1. $a + 3 = 6$

2. $2x - 1 = 7$

3. $-2x = 6$

4. $r - 3 = -1$

5. $3b - 6 = 6$

6. $100y - 1 = 99$

7. $10 + x = 5$

Solving More Difficult Equations

Equations may have variables with fractional and decimal coefficients. Variables may also appear on both sides of the equal sign. The following examples should help to review how to solve these kinds of equations:

EXAMPLE 1: $2x - 3 = x + 2$

EXAMPLE 2: $\frac{3}{4}y = 15$

EXAMPLE 3: $.25a = a - 1.5$

EXAMPLE 4: $6(x - 2) = 12$

When working with equations such as those above, it is necessary to work on the left side of the equal sign as well as the right side.

To make equations easier to work with, elements of the equation must be moved across the equal sign from one side to the other. The goal is to place all of the terms having a variable on one side of the equation and all of the terms not having a variable on the other. In doing this, obey one simple rule: *When moving a term to the other side of the equation, reverse its sign.*

Example 1 would be solved like this:

SOLUTION 1: Solve for x: $2x - 3 = x + 2$

1. Put all terms containing x on the left side of the equal sign. The others go on the right. Reverse the signs of those terms moved from one side to the other.
2. $2x - x = 2 + 3$
3. Simplify: $x = 5$. The equation is thus solved.

In some cases, multiplication and division may be involved, as in example 2. Example 2 would be solved like this:

SOLUTION 2: Solve for y: $\frac{3}{4}y = 15$.

1. The term having the variable is already on the left, and the other is already on the right.
2. Divide both sides of the equation by the coefficient of the variable: $\frac{\frac{3}{4}y}{\frac{3}{4}} = \frac{15}{\frac{3}{4}}$
3. $y = 20$

You may have been able to solve this problem without calculations. By thinking about what number 15 was three quarters of, you may have figured out that y was equal to 20.

Example 3 would be solved like this:

SOLUTION 3: Solve for a: $.25a = a - 1.5$

1. Put the terms with the variable on the left; those without, on the right. Reverse the sign of those that cross the equal sign.
2. $.25a - a = -1.5$
3. Combine: $-.75a = -1.5$
4. Divide both sides by the coefficient of the variable:

$$\frac{-.75a}{-.75} = \frac{-1.5}{-.75}$$

$$a = 2$$

Example 4 would be solved like this:

SOLUTION 4: Solve for x: $6(x - 2) = 12$

1. Remove the grouping symbol by multiplying by 6: $6x - 12 = 12$
2. Move -12 to the right and change its sign: $6x = 12 + 12$
3. Combine: $6x = 24$
4. Divide both sides by the coefficient of the variable:

$$\frac{6x}{6} = \frac{24}{6}$$

$$x = 4$$

Try the following problems. You may be able to solve some of them in your head without calculating on paper. The answers are on page 292.

EXERCISE 43

1. $\frac{1}{4}x - 1 = 2$

2. $\frac{1}{x - 2} = 1$

3. $2x - 2 = 4x - 10$

4. $\frac{7}{x} = 14$

5. $3.2x = 64$

6. $5(x - 3) = x + 9$

7. $\frac{3}{4}x = 20$

8. $4a + 3 = 3a - \frac{1}{2}$

9. $3b = b$

10. $6m - 1 = m + 4$

GEOMETRY

Geometry is that part of mathematics that studies lines, curves, and angles and the various shapes they create when placed together in different ways. Usually, geometry is divided into two subgroups: *plane geometry* and *solid geometry*.

Plane geometry studies any shapes and angles that can be drawn in one plane. This means that shapes that can be measured in only one or two dimensions, or directions, are studied. For example:

- A line has only one dimension, its length.
- A triangle, a square, or a circle drawn on a piece of paper can be measured in only two directions, or dimensions: length and width.

Solid geometry studies shapes that have three dimensions: length, width, and thickness. For example:

- An object such as a brick or a shoebox is a rectangular solid that can be measured in three directions or dimensions: length, width, and height.
- Cubes, cones, spheres, cylinders, pyramids, or tetrahedrons are examples of shapes that are three dimensional and as such require the use of the principles of solid geometry.

First we will review some basics of plane geometry.

Points, Lines, and Angles

A *point* is an exact location and has no dimensions.

By placing lots of points in a row, we build a *line*. A line has infinite length in both directions, and has a symbol like this:

The arrowhead at each end indicates that the line is infinite. Usually, we select two points on the line, give them names, and name the line the same way:

A B $= \overleftrightarrow{AB}$ read: "line *AB*"

Note that we need a minimum of two points to make a line. There is no *maximum* number of points on a line, however.

A *ray* is a line that has one endpoint, and goes infinitely in one direction. We refer to a ray by its endpoint and one other point along it.

A B $= \overrightarrow{AB}$ read: "ray *AB*"

A *line segment* is a piece of a line having two endpoints. We name it by naming the endpoints:

A B $= \overline{AB}$ read: "line segment *AB*"

Because their length is infinite, lines and rays cannot be measured. Line segments, on the other hand, are finite and *can* be measured.

Angles

Where lines, line segments, or rays meet or cross each other, *angles* are formed. The simplest angle is that formed by two rays having the same endpoint but going in different directions. The endpoint that these two rays share is called the *vertex* of the angle.

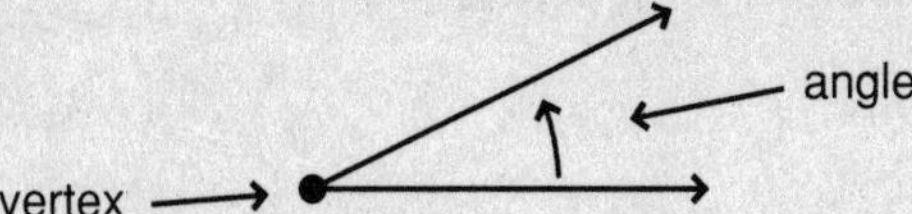

Angles are measured in units called *degrees*. A degree is $\frac{1}{360}$ of a complete revolution around the point called the vertex.

For example, the drawings below show one ray of an angle going through one complete revolution around the vertex. In each case, the measure of the angle is shown.

a.
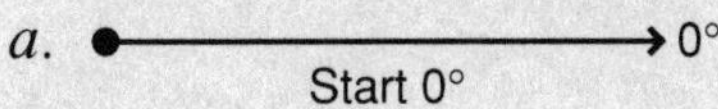

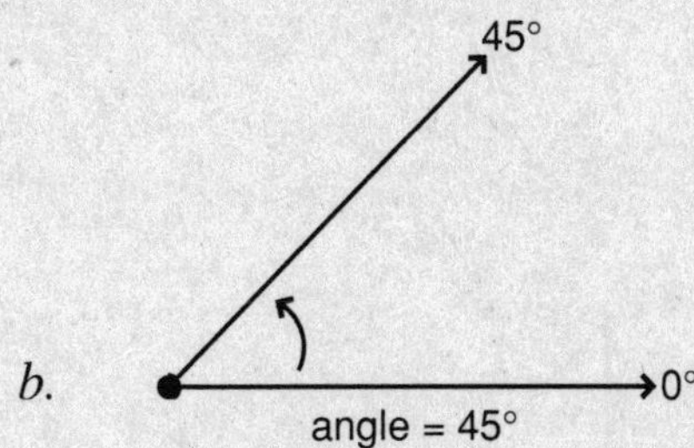

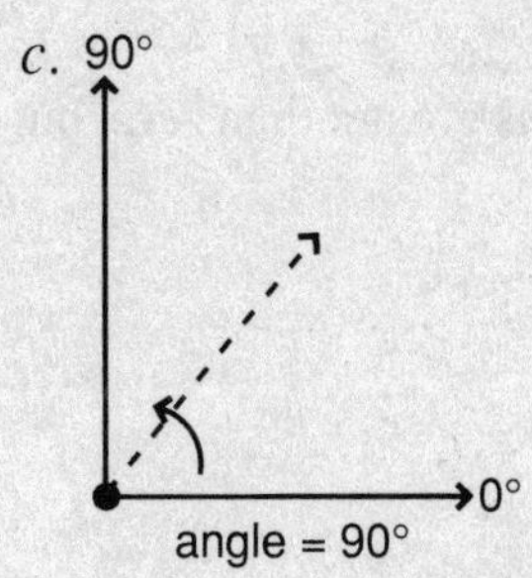

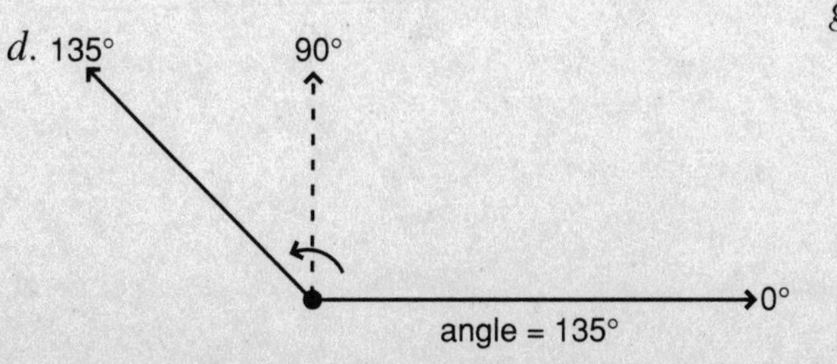

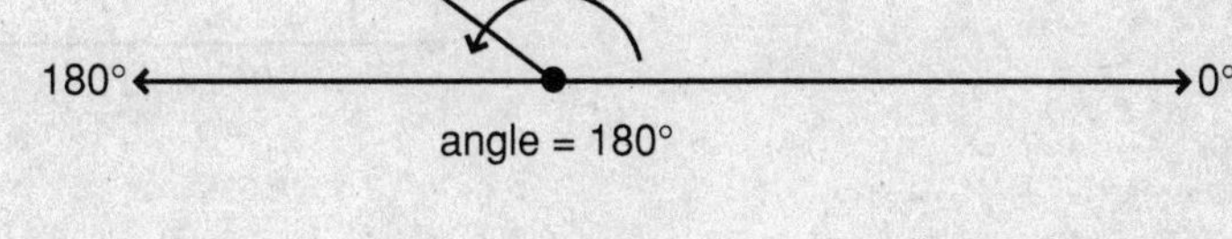

f.
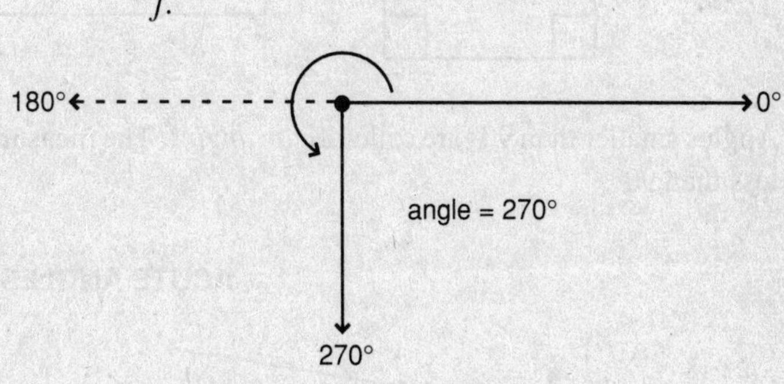

g.
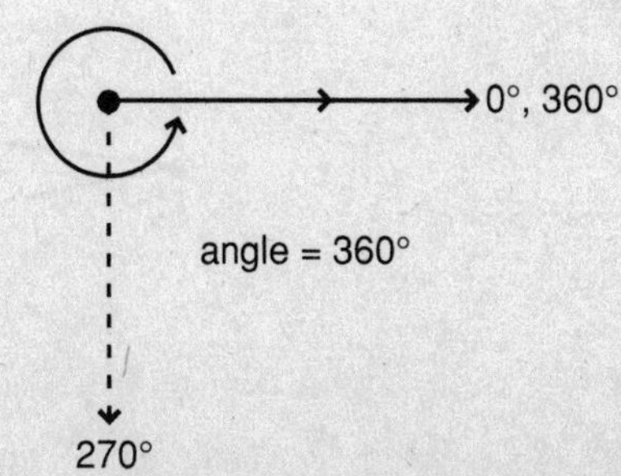

The sequence on the previous page should remind you of a number of rules:

- Each complete revolution around the vertex creates an angle of 360°.
- Angles are measured counterclockwise.
- The measure of the angle is the same, no matter how long the rays are. The tips of each ray have the same angle between them as do two points closer to the vertex.

Kinds of Angles

A 90° angle is also called a *right angle*. Squares, rectangles, and some triangles have right angles.

RIGHT ANGLES

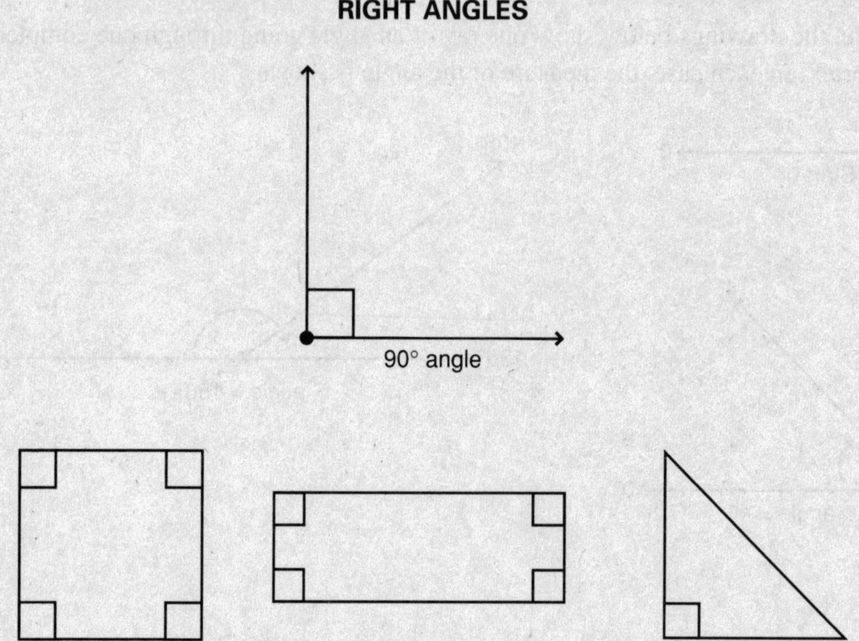

Angles smaller than 90° are called *acute angles*. The measure of an acute angle is greater than zero, but less than 90°.

ACUTE ANGLES

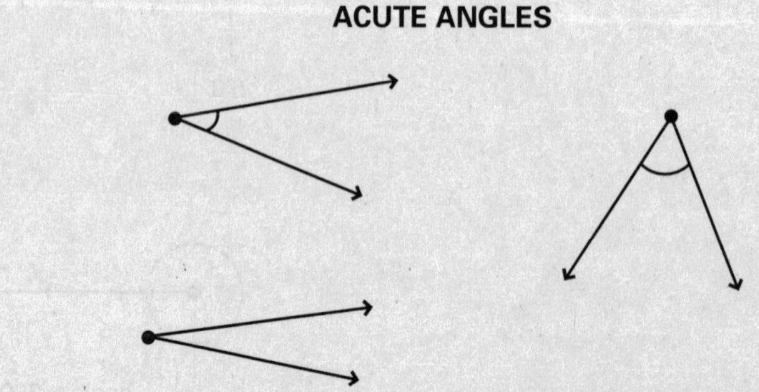

An angle that measures greater than 90° but less than 180° is called an *obtuse angle*.

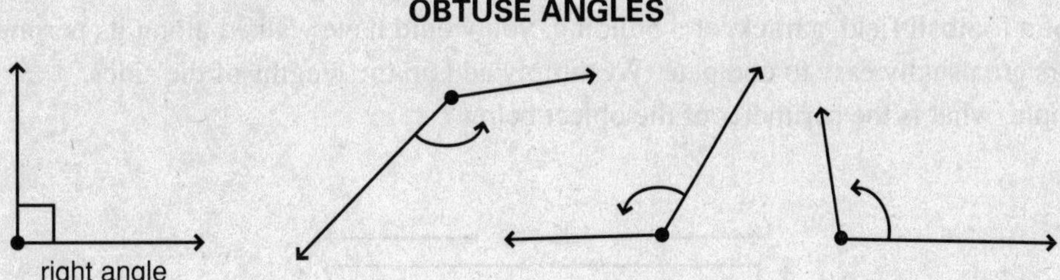

An angle equivalent to 180° is a *straight angle*. Lines may be thought of as straight angles.

Angles whose sum is 180° are *supplementary angles*. For example, the sum of 60° and 120° is 180°. Each angle is a supplement of the other.

A line intersecting a straight angle cuts it into supplementary angles.

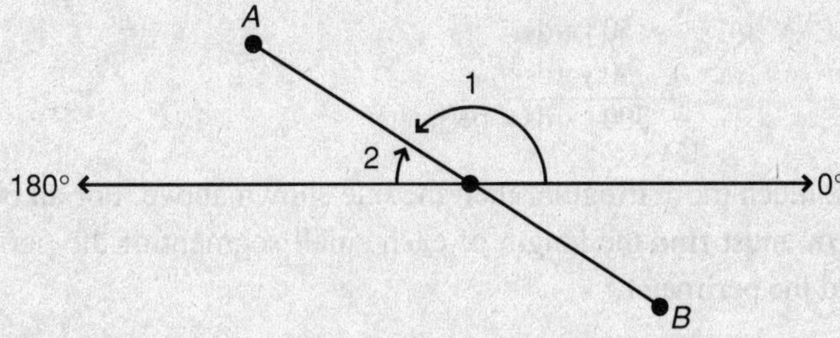

Angle 1 and angle 2 are supplementary angles.

Angles whose sum is 90° are *complementary angles*. For example, the sum of 60° and 30° is 90°. Each angle is a complement of the other.

For the following problems, state whether the angle is acute or obtuse. If it is obtuse, name its supplement. If it is acute, name its supplement and complement. The answers are on page 292.

EXERCISE 44

1. 170°

2. 30°

3. 142°

4. 60°

5. 90°

6. 27°

7. 135°

8. 95°

9. 57°

10. 45°

Perimeter

The *perimeter* of an object is the distance around it. For example, if you walked all the way around the "outside" of a football field, a track, or a building, you would have walked along its perimeter.

Perimeters are usually easy to compute. We simply add up the lengths of the sides.

For example, what is the perimeter of the object below?

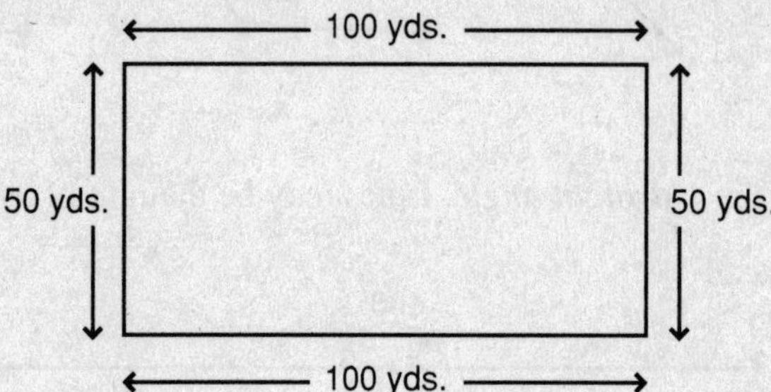

Just add the length of each side:

$$\begin{array}{rl} & 100 \text{ yards} \\ & 100 \text{ yards} \\ & 50 \text{ yards} \\ + & 50 \text{ yards} \\ \hline & 300 \text{ yards} = \text{perimeter} \end{array}$$

Frequently, objects are much more irregular than the one shown above. For an object such as the one below, for example, you must find the length of each small segment of the perimeter. Then add the lengths together to find the perimeter.

The perimeter of a circle is called its *circumference,* which is computed in a special way.

Ancient Greek mathematicians discovered an important fact about circles. No matter how large the circle was, they found that its circumference (perimeter) was almost exactly 3.14 times its diameter. They named the number by which they multiplied a circle's diameter to get its circumference *pi*. We use the value 3.14, or the fraction $\frac{22}{7}$, to represent pi, although its value is slightly larger. The symbol π stands for pi.

To find the perimeter (circumference) of this circle:

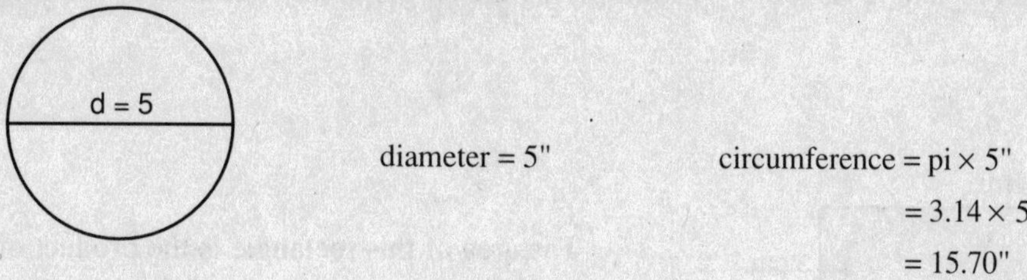

We can also work backward to find the diameter of a circle from its circumference. For example, if the circumference of a circle is 21.98 inches, what is its diameter?

Because the circumference is the product of π and the diameter, divide the circumference by π to find the diameter.

$$21.98 \div 3.14 = 7'' \text{ (diameter)}$$

Find the circumference or diameter for circles having the following dimensions. The answers are on page 292.

EXERCISE 45

1. d = 3.5"

2. d = 5.0"

3. c = 22"

4. $d = 2\frac{1}{2}''$

5. c = 31.4"

6. c = 15.7"

Area of Plane Figures

When a plane figure such as a rectangle, triangle, or circle lies flat, it covers a certain amount of area. When it is necessary to buy carpeting, grass seed, paint, and many other things, the area of the place to be covered must be calculated.

Area is always measured in square units, such as square inches, square feet, square yards, or square miles. Metric system units for area include square centimeters, square meters, and square kilometers. Generally, the unit of measurement to be used is based upon the area of the object being measured.

For example:

- The area of a city would be measured in square miles or square kilometers.
- The area of a football field would be measured in square yards or square meters.
- The area of this page would be measured in square inches or square centimeters.

When calculating area, it is most important to remember that you are dealing with *square units*. Area is always given in square inches, square meters, and so on.

Area of Squares and Rectangles

The area of squares and rectangles is found by multiplying the length of any one side by the length of the side adjoining it.

For example:

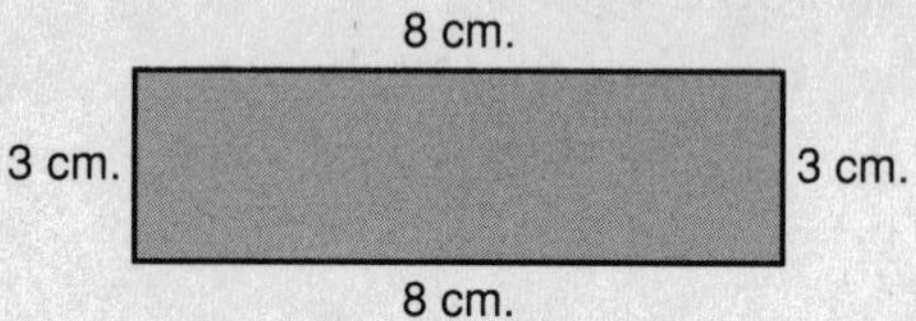

The area of this rectangle is the product of 8 cm. × 3 cm. = 24 sq. cm.

The area of any rectangle can be found by multiplying the length of its longest side by the length of its shortest side.

Area of a rectangle = length times width

A = l × w

The area of squares is calculated the same way. You just have to remember that the sides of a square are all the same length. If you know the length of one side, you know the lengths of all the sides.

For example:

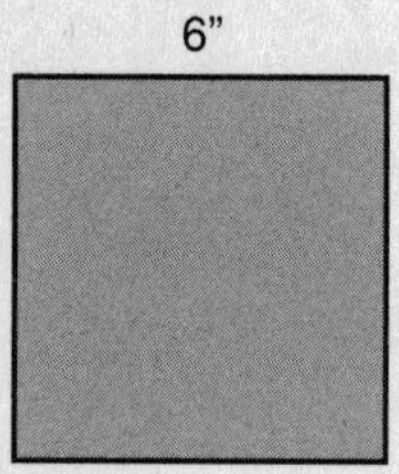

The area of the square is 6 in. × 6 in. = 36 sq. in.

Find the area of the rectangles or squares having the following dimensions. The answers are on page 292.

EXERCISE 46

1. 3" long, 2" wide

2. 3 feet 6" long, 2 feet wide

3. 10 cm. long, 10 cm. wide

4. $1\frac{1}{2}$ miles long, $\frac{3}{5}$ miles wide

5. 12" long, 12" wide*

6. 3' long, 3' wide**

7. $\frac{1}{2}$" wide, 10" long

8. $\frac{3}{4}$" wide by $\frac{3}{4}$" long

*144 sq. in. equals 1 sq. ft.

**9 sq. ft. equals 1 sq. yd.

Area of Triangles

Triangles may be:

- *acute,* if each of their angles is less than 90°:

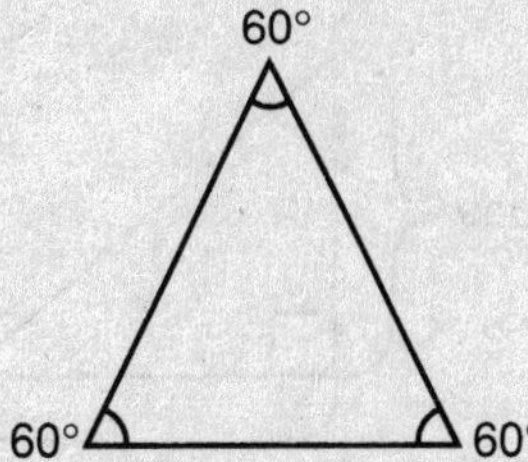

If each angle is 60°, the triangle is called *equilateral,* because all angles are equal in measure.

- *right,* if one angle is 90°:

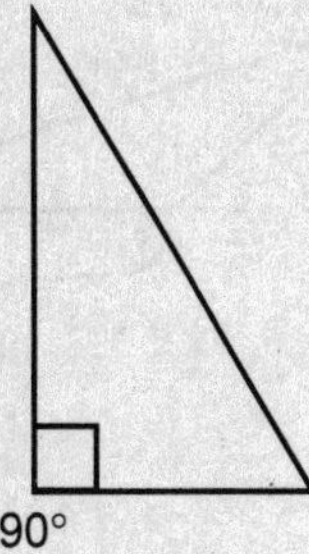

- *obtuse,* if one angle is larger than 90°:

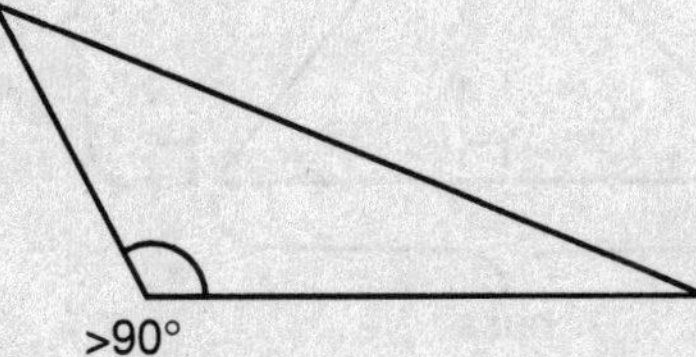

Familiarize yourself with these kinds of triangles, because finding their area requires you to be very careful about one thing: *measuring the altitude correctly.*

We find the area of triangles by using the following formula:

Area = one half the product of the base and the altitude

$$A = \frac{1}{2} \times b \times a \text{ or } A = \frac{1}{2}ba$$

The *altitude* of a triangle is the distance from a point on the base to a point directly above, or perpendicular to, the base.

These drawings show how to measure altitude correctly.

In a right triangle:

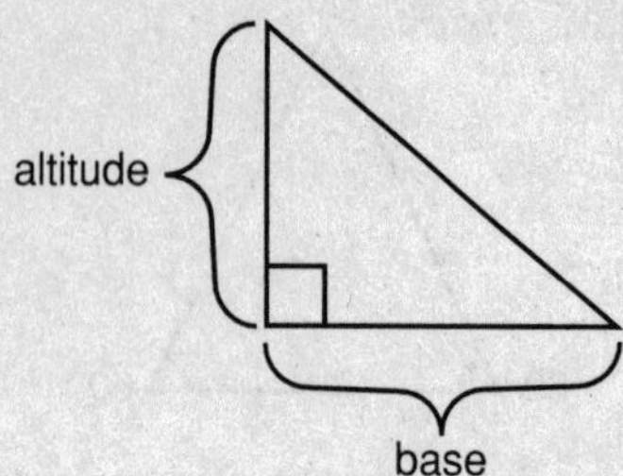

In an obtuse triangle:

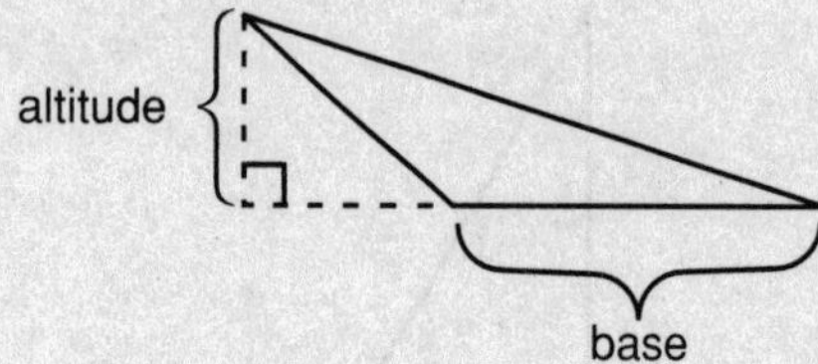

In an acute triangle:

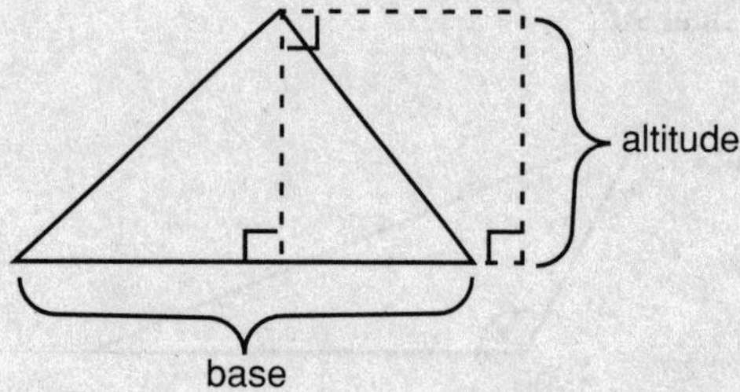

Notice that in each case, the altitude or height of a triangle *must* be measured along a line that makes a right angle with the base.

Example: Find the area of the triangle shown below.

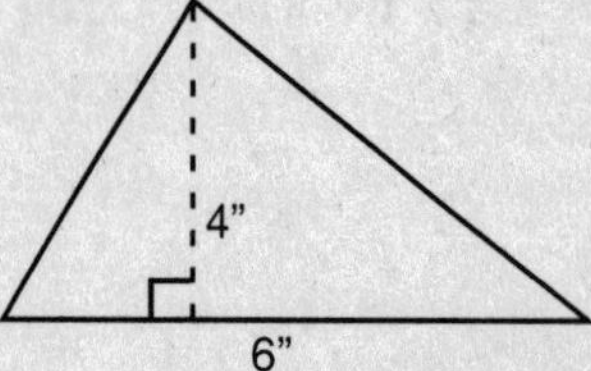

SOLUTION: $A = \frac{1}{2}ba$

$A = \frac{1}{2} \cdot 4" \cdot 6"$

$A = 12$ sq. in.

Find the areas of the triangles whose dimensions are given below. The answers are on page 293.

EXERCISE 47

1. b = 16", a = 8"
2. $b = 4\frac{1}{2}$ feet, a = 2 feet
3. b = 11.5 cm., a = 4.5 cm.
4. b = 2.4 feet, a = 6.3 feet
5. b = 8 inches, a = 2.5 feet
6. $b = 1\frac{2}{3}$ yds., $a = 3\frac{1}{4}$ yds.

Area of Parallelograms and Trapezoids

A *parallelogram* is a four-sided figure with opposite sides parallel to each other. **The area of a parallelogram can be found by multiplying the length of the base by the altitude.**

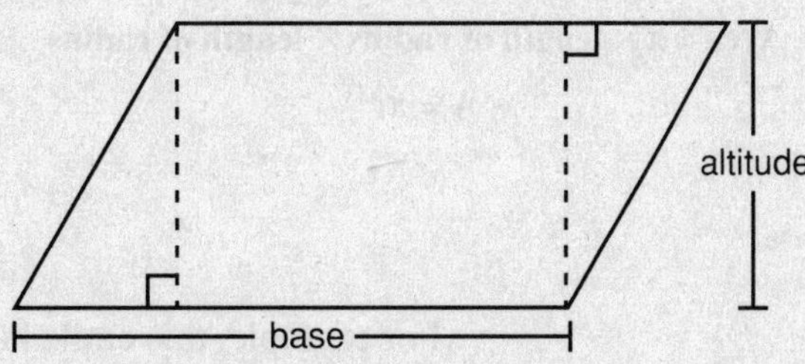

Area = base × altitude

A = b × a *or* A = ba

Here again, you *must* be careful to measure the altitude perpendicular to the base, just as you did when finding the areas of triangles.

A *trapezoid* is a four-sided figure with one pair of sides parallel, and one pair nonparallel. The parallel sides are called the *bases,* and we find the area as follows:

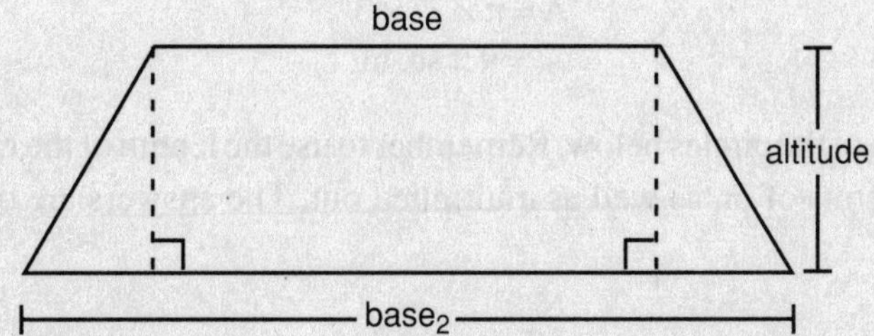

$$\textbf{Area} = \frac{1}{2} \times \textbf{altitude} \times \textbf{(length of base 1 + length of base 2)}$$

$$A = \frac{1}{2} \times a \times (b_1 + b_2) \text{ or } A = \frac{1}{2}a(b_1 + b_2)$$

Be sure to measure the altitude of the trapezoid along a line that makes a right angle with the base.

Find the areas of the following parallelograms and trapezoids. "P" means parallelogram; "T" means trapezoid. The answers are on page 293.

EXERCISE 48

1. P: b = 6", a = 4"

2. P: b = 5", a = 2"

3. T: b_1 = 10", b_2 = 15", a = 3"

4. T: b_1 = 20 cm., b_2 = 40 cm., a = 6 cm.

5. P: b = 4.125 ft., a = 3.34 ft.

6. T: b_1 = 5", b_2 = 7", a = 3"

Area of a Circle

The area of a circle is easily calculated, if you remember two things:

- Use the number pi ($\pi = 3.14$, or $\frac{22}{7}$).
- Use the radius of the circle in the calculation instead of the diameter. The radius is one half of the diameter: $r = \frac{d}{2}$.

To find the area of a circle, use the following formula:

$$\textbf{Area} = \pi \times \textbf{length of radius} \times \textbf{length of radius}$$

$$\mathbf{A = \pi r^2}$$

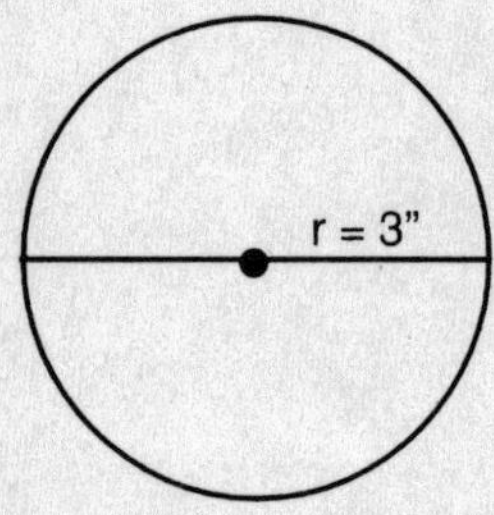

For example, this circle has a radius of 3". Thus, its area is:

$$\begin{aligned} A &= \pi r^2 \\ &= 3.14 \times 3" \times 3" \\ &= 28.26 \text{ sq. in.} \end{aligned}$$

Sometimes, to avoid the extra calculation, areas of circles are written in pi. In the example above, we would write:

$$\begin{aligned} A &= \pi \times 3" \times 3" \\ &= 9\pi \text{ sq. in.} \end{aligned}$$

Practice finding the areas of the circles below. Remember to use the length of the radius in the calculation. Write your answers in terms of pi, as well as multiplied out. The answers are on page 293.

EXERCISE 49

1. r = 2.17 inches
2. r = 3.5 cm.
3. d = 10 feet
4. d = 20 yds.
5. r = 22 inches
6. d = 11 inches
7. r = $\frac{1}{2}$ cm.
8. d = 100 cm.
9. c = 31.4 inches
10. c = 125.6 miles

Volume of Solid Figures

Three-dimensional figures such as cubes, cones, spheres, and rectangular solids take up space. The amount of space an object or substance takes up is called its *volume*.

Because we purchase items and plan the sizes of buildings, homes, ships, and so forth according to our needs for a certain volume of something, volume is one of the most important measurements that we make. In this section, you will review how to calculate the volume of certain easy-to-measure shapes.

Volume of Rectangular Solids

A familiar rectangular solid is a shoe box. Its volume is calculated by multiplying its length times its width times its thickness or depth. The formula is:

volume = l × w × h *or* **V = lwh**

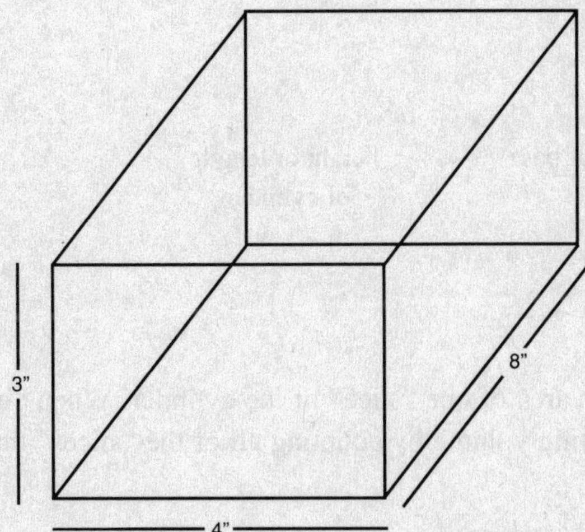

For example, the box shown to the left has the volume:

V = 3" × 4" × 8"
= 96 cu. in.

Notice that we multiplied the measurement of each dimension of the box only once. The units that we use in measuring volume are *cubic* units.

A special rectangular solid is a *cube*. A cube has all of its dimensions the same length, so you need only the length of one edge to find its volume.

For example, the drawing below shows a cube with an edge 4" long.

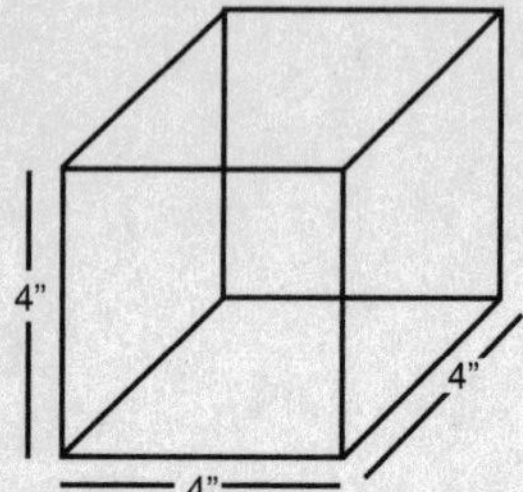

Its volume is calculated:
V = 4" × 4" × 4"
= 64 cu. in.

When you are calculating the volume of rectangular solids, shoe boxes, rooms, and so forth, be certain that you have measurements for each dimension before you calculate.

Volume of a Cylinder

Cylinders are objects we deal with all the time. Soft drink cans and many other containers, as well as pipes and smokestacks, are cylinders.

In many ways, a cylinder resembles a stack of coins, or a stack of round, thin objects such as cocktail coasters, or slices of bologna. By thinking of a cylinder as a stack of slices or coins, its is easy to remember how to calculate its volume.

The volume of a cylinder can be calculated by first finding the area of the circular base, and multiplying that value by the height.

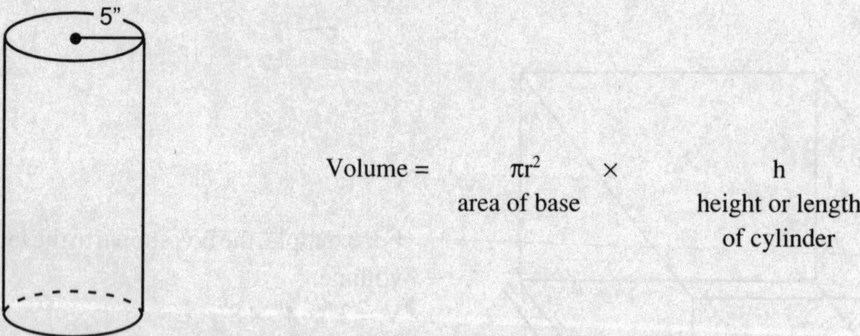

By finding the area of the base, you are finding the area of one "slice" of the cylinder. When you multiply that by the height or length, you are calculating volume by counting all of the "slices" that you could make.

For example, find the volume of the cylinder below:

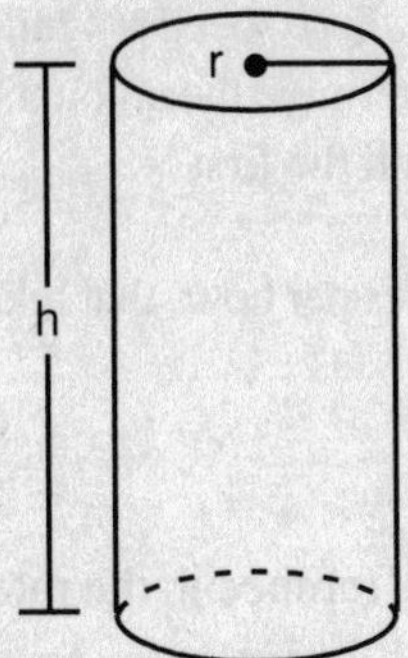

The radius of the base is 5". The height, or length, is 10".

$V = \pi r^2 h$
$V = \pi \times 5" \times 5" \times 10"$
$V = \pi \times 250$ cu. in.
$= 3.14 \times 250$ cu. in.
Volume = 785 cu. in.

As with area, you may find that the answer can be left in terms of pi. That is, it may not be necessary to multiply by 3.14. In the example above, the answer *V = 250π cubic inches* is acceptable.

Find the volumes of the cylinders below. Volume = $\pi r^2 h$. State your answers in terms of pi, as well as multiplied out. The answers are on page 293.

EXERCISE 50

1. r = 1", h = 1"
2. r = 2", h = 2"
3. r = 3.5", h = 6.20"
4. r = 1 ft., h = 2 ft.
5. r = 1.1 cm., h = 3.2 cm.
6. r = 10", h = 1"
7. r = .25", h = 1"
8. r = 20 cm., h = 70 cm.
9. r = .5", h = 1.0"
10. r = x", h = y"

WORD PROBLEMS

Two very common kinds of word problems that you will encounter on high school entrance examinations are *rate, time, and distance problems* and *work problems.*

Rate, Time, and Distance Problems

The basic formula used in solving problems for distance is:

d = rt (distance = rate × time)

Use this form when you know rate (speed) and time.

To find rate, use:

$$r = \frac{d}{t} \text{ (rate = distance ÷ time)}$$

To find time, use:

$$t = \frac{d}{r} \text{ (time = distance ÷ rate)}$$

Study the following problems:

EXAMPLE: Two hikers start walking from the city line at different times. The second hiker, whose speed is 4 miles per hour, starts 2 hours after the first hiker, whose speed is 3 miles per hour. Determine the amount of time and distance that will be consumed before the second hiker catches up with the first.

SOLUTION: Because the first hiker has a 2-hour head start and is walking at the rate of 3 miles per hour, that hiker is 6 miles from the city line when the second hiker starts.

$$\text{Rate} \times \text{Time} = \text{Distance}$$

Subtracting 3 miles per hour from 4 miles per hour gives us 1 mile per hour, or the difference in the rates of speed of the two hikers. In other words, the second hiker gains 1 mile on the first hiker in every hour.

Since there is a 6-mile difference to cut down and it is cut down 1 mile every hour, it is clear that the second hiker will need 6 hours to overtake the first.

In this time, the second hiker will have traveled $4 \times 6 = 24$, or 24 miles. The first hiker will have been walking 8 hours, because of the 2-hour headstart, $8 \times 3 = 24$, or 24 miles.

EXAMPLE: The same two hikers start walking toward each other along a road connecting two cities that are 60 miles apart. Their speeds are the same as in the preceding problems, 3 and 4 miles per hour, respectively. How much time will elapse before they meet?

SOLUTION: In each hour of travel toward each other, the hikers will cut down a distance equal to the sum of their speeds, $3 + 4 = 7$ miles per hour. To meet they must cut down 60 miles, and at 7 miles per hour this would be:

$$\frac{D}{R} = T \qquad \frac{60}{7} = 8\frac{4}{7} \text{ hours}$$

The problem might also have asked: "How much distance must the slower hiker cover before the two hikers meet?" In such a case we should have gone through the same steps plus one additional step:

The time consumed before meeting was $8\frac{4}{7}$ hours. To find the distance covered by the slower hiker, we merely multiply his rate by the time elapsed:

$$\text{R} \times \text{T} = \text{D} \qquad 3 \times 8\frac{4}{7} = 25\frac{5}{7}$$

Solve the problems below, using the formula for rate, time, and distance problems. The answers are on page 293.

EXERCISE 51

1. Matt walked 3 miles in $\frac{3}{4}$ of an hour. At what rate of speed did he walk in miles per hour?

2. A commuter train travels the distance from Acton to Boston in 1 hour and 10 minutes. If the train is traveling at an average speed of 48 miles per hour, what is the distance between the two cities?

3. Paddling 7 miles upstream, Sarah and her brother averaged 2 miles per hour. On the way back, their rate of speed was $3\frac{1}{2}$ miles per hour. How long did it take them to make the round trip?

4. Two cars begin driving toward each other from towns that are 150 miles apart. The first car is traveling 45 miles per hour, and the second is traveling 55 miles per hour. If each leaves at 2:15 PM, when will the two cars pass on the road?

Work Problems

Work problems generally involve two or more workers doing a job at different rates. The aim of work problems is to predict how long it will take to complete a job if the number of workers is increased or decreased. Work problems may also involve determining how fast pipes can fill or empty tanks. Study the examples in this section carefully.

EXAMPLE: If A does a job in six days, and B does the same job in three days, how long will it take the two of them, working together, to do the job?

SOLUTION: Problems of this sort can be done using fractions.

Step 1. Write the amount of the job each worker does each day as a fraction.

A does $\frac{1}{6}$ of the job in one day.

B does $\frac{1}{3}$ of the job in one day.

Step 2. Write the amount of the job completed by both workers in one day.

A $\frac{1}{6}$ of job

B $\frac{1}{3}$ of job

$$A + B = \frac{1}{6} + \frac{1}{3} = \frac{1}{2}$$

One half of the job is completed in one day by both workers working together.

Step 3. Compare the result from Step 2 to how much work has to be done. Because one half of the job is finished in one day, it will take two days for both workers to finish the job working together.

In general, if you are given the amount of time that a job takes, you must find the reciprocal of that time to find out how much of the job is completed in one day, one hour, and so on.

For example, if a job takes $2\frac{1}{2}$, or $\frac{5}{2}$ days, you could do $\frac{2}{5}$ of the job in one day.

If a job takes $4\frac{1}{2}$ hours, you could do $\frac{2}{9}$ of the job in one hour.

If you are given the fraction of the job completed in one day, find the reciprocal of the fraction to determine how long the whole job will take.

For example, if $\frac{2}{3}$ of a lawn can be mowed in an hour, the whole lawn will take $\frac{3}{2}$, or $1\frac{1}{2}$, hours to mow.

If $\frac{3}{4}$ of a job can be done in one day, the whole job can be done in $\frac{4}{3}$, or $1\frac{1}{3}$, days.

EXAMPLE: A and B, working together, do a job in $4\frac{1}{2}$ days. B, working alone, is able to do the job in 10 days. How long would it take A to do the job working alone?

SOLUTION: *Step 1.* The whole job takes $4\frac{1}{2}$, or $\frac{9}{2}$, days. B, working alone, can do $\frac{1}{10}$ of the job in one day.

Step 2. To find the work done by A in one day, subtract B's work from the amount of work done by the two workers together in one day:

$$\frac{2}{9} - \frac{1}{10} = \frac{20 - 9}{90} = \frac{11}{90}$$

$\frac{11}{90}$ represents the portion of the total job done by A in one day.

Step 3. Taking the reciprocal, find how long it would take A to do the entire job.

$$\frac{90}{11} = 8\frac{2}{11} \text{ days}$$

EXAMPLE: If A can do a job in 6 days that B can do in $5\frac{1}{2}$ days and C can do in $2\frac{1}{5}$ days, how long would the job take if A, B, and C were working together?

SOLUTION: A does the job in 6 days: $\frac{1}{6}$ of the job in 1 day.

B does the job in $5\frac{1}{2}$ days: $\frac{2}{11}$ of the job in 1 day.

C does the job in $2\frac{1}{5}$ days: $\frac{5}{11}$ of the job in 1 day.

Add the work done by A, B, and C in one day to find the work done by all three in one day:

$$\frac{1}{6} + \frac{2}{11} + \frac{5}{11} = \frac{11}{66} + \frac{12}{66} + \frac{30}{66} = \frac{53}{66}$$

Find the reciprocal of $\frac{53}{66}$ in order to find how long the total job would take:

$$\frac{66}{53} = 1\frac{13}{53} \text{ days}$$

EXAMPLE: One pipe can fill a pool in 20 minutes, a second can fill the pool in 30 minutes, and a third can fill it in 10 minutes. How long would it take the three together to fill the pool?

SOLUTION: First pipe fills the pool in 20 minutes: $\frac{1}{20}$ of pool in 1 minute.

Second pipe fills the pool in 30 minutes: $\frac{1}{30}$ of pool in 1 minute.

Third pipe fills the pool in 10 minutes: $\frac{1}{10}$ of pool in 1 minute.

Add the three fractions together to determine what part of the pool will be filled in one minute when the three pipes are working together.

$$\frac{1}{20} + \frac{1}{30} + \frac{1}{10} = \frac{3}{60} + \frac{2}{60} + \frac{6}{60} = \frac{11}{60}$$

If $\frac{11}{60}$ of the pool is filled in one minute, the reciprocal of the fraction will tell us how many minutes will be required to fill the whole pool.

$$\frac{60}{11} = 5\frac{5}{11} \text{ min.}$$

Solve the problems below using the solution steps shown for work problems. The answers may be found on page 293.

EXERCISE 52

1. Michelle and Barb can complete a job in 2 hours when working together. If Michelle requires 6 hours to do the job alone, how many hours does Barb need to do the job alone?

2. If John can do $\frac{1}{4}$ of a job in $\frac{3}{4}$ of a day, how many days will it take him to do the entire job?

3. It takes 1 and $\frac{3}{4}$ hours to fill a new underground gasoline storage tank. What part of the tank would be full if the gasoline had been shut off after 1 hour?

4. Mary can clean the house in 6 hours. Her younger brother Jim can do the same job in 9 hours. In how many hours can they do the job if they work together?

ANSWERS TO MATH EXERCISES

Exercise 1

1. 1,228
2. 289
3. 21,136
4. 34,361
5. 513
6. 1,520
7. 902
8. 138,021
9. 3,289
10. 289

Exercise 2

1. seventy-six ten-thousandths
2. eleven and three tenths
3. one thousand four hundred two and six hundred thirty-nine thousandths
4. seven thousand two hundred twenty-two dollars and ninety-three cents
5. fifty one-hundredths (five tenths)
6. five one-hundredths
7. sixteen and two thousand one hundred sixty-three ten-thousandths
8. twenty-nine hundred-thousandths
9. three and six ten-thousandths
10. sixty-two and three hundred ninety-one thousandths

Exercise 3

1. .5
2. 5.12
3. .07
4. equal
5. 10.7
6. 7.62
7. 3.009
8. equal

Exercise 4

1. 67.323
2. 5.1392
3. 110.0262
4. 103.7217
5. .0923
6. 9,666.988
7. 14.1854
8. 95.653
9. 790.3
10. 10.0

Exercise 5

1. lowest terms
2. $\frac{2}{3}$
3. $\frac{1}{6}$
4. lowest terms
5. $\frac{2}{3}$
6. $\frac{7}{8}$
7. $\frac{3}{8}$
8. lowest terms
9. $\frac{1}{12}$
10. $\frac{1}{6}$

Exercise 6

1. $\frac{20}{32}, \frac{25}{40}, \frac{10}{16}$
2. $\frac{28}{36}, \frac{63}{81}$
3. $\frac{12}{15}, \frac{16}{20}, \frac{36}{45}$
4. $\frac{4}{6}, \frac{18}{27}, \frac{22}{33}$
5. $\frac{2}{28}, \frac{3}{42}, \frac{6}{84}$
6. $\frac{15}{18}, \frac{20}{24}, \frac{30}{36}$
7. $\frac{26}{52}, \frac{38}{76}$
8. $\frac{12}{21}, \frac{20}{35}, \frac{28}{49}$
9. $\frac{6}{22}, \frac{24}{88}$
10. $\frac{4}{26}, \frac{8}{52}$

Exercise 7

1. $\frac{31}{8}$
2. $\frac{29}{10}$
3. $\frac{179}{15}$
4. $\frac{23}{3}$
5. $\frac{7}{4}$
6. $3\frac{1}{7}$
7. $5\frac{1}{3}$
8. $5\frac{5}{8}$
9. $4\frac{1}{2}$
10. $5\frac{1}{12}$

Exercise 8

1. C.D. = 20; $\frac{37}{20} = 1\frac{17}{20}$
2. C.D. = 8; $\frac{5}{8}$
3. C.D. = 21; $\frac{127}{21} = 6\frac{1}{21}$
4. C.D. = 36; $\frac{61}{36} = 1\frac{25}{36}$
5. C.D. = 72; $\frac{179}{72} = 3\frac{37}{72}$
6. C.D. = 39; $\frac{53}{39} = 1\frac{14}{39}$
7. C.D. = 63; $\frac{96}{63} = \frac{32}{21} = 1\frac{11}{21}$
8. C.D. = 8; $\frac{15}{8} = 1\frac{7}{8}$
9. C.D. = 6; $\frac{45}{6} = 7\frac{3}{6} = 7\frac{1}{2}$
10. C.D. = 143; $\frac{61}{143}$

Exercise 9

1. 605
2. 779
3. 321
4. 58,991
5. 190
6. 8,301
7. 8,868
8. 771
9. 889
10. 113,992

Exercise 10

1. 15.1798
2. .7676
3. .159
4. .156
5. 4.14
6. 24.848
7. 784.13
8. 37.5177
9. 29.827
10. 63.4215

Exercise 11

1. $\frac{11}{16}$
2. $\frac{1}{9}$
3. $\frac{91}{80} = 1\frac{11}{80}$
4. $\frac{302}{32} = 9\frac{14}{32} = 9\frac{7}{16}$
5. $\frac{23}{12} = 1\frac{11}{12}$
6. $\frac{9}{28}$
7. $\frac{139}{20} = 6\frac{19}{20}$
8. $\frac{1}{12}$
9. $\frac{28}{15} = 1\frac{13}{15}$
10. $\frac{47}{12} = 3\frac{11}{12}$

Exercise 12

1. 21,054
2. 462
3. 422,408
4. 69,632
5. 693,976
6. 369,600
7. 2,540,450
8. 25,606
9. 126,256
10. 94,792,384

Exercise 13

1. 2.6968869
2. 10,020.72
3. 53,389.468
4. 1.164
5. 2.6248
6. 163,930.66
7. .0009384
8. 117.432
9. 44.55703
10. 4,638.26

Exercise 14

1. $\frac{57}{48} = 1\frac{9}{48} = 1\frac{3}{16}$
2. $\frac{36}{70} = \frac{18}{35}$
3. $\frac{120}{5} = 24$
4. $\frac{429}{22} = 19\frac{11}{22} = 19\frac{1}{2}$
5. $\frac{72}{33} = 2\frac{6}{33} = 2\frac{2}{11}$
6. $\frac{300}{5} = 60$
7. $\frac{48}{1125} = \frac{16}{375}$
8. $\frac{3717}{72} = 51\frac{45}{72} = 51\frac{5}{8}$
9. $\frac{6}{24} = \frac{1}{4}$
10. $\frac{90}{40} = 2\frac{1}{4}$

Exercise 15

1. 180
2. 1.4
3. 15
4. 21
5. 2.3
6. 25
7. 2.5
8. 30

Exercise 16

1. 196
2. 13
3. $\frac{11}{9}$
4. 2.4
5. 10,000
6. 625
7. 400
8. $\frac{1}{2}$
9. 12
10. 6.25

Exercise 17

1. 82.277 or $82\frac{13}{47}$
2. 42.50 or $42\frac{1}{2}$
3. .379
4. 41.439 or $41\frac{61}{139}$
5. 10.855
6. 40.49
7. .817
8. 1.977
9. .844
10. 40.208 or $40\frac{5}{24}$

Exercise 18

1. .305
2. 5.760
3. 131.297
4. 17,902.394
5. .085
6. .737
7. .0098
8. 5.308
9. 141.626
10. .0019

Exercise 19

1. $\frac{21}{16} = 1\frac{5}{16}$
2. $\frac{38}{20} = 1\frac{18}{20} = 1\frac{9}{10}$
3. $\frac{78}{144} = \frac{13}{24}$
4. $\frac{72}{1064} = \frac{9}{133}$
5. $\frac{144}{255} = \frac{48}{85}$
6. $\frac{3111}{3} = 1037$
7. $\frac{4}{30} = \frac{2}{15}$
8. $\frac{16}{63}$
9. $\frac{3}{16}$
10. $\frac{20}{30} = \frac{2}{3}$

Exercise 20

1. .80
2. $\frac{3}{4}$
3. .28
4. .333
5. $\frac{87}{200}$
6. $\frac{9}{50}$
7. .30
8. $\frac{9}{20}$
9. $\frac{1}{8}$
10. .26

Exercise 21

1. 3.27
2. 1.02
3. 8.2
4. $\frac{216}{12} = 18$
5. 3.31
6. 25.294
7. –1.15
8. .711
9. $\frac{261}{70} = 3\frac{51}{70}$
10. 21.95

Exercise 22

1. Wednesday, 10 miles farther, 10% farther
2. Thursday, 40 miles farther, 40% farther
3. Friday, 0 miles farther, 0% farther
4. Saturday, 1 mile less, 1% less
5. Sunday, 10 miles less, 10% less

Exercise 23

1. 50% larger
2. 27% smaller
3. 20% smaller
4. 99% smaller
5. 99.5% smaller
6. 100% larger
7. 350% larger
8. 99.99% smaller

Exercise 24

1. $.10 \times 8 = .8$
2. $.25 \times 60 = 15$
3. $.11 \times 10 = 1.1$
4. $.01 \times 350 = 3.50$
5. $.99 \times 80 = 79.2$
6. $.33 \times 33 = 10.89$
7. $.75 \times 112 = 84$
8. $.50 \times 200 = 100$

Exercise 25

1. .01
2. .012
3. .005
4. 5%
5. .1% or $\frac{1}{10}$ of one percent
6. .3% or $\frac{3}{10}$ of one percent
7. .015
8. 1.5%
9. .15
10. .01% or $\frac{1}{100}$ of one percent

Exercise 26

1. 50%; 150%
2. 100%; 200%
3. 50%; 150%
4. 32%; 132%
5. 20%; 120%
6. 50%; 150%
7. 50%; 150%
8. $33\frac{1}{3}\%$; $133\frac{1}{3}\%$
9. 0%; 100%
10. 900%; 1000%

Exercise 27

1. $\frac{21}{32}$ or .656
2. $\frac{3}{8}$ or .375
3. $\frac{4}{15}$ or .267
4. $\frac{243}{200}$ or 1.215
5. $2\frac{2}{9}$ or 2.22
6. $1\frac{11}{50}$ or 1.22

Exercise 28

1. 12.6
2. .1875
3. 1.875
4. 50%
5. 400%
6. $16\frac{2}{3}\%$
7. .0525
8. 240
9. 78
10. 90
11. 1.25
12. 66.6%
13. 150
14. 69.33

Exercise 29

1. 10 • 10 • 10 • 10 • 10 • 10 • 10
2. 1 • 1 • 1
3. 3 • 3
4. $\frac{1}{2} \bullet \frac{1}{2} \bullet \frac{1}{2} \bullet \frac{1}{2}$
5. (.45) (.45) (.45) (.45) (.45)
6. 11 • 11
7. 0 • 0
8. x • x • x
9. b • b • b • b • b • b • b • b
10. (ab) (ab) (ab) (ab) (ab)

Exercise 30

1. $1^{3-2} = 1$
2. $6^{10-8} = 6^2$
3. $15^{5+3} = 15^8$
4. $M^{3+3} = M^6$
5. $10^{10-8} = 10^2$
6. $3^{6+2} = 3^8$
7. $a^{2+3} = a^5$
8. $100^{10-9} = 100^1 = 100$
9. $\left(\frac{3}{4}\right)^{3+2} = \left(\frac{3}{4}\right)^5$
10. $8^{5-4} = 8^1 = 8$
11. $a^{5-3} = a^2$
12. $\left(\frac{1}{2}\right)^{5-4} = \frac{1^1}{2} = \frac{1}{2}$
13. x^{3+a}
14. y^{b-c}

Exercise 31

1. –11
2. 1.3995
3. .999
4. 31
5. $2\frac{4}{15}$
6. –10.75
7. $-1\frac{3}{8}$
8. –120.25
9. –1.7498
10. 0

Exercise 32

1. –1
2. 2
3. –4.6
4. 9.1
5. 7.652
6. 2
7. –.0029
8. –5.5
9. $10\frac{1}{6}$
10. 0

Exercise 33

1. 30
2. 3.25
3. $-\frac{9}{8} = -1\frac{1}{8}$
4. $-\frac{4}{21}$
5. –.09
6. $-\frac{5}{12}$
7. 35.3298
8. $-100\frac{3}{8}$
9. –.0325
10. $-\frac{5}{9}$

Exercise 34

1. -15
2. -2
3. -2.15
4. $-.007$
5. -12.2
6. $\frac{1}{2}$ or $.5$
7. -7
8. 200.02
9. -1
10. 400

Exercise 35

1. $9a$
2. $34x$
3. $3m + 4r + 3s$
4. b
5. $.5r + s$
6. $1\frac{1}{15}m - \frac{1}{2}t$
7. $-1.039S$
8. $-15.75k$ or $-15\frac{3}{4}k$
9. $2x - 3y - 4z$
10. $.4p - 40r$

Exercise 36

1. $-7d$
2. $3\frac{1}{2}x$
3. $-2b - 6y$
4. 0
5. $-3.50m$
6. $-.001x$
7. $-7.483f$
8. $-\frac{1}{8}r$
9. $-2r - 3p$
10. $2x$

Exercise 37

1. $6x^2$
2. $1\frac{1}{3}y^2$
3. $-4.8a^2$
4. $-6z^3$
5. $1.03121r^3$
6. $-5.84f^4$
7. $\frac{5}{21}z^3$
8. $-\frac{5}{64}m^3$
9. $-2.222x^4$
10. $-71.71b^4$

Exercise 38

1. $14xy$
2. $2\frac{1}{4}a^2b^2$
3. $1.56df$
4. $22.5x^2y$
5. $-22.08a^2b$
6. $-100a^2bc$
7. $-6\frac{1}{2}qr^2$
8. $-x^2y^2z^2$
9. $24x^2y^2z$
10. $-30abc$

Exercise 39

1. $10c$
2. -5
3. $-2y$
4. $-2ab$
5. $-2ab$
6. $-3a$
7. $-3x^2$
8. $-.1y$
9. $4r$
10. -2

Exercise 40

1. 1
2. -7
3. $a + b - 4$
4. 2
5. -9
6. $2a + b - 6$

Exercise 41

1. 3
2. –7
3. 1
4. 256
5. $5\frac{1}{2}$
6. a^2
7. $\frac{7}{9}$
8. 5.25
9. 102.4
10. 4

Exercise 42

1. $a = 3$
2. $x = 4$
3. $x = -3$
4. $r = 2$
5. $b = 4$
6. $y = 1$
7. $x = -5$

Exercise 43

1. $x = 12$
2. $x = 3$
3. $x = 4$
4. $x = \frac{1}{2}$
5. $x = 20$
6. $x = 6$
7. $x = 26\frac{2}{3}$
8. $a = -3\frac{1}{2}$
9. $b = 0$
10. $m = 1$

Exercise 44

1. obtuse; 10°
2. acute; 150°, 60°
3. obtuse; 38°
4. acute; 120°, 30°
5. right; 90°, no complement
6. acute; 153°, 63°
7. obtuse; 45°
8. obtuse; 85°
9. acute; 123°, 33°
10. acute; 135°, 45°

Exercise 45

1. 10.99"
2. 15.7"
3. 7"
4. $7\frac{6}{7}$"
5. 10"
6. 5"

Exercise 46

1. 6 sq. in.
2. 7 sq. ft.
3. 100 sq. cm.
4. $\frac{9}{10}$ sq. mi.
5. 144 sq. in., or 1 sq. ft.
6. 9 sq. ft., or 1 sq. yd.
7. 5 sq. in.
8. $\frac{9}{16}$ sq. in.

Exercise 47

1. 64 sq. in.
2. $4\frac{1}{2}$ sq. ft.
3. 25.875 sq. cm.
4. 7.56 sq. ft.
5. $\frac{5}{6}$ sq. ft. or 120 sq. in.
6. $2\frac{17}{24}$ sq. yd.

Exercise 48

1. 24 sq. in.
2. 10 sq. in.
3. $37\frac{1}{2}$ sq. in.
4. 180 sq. cm.
5. 13.7775 sq. ft.
6. 18 sq. in.

Exercise 49

1. 4.71 π sq. in., or 14.79 sq. in.
2. 12.25 π sq. cm., or 38.47 sq. cm.
3. 25 π sq. ft., or 78.5 sq. ft.
4. 100 π sq. yds., or 314 sq. yds.
5. 484 π sq. in., or 1519.76 sq. in.
6. 30.25 π sq. in., or 94.985 sq. in.
7. $\frac{1}{4}$ π sq. cm. or .785 sq. cm.
8. 2500 π sq. cm., or 7850 sq. cm.
9. r = 5; A = 25 π sq. in., or 78.5 sq. in.
10. r = 20; A = 400 π sq. mi., 1256 sq. mi.

Exercise 50

1. π cu. in., or 3.14 cu. in.
2. 8 π cu. in., or 25.12 cu. in.
3. 75.95 π cu. in.; 238.48 cu. in.
4. 2 π cu. ft.; 6.28 cu. ft.
5. 3.872 π cu. cm.; 12.158 cu. cm.
6. 100 π cu. in.; 314 cu. in.
7. .0625 π cu. in.; .19625 cu. in.
8. 28,000 π cu. cm.; 87,920 cu. cm.
9. .25 π cu. in.; .785 cu. in.
10. πx^2y cu. in; $3.14x^2y$ cu. in.

Exercise 51

1. 4 miles per hour
2. 56 miles
3. $5\frac{1}{2}$ hours
4. 3:45 PM

Exercise 52

1. 3 hours
2. 3 days
3. $\frac{4}{7}$
4. $3\frac{3}{5}$ hours

HOW DO I ESTIMATE THE ANSWER?

In multiple-choice math questions, the answer is in front of you. You don't need to calculate it; you only need to recognize it. The problem may be much simpler than it looks or reads. In fact, if it looks as if the calculation will be very long or complicated, you are probably heading down the wrong track. High school entrance exams are not meant to be tests of your computational skills; they are testing your understanding of concepts and ability to apply that understanding. Leave your pencil on the desk for a moment and start with common sense:

EXAMPLE: 3.01 + 10.73 + 2.01 + .781 =

(A) 13.522

(B) 16.531

(C) 20.860

(D) 36.036

Note that in this case it is best *not* to proceed by writing down the numbers to be added, adding them, and then checking your answer against those supplied. Calculating the answer in this way would waste valuable time that could be used later on.

A question such as the one above is best answered in the following manner:

---

1. Read the question, and note that it is a decimal addition problem. DON'T CALCULATE YET.
2. Read the possible answers; notice the range they cover.
3. Estimate the sum of the four numbers as 3 + 11 + 2 + 1 = 17
4. Note that answer **(B)** is the only answer anywhere near a sum of 17. Choose it as the correct answer.

AVOID THE TRAPS!

Don't get bogged down in calculations. Estimate wherever you can.

Or, even simpler:

---

1. Read the question and note that it is a decimal addition problem. DON'T CALCULATE YET.
2. Look at the four addends. Note that three have digits two places to the right of the decimal point and that only one has a digit in the thousandths place. That digit is a "1".
3. Look at the four answer choices. Concentrate on the digit in the thousandths place.
4. Choose **(B)** as the only possible correct answer, and move on quickly to the next question.

WHEN MUST I CALCULATE?

There will be some problems that will require you to use a pencil and paper (no calculators, alas!). You may be able to estimate an answer to those questions, but the choices given will make estimating too risky.

We suggest you calculate the answer when:

- the answer choices differ only very slightly.
- the problem requires three or more steps, making it difficult to remember accurately your intermediate steps.
- you have to change larger units into smaller ones, or vice versa, for purposes of calculation. It is easy to lose track of units within the English system of measurements when working with time, units of measurement, and so on.

LEARNING EXERCISES: MATHEMATICS

The questions in this section are arranged in boxes called "frames." The answer for each frame will be found in the box to the left of the question frame.

First, cover the answer boxes with a strip of paper. Circle your answer to the question. Then, move the paper down to expose the answer to that question.

EXPLANATION	PROBLEM
1. **(C)** The reciprocal of a fraction is the fraction "turned upside down." $1\frac{2}{3}$ is equivalent to $\frac{5}{3}$. The reciprocal of $\frac{5}{3}$ is $\frac{3}{5}$. The correct answer is (C). Choice (D) is a distractor. Because x has a precise value in the problem, we must choose an answer having a precise value.	**1.** Where $x = 1\frac{2}{3}$, the reciprocal of x equals (A) $\frac{2}{3}$ (B) $\frac{5}{3}$ (C) $\frac{3}{5}$ (D) $\frac{1}{x}$
2. **(B)** The product of any number and its reciprocal is 1. Therefore, $\frac{7}{16} \bullet \frac{16}{7} = 1$, and (B) is the correct choice. Even if you didn't know this rule, you could have examined the answers and eliminated both (A), because the product was greater than 1, and (D), because the product was less than 1. Answer (C) is equivalent to (B), but because it is *not* in lowest terms, it is a second choice.	**2.** The product of $\frac{7}{16}$ and a number x is 1. The number is (A) $1\frac{7}{16}$ (B) $\frac{16}{7}$ (C) $\frac{32}{14}$ (D) 1

EXPLANATION	PROBLEM
3. (A) This problem looks much harder than it really is. The numerator of this complex fraction is the same as the denominator. When numerator and denominator are equivalent, the fraction is equal to 1. (A) is the correct answer.	**3.** $\dfrac{\frac{1}{x}+1}{1+\frac{1}{x}}$ is equivalent to (A) 1 (B) $\dfrac{1}{x}$ (C) $\dfrac{1}{x}+2$ (D) $1+x$
4. (D) This is a complex fraction requiring all of your skills in working with fractions. To estimate the correct answer, note that the numerator is slightly larger than 1 $\left(\frac{2}{3}+\frac{3}{8}>1\right)$, and the denominator is equivalent to $\frac{4}{16}-\frac{3}{16}$, or $\frac{1}{16}$. Therefore, a number slightly larger than 1 divided by $\frac{1}{16}$ is slightly larger than 16. The closest answer is (D) $\frac{50}{3}$, which is equivalent to $16\frac{2}{3}$. To solve the problem by calculation, simplify the numerator and denominator, and then divide.	**4.** $\dfrac{\frac{2}{3}+\frac{3}{8}}{\frac{1}{4}-\frac{3}{16}}$ equals (A) $15\frac{2}{3}$ (B) $\dfrac{25}{16}$ (C) $\dfrac{13}{32}$ (D) $\dfrac{50}{3}$
5. (B) This is a problem in which you must substitute the values given into the formula. Once you do that, it is a simple problem. $L=\frac{3}{4}\bullet 2\bullet 7\bullet \frac{1}{2}$ $=\dfrac{3\bullet 2\bullet 7\bullet 1}{4\bullet 2}=\dfrac{42}{8}=\dfrac{21}{4}$ Therefore, (B) is the correct answer. The other answers would have resulted if you had forgotten to multiply one of the numbers in the numerator. Answer (D) might have been chosen by someone who didn't know what to do but thought the most difficult-looking answer would be the best.	**5.** In the formula $L=\frac{3}{4}bxh$, if $b=2$, $x=7$, and $h=\frac{1}{2}$, L equals (A) $\dfrac{21}{2}$ (B) $\dfrac{21}{4}$ (C) $\dfrac{21}{8}$ (D) $\dfrac{7x}{4}$

EXPLANATION	PROBLEM
6. **(A)** The sum of the angles of a triangle is always 180°. The correct answer, therefore, is (A), because 45° + 75° + 60° = 180°. Answers (B), (C), and (D) give sums larger or smaller than 180° when added to 45° and 75°.	**6.** Two angles of a triangle are 45° and 75°. What is the measure of the third angle? (A) 60° (B) 35° (C) 180° (D) 45°
7. **(C)** Note that the base of the triangle is the same as the diameter of the circle. Because ΔABC is isosceles, its altitude is the same length as the radius of the circle. Use the formula for the area of a triangle, and substitute the correct values: $A = \frac{1}{2}ba$ $= \frac{1}{2} \bullet 10 \bullet 5$ $= 25 \text{ cm}^2$ The correct answer, then, is (C). (A) is the area of the circle.	**7.** 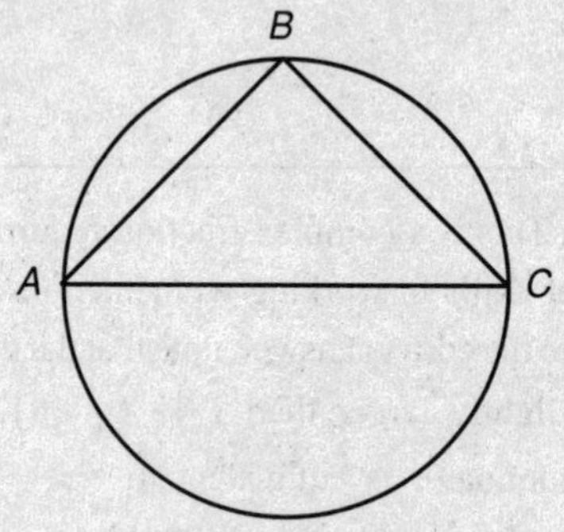 B A C Isosceles ΔABC is inscribed in a circle that has a diameter of 10 centimeters. The area of the triangle is (A) 78.5 sq. cm. (B) 12.5 sq. cm. (C) 25 sq. cm. (D) 50 sq. cm.
8. **(D)** These measurements describe a large rectangular room 30 feet high. Use the formula V = 1 • w • h to find the volume: V = 75 feet • 50 feet • 30 feet = 112,500 cubic feet The correct answer is (D). Answers (B) and (C) use the wrong units. Volume is always measured in *cubic* units.	**8.** The volume of a small warehouse measuring 75 feet long, 50 feet wide, and 30 feet high is (A) 1,112,500 cubic feet (B) 112,500 square feet (C) 112,500 feet (D) 112,500 cubic feet

EXPLANATION	PROBLEM
9. (A) A store markup of 100% would exactly double the price. An 80% markup almost doubles the price. The \$14 jeans are priced at almost double their cost to the store. By estimation, the best answer is (A). To figure precisely, remember that an 80% markup is the equivalent of multiplying the cost by 180%, or 1.80. cost • 1.80 = 14.00 cost = 14.00 ÷ 1.80 cost = \$7.78	**9.** A department store marks up its clothing 80% over cost. If it sells blue jeans for \$14, how much did the store pay for them? (A) \$7.78 (B) \$17.50 (C) \$11.20 (D) \$1.12
10. (B) Reduce the \$14.00 price by 25%. 25% of 14.00 = \$14 × .25 = \$3.50 \$14.00 – 3.50 = \$10.50 (new price) Therefore, (B) is the correct answer. Answer (A) indicates a reduction of only twenty-five cents. Answer (C) represents a reduction *to* 25% of the original price, or a 75% decrease in price.	**10.** The same store puts the same \$14 jeans on sale at a 25% discount. What is the new selling price? (A) \$13.75 (B) \$10.50 (C) \$3.50 (D) \$13.65
11. (D) Substitute .25 into the problem. $= (.25)^2 + \sqrt{.25}$ $= .0625 + .5$ $= .5625$ The correct answer is (D). This might be a good time to review the table of squares and square roots on pages 239 and 240. Answer (A) would have resulted if you had squared .25, gotten .625, and added it to .5. $(.25)^2 = .0625$. Answer (B) would have resulted if you had squared .25 correctly, but thought the square root of .25 was .05. Answer (C) would have resulted if you had made errors in both steps.	**11.** If $y = .25$, the value of $y^2 + \sqrt{y}$ is (A) 1.125 (B) .1125 (C) .6750 (D) .5625

EXPLANATION

12. **(C)** The finance charge will be the sum of $1\frac{1}{2}\%$ of \$500, plus 1% of \$250. You can write this as follows:

$$(.015 \bullet 500) + (.01 \bullet 250)$$

$$= 7.50 + 2.50 = \$10.00$$

Answer (C) is correct. You can estimate the answer if you remember that percent means "hundredths of." One one hundredth of \$500 is \$5.00; one one hundredth of \$250 is \$2.50. The only answer near this sum is (C). Answers (B) and (D) would have resulted if you had misplaced a decimal point.

PROBLEM

12. The monthly finance charge on a charge account is $1\frac{1}{2}\%$ on the unpaid amount up to \$500, and 1% on the unpaid amount over \$500. What is the finance charge on an unpaid amount of \$750?

(A) \$22.50

(B) \$1.00

(C) \$10.00

(D) \$100.00

---

13. **(B)** Begin removing the *innermost* grouping symbols, rewriting each time a set of symbols is removed.

Step 1. 1 – [5 + (3 – 2)]

Step 2. 2 – [5 + 1]

Step 3. 1 – [6]

Step 4. 1 – 6 = –5

Answer (B) is correct. A minus sign in front of a bracket or parenthesis reverses the sign of the number inside. A positive sign does not.

13. Simplify: 1 – [5 + (3 – 2)]

(A) –3

(B) –5

(C) 6

(D) 0

---

14. **(A)**

Step 1. –3 – [–2 + (5 – 6) – 3]

Step 2. –3 – [–2 + (–1) – 3]

Step 3. –3 – [–2 – 1 – 3]

Step 4. –3 – [–6]

Step 5. –3 + 6 = +3

A minus sign in front of a bracket or parenthesis reverses the sign of the number inside. A positive sign does not.

14. Simplify:

–3 – [–2 + (5 – 6) – 3]

(A) +3

(B) –1

(C) +1

(D) –3

EXPLANATION	PROBLEM
15. (B) Each point on the line has a coordinate on the horizontal axis and one on the vertical axis. The coordinates of points located at the lower right part of the graph are low cost per item and large numbers of items manufactured. Therefore, interpret this graph to mean that where larger numbers of items are manufactured, the cost per item is lower. The correct answer is (B).	**15.** 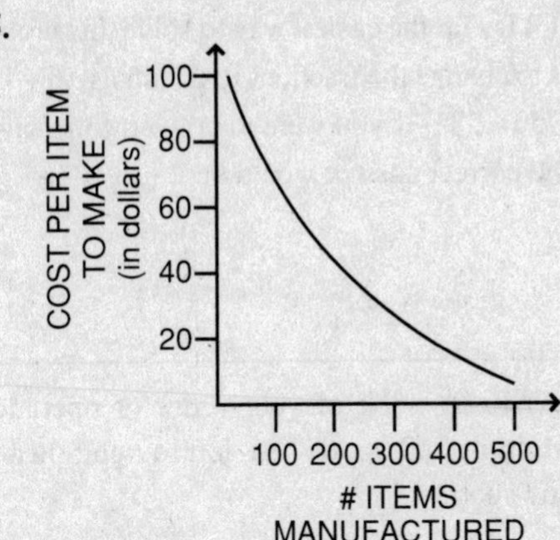 The graph above shows (A) more items cost more money to make (B) by making more items, the production cost per item is lower (C) there is a limit to the number of items that can be made (D) none of the above
16. (B) Find 300 on the horizontal axis. Draw a vertical line upward until you touch the line. Move horizontally from this point on the line to the vertical axis. Note that you touch the vertical axis at a point roughly equivalent to \$28. The correct answer is (B). We suggest you use a straight edge to sketch your line.	**16.** Based upon the graph above, what is the cost per item if 300 items are manufactured? (A) \$40 (B) \$28 (C) \$20 (D) >\$20
17. (B) Find 100 on the horizontal axis and follow the same procedure as above. The coordinate on the vertical axis is approximately \$75.	**17.** If the company produced only 100 items, approximately how much would each item cost? (A) \$100 (B) \$75 (C) \$10 (D) \$60
18. (D) Find the approximate location of \$5–\$10 on the vertical axis. Try to follow a horizontal path across until you hit the line of the graph. Note that your path does not intersect the line. Therefore, the graph does not predict the information asked for. The correct answer is (D).	**18.** How many items would have to be manufactured to bring the cost to between \$5 and \$10 per item? (A) fewer than 100 (B) 1000 (C) 2,000 (D) insufficient information available

EXPLANATION	PROBLEM
19. (C) By far the easiest way to solve this problem is to change the fractions to decimals: .6 + 1.5 + .75 = 2.85. If you were to convert to fractions, the correct answer would be $2\frac{17}{20}$.	**19.** $.6 + 1\frac{1}{2} + \frac{3}{4} =$ (A) 2.31 (B) 2.52 (C) 2.85 (D) $2\frac{13}{20}$
20. (A) Keep track of your order of operations. Multiply and divide first, left to right; then add and subtract. $\left(\frac{2}{3} \bullet \frac{3}{2}\right) + \left(\frac{1}{4} \div \frac{1}{3}\right) - \frac{7}{12}$ $1 + \frac{3}{4} - \frac{7}{12} = \frac{14}{12} = \frac{7}{6}$	**20.** $\frac{2}{3} \bullet \frac{3}{2} + \frac{1}{4} \div \frac{1}{3} - \frac{7}{12} =$ (A) $\frac{7}{6}$ (B) $2\frac{2}{3}$ (C) $\frac{19}{6}$ (D) none of the above
21. (B) Be careful in counting places and in positioning the decimal point.	**21.** 6 ÷ .0006 = (A) .0036 (B) 10,000 (C) 60,000 (D) 100,000
22. (C) The area of the shaded portion is equal to the area of the square, less the area of the circle. The length of the side of the square is equal to the diameter of the circle. Therefore, using $\frac{22}{7}$ for pi: $(4" \times 4") - (\pi 2^2) = 16$ sq. in. $- \frac{88}{7}$ sq. in. $= 3\frac{3}{7}$ sq. in. The correct answer is (C). If you answered (D) $4\frac{3}{7}$, check your skills in subtracting fractions from whole numbers.	**22.** 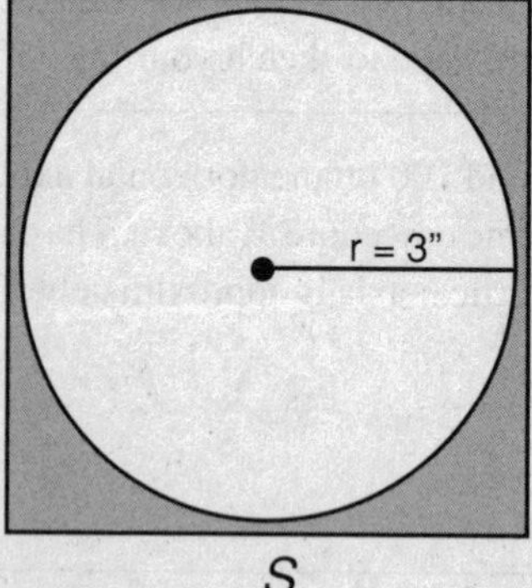 S The square above has a side 4" long. The area of the shaded portion is (A) $\frac{22}{7}$ sq. in. (B) 16 sq. in. (C) $3\frac{3}{7}$ sq. in. (D) $4\frac{3}{7}$ sq. in.

EXPLANATION	PROBLEM
23. **(C)** The long way to solve this problem is to multiply both the numerator and denominator out, and then divide. If you notice that 100^4 can also be written as 10^8, the answer is obviously (C). $100^4 = 10^2 \bullet 100^3 = 10^2 \bullet 10^2 \bullet 100^2 = 10^2 \bullet 10^2 \bullet 10^2 \bullet 100 = 10^2 \bullet 10^2 \bullet 10^2 \bullet 10^2 = 10^8$	**23.** Evaluate: $\frac{100^4}{10^8}$ (A) 10^2 (B) 1000 (C) 1 (D) 10^{12}
24. **(B)** Substitute 3 for x. The problem, then, is to compute 3^5. $3^5 = 3 \bullet 3 \bullet 3 \bullet 3 \bullet 3$ $= 243$ The correct answer is (B). Answer (C) would have resulted if you had multiplied 5×3, instead of 3 times itself 5 times.	**24.** What is the value of x^5, if $x = 3$? (A) 81 (B) 243 (C) 15 (D) 35
25. **(B)** For each teacher, there are 14 students. Because there are 14 teachers, there must be 14×14, or 196, students.	**25.** The ratio of teachers to students in a certain school is 1:14. If there are fourteen teachers in the school, how many students are there? (A) 14 (B) 196 (C) 206 (D) 176
26. **(C)** The ratio of men to women is 15:12, but this ratio must be expressed in lowest terms. Because 15 and 12 have 3 as a common factor, the ratio expressed correctly is 5:4. Answer (C) is the correct choice. The ratio of women to men is 12:15 or 4:5.	**26.** Of 27 people in a certain group, fifteen are men and twelve are women. What is the ratio of men to women? (A) 15:12 (B) 12:15 (C) 5:4 (D) 27:12

EXPLANATION	PROBLEM
27. **(B)** To find the perimeter, we add up the dimensions of all of the sides. Note that there are some parts that have not been assigned measurements, so we have to infer that they are the same as those corresponding parts whose measurements have been designated. Beginning at the bottom and moving clockwise, the dimensions are: 5" + 7" + 1" + 3" + 3" + 3" +1" + 7" These equal 30 inches. The correct answer is (B). If you chose (A), (D), or (C), you failed to add up all of the segments.	**27.** 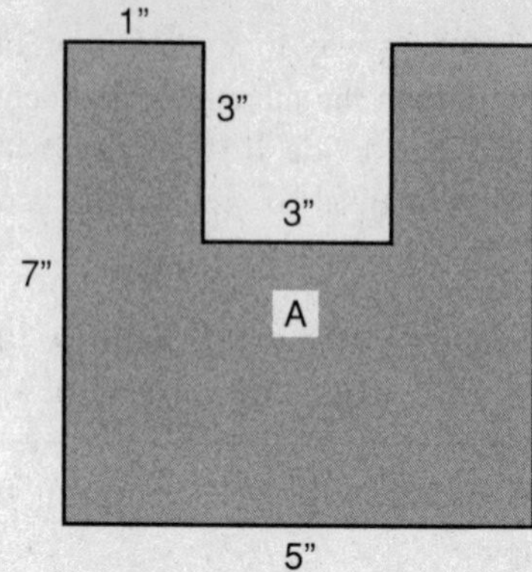 The perimeter of figure A is (A) 19 in. (B) 30 in. (C) 23 sq. in. (D) 19 sq. in.
28. **(A)** The area is most easily found by multiplying the length of the figure by its width, and then subtracting the area of the small 3" × 3" square. (7" × 5") – (3" × 3") = area 35 sq. in. – 9 sq. in. = 26 sq. in. Shapes such as this are often used for irregular pieces of carpeting or covering. **29.** **(B)** The surface of a rectangular solid such as a brick is found by calculating the area of each face of the brick and finding the sum of the areas of the faces. The brick has six faces: Two faces 6" × 3"; total 36 sq. in. Two faces 6" × 2"; total 24 sq. in. Two faces 3" × 2"; total 12 sq. in. Total 72 sq. in. The correct answer is (B). Answer (D) is wrong because it is not written in square units.	**28.** The area of figure A is (A) 26 sq. in. (B) 19 sq. in. (C) 44 sq. in. (D) 30 sq. in. **29.** The surface area of a brick with the dimensions 6" × 3" × 2" is (A) 36 sq. in. (B) 72 sq. in. (C) 128 sq. in. (D) 72 in.

EXPLANATION	PROBLEM
30. **(D)** Calculate the surface area of the cube. It has six faces, each 2" × 2". Its surface area, then, is 6 × 4 sq. in. or 24 sq. in. Its volume is found by multiplying its length × width × height, or 2" × 2" × 2" = 8 cu. in. The ratio of surface area to volume is 24:8, or 3:1.	**30.** The ratio of surface area to volume of a cube having an edge of two inches is (A) 2:3 (B) 1:3 (C) 6:1 (D) 3:1
31. **(C)** The Pythagorean Theorem is used to find the length of the sides of right triangles. The square of the length of the longest side (the hypotenuse) is equal to the sum of the squares of the other two sides. Once we know the square of the length of the longest side, it is easy to find the length. $(\overline{AC})^2 = (\overline{AB})^2 + (\overline{BC})^2$ $(\overline{AC})^2 = 3^2 + 4^2$ $(\overline{AC})^2 = 25$ $\overline{AC} = \sqrt{25} = 5$	**31.** 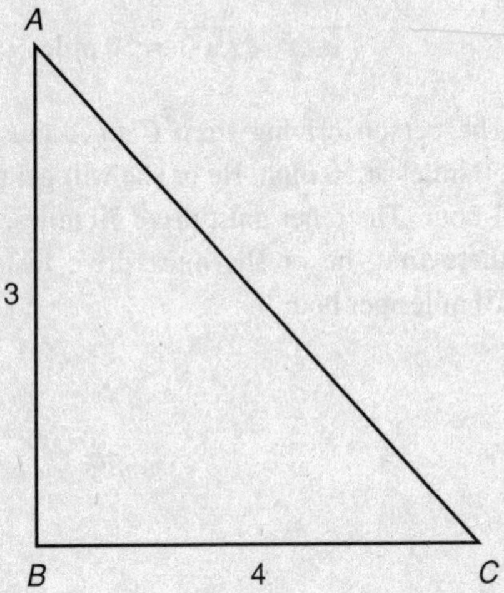 A, 3, B, 4, C The length of $\overline{AC}$ in the triangle above is (A) 4.5 (B) 3.5 (C) 5 (D) 4

EXPLANATION	PROBLEM

32. **(D)** This is a two-step problem. First, find the length of the hypotenuse, so you know how far the other person is driving.

$$(\overline{AC})^2 = (\overline{AB})^2 + (\overline{BC})^2$$
$$= (40)^2 + (30)^2$$
$$= 1600 + 900$$
$$\overline{AC} = \sqrt{2500} = 50 \text{ miles}$$

The person driving from C to A must drive 50 miles at 50 mph. He or she will get there in 1 hour. The other must drive 70 miles. To get there first, he or she must drive faster than 70 miles per hour.

32.

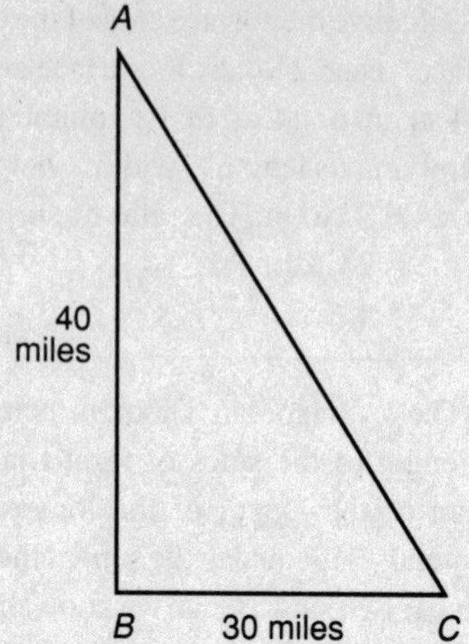

Two drivers begin at point C simultaneously. One drives from C to B to A. The other drives directly to A at 50 mph. How fast must the first person drive to get to A first?

(A) less than 50 mph

(B) less than 60 mph

(C) less than 70 mph

(D) more than 70 mph

33. **(B)** This is a simple division problem. Divide 1.0 by .25. The correct answer is (B). Here is another way to solve this problem. Since .25 = $\frac{1}{4}$, the reciprocal of $\frac{1}{4}$ is 4.

33. If $x = .25$, $\frac{1}{x} =$

(A) $\frac{1}{25}$

(B) 4

(C) $\frac{1}{4}$

(D) 1

EXPLANATION	PROBLEM
34. **(C)** A straight line represents a "straight angle" of 180°. An angle of 60° is given, so $\angle C$ must be 120° to complete the line. Knowing that all the angles in a triangle added together equal 180°, $\angle A + \angle B + \angle C = 180°$; $\angle A + 35° + 120° = 180°$; $\angle A = 180° - 155°$; $\angle A = 25°$	**34.** 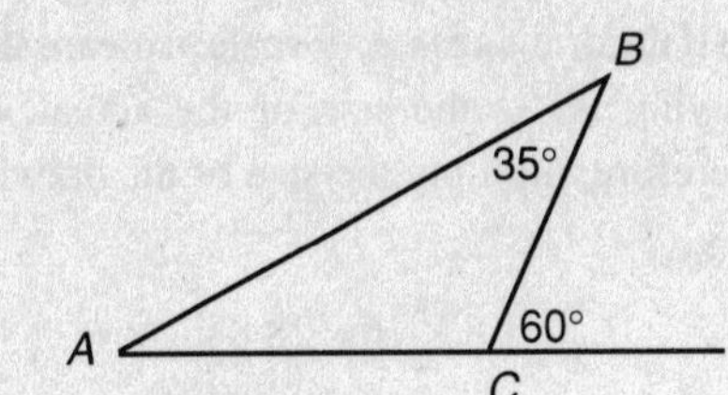 The measure of angle A is (A) 15° (B) 20° (C) 25° (D) 35°
35. **(B)** The boy's age is M years. His older brother is $M + 6$ years old, and his younger sister is $M - 4$ years old. Adding the three ages together, $M + (M + 6) + (M - 4) = 3M + 2$ The correct answer is (B).	**35.** A boy M years old has a brother six years older and a sister four years younger. The combined age of the three is (A) $M + 10$ (B) $3M + 2$ (C) $3M - 2$ (D) $2M - 6$
36. **(D)** This is a *literal problem* requiring you to "think without numbers." Creating mental pictures may help you solve this type of problem. If each person in a group makes L number of things, the group's output will be the product of the number of people in the group and the number of things each makes. Answer (D) represents the product and is the correct choice.	**36.** If A number of people each make L things, the total number of things made is (A) $A \div L$ (B) $A + L$ (C) $A - L$ (D) AL
37. **(A)** This problem asks you to find speed or rate. Speed or rate is found by dividing the distance traveled by the time required. The choice in which distance is divided by time is (A).	**37.** If a man runs M miles in T hours, his speed is (A) $M \div T$ (B) $M + T$ (C) $M - T$ (D) MT
38. **(B)** R rooms each with S square feet contain a total of RS square feet. Because there are 144 square inches in each square foot, the rooms contain $144RS$ square inches.	**38.** How many square inches are there in R rooms, each having S square feet? (A) RS (B) $144RS$ (C) $9 \div RS$ (D) $S + R$

EXPLANATION	PROBLEM
39. **(B)** If the drawing is at $\frac{1}{16}$ scale, it means that the drawing is $\frac{1}{16}$ the size of the actual wheel. Therefore, multiply the size of the drawing by 16. $1.8 \times 16 = 28.8$ inches Answer (B) is correct.	**39.** The drawing of a wheel in a book is done at $\frac{1}{16}$ scale. If the drawing is 1.8 inches in diameter, how big is the wheel? (A) 32" (B) 28.8" (C) 24" (D) .1125"
40. **(B)** A scale of 1:24,000 means that 1 inch on the map equals 24,000 inches on the ground. 24,000 inches equals 2,000 feet. Therefore, (B) is the correct answer.	**40.** One of the scales used in drawing topographic maps is 1:24,000. On a scale of this sort, one inch on the map would equal how much distance on the ground? (A) one inch (B) 2,000 feet (C) 24,000 feet (D) one mile
41. **(C)** If two inches equals 24 feet, one inch equals 12 feet. A line representing 72 feet, therefore, must be six inches long ($72 \div 12 = 6$).	**41.** On a blueprint, two inches represents 24 feet. How long must a line be to represent 72 feet? (A) 36 inches (B) 12 inches (C) 6 inches (D) 4 inches
42. **(A)** In this problem, the bases are the same, so you must subtract the exponent of the divisor from that of the dividend to find the answer. $5^5 \div 5^3 = 5^{5-3} = 5^2 = 25$ Therefore, (A) is the correct answer. Note that the bases must be identical and the exponents must be subtracted. You can check this answer by multiplying each number out and dividing. $\frac{5^5}{5^3} = \frac{3125}{125} = 25$	**42.** $\frac{5^5}{5^3} =$ (A) 25 (B) $1\frac{2}{3}$ (C) 3,000 (D) none of the above
43. **(B)** When multiplying, if the bases are identical, add the exponents. $X^3 \bullet X^2 = X^5$ Note that because we are multiplying, the coefficient remains 1.	**43.** $X^3 \bullet X^2 =$ (A) X^6 (B) X^5 (C) $2X^5$ (D) $2X^6$

EXPLANATION	PROBLEM
44. **(C)** This problem requires two steps. First, find the smallest number that 14 and 12 go into evenly (the least common multiple, or LCM). Secondly, add that number to 1:00 and convert to time of day. The LCM of 14 and 12 is 84. Both events will occur simultaneously 84 minutes past 1:00 or 2:24 PM.	**44.** Event *A* occurs every 14 minutes and event *B* every 12 minutes. If they both occur at 1:00 PM, when will be the next time that both occur together? (A) 2:12 PM (B) 1:48 PM (C) 2:24 PM (D) 3:48 PM
45. **(C)** Here, three events occur periodically, so we must find the LCM of 4, 11, and 33, and add that number to 1950. That year will be the next common occurrence. The LCM of 4, 11, and 33 is 132. 1950 + 132 = 2082. Therefore, answer (C) is correct.	**45.** Event *A* occurs every 4 years, event *B* every 11 years, and event *C* every 33 years. If they last occurred together in 1950, when will they next occur simultaneously? (A) 3402 (B) 1983 (C) 2082 (D) 6804
46. **(D)** In the whole number system, every other number is odd, and every other is even. If x is odd, $x + 1$ is even, $x + 2$ is odd, $x + 3$ is even, and so forth. Also, if x is odd, $x - 1$ is even, $x - 2$ is odd, and $x - 3$ is even. If an even or odd number is doubled, the outcome is even. Therefore, if x is odd, $2x + 1$ is odd, $x - 2$ is odd, and $4x - 3$ is odd. Answer (D) is correct.	**46.** If x is an odd whole number, which of the following also represents an odd number? (A) $2x + 1$ (B) $x - 2$ (C) $4x - 3$ (D) all of the above
47. **(C)** Arrange the periods of time in columns and add as you would add whole numbers. 4 hr. 17 min. 3 hr. 58 min. 45 min. + 7 hr. 12 min. 14 hr. 132 min. We know there are 60 minutes in each hour. Therefore, 132 minutes equals 2 hours 12 minutes. The correct answer for this addition is 16 hours 12 minutes, or answer (C). When working with units that measure time, volume, and length, it is usually best to represent the answer using as many larger units as possible. That's why 16 hours 12 minutes is preferable to 14 hours 132 minutes as an answer.	**47.** The sum of 4 hours 17 minutes, 3 hours 58 minutes, 45 minutes, and 7 hours 12 minutes is (A) 15 hr. 32 min. (B) 17 hr. 32 min. (C) 16 hr. 12 min. (D) 14 hr. 50 min.

EXPLANATION	PROBLEM
48. (A) You do not have to calculate this answer. If eight people are sharing equally of 8 pounds and some ounces of fruit, each person would receive 1 pound and a few ounces. Only choice (A) is possible.	**48.** If 8 lb. 12 oz. of fruit were to be divided among eight people, how much would each receive? (A) 1 lb. 1.5 oz. (B) 10.5 oz. (C) 2.0 lb. (D) 13.5 oz.
49. (B) This is a subtraction problem. You must find the difference between the lengths of time required to finish the race. As with other problems involving units of measurement, you must work carefully. 3 hr. 2 min. 24 sec. – 2 hr. 12 min. 38 sec. Because 38 seconds is larger than 24 seconds and 12 minutes is larger than 2 minutes, borrow from the minutes column and the hour column and rewrite the problem as follows: 2 hr. 61 min. 84 sec. – 2 hr. 12 min. 38 sec. 0 hr. 49 min. 46 sec. Therefore, answer (B) is correct.	**49.** How much faster does a runner who finishes a marathon in 2 hours, 12 minutes, 38 seconds complete the race than a runner who finishes in 3 hours, 2 minutes, 24 seconds? (A) 48 min. 56 sec. (B) 49 min. 46 sec. (C) 1 hr. 51 min. 22 sec. (D) 1 hr. 26 min. 12 sec.
50. (A) The first 6 is in the billions place; the second, in the hundred-thousands place. If you had trouble with this problem, review the sections on how to read numbers and determine place values in your math textbook.	**50.** In the number 6,000,600,000, there are (A) 6 billions and 6 hundred thousands (B) 6 millions and 6 thousands (C) 6 billions and 6 millions (D) 6 millions and 60 thousands

EXPLANATION	PROBLEM

51. (C) This graph contains a line that has points with coordinates (1,1), (2,2), (3,3), and (4,4). From one point to another the value of the x-coordinate changes just as much as the value of the y-coordinate. Therefore, (C) is the correct answer. This line is at a 45° angle from the x-axis and will be created whenever the x- and y-coordinates are equal.

51.

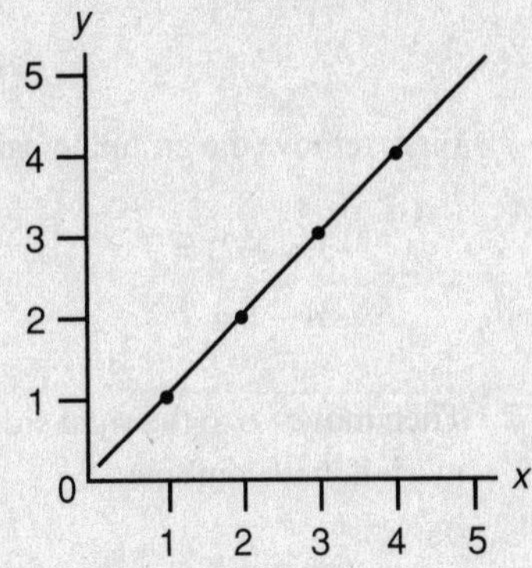

The graph above shows

(A) x increasing faster than y

(B) y increasing faster than x

(C) x increasing as fast as y

(D) no relationship between x and y

52. (D) This is a simple subtraction problem designed to test how carefully you can subtract. It is possible to calculate the correct answer without pencil and paper. 999,999 is only 1 less than a million, and 1,001,000 is 1,000 greater than a million. The difference, then, is 1,000 + 1, or 1,001. Or, you may figure the problem in the following way:

$$\begin{array}{r} 1{,}001{,}000 \\ -\ \ 999{,}999 \\ \hline 1{,}001 \end{array}$$

52. The difference between 1,001,000 and 999,999 is

(A) 101,001

(B) 1,999

(C) 10,001

(D) 1,001

53. (A) This equation can be solved in two steps.

Step 1. Move –6 to the right side and change the sign.

$$3x = 2 + 6$$
$$3x = 8$$

Step 2. Divide by the coefficient of the variable.

$$\frac{3x}{3} = \frac{8}{3}$$
$$x = \frac{8}{3}$$

53. If $3x - 6 = 2$, find x.

(A) $\frac{8}{3}$

(B) 8

(C) $-\frac{4}{3}$

(D) $\frac{2}{3}$

EXPLANATION	PROBLEM
54. (C) *Step 1.* First, remove the grouping parentheses. $-3(y+2)=9$ $-3y-6=9$ *Step 2.* Then move −6 to the right side, change its sign, and combine. $-3y=9+6$ $-3y=15$ *Step 3.* Divide through by the coefficient of the variable. $\frac{-3y}{-3}=\frac{15}{-3}\quad y=-5$	**54.** If $-3(y+2)=9$, find y (A) −3 (B) 15 (C) −5 (D) 3
55. (A) To solve this problem, simply plug in the values given and multiply. *Step 1.* $-4xy^2z^3$ *Step 2.* $-4\left(\frac{1}{3}\right)(-2)^2(1)^3$ *Step 3.* $-4\left(\frac{1}{3}\right)(4)(1)$ *Step 4.* $\left(-\frac{4}{3}\right)(4)=-\frac{16}{3}$	**55.** Evaluate the expression below if $x=\frac{1}{3}$, $y=-2$, and $z=1$. $-4xy^2z^3=$ (A) $-\frac{16}{3}$ (B) −16 (C) $\frac{16}{3}$ (D) $4\frac{2}{3}$
56. (B) Here again, simply plug in the values and multiply the fractions. *Step 1.* $A=\frac{1}{2}bh$ *Step 2.* $A=\frac{1}{2}\bullet\frac{1}{4}\bullet 2$ *Step 3.* $A=\frac{2}{8}=\frac{1}{4}$ If you had trouble with these fractions, review multiplication of fractions.	**56.** What is the value of the expression $A=\frac{1}{2}bh$, when $h=2$ and $b=\frac{1}{4}$? (A) $A=\frac{1}{3}$ (B) $A=\frac{1}{4}$ (C) $A=\frac{1}{6}$ (D) $A=\frac{2}{5}$

EXPLANATION	PROBLEM
57. **(C)** When simplifying, begin with the innermost grouping symbols first, and work your way outward. *Step 1.* $-6 - [2 - (3a - b) + b] + a$ *Step 2.* $-6 - [2 - 3a + b + b] + a$ *Step 3.* $-6 - [2 - 3a + 2b] + a$ *Step 4.* $-6 - 2 + 3a - 2b + a$ *Step 5.* $-8 + 4a - 2b$	**57.** Simplify $-6 - [2 - (3a - b) + b] + a$ (A) $4 - 3a + 2b$ (B) $-6 + 3a + b$ (C) $-8 + 4a - 2b$ (D) $-8 + 3a - b$
58. **(D)** Begin with the innermost parentheses and work your way outward. Note that a minus sign in front of a grouping symbol reverses the signs of all numbers within. *Step 1.* $-2[-4(2 - 1) + (3 + 2)]$ *Step 2.* $-2[-4(1) + (5)]$ *Step 3.* $-2[-4 + 5]$ *Step 4.* $-2[+ 1] = -2$	**58.** Simplify: $-2[-4(2 - 1) + (3 + 2)]$ (A) 18 (B) 2 (C) −18 (D) −2
59. **(C)** This proportion asks you to find the missing element. A proportion is a statement of equality between two ratios, so we know that 5 bears the same relationship to 15 as 6 does to the unknown number. Because 3×5 equals 15, we know 3×6 equals the unknown number. The number, thus, is 18. The completed proportion should read: 5:6 as 15:18. Proportions may also be written with a set of two colons replacing the word "as." In this case, the proportion would read: 5:6::15:18	**59.** 5:6 as 15:? (A) 25 (B) 16 (C) 18 (D) 12
60. **(C)** *Step 1.* To find the correct ratio, write it as: $\frac{\text{6 inches}}{\text{6 feet}}$ *Step 2.* Rewrite each quantity in inches. $\frac{\text{6 inches}}{\text{72 inches}}$ *Step 3.* Reduce the ratio. $\frac{6}{72} = \frac{1}{12} = 1{:}12$	**60.** The ratio of the six inches to six feet is (A) 1:6 (B) 12:1 (C) 1:12 (D) 24:1

CHAPTER 12

Quantitative Ability

PLAN A: ACCELERATED

- ***Read*** the chapter
- ***Study*** "What Smart Test-Takers Know"
- ***Do*** Practice Tests 1 to 5 for ISEE or 6 to 10 for SSAT

PLAN B: TOP SPEED

- ***Read*** "How Do You Solve Multiple-Choice Math Questions?"
- ***Study*** "What Smart Test-Takers Know"

You'll Find the Answers to These Questions

What makes multiple-choice math easier?
How do you solve multiple-choice quantitative ability questions?
What do smart test-takers know about multiple-choice math questions?

WHAT MAKES MULTIPLE-CHOICE MATH EASIER?

How can one kind of quantitative ability question possibly be easier than another? Well, multiple-choice math is easier than the math tests you take in school. Why? Simple. Because it's multiple choice, the correct answer is always on the page in front of you. So even if you are estimating, you'll be able to narrow down the choices and improve your guessing odds.

Some multiple-choice questions require no calculation at all; the correct answer is based upon your grasp of the concepts introduced by the question. Some questions are straight calculations; others are presented in the form of word problems. Some include graphs, charts, or tables that you will be asked to interpret. All the questions have either four (ISEE) or five (SSAT) answer choices. These choices are arranged in order by size from smallest to largest or from largest to smallest.

HOW DO YOU SOLVE MULTIPLE-CHOICE QUANTITATIVE ABILITY QUESTIONS?

Multiple-Choice Math: Getting It Right

1. Read the question carefully and determine what's being asked.
2. Decide which math principles apply and use them to solve the problem.
3. Look for your answer among the choices. If it's there, mark it and go on.

4. If the answer you found is not there, recheck the question and your calculations.

5. If you still can't solve the problem, eliminate obviously wrong answers and take your best guess.

Now let's try out these steps on a couple of multiple-choice math questions.

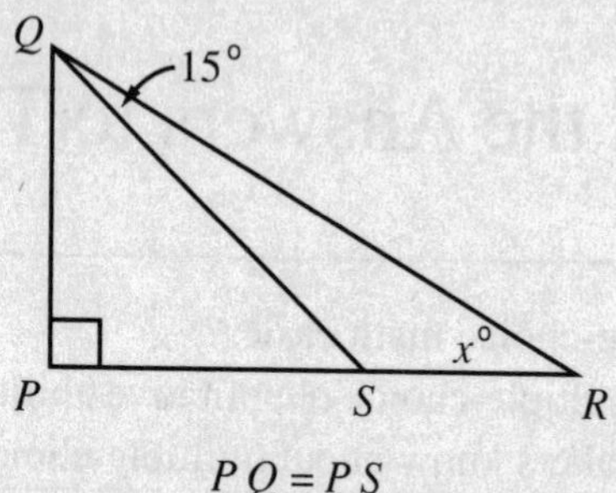

$PQ = PS$

In the figure above, $x =$

(A) 15

(B) 30

(C) 40

(D) 60

(E) 75

1. The problem asks you to find the measure of one angle of right triangle *PQR*.

2. Two math principles apply: (1) the sum of the measures, in degrees, of the angles of a triangle is 180, and (2) 45-45-90 right triangles have certain special properties. Because $PQ = PS$, *PQS* is a 45-45-90 right triangle. Therefore, angle $PQS = 45°$ and angle $PQR = 45 + 15 = 60°$. Therefore, angle $x = 180 - 90 - 60 = 30°$.

3. The correct answer, 30, is choice (B).

If x and y are negative numbers, which of the following is negative?

(A) xy

(B) $(xy)^2$

(C) $(x - y)^2$

(D) $x + y$

(E) $\frac{x}{y}$

1. The problem asks you to pick an answer choice that is a negative number.
2. The principles that apply are those governing operations with signed numbers. Because x and y are negative, both (A) and (E) must be positive. As for (B) and (C), so long as neither x nor y is zero, those expressions must be positive. (Any number other than zero squared gives a positive result.) (D), however, is negative because it represents the sum of two negative numbers.
3. By applying the rules governing signed numbers to each answer choice, you can determine that choices (A), (B), (C), and (E) can only be positive numbers.

Therefore, the correct answer must be choice (D). If you have trouble working with letters, try substituting easy numbers for x and y in each choice.

WHAT SMART TEST-TAKERS KNOW

Some of these you've heard before, some will be new to you. Whatever the case, read them, learn them, love them. They will help you.

TESTSMARTS

Look for shortcuts. Math problems test your math reasoning, not your ability to make endless calculations. If you find yourself calculating too much, you've probably missed a shortcut that would have made your work easier.

THE QUESTION NUMBER TELLS YOU HOW HARD THE QUESTION WILL BE.

Just as in most of the other test sections, the questions go from easy to hard as you work toward the end. The first third of the questions are easy, the middle third are average but harder, and the final third get more and more difficult. Take a look at these three examples. Don't solve them yet (you'll be doing that in a couple of minutes), just get an idea of how the level of difficulty changes from Question 1 to Question 12 to Question 25.

1. If $x - 2 = 5$, then $x =$

   (A) -10

   (B) -3

   (C) $\frac{5}{2}$

   (D) 3

   (E) 7

12. For how many integers x is $-7 < 2x < -5$?

   (A) None

   (B) One

   (C) Two

   (D) Three

   (E) Indefinite number

25. In a set of five books, no two of which have the same number of pages, the longest book has 150 pages and the shortest book has 130 pages. If x pages is the average (arithmetic mean) of the number of pages in the five-book set, which of the following best indicates all possible values of x and only possible values of x?

   (A) $130 < x < 150$

   (B) $131 < x < 149$

   (C) $133 < x < 145$

   (D) $134 < x < 145$

   (E) $135 < x < 145$

Can you see the difference? You can probably do Question 1 with your eyes closed. For Question 12 you probably have to open your eyes and do some calculations on scratch paper. Question 25 may cause you to wince a little, and then get started on some heavy-duty thinking.

EASY QUESTIONS HAVE EASY ANSWERS. DIFFICULT QUESTIONS DON'T.

Duh, but with an explanation. The easy questions are straightforward and don't have any hidden tricks. The obvious answer is almost always the correct answer. So for Question 1 the answer is indeed choice (E).

When you hit the difficult stuff, you have to think harder. The information is not straightforward and the answers aren't obvious. You can bet that your first-choice, easy answer will be wrong. If you don't believe it, let's take a look at the solution for difficult Question 25.

AVOID THE TRAPS!

Beware of the obvious. Don't be fooled by what look like obvious answers to difficult questions. The answers to difficult questions require some digging. They never jump out at you.

25. In a set of five books, no two of which have the same number of pages, the longest book has 150 pages and the shortest has 130 pages. If x pages is the average (arithmetic mean) of the number of pages in the five-book set, which of the following best indicates all possible values of x and only possible values of x?

    (A) $130 < x < 150$

    (B) $131 < x < 149$

    (C) $133 < x < 145$

    (D) $134 < x < 145$

    (E) $135 < x < 145$

Yes, it's difficult mostly because the process you have to use to find the solution is difficult. Let's start by eliminating answer choices. Choice (A) is a bad guess. You see the same info as you see in the word problem so you figure it's got to be right. Wrong. All it does is say that the shortest book is 130 pages, the longest book is 150 pages, and the average is between 130 and 150. Simple and wrong.

Choice (B) illustrates the reasoning that "no two books have the same number of pages, so the average must be one page more than the shortest book and one page less than the longest." Remember, it's a difficult question, it's just not that easy an answer.

OK then, let's skip to the correct answer, which is (E), and find out how we got there. First, you want to find the minimum value for x so you assume that the other three books contain 131, 132, and 133 pages. So the average would be

$$\frac{130+131+132+133+150}{5} = \frac{676}{5} = 135.2$$

So x must be more than 135. Now assume that the other three books contain 149, 148, and 147 pages. Then the average length of all five books would be

$$\frac{150+149+148+147+130}{5} = \frac{724}{5} = 144.8$$

Then x would be greater than 135 but less than 145.

WHEN GUESSING AT HARD QUESTIONS, YOU CAN TOSS OUT EASY ANSWERS.

Now that you know the difficult questions won't have easy or obvious answers, use a guessing strategy. (Use all the help you can get!) When you have less than a clue about a difficult question, scan the answer choices and eliminate the ones that seem easy or obvious, such as any that just restate the information in the question. Ditch those and then take your best guess.

QUESTIONS OF AVERAGE DIFFICULTY WON'T HAVE TRICK ANSWERS.

Let's look again at Question 12:

12. For how many integers x is $-7 < 2x < -5$?
    - (A) None
    - (B) One
    - (C) Two
    - (D) Three
    - (E) Indefinite number

This is a bit more difficult than Question 1, but it's still pretty straightforward. There is only one integer between –7 and –5, and that's –6. There's also only one value for integer x so that $2x$ equals –6, and that is –3. Get it? $2(-3) = -6$. So, (B) is the correct answer. Trust your judgment and your reasoning; no tricks here.

IT'S SMART TO TEST ANSWER CHOICES.

Every standard multiple-choice math problem includes four (ISEE) or five (SSAT) answer choices. One of them has to be correct; the others are wrong. This means that it's always possible to solve a problem by testing each of the answer choices. Just plug each choice into the problem and sooner or later you'll find the one that works! Testing answer choices can often be a much easier and surer way of solving a problem than attempting a lengthy calculation.

WHEN TESTING CHOICES, IT'S SMART TO START NEAR THE MIDDLE.

Remember, the answer is somewhere right in front of you. If you test all the answer choices, you'll find the right one. However, the smart place to start is always as close to the middle as possible. Why? Because the quantities in the choices are always arranged in order, either from smallest to largest or the other way around. If you start at the middle and it's too large, you'll just have to concentrate on the smaller choices. There, you've knocked off some choices in a heartbeat. Let's give it a "test" run, so to speak . . .

> If a rectangle has sides of $2x$ and $3x$ and an area of 24, what is the value of x?
>
> (A) 2
>
> (B) 3
>
> (C) 4
>
> (D) 5
>
> (E) 6

You know that one of these is right. Get started by testing (C), and assume that $x = 4$. Then the sides would have lengths $2(4) = 8$ and $3(4) = 12$ and the rectangle would have an area of $8 \times 12 = 96$. Because 96 is larger than 24 (the area in the question), start working with the smaller answer choices. (Which means, of course, that you can immediately forget about (D) and (E). Great!)

When you plug 3 into the figuring, you get $2(3) = 6$ and $3(3) = 9$ and $6 \times 9 = 54$; still too large. The only choice left is (A), and it works.

Now try this testing business with a more difficult question:

> A farmer raises chickens and cows. If her animals have a total of 120 heads and a total of 300 feet, how many chickens does the farmer have?
>
> (A) 50
>
> (B) 60
>
> (C) 70
>
> (D) 80
>
> (E) 90

Here goes—starting with (C). If the farmer has 70 chickens, she has 50 cows. (You know the farmer has 120 animals, because they each have only one head, right?) So now you're talking about $70 \times 2 = 140$ chicken feet and $50 \times 4 = 200$ cow feet, for a grand total of 340 animal feet. Well, that's more than the 300 animal feet in the question. How will you lose some of those feet? First, assume that the farmer has more chickens and fewer cows (cows have more feet than chickens do). Give (D)—80—a try. Test $80 \times 2 = 160$ and $40 \times 4 = 160$; your total is 320 feet, which is closer but not quite right. The only answer left is (E), and that's the correct one. Check it out: $90 \times 2 = 180$ and $30 \times 4 = 120$ and the total is . . . 300!

IT'S EASIER TO WORK WITH NUMBERS THAN WITH LETTERS.

Because numbers are more meaningful than letters, try plugging them into equations and formulas in place of variables. This technique can make problems much easier to solve. Here are some examples:

If $x - 4$ is 2 greater than y, then $x + 5$ is how much greater than y?

(A) 1

(B) 3

(C) 7

(D) 9

(E) 11

TESTSMARTS

Leave a paper trail! If you need to set up an equation, jot it down in your test booklet. That way, if you come back to recheck your work, you'll know what you were originally thinking.

Choose any value for x. Let's say you decide to make $x = 4$. All right, $4 - 4 = 0$, and 0 is 2 greater than y. So $y = -2$. If $x = 4$, then $x + 5 = 4 + 5 = 9$, and so $x + 5$ is 11 more than y. Therefore, the correct answer is choice (E).

The unit cost of pens is the same regardless of how many pens are purchased. If the cost of p pens is d dollars, what is the cost, in dollars, of x pens?

(A) xd

(B) xpd

(C) $\frac{xd}{p}$

(D) $\frac{xp}{d}$

(E) $\frac{pd}{x}$

Time to plug in some real numbers, because you need real money to buy anything, including pens. Say that four pens (p) cost \$2.00 (d), so each pen (x) would cost 50 cents. And say that you really only need one pen, so you're spending only \$0.50. Then $p = 4$, $d = 2$, and $x = 1$, and the right answer would be 0.5. Now, start using these numbers with the answer choices:

(A) $xd = (1)(2) = 2$ (Nope.)

(B) $xpd = (1)(4)(2) = 8$ (Nope, again.)

(C) $\frac{xd}{p} = \frac{(1)(2)}{4} = 0.5$ (Yes, there it is.)

(D) $\frac{xp}{d} = \frac{(1)(4)}{2} = 2$ (Nope.)

(E) $\frac{pd}{x} = \frac{(4)(2)}{1} = 8$ (Nope.)

If a question asks for an odd integer or an even integer, go ahead and pick any odd or even integer you like.

IT'S OK TO WRITE IN YOUR TEST BOOKLET, SO USE IT FOR SCRATCH WORK.

The test booklet is yours, so feel free to use it for your scratch work. Also, go ahead and mark up any diagrams with length or angle information; it helps. But don't waste time trying to redraw diagrams; it's just not worth it.

A REALITY CHECK CAN HELP YOU ELIMINATE ANSWERS THAT CAN'T POSSIBLY BE RIGHT.

Knowing whether your calculations should produce a number that's larger or smaller than the quantity you started with can point you toward the right answer. It's also an effective way of eliminating wrong answers. Here's an example:

> Using his bike, Daryl can complete a paper route in 20 minutes. Jennifer, who walks the route, can complete it in 30 minutes. How long will it take the two kids to complete the route if they work together, one starting at each end of the route?
>
> (A) 8 minutes
>
> (B) 12 minutes
>
> (C) 20 minutes
>
> (D) 30 minutes
>
> (E) 45 minutes

Immediately you can see that choices (C), (D), and (E) are impossible because the two kids working together will have to complete the job in less time than either one of them working alone. In fact, the correct answer is choice (B), 12 minutes.

	Daryl	Jennifer
$\dfrac{\text{Time actually spent}}{\text{Time needed to do entire job alone}}$	$\dfrac{x}{20}$	$\dfrac{x}{30}$

$$\frac{x}{20}+\frac{x}{30}=1$$

Multiply by 60 to clear fractions:

$$3x + 2x = 60$$
$$5x = 60$$
$$x = 12$$

TESTSMARTS

Circle what's asked. For multiple-choice math questions, circle what's being asked so that you don't pick a wrong answer by mistake. That way, for example, you won't pick an answer that gives a perimeter when the question asks for an area.

YOUR EYE IS A GOOD ESTIMATOR.

Figures in the standard multiple-choice math section are always drawn to scale unless you see the warning "Note: Figure not drawn to scale." That means you can sometimes solve a problem just by looking at the picture and estimating the answer. Here's how this works:

In the rectangle $PQRS$ shown, TU and WV are parallel to SR. If $PS = 6$, $UV = 1$, and PR (not shown) = 10, what is the area of rectangle $TUVW$?

(A) 8

(B) 12

(C) 16

(D) 24

(E) 32

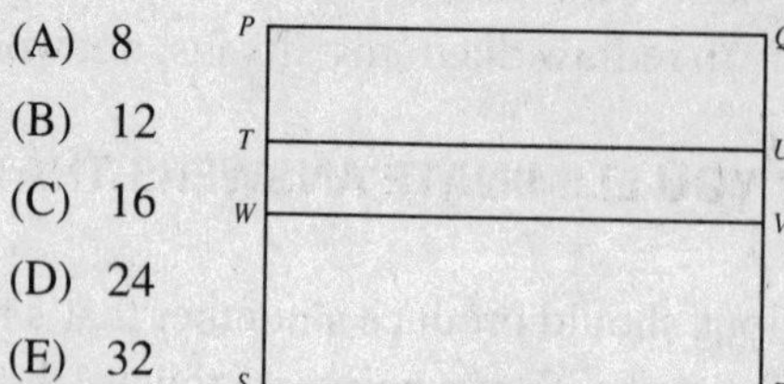

To solve the problem, you will need to find the length of TU. You can do this by using the Pythagorean Theorem. The triangle PSR has sides of 6 and 10, so $SR = 8$. Because $TU = SR$, $TU = 8$, so the area of the small rectangle is equal to $1 \times 8 = 8$.

As an alternative, you could simply estimate the length of TU. TU appears to be longer than PS (6), and TU must be shorter than PR (10). Therefore, TU appears to be approximately 8. And the area must be approximately $1 \times 8 = 8$. Is that sufficiently accurate to get the right answer? Look at the choices. (A) is 8, and it's the only choice that is even close to 8.

IF SOME QUESTIONS ALWAYS GIVE YOU TROUBLE, SAVE THEM FOR LAST.

You know which little demons haunt your math skills. If you find questions that you know will give you nightmares, save them for last. They will take up a lot of your time, especially if you're panicking, and you can use that time to do more of the easier questions.

PRACTICE MULTIPLE-CHOICE MATHEMATICS TESTS

TEST 1 — 12 MINUTES

Directions: Each of the following questions has four suggested answers. Decide which one is best. Circle the letter that appears before your answer.

1. In the simplest form, –11 – (–2) is
   (A) 7
   (B) 9
   (C) –9
   (D) –11

2. Find the average of 6.47, 5.89, 3.42, .65, and 7.09.
   (A) 3.920
   (B) 4.704
   (C) 4.705
   (D) 5.812

3. Change 0.03125 to a common fraction.
   (A) $\frac{3}{64}$
   (B) $\frac{1}{16}$
   (C) $\frac{1}{64}$
   (D) $\frac{1}{32}$

4. A roll of carpeting will cover 224 square feet of floor space. How many rolls will be needed to carpet a room 36' × 8' and another 24' × 9'?
   (A) 2.25
   (B) 2.50
   (C) 4.25
   (D) 4.50

5. After deducting a discount of 30%, the price of a coat was $35.00. The regular price of the coat was
   (A) $24.50
   (B) $42.00
   (C) $50.00
   (D) $116.67

6. Find the sum of –16, 14, –38, 26, and 20.
   (A) 6
   (B) 4
   (C) 0
   (D) –6

7. The number of cubic feet of soil needed for a flower box 3 feet long, 8 inches wide, and 1 foot deep is
   (A) 24
   (B) 12
   (C) $4\frac{2}{3}$
   (D) 2

8. Using exponents, write 359 in expanded form
   (A) $(3 \times 10^2) + (5 \times 10) + 9$
   (B) $(3^2 \times 10) + (5^2 \times 10) + 9$
   (C) $(3 \times 10^2) + (5 \times 10 \times 3^2)$
   (D) $(3 \times 10^3) + (5 \times 10 + 3^2)$

9. The scale of a certain map is 4 inches = 32 miles. The number of inches that would represent 80 miles is
   (A) 16
   (B) 12
   (C) 10
   (D) 8

10. 15 is 20% of
    (A) 3
    (B) 18
    (C) 35
    (D) 75

11. The bar graph below shows the population of a town during a 30-year period. By what number of people did the population decrease between 1960 and 1970?

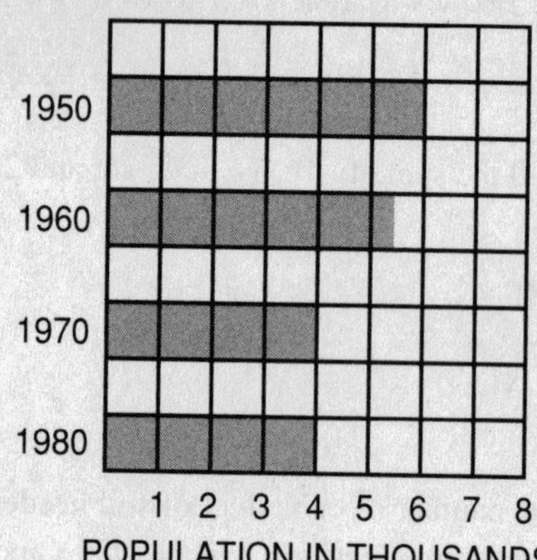

(A) 1,000
(B) 1,500
(C) 2,500
(D) 15,000

12. Which of these fractions is greater than $\frac{9}{17}$?

(A) $\frac{6}{13}$
(B) $\frac{13}{25}$
(C) $\frac{11}{20}$
(D) $\frac{1}{2}$

13. If $y = x - 4$, then $y - 2 =$

(A) $x - 6$
(B) $x + 2$
(C) $x - 2$
(D) $x + 6$

14. $19\frac{2}{3} - 7\frac{1}{4} =$

(A) $12\frac{1}{4}$
(B) $12\frac{1}{3}$
(C) $12\frac{5}{12}$
(D) $12\frac{3}{4}$

15. If $a - b = 7$ and a and b are both positive integers, what is the minimum possible value of $a + b$?

(A) 11
(B) 9
(C) 8
(D) 0

TEST 2 — 12 MINUTES

Directions: Each of the following questions has four suggested answers. Decide which one is best. Circle the letter that appears before your answer.

1. The sum of $\frac{2}{3}$, $\frac{1}{8}$, $\frac{5}{6}$, and $3\frac{1}{2}$ is

(A) $4\frac{1}{3}$

(B) $4\frac{3}{4}$

(C) $5\frac{1}{8}$

(D) $5\frac{3}{8}$

2. A store sold suits for $65.00 each. The suits cost the store $50.00 each. The percentage of increase of selling price over cost is

(A) 40%

(B) $33\frac{1}{2}$%

(C) $33\frac{1}{3}$%

(D) 30%

3. 72 divided by .0009 =

(A) .125

(B) 80

(C) 800

(D) 80,000

4. What is the simple interest on $460.00 for two years at $2\frac{1}{2}$%?

(A) $20.00

(B) $23.00

(C) $25.00

(D) $28.00

5. A house plan uses the scale $\frac{1}{4}$ inch = 1 foot, and, in the drawing, the living room is 7 inches long. If the scale is changed to 1 inch = 1 foot, what will the length of the living room be in the new drawing?

(A) 18 in.

(B) 28 in.

(C) 30 in.

(D) 36 in.

6. During his summer vacation, a boy earned $14.50 per day and saved 60% of his earnings. If he worked 45 days, how much did he save?

(A) $287.93

(B) $391.50

(C) $402.75

(D) $543.50

7. $\frac{27}{64}$ expressed as a percent is

(A) 40.625%

(B) 42.188%

(C) 43.750%

(D) 45.313%

8. If the formula for the area of a circle is πr^2, find the area of a circle that has a diameter 8 inches long.

(A) 50.24 sq. in.

(B) 100.48 sq. in.

(C) 102.34 sq. in.

(D) 200.96 sq. in.

9. If $8 > x > 5$ and $3 > y > -2$, then

(A) $x < y$

(B) $x \leq y$

(C) $x \geq y$

(D) $x > y$

10. $5^3 \times 3^4 =$

(A) $5 \times 3 \times 3 \times 4$

(B) $5 \times 5 \times 5 \times 3 \times 3 \times 3$

(C) $5 \times 5 \times 5 \times 3 \times 3 \times 3 \times 3$

(D) $5 \times 5 \times 5 \times 5 \times 3 \times 3 \times 3$

11. If $a + b = 200°$, and $c + d + e + f = 140°$, what is the number of degrees in angle g?

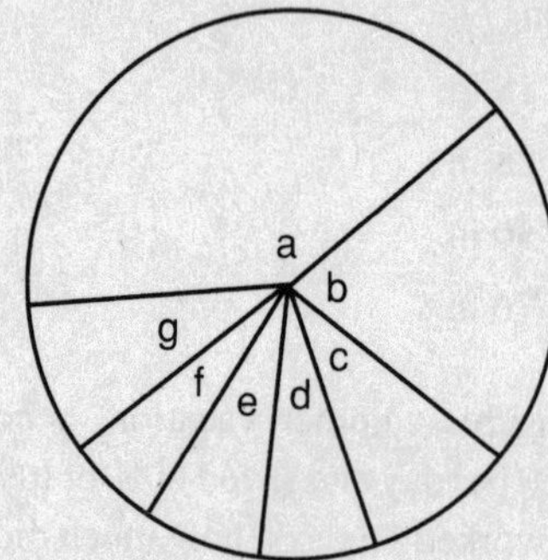

(A) 10°

(B) 20°

(C) 30°

(D) 45°

12. If a steel bar is 0.39 feet long, its length in *inches* is

(A) less than 4

(B) between 4 and $4\frac{1}{2}$

(C) between $4\frac{1}{2}$ and 5

(D) between 5 and 6

13. The graph below shows the number of hours in each 8-hour working day that Mr. Smith spent on the telephone last week. What fraction represents the average of the part of the day Mr. Smith spends on the telephone?

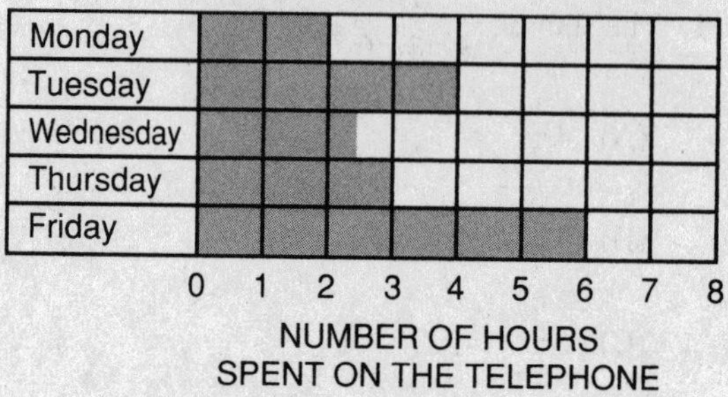

Monday
Tuesday
Wednesday
Thursday
Friday

0 1 2 3 4 5 6 7 8

NUMBER OF HOURS
SPENT ON THE TELEPHONE

(A) $\frac{3}{8}$

(B) $\frac{7}{16}$

(C) $\frac{4}{5}$

(D) $\frac{72}{24}$

14. Multiply $(10a^3)(5a)$.

(A) $14a^3$

(B) $50a^4$

(C) $40a^3$

(D) $15a^4$

15. The formula for the area of a triangle is $A = \frac{1}{2}bh$. Find A if b = 12 and h = 10.

(A) 22

(B) 32

(C) 50

(D) 60

TEST 3 — 12 MINUTES

Directions: Each of the following questions has four suggested answers. Decide which one is best. Circle the letter that appears before your answer.

1. Find the hypotenuse of a right triangle if the legs are 6 and 8.
   (A) 8
   (B) 9
   (C) 10
   (D) 11

2. One man earns $24,000 per year. Another earns $1,875 per month. How much more does the first man make in a year than the second man?
   (A) $2,500
   (B) $2,000
   (C) $1,500
   (D) $1,000

3. The square root of 53 is closest to
   (A) 8
   (B) 7
   (C) 6.5
   (D) 6

4. Solve for x: $4x - 8 = 16$
   (A) 4
   (B) 6
   (C) 8
   (D) 10

5. A library contains 60 books on arts and crafts. If this is .05% of the total number of books on the shelves, how many books does the library own?
   (A) 1,200
   (B) 12,000
   (C) 120,000
   (D) 1,200,000

6. The graph below represents Ms. Lawson's monthly budget. What percentage of her salary does she spend on things other than housing costs?

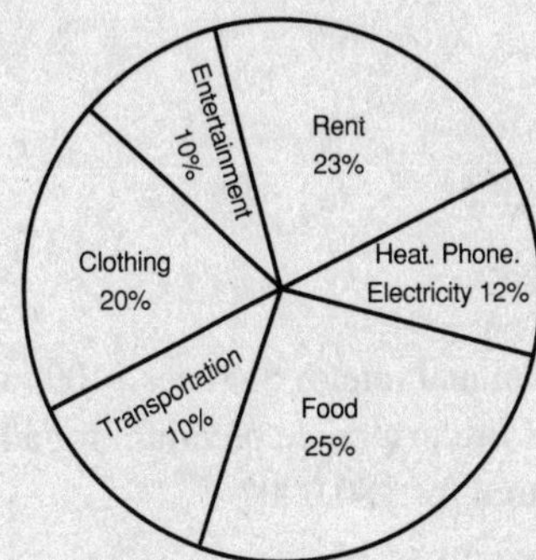

   (A) 35%
   (B) 40%
   (C) 52%
   (D) 65%

7. Find the length in inches of diagonal $\overline{DB}$ in the rectangle below.

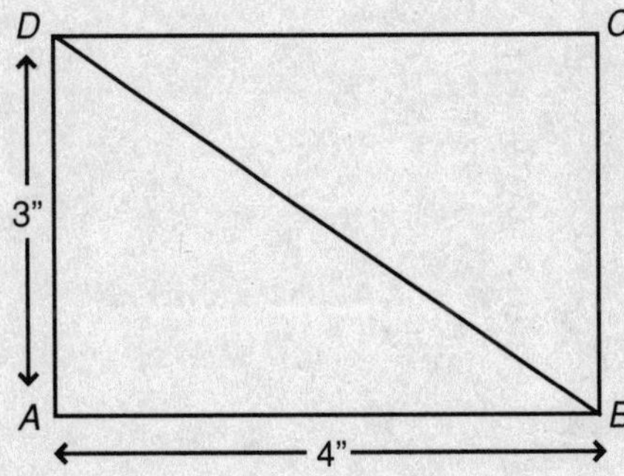

   (A) 5
   (B) 7
   (C) 9
   (D) 11

8. A woman borrowed \$5,000 and agreed to pay $11\frac{1}{2}$% simple interest. If she repaid the loan in 6 months, how much interest would she pay?

(A) \$287.50

(B) \$575.00

(C) \$2,875.00

(D) \$5,750.00

9. Solve for x: $2x^2 - 6 = 44$

(A) –5

(B) 5

(C) 12.5

(D) 25

10. At an annual rate of \$.40 per \$100, what is the annual fire insurance premium for a house that is insured for \$80,000?

(A) \$3.20

(B) \$32

(C) \$320

(D) \$3,200

11. Simplify: $\frac{2}{3} + (\frac{3}{4} \times \frac{2}{9}) - \frac{1}{6}$

(A) $\frac{3}{4}$

(B) $\frac{1}{2}$

(C) $\frac{1}{3}$

(D) $\frac{2}{3}$

12. Which of the following is true?

(A) $\frac{2}{3} > \frac{7}{10}$

(B) $\frac{2}{7} > \frac{1}{3}$

(C) $\frac{5}{7} < \frac{8}{9}$

(D) $\frac{2}{9} < \frac{1}{5}$

13. Find the missing term in the proportion $x{:}5 = 24{:}30$.

(A) 3

(B) 4

(C) 6

(D) 8

14. A distance of 25 miles is represented on a map by $2\frac{1}{2}$ inches. On the map, how many miles are represented by one inch?

(A) 6

(B) 8

(C) 10

(D) 12

15. If the school tax rate in a community is \$33.50 per \$1,000 of assessed valuation, find the amount of tax on property assessed at \$50,000.

(A) \$167.50

(B) \$420.02

(C) \$1,675.00

(D) \$4,200.02

TEST 4 — 12 MINUTES

Directions: Each of the following questions has four suggested answers. Decide which one is best. Circle the letter that appears before your answer.

1. A junior high school established a school savings account, and the eighth grade saved $990. If this was 45% of the total amount saved by the school, find the total amount.

(A) $220

(B) $1,210

(C) $2,100

(D) $2,200

2. A team won 25 games and lost 8. What is the ratio of the number of games won to the number of games played?

(A) 33:25

(B) 25:33

(C) 58:25

(D) 25:58

3. A circular flower garden has a diameter of 21 feet. How many feet of fencing will be required to enclose this garden?

(A) 72

(B) 66

(C) 60

(D) $20\frac{1}{2}$

4. Solve for x: $7x - 4 = 115$

(A) 17

(B) 19

(C) 21

(D) 22

5. The best approximate answer for $1.2507623 \times 72.964896$ is

(A) 100

(B) 90

(C) 70

(D) 9

6. $3\frac{1}{2} \times 2\frac{1}{4} =$

(A) $5\frac{3}{4}$

(B) $6\frac{1}{8}$

(C) $6\frac{2}{8}$

(D) $7\frac{7}{8}$

7. The area of a rectangular room is 1,000 square feet. If the width of the room is 25 feet, what is the length of the room?

(A) 30 feet

(B) 35 feet

(C) 40 feet

(D) 45 feet

8. An order for 345 machine bolts at $4.15 per hundred will cost

(A) $.1432

(B) $1.14

(C) $14.32

(D) $143.20

9. On the first day of its drive, a junior high school raised $40, which was $33\frac{1}{3}\%$ of its quota. How much was the quota?

(A) $120

(B) $100

(C) $80

(D) $68

10. According to the 1950 census, 14,830,192 people were then living in New York State. Round this number off to the nearest thousand.

(A) 14,000

(B) 148,300

(C) 1,483,000

(D) 14,830,000

11. Simplify: $x - [8 - (x - 2)]$

(A) -10

(B) $2x - 10$

(C) $2x + 10$

(D) $2x - 6$

12. Sharon made a circle graph and drew an angle of 45° to show the number of pupils in her grade who had earned an A in mathematics. What percent of her grade earned an A?

(A) 10%

(B) $12\frac{1}{2}\%$

(C) $16\frac{2}{3}\%$

(D) 20%

Questions 13–15 pertain to the graph below.

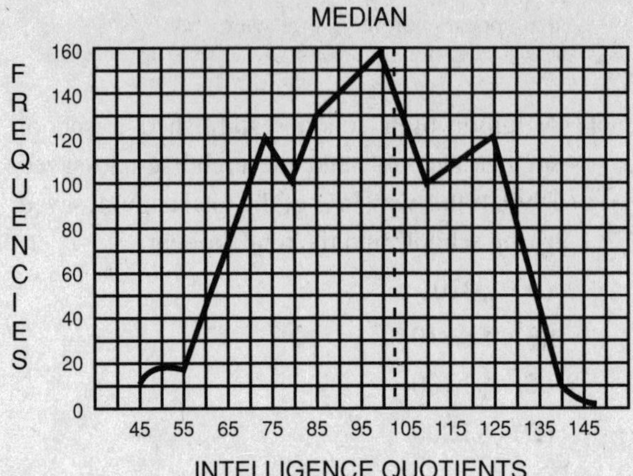

13. The number of pupils having the highest intelligence quotient (I.Q.) is about

(A) 5

(B) 20

(C) 145

(D) 160

14. The number of pupils having an I.Q. of 80 is identical with the number of pupils having an I.Q. of

(A) 68

(B) 100

(C) 110

(D) 128

15. The intelligence quotient that has the greatest frequency is

(A) 95

(B) 100

(C) 105

(D) 160

TEST 5 — 12 MINUTES

Directions: Each of the following questions has four suggested answers. Decide which one is best. Circle the letter that appears before your answer.

1. $0.16\frac{3}{4}$ written as a percent is

(A) $16\frac{3}{4}\%$

(B) $16.\frac{3}{4}\%$

(C) $0.016\frac{3}{4}\%$

(D) $0.0016\frac{3}{4}\%$

2. The area of the shaded portion of the rectangle below is

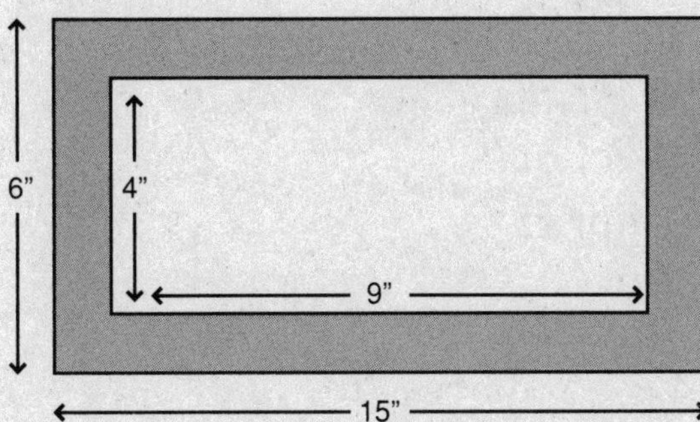

(A) 90 sq. in.

(B) 54 sq. in.

(C) 45 sq. in.

(D) 36 sq. in.

3. The ratio of 16:36 is

(A) 3:5

(B) 3:21

(C) 4:8

(D) 4:9

4. 595 written in expanded form with exponents is

(A) $(5 \times 10) + (9 \times 10) + (5 \times 1)$

(B) $(5 \times 10^2) + (9 \times 10) + 5$

(C) $(5 \times 10^2) + (9 \times 10) + (5 \times 1)$

(D) $(5 \times 10^2) + (3^2 \times 10) + 5$

5. Jane saved $5 by buying a jacket at a sale where a 25% discount was given. What was the original price of the jacket?

(A) $14.00

(B) $16.00

(C) $18.00

(D) $20.00

6. How many square yards are there in the area of a rug that is 15 feet long and 12 feet wide?

(A) 18

(B) 20

(C) 22

(D) 24

7. Solve for x: $3x^2 + 15 = 90$

(A) 75

(B) 60

(C) 25

(D) 5

8. A scale drawing of a bird is $\frac{1}{8}$ actual size. If the drawing is $\frac{3}{4}$ inches high, find in inches the height of the real bird.

(A) 2

(B) 4

(C) 6

(D) 8

9. Find the sum of −8, 17, 29, −12, −3, and 5.

(A) −18

(B) 28

(C) 29

(D) 33

10. If a man walks $\frac{2}{5}$ mile in 5 minutes, what is his average rate of walking in miles per hour?

(A) 4

(B) $4\frac{1}{2}$

(C) $4\frac{4}{5}$

(D) $5\frac{1}{5}$

11. Solve for x: $\frac{x}{2} + 3 = 15$

(A) 18

(B) 20

(C) 22

(D) 24

12. On a map, 1 inch represents 500 miles. How many miles apart are two places that are $1\frac{1}{2}$ inches apart on the map?

(A) 750

(B) 1,000

(C) 1,250

(D) 1,500

13. $(6 \times 10^3) + (8 \times 10^2) + (7 \times 10) + 3$ is equal to

(A) 6,873

(B) 60,873

(C) 68,730

(D) 600,873

14. A salesman received a salary of $150 a week plus 5% commission on his total weekly sales. During one week his total sales amounted to $1,800. How much did he earn that week?

(A) $90

(B) $240

(C) $330

(D) $340

15. If a car averages 18 miles to a gallon of gasoline, how many gallons of gasoline will be used on a trip of 369 miles?

(A) 18

(B) $20\frac{1}{2}$

(C) $21\frac{3}{4}$

(D) 22

TEST 6 — 15 MINUTES

Directions: Each question below has five suggested answers. Decide which one is best. Circle the letter that appears before your answer.

1. A boy's quarterly test marks were 67, 74, 86, and 89. What was the average of his test marks?

(A) 75

(B) 79

(C) 81

(D) 84

(E) 85

2. What fraction is equal to 2.5%?

(A) $\frac{1}{400}$

(B) $\frac{1}{40}$

(C) $\frac{1}{4}$

(D) $2\frac{1}{4}$

(E) $2\frac{1}{2}$

3. To the nearest tenth, find the square root of 48.

(A) 5.9

(B) 6.5

(C) 6.9

(D) 7.2

(E) 7.3

4. Solve for x: $x + 2\frac{1}{2} = 5$

(A) $-2\frac{1}{2}$

(B) 2

(C) $2\frac{1}{2}$

(D) 3

(E) $7\frac{1}{2}$

5. Simplify: $\frac{68}{204}$

(A) $\frac{1}{6}$

(B) $\frac{2}{9}$

(C) $\frac{4}{12}$

(D) $\frac{1}{3}$

(E) $\frac{3}{8}$

6. Using a scale of $\frac{1}{8}$ inch = 1 foot, what length line would be needed to represent 23 feet?

(A) $2\frac{3}{8}$

(B) $2\frac{7}{8}$

(C) 3

(D) $3\frac{1}{8}$

(E) $3\frac{3}{8}$

7. Which of these fractions is equal to $\frac{1}{4} - \frac{2}{3}$?

(A) $\frac{5}{12}$

(B) $\frac{3}{10}$

(C) $-\frac{3}{10}$

(D) $-\frac{5}{12}$

(E) $-\frac{7}{12}$

8. The formula for finding the area of a triangle is $A = \frac{1}{2}bh$. Find the area of the triangle below.

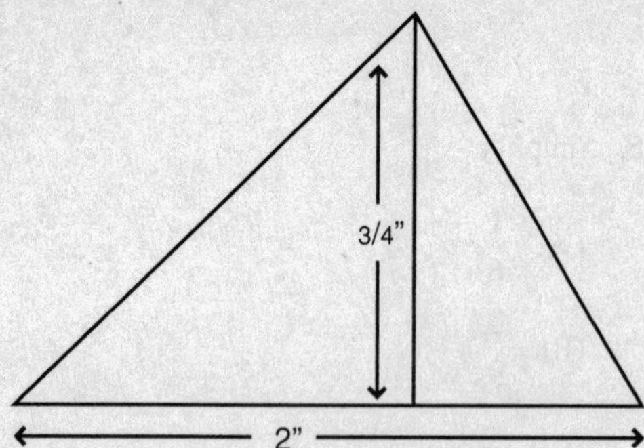

(A) 3 sq. in.

(B) $2\frac{1}{2}$ sq. in.

(C) $1\frac{1}{2}$ sq. in.

(D) 1 sq. in.

(E) $\frac{3}{4}$ sq. in.

9. Solve for x: $\frac{x}{9} = 27$

(A) 272

(B) 243

(C) 181

(D) 81

(E) 3

10. A salesperson gets a commission of 4% on her sales. If she wants her commission to amount to $40, she will have to sell merchandise totaling

(A) $10

(B) $100

(C) $160

(D) $1,000

(E) $10,000

11. Using the formula $A = \pi r^2$, find the area of a circle whose diameter is 14 feet.

(A) 154 sq. ft.

(B) 256 sq. ft.

(C) 286 sq. ft.

(D) 544 sq. ft.

(E) 615.4 sq. ft.

12. Using the formula $V = lwh$, find the volume of a rectangular solid whose dimensions are $l = 46$ ft., $w = 38$ ft., $h = 40$ ft.

(A) 89,176 cu. ft.

(B) 79,507 cu. ft.

(C) 75,380 cu. ft.

(D) 69, 920 cu. ft.

(E) 7,538 cu. ft.

13. The standing of a seventh grade baseball team that won ten games and lost five games is

(A) .667

(B) .500

(C) .333

(D) .250

(E) .200

14. If $x = 10$, which of the following statements is true?

(A) $x^2 < 2x$

(B) $x^2 = 15x - 50$

(C) $3x > x^3$

(D) $x^3 = x^2 + 2x$

(E) $x^3 < x^2 + x^2$

15. 921 written in expanded exponential form is

(A) $(9 \times 10^2) + (2 \times 10) + 21$

(B) $(9 \times 100) + (2 \times 10) + 1$

(C) $(9 \times 10^3) + (2 \times 10) + 1$

(D) $(9 \times 10^3) + (2 \times 0^2) + 1$

(E) $(9 \times 10^3) + (2 \times 10) + 1$

TEST 7 — 15 MINUTES

Directions: Each question below has five suggested answers. Decide which one is best. Circle the letter that appears before your answer.

1. How many degrees are in angle *A* of the triangle below?

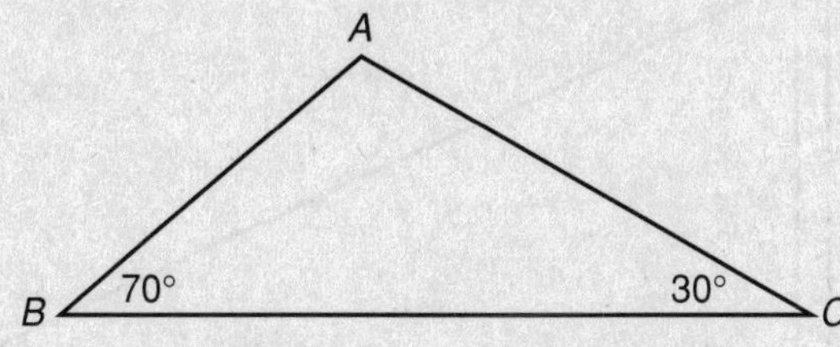

(A) 60°

(B) 70°

(C) 80°

(D) 90°

(E) 100°

2. What is the cost of nine ounces of cheese at $.80 per pound?

(A) $.36

(B) $.45

(C) $.48

(D) $.52

(E) $.55

3. A man borrowed $3,600 for one month at an annual rate of 5%. How much interest did he owe?

(A) $ 5.00

(B) $ 7.50

(C) $12.50

(D) $15.00

(E) $30.00

4. One piece of wire is 25 feet 8 inches long and another is 18 feet 10 inches long. What is the difference in length?

(A) 6 ft. 10 in.

(B) 6 ft. 11 in.

(C) 7 ft. 2 in.

(D) 7 ft. 4 in.

(E) 7 ft. 5 in.

5. The ratio of 24 to 64 is

(A) 8:3

(B) 24:100

(C) 3:8

(D) 64:100

(E) 8:12

6. Express algebraically the perimeter of the figure below.

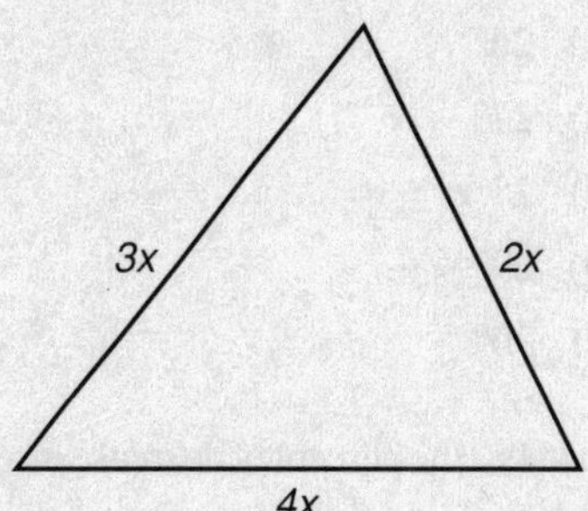

(A) $3x$

(B) $5x$

(C) $7x$

(D) $9x$

(E) $24x$

7. If three times a certain number increased by 4 is equal to 19, what is the number?

(A) 10

(B) 8

(C) 7

(D) 6

(E) 5

Questions 8–10 pertain to the graph below.

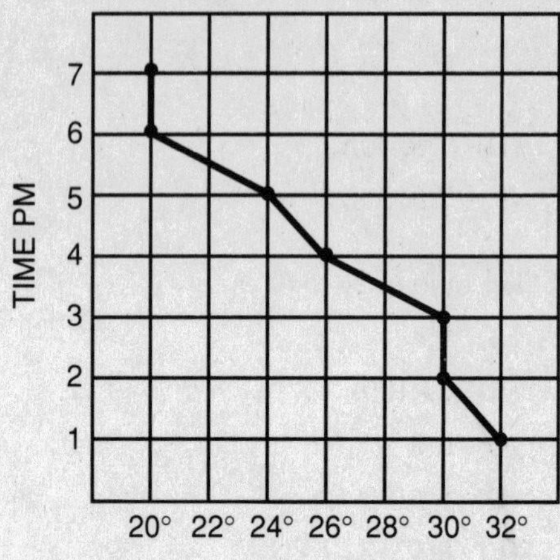

8. What was the approximate temperature at 3:30 PM?

(A) 26°
(B) 27°
(C) 28°
(D) 29°
(E) 30°

9. What was the percent of decrease in temperature between 2 and 5 PM?

(A) 50%
(B) 45%
(C) 38%
(D) 25%
(E) 20%

10. The ratio of the rate of temperature decrease between 1 and 3 PM and 4 and 7 PM is

(A) 2:3
(B) 3:4
(C) 1:4
(D) 1:3
(E) 3:5

11. If a box of 24 candy bars is bought for $.80, and the bars are sold for $.05 each, what is the percent of profit on the cost?

(A) 25%
(B) 30%
(C) 45%
(D) 50%
(E) 75%

12. Find the length of the diagonal in the rectangle below.

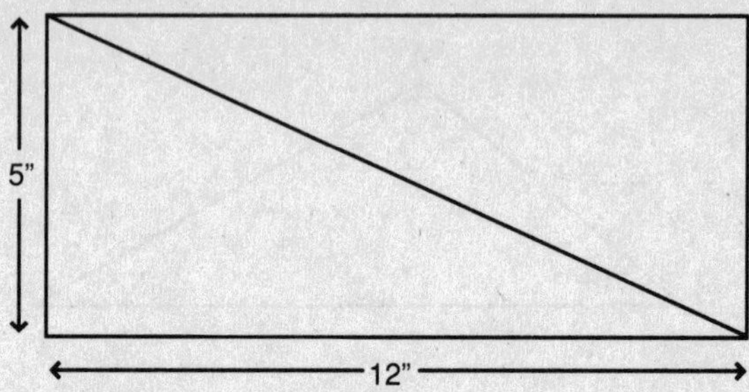

(A) 12"
(B) 13"
(C) 16"
(D) 17"
(E) 20"

13. Multiply: (–8)(+6)

(A) –2
(B) –14
(C) –48
(D) +24
(E) +48

14. If $x > 9$, then

(A) $x^2 > 80$
(B) $x^2 - 2 = 47$
(C) $x^2 < 65$
(D) $x^2 - 2 < 90$
(E) $x^2 + x < 90$

15. Divide $\frac{7}{8}$ by $\frac{7}{8}$.

(A) $\frac{64}{49}$
(B) 1
(C) $\frac{7}{8}$
(D) $\frac{49}{64}$
(E) 0

TEST 8 — 15 MINUTES

Directions: Each question below has five suggested answers. Decide which one is best. Circle the letter that appears before your answer.

1. If the scale on a map indicates that $1\frac{1}{2}$ inches equals 500 miles, 5 inches on that map represents approximately

(A) 1,800 miles

(B) 1,600 miles

(C) 1,300 miles

(D) 700 miles

(E) 350 miles

2. Change 0.03125 to a common fraction.

(A) $\frac{1}{8}$

(B) $\frac{1}{16}$

(C) $\frac{3}{64}$

(D) $\frac{1}{32}$

(E) $\frac{1}{64}$

3. Solve for x: $2x^2 - 5 = 93$

(A) 7

(B) 9

(C) 12

(D) 36

(E) 49

4. Find the area of the shaded portion of the figure below.

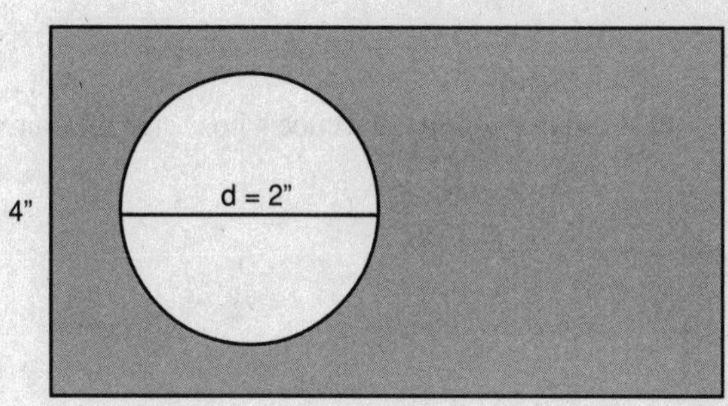

(A) 18.50 sq. in.

(B) 23.98 sq. in.

(C) 25.72 sq. in.

(D) 28.86 sq. in.

(E) 32.24 sq. in.

5. What is the simple interest on a loan of \$20,000 taken for five years at 12% interest?

(A) \$240

(B) \$1,200

(C) \$2,400

(D) \$6,000

(E) \$12,000

6. The sum of $(10^3 + 2) + (3 \times 10^2)$ is

(A) 13,002

(B) 3,102

(C) 1,302

(D) 312

(E) 132

7. A woman whose salary is \$225 per week has 12% deducted for taxes and 5% deducted for Social Security. What is her take-home salary?

(A) \$213.75

(B) \$198.00

(C) \$186.75

(D) \$112.80

(E) \$39.25

8. Find the volume of a cube whose side measures 5 yd.

(A) 25 cu. yd.

(B) 100 cu. yd.

(C) 125 cu. yd.

(D) 225 cu. yd.

(E) 625 cu. yd.

9. $42 \div .06 =$

(A) .07

(B) .7

(C) 7

(D) 70

(E) 700

10. Solve for x: $x - 62 = -18$

(A) 124

(B) 80

(C) 44

(D) –44

(E) –80

11. On a mathematics test, $12\frac{1}{2}$% of a class received marks of D, $37\frac{1}{2}$% received Cs, 25% marks of B, and the remainder received As. What percent of the class received a mark of A?

(A) 20%

(B) 25%

(C) 28%

(D) 30%

(E) $33\frac{1}{3}$%

12. The scale on a blueprint is $\frac{1}{4}$" = 1 foot. A room whose actual dimensions are 28 feet by 14 feet would be what size in the drawing?

(A) 14" × 7"

(B) $8\frac{1}{4}$" × $4\frac{1}{2}$"

(C) $7\frac{1}{2}$" × 3"

(D) 7" × $3\frac{1}{2}$"

(E) 7" × $3\frac{1}{4}$"

13. $(2 \times 10^4 + 1) - (10^3 + 9) =$

(A) 18,992

(B) 16,540

(C) 1,892

(D) 1,654

(E) 992

14. Find the approximate area of a circle whose radius is 21 inches.

(A) 138 sq. in.

(B) 795 sq. in.

(C) 989 sq. in.

(D) 1385 sq. in.

(E) 3725 sq. in.

15. If $x = 3.5$, then

(A) $x^2 > 10$

(B) $4x + 6 = 20$

(C) $x^3 - 5 < 40$

(D) $x^2 + x^2 = 24.50$

(E) $x^3 + x < 50$

TEST 9 — 15 MINUTES

Directions: Each question below has five suggested answers. Decide which one is best. Circle the letter that appears before your answer.

1. One man earns $21,000 per year. Another man earns $1,675 per month. How much more does the first man earn in a year than the second man?

(A) $19

(B) $90

(C) $190

(D) $900

(E) $1900

2. Solve for x: $2x^2 - 2 = 30$

(A) 2

(B) 4

(C) 5

(D) 16

(E) 32

3. By purchasing her coat on sale, Jan saved $25, a savings of $33\frac{1}{3}$%. What was the original price of the coat?

(A) $120

(B) $100

(C) $90

(D) $75

(E) $60

4. Find the volume of a cube whose edge is 4 inches long.

(A) 32 cu. in.

(B) 48 cu. in.

(C) 64 cu. in.

(D) 84 cu. in.

(E) 96 cu. in.

5. Which of the following has the same value as .5%?

(A) $\frac{1}{2}\%$

(B) $\frac{1}{5}\%$

(C) $\frac{1}{20}\%$

(D) $\frac{1}{50}\%$

(E) $\frac{1}{500}\%$

6. On a map, $1\frac{1}{2}$ inches represents 25 miles. How many miles apart are two places that are $3\frac{3}{4}$ inches apart on the map?

(A) 50 miles

(B) 55.5 miles

(C) 60 miles

(D) 62.5 miles

(E) 67.5 miles

7. Find the sum of –11, –22, 60, 2 and –36.

(A) –131

(B) –7

(C) 0

(D) 7

(E) 131

8. A certain department store arrives at its retail prices by using a 150% mark-up of wholesale prices. If a dress cost the store $30 wholesale, what will its retail price be?

(A) $75

(B) $70

(C) $65

(D) $60

(E) $45

9. Find the difference between $(3^4 + 4)$ and $(4^3 + 1)$.

(A) 21

(B) 20

(C) 18

(D) 14

(E) 3

10. Solve for x: $\frac{x}{12} = 7.5$

(A) 78

(B) 80

(C) 84

(D) 90

(E) 102

11. A woman bought groceries totaling $22.73 and gave the clerk three ten-dollar bills and three pennies. How much change did she receive?

(A) $8.30

(B) $8.20

(C) $7.30

(D) $7.27

(E) $7.20

12. Find the total surface area for a rectangular solid with these dimensions: l = 8", w = 4", h = 8".

(A) 64 sq. in.

(B) 128 sq. in.

(C) 256 sq. in.

(D) 320 sq. in.

(E) 512 sq. in.

13. A woman bought a lamp for $16.75. She returned it the next day and chose a lamp that cost $18.95. She gave the clerk a five-dollar bill to pay the difference in price. How much change did she get?

(A) $2.10

(B) $2.30

(C) $2.40

(D) $2.60

(E) $2.80

14. A boy sold $60 worth of magazine subscriptions, for which he was paid $18. What rate of commission was he paid?

(A) 20%

(B) 30%

(C) 40%

(D) 50%

(E) 60%

15. Which consecutive integers for x and y would make this statement true?

$x < \sqrt{200} < y$

(A) 100 and 101

(B) 40 and 50

(C) 27 and 33

(D) 14 and 15

(E) 10 and 11

TEST 10 — 15 MINUTES

Directions: Each of the following questions has five suggested answers. Decide which one is best. Circle the letter that appears before your answer.

1. Last year the enrollment in a kindergarten was 150 pupils. This year the enrollment is 180 pupils. What was the percent of the increase in enrollment?

(A) 10%

(B) 15%

(C) 20%

(D) 25%

(E) 30%

2. The dimensions of a room are: l = 15 feet, w = 12 feet, and h = 8 feet. How many square feet of wallpaper will be required to cover the walls of this room?

(A) 192 sq. ft.

(B) 216 sq. ft.

(C) 240 sq. ft.

(D) 432 sq. ft.

(E) 648 sq. ft.

3. If $a = 8$ and $b = 3$, find the value of $4a + 3b^2$.

(A) 39

(B) 41

(C) 59

(D) 66

(E) 70

4. Model trains are built on a scale of 1 inch = 1 foot. If a particular model train is 3 feet $7\frac{1}{2}$ inches long, how many yards long would the actual train be?

(A) 14.5

(B) 28

(C) 36

(D) 43.5

(E) 57.75

5. A recipe calls for $1\frac{1}{2}$ cups of sugar. It is necessary to make eight times the recipe for a church supper. If 2 cups of sugar equal one pound, how many pounds of sugar will be needed to make the recipe for the supper?

(A) 4

(B) 6

(C) 8

(D) 10

(E) 12

6. The tax rate, in decimal form, for a certain community was .029 of the assessed valuation. Express this tax rate in dollars per $1,000 of the assessed valuation.

(A) $25 per $1,000

(B) $29 per $1,000

(C) $32 per $1,000

(D) $34 per $1,000

(E) $290 per $1,000

7. Which of the following is a member of the solution set of $x - y > 10$?

(A) (8, –3)

(B) (6, –3)

(C) (3, –7)

(D) (–3, 7)

(E) (–6, 3)

8. Find the area of the triangle pictured below.

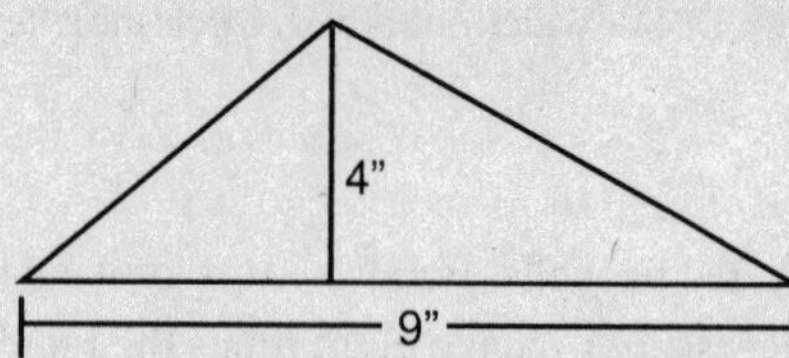

(A) 72 sq. in.

(B) 40 sq. in.

(C) 36 sq. in.

(D) 32 sq. in.

(E) 18 sq. in.

9. Solve for x: $\frac{x^2}{2} = 18$

(A) 72

(B) 36

(C) 9

(D) 8

(E) 6

10. The daily almanac report for one day during the summer stated that the sun rose at 6:14 AM and set at 6:06 PM. Find the number of hours and minutes in the time between the rising and setting of the sun on that day.

(A) 11 hr. 2 min.

(B) 11 hr. 48 min.

(C) 11 hr. 52 min.

(D) 12 hr. 8 min.

(E) 12 hr. 48 min.

11. Express 894 in expanded form, using exponents

(A) $(8 \times 10^2) + (9 \times 10) + 4$

(B) $(8 \times 10) + (9 \times 10) + 4$

(C) $(9^2 + 8) + 4$

(D) $(8 \times 10^3) + (9 \times 10^2) + 4$

(E) $(8^2 + 3^3) + 2^2$

12. The price of eggs increased from 50 cents to 60 cents a dozen. What was the percent of increase in price?

(A) 10%

(B) 15%

(C) 20%

(D) 25%

(E) 30%

13. Tom spent 2 hours and 30 minutes studying for three classes. What was the average time in minutes that he spent in studying for each class?

(A) 30

(B) 40

(C) 45

(D) 50

(E) 55

14. Find the perimeter of a parallelogram whose dimensions are l = 16 inches, w = 12 inches.

(A) 24 in.

(B) 28 in.

(C) 38 in.

(D) 56 in.

(E) 63 in.

15. Approximate the square root of 91 to the nearest tenth.

(A) 9.9

(B) 9.5

(C) 9.1

(D) 8.9

(E) 8.5

Practice Multiple-Choice Mathematics Tests

Answer Key

TEST 1

1. **C**	4. **A**	7. **D**	10. **D**	13. **A**
2. **B**	5. **C**	8. **A**	11. **B**	14. **C**
3. **D**	6. **A**	9. **C**	12. **C**	15. **B**

TEST 2

1. **C**	4. **B**	7. **B**	10. **C**	13. **B**
2. **D**	5. **B**	8. **A**	11. **B**	14. **B**
3. **D**	6. **B**	9. **D**	12. **C**	15. **D**

TEST 3

1. **C**	4. **B**	7. **A**	10. **C**	13. **B**
2. **C**	5. **C**	8. **A**	11. **D**	14. **C**
3. **B**	6. **D**	9. **B**	12. **C**	15. **C**

TEST 4

1. **D**	4. **A**	7. **C**	10. **D**	13. **A**
2. **B**	5. **B**	8. **C**	11. **B**	14. **C**
3. **B**	6. **D**	9. **A**	12. **B**	15. **B**

TEST 5

1. **A**	4. **D**	7. **D**	10. **C**	13. **A**
2. **B**	5. **D**	8. **C**	11. **D**	14. **B**
3. **D**	6. **B**	9. **B**	12. **A**	15. **B**

TEST 6

1. **B**	4. **C**	7. **D**	10. **D**	13. **A**
2. **B**	5. **D**	8. **E**	11. **A**	14. **B**
3. **C**	6. **B**	9. **B**	12. **D**	15. **C**

TEST 7

1. **C**	4. **A**	7. **E**	10. **D**	13. **C**
2. **B**	5. **C**	8. **C**	11. **D**	14. **A**
3. **D**	6. **D**	9. **E**	12. **B**	15. **B**

TEST 8

1. **B**	4. **D**	7. **C**	10. **C**	13. **A**
2. **D**	5. **E**	8. **C**	11. **B**	14. **D**
3. **A**	6. **C**	9. **E**	12. **D**	15. **E**

TEST 9

1. **D**	4. **C**	7. **B**	10. **D**	13. **E**
2. **B**	5. **A**	8. **A**	11. **C**	14. **B**
3. **D**	6. **D**	9. **B**	12. **C**	15. **D**

TEST 10

1. **C**	4. **A**	7. **A**	10. **C**	13. **D**
2. **D**	5. **B**	8. **E**	11. **A**	14. **D**
3. **C**	6. **B**	9. **E**	12. **C**	15. **B**

CHAPTER 13

Quantitative Comparisons

PLAN A: ACCELERATED

- ***Read*** the chapter
- ***Study*** "What Smart Test-Takers Know"
- ***Read*** "Learning Exercises"
- ***Do*** "Practice Tests"

PLAN B: TOP SPEED

- ***Read*** "How Do You Solve Quantitative Comparisons?"
- ***Study*** "What Smart Test-Takers Know"
- ***Do*** "Practice Tests"

You'll Find Answers to These Questions

What are these strange-looking questions?
How do you solve quantitative comparisons?
What do smart test-takers know about quantitative comparisons?

WHAT ARE THESE STRANGE-LOOKING QUESTIONS?

You picked up this book. You flipped through some pages. You got to this chapter and thought, "What the heck am I supposed to do with these weird questions? What do they want from me now?" Well, quantitative comparisons are not quite as wacky as they look. You can recognize quantitative comparison questions easily because they look very different from other math questions. Each one has two side-by-side boxes containing quantities that you must compare. Then you choose the correct answers from choices (A) through (D).

There are some good things to remember about these. First, the choices are always the same (check out the sample directions below). Second, you don't actually have to solve a problem. The questions are really testing knowledge of mathematical principles rather than your calculating skills. Third, sometimes the testing folks give you a little help and provide a diagram or other information centered above the boxes with the information you are comparing.

HOW DO YOU SOLVE QUANTITATIVE COMPARISONS?

Your estimating and comparison skills, as well as the four steps shown below, will help you cope with these questions. Once you get used to the choices, things can move pretty quickly.

Quantitative Comparisons: Getting It Right

1. Memorize the answer choices.
2. For each question, compare the boxed quantities.
3. Consider all possibilities for any variables.
4. Choose your answer.

Now let's look at these steps in more detail.

1. Don't just learn the directions, try to memorize the answer choices. (Remember, they are always the same.) Then you can save time because you won't need to refer to them for every question.
2. Even though there are two quantities in each question, deal with one at a time. If there is extra information above the boxes, see how each quantity relates to it. Then do any figuring you need to do. (There won't be much.)
3. Consider all possibilities for any unknowns. Think what would happen if special numbers such as 0, negative numbers, or fractions were put into play.
4. Choose your answer. You shouldn't have to do involved calculations to get to the answer. If you're calculating endlessly, you've probably missed the mathematical principle the question is asking about.

Column A	Column B

The price of a pound of cheese increased from \$2.00 to \$2.50.

The percent increase in the price of cheese	25%

1. You already know the answer choices.
2. The centered information tells you that cheese increased in price from \$2.00 to \$2.50 per pound. Column A asks for the percent increase, which is $\frac{\$0.50}{\$2.00} = 25\%$. Column B requires no calculation, and it's equal to Column A.
3. There are no variables, so go on to Step 4.
4. Since the two columns are equal, the answer is choice (C).
5. Mark choice (C) on the answer sheet.

Column A	Column B
$x^2 + y^2$	$(x + y)^2$

TESTSMARTS

Variables stay constant. A variable that appears in both columns has the same meaning in each column.

1. You already know the answer choices.
2. The expression in Column B is $(x + y)^2 = x^2 + 2xy + y^2$. This is the same as the expression in Column A with the addition of the middle term $2xy$.
3. The terms x and y are variables that can be positive or negative or zero. For example, if x were 1 and y were 2, Column A would be $1^2 + 2^2 = 5$ and Column B would be $(1 + 2)^2 = 9$. The correct answer would then be choice (B). But if x were -1 and y were 2, Column A would be $-1^2 + 2^2 = 5$ and Column B would be $(-1 + 2)^2 = 1^2 = 1$. This time the correct answer would be choice (A).
4. Any time more than one answer can be true for a comparison—as is the case here—then the answer to that question must be choice (D), "the relationship cannot be determined from the information given."
5. Mark choice (D) on the answer sheet.

Remember that many quantitative comparisons can be solved without doing any calculating at all. In many cases, you should be able to arrive at the correct answer simply by applying your knowledge of basic math rules and principles. Look at these examples:

AVOID THE TRAPS!

Figures can be deceiving. If a figure carries a warning that it is not drawn to scale, don't depend on estimating or measuring to help you solve the question.

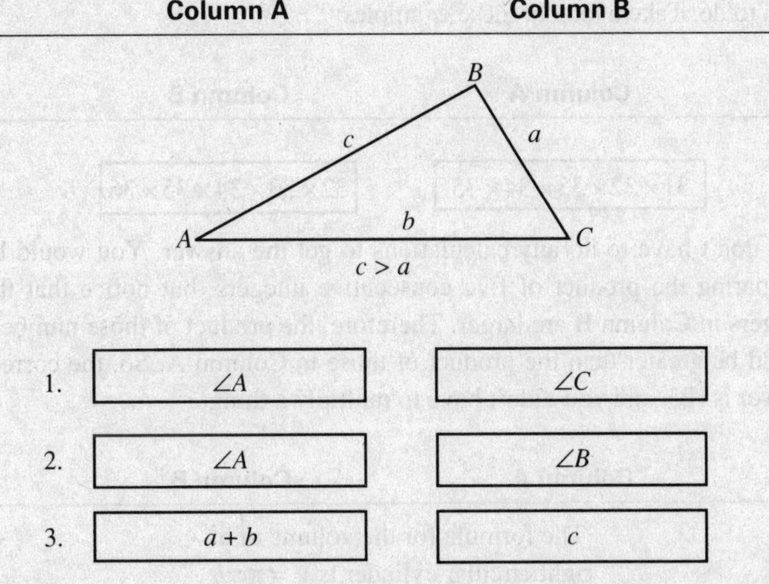

1. If two sides of a triangle are unequal, the angles opposite them are unequal, and the larger angle is opposite the longer side. So, the answer for this question is (B).
2. Because we can't really tell whether a or b is greater, we can't tell which angle is greater, so (D) is the correct answer.
3. The sum of any two sides of a triangle must always be greater than the length of the third side. The only answer for this question is (A).

What Smart Test-Takers Know

Quantitative comparisons may look complex, but if you come at them from the right angle (pardon the pun), you can streamline the answering process.

A COMPARISON IS FOREVER.

In quantitative comparisons, choice (A) is correct only if the quantity is *always* greater than that in Column B. The reverse is true of choice (B); it must *always* be greater than the information in Column A. If you choose (C), it means that the two quantities are *always* equal. The condition must hold true regardless of what number you plug in for a variable.

THE HIGHER THE NUMBER, THE TOUGHER THE CHOICE.

Just like the other sets of questions, quantitative comparisons go from easy to difficult as you progress through the section.

QUANTITATIVE COMPARISONS ARE NOT ABOUT CALCULATING.

If you find yourself calculating up a storm on a quantitative comparison, you've probably missed the boat. There's sure to be a simpler, shorter way to solve the problem. Find a way to reduce the amount of actual math you need to do. Take a look at these examples:

Column A	Column B
$31 \times 32 \times 33 \times 34 \times 35$	$32 \times 33 \times 34 \times 35 \times 36$

You don't have to do any calculations to get the answer. You would be comparing the product of five consecutive integers, but notice that the integers in Column B are larger. Therefore, the product of those numbers would be greater than the product of those in Column A. So, the correct answer is (B), and you didn't have to multiply a thing.

Column A	Column B
The formula for the volume of a right circular cylinder is $V = \pi r^2 h$	
The volume of a right circular cylinder with $r = 3$ and $h = 6$	The volume of a right circular cylinder with $r = 6$ and $h = 3$

You might think that for this question you absolutely have to do the complete calculations to find the volume of each cylinder. But you don't! Take a look at how simply this problem can be solved.

Volume $A = \pi(3^2)(6) = (3.14)(3)(3)(6)$

Volume $B = \pi(6^2)(3) = (3.14)(6)(6)(3)$

Since you're doing the same operation for both formulas—multiplying by 3.14—that cancels out. So the problem then shifts to the other factors: Which is larger, $(3^2)(6)$ or $(6^2)(3)$? At this point you should be able to see that the second one is larger. If you still need to take it another step, multiply $(3^2)(6) = (9)(6) = 54$ and then $(6^2)(3) = (36)(3)$. You don't have to finish because you can see that (36)(3) is larger than 54.

IF THE MATH IS NOT DIFFICULT, YOU SHOULD DO IT.

Column A	Column B
(0.6) (0.6)	$\frac{36}{100}$

Do this simple math and you've got a guaranteed correct answer. They both equal 0.36, so your choice is (C).

WHEN THE CENTERED INFORMATION HAS UNKNOWNS, YOU SHOULD SOLVE FOR THE UNKNOWNS.

Column A	Column B

$$3x = 12$$
$$4y = 20$$

x	y

You need to know what each of the unknowns is, so you have to solve for both. The correct answer is (B).

IT PAYS TO SIMPLIFY.

$$\frac{(8)(45)(17)}{(462)(8)} \qquad \frac{(17)(9)(42)}{(231)(16)}$$

There are a couple of things to notice here that will help you simplify the problem. First, both denominators are really the same: 462 is 231×2, so the denominators become (231)(2)(8). Next, the (17)s in both numerators cancel each other out. Now, all you have to do is figure out the results of (8)(45) and (9)(42), compare, and mark the correct answer. (It's (B), by the way.)

HERE'S THE ANSWER

Do I have to actually do all the calculations?

No, for most of the questions you can estimate or use your knowledge of basic mathematical principles to make your comparisons.

YOU CAN SIMPLIFY BY ADDING OR SUBTRACTING THE SAME VALUE IN EACH COLUMN.

Column A	Column B
$4x + 5$	$3x + 6$

Let's start by saying that the correct answer is (D). You might not see that right away, so we'll show you why it's true. The first thing you do is subtract 5 from both sides. The result is $4x$ and $3x + 1$. Now subtract $3x$ from both sides; you end up with x and 1. Since you don't know what x is, you can't know if it is larger or smaller than 1. That's why (D) is the correct answer.

YOU CAN SIMPLIFY BY MULTIPLYING OR DIVIDING EACH SIDE BY THE SAME POSITIVE NUMBER.

Column A	Column B
$9^{99} – 9^{98}$	9^{98}

You begin to simplify by dividing both sides by 9^{98}.

$\frac{9^{99} - 9^{98}}{9^{98}}$	$\frac{9^{98}}{9^{98}}$
$9^1 – 9^0$	9^0
9–1	1
8	1

This proves that the quantity in Column A is larger, even though you haven't solved for the exact quantity. Your correct answer is (A).

YOU HAVE TO CONSIDER ALL THE POSSIBILITIES.
When there are unknowns in the quantities being compared, you have to remember to consider all possibilities for what those unknowns might be. For example, an unknown might be 1, 0, a fraction, or a negative number. In each of these cases, the number has special properties that will affect your calculations. Or, unless otherwise stated, two unknowns could even be equal.

AN UNKNOWN MIGHT BE A ZERO.

Zero has special properties that come into play when you plug it in for an unknown.

TESTSMARTS

Common knowledge. The information centered above the two columns applies to both columns.

Column A	Column B
$x > 0, y > 0, z = 0$	
$3z(2x + 5y)$	$3x(2z + 5y)$

If $z = 0$, then $3z = 0$ and the product of Column A is 0. In Column B, though, $2z = 0$, so it comes out of the equation. The product will be $(3x)(5y)$, which will be a positive number. This means that (B) is the correct answer choice.

Column A	Column B
$x < 0, y > 0, z = 0$	
$3z(2x + 5y)$	$3x(2z + 5y)$

Again, the product of Column A is 0, because $3z$ still equals 0. The change comes in Column B. Because x is less than 0, $3x$ will be negative and $5y$ will be positive, so the product will be a negative number. This time, (A) is the correct answer.

AN UNKNOWN MIGHT BE A NEGATIVE NUMBER.

Column A	Column B
$3x = 4y$	
x	y

Don't think that (A) is the correct answer, even though if x and y are positive, x is greater than y. What if x and y are negative, as in $3(-4) = 4(-3)$; then y is greater than x. And if x and y are both zero, both columns are equal. Since you have no way of knowing what the values are, the correct answer is (D).

AN UNKNOWN MIGHT BE A FRACTION.

Column A	Column B
$x > 0$ and $x \neq 1$	
x^2	x

The correct answer to this comparison is (D). If x is larger than 1, then x^2 is larger than x. But if x is between 0 and 1—a fraction—then x^2 is smaller than x.

FRACTIONS CAN PLAY TRICKS.

Remember that a proper fraction raised to a power is smaller than the fraction itself.

Column A	Column B
$\frac{27}{41}$	$\left(\frac{27}{41}\right)^{15}$

If you keep the math principle in mind, you don't even have to think about doing these calculations. Since each successive multiplication would result in a smaller fraction, Column A will always be larger than Column B, so your answer is (A).

HERE'S THE ANSWER

What's an easy way to remember the directions for quantitative comparisons?

Just keep this key in mind:

A = A is bigger
B = B is bigger
C = Columns are equal
D = Determination impossible

IN QUANTITATIVE COMPARISONS, FIGURES ARE NOT NECESSARILY DRAWN TO SCALE.

Column A **Column B**

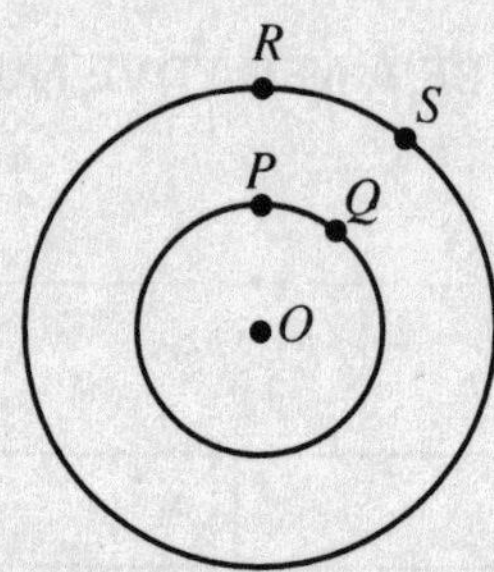

Minor arcs PQ and RS have equal length and each circle has center O.
Note: Figure not drawn to scale.

Column A	Column B
Degree measure of angle POQ	Degree measure of angle ROS

In the figure, angles POQ and ROS seem to be equal, but remember the warning. You're told that the figure is not drawn to scale, so don't be fooled.

The correct answer is (A), which you can see proved by this figure, which is drawn to scale.

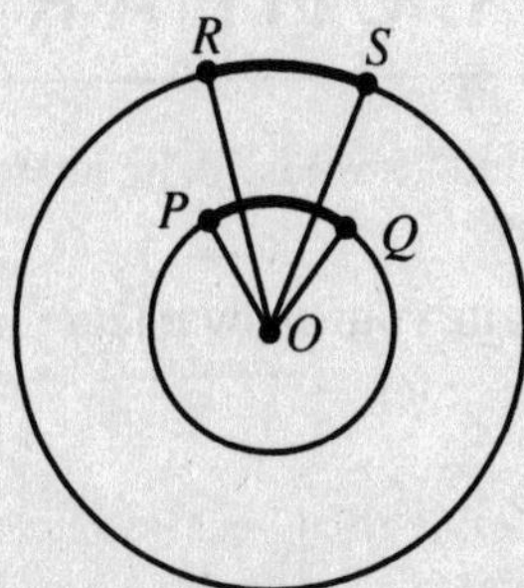

PLUGGING IN NUMBERS CAN HELP.
If you're stuck on a comparison with unknowns, try substituting numbers. Choose the numbers at random and plug them into the equations. Do this with three different substitutions and see if there is any consistent result. It's not a guarantee, but it's definitely worth a shot.

STRATEGIC GUESSING CAN RAISE YOUR SCORE.
When all else fails, call up your guessing skills. Here's how you can tip the scales in your favor, even if it's only a little bit:

- If a comparison involves only numbers without any unknowns, chances are that you'll be able to figure out the quantities and make a comparison. So in this situation, don't guess (D).
- If the comparison does contain an unknown or a figure, as a last resort guess (D).

LEARNING EXERCISES: QUANTITATIVE COMPARISONS

The questions in this section are arranged in boxes called "frames." The answer for each frame will be found in the box to the left of the question frame.

First, cover the answer boxes with a strip of paper. Write your answer letter in the margin. Then, move the paper down to expose the answer to that question.

Directions: For each of the following questions, two quantities are given—one in Column A, the other in Column B. Compare the two quantities and mark your answer sheet as follows:

(A) if the quantity in Column A is greater
(B) if the quantity in Column B is greater
(C) if the quantities are equal
(D) if the relationship cannot be determined from the information given.

Notes:

- In some questions, information concerning one or both of the quantities to be compared is centered above the entries in the two columns.
- A symbol that appears in any column has the same meaning in Column A as it does in Column B.
- Letters such as *x, y, a, b, k,* and *m* stand for real numbers.

EXPLANATION	PROBLEM
1. (B) The given information, $a > 0$ and $x > 0$, informs us that both a and x are positive numbers. The sum of two positive numbers is always greater than their difference.	**1.** Column A / Column B $a > 0$ $x > 0$ Column A: $a - x$ Column B: $a + x$
2. (A) The numbers in Column A are respectively larger than the numbers in Column B; therefore, their average must be greater.	**2.** Column A: The average of 17, 19, 21, 23 Column B: The average of 16, 18, 20, 22
3. (B) $\frac{5}{100} = \frac{x}{34}$, $100x = 170$, $x = 1.7$ $\frac{5}{100} = \frac{34}{x}$, $5x = 3400$, $x = 680$	**3.** Column A: 5% of 34 Column B: The number 34 is 5% of
4. (B) $[5a(4t)]^3 = [-10(12)]^3$ $= (-120)^3$ = negative answer $[4a(5s)]^2 = [-8(1)]^2$ $= (-8)^2$ = positive answer ∴ A positive product is greater than a negative one	**4.** $s = 1$ $t = 3$ $a = -2$ Column A: $[5a(4t)]^3$ Column B: $[4a(5s)]^2$

EXPLANATION	PROBLEM

5. (A)

$b > a$ (given)

$\therefore KR > KT$ (in a triangle, the greater side lies opposite the greater angle)

5. COLUMN A / COLUMN B

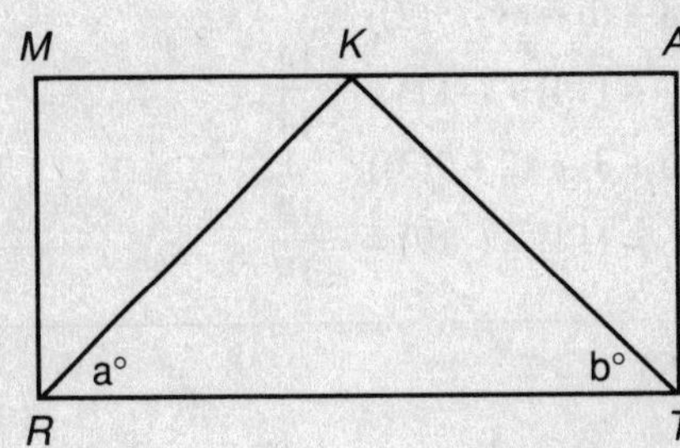

$a < b$

COLUMN A	COLUMN B
KR	KT

6. (D) Because x could be any integer from –2 to 3, the values of the fractions are impossible to determine.

6. $4 > x > -3$

COLUMN A	COLUMN B
$\frac{x}{3}$	$\frac{3}{x}$

7. (A)

$$\frac{2}{3}+\frac{3}{7}=\frac{14}{21}-\frac{9}{21} \qquad \frac{16}{21}-\frac{3}{7}=\frac{16}{21}-\frac{9}{21}$$

$$=\frac{23}{21} \qquad =\frac{7}{21}$$

7.

COLUMN A	COLUMN B
$\frac{2}{3}+\frac{3}{7}$	$\frac{16}{21}-\frac{3}{7}$

8. (C)

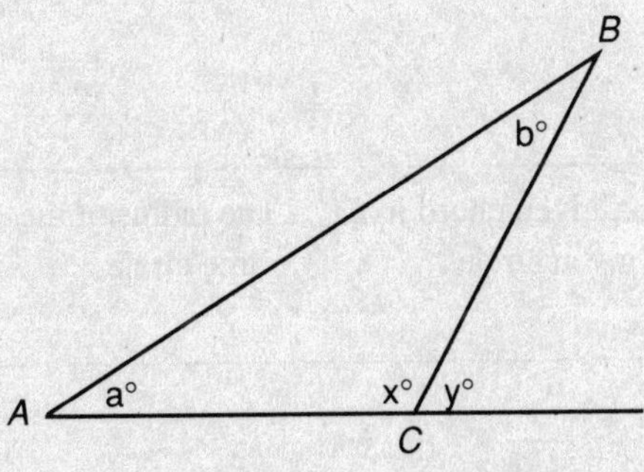

$y = a + b$ (an exterior angle of a triangle is equal to the sum of the two interior remote angles)

8.

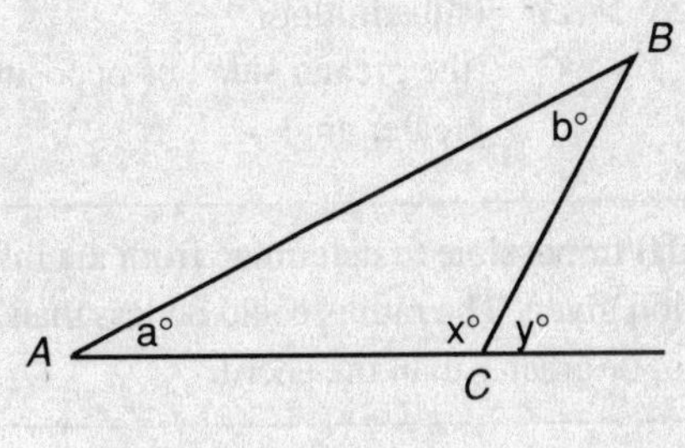

$a > b$

$x < a + b$

COLUMN A	COLUMN B
$a + b$	y

9. (D) There is not enough information, as y could equal 1, which would make both quantities equal; or y could be greater than 1, which would make y^3 greater than y^2. If y were a negative integer, then y^2 would be greater that y^3.

9. y = an odd integer

COLUMN A	COLUMN B
The numerical value of y^2	The numerical value of y^3

EXPLANATION	PROBLEM
	Column A / Column B
10. (B) $(8+6)\div(3-7(2))$ $=(14)\div(-11)=\frac{14}{-11}$ $(6+8)\div(2-7(3))$ $=(14)\div(-19)=\frac{14}{-19}$	**10.** Column A: $(8+6)\div(3-7(2))$ Column B: $(6+8)\div(2-7(3))$
11. (C) $\frac{3}{4}\times\frac{9}{9}=\frac{3}{4}$ $\frac{9}{9}\times\frac{3}{4}=\frac{3}{4}$	**11.** Column A: three-fourths of $\frac{9}{9}$ Column B: $\frac{9}{9}\bullet\frac{3}{4}$
12. (B) 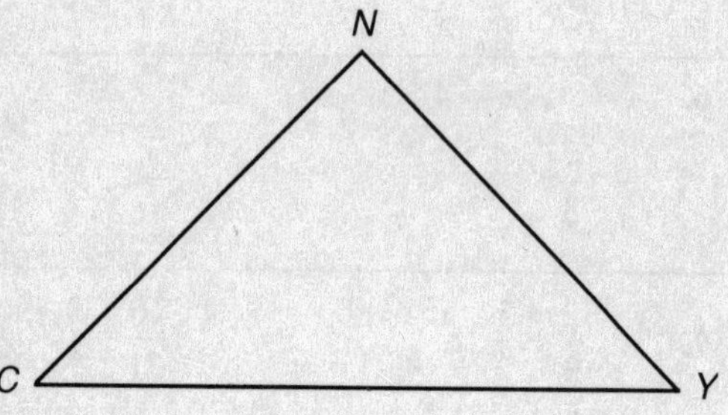 $NC = NY$ (given) $\angle C = \angle Y$ (angles opposite equal sides are equal) $\angle N > \angle C$ (given) $\angle N > \angle Y$ (substitution) $CY > NC$ (the greater side lies opposite the greater angle)	**12.** N C Y $NC = NY$ $\angle N > \angle C$ Column A: NC Column B:  CY
13. (D) Impossible to determine from the information given. The radius could be less than, equal to, or greater than the chord.	**13.** Column A: A given chord in a given circle. Column B: The radius of the same circle.
14. (C) $\frac{1}{\sqrt{9}}=\frac{1}{3}$	**14.** Column A: $\frac{1}{\sqrt{9}}$ Column B: $\frac{1}{3}$
15. (C) $5\left(\frac{2}{3}\right)=\frac{5}{1}\bullet\frac{2}{3}=\frac{10}{3}$ $\left(\frac{5}{3}\right)2=\frac{5}{3}\bullet\frac{2}{1}=\frac{10}{3}$	**15.** Column A: $5\left(\frac{2}{3}\right)$ Column B: $\left(\frac{5}{3}\right)2$

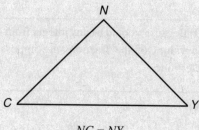

PRACTICE QUANTITATIVE COMPARISONS TESTS

TEST 1—15 MINUTES

Directions: For each of the following questions, two quantities are given—one in Column A, the other in Column B. Compare the two quantities and write your answer in the margin as follows:

(A) if the quantity in Column A is greater
(B) if the quantity in Column B is greater
(C) if the quantities are equal
(D) if the relationship cannot be determined from the information given.

NECESSARY INFORMATION:

- In each question, information concerning one or both of the quantities to be compared is centered above the entries in the two columns.
- A symbol that appears in any column represents the same value in Column A as it does in Column B.
- All numbers used are real numbers: letters such as *x*, *y*, and *t* stand for real numbers.
- Assume that the position of points, angles, regions, and so forth are in the order shown and that all figures lie in a plane unless otherwise indicated.
- Figures are not necessarily drawn to scale.

	Column A		Column B
1.	The average of 18, 20, 22, 24, 26		The average of 19, 21, 23, 25
2.	8 + 14 (8 – 6)		14 + 8 (8 – 6)
3.	6% of 30		The number 30 is 6% of
4.	$\left(\frac{1}{5}\right)^3$		$\left(\frac{1}{5}\right)^2$
5.	2^2		$\sqrt[3]{64}$
6.	(8 – 6)(2 + 7)		$\frac{9+12}{4-6}$
7.		The ratio of girls to boys in a math class is 3:1	
	Ratio of boys to the entire class		$\frac{1}{3}$
8.		A sport jacket priced $48 after a 20% discount	
	Original price of the sport jacket		$60
9.	1^{17}		17^1

	Column A		Column B
10.	A package of meat weighing 1.8 lbs. (unit price 92.6¢ per lb.)		A package of meat weighing 2.3 lbs. (unit price 67.5¢ per lb.)
11.	x	$x - y = -6$ $x + y = -2$	y
12.	The smallest root of the equation	$(x - 6)(x + 4) = 0$	The negative of the greatest root of the equation
13.	x	$\frac{x}{4} = y^2$	y
14.	$3x^2 - 2x + 4$	$x = -1$	$2x^3 + x^2 + 4$
15.	$\frac{y}{4}$	$6 > y > -2$	$\frac{4}{y}$

TEST 2—15 MINUTES

Directions: For each of the following questions, two quantities are given—one in Column A, the other in Column B. Compare the two quantities and write your answer in the margin as follows:

(A) if the quantity in Column A is greater
(B) if the quantity in Column B is greater
(C) if the quantities are equal
(D) if the relationship cannot be determined from the information given.

NECESSARY INFORMATION:

- In each question, information concerning one or both of the quantities to be compared is centered above the entries in the two columns.
- A symbol that appears in any column represents the same value in Column A as it does in Column B.
- All numbers used are real numbers; letters such as x, y, and t stand for real numbers.
- Assume that the position of points, angles, regions, and so forth are in the order shown and that all figures lie in a plane unless otherwise indicated.
- Figures are not necessarily drawn to scale.

	Column A		Column B
1.		$x < 0$ $y < 0$	
	$x + y$		$x - y$
2.		$t < 0$	
	t^3		t^2
3.		$\frac{a}{b} = \frac{c}{d}$	
	$a + b$		$c + d$

4.

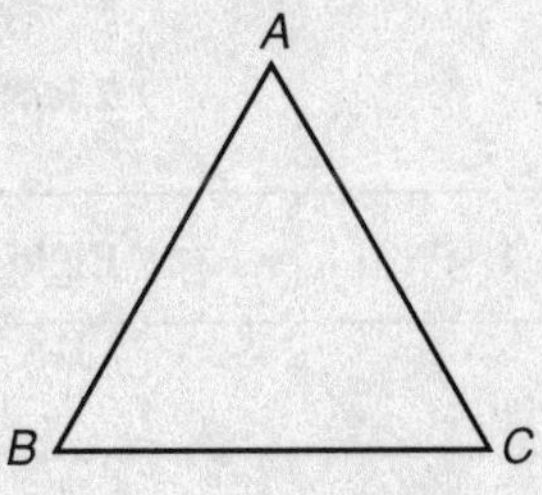

$AB = AC$
$\angle A < \angle B$

Column A	Column B
BC	AB

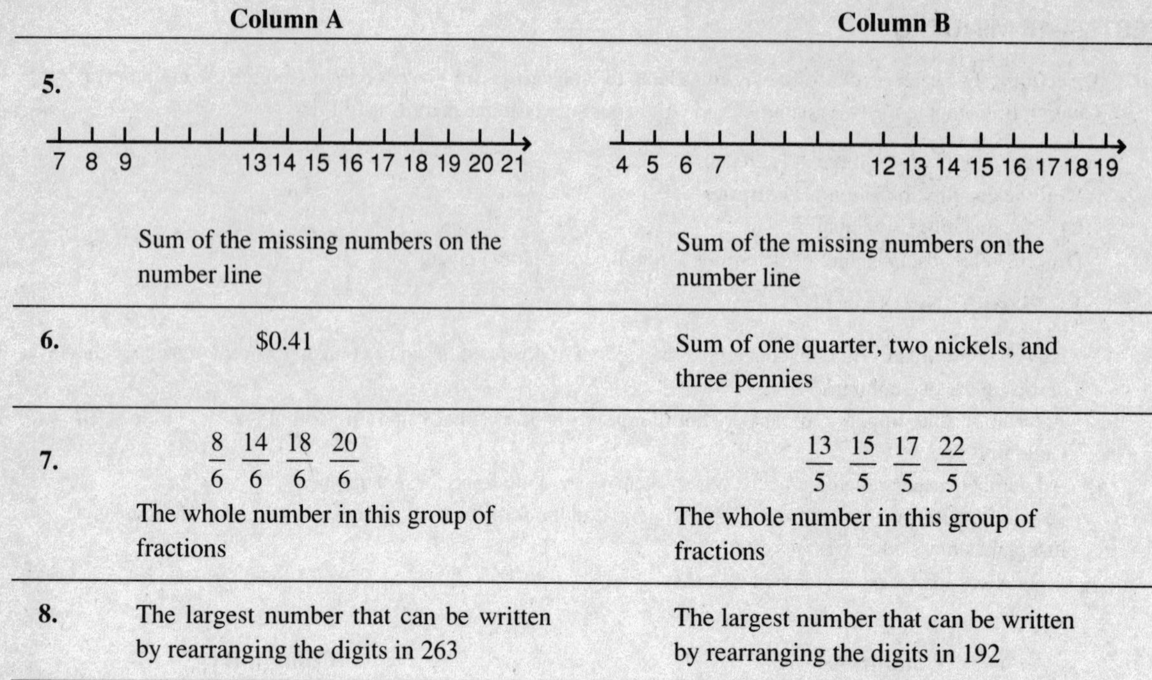

	Column A	Column B
5.	7 8 9 13 14 15 16 17 18 19 20 21 (number line) Sum of the missing numbers on the number line	4 5 6 7 12 13 14 15 16 17 18 19 (number line) Sum of the missing numbers on the number line
6.	\$0.41	Sum of one quarter, two nickels, and three pennies
7.	$\frac{8}{6}$ $\frac{14}{6}$ $\frac{18}{6}$ $\frac{20}{6}$ The whole number in this group of fractions	$\frac{13}{5}$ $\frac{15}{5}$ $\frac{17}{5}$ $\frac{22}{5}$ The whole number in this group of fractions
8.	The largest number that can be written by rearranging the digits in 263	The largest number that can be written by rearranging the digits in 192

9.

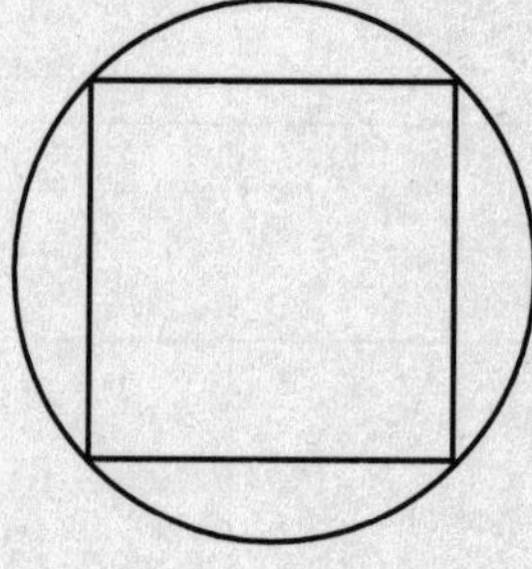

	Column A	Column B
9.	Circumference of the circle	Perimeter of the square
10.	2 more than $\frac{1}{3}$ of 63	2 less than $\frac{1}{3}$ of 66
11.	Two eights plus three	Eight twos plus three
12.	$4 \times 4 \times 6$	$6 \times 6 \times 4$
13.	The average of the numbers 2, 7, 9	The average of the numbers 3, 5, 9

Column A	Column B

14.

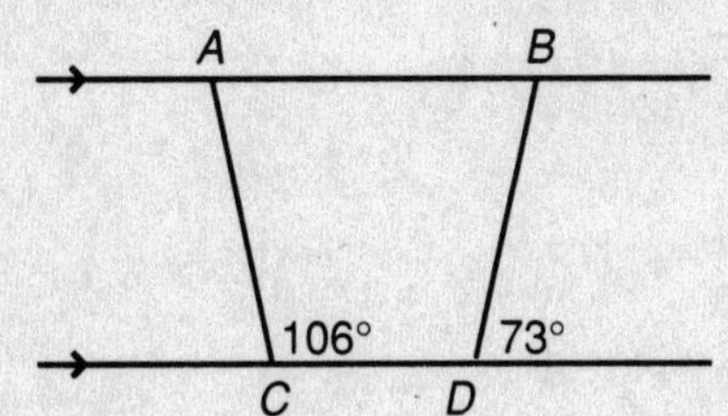

AC	*BD*

15.

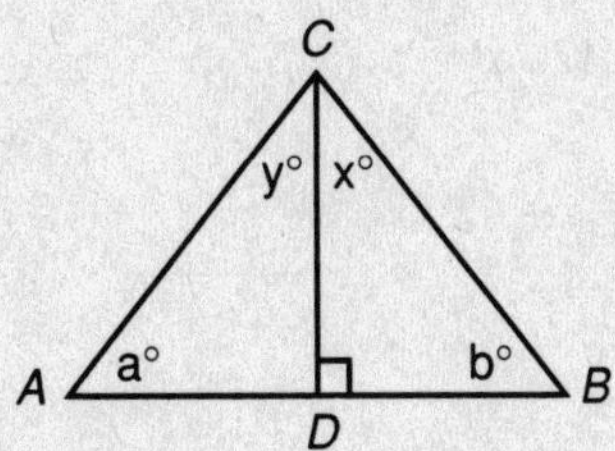

x	y

Practice Quantitative Comparisons Tests

Answer Key

TEST 1

1. **C**	4. **B**	7. **B**	10. **A**	13. **D**
2. **A**	5. **C**	8. **C**	11. **B**	14. **A**
3. **B**	6. **A**	9. **B**	12. **A**	15. **D**

TEST 2

1. **B**	4. **B**	7. **C**	10. **A**	13. **A**
2. **B**	5. **B**	8. **B**	11. **C**	14. **B**
3. **D**	6. **A**	9. **A**	12. **B**	15. **A**

What You Must Know About High School Entrance Exams—Mathematics Questions

Review this page the night before you take your high school entrance exam. It will help you get the answers to your math questions.

Multiple-Choice Questions—Both Exams

- These steps will help you solve multiple-choice math questions:
    1. Read the question carefully and determine what's being asked.
    2. Decide which math principles apply, and use them to solve the problem.
    3. Look for your answer among the choices. If it's there, mark it and go on.
    4. If the answer you found is not there, recheck the question and your calculations.
    5. If you still can't solve the problem, eliminate obviously wrong answers and take your best guess.
- The questions in the multiple-choice math section go from easy to hard, and the answer choices generally go from smallest to largest or from largest to smallest.
- If a certain kind of math question always gives you trouble, save it for last.

Quantitative Comparison Questions—ISEE Only

- Remember these steps as you work through the questions in this section:
    1. Memorize the answer choices.
    2. For each question, compare the boxed quantities.
    3. Consider all possibilities for any variables.
    4. Choose your answer.
- The quantitative comparison questions usually require less reading and computation than the standard multiple-choice questions.
- You don't actually have to solve the problem; you just need to determine which expression, if any, is greater.
- Quantitative comparison questions go from easy to hard.

PART

SEVEN

EVERYTHING YOU NEED!

The Writing Sample

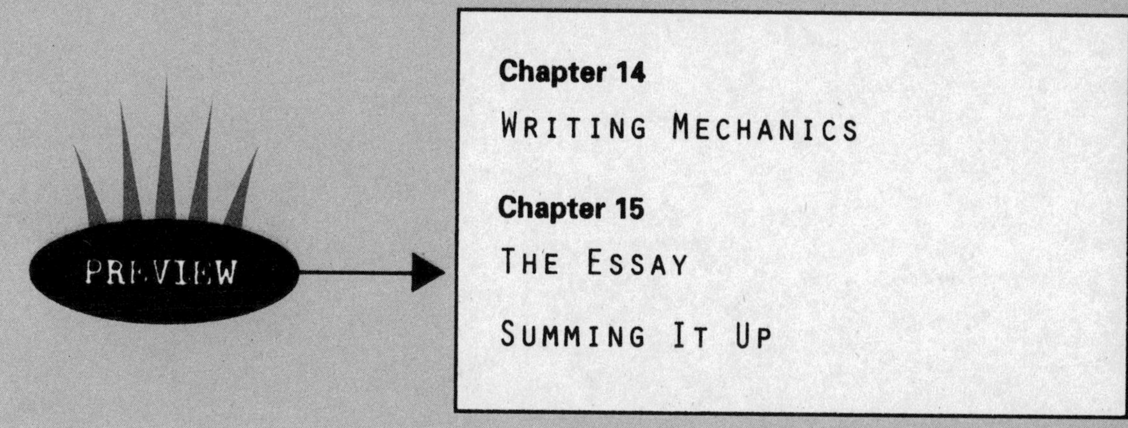

CHAPTER 14

Writing Mechanics

PLAN A: ACCELERATED

- ***Read*** the chapter

PLAN B: TOP SPEED

- ***Read*** "Why Should I Care about Writing Mechanics?"
- ***Skim*** the rest of the chapter

You'll Find Answers to These Questions

Why should I care about writing mechanics?
What are the rules of spelling?
What are the rules of punctuation?
What are the rules for capitalization?
What are the rules of grammar?
What is correct English usage?
How can I improve my writing?

WHY SHOULD I CARE ABOUT WRITING MECHANICS?

You have asked a good question. Neither the SSAT nor the ISEE includes test questions that directly measure spelling, grammar, English usage, punctuation, or capitalization, although some of the Catholic high school entrance exams and other less commonly used private secondary school admissions tests do so.

You won't have to take a test of your knowledge of writing mechanics, but you will have to submit a writing sample in the form of an essay on an assigned topic. The essay tests far more than mechanics. It shows your ability to organize and convey your thoughts. Your essay will not be scored. It will be photocopied and sent to the schools to which you apply. The essay will give the school an overall impression of your maturity and power of self-expression.

Clear thinking and a good vocabulary are important aspects of a well-written essay. Correct spelling, capitalization, punctuation, grammar, and English usage also do much for the quality of an essay. This chapter gives you some of the most important rules to help you through the mechanics of your essay writing and some practical exercises to help you put to use the information you are learning.

HERE'S THE ANSWER

How will writing mechanics affect my test score?

Writing mechanics will have no effect on your test score, but they will affect the overall quality of your writing sample. You want your essay to make a good impression.

WHAT ARE THE RULES OF SPELLING?

Rule 1

If a one-syllable word ends with a short vowel and one consonant,

- DOUBLE THE FINAL CONSONANT before adding a suffix that begins with a vowel.
- DO NOT DOUBLE THE FINAL CONSONANT before adding a suffix that begins with a consonant *or* if the word has two vowels before the consonant or ends in two consonants.

DOUBLE THE FINAL CONSONANT

-er	-er, -est	-y	-en	-ing	-ed
blotter	biggest	baggy	bidden	budding	rubbed
chopper	dimmer	blurry	bitten	quitting	scarred
clipper	fattest	funny	fatten	clipping	skipped
fitter	flatter	furry	flatten	dropping	stabbed
hopper	gladdest	muddy	gladden	fanning	stepped
plotter	grimmer	sloppy	hidden	fretting	stopped
quitter	hottest	starry	madden	grinning	tanned
shipper	madder	stubby	sadden	gripping	nodded
shopper	reddest	sunny	trodden	hopping	plotted

DO NOT DOUBLE THE FINAL CONSONANT

-ing, -ed, -er	-ly	-ness	-ful	-y
acting	badly	baseness	boastful	dirty
burned	dimly	bigness	baleful	dusky
cooker	gladly	coldness	doleful	fishy
climber	madly	dimness	fitful	frosty
coasting	manly	fatness	fretful	leafy
farmer	nearly	grimness	masterful	misty
feared	sadly	sadness	sinful	rainy
feasting	thinly	redness		soapy
quoted	trimly	wetness		weedy

Rule 2

If a word of more than one syllable ends with a short vowel and one consonant,

- DOUBLE THE FINAL CONSONANT before adding a suffix that begins with a vowel if the accent is on the last syllable.
- DO NOT DOUBLE THE FINAL CONSONANT if the accent is not on the last syllable or if the suffix begins with a consonant.

DOUBLE THE FINAL CONSONANT

-ing, ed	**-ence, -ent**	**-ance**	**-at**
befitting	abhorrence	acquittance	acquittal
befogged	concurrent	admittance	transmittal
committing	excellence	remittance	noncommittal
compelled	intermittent	transmittance	
controlling	occurrence		
disbarred	recurrent		
impelling			
incurred			
omitting	**-er**	**-en**	**-able**
permitted			
propelling	beginner	forbidden	controllable
regretted	propeller	forgotten	forgettable
submitting	transmitter		regrettable

DO NOT DOUBLE THE FINAL CONSONANT

ENDING IN TWO CONSONANTS	TWO VOWELS BEFORE THE FINAL CONSONANT	ACCENT NOT ON THE FINAL SYLLABLE	SUFFIX BEGINS WITH A CONSONANT
-ing, -ed	**-ing, -ed**	**-ing, -ed**	**-ment**
consenting	concealing	benefiting	allotment
converted	contained	blossomed	annulment
demanding	detaining	differed	commitment
diverted	disdained	gathered	deferment
requesting	refraining	limiting	equipment
subsisted	remounted	profited	interment
supplanting	restraining	quarreling	preferment
supported	retained	soliciting	
transcending	revealing	summoned	

Rule 3

If a word ends with a silent e,

- DROP THE E before adding a suffix that begins with a vowel.
- DO NOT DROP THE E before a suffix that begins with a consonant.

DROP THE SILENT E

-ing, -ed	**-able**	**-ation**	**-ive**
achieving	believable	admiration	abusive
balanced	debatable	continuation	appreciative
believing	desirable	declaration	creative
capsized	endurable	derivation	decorative
relieved	excitable	duplication	expensive
revolving	imaginable	exhalation	exclusive
telephoned	measurable	inclination	illustrative
trembling	observable	inhalation	intensive
trembled	pleasurable	quotation	repulsive

DO NOT DROP THE SILENT E

-ful	**-ment**	**-ly**	**-ness**
careful	achievement	accurately	completeness
disgraceful	amusement	affectionately	cuteness
distasteful	announcement	bravely	fineness
fateful	engagement	extremely	genuineness
hopeful	enlargement	genuinely	lameness
prideful	enslavement	immediately	lateness
tasteful	entanglement	intensely	likeness
vengeful	management	intimately	ripeness
wasteful	replacement	sincerely	wideness

EXCEPTIONS

acknowledgment	changeable	judgment	peaceable
acreage	chargeable	manageable	pronounceable
advantageous	duly	noticeable	replaceable
argument	dyeing	outrageous	serviceable
awful	exchanging		

Rule 4

To make a word plural,

- ADD -ES to words ending in s, x, l, ch, or sh.
- ADD -S to all other words.

ADD -S		ADD -ES	
advantages	croutons	annexes	fizzes
angles	distances	birches	hoaxes
beacons	effects	brushes	marshes
briquets	rings	caresses	witnesses
candles		coaches	

Rule 5

If a word ends with a y that has a vowel sound,

- CHANGE THE Y TO I before adding any suffix except one that begins with the letter i.
- DO NOT CHANGE THE Y if it is preceded by another vowel, or if the suffix begins with i.

CHANGE THE Y TO I

-er, -est, -ly, -ness	-ous	-ance, -ant	-able, -ful
craftier	ceremonious	alliance	beautiful
daintiest	harmonious	appliance	fanciful
healthier	industrious	compliant	justifiable
heavily	injurious	defiant	merciful
moldiness	luxurious	pliant	pitiable
moodiest	melodious	reliance	pliable
murkiness	mysterious		
steadily	studious		
sleepiness	victorious		

DO NOT CHANGE THE Y		EXCEPTIONS
-ing	-ly, -ness	-ous
allying	dryly	beauteous
applying	dryness	bounteous
complying	shyly	duteous
defying	shyness	miscellaneous
fortifying	slyly	piteous
justifying	slyness	plenteous
pitying	spryly	
multiplying	wryly	
supplying		

Rule 6

Put i before e,
Except after c,
Or when sounded like a,
As in *neighbor* or *weigh*.

I BEFORE E	EXCEPT AFTER C	OR SOUNDS LIKE A	EXCEPTIONS
achieve	conceit	deign	ancient
believe	conceive	eight	conscience
fiend	ceiling	freight	deficient
fierce	deceit	inveigh	efficient
grief	deceive	neighbor	foreign
relieve	perceive	reign	glacier
reprieve	receipt	skein	heifer
retrieve	receive	vein	leisure
sieve		weigh	proficient
			weird

Rule 7

The suffix -ful never has two l's. When -ful is added to a word, the spelling of the base word does not change.

EXAMPLES		
careful	disdainful	distasteful
forceful	grateful	hopeful
masterful	powerful	sorrowful

Rule 8

When the suffix -ly is added to a word, the spelling of the base word does not change.

EXAMPLES				
coyly	quickly	frankly	swiftly	forcefully

EXCEPTIONS

When -ly is added to a word ending with -le, the e is replaced by a y.

forcibly	despicably	illegibly
indelibly	probably	suitably

When the base word ends with a y following a consonant, the y is changed to i before -ly.

busily	daintily	heavily
luckily	merrily	sleepily

Rule 9

When a syllable ends in a long vowel sound, that sound is made by the vowel alone: OPEN SYLLABLE.

A long vowel sound occurring in a one-syllable word, or in a syllable that ends with a consonant, is usually spelled by a vowel team: CLOSED SYLLABLE.

OPEN SYLLABLE	CLOSED SYLLABLE
recent	sublime
premium	infantile
sequence	crayon
stationary	attainment
fatality	cavalcade
abrasion	genteel
motivate	intercede
custodian	sincere
component	ridicule
proprietor	vestibule
microbe	clapboard
cyclone	disclose
cucumber	telescope
humane	growth

SPELLING DEMONS

aberration
abscess
abundance
accessible
accumulation
acquaint
adjunct
aggravate
alleged
amendment
ancient
anecdote
annoyance
apparatus
arraignment
ascertain
assessment

beleaguered
bureau

character
column
committal
committee
community
confectionery
correlation
crystallized
currency

deferred
derogatory
desecrated
dilapidated
disappearance
dissatisfied
distinguished

ecstasy
embarrass
eminent
emphasis
emphatically
essential
exaggerate
exceed
exhortation
existence

fascinated
feudal
financier

harassment
hearth
heritage
hindrance

imminent
impartiality
incongruous
indict
inimitable
irreparably

jeopardy
journal
judgment

laboratory
lacquer
liquidate

maneuver
masquerade
matinee
mechanical
medieval
memoir
mischievous

negligible
nickel

occasionally
occur
official

pamphlet
panicky
parliamentary
patient
peculiar
picnicking
pneumonia
possession
precious
presumptuous
publicity
punctilious

regrettable
rehearsal
relevant
repetitious
resilience
rhetorical
rhythm

sacrilegious
scissors
separate
sophomore
source
sovereign
specialized
specifically
staunch
subversive
surgeon
symmetrical

temperamental
thorough
tomorrow
transient

vacillate
vacuum
vengeance

whether
wholly
wield
yacht

LEARNING EXERCISES: SPELLING

Directions: In the following exercise you find a group of four words. One of these four is spelled correctly. You are to find the correctly spelled word. In the answer frames, you find the letter of the correct answer and a reference to one of the spelling rules you just learned. The correctly spelled word in that exercise follows the rule mentioned in the answer frame.

ANSWER	QUESTION	
1. **(A)** See Rule 6 and the Demons list.	**1.** (A) transient (B) transeint	(C) transent (D) transint
2. **(B)** See the Demons list.	**2.** (A) heratage (B) heritage	(C) heiritage (D) heretage
3. **(B)** See Rule 6.	**3.** (A) retreivable (B) retrievable	(C) retrievible (D) retreivible
4. **(B)** See Rule 6, Exceptions.	**4.** (A) foriegn (B) foreign	(C) foureign (D) fouriegn
5. **(C)** See Rule 4.	**5.** (A) witneses (B) wittnesses	(C) witnesses (D) wittneses
6. **(B)** See Rule 3.	**6.** (A) priceing (B) pricing	(C) priseing (D) prising
7. **(A)** See Rule 1.	**7.** (A) intermittent (B) intermitant	(C) intermittant (D) intermitent
8. **(A)** See Rule 7.	**8.** (A) disgracefully (B) disgracefull	(C) disgracful (D) disgracefuly
9. **(C)** See Rule 5.	**9.** (A) complyeing (B) complieing	(C) complying (D) compling
10. **(D)** See Rules 6 and 3.	**10.** (A) acheivment (B) achievment	(C) acheivement (D) achievement

Directions: In the following exercise you find a group of three words, plus choice (D), NO ERROR. You have to decide whether one of the three words is misspelled. The incorrectly spelled word is spelled correctly in the answer frame. You are referred back to the spelling rules, if necessary.

ANSWER	QUESTION	
11. **(A)** nuisance	**11.** (A) nuisanse (B) obedience	(C) nonsense (D) NO ERROR
12. **(C)** martial	**12.** (A) confidential (B) initial	(C) marsial (D) NO ERROR

ANSWER	QUESTION	
13. (C) Wednesday	**13.** (A) Saturday (B) Thursday	(C) Wendsday (D) NO ERROR
14. (B) arousing See Rule 3.	**14.** (A) confessing (B) aroussing	(C) caressing (D) NO ERROR
15. (D)	**15.** (A) medicine (B) feminine	(C) paraffin (D) NO ERROR
16. (C) leisure See Rule 6.	**16.** (A) pleasure (B) measure	(C) liesure (D) NO ERROR
17. (A) library	**17.** (A) libary (B) contemporary	(C) canary (D) NO ERROR
18. (D)	**18.** (A) prosperity (B) university	(C) susceptibility (D) NO ERROR
19. (D)	**19.** (A) immaterial (B) immeasurable	(C) implicit (D) NO ERROR
20. (A) occasionally See the Demons List.	**20.** (A) ocassionaly (B) necessarily	(C) recommended (D) NO ERROR
21. (C) mutiny See Rule 9.	**21.** (A) feudal (B) fugitive	(C) muetiny (D) NO ERROR
22. (A) donkeys See Rule 5.	**22.** (A) donkies (B) territories	(C) secretaries (D) NO ERROR
23. (B) *Shelves* is the plural form of the word *shelf*.	**23.** (A) squashes (B) shelfs	(C) lenses (D) NO ERROR
24. (A) blameless See Rule 3.	**24.** (A) blamless (B) nervous	(C) immensity (D) NO ERROR
25. (A) concurrence See Rule 2.	**25.** (A) concurence (B) remittance	(C) appearance (D) NO ERROR
26. (C) steadily See Rule 8, Exceptions.	**26.** (A) gracefully (B) intimately	(C) steadyly (D) NO ERROR

ANSWER	QUESTION	
27. (B) weird See Rule 6, Exceptions.	**27.** (A) deficient (B) wierd	(C) financier (D) NO ERROR
28. (D)	**28.** (A) forcible (B) irascible	(C) tyrannical (D) NO ERROR
29. (C) dryness See Rule 5.	**29.** (A) driest (B) dryly	(C) driness (D) NO ERROR
30. (A) embargoes	**30.** (A) embargos (B) topazes	(C) sheaves (D) NO ERROR

Directions: In the following exercise you find a group of four words. One of these four is spelled incorrectly. You are to find the incorrectly spelled word. It is spelled correctly in the answer frame. You are referred back to the spelling rules, if necessary.

ANSWER	QUESTION	
31. (B) arraignment See the Demons List.	**31.** (A) heinous (B) arrainment	(C) bureau (D) repetitious
32. (C) deliberation	**32.** (A) corrugated (B) regrettable	(C) deliberasion (D) yacht
33. (A) possession See the Demons List.	**33.** (A) posession (B) blamable	(C) bookkeeping (D) whether
34. (D) irrelevant	**34.** (A) mediocrity (B) dilapidated	(C) derogatory (D) irelevant
35. (A) sovereign See the Demons List.	**35.** (A) soverein (B) mischievous	(C) harassment (D) masquerade
36. (C) presumptuous See the Demons List.	**36.** (A) anemia (B) equilibrium	(C) presumptious (D) baccalaureate
37. (A) vengeance See the Demons List.	**37.** (A) vengance (B) punctilious	(C) vacillation (D) resilience
38. (D) beleaguered See the Demons List.	**38.** (A) beatitude (B) aggravation	(C) description (D) beleagered

ANSWER	QUESTION	
39. (B) imminent See the Demons List.	**39.** (A) inimitable (B) iminent	(C) eminent (D) impartial
40. (A) recognizable See Rule 3.	**40.** (A) recognizeable (B) incongruity	(C) temperamentally (D) complacency

WHAT ARE THE RULES OF PUNCTUATION?

1. Apostrophe (')

The apostrophe is used

1. *to indicate possession*

   Bob's hat; Burns' poems; Jones's houses;

NOTE: Use *apostrophe only* (without the *s*) for certain words that end in *s:*

a. When *s* or *z* sound comes before the final *s*
   Moses' journey
   Cassius' plan

b. after a plural noun
   girls' shoes
   horses' reins

Where to place the Apostrophe

EXAMPLE:

These (ladie's, ladies') blouses are on sale.

The apostrophe means *belonging to everything to the* left *of the apostrophe*.
ladie's means *belonging to ladie* (no such word)
ladies' means *belonging to ladies* (correct)

EXAMPLE:

These (childrens', children's) coats are size 8.

One cannot say *belonging to childrens* (childrens'); therefore, children's (belonging to children) is correct.

ALSO NOTE:

a. When two or more names comprise one firm, possession is indicated in the last name.
   Lansdale, Jackson, and Roosevelt's law firm.
   Sacks and Company's sale.

b. In a compound noun, separated by hyphens, the apostrophe belongs in the last syllable—*father-in-law's*.

Note that the *plurals* of compound nouns are formed by adding the *s* (no apostrophe, of course) to the *first* syllable: I have three *brothers-in-law*.

The apostrophe has two other uses besides indicating possession:

2. *for plurals of letters and figures*
   three d's; five 6's

3. *to show that a letter has been left out*
   let's (for let us)

NOTE A: ours, yours, his, hers, its, theirs, and whose—all are possessive but have no apostrophe.

NOTE B: The apostrophe is omitted occasionally in titles: Teachers College, Actors Equity Association.

2. Colon (:)

The colon is used

1. *after such expressions as "the following," "as follows," and their equivalents*

   The sciences studied in high schools are as follows: biology, chemistry, and physics.

2. *after the salutation in a business letter*

   Gentlemen:
   Dear Mr. Jones:

NOTE: A comma (see below) is used after the salutation in a friendly letter:
   Dear Ted,

The semicolon is *never* used in a salutation.

3. Comma (,)

In general, the comma is used in writing just as you use a pause in speaking. Here are the specific situations in which commas are used:

1. *direct address*

   Mr. Adams, has the report come in yet?

2. *apposition*

   Sam, our buyer, gave us some good advice.

3. *parenthetical expressions*
   We could not, however, get him to agree.
4. *complimentary closing of a letter*
   Sincerely,
   Truly yours,
5. *dates, addresses*
   November 11, 1918
   Cleveland, Ohio
6. *series*
   We had soup, salad, ice cream, and milk for lunch.

NOTE: Comma before the *and* in a series is optional.

7. *phrase or clause at beginning of sentence (if longer than four words)*
   As I left the room to go to school, my mother called me.
8. *separating two independent clauses joined by a conjunction*
   We asked for Mr. Smith, but he had already left for home.
9. *clarity*
   After planting, the farmer had his supper.
10. *direct quotation*
    Mr. Arnold blurted out, "This is a fine mess!"
11. *modifier expressions that do not restrict the meaning of the thought which is modified*
    Air travel, which may or may not be safe, is an essential part of our way of life.

NOTE: Travel that is on the ground is safer than air travel. (NO COMMAS)

4. Dash (—)

The dash is about twice as long as the hyphen. The dash is used

1. *to break up a thought*
   There are five—remember I said five—good reasons to refuse their demands.
2. *instead of parentheses*
   A beautiful horse—Black Beauty is its name—is the hero of the book.

5. Exclamation Mark (!)

The exclamation mark is used after an expression of *strong feeling:*

Ouch! I hurt my thumb.

6. Hyphen (-)

The hyphen divides a word:
mother-in-law

NOTE: When written out, numbers from twenty-one through ninety-nine are hyphenated.

7. Parentheses ()

1. Parentheses set off that part of the sentence that is not absolutely necessary to the completeness of the sentence:
   I was about to remark (this may be repetition) that we must arrive there early.
2. Parentheses are also used to enclose or to set off figures, letters, signs, and dates in a sentence:
   Shakespeare (1564–1616) was a great dramatist.
   The four forms of discourse are a) narration b) description c) exposition d) argument.

8. Period (.)

The period is used

1. *after a complete thought unit*
   The section manager will return shortly.
2. *after an abbreviation*
   Los Angeles, Calif.

9. Question Mark (?)

The question mark is used after a *request for information:*

When do you leave for lunch?

10. Quotation Marks (" ")

Quotation marks are used

1. *to enclose what a person says directly*

   "No one could tell," she said, "that it would occur."

   He exclaimed, "This is the end!"

   "Don't leave yet," the boss told her.

2. *to enclose a title*

   I have just finished reading "Arrowsmith."

11. Semicolon (;)

The semicolon is not used much. It is to be avoided where a comma or a period will suffice. Following, however, are the common uses of the semicolon:

1. *to avoid confusion with numbers*

   Add the following: $1.25; $7.50; and $12.89.

2. *before explanatory words or abbreviations—namely, e.g., etc.*

   We are able to supply you with two different gauges of nylon stockings; namely, 45 and 51.

NOTE: The semicolon goes before the expression "namely." A comma follows the expression.

3. *to separate short statements of contrast*

   War is destructive; peace is constructive.

WHAT ARE THE RULES FOR CAPITALIZATION?

Capitalize:

1. *the first word of a sentence*
   With cooperation, a depression can be avoided.
2. *all proper names*
   America, Sante Fe Chief, General Motors, Abraham Lincoln.
3. *days of the week and months*
   The check was mailed on *Thursday*.

NOTE: The seasons are not capitalized.
Example: In Florida, *winter* is mild.

4. *the word* dear *when it is the first word in the salutation of a letter*
   Dear Mr. Jones:
   but
   My *dear* Mr. Jones:
5. *the first word of the complimentary close of a letter*
   Truly yours,
   Very truly yours,
6. *the first and all other important words in a title*
   The Art of *Salesmanship*
7. *a word used as part of a proper name*
   William *Street* (but—That *street* is narrow.)
   Morningside *Terrace* (but—We have a *terrace* apartment.)
8. *titles, when they refer to a particular official or family member*
   The report was read by *Secretary* Marshall.
   (but—Miss Shaw, our *secretary*, is ill.)
   Let's visit *Uncle* Harry.
   (but—I have three *uncles*.)
9. *points of a compass, when they refer to particular regions of a country*
   We're going *South* next week. (but—New York is *south* of Albany.)

NOTE: Write: the Far West, the Pacific Coast, the Middle East, etc.

10. *the first word of a direct quotation*
    It was Alexander Pope who wrote, "*A* little learning is a dangerous thing."

NOTE: When a direct quotation sentence is broken, the *first* word of the *second half* of the sentence is not capitalized.

"Don't phone," Lilly told me, "*because* they're not in yet."

WHAT ARE THE RULES OF GRAMMAR?

The rules of grammar govern the ways in which parts of speech are organized in a sentence. There are rules concerning word endings, word order, and which words may be used together. You must know the parts of speech in order to follow the rules of grammar.

Parts of Speech

A **NOUN** is the name of a person, place, thing, or idea:

teacher city desk democracy

PRONOUNS substitute for nouns:

he they ours those

An **ADJECTIVE** describes a noun:

warm quick tall blue

A **VERB** expresses action or a state of being:

yell interpret feel are

An **ADVERB** modifies a verb, an adjective, or another adverb:

fast slowly friendly well

CONJUNCTIONS join words, sentences, and phrases:

and but or

A **PREPOSITION** shows position in time or space:

in during after behind

Nouns

There are different kinds of nouns.

Common nouns are general:

house girl street city

Proper nouns are specific:

White House Jane Main Street New York

Collective nouns name groups:

team crowd organization Congress

Nouns have *cases:*

Nominative—the subject, noun of address, or predicate noun

Objective—the direct object, indirect object, or object of the preposition

Possessive—the form that shows possession

Pronouns

The **antecedent of the pronoun** is the noun to which a pronoun refers. A pronoun must agree with its antecedent in gender, person, and number.

There are several kinds of pronouns. (Pronouns also have cases.)

Demonstrative pronoun: this, that, these, those

Indefinite pronoun: all, any, nobody

Interrogative pronoun: who, which, what

Personal pronoun:

		NOMINATIVE	OBJECTIVE	POSSESSIVE
SINGULAR	1st person	I	me	my, mine
	2nd person	you	you	your, yours
	3rd person	he, she, it	him, her, it	his, hers
PLURAL	1st person	we	us	our, ours
	2nd person	you	you	your, yours
	3rd person	they	them	their, theirs

Adjectives

Adjectives answer the questions "Which one?"; "What kind?"; and "How many?"

There are three uses of adjectives:

A **noun modifier** is usually placed directly before the noun it describes: He is a *tall* man.

A **predicate adjective** follows an inactive verb and modifies the subject: She is *happy*. I feel *terrible*.

Article or **noun marker** are other names for these adjectives: *the, a, an*.

Adverbs

Adverbs answer the questions "Why?"; "How?"; "Where?"; "When?"; and "To what degree?"

Adverbs should not be used to modify nouns.

TWENTY PRINCIPLES OF GRAMMAR

1. The subject of a verb is in the nominative case even if the verb is understood and not expressed.
2. The word *who* is in the nominative case. *Whom* is in the objective case.
3. The word *whoever* is in the nominative case. *Whomever* is in the objective case.
4. Nouns or pronouns connected by a form of the verb *to be* should always be in the nominative case.
5. The object of a preposition or of a transitive verb should use a pronoun in the objective case.
6. It is unacceptable to use the possessive case in relation to inanimate objects.
7. A pronoun agrees with its antecedent in person, number, gender, and case.
8. A noun or pronoun linked with a gerund should be in the possessive case.
9. *Each, every, everyone, everybody, anybody, either, neither, no one, nobody,* and similar words are singular and require the use of singular verbs and pronouns.
10. When modifying the words *kind* and *sort,* the words **this** and **that** always remain in the singular.
11. The word *don't* is not used with third person singular pronouns or nouns.
12. A verb agrees in number with its subject. A verb should not be made to agree with a noun that is part of a phrase following the subject.
13. The number of the verb is not affected by the addition to the subject of words introduced by *with, together with, no less than, as well as,* and so on.
14. Singular subjects joined by the words *nor* and *or* take a singular verb.
15. A subject consisting of two or more nouns joined by the word *and* takes a plural verb.
16. A verb should agree in number with the subject, not with the predicate noun.
17. In *there is* and *there are*, the verb should agree in number with the noun that follows it.
18. An adjective should not be used to modify a verb.
19. Statements equally true in the past and in the present are usually expressed in the present tense.
20. The word *were* is used to express a condition contrary to fact or a wish.

LEARNING EXERCISES: PRINCIPLES OF GRAMMAR

Directions: Each of the sentences on the following pages is grammatically incorrect. Rewrite each sentence correctly. The answer box provides the correctly written sentence and refers to the Principle of Grammar that governs that sentence.

ANSWER	QUESTION
1. They are as old as we (are). *See Principle 1.*	**1.** They are as old as us.
2. Who do you suppose paid us a visit? *See Principle 2.*	**2.** Whom do you suppose paid us a visit?
3. Punish whoever is guilty. *See Principle 3.*	**3.** Punish whomever is guilty.
4. It is I. *See Principle 4.*	**4.** It is me.
5. Can it be they? *See Principle 4.*	**5.** Can it be them?
6. It would be impossible for you and me. *See Principle 5.*	**6.** It would be impossible for you and I.
7. He had difficulty with the management of the store. *See Principle 6.*	**7.** He had difficulty with the store's management.
8. I, who am older, know better than you. *See Principle 7.*	**8.** I, who's older, know better than you.
9. Is there any criticism of Arthur's going? *See Principle 8.*	**9.** Is there any criticism of Arthur going?
10. Everybody tried his (or her) hardest. *See Principle 9.*	**10.** Everybody tried their hardest.
11. I do not like this sort of cake. *See Principle 10.*	**11.** I do not like these sort of cakes.
12. She doesn't like to engage in such activity. *See Principle 11.*	**12.** She don't like to engage in such activity.
13. The use of liquors is dangerous. *See Principle 12.*	**13.** The use of liquors are dangerous.
14. The district attorney, as well as many of his aides, has been involved in the investigation. *See Principle 13.*	**14.** The district attorney, as well as many of his aides, have been involved in the investigation.

ANSWER	QUESTION
15. Either the fifth or the seventh of the courses they have laid open is to be accepted. *See Principle 14.*	**15.** Either the fifth or the seventh of the courses they had laid open are to be accepted.
16. The fighting and wrestling of the two men are excellent. *See Principle 15.*	**16.** The fighting and wrestling of the two men is excellent.
17. The worst feature of the play was the abominable actors. *See Principle 16.*	**17.** The worst feature of the play were the abominable actors.
18. There are present a child and two dogs. *See Principle 17.*	**18.** There is present a child and two dogs.
19. He spoke slowly and carefully. *See Principle 18.*	**19.** He spoke slow and careful.
20. He said that Venus is a planet. *See Principle 19.*	**20.** He said that Venus was a planet.
21. I wish I were a clown. *See Principle 20.*	**21.** I wish I was a clown.

WHAT IS CORRECT ENGLISH USAGE?

Correct English usage refers to word choice. Correct English usage means using the right word with the specific meaning intended. Many English words are easily confused and misused. Here is a list of commonly misused words and examples of how to use them correctly.

accede—means *to agree with.*
concede—means *to yield,* but not necessarily in agreement.
exceed—means *to be more than.*

We shall *accede* to your request for more evidence.

To avoid delay, we shall *concede* that more evidence is necessary.

Federal expenditures now *exceed* federal income.

access—means *availability.*
excess—means *too much.*

The lawyer was given *access* to the grand jury records.

The expenditures this month are far in *excess* of income.

accept—means *to take when offered.*
except—means *excluding.* (preposition)
except—means *to leave out.* (verb)

The draft board will *accept* all seniors as volunteers before graduation.

All eighteen-year-olds *except* seniors will be called.

The draft board will *except* all seniors until after graduation.

adapt—means *to adjust or change.*
adopt—means *to take as one's own.*
adept—means *skillful.*

Children can *adapt* to changing conditions very easily.

The war orphan was *adopted* by the general's family.

Proper instruction makes children *adept* in various games.

NOTE: adapt *to,* adopt *by,* adept *in* or *at.*

adapted to—implies *original or natural suitability.*

The gills of the fish are *adapted* to underwater breathing.

adapted for—implies *created suitability.*

Atomic energy is constantly being *adapted for* new uses.

adapted from—implies *changed to be made suitable.*

Many of Richard Wagner's opera librettos were *adapted from* old Norse sagas.

addition—means *the act or process of adding.*
edition—means *a printing of a publication.*

In *addition* to a dictionary, she always used a thesaurus.

The first *edition* of Shakespeare's plays appeared in 1623.

advantage—means *a superior position.*
benefit—means *a favor conferred* or *earned* (as a profit).

He had an *advantage* in experience over his opponent.

The rules were changed for his *benefit.*

NOTE: to *take* advantage *of,* to *have* an advantage *over.*

adverse—(pronounced AD-verse) means *unfavorable.*
averse—(pronounced a-VERSE) means *disliking.*

He took the *adverse* decision in poor taste.

Many students are *averse* to criticism by their classmates.

advise—means *to give advice. Advise* is losing favor as a synonym for *notify.*

Acceptable: The teacher will *advise* the student in habits of study.

Unacceptable: We are *advising* you of a delivery under separate cover. (SAY: *notifying*)

affect—means *to influence.* (verb)
effect—means *an influence.* (noun)
effect—means *to bring about.* (verb)

Your education must *affect* your future.

The *effect* of the last war is still being felt.

A diploma *effected* a tremendous change in her attitude.

NOTE: *Affect* also has a meaning of *pretend.* She had an *affected* manner.

after—is unnecessary with the *past* participle.

SAY: *After* checking the timetable, I left for the station.
DON'T SAY: *After having checked* (omit *after*) the timetable, I left for the station.

ain't—is an *unacceptable* contraction for *am not, are not,* or *is not.*

aisle—is *a passageway* between seats.
isle—is *a small island.* (Both words rhyme with *pile.*)

all ready—means *everybody* or *everything ready.*
already—means *previously.*
They were *all ready* to write when the teacher arrived.
They had *already* begun writing when the teacher arrived.

alright—is *unacceptable.*
all right—is *acceptable.*

all-round—means *versatile* or *general.*
all around—means *all over a given area.*
Rafer Johnson, decathlon champion, is an *all-round* athlete.
The police were lined up for miles *all around.*

all together—means *everybody* or *everything together.*
altogether—means *completely.*
The boys and girls sang *all together.*
This was *altogether* strange for a person of that type.

all ways—means *in every possible way.*
always—means *at all times.*
She was in *all ways* acceptable to the voters.
His reputation had *always* been spotless.

allude—means *to make a reference to.*
elude—means *to escape from.*
Only incidentally does Coleridge *allude* to Shakespeare's puns.
It is almost impossible for one to *elude* tax collectors.

allusion—means *a reference.*
illusion—means *a deception of the eye or mind.*
The student made *allusions* to his teacher's habits.
Illusions of the mind, unlike those of the eye, cannot be corrected with glasses.

alongside of—means *side by side with.*
Bill stood *alongside of* Barb.

alongside—means *parallel to the side.*
Park the car *alongside* the curb.

alot—is *unacceptable.* It should always be written as two words: *a lot.*

among—is used with *more than two persons or things.*
NOTE: *Amongst* should be avoided.

between—is *used* with *two persons or things.*
The inheritance was equally divided *among* the four children.
The business, however, was divided *between* the oldest and the youngest one.

amount—applies to quantities *that cannot be counted one by one.*
number—applies to quantities *that can be counted one by one.*
A large *amount* of grain was delivered to the storehouse.
A large *number* of bags of grain was delivered.

annual—means *yearly.*
biannual—means *twice a year.* (*Semiannual* means the same.)
biennial—means *once in two years* or *every two years.*

anywheres—is *unacceptable.*
anywhere—is *acceptable.*
SAY we can't find it *anywhere.*
ALSO SAY *nowhere* (NOT nowheres), *somewhere* (NOT somewheres)

aren't I—is colloquial. Its use is to be discouraged.
SAY: *Am I not* entitled to an explanation? (preferred to *Aren't I …*)

as—(used as a conjunction) is followed by a verb.
like—(used as a preposition) is NOT followed by a verb.
Do *as* I do, not *as* I say.
Try not to behave *like* a child.
Unacceptable: He acts *like* I do.

as far as—expresses *distance.*
so far as—indicates *a limitation.*
We hiked *as far as* the next guest house.
So far as we know, the barn was adequate for a night's stay.

as good as—should be used *for comparisons only.*
This motel is *as good as* the next one.
NOTE: *As good as* does NOT mean *practically.*
Unacceptable: They *as good as* promised us a place in the hall.
Acceptable: They *practically* promised us a place in the hall.

as if—is correctly used in the expression, "He talked *as if* his jaw hurt him."
Unacceptable: "He talked *like* his jaw hurt him."

ascared—no such word. It is *unacceptable* for *scared.*
The child was *scared* of ghosts. (NOT *ascared*).

ascent—is *the act of rising.*
assent—means *approval.*
The *ascent* to the top of the mountain was perilous.
Congress gave its *assent* to the President's emergency directive.

assay—means to analyze or examine.
essay—means a short literary composition.
The chemist *assayed* the content of the ore.
The candidate expressed her views in an *essay.*

attend to—means *to take care of.*
tend to—means *to be inclined to.*
One of the clerks will *attend to* mail in my absence.
Inactive people *tend* to gain weight.

back—should NOT be used with such words as *refer* and *return* since the prefix *re* means *back.*
Unacceptable: Refer *back* to the text, if you have difficulty recalling the facts.

backward / **backwards** — Both are *acceptable* and may be used interchangeably as an adverb.
We tried to run *backward.* (or *backwards*)
Backward as an adjective means *slow in learning.* (DON'T say backwards in this case)
A *backward* pupil should be given every encouragement.

berth—is *a resting place.*
birth—means *the beginning of life.*
The new liner was given a wide *berth* in the harbor.
He was a fortunate man from *birth.*

beside—means *close to.*
besides—refers *to something that has been added.*
He lived *beside* the stream.
He found wild flowers and weeds *besides.*

better—means *recovering.*
well—means *completely recovered.*
She is *better* now than she was a week ago.
In a few more weeks, she will be *well.*

both—means *two considered together.*
each—means *one of two or more.*
Both of the applicants qualified for the position.
Each applicant was given a generous reference.
NOTE: Avoid using such expressions as the following:
Both girls had a new typewriter. (Use *each girl* instead.)
Both girls tried to outdo the other. (Use *each girl* instead.)
They are *both* alike (Omit *both*).

breath—means *an intake of air.*
breathe—means *to draw air in and give it out.*
breadth—means *width.*
Before you dive in, take a very deep *breath.*
It is difficult to *breathe* under water.
In a square, the *breadth* should be equal to the length.

bring—means *to carry toward the person who is speaking.*
take—means *to carry away from the speaker.*
Bring the books here.
Take your raincoat with you when you go out.

broke—is the past tense of *break.*
broke—is *unacceptable* for *without money.*
He *broke* his arm.
"Go for broke" is a slang expression widely used in gambling circles.

bunch—refers to *things.*
group—refers to *persons* or *things.*
This looks like a delicious *bunch* of bananas.
What a well-behaved *group* of children!
NOTE: The colloquial use of bunch applied to *persons* is to be discouraged.
A *bunch* of the boys were whooping it up. (*Number* is preferable.)

certainly—(and *surely*) is an *adverb.*
sure—is an *adjective.*
He was *certainly* learning fast.
Unacceptable: He *sure* was learning fast.

cite—means *to quote.*
sight—refers to *vision* or appearance.
site—means *a place for a building.*

He was fond of *citing* from the Scriptures.
The *sight* of the wreck was appalling.
The Board of Education is seeking a *site* for the new school.

coarse—means *vulgar or harsh.*
course—means a *path* or a *study.*

We were shunned because of his *coarse* behavior.
The ship took its usual *course.*
Which *course* in English are you taking?

come to be—should NOT be replaced with the expression *become to be,* since *become* means *come to be.*

True freedom will *come to be* when all tyrants have been overthrown.

comic—means *intentionally funny.*
comical—means *unintentionally funny.*

A clown is a *comic* figure.
The peculiar hat she wore gave her a *comical* appearance.

conscience—means *sense of right.*
conscientious—means *faithful.*
conscious—means *aware.*

People's *conscience* prevents them from becoming completely selfish.
We all depend on him because he is *conscientious.*
The injured woman was completely *conscious.*

considerable—is properly used *only as an adjective,* NOT as a noun.

cease—means *to end.*
seize—means *to take hold of.*

Will you please *cease* making those sounds?
Seize him by the collar as he comes around the corner.

cent—means *a coin.*
scent—means *an odor.*
sent—is the past tense of *send.*

The *one-cent* postal card is a thing of the past.
The *scent* of roses is pleasing.
We were *sent* to the rear of the balcony.

calendar—is *a system of time.*
calender—is *a smoothing and glazing machine.*
colander—is *a kind of sieve.*

In this part of the world, most people prefer the twelve-month *calendar.*
In ceramic work, the potting wheel and the *calender* are indispensable.
Garden-picked vegetables should be washed in a *colander* before cooking.

can—means *physically able.*
may—implies *permission.*

I *can* lift this chair over my head.
You *may* leave after you finish your work.

cannot help—must be followed by an *-ing* form.

We cannot help *feeling* (NOT *feel*) distressed about this.
NOTE: *cannot help but is unacceptable.*

can't hardly—is a *double negative.* It is *unacceptable.*

SAY: The child *can hardly* walk in those shoes.

capital—is *the city.*
capitol—is *the building.*

Paris is the *capital* of France.
The Capitol in Washington is occupied by the Congress. (The Washington *Capitol* is capitalized.)
NOTE: *Capital* also means wealth.

compare to—means *to liken to something which has a different form.*
compare with—means *to compare persons or things with each other when they are of the same kind.*
contrast with—means *to show the difference between two things.*

A minister is sometimes *compared to* a shepherd.
Shakespeare's plays are often *compared with* those of Marlowe.
The writer *contrasted* the sensitivity of the dancer *with* the grossness of the pugilist.

complement—means *a completing part.*
compliment—is *an expression of admiration.*

Her wit was a *complement* to her beauty.
He *complimented* her sense of humor.

consul—means *a government representative.*
council—means *an assembly that meets for deliberation.*

counsel—means *advice.*
Americans abroad should keep in touch with their *consuls.*
The City *Council* enacts local laws and regulations.
The defendant heeded the *counsel* of his friends.

convenient to—should be followed by a *person.*
convenient for—should be followed by a *purpose.*
Will these plans be *convenient to* you?
You must agree that they are *convenient for* the occasion.

copy—is *an imitation of an original work.* (not necessarily an exact imitation)
facsimile—is *an exact imitation of an original work.*
The counterfeiters made a crude *copy* of the hundred-dollar bill.
The official government engraver, however, prepared a *facsimile* of the bill.

could of—is *unacceptable.* (*Should of* is also *unacceptable.*)
could have—is *acceptable.* (*Should have* is *acceptable.*)
Acceptable: You *could have* done better with more care.
Unacceptable: I *could of* won.
ALSO AVOID: *must of, would of.*

decent—means *suitable.*
descent—means *going down.*
dissent—means *disagreement.*
The *decent* thing to do is to admit your fault.
The *descent* into the cave was treacherous.
Two of the nine justices filed a *dissenting* opinion.

deduction—means *reasoning from the general (laws or principles) to the particular (facts).*
induction—means *reasoning from the particular (facts) to the general (laws or principles).*
All humans are mortal. Since John is human, he is mortal. *(deduction)*
There are 10,000 oranges in this truckload.
I have examined 100 from various parts of the load and find them all of the same quality. I conclude that the 10,000 oranges are of this quality. *(induction)*

delusion—means *a wrong idea* that will probably influence action.
illusion—means *a wrong idea* that will probably *not* influence action.
People were under the *delusion* that the earth was flat.
It is just an *illusion* that the earth is flat.

desert—(pronounced DEZZ-ert) means *an arid area.*
desert—(pronounced di-ZERT) means *to abandon;* also *a reward or punishment.*
dessert—(pronounced di-ZERT) means *the final course of a meal.*
The Sahara is the world's most famous *desert.*
A husband must not *desert* his wife.
Execution was a just *desert* for his crime.
We had plum pudding for *dessert.*

different from—is *acceptable.*
different than—is *unacceptable.*
Acceptable: Jack is *different from* his brother.
Unacceptable: Florida's climate is *different than* New York's climate.

doubt that—is *acceptable.*
doubt whether—is *unacceptable.*
Acceptable: I *doubt that* you will pass this term.
Unacceptable: We *doubt whether* you will succeed.

dual—means *relating to two.*
duel—means *a contest between two persons.*
Dr. Jekyl had a *dual* personality.
Alexander Hamilton was fatally injured in a *duel* with Aaron Burr.

due to—is *unacceptable* at the beginning of a sentence. Use *because of, on account of,* or some similar expression instead.
Unacceptable: Due to the rain, the game was postponed.
Acceptable: Because of the rain, the game was postponed.
Acceptable: The postponement was *due to* the rain.

each other—refers to *two persons.*
one another—refers to *more than two persons.*
The two girls have known *each other* for many years.
Several of the girls have known *one another* for many years.

either ... or—is used when referring to choices.
neither ... nor—is the *negative* form.

Either you *or* I will win the election.

Neither Bill *nor* Barb is expected to have a chance.

eliminate—means *to get rid of.*
illuminate—means *to supply with light.*

Let us try to *eliminate* the unnecessary steps.

Several lamps were needed to *illuminate* the corridor.

emerge—means *to rise out of.*
immerge—means *to sink into.* (also **immerse**)

The swimmer *emerged* from the pool.

The laundress *immerged* the dress in the tub of water.

emigrate—means *to leave one's country for another.*
immigrate—means *to enter another country.*

The Norwegians *emigrated* from Norway in the mid-1860s.

Many of the Norwegian *immigrants* settled in the Middle West.

everyone—is written as one word when it is a *pronoun.*
every one—(two words) is used when each individual is stressed.

Everyone present voted for the proposal.

Every one of the voters accepted the proposal.

NOTE: *Everybody* is written as one word.

everywheres—is *unacceptable.*
everywhere—is *acceptable.*

We searched *everywhere* for the missing book.

NOTE: *Everyplace* (one word) is likewise *unacceptable.*

feel bad—means *to feel ill.*
feel badly—means *to have a poor sense of touch.*

I *feel bad* about the accident I saw.

The numbness in his limbs caused him to *feel badly.*

feel good—means *to be happy.*
feel well—means *to be in good health.*

I *feel* very *good* about my recent promotion.

Spring weather always made me *feel well.*

flaunt—means *to make a display of.*

Mary *flouted* the authority of the principal.

Hester Prynne *flaunted* her scarlet "A."

flout—means *to insult.*

formally—means *in a formal way.*
formerly—means *at an earlier time.*

The letter of reference was *formally* written.

Max was *formerly* a delegate to the convention.

former—means *the first of two.*
latter—means *the second of two.*

The *former* half of the book was in prose.

The *latter* half of the book was in poetry.

forth—means *forward.*
fourth—*comes after third.*

They went *forth* like warriors of old.

The *Fourth* of July is our Independence Day.

NOTE: spelling of *forty* (40) and *fourteen* (14).

get—is a verb that strictly means *to obtain.*

Please *get* my bag.

There are many slang forms of GET that should be avoided: AVOID: Do you *get* me? (SAY: Do you *understand* me?) AVOID: You can't *get* away with it. (SAY: You won't *avoid* punishment if you do it.) AVOID: *Get* wise to yourself. (SAY: *Use* common sense.) AVOID: We didn't *get* to go. (SAY: We didn't *manage* to go.)

got—means *obtained.*

He *got* the tickets yesterday.

AVOID: You've *got* to do it. (SAY: You *have* to do it.)

AVOID: We *have got* no sympathy for them. (SAY: We *have* no sympathy for them.)

AVOID: They have *got* a great deal of property. (SAY: They *have* a great deal of property.)

hanged—is used in reference to a *person.*
hung—is used in reference to a *thing.*

The prisoner was *hanged* at dawn.

The picture was *hung* above the fireplace.

however—means *nevertheless.*
how ever—means *in what possible way.*

We are certain, *however,* that you will like this class.

We are certain that, *how ever* you decide to study, you will succeed.

if—introduces a *condition.*
whether—introduces a *choice.*

I shall go to Europe *if* I win the prize.

He asked me *whether* I intended to go to Europe. (not *if*)

if it was—implies that *something might have been true in the past.*
if it were—implies *doubt,* or indicates *something that is contrary to fact.*

If your book was there last night, it is there now.

If it were summer now, we would all go swimming.

in—usually refers to *a state of being.* (no motion)
into—is used for *motion from one place to another.*

The records are *in* that drawer.

I put the records *into* that drawer.

NOTE: "We were walking in the room" is correct even though there is motion. The motion is *not* from one place to another.

irregardless—is *unacceptable.*
regardless—is *acceptable.*

Unacceptable: Irregardless of the weather, I am going to the game.

Acceptable: Regardless of his ability, he is not likely to win.

its—means *belonging to it.*
it's—means *it is.*

The house lost *its* roof.

It's an exposed house, now.

kind of
sort of } are *unacceptable* for *rather.*

SAY: We are *rather* disappointed in you.

last—refers to *the final member in a series.*
latest—refers to *the most recent in time.*
latter—refers to *the second of two.*

This is the *last* bulletin. There won't be any other bulletins.

This is the *latest* bulletin. There will be other bulletins.

Of the two most recent bulletins, the *latter* is more encouraging.

lay—means *to place.*
lie—means *to recline.*

Note the forms of each verb:

TENSE	LIE (RECLINE)
Present	The child *is lying* down.
Past	The child *lay* down.
Pres. Perf.	The child *has lain* down.

TENSE	LAY (PLACE)
Present	The chicken *is laying* an egg.
Past	The chicken *laid* an egg.
Pres. Perf.	The chicken *has laid* an egg.

lightening—is the present participle of *to lighten.*
lightning—means *the flashes of light accompanied by thunder.*

Leaving the extra food behind resulted in *lightening* the pack.

Summer thunderstorms produce startling *lightning* bolts.

many—refers to *a number.*
much—refers to *a quantity* in *bulk.*

How *many* inches of rain fell last night?

I don't know; but I would say *much* rain fell last night.

may—is used in the *present tense.*
might—is used in the *past tense.*

We are hoping that they *may* come today.

He *might* have done it if you had encouraged him.

it's I—is always *acceptable.*
it's me—is *acceptable* only in colloquial speech or writing.

It's him
This is her
It was them } always *unacceptable*

It's he
This is she
It was they } always *acceptable*

noplace—as a solid word, is *unacceptable* for *no place* or *nowhere.*

Acceptable: You now have *nowhere* to go.

number—is singular *when the total is intended.*

The *number* (of pages in the book) is 500.

number—is plural *when the individual units are referred* to.

A *number of pages* (in the book) were printed in italic type.

of any—(and *of anyone*) is *unacceptable* for *of all.*
SAY: Hers was the highest mark *of all.*
(NOT *of any* or *of anyone*)

off of—is *unacceptable.*
SAY: He took the book *off* the table.

out loud—is *unacceptable* for *aloud.*
SAY: Jane read *aloud* to her family every evening.

outdoor—(and *out-of-door*) is an adjective.
outdoors—is an adverb.
We spent most of the summer at an *outdoor* music camp.
Most of the time we played string quartets *outdoors.*
NOTE: *Out-of-doors* is *acceptable* in either case.

people—comprise *a united* or *collective group of individuals.*
persons—are *individuals that are separate and unrelated.*
Only five *persons* remained in the theater after the first act.
The *people* of New York City have enthusiastically accepted "Shakespeare-in-the-Park" productions.

persecute—means *to make life miserable for someone.* (Persecution is illegal.)
prosecute—means *to conduct a criminal investigation.* (Prosecution is legal.)
Some people insist upon *persecuting* other ethnic groups.
The District Attorney is *prosecuting* the racketeers.

precede—means *to come before.*
proceed—means *to go ahead.* (*Procedure* is the noun.)
supersede—means *to replace.*
What were the circumstances that *preceded* the attack?
We can then *proceed* with our plan for resisting a second attack.
It is then possible that Plan B will *supersede* Plan A.

principal—means *chief* or *main* (as an adjective); *a leader* (as a noun).
principle—means *a fundamental truth* or *belief.*
His *principal* supporters came from among the peasants.
The *principal* of the school asked for cooperation from the staff.
Humility was the guiding *principle* of Buddha's life.
NOTE: *Principal* may also mean *a sum placed at interest.*
Part of her monthly payment was applied as interest on the *principal.*

sit—means *take a seat.* (intransitive verb)
set—means *place.* (transitive verb)
Note the forms of each verb:

TENSE	SIT (TAKE A SEAT)
Present	He *sits* on a chair.
Past	He *sat* on the chair.
Pres. Perf.	He *has sat* on the chair.

TENSE	SET (PLACE)
Present	He *sets* the lamp on the table.
Past	He *set* the lamp on the table.
Pres. Perf.	He *has set* the lamp on the table.

some time—means *a portion of time.*
sometime—means *at an indefinite time in the future.*
sometimes—means *occasionally.*
I'll need *some time* to make a decision.
Let us meet *sometime* after twelve noon.
Sometimes it is better to hesitate before signing a contract.

somewheres—is *unacceptable.*
somewhere—is *acceptable.*

stationary—means *standing still.*
stationery—means *writing materials.*
In ancient times people thought the earth was *stationary.*
We bought writing paper at the *stationery* store.

stayed—means *remained.*
stood—means *remained upright* or *erect.*
The army *stayed* in the trenches for five days.
The soldiers *stood* at attention for one hour.

sure—for *surely* is *unacceptable.*
SAY: You *surely* (NOT *sure*) are not going to write that!

take in—is *unacceptable* in the sense of *deceive* or *attend.*
SAY: We were *deceived* (NOT *taken in*) by his oily manner.
We should like to *attend* (NOT *take in*) a few plays during our vacation.

their—means *belonging to them.*
there—means *in that place.*
they're—means *they are.*
We took *their* books home with us.
You will find your books over *there* on the desk.
They're going to the ballpark with us.

theirselves—is *unacceptable* for *themselves.*
SAY: Most children of school age are able to care for *themselves* in many ways.

these kind—is *unacceptable.*
this kind—is *acceptable.*
I am fond of *this kind* of apples.
NOTE: *These kinds* would also be *acceptable.*

through—meaning *finished* or *completed is unacceptable.*
SAY: We'll finish (NOT *be through with*) the work by five o'clock.

try to—is *acceptable.*
try and—is *unacceptable.*
Try to come (NOT *try and* come).
NOTE: *plan on going* is *unacceptable.*
plan to go is *acceptable.*

two—is the *numeral* 2.
to—means *in the direction of.*
too—means *more than* or *also.*
There are *two* sides to every story.
Three *twos* (or 2's) equal six.
We shall go *to* school.
We shall go, *too.*
The weather is *too* hot for school.

was / **were**—If something is contrary to fact (not a fact), use *were* in every instance.
I wish I *were* in Bermuda.
Unacceptable: If he *was* sensible, he wouldn't act like that.
(SAY: If he *were* ...)

ways—is *unacceptable* for *way.*
SAY: We climbed a little *way* (NOT *ways*) up the hill.

went and took—(*went and stole,* and so on) is *unacceptable.*
SAY: They *stole* (NOT *went and stole*) our tools.

when—(and *where*) should NOT be used to introduce a definition of a noun.
SAY: A tornado *is* a twisting, high wind on land (NOT *is when a twisting, high wind is on land*).
A pool *is a place for swimming.* (NOT *is where people swim*)

whereabouts—is *unacceptable* for *where.*
SAY: *Where* (NOT *whereabouts*) do you live?
NOTE: *Whereabouts* as a noun meaning a place is *acceptable.*
Do you know his *whereabouts?*

whether—should NOT be preceded by *of* or *as to.*
SAY: The President will consider the questions *whether* (NOT *of whether*) it is better to ask for or demand higher taxes now.
He inquired *whether* (NOT *as to whether*) we were going or not.

which—is used *incorrectly* in the following expressions:
He asked me to stay, *which* I did. (CORRECT: He asked me to stay and I did.)
It has been a severe winter, *which* is unfortunate. (CORRECT: Unfortunately, it has been a severe winter.)
You did not write; besides *which* you have not telephoned. (CORRECT: Omit *which*)

while—is *unacceptable* for *and* or *though.*
SAY: The library is situated on the south side; (OMIT *while*) the laboratory is on the north side.
Though (NOT *while*) I disagree with you, I shall not interfere with your right to express your opinion.
Though (NOT *while*) I am in my office every day, you do not attempt to see me.

who / **whom** — The following is a method (without going into grammar rules) for determining when to use WHO or WHOM.

"Tell me (*Who, Whom*) you think should represent our company?"

STEP ONE: Change the who—whom part of the sentence to its natural order.

"You think (*who, whom*) should represent our company?"

STEP TWO: Substitute HE for WHO, HIM for WHOM.

"You think (he, him) should represent our company?"

You would say *he* in this case.

THEREFORE: "Tell me WHO you think should represent the company?" is correct.

who is / **who am** — Note these constructions:

It is I who *am* the most experienced.
It is he who *is* ...
It is he or I who *am* ...
It is I or he who *is* ...
It is he and I who *are* ...

whose—means *of whom.*

who's—means *who is.*

Whose is the notebook?
Who's in the next office?

would have—is *unacceptable* for *had.*

SAY: I wish you *had* (NOT *would have*) called earlier.

you all—is *unacceptable* for *you* (plural).

SAY: We welcome *you,* the delegates from Ethiopia.
You are all welcome, delegates of Ethiopia.

HOW CAN I IMPROVE MY WRITING?

Written communication starts with the sentence. A group of related sentences forms a paragraph. A series of connected paragraphs becomes a composition.

The first step in improving your writing is to know what makes a good sentence.

What is a sentence?

A sentence must have a subject and an action word or verb. In addition, a sentence must express a complete thought.

EXAMPLES OF SENTENCES: Bob walks.
Eric swims.

Other words can be added to make these sentences more descriptive.

IMPROVED SENTENCES: Bob walks briskly.
Eric swims rapidly.

Adding phrases that tell more about the subject or the verb can make these same two sentences even more interesting.

GOOD SENTENCES: Bob walks briskly down the road.
Eric swims rapidly across the pool.

The addition of another phrase at either the beginning or the end of these sentences provides an even clearer picture of Bob and Eric.

BETTER SENTENCES: In a hurry to get to school on time, Bob walks briskly down the road.
Eric swims rapidly across the pool, attempting to overtake his opponent.

The more you can practice writing clear, descriptive sentences, the better you will become at writing them.

The second step in improving your writing is to learn what makes a good paragraph.

What is a paragraph?

A paragraph is a group of sentences that develops one main idea. Usually this main idea or topic is stated in the first sentence of the paragraph. The rest of the paragraph can provide details about the topic or it can clarify the topic by providing specific examples.

There are no rules for determining the length of a paragraph. However, it is a good idea to make most paragraphs in a composition or report at least three sentences long.

EXAMPLE OF A PARAGRAPH DEVELOPED BY DETAILS

> The man opened the door cautiously and slipped quietly into the crowded waiting room. He was dressed in a clean but well-worn overcoat and sneakers that had seen better days. On his head was a black knitted cap, pulled down to cover his forehead and ears.

Every sentence in this paragraph provides additional details about the topic—the man.

EXAMPLE OF A PARAGRAPH DEVELOPED BY EXAMPLES

Intramural sports are a valuable part of the high school curriculum. A sports program provides a constructive outlet for the energy that has been stored up during the school day. Practice sessions or games take up the time that might otherwise be spent hanging out on street corners looking for trouble. Tossing a basketball around the gym provides an acceptable alternative to tossing rocks at street lights or store windows.

Each sentence in this paragraph provides a specific example of the value of intramural sports.

A new paragraph indicates a change. Start a new paragraph to show a change in:

1. the **time,** the **place,** or the **action** in a story
2. the **mood** or **point of view** in a description
3. **ideas** or **steps** in an explanation
4. **speakers** in a conversation

CONNECTING PARAGRAPHS

Just as you must provide for an orderly flow of sentences within a paragraph, you must also provide for a logical transition from paragraph to paragraph in any composition or report.

The three most common means of connecting paragraphs are:

1. **Repetition** of a key word or phrase introduced in one paragraph and expanded upon in the next paragraph.
2. **Use of pronouns** that refer to a person or an idea mentioned in the previous paragraph.

   Examples of pronouns: he, she, they, this, that, these, those, such, both, all.
3. **Use of transitional words and phrases** to illustrate the relationship of one topic to another.

   Examples of transitional words and phrases: although, as a result, consequently, for example, in comparison, in contrast, in fact, nevertheless, therefore, thus.

EXAMPLE OF PARAGRAPHS CONNECTED BY REPETITION OF A KEY WORD

Last summer our whole family piled into the car and drove to Disney World in Florida. Although we had heard about the amusement park from friends who had already been there, this would be our first experience at a Disney park. We were all eager to get there, but we really did not know what to expect.

Our first day at Disney World went beyond any expectations we might have had . . .

These paragraphs are connected by the use of forms of the same word. *Expect* in paragraph 1 is repeated as *expectations* in paragraph 2, allowing one thought to flow from the first paragraph to the second. The second paragraph will continue with specific things the family did at Disney World.

EXAMPLE OF PARAGRAPHS CONNECTED BY TRANSITIONAL WORDS

Teenage alcoholism is a serious problem today. It is a problem that affects young people of all types, regardless of ethnic background or socio-economic level. Alcoholism shows no discrimination in choosing its victims.

Although the problem is far from being solved, steps are being taken by both families and schools to deal with alcoholism among teens . . .

These paragraphs are connected by the use of the transitional word *although* and the repetition of the key word *problem.* The second paragraph will continue by detailing some of the steps that are being taken to combat alcoholism.

CHAPTER 15

The Essay

You'll Find Answers to These Questions

What is the purpose of the essay?
How do you write an essay under time pressure?
What do smart test-takers know about essay writing?

PLAN A: ACCELERATED

- ***Read*** the chapter
- ***Study*** "How Do You Write an Essay under Time Pressure?"
- ***Study*** "What Smart Test-Takers Know"
- ***Write*** an essay in Exercise 1 only
- ***Read*** the sample essay answer

PLAN B: TOP SPEED

- ***Skim*** the chapter
- ***Read*** "How Do You Write an Essay under Time Pressure?"
- ***Study*** "What Smart Test-Takers Know"
- ***Write*** an essay in Exercise 2 only
- ***Read*** the sample essay answer

WHAT IS THE PURPOSE OF THE ESSAY?

The essay on your high school entrance exam serves as a writing sample. Its purpose is to show the school admissions committee how well you express yourself in writing. The school is interested in how you organize your thoughts and how you convey those thoughts to a reader. The essay is not graded and does not count toward your test score. Each school that receives your test score also receives a copy of your essay.

The SSAT Essay

The SSAT essay is the first part of the SSAT exam. You have 25 minutes to read the essay topic, choose a position, organize your essay, and write.

The ISEE Essay

The ISEE essay is the last part of the ISEE exam. You will be given 30 minutes to read the essay topic, decide what to say, organize, and write.

HERE'S THE ANSWER

How important is the essay to my score?

The essay does not count towards your score at all. In fact, the essay is not even graded.

The essay does count towards the impression you make on the school. Admissions officers read your essay to learn about how well you write.

HOW DO YOU WRITE AN ESSAY UNDER TIME PRESSURE?

To write a coherent, correct essay in 25 or 30 minutes, follow these steps:

Essay Writing: Getting It Right:

1. Read the question to find out exactly what it asks you to do.
2. Choose a point of view or decide how to answer the question.
3. Outline your essay. You will probably want four paragraphs: an introduction, two paragraphs for two supporting ideas or illustrations, and a conclusion.
4. Write the essay.
5. Proofread. Correct errors in punctuation, spelling, grammar, and word choice.
6. If needed, make phrasing changes as neatly as possible.

Now let's try these steps on a couple of sample topics:

Topic: Every student should be required to complete 60 hours of community service during his or her high school years. Do you agree or disagree?

1. This question is asking you to choose sides, then support your position.
2. You must now decide whether you want to write in favor or in opposition. Choose the side that you will find easier to defend with strong examples; which side you choose does not matter. The question is not really seeking your opinion. For this exercise, let's disagree.
3. Introduction: Community service should not be compulsory.

   Point 1: Involuntary activities are never performed well.

   A. Beneficiaries suffer from half-hearted service.

   B. Student is resentful and gains no satisfaction.

   Point 2: Teenagers must learn to arrange priorities and manage their time for their own benefit.

   A. Some poor students can not afford to give up so much study time.

   B. Many beneficial extracurricular activities compete for precious time.

   C. Some students must hold part-time jobs to help their families.

   Conclusion: Community service should be encouraged.
4. Write the essay.
5. Proofread. Ask yourself these questions:
   - Does each paragraph have a topic sentence? Is the topic sentence well developed within the paragraph?
   - Is my language colorful and descriptive? Have I varied my sentence structure?

- Do I make a convincing argument for my position?
- How is my spelling? Is my punctuation correct? What about my grammar?

6. Refine the essay if necessary. Remember: neatness counts.

TESTSMARTS

Answer the question. You get no credit for an essay that does not do what is asked for.

Topic: If you were in charge of planning your family's next two-week vacation, where would you go and what would you do? Why?

1. This question is asking you to tell about a place you want to see or an activity you especially enjoy and to explain why this appeals to you.
2. You must name a place to which you would like to go or, if yours will be a stay-close-to-home vacation, an activity or series of activities. If you have an ideal vacation in mind, describe it. You might also describe a vacation you have already taken. The readers are not interested in the vacation you choose; they want to know how you write about it. For this exercise, let's choose a summer vacation in eastern Canada.
3. Introduction: Canada is a nearby neighbor with much to offer in terms of culture and vacation activities.

   Paragraph: We should know more about our closest neighbor and trading partner.

   A. People speak English; easy to learn about lifestyles and ideas.

   B. Easy to get to; can drive; no passport needed.

   Paragraph: Canada offers scenic beauty, recreational activities, and foreign culture.

   A. Nova Scotia, Prince Edward Island, and Laurentians all scenic.

   B. Hiking and water sports available.

   C. Montreal and Quebec offer food, architecture, general feel of French cities.

   Conclusion: Summer vacation in Canada will be interesting, fun, and not too expensive.
4. Write the essay.
5. Proofread. Ask yourself these questions:
   - Does each paragraph have a topic sentence? Is the topic sentence well developed within the paragraph?
   - Is my language colorful and descriptive? Have I varied my sentence structure?
   - Do I make a convincing argument? Does my vacation sound appealing?
   - How is my spelling? Is my punctuation correct? What about my grammar?
6. Refine the essay if necessary. Remember: neatness counts.

   Be certain your writing is legible.

What Smart Test-Takers Know

TESTSMARTS

Organize before you begin. Your first draft is your only draft. There is no time for rewrite.

PLANNING COMES FIRST.

Do not even think about beginning to write until you have carefully read the essay topic and have answered these questions for yourself.

What must I prove?
How many things am I being asked to do?
How many paragraphs will I need for this?

If you are asked to discuss advantages and disadvantages, you must represent both sides.

If you are asked for your opinion, you must state it clearly and must support your position with good reasons.

If you are asked to support your statements with a specific number of examples from your own experience, from history, or from literature, you must provide the requested number of examples from the appropriate sources.

Jot down your ideas on the topic. Think of what you want to say, and sketch out your points and supporting statements. As good descriptive words or phrases pop into your head, write them down on the same scratch paper. Don't let any thoughts get away. You'll want to refer to your list of ideas as you write so that you don't have to squeeze ideas between the lines after you have written your essay.

Allow yourself 2 to 3 minutes for planning.

OUTLINES ARE IMPORTANT.

No matter how little time you have, an outline will save you time in the end. The outline is a framework for your essay to hang on. Your outline consists of specific details in the order in which you would like them to appear in the essay. Your outline will not be sent to the schools, so you do not need to be concerned with complete sentences, with spelling and punctuation, nor with legibility for anyone but yourself.

This is a typical outline plan:

I. Introductory paragraph
   A. Topic sentence (rephrase or state your position on the question)
   B. Sentence that introduces second paragraph
   C. Sentence that introduces third paragraph
   D. Optional sentence leading into second paragraph.

II. The first point you have to make
    A. Topic sentence
    B. First idea that supports this point
        1. Detail or illustration—experience, citing of example
        2. Detail or illustration
    C. Second idea supporting first point
        1. Detail or illustration
        2. Detail or illustration
    D. Optional summary of points made in the paragraph
III. The second point you have to make
    A. Topic sentence
    B. First idea that supports this point
        1. Detail or illustration
        2. Detail or illustration
    C. Second idea that supports this point
        1. Detail or illustration
        2. Detail or illustration
    D. Optional summary
IV. Conclusion to the essay
    A. Topic sentence rephrasing the question
    B. Sentence summarizing second paragraph
    C. Sentence summarizing third paragraph
    D. Overall conclusion that makes your point

Spend 3 to 5 minutes drafting your outline.

TOPIC SENTENCES ARE A MUST.

In a way, writing a good topic sentence is like aiming a gun: If the topic sentence is aimed correctly, the whole paragraph will hit its mark and prove your point.

- Every paragraph must have a topic sentence.
- The topic sentence expresses the main idea—the topic—of the paragraph.
- The topic sentence must join all the ideas expressed in the paragraph.
- The topic sentence must be limited enough to be developed within a single paragraph.
- The topic sentence must be broad enough to encompass all the ideas that you plan to express in that paragraph.
- The more specific your topic sentence, the more detailed and descriptive your paragraph will be.

A GOOD TOPIC SENTENCE IS CRUCIAL.

Remember: A topic sentence has an idea that can be fully proven in one paragraph. For example, the sentence "You can learn a lot about human nature just by observing people" is so broad that it cannot be proven in one single paragraph. But if we write

"You can learn a lot about human nature by watching people at a bus station"

or

"You can learn a lot about human nature by watching people at the beach" we have a topic that we can prove in one paragraph.

Another way to look at topic sentences is through the controlling idea. This is a key word or group of words that expresses the basic idea of the sentence. When the controlling idea is clear, the entire sentence will be specific and clear.

Example: An encyclopedia is a handy book for students.

"Handy" is the controlling idea. In the paragraph that follows, you will explain *how* the encyclopedia is handy.

Example: Traveling by train has several advantages over traveling by car.

"Several advantages" is the controlling idea. The paragraph will detail these advantages.

Example: Good English is clear, appropriate, and vivid.

"Clear, appropriate, and vivid" is the controlling idea. The paragraph will offer illustrations of clear, appropriate, and vivid English.

DESCRIPTIVE WORDS MAKE WRITING INTERESTING.

To prove your point and make your writing interesting, you have to use specific words and phrases.

His face was _____ with fright.

colorless scarlet chalky pale

"Chalky" is the best word for in addition to color—a pale, dry white—it implies a texture—dry and lifeless. "Scarlet" is incorrect because your face does not become scarlet (red) when you are afraid. "Colorless" and "pale" are too vague. "Chalky" is the most descriptive word and the one that makes this sentence most effective.

The sun is high and hot; the air is sultry; it is _____ time.

siesta sleep nap rest

"Siesta" describes a nap that is taken when it is very warm during the middle of the day and is thus the most precise word. Then would come:

nap (a short sleep)
sleep (a type of rest)
rest (any sitting down and relaxing)

PROOFREADING CAN RAISE YOUR SCORE.

Writing your essay should take you about 15 minutes. Do not use up all the time writing the essay. Keep track of how much time is left and allow the last few minutes, at least 3 minutes, to check over what you said. Make sure of the following:

- Did I answer the question?
- Did I provide good, specific details to support my ideas?
- Did I organize my answer in the best possible way to make my point clearly?
- Did I make any errors in spelling, grammar, punctuation, or word use?

Proofreading time is time well spent. Check over what you said, being sure to read what is really there and not what you think is there. Do not read too quickly or you may miss obvious errors. If you find that a sentence might be improved by different phrasing or that a line is illegible, rewrite more clearly at the bottom of the page, cross out the offending portion neatly, and indicate by arrows where the substitution should be inserted.

TESTSMARTS

Make it legible. If they can't read it, it won't count.

EXERCISES: ESSAY WRITING

Exercise 1

Choose the essay topic appropriate to your exam and write an essay.

SSAT STYLE TOPIC. 25 MINUTES

Some educators suggest that all elementary, middle school, and high school students should be required to wear school uniforms. What do you think?

ISEE STYLE TOPIC. 30 MINUTES

Tell about a time when you felt a very strong emotion. What was it? Why did you feel it?

Exercise 2

You are already familiar with the following essay topics, what they require of you, and how they might be organized. Choose the topic appropriate to your exam and write your own essay.

SSAT STYLE TOPIC. 20 MINUTES

Every student should be required to complete 60 hours of community service during his or her high school years. Do you agree or disagree?

ISEE STYLE TOPIC. 25 MINUTES

If you were in charge of planning your family's next two-week vacation, where would you go and what would you do? Why?

Model Essay Answers

Exercise 1

SSAT STYLE TOPIC.

Many people have suggested that all students be required to wear uniforms to school. Some students object to this idea because it takes away their individuality, but I think there are a number of reasons why school uniforms might be a good idea.

Over the past few years, there have been no dress guidelines and no dress codes in our schools. Some students just naturally dress neatly and appropriately, but others are truly sloppy. When people dress in sloppy clothing, they tend to be too relaxed. This leads to sloppy thinking. Pretty soon they lose respect for school and teachers and the whole learning process. School uniforms would remind these students that they are in school for a purpose. I think that if everyone were dressed in the same uniform there would be more school spirit too. Students would all feel as if they were part of something important.

Some students, especially girls, worry too much about their clothes and how they look. They bother their parents to spend too much on clothes, often more than their families can afford, and are always trying to compete. I have heard about boys fighting over "status" clothes. There have been cases of stealing fancy jackets and sneakers and even some knifings. School uniforms might cost more, but each student needs only two or three of them. This would take the pressure off poorer families. If everyone dressed alike, there would be no competition. A special benefit that educators probably haven't thought of is that of extra sleep. With no choice of what to wear, it will be much quicker to dress and get out in the morning.

I think we should try out school uniforms. I expect that discipline, paying attention, and school spirit will go up while squabbles about appearance and fights over clothing will go down. And I think that many students will be happier without the competition, and parents will be happier too.

ISEE STYLE TOPIC.

On October 15th of last year my grandmother died. Grandmother had been sick and in pain for some months, so her death was not a surprise and in some ways it was a relief and a blessing. But I was unbelievably saddened when she died. I had never felt this type or degree of sadness before.

My grandmother was an extraordinary woman. Her own parents died when she was a teenager, and she raised two younger sisters alone. Then her husband died while she was still in her thirties, leaving her with my mother, then only seven years old, and my uncle, then only nine. Still, she maintained a sense of humor and great dignity. As I grew up, my grandmother was always there for me. She listened to my joys and problems and always gave me good advice. She was never judgmental but always gave me unconditional love and much warmth. I will miss her a lot.

Part of my sadness, I think, was sadness for my mother who is now an orphan herself. She and my grandmother were always very close. Grandmother was the last family member of her generation. There is now a void in the family, and celebrations will always have an empty place.

I loved my grandmother very much, and now she is gone. I was very, very sad when she died. I have overcome that sadness by now, but many little things remind me of her. Every once in a while something happens and I first think that I must tell grandma—that she will be interested or amused. Then I remember that grandma is gone, and I feel a twinge of sadness again.

Exercise 2

SSAT STYLE TOPIC

The school board has been debating about a proposed new graduation requirement. They are suggesting that every student be required to complete 60 hours of community service during the high school years. I think that community service is a noble concept but that it should not be compulsory.

A student who is forced to perform an activity against his or her will is unlikely to perform it well. The very fact of the coercion almost guarantees a half-hearted approach. Community service not done well is hardly service at all. Yet, someone thinks that service is being performed. Then the intended beneficiaries suffer from the lack of service. Community service is supposed to be ennobling. Yet the student who is forced to perform this service is resentful and gains no satisfaction from it.

There are more downsides to compulsory community service. Students must learn to arrange their own priorities and to manage their own time. Some poor students can not afford to give up so much study time, yet they are not permitted to devote the study time they would like because of the required community service. Other students must hold part-time paid jobs to help out their families or to have any spending money for themselves. Community service to the extent proposed would be a hardship for them. Still other students are so deeply into extracurriculars—sports, music, drama, or religious studies—that compulsory community service would cut into study time or sleep time.

Community service is certainly a worthwhile goal, and all students should be encouraged to engage in some service that suits their interests, abilities, and time schedule. However, I don't think that compulsory community service is a good idea. School administrators and teachers should instead help students devise creative forms of community service that the students will want to fit into their busy lives.

ISEE STYLE TOPIC

Canada is a foreign country, yet it is only an automobile drive away from many states in the northern part of the United States. Included within Canada are rivers, lakes, mountains, and seacoast along with interesting cities. It should be easy to plan a Canadian vacation.

The United States shares its borders with only two countries—Mexico to the south and Canada to the north. We really should know more about these neighbors. Since I live in New England, Canada is the easiest for my family to visit. We can drive to Canada's northeast in one day and need no passports. Best of all, nearly all Canadians speak English so it should be easy to get around and easy to learn about lifestyles and ideas.

Because Canada is so big, it offers every kind of vacation. Nova Scotia and Prince Edward Island are filled with quaint fishing villages and spectacular seacoast scenery. They are probably cold for ocean swimming, but great for hiking. The Laurentian Mountains are known for skiing, but their lakes offer all sorts of water sports and we might camp in the mountains. And to vary the vacation, we should visit the cities of Montreal and Quebec which retain much French influence. I am looking forward to real French food.

For a summer vacation that will be fun, not too expensive, and educational besides, Canada can't be beat. It should not be too hard to convince my family.

What You Must Know About The Writing Sample

Review this page the night before you take your exam. It will help you write an impressive essay.

- The essay does not count towards your score, but it does influence the admissions committee.
- Follow these steps:

  1. Read the question to find out exactly what it asks you to do.
  2. Choose a point of view or decide how to answer the question.
  3. Outline your essay. Sketch in and organize the ideas that you want to include in each paragraph.
  4. Write the essay, paying attention to mechanics.
  5. Proofread. Correct errors in punctuation, spelling, grammar, and word choice.
  6. Make changes and refinements as neatly as possible.

- Remember: Your essay must be legible. Watch your handwriting.

PART

EIGHT

EVERYTHING YOU NEED!

Four Practice Examinations

- Making The Best of The Practice Exams
- Secondary School Admission Test Practice Exam 1
- Secondary School Admission Test Practice Exam 2
- Independent School Entrance Examination Practice Exam 1
- Independent School Entrance Examination Practice Exam 2

PLAN A: ACCELERATED

- ***Take*** one practice SSAT or ISEE, as appropriate
- ***Study*** the explanatory answers

PLAN B: TOP SPEED

- ***Take*** one practice SSAT or ISEE, as appropriate
- ***Check*** your answers against the "Answer Key"
- ***Skim*** the explanatory answers

MAKING THE BEST USE OF THE PRACTICE EXAMS

Get the most benefit you can from the practice exams. Take them under battle conditions, or as close to actual exam conditions as possible.

Setting

Find a quiet room where you will not be disturbed during the three hours the exam will take. Set yourself up with a good light, a desk or desk-height table, and a straight-backed wooden chair. If you will be taking a morning exam, be sure to take your sample exams in the morning so as to exactly duplicate your testing conditions.

Timing

Use a stopwatch, portable kitchen timer, or clock to time yourself. Be accurate in your timing, stopping promptly when time for a section is up. If you have a great many questions left, you may return to the practice exams and try those questions later just for the extra practice. But you must not count in your score any questions that you answer outside of the time limit.

Allow yourself one 10-minute break between Sections 2 and 3.

Answer sheets

Tear the appropriate answer sheet out of the book before you begin a practice exam. Mark all your answers with a medium lead, #2, pencil.

Answer keys and explanations

You will find answers to all exam questions in the answer key following each practice exam. Explanations appear directly after each complete answer key. Make a point of studying all the explanations—even explanations for questions you answered correctly. Explanations can introduce new concepts or suggest alternative approaches to questions. Remember, too, that your dictionary, school textbooks, and teachers are there to help.

Scoring

Convert your scores into percentages so that you can compare them with your scores on the diagnostic exam and can monitor your progress.

Note: The practice exams are NOT actual exams. The actual exams are copyrighted and cannot be reproduced. The practice exams, however, do accurately reflect the format and types of questions you may expect to see on your exam.

TEAR HERE

Secondary School Admission Test Practice Exam 1

Answer Sheet

SECTION ONE: VERBAL

1. Ⓐ Ⓑ Ⓒ Ⓓ Ⓔ	13. Ⓐ Ⓑ Ⓒ Ⓓ Ⓔ	25. Ⓐ Ⓑ Ⓒ Ⓓ Ⓔ	37. Ⓐ Ⓑ Ⓒ Ⓓ Ⓔ	49. Ⓐ Ⓑ Ⓒ Ⓓ Ⓔ
2. Ⓐ Ⓑ Ⓒ Ⓓ Ⓔ	14. Ⓐ Ⓑ Ⓒ Ⓓ Ⓔ	26. Ⓐ Ⓑ Ⓒ Ⓓ Ⓔ	38. Ⓐ Ⓑ Ⓒ Ⓓ Ⓔ	50. Ⓐ Ⓑ Ⓒ Ⓓ Ⓔ
3. Ⓐ Ⓑ Ⓒ Ⓓ Ⓔ	15. Ⓐ Ⓑ Ⓒ Ⓓ Ⓔ	27. Ⓐ Ⓑ Ⓒ Ⓓ Ⓔ	39. Ⓐ Ⓑ Ⓒ Ⓓ Ⓔ	51. Ⓐ Ⓑ Ⓒ Ⓓ Ⓔ
4. Ⓐ Ⓑ Ⓒ Ⓓ Ⓔ	16. Ⓐ Ⓑ Ⓒ Ⓓ Ⓔ	28. Ⓐ Ⓑ Ⓒ Ⓓ Ⓔ	40. Ⓐ Ⓑ Ⓒ Ⓓ Ⓔ	52. Ⓐ Ⓑ Ⓒ Ⓓ Ⓔ
5. Ⓐ Ⓑ Ⓒ Ⓓ Ⓔ	17. Ⓐ Ⓑ Ⓒ Ⓓ Ⓔ	29. Ⓐ Ⓑ Ⓒ Ⓓ Ⓔ	41. Ⓐ Ⓑ Ⓒ Ⓓ Ⓔ	53. Ⓐ Ⓑ Ⓒ Ⓓ Ⓔ
6. Ⓐ Ⓑ Ⓒ Ⓓ Ⓔ	18. Ⓐ Ⓑ Ⓒ Ⓓ Ⓔ	30. Ⓐ Ⓑ Ⓒ Ⓓ Ⓔ	42. Ⓐ Ⓑ Ⓒ Ⓓ Ⓔ	54. Ⓐ Ⓑ Ⓒ Ⓓ Ⓔ
7. Ⓐ Ⓑ Ⓒ Ⓓ Ⓔ	19. Ⓐ Ⓑ Ⓒ Ⓓ Ⓔ	31. Ⓐ Ⓑ Ⓒ Ⓓ Ⓔ	43. Ⓐ Ⓑ Ⓒ Ⓓ Ⓔ	55. Ⓐ Ⓑ Ⓒ Ⓓ Ⓔ
8. Ⓐ Ⓑ Ⓒ Ⓓ Ⓔ	20. Ⓐ Ⓑ Ⓒ Ⓓ Ⓔ	32. Ⓐ Ⓑ Ⓒ Ⓓ Ⓔ	44. Ⓐ Ⓑ Ⓒ Ⓓ Ⓔ	56. Ⓐ Ⓑ Ⓒ Ⓓ Ⓔ
9. Ⓐ Ⓑ Ⓒ Ⓓ Ⓔ	21. Ⓐ Ⓑ Ⓒ Ⓓ Ⓔ	33. Ⓐ Ⓑ Ⓒ Ⓓ Ⓔ	45. Ⓐ Ⓑ Ⓒ Ⓓ Ⓔ	57. Ⓐ Ⓑ Ⓒ Ⓓ Ⓔ
10. Ⓐ Ⓑ Ⓒ Ⓓ Ⓔ	22. Ⓐ Ⓑ Ⓒ Ⓓ Ⓔ	34. Ⓐ Ⓑ Ⓒ Ⓓ Ⓔ	46. Ⓐ Ⓑ Ⓒ Ⓓ Ⓔ	58. Ⓐ Ⓑ Ⓒ Ⓓ Ⓔ
11. Ⓐ Ⓑ Ⓒ Ⓓ Ⓔ	23. Ⓐ Ⓑ Ⓒ Ⓓ Ⓔ	35. Ⓐ Ⓑ Ⓒ Ⓓ Ⓔ	47. Ⓐ Ⓑ Ⓒ Ⓓ Ⓔ	59. Ⓐ Ⓑ Ⓒ Ⓓ Ⓔ
12. Ⓐ Ⓑ Ⓒ Ⓓ Ⓔ	24. Ⓐ Ⓑ Ⓒ Ⓓ Ⓔ	36. Ⓐ Ⓑ Ⓒ Ⓓ Ⓔ	48. Ⓐ Ⓑ Ⓒ Ⓓ Ⓔ	60. Ⓐ Ⓑ Ⓒ Ⓓ Ⓔ

SECTION TWO: QUANTITATIVE

1. Ⓐ Ⓑ Ⓒ Ⓓ Ⓔ	6. Ⓐ Ⓑ Ⓒ Ⓓ Ⓔ	11. Ⓐ Ⓑ Ⓒ Ⓓ Ⓔ	16. Ⓐ Ⓑ Ⓒ Ⓓ Ⓔ	21. Ⓐ Ⓑ Ⓒ Ⓓ Ⓔ
2. Ⓐ Ⓑ Ⓒ Ⓓ Ⓔ	7. Ⓐ Ⓑ Ⓒ Ⓓ Ⓔ	12. Ⓐ Ⓑ Ⓒ Ⓓ Ⓔ	17. Ⓐ Ⓑ Ⓒ Ⓓ Ⓔ	22. Ⓐ Ⓑ Ⓒ Ⓓ Ⓔ
3. Ⓐ Ⓑ Ⓒ Ⓓ Ⓔ	8. Ⓐ Ⓑ Ⓒ Ⓓ Ⓔ	13. Ⓐ Ⓑ Ⓒ Ⓓ Ⓔ	18. Ⓐ Ⓑ Ⓒ Ⓓ Ⓔ	23. Ⓐ Ⓑ Ⓒ Ⓓ Ⓔ
4. Ⓐ Ⓑ Ⓒ Ⓓ Ⓔ	9. Ⓐ Ⓑ Ⓒ Ⓓ Ⓔ	14. Ⓐ Ⓑ Ⓒ Ⓓ Ⓔ	19. Ⓐ Ⓑ Ⓒ Ⓓ Ⓔ	24. Ⓐ Ⓑ Ⓒ Ⓓ Ⓔ
5. Ⓐ Ⓑ Ⓒ Ⓓ Ⓔ	10. Ⓐ Ⓑ Ⓒ Ⓓ Ⓔ	15. Ⓐ Ⓑ Ⓒ Ⓓ Ⓔ	20. Ⓐ Ⓑ Ⓒ Ⓓ Ⓔ	25. Ⓐ Ⓑ Ⓒ Ⓓ Ⓔ

SECTION THREE: READING COMPREHENSION

1. Ⓐ Ⓑ Ⓒ Ⓓ Ⓔ	9. Ⓐ Ⓑ Ⓒ Ⓓ Ⓔ	17. Ⓐ Ⓑ Ⓒ Ⓓ Ⓔ	25. Ⓐ Ⓑ Ⓒ Ⓓ Ⓔ	33. Ⓐ Ⓑ Ⓒ Ⓓ Ⓔ
2. Ⓐ Ⓑ Ⓒ Ⓓ Ⓔ	10. Ⓐ Ⓑ Ⓒ Ⓓ Ⓔ	18. Ⓐ Ⓑ Ⓒ Ⓓ Ⓔ	26. Ⓐ Ⓑ Ⓒ Ⓓ Ⓔ	34. Ⓐ Ⓑ Ⓒ Ⓓ Ⓔ
3. Ⓐ Ⓑ Ⓒ Ⓓ Ⓔ	11. Ⓐ Ⓑ Ⓒ Ⓓ Ⓔ	19. Ⓐ Ⓑ Ⓒ Ⓓ Ⓔ	27. Ⓐ Ⓑ Ⓒ Ⓓ Ⓔ	35. Ⓐ Ⓑ Ⓒ Ⓓ Ⓔ
4. Ⓐ Ⓑ Ⓒ Ⓓ Ⓔ	12. Ⓐ Ⓑ Ⓒ Ⓓ Ⓔ	20. Ⓐ Ⓑ Ⓒ Ⓓ Ⓔ	28. Ⓐ Ⓑ Ⓒ Ⓓ Ⓔ	36. Ⓐ Ⓑ Ⓒ Ⓓ Ⓔ
5. Ⓐ Ⓑ Ⓒ Ⓓ Ⓔ	13. Ⓐ Ⓑ Ⓒ Ⓓ Ⓔ	21. Ⓐ Ⓑ Ⓒ Ⓓ Ⓔ	29. Ⓐ Ⓑ Ⓒ Ⓓ Ⓔ	37. Ⓐ Ⓑ Ⓒ Ⓓ Ⓔ
6. Ⓐ Ⓑ Ⓒ Ⓓ Ⓔ	14. Ⓐ Ⓑ Ⓒ Ⓓ Ⓔ	22. Ⓐ Ⓑ Ⓒ Ⓓ Ⓔ	30. Ⓐ Ⓑ Ⓒ Ⓓ Ⓔ	38. Ⓐ Ⓑ Ⓒ Ⓓ Ⓔ
7. Ⓐ Ⓑ Ⓒ Ⓓ Ⓔ	15. Ⓐ Ⓑ Ⓒ Ⓓ Ⓔ	23. Ⓐ Ⓑ Ⓒ Ⓓ Ⓔ	31. Ⓐ Ⓑ Ⓒ Ⓓ Ⓔ	39. Ⓐ Ⓑ Ⓒ Ⓓ Ⓔ
8. Ⓐ Ⓑ Ⓒ Ⓓ Ⓔ	16. Ⓐ Ⓑ Ⓒ Ⓓ Ⓔ	24. Ⓐ Ⓑ Ⓒ Ⓓ Ⓔ	32. Ⓐ Ⓑ Ⓒ Ⓓ Ⓔ	40. Ⓐ Ⓑ Ⓒ Ⓓ Ⓔ

SECTION FOUR: QUANTITATIVE

1. Ⓐ Ⓑ Ⓒ Ⓓ Ⓔ	6. Ⓐ Ⓑ Ⓒ Ⓓ Ⓔ	11. Ⓐ Ⓑ Ⓒ Ⓓ Ⓔ	16. Ⓐ Ⓑ Ⓒ Ⓓ Ⓔ	21. Ⓐ Ⓑ Ⓒ Ⓓ Ⓔ
2. Ⓐ Ⓑ Ⓒ Ⓓ Ⓔ	7. Ⓐ Ⓑ Ⓒ Ⓓ Ⓔ	12. Ⓐ Ⓑ Ⓒ Ⓓ Ⓔ	17. Ⓐ Ⓑ Ⓒ Ⓓ Ⓔ	22. Ⓐ Ⓑ Ⓒ Ⓓ Ⓔ
3. Ⓐ Ⓑ Ⓒ Ⓓ Ⓔ	8. Ⓐ Ⓑ Ⓒ Ⓓ Ⓔ	13. Ⓐ Ⓑ Ⓒ Ⓓ Ⓔ	18. Ⓐ Ⓑ Ⓒ Ⓓ Ⓔ	23. Ⓐ Ⓑ Ⓒ Ⓓ Ⓔ
4. Ⓐ Ⓑ Ⓒ Ⓓ Ⓔ	9. Ⓐ Ⓑ Ⓒ Ⓓ Ⓔ	14. Ⓐ Ⓑ Ⓒ Ⓓ Ⓔ	19. Ⓐ Ⓑ Ⓒ Ⓓ Ⓔ	24. Ⓐ Ⓑ Ⓒ Ⓓ Ⓔ
5. Ⓐ Ⓑ Ⓒ Ⓓ Ⓔ	10. Ⓐ Ⓑ Ⓒ Ⓓ Ⓔ	15. Ⓐ Ⓑ Ⓒ Ⓓ Ⓔ	20. Ⓐ Ⓑ Ⓒ Ⓓ Ⓔ	25. Ⓐ Ⓑ Ⓒ Ⓓ Ⓔ

SSAT Practice Exam 1

Part I: Writing Sample

TIME—25 MINUTES

Directions: Write a convincing, legible essay supporting your opinion on the following proposal.

Topic: The state legislature is debating a proposal to raise the minimum driving age from 16 to 18 to reduce the accident rate. Do you think that this is a good idea? Give specific reasons.

Part II: Multiple Choice

SECTION ONE: VERBAL

60 QUESTIONS • TIME—25 MINUTES

The Verbal Section consists of two different types of questions. There are directions for each type of question.

Directions: Each question shows a word in capital letters followed by five words or phrases. Choose the word or phrase whose meaning is most similar to the word in capital letters. Mark the appropriate space on your answer sheet.

1. DETER
(A) halt
(B) steer
(C) sting
(D) turn
(E) hinder

2. HOSTILE
(A) friendly
(B) unfriendly
(C) suspicious
(D) indifferent
(E) doubtful

3. UTILIZE
(A) make use of
(B) utilities
(C) modernize
(D) sing
(E) undo

4. ABDICATE
(A) resign
(B) explain
(C) remorse
(D) disprove
(E) control

5. PROMINENT
(A) disturbing
(B) secret
(C) outstanding
(D) extravagant
(E) surreptitious

6. BOUNDARY
(A) hovel
(B) limit
(C) ceiling
(D) map
(E) seam

GO ON TO THE NEXT PAGE

7. ILLITERATE
(A) unable to vote
(B) unmanageable
(C) sickly
(D) unable to read
(E) unclean

8. ORATOR
(A) professor
(B) poet
(C) speaker
(D) ear
(E) student

9. CORROBORATE
(A) confirm
(B) understand
(C) cooperate
(D) agree
(E) disagree

10. RATIFY
(A) delete
(B) consider
(C) approve
(D) examine
(E) assess

11. PERILOUS
(A) careless
(B) conniving
(C) irregular
(D) estranged
(E) hazardous

12. STATIONARY
(A) paper
(B) moving
(C) immobile
(D) position
(E) mobile

13. TRANSCRIBE
(A) copy
(B) illustrate
(C) circulate
(D) request
(E) author

14. PROFICIENT
(A) well-known
(B) professional
(C) adept
(D) practice
(E) prolific

15. DECEIVE
(A) rearrange
(B) mislead
(C) pretend
(D) stun
(E) examine

16. AGILE
(A) strong
(B) similar
(C) anxious
(D) rested
(E) nimble

17. DURATION
(A) area
(B) temptation
(C) term
(D) wait
(E) former

18. AMBIGUOUS
(A) unclear
(B) adhere
(C) aspire
(D) afflict
(E) certain

19. PREROGATIVE
(A) command
(B) choice
(C) prerequisite
(D) conviction
(E) haggard

20. INTRIGUING
(A) business
(B) furtive
(C) mystery
(D) fascinating
(E) boorish

21. CLANDESTINE
(A) overt
(B) dated
(C) exclusive
(D) fortunate
(E) secret

22. BOUNTEOUS
(A) elastic
(B) industrious
(C) abundant
(D) mutinous
(E) energetic

23. DIVERGE
(A) annoy
(B) change course
(C) stay
(D) analyze
(E) distract

24. BENIGN
(A) gentle
(B) blessed
(C) initial
(D) virulent
(E) malignant

25. CAUCUS
(A) dispersal
(B) corpse
(C) meeting
(D) partnership
(E) cosmetic

26. DISSEMINATE
(A) collate
(B) strip
(C) collect
(D) disagree
(E) spread

27. CHAGRIN
(A) delight
(B) alter
(C) embarrass
(D) wreck
(E) anger

28. VALOR
(A) courage
(B) disclosure
(C) treason
(D) hate
(E) foreboding

29. NONCHALANT
(A) interested
(B) caring
(C) impoverished
(D) indifferent
(E) persecuted

30. LIAISON
(A) permission
(B) laziness
(C) scarf
(D) remedy
(E) association

GO ON TO THE NEXT PAGE

Directions: The following questions ask you to find relationships between words. Read each question and then choose the answer that best completes the meaning of the sentence. Mark the appropriate space on your answer sheet.

31. Beg is to borrow as offer is to

(A) lender
(B) bank
(C) lend
(D) repay
(E) security

32. Lazy is to inert as resist is to

(A) refuse
(B) reply
(C) respond
(D) active
(E) insist

33. Cylinder is to circle as pyramid is to

(A) sphere
(B) point
(C) triangle
(D) angle
(E) height

34. Crocodile is to reptile as kangaroo is to

(A) amphibian
(B) marsupial
(C) opossum
(D) canine
(E) tail

35. Milliliter is to quart as

(A) pound is to gram
(B) millimeter is to yard
(C) inch is to yard
(D) pint is to quart
(E) foot is to yard

36. Destroy is to demolish as

(A) win is to lose
(B) candid is to secret
(C) amend is to change
(D) establish is to abolish
(E) attempt is to succeed

37. Plaintiff is to defendant as

(A) plain is to ordinary
(B) lawyer is to courtroom
(C) professor is to college
(D) complain is to complainant
(E) prosecute is to defend

38. Fundamental is to frivolous as

(A) fantasy is to fiction
(B) nonfiction is to fact
(C) regulation is to rule
(D) truth is to nonsense
(E) strange is to common

39. Wild is to wolf as domestic is to

(A) dog
(B) coyote
(C) pet
(D) cat
(E) animal

40. Hammer is to carpenter as

(A) awl is to cobbler
(B) computer is to printer
(C) saw is to timber
(D) author is to typewriter
(E) scale is to musician

41. Subject is to predicate as senator is to
   (A) congress
   (B) president
   (C) capitol
   (D) representative
   (E) senate

42. Pungent is to odor as
   (A) intense is to emotion
   (B) pervade is to atmosphere
   (C) infect is to spread
   (D) proverb is to paragraph
   (E) resent is to denial

43. Exploit is to adventure as
   (A) rule is to governor
   (B) safari is to expedition
   (C) school is to field trip
   (D) attack is to hunt
   (E) chase is to escape

44. Spread is to scatter as separate is to
   (A) integrate
   (B) distribute
   (C) reap
   (D) group
   (E) displace

45. Exuberant is to mood as adroit is to
   (A) proficient
   (B) adept
   (C) hand
   (D) dexterous
   (E) movement

46. Defiance is to opposition as exertion is to
   (A) expert
   (B) vigor
   (C) endeavor
   (D) restraint
   (E) challenge

47. Food is to nutrition as light is to
   (A) watt
   (B) bulb
   (C) electricity
   (D) reading
   (E) vision

48. Perpetuity is to impermanence as interminable is to
   (A) impertinent
   (B) brief
   (C) incessant
   (D) eternal
   (E) occasional

49. Erratic is to predictable as exorbitant is to
   (A) reasonable
   (B) productive
   (C) absorbent
   (D) small
   (E) implicit

50. Comment is to speech as
   (A) question is to answer
   (B) exclamation is to statement
   (C) written is to spoken
   (D) prose is to essay
   (E) note is to letter

51. Flammable is to inflammable as
   (A) persistent is to important
   (B) opportune is to inopportune
   (C) relevant is to incoherent
   (D) truculent is to intrusion
   (E) impartial is to disinterested

52. Tailor is to pattern as builder is to
   (A) architect
   (B) contractor
   (C) foundation
   (D) construct
   (E) blueprint

GO ON TO THE NEXT PAGE

53. Impeach is to dismiss as
   (A) arraign is to indict
   (B) accuse is to charge
   (C) imprison is to jail
   (D) plant is to sow
   (E) absent is to present

54. Speedy is to greyhound as
   (A) wool is to lamb
   (B) shark is to voracious
   (C) clever is to fox
   (D) mammal is to whale
   (E) fin is to fish

55. Exhale is to lung as
   (A) exhume is to corpse
   (B) pump is to heart
   (C) think is to brain
   (D) perspire is to skin
   (E) taste is to tongue

56. Celebrate is to birth as
   (A) grieve is to death
   (B) announce is to birthday
   (C) crime is to penalty
   (D) joy is to lament
   (E) party is to graduation

57. Recommend is to urge as
   (A) request is to plead
   (B) refuse is to deny
   (C) harass is to bother
   (D) cajole is to insult
   (E) apply is to receive

58. Weeping is to tears as breathing is to
   (A) air
   (B) lungs
   (C) nose
   (D) mouth
   (E) carbon dioxide

59. Plane is to air pocket as
   (A) vehicle is to rut
   (B) hangar is to airport
   (C) ground is to sky
   (D) safety is to danger
   (E) horse is to reins

60. Arbitrate is to dispute as
   (A) solve is to mystery
   (B) regard is to problem
   (C) exacerbate is to problem
   (D) organize is to labor
   (E) management is to union

STOP

END OF SECTION ONE. IF YOU HAVE ANY TIME LEFT, GO OVER YOUR WORK IN THIS SECTION ONLY. DO NOT WORK IN ANY OTHER SECTION OF THE EXAM.

SECTION TWO: QUANTITATIVE

25 QUESTIONS • TIME—25 MINUTES

Directions: Calculate the answer to each of the following questions. Select the answer choice that is best, and mark the appropriate letter on your answer sheet.

1. $1\frac{1}{2} + .750 + .1010 =$

(A) 1.001

(B) 2.051

(C) 2.055

(D) 2.351

(E) 2.551

2. Evaluate: $\frac{2^{12}}{2^8}$

(A) 2^{20}

(B) 16

(C) 8

(D) 2

(E) 1^{20}

3. 503.384 ÷ 62.3 =

(A) 7.08

(B) 7.68

(C) 8.08

(D) 9.08

(E) 10.08

4. $\dfrac{1\frac{3}{4} - \frac{1}{8}}{\frac{1}{8}}$

(A) 1

(B) 2

(C) 12

(D) 13

(E) 14

5. 2.01 ÷ 1.02 =

(A) .507

(B) 1.83

(C) 1.97

(D) 2.0001

(E) 3.03

6. $-3 - [(2 - 1) - (3 + 4)] =$

(A) 12

(B) 6

(C) 3

(D) –6

(E) –9

7. 3,003 – 699 =

(A) 2,294

(B) 2,304

(C) 2,314

(D) 2,404

(E) 2,414

8. If $a = 5$ and $b = \frac{1}{5}$, then the value of a, expressed in terms of b is

(A) $25b$

(B) $20b$

(C) $5\frac{1}{5}b$

(D) $5b$

(E) $\frac{1}{25}b$

9. 140% of 70 is

(A) .98

(B) 9.8

(C) 98

(D) 150

(E) 9,800

GO ON TO THE NEXT PAGE

10. 5 gallons 2 quarts 1 pint
− 1 gallon 3 quarts

(A) 2 gal. 2 qt. 1 pt.
(B) 2 gal. 6 qt. 2 pt.
(C) 3 gal. 3 qt. 1 pt.
(D) 4 gal. 3 qt. 1 pt.
(E) 4 gal. 9 qt. 1 pt.

11. In the fraction $\frac{xy}{z}$, if the value of z is doubled and the value of x is halved, the value of the fraction is

(A) multiplied by four
(B) decreased by $\frac{1}{2}$
(C) increased by $\frac{1}{2}$
(D) doubled
(E) divided by four

12. 20 is eight percent of

(A) 1.60
(B) 160
(C) 200
(D) 250
(E) 400

13. How much larger than 80 is 100?

(A) 18%
(B) 20%
(C) 25%
(D) 35%
(E) 40%

14. If $\frac{3}{8}$" on a scale drawing is equivalent to one foot at full scale, what distance on the drawing will stand for forty inches?

(A) $\frac{1}{8}$ inches
(B) $\frac{7}{8}$ inches
(C) $1\frac{1}{4}$ inches
(D) $2\frac{1}{3}$ inches
(E) $8\frac{8}{9}$ inches

15. $6 \div \frac{1}{3} + \frac{2}{3} \times 9 =$

(A) $\frac{2}{3}$
(B) 11
(C) 24
(D) 54
(E) 168

16. If $x - 3 < 12$, x may be

(A) less than 15
(B) greater than 16
(C) equal to 15
(D) less than 18
(E) equal to 18

17. If $a = 9, b = 2$, and $c = 1$, the value of $\sqrt{a + 3b + c}$ is

(A) 16
(B) 7
(C) 6
(D) 4
(E) 2

18. In the fraction $\frac{1}{\Delta - 2}$, Δ can be replaced by all of the following except

(A) +3
(B) +2
(C) 0
(D) −1
(E) −2

19. .10101 ÷ 10 is equivalent to

(A) .0010101
(B) .0100

(C) .010101

(D) .1001

(E) 1.0101

20. David walked from his home to town, a distance of 5 miles, in one hour. The return trip took two hours because he made several stops along the way. What was his average rate of speed (in miles per hour) for the entire walk?

(A) $\frac{3}{10}$ mph

(B) $1\frac{1}{2}$ mph

(C) $1\frac{2}{3}$ mph

(D) $3\frac{1}{3}$ mph

(E) 4 mph

21. 7 is to 21 as $\frac{2}{3}$ is to

(A) 3

(B) 2

(C) $\frac{4}{3}$

(D) 1

(E) $\frac{5}{9}$

22. If $n = \sqrt{85}$, then

(A) $9 > n > 8$

(B) $n = 9.5$

(C) $10 > n > 9$

(D) $8 < n < 9$

(E) $n^2 > 100$

23.

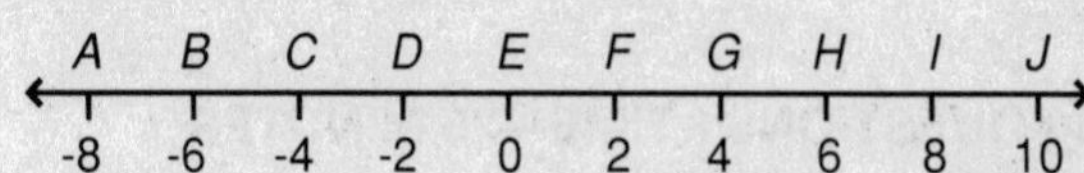

The sum of which points on the number line above would be equal to zero?

(A) B, D, E, I

(B) C, D, G, H

(C) A, C, F, I

(D) D, E, F, G

(E) B, C, H, I

24. How many fourths are there in $\frac{5}{6}$?

(A) $\frac{5}{24}$

(B) $\frac{7}{12}$

(C) $1\frac{1}{2}$

(D) 2

(E) $3\frac{1}{3}$

25. The average of –10, 6, 0, –3, and 22 is

(A) 4

(B) 3

(C) 2

(D) –3

(E) –6

STOP

END OF SECTION TWO. IF YOU HAVE ANY TIME LEFT, GO OVER YOUR WORK IN THIS SECTION ONLY. DO NOT WORK IN ANY OTHER SECTION OF THE EXAM.

SECTION THREE: READING COMPREHENSION

40 QUESTIONS • TIME—25 MINUTES

Directions: Read each passage carefully. Then decide which of the possible responses is the best answer to each question. Mark the appropriate space on your answer sheet.

As recently as the 1860s, most people believed that the earth, and humanity with it, was created a mere 6,000 to 7,000 years ago. For centuries, beautifully worked flints were regarded as the work of elves, a notion once far more plausible than the idea that humans roamed the world's wildernesses in small bands long before the days of the Greek and Roman Empires. Even when these stones were accepted as man-made tools, they were attributed to the Romans or Early Britons.

Today, we think in wider terms, but the older ideas about humanity's beginnings faded slowly. During the late eighteenth and early nineteenth centuries, excavators, mainly enthusiastic amateurs, began to associate fossil remains of men and extinct animals with the stone tools. Still, most geologists continued to think in Biblical terms, maintaining that these associations were merely coincidental. They believed the Flood had mixed the bones of ancient animals with the tools and remains of recent humans. These theories finally crumbled as archaeologists began to find bones and tools together in unflooded, undisturbed deposits, including a number of important sites on the banks of the Sommes River. British investigators came to check the French deposits, were convinced, and announced their conclusions in 1859. This was the same year that Darwin published *On the Origin of Species,* the date that marks the beginning of modern research into human evolution.

1. All of the following types of archaeological evidence were mentioned except:

(A) carbon dating

(B) fossils

(C) extinct animal remains

(D) man-made objects

(E) flint

2. The turning point in scientific theories about the age of humanity's existence on earth was

(A) the discovery in France of the remains of extinct animals and humans together in an unflooded area

(B) the publication of Darwin's *On the Origin of Species*

(C) new theological research of the Bible

(D) new theories about the Flood and its effects on humanity

(E) evidence left by the Greeks, Romans, and early Britons

3. In the early nineteenth century

(A) elves made flints in caves

(B) small bands of Romans roamed the earth

(C) geologists dated humanity's early existence to 1859

(D) stones were accepted as ancient tools and artifacts of 20,000-year-old man

(E) most people believed that humanity's existence was 6,000–7,000 years old.

Next morning, I saw for the first time an animal that is rarely encountered face to face. It was a wolverine. Though relatively small, rarely weighing more than 40 pounds, he is, above all animals, the one most hated by the Indians and trappers. He is a fine tree climber and a relentless destroyer. Deer, reindeer, and even moose *succumb* to his attacks. We sat on a rock and watched him come, a bobbing rascal in blackish-brown. Because the male wolverine occupies a very large hunting area and fights to the death any male that intrudes on his domain, wolverines are always scarce, and in order to avoid extinction need all the protection that humans can give. As a trapper, Henry wanted me to shoot him, but I refused, for this is the most fascinating and little known of all our wonderful predators. His hunchback gait was awkward and ungainly, lopsided yet tireless.

4. Wolverines are very scarce because

(A) they suffer in the survival of the fittest

(B) they are afraid of all humankind

(C) they are seldom protected by man

(D) trappers take their toll of them

(E) their food supply is limited

5. The author of this selection is most probably

(A) a conscious naturalist

(B) an experienced hunter

(C) an inexperienced trapper

(D) a young Indian

(E) a farmer

6. The word *succumb* as used in the fifth sentence means

(A) outmaneuver

(B) surrender

(C) overcome

(D) invite

(E) repel

When Jason, the son of the dethroned king of Solcus, was a little boy, he was sent away from his parents and placed under the queerest schoolmaster that ever you heard of. This learned person was one of the people, or *quadrupeds*, called Centaurs. He lived in a cavern and had the body and legs of a white horse, with the head and shoulders of a man. His name was Chiron; and, in spite of his odd appearance, he was a very excellent teacher and had several scholars who afterward did him credit by making great figures in the world. The famous Hercules was one, and so was Achilles, and Philoctetes, likewise, and Aesculapius, who acquired immense repute as a doctor. The good Chiron taught his pupils how to play upon the harp and how to cure diseases and how to use the sword and shield, together with various other branches of education in which the lads of those days used to be instructed, instead of writing and arithmetic.

—from *The Golden Fleece*
by Nathaniel Hawthorne

7. The main purpose of this passage is to

(A) describe Jason

(B) describe Chiron

(C) describe Jason's education

(D) explain Jason's family relationships

(E) name the scholars taught by Chiron

8. The word *quadruped* probably means

(A) a creature with four feet

(B) a creature with two feet

(C) a strange schoolmaster

(D) a learned person

(E) a scholar

9. Chiron

(A) taught writing and arithmetic to his pupils

(B) acquired a reputation as a doctor

(C) instructed the Centaurs

(D) was the son of Solcus

(E) had the body and legs of a horse and the head and shoulders of a man

The kangaroo is found nowhere in the world but in Australasia. Ages ago, when that part of our earth was cut off from the Asian mainland, this fantastic animal from nature's long-ago was also isolated. There are about two dozen species distributed through Australia, southward to Tasmania and northward to New Guinea and neighboring islands. Some are no bigger than rabbits; some can climb trees. They are known by a variety of picturesque names: wallabies, wallaroos, potoroos, boongaries, and paddymelons. But the kangaroo—the one that is Australia's national symbol—is the great gray kangaroo of the plains, admiringly known throughout the island continent as the Old Man, and also as Boomer, Forester, and Man of the Woods. His

GO ON TO THE NEXT PAGE

smaller mate, in Australian talk, is called a flyer. Their baby is known as Joey.

A full-grown kangaroo stands taller than a man, and commonly weighs 200 pounds. Even when he sits in his favorite position, reposing on his haunches and tilting back on the propping support of his "third leg"—his tail—his head is five feet or more above the ground. His huge hind legs, with steel-spring power, can send him sailing over a ten-foot fence with ease, or in a fight can beat off a dozen dogs. A twitch of his tail can break someone's leg like a match stick.

Kangaroos provide an endless supply of tall tales to which wide-eyed visitors are treated in the land Down Under. The beauty of the tall tales about the kangaroo is that they can be almost as tall as you please and still be close to fact.

10. Kangaroos are found only

(A) in Australia

(B) in Australasia

(C) on the Asian mainland

(D) in Tasmania

(E) on New Guinea

11. A female kangaroo is called

(A) a wallaby

(B) a potoroo

(C) a Joey

(D) a flyer

(E) the Old Man

12. The amazing jumping power of the kangaroo is chiefly due to

(A) the power of the hind legs

(B) the support of the tail

(C) the kangaroo's size

(D) the kangaroo's weight

(E) the kangaroo's tilted sitting position

13. Which statement is *true* according to the passage?

(A) The name "Old Man" shows the people's dislike of kangaroos.

(B) Visitors to Australia hear very little about kangaroos.

(C) A kangaroo's tail is a powerful weapon.

(D) The most widely known species of kangaroo is no larger than a rabbit.

(E) Kangaroos have three legs.

14. The author believes that the stories told about kangaroos are generally

(A) harmful

(B) true

(C) suspicious

(D) beautiful

(E) ancient

What is a cord of wood? Some people say the cord is the most elastic unit of measure ever devised by the mind of humans. A "standard" cord is a pile of stacked wood $4 \times 4 \times 8$ feet; that's 128 cubic feet. How much of this is wood? That depends on what kind of wood, the size and straightness of the sticks, and who does the piling. Small crooked sticks, cut from hardwood limbs and piled by one of those cordwood artists who know how to make air spaces, may contain less than 30 cubic feet of solid wood per cord. Smooth, round wood such as birch or spruce, in sizes eight inches and better, will average 100 cubic feet or more per cord. That's with the bark on. Peeled wood will make 10 to 12 percent more cubic volume in the same sized stack.

The heating value of wood varies enormously with the kind of tree. Black locust, white oak, hickory, black birch, and ironwood are the best. A cord of any of these woods, when seasoned, is worth approximately a ton of coal. Beech, yellow birch, sugar maple, ash, and red oak are next. White birch, cherry, soft maple, sycamore, and elm are comparatively poor fuel woods, with basswood, butternut, poplar, and the softwoods at the bottom of the scale.

15. The title that best expresses the main idea of this selection is

(A) Fuels

(B) The Value of a Cord of Wood

(C) Kinds of Trees

(D) Standard Measures
(E) Modern Heating

16. A standard cord of wood
(A) always contains 128 cubic feet of wood
(B) will average 100 cubic feet of wood
(C) contains less than 30 cubic feet of solid wood
(D) is stacked wood in a pile 4 × 4 × 8 feet
(E) is measured by weight of the wood per foot

17. Removal of the bark before stacking
(A) increases the cubic volume of wood in a cord
(B) makes the stacking easier
(C) allows more air spaces in a cord of wood
(D) prevents seasoning of wood
(E) decreases the measurements of the wood

18. The amount of heat supplied by wood depends upon
(A) the person who has piled the wood
(B) the type of tree from which the wood came
(C) the way the wood was cut
(D) the straightness of the sticks
(E) the amount of bark left on the wood

19. The most valuable fuel woods come from
(A) all kinds of birches and oaks
(B) any kind of wood that is well-seasoned
(C) home-grown beech, maple, cherry, and elm trees
(D) hickory, ironwood, black birch, black locust, and white oak
(E) sycamore, ash, butternut, and poplar that have been sprayed

Eight of the city's twelve workers in Venetian glass recently finished one of the most unusual murals ever made for a New York skyscraper. It is an abstract, the creation of Hans Hofmann, a 77-year-old German-born painter.

The mural covers 1,200 square feet of the outer wall of the elevator shaft in the William Kaufman Building at 711 Third Avenue. More than a half-million tiles in close to 500 shades of color have gone into it. Blue, red, and yellow are the chief colors. Each tile was made in Venice and is somewhat less than postage-stamp size. Each is beaten into a special everlasting concrete with a kind of flat wooden hand tool used for nothing else.

Mr. Hofmann did the original color sketch about one-sixth of the final size. This was photographed, and from the negative an enlargement was hand-colored by the artist, cut into sections, and sent in that form to the Vincent Foscato plant in Long Island City, which specializes in Venetian glass tile, or mosaic. There the Venetian specialists, whose trade has been handed down through families through the centuries, set each mosaic into place on the cartoon section, with painstaking fidelity to Mr. Hofmann's color rendering. Although Mr. Foscato's plant keeps 1,400 shades of the glass mosaic, it had to have twelve additional shades specially made in Venice to match the sketch coloring for perfect blending. When all the sections had been filled and approved, they were carried by truck to the building lobby, the walls were covered with a special cement, and the workers carefully beat each bit into place.

20. The best title for this selection would be
(A) Picture by German Artist to Hang in New York
(B) New Mosaic Designed by Vincent Foscato
(C) Unusual Photograph Decorates New York Building
(D) Venetian-Glass Mural Installed in Skyscraper
(E) The William Kaufman Building

GO ON TO THE NEXT PAGE

21. The original design was
   (A) painted on the wall of the Kaufman building
   (B) a fraction of the size of the finished mural
   (C) imported from Venice
   (D) larger than the finished mural
   (E) projected on a large sheet of paper

22. Mr. Hofmann
   (A) learned from his father how to do mosaic work
   (B) is a native of New York
   (C) is a painter
   (D) lives in Long Island City
   (E) is a Venetian-glass specialist

23. In making the mural
   (A) the shades of tile that the Foscato plant had in stock were not adequate
   (B) 1,412 shades were needed
   (C) half a million colors were used
   (D) over 500 shades of color were used
   (E) 1,400 specialists were consulted

24. Mr. Hofmann
   (A) took a color photograph of his painting
   (B) used only the most unusual shades of red, blue, and green
   (C) had no further connection with the work after making the original sketch
   (D) died shortly before the mural was completed
   (E) colored the enlarged reproduction of the original

25. Of the tiles used
   (A) some were made of special colors by Mr. Foscato
   (B) all were made by the workers who put the mural in place
   (C) all were made in Italy
   (D) all were made in New York
   (E) many were made by a wooden hand tool

26. The mosaic was assembled by
   (A) Hans Hofmann
   (B) an artist specializing in Venetian glass
   (C) Vincent Foscato of Long Island
   (D) workers in the Foscato plant
   (E) Venetian workers

The history of modern pollution problems shows that most have resulted from negligence and ignorance. We have an appalling tendency to interfere with nature before all of the possible consequences of our actions have been studied in-depth. We produce and distribute radioactive substances, *synthetic* chemicals, and many other potent compounds before fully comprehending their effects on living organisms. Our education is dangerously incomplete.

It is often argued that the purpose of science is to move into unknown territory, to explore, and to discover. It can be said that similar risks have been taken before, and that these risks are necessary to technological progress.

These arguments overlook an important element. In the past, risks taken in the name of scientific progress were restricted to a small place and a brief period of time. The effects of the processes we now strive to master are neither localized nor brief. Air pollution covers vast urban areas. Ocean pollutants have been discovered in nearly every part of the world. Synthetic chemicals spread over huge stretches of forest and farmland may remain in the soil for decades. Radioactive pollutants will be found in the biosphere for generations. The size and persistence of these problems have grown with the expanding power of modern science.

One might also argue that the hazards of modern pollutants are small compared to the dangers associated with other human activity. No estimate of the actual harm done by smog, fallout, or chemical residues can obscure the reality that the risks are being taken before being fully understood.

The importance of these issues lies in the failure of science to predict and control human intervention into natural processes. The true measure of the danger is represented by the hazards we will encounter if we enter the new age of technology without first evaluating our responsibility to the environment.

27. According to the author, the major cause of pollution is the result of

(A) designing synthetic chemicals to kill living organisms

(B) a lack of understanding of the history of technology

(C) scientists who are too willing to move into unknown territory

(D) changing our environment before understanding the effects of these changes

(E) not passing enough laws

28. The author believes that the risks taken by modern science are greater than those taken by earlier scientific efforts because

(A) the effects may be felt by more people for a longer period of time

(B) science is progressing faster than ever before

(C) technology has produced more dangerous chemicals

(D) the materials used are more dangerous to scientists

(E) the problems are greater

29. The author apparently believes that the problem of finding solutions to pollution depends on

(A) the removal of present hazards to the environment

(B) the removal of all potential pollutants from their present uses

(C) overcoming technical difficulties

(D) the willingness of scientists to understand possible dangers before using new products in the environment

(E) a new age of science that will repair the faults of our present technology

30. The author seems to feel that the attitude of scientists toward pollution has been

(A) naive

(B) concerned

(C) confused

(D) ignorant

(E) nonchalant

31. The word *synthetic* means

(A) new

(B) unsafe

(C) polluting

(D) man-made

(E) progressive

A third of our lives is spent in the mysterious state of sleep. Throughout our history, we have attempted to understand this remarkable experience. Many centuries ago, for example, sleep was regarded as a type of anemia of the brain. Alemaeon, a Greek scientist, believed that blood retreated into the veins, and the partially starved brain went to sleep. Plato supported the idea that the soul left the body during sleep, wandered the world, and woke up the body when it returned.

Recently, more scientific explanations of sleep have been proposed. According to one theory, the brain is put to sleep by a chemical agent that accumulates in the body when it is awake. Another theory is that weary branches of certain nerve cells break connections with neighboring cells. The flow of impulses required for staying awake is then disrupted. These more recent theories have had to be subjected to laboratory research.

Why do we sleep? Why do we dream? Modern sleep research is said to have begun in the 1950s, when Eugene Aserinsky, a graduate student at the University of Chicago, and Nathaniel Kleitman, his professor, observed periods of rapid eye movements (REMs) in sleeping subjects. When awakened during these REM periods, subjects almost always remembered

GO ON TO THE NEXT PAGE

dreaming. On the other hand, when awakened during non-REM phases of sleep, the subjects rarely could recall their dreams.

Guided by REMs, it became possible for investigators to "spot" dreaming from outside and then awaken the sleepers to collect dream stories. They could also alter the dreamers' experiences with noises, drugs, or other *stimuli* before or during sleep.

Since the mid-1950s, researchers have been drawn into sleep laboratories. There, bedrooms adjoin other rooms that contain recorders known as electroencephalograph (EEG) machines.

The EEG amplifies signals from sensors on the face, head, and other parts of the body, which together yield tracings of respiration, pulse, muscle tension, and changes of electrical potential in the brain that are sometimes called brain waves. These recordings supply clues to the changes of the sleeping person's activities.

32. The main purpose of this passage is to

(A) describe early beliefs about sleep

(B) compare modern scientific theories to early ideas about sleep

(C) point out the importance of REMs in human sleep

(D) describe modern research techniques

(E) give a short history of human's interest in sleep

33. This passage implies that the importance of the research of Aserinsky and Kleitman was mainly in the

(A) reports they published

(B) problems they attacked

(C) information they observed and recorded

(D) understandings they uncovered

(E) conclusions they drew for treatment of sleep disorders

34. All of the following were mentioned as possible causes of sleep *except*

(A) exhausted nerve endings

(B) a build-up of certain body chemicals

(C) recurrent periods of rapid eye movement

(D) the absence of the conscious spirit

(E) the departure of the soul from the body

35. In paragraph 4, the word *stimuli* means

(A) substances that make a person more alert

(B) drugs

(C) sleep inducing

(D) comatose

(E) things that cause the body to react in a certain way

As he threw his head back in the chair, his glance happened to rest upon a bell, a disused bell, that hung in the room and communicated, for some purpose now forgotten, with a chamber in the highest story of the building. It was with great astonishment, and with a strange *inexplicable* dread, that, as he looked, he saw this bell begin to swing. Soon it rang out loudly, and so did every bell in the house.

This was succeeded by a clanking noise, deep down below as if some person were dragging a heavy chain over the casks in the wine merchant's cellar. Then he heard the noise much louder on the floors below; then coming up the stairs; then coming straight toward his door.

It came in through the heavy door, and a *specter* passed into the room before his eyes. And upon its coming in, the dying flame leaped up, as though it cried, "I know him! Marley's ghost!"

—from *A Christmas Carol*
by Charles Dickens

36. The word *inexplicable* means

(A) explaining in simple terms

(B) not able to be taken out of

(C) without an expressed reason

(D) eerie

(E) incapable

37. The bell that began ringing
   (A) was large and heavy
   (B) did so by itself
   (C) could be rung from another room
   (D) was attached to every bell in the house
   (E) rested first on his glance

38. The man who was listening to the bell
   (A) dragged a chain across the wine casks
   (B) sat perfectly still
   (C) was apparently very frightened
   (D) was Marley's ghost
   (E) was quite curious

39. The word *specter* probably means
   (A) a long-handled sword
   (B) a bright light
   (C) a hazy, recognizable vision
   (D) strange noises
   (E) clanking chains

40. The man in the story
   (A) first heard noises in his room
   (B) is probably a wine merchant
   (C) had been asleep
   (D) recognized Marley's ghost
   (E) set the room on fire

STOP

END OF SECTION THREE. IF YOU HAVE ANY TIME LEFT, GO OVER YOUR WORK IN THIS SECTION ONLY. DO NOT WORK IN ANY OTHER SECTION OF THE EXAM.

SECTION FOUR: QUANTITATIVE

25 QUESTIONS • TIME—25 MINUTES

Directions: Each question below is followed by five possible answers. Select the one that is best, and mark the appropriate letter on your answer sheet.

1. In two hours, the minute hand of a clock rotates through an angle of

(A) 60°

(B) 90°

(C) 180°

(D) 360°

(E) 720°

2. Which of the following fractions is less than one third?

(A) $\frac{22}{63}$

(B) $\frac{4}{11}$

(C) $\frac{15}{46}$

(D) $\frac{33}{98}$

(E) $\frac{102}{303}$

3.

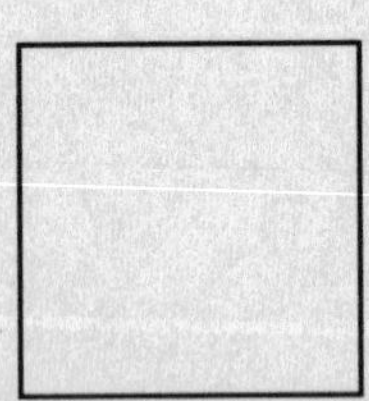

The length of each side of the square above is $\frac{2x}{3} + 1$. The perimeter of the square is

(A) $\frac{8x}{3} + 4$

(B) $\frac{8x + 4}{3}$

(C) $\frac{2x}{3} + 4$

(D) $\frac{2x}{3} + 16$

(E) $\frac{4x}{3} + 2$

4.

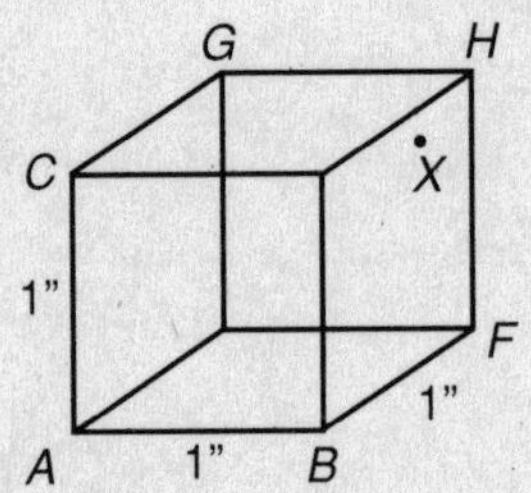

The diagram shows a cube.

The distance from A to D is

(A) 2 inches

(B) $\sqrt{3}$ inches

(C) $\sqrt{2}$ inches

(D) 1 inch

(E) $\frac{1}{\sqrt{2}}$ inches

5. A motorist travels 120 miles to his destination at an average speed of 60 miles per hour and returns to the starting point at an average speed of 40 miles per hour. His average speed for the entire trip is

(A) 53 miles per hour

(B) 52 miles per hour

(C) 50 miles per hour

(D) 48 miles per hour

(E) 45 miles per hour

6. A snapshot measures $2\frac{1}{2}$ inches by $1\frac{7}{8}$ inches. It is to be enlarged so that the longer dimension will be 4 inches. The length of the enlarged shorter dimension will be

(A) $2\frac{1}{2}$ inches

(B) $2\frac{5}{8}$ inches

(C) 3 inches

(D) $3\frac{3}{8}$ inches

(E) $3\frac{5}{8}$ inches

7. From a piece of tin in the shape of a square 6 inches on a side, the largest possible circle is cut out. Of the following, the ratio of the area of the circle to the area of the original square is closest in value to

(A) $\frac{4}{5}$

(B) $\frac{2}{3}$

(C) $\frac{3}{5}$

(D) $\frac{7}{9}$

(E) $\frac{3}{4}$

8. If the outer diameter of a metal pipe is 2.84 inches and the inner diameter is 1.94 inches, the thickness of the metal is

(A) .45 in.

(B) .90 in.

(C) 1.42 in.

(D) 1.94 in.

(E) 2.39 in.

9. A sportswriter claims that her football predictions are accurate 60% of the time. During football season, a fan kept records and found that the writer was inaccurate for a total of 16 games, although she did maintain her 60% accuracy. For how many games was the sportswriter accurate?

(A) 5

(B) 15

(C) 24

(D) 40

(E) 60

10. In a certain boys' camp, 30% of the boys are from New York State and 20% of these are from New York City. What percent of the boys in the camp are from New York City?

(A) 60%

(B) 50%

(C) $33\frac{1}{3}$%

(D) 10%

(E) 6%

11.

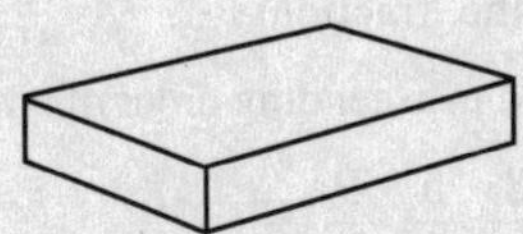

A unit block for construction is $1 \times 2 \times 3$ inches. What is the number of whole blocks required to cover an area 1 foot long by $1\frac{1}{4}$ feet wide with *one layer* of blocks?

(A) 30 blocks

(B) 60 blocks

(C) 72 blocks

(D) 90 blocks

(E) 180 blocks

GO ON TO THE NEXT PAGE

12. If the number of square inches in the area of a circle is equal to the number of inches in its circumference, the diameter of the circle is
    (A) 4 inches
    (B) 2 inches
    (C) 1 inch
    (D) π inches
    (E) 2π inches

13. The least common multiple of 20, 24, and 32 is
    (A) 240
    (B) 480
    (C) 960
    (D) 1,920
    (E) 15,360

14. If $9x + 5 = 23$, the numerical value of $18x + 5$ is
    (A) 46
    (B) 41
    (C) 38
    (D) 36
    (E) 32

15. When the fractions $\frac{2}{3}$, $\frac{5}{7}$, $\frac{8}{11}$, and $\frac{9}{13}$ are arranged in ascending order of size, the result is
    (A) $\frac{8}{11}, \frac{5}{7}, \frac{9}{13}, \frac{2}{3}$
    (B) $\frac{5}{7}, \frac{8}{11}, \frac{2}{3}, \frac{9}{13}$
    (C) $\frac{2}{3}, \frac{8}{11}, \frac{5}{7}, \frac{9}{13}$
    (D) $\frac{2}{3}, \frac{9}{13}, \frac{5}{7}, \frac{8}{11}$
    (E) $\frac{9}{13}, \frac{2}{3}, \frac{8}{11}, \frac{5}{7}$

16. If a cubic inch of a metal weighs 2 pounds, a cubic foot of the same metal weighs
    (A) 8 pounds
    (B) 24 pounds
    (C) 96 pounds
    (D) 288 pounds
    (E) 3,456 pounds

17. A micromillimeter is defined as one millionth of a millimeter. A length of 17 micromillimeters may be represented as
    (A) .00017 mm.
    (B) .000017 mm.
    (C) .0000017 mm.
    (D) .00000017 mm.
    (E) .000000017 mm.

18. To find the radius of a circle whose circumference is 60 inches,
    (A) multiply 60 by π
    (B) divide 60 by 2π
    (C) divide 30 by 2π
    (D) divide 60 by π and extract the square root of the result
    (E) multiply 60 by $\frac{\pi}{2}$

19. A carpenter needs four boards, each 2 feet 9 inches long. If wood is sold only by the foot, how many feet must he buy?
    (A) 9
    (B) 10
    (C) 11
    (D) 12
    (E) 13

20. The approximate distance, S, in feet that an object falls in t seconds when dropped from a height can be found by using the formula $S = 16t^2$. In 8 seconds the object will fall
    (A) 256 feet
    (B) 1,024 feet
    (C) 1,084 feet
    (D) 2,048 feet
    (E) 15,384 feet

21. Event A occurs every four minutes, event B every six minutes, and event C every fifteen minutes. If they occur simultaneously at noon, when is the next time all three events will occur together again?

(A) 1:00 PM

(B) 1:30 PM

(C) 3:00 PM

(D) 6:00 PM

(E) 12:00 AM

22. The number of telephones in Adelaide, Australia is 48,000. If this represents 12.8 telephones per 100 persons, the population of Adelaide to the nearest thousand is

(A) 128,000

(B) 375,000

(C) 378,000

(D) 556,000

(E) 575,000

23. One person can load a truck in 25 minutes, a second can load it in 50 minutes, and a third can load it in 10 minutes. How long would it take the three together to load the truck?

(A) $5\frac{3}{11}$ minutes

(B) $6\frac{1}{4}$ minutes

(C) $8\frac{1}{3}$ minutes

(D) 10 minutes

(E) $28\frac{1}{3}$ minutes

Questions 24 and 25 refer to the following graph.

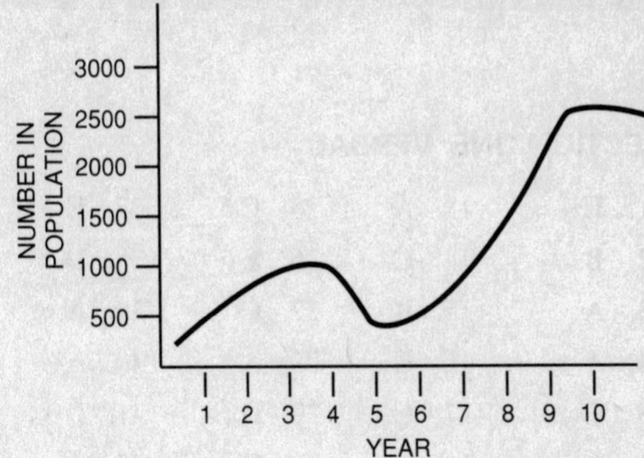

24. During which years did the population increase at the fastest rate?

(A) years 5–7

(B) years 1–3

(C) years 4–5

(D) years 7–9

(E) years 9–10

25. During which year did the size of the population decrease the most?

(A) years 4–5

(B) years 3–4

(C) years 9–10

(D) years 1–2

(E) years 4–6

STOP

END OF SECTION FOUR. IF YOU HAVE ANY TIME LEFT, GO OVER YOUR WORK IN THIS SECTION ONLY. DO NOT WORK IN ANY OTHER SECTION OF THE EXAM.

Answer Key

SECTION ONE: VERBAL

1. E	13. A	25. C	37. E	49. A
2. B	14. C	26. E	38. D	50. E
3. A	15. B	27. C	39. A	51. E
4. A	16. E	28. A	40. A	52. E
5. C	17. C	29. D	41. D	53. A
6. B	18. A	30. E	42. A	54. C
7. D	19. B	31. C	43. B	55. D
8. C	20. D	32. A	44. B	56. A
9. A	21. E	33. C	45. E	57. A
10. C	22. C	34. B	46. E	58. E
11. E	23. B	35. B	47. E	59. A
12. C	24. A	36. C	48. B	60. A

SECTION TWO: QUANTITATIVE

1. D	6. C	11. E	16. A	21. B
2. B	7. B	12. D	17. D	22. C
3. C	8. A	13. C	18. B	23. A
4. D	9. C	14. C	19. C	24. E
5. C	10. C	15. C	20. D	25. B

SECTION THREE: READING

1. A	9. E	17. A	25. C	33. C
2. A	10. B	18. B	26. D	34. C
3. E	11. D	19. D	27. D	35. E
4. A	12. A	20. D	28. A	36. C
5. A	13. C	21. B	29. D	37. B
6. B	14. B	22. C	30. E	38. C
7. B	15. B	23. A	31. D	39. C
8. A	16. D	24. C	32. E	40. D

SECTION FOUR: QUANTITATIVE

1. **E**
2. **C**
3. **A**
4. **C**
5. **D**
6. **C**
7. **D**
8. **A**
9. **C**
10. **E**
11. **A**
12. **A**
13. **B**
14. **B**
15. **D**
16. **E**
17. **B**
18. **B**
19. **C**
20. **B**
21. **A**
22. **B**
23. **B**
24. **D**
25. **A**

Explanatory Answers

Part I: WRITING SAMPLE

Example of a well-written essay.

The proposal to raise the minimum licensing age from 16 to 18 should be rejected for a number of reasons. There are no solid statistics proving that youths cause the accidents that they are involved in, so the 16- and 17-year-old age group should not be penalized for those accidents. Also, for many young people, use of a car is an absolute necessity.

Legislators should ask themselves why 16 to 18 year old drivers tend to be involved in accidents. I think that the main cause of these accidents is lack of experience. If a study were made, I suspect that it would show that new drivers of any age tend to have accidents. Raising the licensing age would only raise the age of drivers involved in accidents. A better cure might be driving education programs that stress judgment on the road and a requirement for a longer period of driving under supervision before licensing.

Raising the driving age would create a real financial hardship for some teenagers and their families. Many working parents count on their high schoolers to transport younger children in the afternoon and to run errands. Other teens have part-time jobs in locations that can be reached only by car. Attempting to solve the accident problem by creating financial problems does not seem logical.

Raising the licensing age could actually lead to a higher accident rate. Teenagers who have to drive would drive anyway, but without benefit of driver education or the testing that is required for getting that license. Untrained, untested teenage drivers would be a menace on the roads. The 16-year minimum should be retained for the safety of all.

Part II: EXPLANATORY ANSWERS

SECTION ONE: VERBAL

Synonyms

1. **(E)** To DETER is to *discourage* a person or group from doing something. Fear of retaliation may deter our enemies from attacking.
2. **(B)** HOSTILE means *antagonistic* or *unfriendly*. It is the nature of cats to be hostile to dogs.
3. **(A)** To UTILIZE is to *make practical use of*. You can utilize the microwave for quick defrosting.
4. **(A)** To ABDICATE is to *give up formally* or to *resign*. King Edward abdicated from the English throne to marry a divorced woman.
5. **(C)** PROMINENT means *sticking out, noticeable*, or *outstanding*. Jimmy Durante had a prominent nose.
6. **(B)** A BOUNDARY is a *border*. Mexico shares a boundary with the state of Texas.
7. **(D)** ILLITERATE means *unable to read*. One who is literate is educated and is able to read. The prefix *il-* creates the negative. Many of the homeless are unemployable because they are illiterate.
8. **(C)** An ORATOR is *one who speaks*. (Can you see the root *oral?*) The keynote speaker at the convention was a superb orator.
9. **(A)** To CORROBORATE is to *strengthen*, to *support*, or to *confirm*. The bloody knife served to corroborate the eyewitness's testimony.
10. **(C)** To RATIFY is to *give official sanction to* or to *approve*. If three more states ratify the proposed amendment, it will become a part of our Constitution.

11. **(E)** PERILOUS means *risky* or *dangerous*. Construction of skyscrapers is perilous work.

12. **(C)** STATIONARY means *not moving* or *not movable*. It is the adjective form of the noun *station*. Choice (A) refers to the homophone *stationery*. Unlike Easter, Christmas is a stationary holiday; it always occurs on the same date.

13. **(A)** To TRANSCRIBE is to *write out in full* or to *make a recording*. The court stenographer transcribed the full proceedings of the trial.

14. **(C)** PROFICIENT means *highly skilled, competent*, or *adept*. The concert pianist is proficient at the art.

15. **(B)** To DECEIVE is to *make a person believe what is not true*. The purpose of a lie is to deceive.

16. **(E)** AGILE means *deft, active*, and *lively*. Prize-winning gymnasts are always agile.

17. **(C)** The DURATION is the *time that a thing continues or lasts*. The duration of a school semester is a four-month term.

18. **(A)** AMBIGUOUS means *having two meanings* or *being vague and uncertain*. The prefix *ambi-* means *both* and implies that both possible interpretations might be correct and therefore neither is clear. Her ambiguous answer left us uncertain as to whether she meant "Yes" or "No."

19. **(B)** A PREROGATIVE is a *right, privilege*, or *special advantage*. The aged and the disabled have the prerogative of sitting at the front of the bus.

20. **(D)** That which is INTRIGUING excites *interest* and *curiosity* and is *fascinating*. His interpretation of the event presents an intriguing new theory.

21. **(E)** CLANDESTINE means *surreptitious* or *secret*, usually for some illicit reason or purpose. The married man had clandestine meetings with his mistress.

22. **(C)** BOUNTEOUS means *plentiful, generous*, and *abundant*. At the end of a favorable growing season, we had a bounteous harvest.

23. **(B)** To DIVERGE is to *move off in different directions* or to *become different*. Parallel lines do not diverge.

24. **(A)** BENIGN means *good-natured, kindly*, or *harmless*. When applied to a tumor, *benign* means *harmless* as opposed to *malignant*, which implies *life-threatening*. The Pope faced his audience with a benign smile.

25. **(C)** A CAUCUS is a *meeting of people with similar goals*, usually a group of people within a larger group. The Black Congressional caucus meets periodically to discuss minority issues.

26. **(E)** To DISSEMINATE is to *scatter widely*. It is important that we disseminate information about the transmission of AIDS.

27. **(C)** CHAGRIN is *embarrassment* or *humiliation*. The bettor was chagrined that the horse he had praised so loudly came in last.

28. **(A)** VALOR is *high value, courage*, or *bravery*. The soldiers defended the Alamo with valor.

29. **(D)** NONCHALANT means *without enthusiasm* or *indifferent*. The student was so nonchalant about her award that she did not even tell her parents.

30. **(E)** A LIAISON is a *linking up* or a *connection*. The liaison of allies from a number of countries led to defeat of the enemy forces.

Analogies

31. **(C)** The relationship is not of precise synonyms, but it is close. Both *beg* and *borrow* have to do with *ask for* and *take*. Both *offer* and *lend* have to do with *give*. *Repay* also has to do with *give* but it implies a previous activity not implied in the relationship of *beg* and *borrow*.

32. **(A)** One who is *lazy* is *inert*. One who *resists*, *refuses*. The relationship is one of characteristics or even synonyms.

33. **(C)** A *circle* is the base of a *cylinder;* a *triangle* is the base of a *pyramid*. We have explained this as a part-to-whole relationship. The actual statement of the analogy is whole-to-part.

34. **(B)** This is a true part-to-whole analogy. A *crocodile* is part of a larger group, *reptiles*. A *kangaroo* is part of a larger group, *marsupials*.

35. **(B)** This is another part-to-whole relationship. A *quart* is roughly equivalent to a liter, and a *milliliter* is 1/1000 of a liter. A *yard* is roughly equivalent to a meter, and a *millimeter* is 1/1000 of a meter. Choice (A) reverses the relationship. The other choices do not move from metric to American measures.

36. **(C)** These are true synonyms.

37. **(E)** These are true antonyms.

38. **(D)** In neither set are the terms true antonyms, but they clearly have opposite connotations. Choice (E) also offers opposite connotations, but the order of the terms is reversed.

39. **(A)** Wild is a characteristic of *wolf* as *domestic* is a characteristic of both *dog* and *cat*. You must narrow further to choose the best answer. *Dog* is the domestic counterpart of *wolf*, so *dog* creates the best analogy.

40. **(A)** This is a purpose relationship. A *hammer* is a tool used by a *carpenter;* an *awl* is a tool used by a *cobbler*. Choice (D) reverses the order of tool and its user.

41. **(D)** This is a part-to-part relationship. Both subject and predicate are parts of a sentence; both senator and representative are parts of the congress. (A) is an incorrect answer because a senator's relationship to congress is that of part-to-whole.

42. **(A)** This is an association relationship. *Pungent* is an adjective used to describe a degree of *odor*. *Intense* is an adjective used to describe a degree of *emotion*.

43. **(B)** The analogy is based on synonyms.

44. **(B)** All four terms are synonyms.

45. **(E)** The relationship is one of association or characteristic. *Exuberant* is an adjective used to describe *mood; adroit* is an adjective used to describe *movement*.

46. **(E)** *Opposition* leads to *defiance; challenge* leads to *exertion*. The actual statement of the analogy is effect and its cause.

47. **(E)** This is a true cause-and-effect relationship. *Food* promotes *nutrition; light* promotes *vision*. Light does not promote any of the other choices.

48. **(B)** The relationship is that of true antonyms. The false choices are synonyms or partial antonyms making this a very difficult analogy question.

49. **(A)** This antonym relationship is easier to see at a glance.

50. **(E)** This may be either a part-to-whole relationship or an analogy of degree. Either a *comment* is part of a *speech* and a *note* is part of a *letter* or a *comment* is much shorter than a *speech* and a *note* is much shorter than a *letter*.

51. **(E)** Be careful. *Flammable* and *inflammable* are synonyms; both mean *easily inflamed. Disinterested* means *impartial*.

52. **(E)** This is a purpose relationship. A *tailor* follows a *pattern* to construct a piece of clothing; a *builder* follows a *blueprint* to construct a building.

53. **(A)** The relationship is sequential. *Impeachment* (accusation) comes before *dismissal. Arraignment* (accusation) comes before *indictment* (placement of charges).

54. **(C)** The relationship is of characteristic to animal. Choice (B) reverses the relationship.

55. **(D)** All choices except (A) involve the activity of a bodily organ, so you must think further. Both *exhalation* and *perspiration* involve giving off something from within the body.

56. **(A)** You *celebrate* a *birth;* you *grieve* over a *death*. The analogy states the effect and its cause.

57. **(A)** This is an analogy of degree. To *urge* is to *recommend* strongly; to *plead* is to *request* strongly. Choice (B) offers synonyms of equal degree; choice (C) reverses the order.

58. **(E)** This is a cause-and-effect relationship. When one *weeps*, one gives off *tears;* when one *breathes*, one gives off *carbon dioxide*.

59. **(A)** The relationship is hard to categorize but easy to spot. An *air pocket* makes a *plane* bounce; a *rut* has the same effect on a *vehicle*.

60. **(A)** This is a verb-to-noun relationship. *Arbitrate* is what one does to a *dispute; solve* is what must be done to a *mystery*.

SECTION TWO: QUANTITATIVE

1. **(D)** Change $1\frac{1}{2}$ to the decimal 1.50 and add.

$$\begin{array}{r} 1.50 \\ .750 \\ \underline{.1010} \\ 2.351 \end{array}$$

2. **(B)** When dividing numbers having the same base, simply subtract the exponents.

$$\frac{2^{12}}{2^8} = 2^{12-8} = 2^4 = 16$$

3. **(C)**

$$62.3\overline{)503.384} = 8.08$$

4984
4984
4984
0

4. **(D)** Simplify the numerator of the fraction, and then divide.

$$\frac{1\frac{3}{4}-\frac{1}{8}}{\frac{1}{8}} = \frac{1\frac{6}{8}-\frac{1}{8}}{\frac{1}{8}}$$

$$= \frac{1\frac{5}{8}}{\frac{1}{8}} = 1\frac{5}{8} \bullet \frac{8}{1}$$

$$= \frac{13}{8} \bullet \frac{8}{1} = 13$$

5. **(C)**

$$1.02\overline{)2.010000} = 1.970$$

102
990
918
720
714
60

6. **(C)** Begin working with the innermost parentheses and work your way out.

$-3 - [(2 - 1) - (3 + 4)]$
$= -3 - [(1) - (7)]$
$= -3 - [1 - 7]$
$= -3 - [-6]$
$= -3 + 6$
$= 3$

7. **(B)** This is a good problem to do in your head. Mentally subtract 700 from 3,003 and get 2303. Then look at the answers carefully and note that only (B) is close to your estimate.

3,003
− 699
2,304

8. **(A)** The problem states that $a = 5$ and $b = \frac{1}{5}$; $\frac{1}{5}$ is $\frac{1}{25}$ of 5. Therefore, the value of a expressed in terms of b is $25 \times \frac{1}{5} = 5$, or $25b$.

9. **(C)** This is a good problem to do in your head. Note that 10% of 70 is 7. 140%, then, is 14×7, or 98.

10. **(C)** Borrow a gallon and add it to 2 quarts. Rewrite the problem. Remember that you borrowed.

4 gallons 6 quarts 1 pint
− 1 gallon 3 quarts 0 pints
3 gallons 3 quarts 1 pint

11. **(E)** By doubling the denominator of a fraction, we actually divide it by two. By halving one of the factors in the numerator, we also halve the value of the fraction. By doing both, we have actually divided the original value by four. Plug in some values for x, y, and z, and try this.

12. **(D)** This is a good problem to estimate. Since 8% is slightly less than $\frac{1}{12}$, you can multiply 20 by 12 to approximate the answer. Note that 250 is close enough to your 240 estimate. To be precise: $20 \div .08 =$

$$.08\overline{)20.00} = 250.$$

16
40
40
0

13. **(C)** 100 is 20 larger than 80. 20 is one fourth, or 25%, of 80. Therefore, 125% of 80 is equivalent to 100.

14. **(C)** Forty inches equals $3\frac{1}{3}$ feet. Since $\frac{3}{8}$" equals 1 foot,

$$3\frac{1}{3}\text{ feet} = 3\frac{1}{3} \bullet \frac{3}{8}$$
$$= \frac{10}{3} \bullet \frac{3}{8}$$
$$= \frac{10}{8}$$
$$= 1\frac{1}{4}"$$

15. **(C)** Bracket the multiplication and division first, and solve the problem.

$$(6 \div \frac{1}{3}) + (\frac{2}{3} \times 9)$$
$$= 18 + 6$$
$$= 24$$

16. **(A)** Since $x-3<12$, x can be any number less than 15.

17. **(D)** Substitute the values into the expression.

$$\sqrt{9+3(2)+1}$$
$$= \sqrt{9+6+1}$$
$$= \sqrt{16}$$
$$= 4$$

18. **(B)** By substituting +2 for the triangle, the denominator of the fraction becomes zero. A denominator of zero has no meaning in mathematics.

19. **(C)** Simply move the decimal point one place to the left and insert a zero in the newly created decimal place.

$$.10101 \div 10 = .010101$$

20. **(D)** The formula for rate is rate = distance ÷ time. In this problem, rate = 10 miles ÷ 3 hours, or $3\frac{1}{3}$ miles per hour.

21. **(B)** 7 is one third of 21, and $\frac{2}{3}$ is one third of 2.

As a proportion:

$$\frac{7}{21} = \frac{\frac{2}{3}}{x}$$

22. **(C)** The square root of 85 is between 9, whose square is 81, and 10, whose square is 100.

23. **(A)** $-6 + -2 + 0 + 8 = 0$

24. **(E)** Simply divide $\frac{5}{6}$ by $\frac{1}{4}$.

$$\frac{5}{6} \div \frac{1}{4} = \frac{5}{6} \bullet \frac{4}{1}$$
$$= \frac{20}{6} = 3\frac{1}{3}$$

25. **(B)** To find the average, find the sum of the addends and divide that sum by the number of addends.

$$-10 + 6 + 0 + -3 + 22 = 15$$
$$15 \div 5 = 3$$

SECTION THREE: READING COMPREHENSION

1. **(A)** This is a detail question that you answer through a process of elimination. (D) and (E) are mentioned in the first paragraph, whereas (B) and (C) may be found in the second sentence of the second paragraph.
2. **(A)** Careful reading will find this detail in the fifth sentence of the second paragraph.
3. **(E)** See the first sentence.
4. **(A)** You must infer this answer from the information given. Because "the male wolverine … fights to the death any male that intrudes on his domain …" only the fittest, the best fighters, survive, and numbers are held down.
5. **(A)** The writer's total fascination with and expertise on the subject of the wolverine leads us to infer that he is a naturalist. The fact that he is carrying a gun in wild country does not necessarily imply that he is a hunter. Prudent naturalists may carry guns for self-defense in the wilderness.
6. **(B)** The wolverine is a destroyer, and even large animals succumb to his attacks. The large animals *are overcome* by the wolverine, but the word *succumb* is an active verb; therefore, what the animals who are overcome do is *surrender*.
7. **(B)** This is a main-idea question. The paragraph describes Chiron.

8. **(A)** The paragraph states that Chiron had the legs of a horse; a horse has four legs. From basic etymology, you know that "quad" means "four" and that "ped" refers to feet.
9. **(E)** Read carefully. The physical description is the only choice supported by the paragraph. The last sentence specifically states that Chiron did *not* teach writing and arithmetic.
10. **(B)** See the first sentence.
11. **(D)** See the next-to-last sentence of the first paragraph.
12. **(A)** The third sentence of the second paragraph gives this information.
13. **(C)** You certainly can infer this from the last sentence of the second paragraph.
14. **(B)** This is the author's meaning in the last sentence, in which the author states that the tall tales are close to fact.
15. **(B)** This is a main-idea question, and you must choose the most inclusive title for the entire selection. The selection discusses the value of a cord of wood—the volume value in the first paragraph and the heating value in the second paragraph.
16. **(D)** This detail question is answered in the third sentence.
17. **(A)** See the last sentence of the first paragraph.
18. **(B)** See the first sentence of the second paragraph.
19. **(D)** See the second sentence of the second paragraph.
20. **(D)** The selection is all about the mural.
21. **(B)** The first sentence of the third paragraph gives this information.
22. **(C)** The second sentence tells us that Mr. Hofmann is a painter. All the other choices confuse other information.
23. **(A)** This is a difficult question requiring concentration on the meanings of statements. The selection tells us that the Foscato plant had 1400 shades in stock yet had to send to Italy for 12 special shades, but it does not say that all 1400 shades in stock were used.
24. **(C)** Find the answer to this question by means of elimination and inference. The passage tells us that Mr. Hofmann made the original sketch, but never mentions any further involvement by him. None of the other choices can be supported by the text.
25. **(C)** The next-to-last sentence of the second paragraph states that each tile was made in Venice. Venice is in Italy.
26. **(D)** In the middle of the third paragraph we learn that the mosaic was assembled—each mosaic was set into place—by specialists in the Foscato plant.
27. **(D)** Read carefully the second sentence of the first paragraph.
28. **(A)** You can infer this answer from the third paragraph in which the author states that "The effects of the processes ... are neither localized nor brief."
29. **(D)** This answer can be inferred from the whole tone of the selection. None of the other choices can be supported by the selection.
30. **(E)** *Nonchalant* means *casually indifferent.* Negligence and ignorance on the part of scientists certainly implies nonchalance.
31. **(D)** *Synthetic* means *not natural* or *man-made.*
32. **(E)** The approach of the entire selection is historical. Each of the other choices focuses on one paragraph, one phase of this history.
33. **(C)** Aserinsky and Kleitman observed, recorded, and reported; they did not explain. Their observations opened lines for future research.
34. **(C)** Rapid eye movement is mentioned as a part of sleep, not as a cause.
35. **(E)** A stimulus is anything that produces some kind of reaction, physical or mental. *Stimuli* is the plural of this Latin word.
36. **(C)** Use word arithmetic. *In* = not; *able* = able to be; *explic* = explained; in other words, without an expressed reason.
37. **(B)** If a disused bell suddenly began to swing, it must have done so all by itself.
38. **(C)** Great astonishment and inexplicable dread certainly imply fright.

39. **(C)** You can get this definition from the last paragraph. A specter is a ghost.

40. **(D)** This is the only choice supported by the selection. The answer is in the last sentence. (A) is incorrect because the man first saw the bell begin to move, and then he heard noises.

SECTION FOUR: QUANTITATIVE

1. **(E)** In one hour, the minute hand of a clock goes around in a complete circle. In two hours, it revolves through two circles. Because each circle consists of 360°, two revolutions equal 720°.

2. **(C)** A fraction is less than $\frac{1}{3}$ if three times the numerator is less than the denominator. Of the fractions listed, only $\frac{15}{46}$ has a numerator that is less than $\frac{1}{3}$ of the denominator.

3. **(A)** The figure is a square, so all four sides are equal in length. The perimeter is the sum of the lengths of the four sides. Each side is $\frac{2x}{3} + 1$.

The sum, then, is $\left(\frac{2x}{3}+1\right) + \left(\frac{2x}{3}+1\right) + \left(\frac{2x}{3}+1\right) + \left(\frac{2x}{3}+1\right) = \frac{8x}{3} + 4$.

You could also multiply $\frac{2x}{3} + 1$ by 4 for the same result.

4. **(C)** The face of the cube is a square, 1" by 1". Use the Pythagorean Theorem to find the length of the diagonal of the square.

$$c^2 = a^2 + b^2$$
$$c^2 = 1^2 + 1^2$$
$$c^2 = 2$$
$$c = \sqrt{2}$$

5. **(D)** The average speed for the entire trip is the total distance (240 miles) divided by the total time (5 hours), which yields 48 mph.

6. **(C)** This is a proportion problem. Set up the proportion as follows:

$$\frac{2\frac{1}{2}}{4} = \frac{1\frac{7}{8}}{?}$$

Substitute x for ?: $\frac{2\frac{1}{2}}{4} = \frac{1\frac{7}{8}}{x}$

Cross-multiply: $\frac{2\frac{1}{2}}{4} \times \frac{1\frac{7}{8}}{x}$ $\quad 2\frac{1}{2}x = 4 \bullet 1\frac{7}{8}$

Divide both sides by the coefficient of x and calculate:

$$\frac{5}{2}x = \frac{60}{8}$$
$$x = \frac{60}{8} \div \frac{5}{2}$$
$$x = \frac{60}{8} \times \frac{2}{5}$$
$$x = 3$$

7. **(D)** To find the ratio of the circle to the area of the square, first find the area of each. Note that the diameter of the circle equals the width of the square.

Area of the square = 6" × 6" = 36 sq. in.

Area of circle = $\pi 3^2 = 9\pi = 9 \bullet \frac{22}{7} = \frac{198}{7} = 28$ sq. in., approximately.

Ratio of the area of the circle to the area of the square: $\frac{28}{36} = \frac{7}{9}$

8. **(A)** The difference is .90 inch, but the outside diameter consists of two thicknesses of metal (one on each side). Therefore, the thickness of the metal is .90 ÷ 2 = .45 inch.

9. **(C)** If 60% of the games were predicted accurately, 40% of the games were predicted inaccurately.

Let x = games played

$.40x = 16$

$x = 40$ games played

$40 - 16 = 24$ games won

Therefore, the sportswriter was accurate for 24 games.

10. **(E)** Thirty percent of the boys are from New York State, and 20% of them (.20 of them) are from New York City. Therefore, (.20 × .30) of the boys in the camp are from New York City.

11. **(A)** An area 1 foot long by $1\frac{1}{4}$ feet wide is 12" × 15", or 180 square inches in area. Each block is 6 square inches in area. Therefore, the number of blocks needed is $\frac{180}{6}$ = 30 blocks. The height of each block is irrelevant to the solution of the problem.

12. **(A)** The area of a circle is equal to πr^2. The circumference of a circle is equal to πd. If the number of inches in each are equal, then $\pi d = \pi r^2$, or the diameter equals the square of the radius. The only value for which the diameter can equal the square of the radius is a diameter of 4".

13. **(B)** The LCM is found by rewriting each number in prime factorization and finding the product of each unique prime factor. 2^2 and 2^3 are not selected because each is a factor of 2^5.

$$20 = 2^2 \bullet 5$$
$$24 = 2^3 \bullet 3$$
$$32 = 2^5$$
$$\text{LCM} = 5 \bullet 3 \bullet 2^5 = 480$$

Trial and error can also give you this answer. None of the other choices can be divided by all three numbers without a remainder.

14. **(B)** If $9x + 5 = 23$, then $9x = 18$, and $x = 2$. Therefore, $18x + 5$ equals $18(2) + 5 = 41$.

15. **(D)** Fractions are most easily compared by comparing cross-products. Start by comparing $\frac{2}{3}$ with $\frac{5}{7}$. The product of 3 and 5 is 15. The product of 7 and 2 is 14. Therefore $\frac{5}{7}$ is larger than $\frac{2}{3}$. Continue this process with the other fractions to be compared.

$$\frac{5}{7} \times \frac{8}{11},\ \text{note}\ \frac{8}{11} > \frac{5}{7}\ \text{and also}\ \frac{8}{11} > \frac{2}{3}$$

$$\frac{8}{11} \times \frac{9}{13},\ \text{note}\ \frac{8}{11} > \frac{9}{13}$$

$$\frac{2}{3} \times \frac{9}{13},\ \text{note}\ \frac{9}{13} > \frac{2}{3}\ \text{and also}\ \frac{9}{13} < \frac{5}{7}.$$

Therefore, $\frac{2}{3} < \frac{9}{13} < \frac{5}{7} < \frac{8}{11}$.

16. **(E)** A cubic foot contains 12" × 12" × 12" or 1,728 cubic inches. If each cubic inch weighs two pounds, the substance weighs 2 • 1,728 or 3,456 pounds. None of the answers is correct.

17. **(B)** 17 millionths in decimals is .000017. The number of places to the right of the decimal point is equal to the number of zeros in the whole number. 17,000,000 has six zeros.

18. **(B)** Because the circumference of a circle is equivalent to π times the diameter, the circumference is also equal to π times twice the radius. Divide the circumference by 2π.

19. **(C)** Four boards, each 2'9" long, total 11 feet. The carpenter must buy 11 feet of wood.

20. **(B)** Find the answer to this problem by substituting the values given into the formula.

$$S = 16t^2$$
$$S = 16(8)^2 = 16(64) = 1{,}024 \text{ feet}$$

21. **(A)** To find the number of minutes that must pass before the events next occur simultaneously, calculate the least common multiple of 4, 6, and 15. The LCM is 60 minutes. If the events last occurred together at noon, the next occurrence will thus be 60 minutes later, or at 1:00 PM.

22. **(B)** By knowing how many telephones are in Adelaide (48,000), and how many serve each group of 100 in the population (12.8), we can find how many groups of 100 are in the population.

48,000 telephones ÷ 12.8 telephones per 100 of population

= 3,750 groups of 100 in the population.

3,750 × 100 = 375,000 people

23. **(B)** The first person does $\frac{1}{25}$th of the job in 1 minute. The second person does $\frac{1}{50}$th of the job in 1 minute. The third person does $\frac{1}{10}$th of the job in 1 minute. Together: $\frac{1}{25} + \frac{1}{50} + \frac{1}{10} = \frac{8}{50}$ or $\frac{4}{25}$th of the job in 1 minute $= \frac{25}{4}$ minutes for the entire job, or $6\frac{1}{4}$ minutes.

24. **(D)** The graph is steepest between years 7 and 9. The population was approximately 1,000 in year 7 and increased to over 2,500 by year 9.

25. **(A)** The size of the population was quite constant from year 3 to year 4 and decreased from year 4 to year 5 from almost 1,000 to 500. Notice that the population was the same in year 3 as in year 7.

SCORE YOURSELF

Check your answers against the correct answer key. Count up the number of answers you got right and the number you got wrong.

Section	No. Right	No. Wrong
Synonyms		
Verbal Analogies		
Total Verbal		
Reading Comprehension		
Quantitative		

Now, for each test subject divide the number of answers you got wrong by 4. Round down for fractions below .5; up from .5. Subtract this number from the number of correct answers in each section to find your raw score. Use this raw score to figure your percentage score on the score sheet below.

Section	Raw Score ÷ No. of questions	× 100 =	%
Synonyms	÷ 30	× 100 =	%
Verbal Analogies	÷ 30	× 100 =	%
Total Verbal	÷ 60	× 100 =	%
Reading Comprehension	÷ 40	× 100 =	%
Quantitative	÷ 50	× 100 =	%

High percentage scores should make you feel very good about yourself, but low percentages do not mean that you are a failure.

Remember:

- Scores are not reported as percentages. A low percentage may translate to a respectable scaled score.
- The same exam is given to students in grades 8 through 12. Unless you have finished high school, you have not been taught everything on the exam. You are not expected to know what you have not been taught.
- You will be compared only to students in your own grade.

Use your scores to plan further study if you have time.

Secondary School Admission Test
Practice Exam 2

Answer Sheet

TEAR HERE

SECTION ONE: VERBAL

1. Ⓐ Ⓑ Ⓒ Ⓓ Ⓔ	13. Ⓐ Ⓑ Ⓒ Ⓓ Ⓔ	25. Ⓐ Ⓑ Ⓒ Ⓓ Ⓔ	37. Ⓐ Ⓑ Ⓒ Ⓓ Ⓔ	49. Ⓐ Ⓑ Ⓒ Ⓓ Ⓔ
2. Ⓐ Ⓑ Ⓒ Ⓓ Ⓔ	14. Ⓐ Ⓑ Ⓒ Ⓓ Ⓔ	26. Ⓐ Ⓑ Ⓒ Ⓓ Ⓔ	38. Ⓐ Ⓑ Ⓒ Ⓓ Ⓔ	50. Ⓐ Ⓑ Ⓒ Ⓓ Ⓔ
3. Ⓐ Ⓑ Ⓒ Ⓓ Ⓔ	15. Ⓐ Ⓑ Ⓒ Ⓓ Ⓔ	27. Ⓐ Ⓑ Ⓒ Ⓓ Ⓔ	39. Ⓐ Ⓑ Ⓒ Ⓓ Ⓔ	51. Ⓐ Ⓑ Ⓒ Ⓓ Ⓔ
4. Ⓐ Ⓑ Ⓒ Ⓓ Ⓔ	16. Ⓐ Ⓑ Ⓒ Ⓓ Ⓔ	28. Ⓐ Ⓑ Ⓒ Ⓓ Ⓔ	40. Ⓐ Ⓑ Ⓒ Ⓓ Ⓔ	52. Ⓐ Ⓑ Ⓒ Ⓓ Ⓔ
5. Ⓐ Ⓑ Ⓒ Ⓓ Ⓔ	17. Ⓐ Ⓑ Ⓒ Ⓓ Ⓔ	29. Ⓐ Ⓑ Ⓒ Ⓓ Ⓔ	41. Ⓐ Ⓑ Ⓒ Ⓓ Ⓔ	53. Ⓐ Ⓑ Ⓒ Ⓓ Ⓔ
6. Ⓐ Ⓑ Ⓒ Ⓓ Ⓔ	18. Ⓐ Ⓑ Ⓒ Ⓓ Ⓔ	30. Ⓐ Ⓑ Ⓒ Ⓓ Ⓔ	42. Ⓐ Ⓑ Ⓒ Ⓓ Ⓔ	54. Ⓐ Ⓑ Ⓒ Ⓓ Ⓔ
7. Ⓐ Ⓑ Ⓒ Ⓓ Ⓔ	19. Ⓐ Ⓑ Ⓒ Ⓓ Ⓔ	31. Ⓐ Ⓑ Ⓒ Ⓓ Ⓔ	43. Ⓐ Ⓑ Ⓒ Ⓓ Ⓔ	55. Ⓐ Ⓑ Ⓒ Ⓓ Ⓔ
8. Ⓐ Ⓑ Ⓒ Ⓓ Ⓔ	20. Ⓐ Ⓑ Ⓒ Ⓓ Ⓔ	32. Ⓐ Ⓑ Ⓒ Ⓓ Ⓔ	44. Ⓐ Ⓑ Ⓒ Ⓓ Ⓔ	56. Ⓐ Ⓑ Ⓒ Ⓓ Ⓔ
9. Ⓐ Ⓑ Ⓒ Ⓓ Ⓔ	21. Ⓐ Ⓑ Ⓒ Ⓓ Ⓔ	33. Ⓐ Ⓑ Ⓒ Ⓓ Ⓔ	45. Ⓐ Ⓑ Ⓒ Ⓓ Ⓔ	57. Ⓐ Ⓑ Ⓒ Ⓓ Ⓔ
10. Ⓐ Ⓑ Ⓒ Ⓓ Ⓔ	22. Ⓐ Ⓑ Ⓒ Ⓓ Ⓔ	34. Ⓐ Ⓑ Ⓒ Ⓓ Ⓔ	46. Ⓐ Ⓑ Ⓒ Ⓓ Ⓔ	58. Ⓐ Ⓑ Ⓒ Ⓓ Ⓔ
11. Ⓐ Ⓑ Ⓒ Ⓓ Ⓔ	23. Ⓐ Ⓑ Ⓒ Ⓓ Ⓔ	35. Ⓐ Ⓑ Ⓒ Ⓓ Ⓔ	47. Ⓐ Ⓑ Ⓒ Ⓓ Ⓔ	59. Ⓐ Ⓑ Ⓒ Ⓓ Ⓔ
12. Ⓐ Ⓑ Ⓒ Ⓓ Ⓔ	24. Ⓐ Ⓑ Ⓒ Ⓓ Ⓔ	36. Ⓐ Ⓑ Ⓒ Ⓓ Ⓔ	48. Ⓐ Ⓑ Ⓒ Ⓓ Ⓔ	60. Ⓐ Ⓑ Ⓒ Ⓓ Ⓔ

SECTION TWO: QUANTITATIVE

1. Ⓐ Ⓑ Ⓒ Ⓓ Ⓔ	6. Ⓐ Ⓑ Ⓒ Ⓓ Ⓔ	11. Ⓐ Ⓑ Ⓒ Ⓓ Ⓔ	16. Ⓐ Ⓑ Ⓒ Ⓓ Ⓔ	21. Ⓐ Ⓑ Ⓒ Ⓓ Ⓔ
2. Ⓐ Ⓑ Ⓒ Ⓓ Ⓔ	7. Ⓐ Ⓑ Ⓒ Ⓓ Ⓔ	12. Ⓐ Ⓑ Ⓒ Ⓓ Ⓔ	17. Ⓐ Ⓑ Ⓒ Ⓓ Ⓔ	22. Ⓐ Ⓑ Ⓒ Ⓓ Ⓔ
3. Ⓐ Ⓑ Ⓒ Ⓓ Ⓔ	8. Ⓐ Ⓑ Ⓒ Ⓓ Ⓔ	13. Ⓐ Ⓑ Ⓒ Ⓓ Ⓔ	18. Ⓐ Ⓑ Ⓒ Ⓓ Ⓔ	23. Ⓐ Ⓑ Ⓒ Ⓓ Ⓔ
4. Ⓐ Ⓑ Ⓒ Ⓓ Ⓔ	9. Ⓐ Ⓑ Ⓒ Ⓓ Ⓔ	14. Ⓐ Ⓑ Ⓒ Ⓓ Ⓔ	19. Ⓐ Ⓑ Ⓒ Ⓓ Ⓔ	24. Ⓐ Ⓑ Ⓒ Ⓓ Ⓔ
5. Ⓐ Ⓑ Ⓒ Ⓓ Ⓔ	10. Ⓐ Ⓑ Ⓒ Ⓓ Ⓔ	15. Ⓐ Ⓑ Ⓒ Ⓓ Ⓔ	20. Ⓐ Ⓑ Ⓒ Ⓓ Ⓔ	25. Ⓐ Ⓑ Ⓒ Ⓓ Ⓔ

SECTION THREE: READING COMPREHENSION

1. Ⓐ Ⓑ Ⓒ Ⓓ Ⓔ	9. Ⓐ Ⓑ Ⓒ Ⓓ Ⓔ	17. Ⓐ Ⓑ Ⓒ Ⓓ Ⓔ	25. Ⓐ Ⓑ Ⓒ Ⓓ Ⓔ	33. Ⓐ Ⓑ Ⓒ Ⓓ Ⓔ
2. Ⓐ Ⓑ Ⓒ Ⓓ Ⓔ	10. Ⓐ Ⓑ Ⓒ Ⓓ Ⓔ	18. Ⓐ Ⓑ Ⓒ Ⓓ Ⓔ	26. Ⓐ Ⓑ Ⓒ Ⓓ Ⓔ	34. Ⓐ Ⓑ Ⓒ Ⓓ Ⓔ
3. Ⓐ Ⓑ Ⓒ Ⓓ Ⓔ	11. Ⓐ Ⓑ Ⓒ Ⓓ Ⓔ	19. Ⓐ Ⓑ Ⓒ Ⓓ Ⓔ	27. Ⓐ Ⓑ Ⓒ Ⓓ Ⓔ	35. Ⓐ Ⓑ Ⓒ Ⓓ Ⓔ
4. Ⓐ Ⓑ Ⓒ Ⓓ Ⓔ	12. Ⓐ Ⓑ Ⓒ Ⓓ Ⓔ	20. Ⓐ Ⓑ Ⓒ Ⓓ Ⓔ	28. Ⓐ Ⓑ Ⓒ Ⓓ Ⓔ	36. Ⓐ Ⓑ Ⓒ Ⓓ Ⓔ
5. Ⓐ Ⓑ Ⓒ Ⓓ Ⓔ	13. Ⓐ Ⓑ Ⓒ Ⓓ Ⓔ	21. Ⓐ Ⓑ Ⓒ Ⓓ Ⓔ	29. Ⓐ Ⓑ Ⓒ Ⓓ Ⓔ	37. Ⓐ Ⓑ Ⓒ Ⓓ Ⓔ
6. Ⓐ Ⓑ Ⓒ Ⓓ Ⓔ	14. Ⓐ Ⓑ Ⓒ Ⓓ Ⓔ	22. Ⓐ Ⓑ Ⓒ Ⓓ Ⓔ	30. Ⓐ Ⓑ Ⓒ Ⓓ Ⓔ	38. Ⓐ Ⓑ Ⓒ Ⓓ Ⓔ
7. Ⓐ Ⓑ Ⓒ Ⓓ Ⓔ	15. Ⓐ Ⓑ Ⓒ Ⓓ Ⓔ	23. Ⓐ Ⓑ Ⓒ Ⓓ Ⓔ	31. Ⓐ Ⓑ Ⓒ Ⓓ Ⓔ	39. Ⓐ Ⓑ Ⓒ Ⓓ Ⓔ
8. Ⓐ Ⓑ Ⓒ Ⓓ Ⓔ	16. Ⓐ Ⓑ Ⓒ Ⓓ Ⓔ	24. Ⓐ Ⓑ Ⓒ Ⓓ Ⓔ	32. Ⓐ Ⓑ Ⓒ Ⓓ Ⓔ	40. Ⓐ Ⓑ Ⓒ Ⓓ Ⓔ

SECTION FOUR: MATHEMATICS

1. Ⓐ Ⓑ Ⓒ Ⓓ Ⓔ	6. Ⓐ Ⓑ Ⓒ Ⓓ Ⓔ	11. Ⓐ Ⓑ Ⓒ Ⓓ Ⓔ	16. Ⓐ Ⓑ Ⓒ Ⓓ Ⓔ	21. Ⓐ Ⓑ Ⓒ Ⓓ Ⓔ
2. Ⓐ Ⓑ Ⓒ Ⓓ Ⓔ	7. Ⓐ Ⓑ Ⓒ Ⓓ Ⓔ	12. Ⓐ Ⓑ Ⓒ Ⓓ Ⓔ	17. Ⓐ Ⓑ Ⓒ Ⓓ Ⓔ	22. Ⓐ Ⓑ Ⓒ Ⓓ Ⓔ
3. Ⓐ Ⓑ Ⓒ Ⓓ Ⓔ	8. Ⓐ Ⓑ Ⓒ Ⓓ Ⓔ	13. Ⓐ Ⓑ Ⓒ Ⓓ Ⓔ	18. Ⓐ Ⓑ Ⓒ Ⓓ Ⓔ	23. Ⓐ Ⓑ Ⓒ Ⓓ Ⓔ
4. Ⓐ Ⓑ Ⓒ Ⓓ Ⓔ	9. Ⓐ Ⓑ Ⓒ Ⓓ Ⓔ	14. Ⓐ Ⓑ Ⓒ Ⓓ Ⓔ	19. Ⓐ Ⓑ Ⓒ Ⓓ Ⓔ	24. Ⓐ Ⓑ Ⓒ Ⓓ Ⓔ
5. Ⓐ Ⓑ Ⓒ Ⓓ Ⓔ	10. Ⓐ Ⓑ Ⓒ Ⓓ Ⓔ	15. Ⓐ Ⓑ Ⓒ Ⓓ Ⓔ	20. Ⓐ Ⓑ Ⓒ Ⓓ Ⓔ	25. Ⓐ Ⓑ Ⓒ Ⓓ Ⓔ

TEAR HERE

SSAT Practice Exam 2

Part I: Writing Sample

TIME—25 MINUTES

Directions: Write a convincing, legible essay supporting your opinion on the topic that follows.

Topic: In some high schools, students must maintain a certain grade point level in order to play on competitive sports teams. At other high schools, anyone who makes the team can play. What is your opinion? Give reasons.

Part II: Multiple Choice

SECTION ONE: VERBAL

60 QUESTIONS • TIME—25 MINUTES

The Verbal Section consists of two different types of questions. There are directions for each type of question.

Directions: Each question shows a word in capital letters followed by five words or phrases. Choose the word or phrase whose meaning is most similar to the word in capital letters. Mark the appropriate space on your answer sheet.

1. AGENDA
(A) receipt
(B) agent
(C) combination
(D) correspondence
(E) schedule

2. CREDIBLE
(A) believable
(B) untrue
(C) correct
(D) suitable
(E) fortunate

3. PLACID
(A) explosive
(B) quiet
(C) public
(D) lenient
(E) crystalline

4. INTERVENE
(A) induce
(B) invert
(C) interfere
(D) solve
(E) intermediary

5. MUNDANE
(A) stupid
(B) extraordinary
(C) worldly
(D) immense
(E) common

6. DEHYDRATED
(A) airless
(B) deflated
(C) pointless
(D) worthless
(E) waterless

GO ON TO THE NEXT PAGE

7. PREVALENT
   (A) predating
   (B) predominant
   (C) preeminent
   (D) prior
   (E) predictive

8. SUCCINCT
   (A) concise
   (B) superfluous
   (C) alert
   (D) despicable
   (E) fearful

9. NOCTURNAL
   (A) by night
   (B) by day
   (C) revolving
   (D) alternating
   (E) frequent

10. EQUITABLE
   (A) preferential
   (B) fair
   (C) unreasonable
   (D) biased
   (E) prejudiced

11. EXPEDITE
   (A) hinder
   (B) harm
   (C) send
   (D) hasten
   (E) block

12. TURBULENT
   (A) authentic
   (B) tranquil
   (C) tamed
   (D) fatal
   (E) violent

13. TENACIOUS
   (A) timid
   (B) thin
   (C) unyielding
   (D) divisive
   (E) stranded

14. PERTINENT
   (A) applicable
   (B) prudent
   (C) irreverent
   (D) irrelevant
   (E) truthful

15. DOGMATIC
   (A) bovine
   (B) canine
   (C) opinionated
   (D) individualistic
   (E) traditional

16. UNSCRUPULOUS
   (A) filthy
   (B) honest
   (C) austere
   (D) unprincipled
   (E) unresolved

17. WILY
   (A) crooked
   (B) narrow
   (C) cunning
   (D) blunt
   (E) broken

18. BLATANT
   (A) insipid
   (B) obvious
   (C) shining
   (D) closed
   (E) secret

19. PRETEXT
(A) excuse
(B) reason
(C) preface
(D) fit
(E) doubt

20. ACUMEN
(A) beauty
(B) poise
(C) keenness
(D) illness
(E) courtesy

21. EVASION
(A) attack
(B) displeasure
(C) enjoyment
(D) avoidance
(E) fatigue

22. INDISPENSABLE
(A) incontrovertible
(B) essential
(C) impetuous
(D) ungovernable
(E) confused

23. OBLITERATE
(A) obligate
(B) subjugate
(C) exhibit
(D) maintain
(E) erase

24. AMIABLE
(A) allied
(B) disjointed
(C) indignant
(D) friendly
(E) introverted

25. WRITHE
(A) strangle
(B) topple
(C) trouble
(D) slide
(E) twist

26. ABATE
(A) let up
(B) continue
(C) forego
(D) placate
(E) intimidate

27. ENDORSEMENT
(A) inscription
(B) approval
(C) standard
(D) editorial
(E) article

28. CONVERT
(A) reform
(B) predict
(C) weave
(D) transform
(E) translate

29. ERUDITE
(A) knowledgeable
(B) meddlesome
(C) eroded
(D) careless
(E) intrusion

30. ENDEAVOR
(A) expectation
(B) attempt
(C) tack
(D) necessity
(E) ability

GO ON TO THE NEXT PAGE

Directions: The following questions ask you to find relationships between words. Read each question, and then choose the answer that best completes the meaning of the sentence. Mark the appropriate space on your answer sheet.

31. None is to little as never is to
- (A) nothing
- (B) infrequently
- (C) negative
- (D) much
- (E) often

32. Receive is to admit as settle is to
- (A) resist
- (B) comfort
- (C) remain
- (D) adjust
- (E) mediate

33. Dishonesty is to distrust as
- (A) violin is to bow
- (B) hand is to paper
- (C) money is to thief
- (D) strange is to odd
- (E) carelessness is to accident

34. Sociologist is to group as
- (A) psychologist is to individual
- (B) doctor is to nurse
- (C) children is to pediatrician
- (D) biologist is to frog
- (E) mathematician is to algebra

35. Generous is to frugal as
- (A) wasteful is to squander
- (B) philanthropist is to miser
- (C) tasteful is to garish
- (D) gratify is to desire
- (E) important is to nonessential

36. Transparent is to translucent as
- (A) water is to milk
- (B) glass is to crystal
- (C) translucent is to opaque
- (D) muddy is to clear
- (E) suspension is to mixture

37. Discontent is to rebellion as
- (A) friction is to spark
- (B) complacent is to revolt
- (C) success is to study
- (D) employment is to retirement
- (E) surgeon is to operation

38. Beaker is to chemist as hammer is to
- (A) nails
- (B) geologist
- (C) construction
- (D) architect
- (E) noise

39. Follow is to lead as dependent is to
- (A) subservient
- (B) supportive
- (C) child
- (D) autonomous
- (E) anonymous

40. State is to country as country is to
- (A) island
- (B) capitol
- (C) continent
- (D) planet
- (E) ocean

41. Accelerator is to motion as
(A) catalyst is to change
(B) inertia is to immobile
(C) ignition is to speed
(D) automobile is to vehicle
(E) experiment is to hypothesis

42. Probable is to certain as
(A) approach is to reproach
(B) steady is to rocky
(C) correct is to accurate
(D) save is to record
(E) plausible is to definite

43. Obstruct is to impede as impenetrable is to
(A) impervious
(B) hidden
(C) merciful
(D) porous
(E) transparent

44. Include is to omit as acknowledge is to
(A) notice
(B) ignore
(C) recognize
(D) greet
(E) know

45. Nucleus is to electron as
(A) Earth is to satellite
(B) Earth is to Sun
(C) constellation is to Sun
(D) neutron is to proton
(E) atom is to neutron

46. Sculptor is to statue as
(A) actor is to play
(B) paint is to artist
(C) composer is to music
(D) orchestra is to conductor
(E) programmer is to computer

47. Dreary is to happy as
(A) light is to graceful
(B) close is to narrow
(C) dearth is to surplus
(D) curtain is to play
(E) interdict is to expect

48. Allow is to restrict as
(A) gain is to success
(B) seeing is to believing
(C) heart is to soul
(D) encourage is to prevent
(E) terrible is to worse

49. Interrupt is to speak as
(A) telephone is to telegraph
(B) interfere is to assist
(C) shout is to yell
(D) intercede is to interfere
(E) intrude is to enter

50. Modesty is to arrogance as
(A) debility is to strength
(B) cause is to purpose
(C) hate is to emotion
(D) finance is to poverty
(E) agility is to stamina

51. Adversity is to happiness as
(A) fear is to misfortune
(B) solace is to sorrow
(C) graduation is to superfluous
(D) vehemence is to serenity
(E) troublesome is to petulant

52. Extortionist is to blackmail as
(A) kleptomaniac is to steal
(B) criminal is to arrest
(C) kidnapper is to crime
(D) businessman is to profit
(E) clerk is to stock

GO ON TO THE NEXT PAGE

53. Monsoon is to rain as
- (A) hurricane is to destruction
- (B) tornado is to wind
- (C) sun is to spring
- (D) famine is to drought
- (E) morning is to dew

54. Introspective is to withdrawn as
- (A) hesitant is to hasty
- (B) quick is to feelings
- (C) introvert is to extrovert
- (D) import is to export
- (E) gregarious is to social

55. Equator is to world as
- (A) boundary is to country
- (B) capitol is to state
- (C) fur is to animal
- (D) waist is to man
- (E) latitude is to longitude

56. Superficial is to surface as
- (A) probing is to deep
- (B) subway is to subterranean
- (C) crust is to Earth
- (D) tepid is to warm
- (E) internal is to external

57. Stagnant is to pond as
- (A) sandy is to river
- (B) noisy is to sheep
- (C) flowing is to stream
- (D) oceanic is to tide
- (E) tidal is to wave

58. Sanctuary is to fortress as
- (A) sanctum is to inner
- (B) shelter is to house
- (C) violent is to peaceful
- (D) guns is to fort
- (E) sanction is to assassinate

59. Mentor is to professor as
- (A) advisor is to counselor
- (B) child is to parent
- (C) learning is to teacher
- (D) mental is to physical
- (E) tooth is to dentist

60. Lucid is to clear as
- (A) sullen is to gloomy
- (B) furtive is to clever
- (C) potent is to weak
- (D) droll is to serious
- (E) pensive is to hanging

STOP

END OF SECTION ONE. IF YOU HAVE ANY TIME LEFT, GO OVER YOUR WORK IN THIS SECTION ONLY. DO NOT WORK IN ANY OTHER SECTION OF THE EXAM.

SECTION TWO: QUANTITATIVE

25 QUESTIONS • TIME—25 MINUTES

Directions: Calculate the answer to each of the following questions. Select the answer choice that is best, and mark the appropriate letter on your answer sheet.

1. $\frac{3}{5} + 1.25 + .004 =$

(A) 1.750

(B) 1.854

(C) 1.9

(D) 2.25

(E) 2.35

2. Evaluate: $\frac{10^6}{10^3}$

(A) 1 billion

(B) 1 million

(C) 1,000

(D) 100

(E) 1^3

3. $71.4 \times 98.2 =$

(A) 4,011.38

(B) 5,321.48

(C) 6,921.38

(D) 7,011.48

(E) 8,231.48

4. $\frac{4\frac{2}{3} + \frac{1}{6}}{\frac{1}{3}} =$

(A) 9

(B) $10\frac{1}{3}$

(C) $12\frac{3}{24}$

(D) $14\frac{1}{2}$

(E) 23

5. $(.25)^2 =$

(A) .00625

(B) .0625

(C) .625

(D) 1.625

(E) 16.25

6. $(3 + 1) + [(2 - 3) - (4 - 1)] =$

(A) 6

(B) 2

(C) 0

(D) –2

(E) –4

7. 10,001 – 8,093

(A) 1,908

(B) 1,918

(C) 2,007

(D) 18,094

(E) 20,007

8. The ratio of 3 quarts to 3 gallons is

(A) 3:1

(B) 1:4

(C) 6:3

(D) 4:1

(E) 1:3

9. 10% of $\frac{1}{5}$ of $50.00 is

(A) $100.00

(B) $5.00

(C) $1.00

(D) 103

(E) $\frac{3}{5}$

GO ON TO THE NEXT PAGE

10. 4 hours 12 minutes 10 sec
− 2 hours 48 minutes 35 sec.

(A) 2 hr. 23 min. 25 sec.
(B) 2 hr. 12 min. 40 sec.
(C) 1 hr. 23 min. 35 sec.
(D) 1 hr. 23 min. 25 sec.
(E) 1 hr. 12 min. 35 sec.

11. If we double the value of a and c in the fraction $\frac{ab}{c}$, the value of the fraction is
(A) doubled
(B) tripled
(C) multiplied by 4
(D) halved
(E) unchanged

12. What percentage of 220 is 24.2?
(A) 909%
(B) 99%
(C) 40%
(D) 27%
(E) 11%

13. 98 reduced by $\frac{5}{7}$ is equivalent to
(A) 28
(B) 33
(C) 66
(D) 70
(E) 85

14. How long should an object $6\frac{1}{2}$ feet long be drawn, if according to the scale, $\frac{1}{4}$ inch equals 1 foot?

(A) $1\frac{3}{4}$ inches
(B) $1\frac{5}{8}$ inches
(C) $\frac{7}{8}$ inches
(D) $\frac{5}{8}$ inches
(E) $\frac{17}{32}$ inches

15. $12\frac{1}{2} \div \frac{1}{2} + \frac{3}{2} \times 4 - 3 =$
(A) 1
(B) $4\frac{3}{4}$
(C) 20
(D) 28
(E) $32\frac{1}{2}$

16. If $y + 2 > 10$, then y may be
(A) larger than 8
(B) larger than 6
(C) larger than 0
(D) equal to 0
(E) unknown

17. If $a = 1$, $b = 2$, $c = 3$, and $d = 5$, the value of $\sqrt{b(d + a) - b(c + a)}$ is
(A) 2
(B) 3.5
(C) 4
(D) $\sqrt{20}$
(E) 50

18. In the fraction $\frac{1}{\Delta}$, Δ could be replaced by all of the following except
(A) 0
(B) 1
(C) 4.2
(D) 9
(E) 10

19. .0515 × 100 is equivalent to
(A) 5,150 ÷ 100
(B) 5.15 × 10
(C) .00515 × 1,000
(D) 510,000 ÷ 10
(E) 5,150 ÷ 10,000

20.

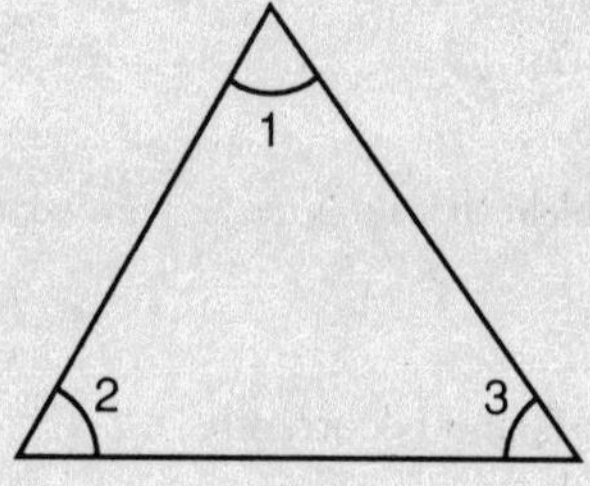

$\angle 2 = 60°$

Figure not necessarily drawn to scale.

(A) $\angle 1 + \angle 3 > 180°$

(B) $\angle 1 > \angle 3$

(C) $\angle 1 = \angle 3$

(D) $\angle 1 - \angle 3 > \angle 2$

(E) $\angle 1 + \angle 3 = 120°$

21. 45 is to _____ as 90 is to .45.

(A) .225

(B) .900

(C) 4.50

(D) 9.00

(E) 22.5

22. If $n = \sqrt{20}$, then

(A) $\sqrt{5} > n > \sqrt{3}$

(B) $3 > n > 2$

(C) $n = 4.5$

(D) $4 < n < 5$

(E) $n > 5$

23.

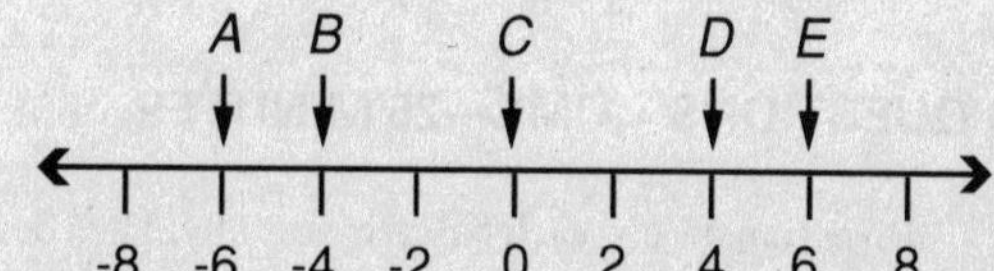

How would you move along the number line above to find the difference between –6 and 4?

(A) from E to B

(B) from A to D

(C) from B to D

(D) from D to A

(E) from B to E

24. How many sixths are there in $\frac{4}{5}$?

(A) $2\frac{3}{8}$

(B) 3

(C) $4\frac{4}{5}$

(D) $5\frac{1}{5}$

(E) 6

25. Four games drew an average of 36,500 people per game. If the attendance at the first three games was 32,000, 35,500, and 38,000, how many people attended the fourth game?

(A) 36,500

(B) 37,000

(C) 39,000

(D) 40,500

(E) 43,000

STOP

END OF SECTION TWO. IF YOU HAVE ANY TIME LEFT, GO OVER YOUR WORK IN THIS SECTION ONLY. DO NOT WORK IN ANY OTHER SECTION OF THE EXAM.

SECTION THREE: READING COMPREHENSION

40 QUESTIONS • TIME—25 MINUTES

Directions: Read each passage carefully. Then decide which of the possible responses is the best answer to each question. Mark the appropriate space on your answer sheet.

Back in the seventeenth century, when Abraham Rycken owned it, Rikers Island was a tiny spit of land in the East River. It became part of New York City in the 1890s and was used as a convenient place to deposit the rock and soil debris of subway construction. Later, the island became the end of the line for the discards of city households, in a landfill operation that went on until Rikers Island reached its present size of 400 acres.

Robert Moses, then New York's Park Commissioner, was looking for ways to supply city parks with shade trees and eliminate the expense of buying them from commercial nurseries. He noted that weeds grew prodigiously in the landfill, thought that trees and plants might do the same, and arranged to clear a few acres for a trial planting. In 1944, the first 287 shrubs and trees were transplanted from the fledgling nursery to the city's parks. The nursery now covers some 115 acres of the island, and several hundred thousand of its shrubs and trees have been planted along city streets, in parks, around housing projects, and around the malls and paths of the United Nations.

1. To obtain plantings for New York City, authorities

(A) buy them from the United Nations

(B) purchase them from commercial nurseries

(C) transplant them from city-owned property

(D) buy them from Robert Moses

(E) grow them in Central Park

2. Rikers Island is currently

(A) 115 acres in area

(B) a landfill operation

(C) owned by Abraham Rycken

(D) 400 acres in area

(E) a dumping ground for subway debris

3. The soil of the island

(A) is volcanic

(B) was enriched by discarded rubbish

(C) was brought in from commercial nurseries

(D) is a combination of mud and rock

(E) was brought in on subways

4. The first plantings were taken from Rikers Island

(A) a decade ago

(B) about 1890

(C) in the seventeenth century

(D) quite recently

(E) in 1944

America's national bird, the bald eagle, which has flown high since the Revolutionary War, may soon be grounded. The eagle population of the United States is decreasing at an alarming rate, and the National Audubon Society has just launched a full-scale survey to find out how many bald eagles are left and what measures are necessary to protect them from extinction. The survey, a year-long project, focuses attention on the bird chosen to appear on the Great Seal of the United States.

When it gained its official status over 200 years ago, the bald eagle was undisputed king of America's skies. Many thousands of the great birds roamed the country, and both the sight of the bald eagle and its piercing scream were familiar to almost every American. Today, naturalists fear that there are less than a thousand of them still in this country.

Nature is partly to blame. Our severe hurricanes have destroyed many eggs, fledglings, and aeries, the eagles' mammoth nests. But man is the chief culprit. Despite legislation passed by Congress in 1940 to protect the *emblematic birds*, thousands of them have been gunned out of the skies by over-eager shooters who perhaps mistook them for large hawks.

The bald eagle was known as the bald-headed eagle when Congress began the search for a seal in 1776. The archaic meaning of bald—white or streaked with white—refers to his head, neck, and tail coloring rather than to any lack of plumage in our fine-feathered friend.

5. The Audubon Society is trying to

(A) rid the country of the bald eagle
(B) have the bald eagle chosen as the national bird of the United States
(C) prevent the extinction of the bald eagle in this country
(D) have Congress pass a law forbidding the shooting of eagles
(E) band more eagles

6. There are now

(A) more eagles in this country than in 1776
(B) fewer eagles here than there were over 200 years ago
(C) many thousands of bald eagles
(D) eagles whose scream is familiar to every American
(E) too many eagles

7. Aeries are

(A) fledglings
(B) eggs
(C) young mammoths
(D) nests
(E) mating areas

8. The eagle is called an *emblematic bird* because it is

(A) bald
(B) decreasing
(C) handsome and powerful
(D) prized by hunters
(E) a symbol of a nation

9. The design for the Great Seal of the United States was first considered

(A) in 1776
(B) in 1783
(C) in 1840
(D) in 1876
(E) at an unknown date

You know, of course, that in China the Emperor is a Chinaman, and all the people around him are Chinamen too. It happened a good many years ago, but that's just why it's worthwhile to hear the story, before it is forgotten. The Emperor's palace was the most splendid in the world; entirely and altogether made of porcelain, so costly, but so brittle, so difficult to handle that one had to be terribly careful. In the garden were to be seen the strangest flowers, and to the most splendid of them silver bells were tied, which tinkled so that nobody should pass by without noticing the flowers. Oh, the Emperor's garden had been laid out very smartly, and it extended so far that the gardener himself didn't know where the end was. If you went on and on, you came into the loveliest forest with high trees and deep lakes. The forest went right down to the sea, which was blue and deep; tall ships could sail right in under

GO ON TO THE NEXT PAGE

the branches of the trees; and in the trees lived a nightingale, which sang so sweetly that even the poor fisherman, who had many other things to do, stopped still and listened when he had gone out at night to take up his nets and then heard the nightingale.

—from *The Nightingale*
by Hans Christian Andersen

10. The author wants to tell this story
- (A) because he can't forget the nightingale
- (B) before it is forgotten
- (C) to teach us about China
- (D) because he is a writer and storyteller
- (E) in order to describe the garden

11. The Emperor's palace was made of
- (A) brick
- (B) silver bells
- (C) high trees
- (D) large stones and boulders
- (E) porcelain

12. Silver bells were tied to flowers in the garden
- (A) to draw attention to their beauty
- (B) to frighten birds and mice away
- (C) to play soft melodies
- (D) to remind the gardener not to pick them
- (E) to sparkle in the sun

13. The Emperor's garden
- (A) was very strange
- (B) was too large to care for
- (C) led into a lovely forest
- (D) housed a rare nightingale
- (E) was a source of pleasure for all in the kingdom

14. The forest
- (A) was dark and threatening
- (B) contained many rare animals
- (C) was an easy place in which to get lost
- (D) housed the nightingale
- (E) was a fisherman's hiding place

An excerpt from a Dead Sea Scroll describing Abraham's *sojourn* in Egypt and the beauty of Sarah, his wife, was recently made public for the first time. The 2,000-year-old scroll, badly preserved and extremely brittle, is the last of seven scrolls found in 1947 in the caves of the Judean desert south of Jericho. Scholars say that this scroll enlarges on the hitherto known Biblical tales of Lamech, Enoch, Noah, and Abraham.

This document of Hebrew University yielded *decipherable* contents only after months of exposure to controlled humidity. The centuries had compressed the leather scroll into a brittle, glued-together mass. After it had been rendered flexible, the scroll was folded into pages. Four complete pages, each with 34 lines of writing, resulted. Besides this, scholars had for their studies large sections of the decipherable writing on five other pages, and readable lines and words on additional pages. Scholars were delighted, for they had almost despaired of recovering the scroll as a readable document. The work of giving new life to the desiccated parchment and of unrolling it was done by an old German expert on ancient materials, under the supervision of two Israeli scholars.

15. The word *sojourn* means
- (A) servitude
- (B) stay
- (C) congruent
- (D) flight
- (E) difficulties

16. *Decipherable* as used in the second paragraph means
- (A) intelligible
- (B) durable
- (C) exciting
- (D) scholarly
- (E) practical

17. The scroll

(A) was found in Egypt

(B) gives new details about persons already known of

(C) is limited to an account of Abraham and Sarah

(D) tells of Abraham's life in the Judean desert

(E) is the first of seven found in 1947

18. The scroll

(A) belongs to an Israeli university

(B) is in Germany

(C) was deciphered by a German specialist

(D) was taken to Jericho

(E) was beautifully preserved

19. The writing on the scroll

(A) was finally legible throughout the document

(B) was legible on only four pages

(C) could be read on several pages

(D) was too damaged by age to be deciphered

(E) was irreparable

The police department of New York City has one branch that many do not know about, although it was established almost a century ago. This is the harbor precinct's 14-boat fleet of police launches, which patrols 578 miles of waters around the city, paying particular attention to the areas containing 500 piers and some 90 boat clubs.

The boats are equipped for various jobs. One boat is an ice-breaker; another is equipped to render aid in the event of an airplane crash at La Guardia Airport. All of the boats are equipped with lifeline guns, heavy grappling irons to raise sunken automobiles, and lasso-sticks to rescue animals in the water. They have power pumps to bail out sinking craft, first-aid kits, extra life preservers, signal flags, and searchlights.

The force of 183 men have all had previous experience with boats. Some of the officers are Navy and Coast Guard veterans. Many of the harbor policemen have ocean-going Master's or Harbor Captain's licenses. All are highly trained in the care and handling of engines and in navigation. All are skilled in giving first aid, and each man is a qualified radio operator and a trained marksman with a revolver.

The work of the police includes many tasks. One duty of this force is to check the operation of the fleet of 43 junk boats that ply their trade in the harbor, buying scrap, rope, and other items for resale ashore. These boats could just as easily be used to smuggle narcotics, gems, aliens, or spies into the country, so they are watched closely by the city's harbor police force. During the last summer, the police launches towed 450 disabled boats and gave some kind of help to thousands of others. The officers also arrest those who break navigation laws or who endanger the safety of bathers by approaching too near the shore in speed boats.

20. The harbor police were

(A) introduced by order of the mayor

(B) first used in the twentieth century

(C) in use before the Civil War

(D) introduced by veterans of World War II

(E) in full force almost 100 years ago

21. The boats used

(A) are uniform in design

(B) can all serve as ice-breakers

(C) are all equipped with deck guns

(D) work at Kennedy Airport

(E) vary in function

22. The harbor police

(A) arrest any man found on a junk boat

(B) prevent the resale of scrap material

(C) regulate the admission of spies

(D) ensure legal traffic in junk

(E) regulate disabled boats

GO ON TO THE NEXT PAGE

23. Their services include
   (A) towing, life-saving, and salvage
   (B) customs collection, towing, and the sending of radio messages
   (C) first aid, the rescue of animals, and fire patrol
   (D) ice-breaking, the collection of junk, and the transportation of aliens
   (E) smuggling, first aid, and rescue

24. The police boats
   (A) have no responsibility for bathers
   (B) unload ships at the piers
   (C) assist boats of all kinds
   (D) warn offenders but do not make arrests
   (E) cannot detain other boats

"There are many things from which I might have derived good, by which I have not profited, I dare say, Christmas among the rest. But I am sure I have always thought of Christmastime, when it has come round—apart from the *veneration* due to its sacred origin, if anything belonging to it *can* be apart from that—as a good time; a kind, forgiving, charitable, pleasant time; the only time I know of, in the long calendar of the year, when men and women seem *by one consent* to open their shut-up hearts freely and to think of people below them as if they really were fellow travelers to the grave, and not another race of creatures bound on other journeys. And therefore, Uncle, though it has never put a scrap of gold or silver in my pocket, I believe that it *has* done me good, and *will* do me good; and I say, God bless it!"

The clerk in the tank involuntarily applauded.

"Let me hear another sound from *you*," said Scrooge, "and you'll keep your Christmas by losing your situation! You're quite a powerful speaker, sir," he added, turning to his nephew. "I wonder you don't go into Parliament."

—from *A Christmas Carol*
by Charles Dickens

25. The word *veneration* probably means
   (A) worship
   (B) disapproval
   (C) agreement
   (D) love
   (E) participation

26. The first speaker
   (A) is a very religious person
   (B) enjoys and celebrates Christmas
   (C) is defending Christmas
   (D) has been fired by Scrooge
   (E) is obviously frightened of Scrooge

27. The first speaker believes that Christmas
   (A) is a pleasant nuisance
   (B) is an excuse for people to throw wild parties
   (C) has been separated from its religious origin
   (D) could be a profitable time of year
   (E) brings out the best in people

28. The phrase *by one consent* is synonymous with
   (A) affirmation
   (B) reaffirmation
   (C) partially
   (D) unanimously
   (E) contractual

29. Scrooge probably is angry with
   (A) the speaker and the clerk
   (B) only the speaker
   (C) only the clerk
   (D) people who celebrate Christmas
   (E) no one

One day recently, a man in a ten-gallon hat appeared at the gate of New York's famous Bronx Zoo. "Just stopped by on my way through town," he told zoo officials. "I've got an animal outside I think you might like to see."

The officials raised their eyebrows and looked at each other meaningfully, but the man in the hat didn't seem to notice. He went on to introduce himself as Gene Holter. "I call it a Zonkey," he said calmly, "because it's a cross between a donkey and a zebra. I've got his parents out there, too."

The zoo officials didn't wait to hear about the parents. They left their desks and started for the gate. Outside, Mr. Holter opened the side door of a huge truck and reached inside. Calmly, he pulled out a gibbon, and hung it, by its tail, from a tree. Then he walked past five ostriches and carried out the baby Zonkey.

Just three weeks old, the only Zonkey in the world had long ears, a face and legs covered with candy stripes, and a body covered with brown baby fuzz. The parents were on hand, too. The father was no ordinary zebra. He was broken to ride, and one of the zoo officials realized a lifelong dream when he jumped on the zebra's back and cantered around.

When last seen, Mr. Holter and his caravan were on their way to Dayton and then to Anaheim, California, where they live year-round.

30. Mr. Holter's manner was

(A) boastful

(B) excitable

(C) demanding

(D) matter-of-fact

(E) personable

31. When Mr. Holter first approached the zoo officials, they

(A) were excited about his announcement

(B) thought he was telling a tall tale

(C) thought he was an interesting person

(D) couldn't wait to realize a lifelong dream

(E) laughed behind his back

32. Mr. Holter probably made a living

(A) as a veterinarian

(B) traveling and showing his animals

(C) breeding animals for scientific experiments

(D) working as a zoo official

(E) filming animals

There is evidence that the usual variety of high blood pressure is, in part, a familial disease. Since families have similar genes as well as similar environment, familial diseases could be due to shared genetic influences, to shared environmental factors, or both. For some years, the role of one environmental factor commonly shared by families, namely dietary salt, has been studied at Brookhaven National Laboratory. The studies suggest that excessive ingestion of salt can lead to high blood pressure in man and animals. Some individuals and some rats, however, consume large amounts of salt without developing high blood pressure. No matter how strictly all environmental factors were controlled in these experiments, some salt-fed animals never develop hypertension, whereas a few rapidly developed very severe hypertension followed by early death. These marked variations were interpreted to result from differences in genetic makeup.

33. The main idea of this article is that

(A) research is desperately needed in the field of medicine

(B) a cure for high blood pressure is near

(C) research shows salt to be a major cause of high blood pressure

(D) a tendency toward high blood pressure may be inherited

(E) some animals never develop high blood pressure

34. According to the article, high blood pressure is

(A) strictly a genetic disease

(B) strictly an environmental disease

(C) due to both genetic and environmental factors

(D) caused only by dietary salt

(E) a more severe form of hypertension

GO ON TO THE NEXT PAGE

The dark and the sea are full of dangers to the fishermen of Norway. A whale may come and destroy the floating chain of corks that edge the nets, break it, and carry it off. Or a storm may come suddenly, unexpectedly, out of the night. The sea seems to turn somersaults. It opens and closes immense caverns with terrible clashes, chasing boats and men who must flee from their nets and the expected catch. Then the men may lift their nets as empty as they set them. At other times the herring may come in such masses that the lines break from the weight when lifted, and the men must return home empty-handed, without lines, nets, or the herring.

But often the nets are full of herring that shine and glisten like silver. Once in awhile, a couple of men will venture in their boats along the net lines to see whether the herring are coming, and when the corks begin to bob and jerk, as if something were hitting the nets to which they are attached, then they know that the herring are there. The nets are being filled, and all the men sit in quiet excitement. They dare only to whisper to each other, afraid to disturb, and quite overcome by the overwhelming generosity of the sea. Eyes shine in happy anticipation; hands are folded in thanks. Then muscles strain with power. It is as though the strength of the body doubled. They can work day and night without a thought of weariness. They need neither food nor rest; the thought of success keeps their vigor up almost endlessly. They will take food and rest when it is all over.

35. The best title for this passage is

(A) Whaling in Norway
(B) The Perils and Rewards of Fishing
(C) Hard Work in Norway
(D) Risky Business
(E) The Generosity of the Sea

36. The fishermen's difficulties include

(A) the eating of the herring by whales
(B) becalming
(C) an attack on the men by the herring
(D) the jerking of the corks
(E) interference by rough seas

37. At the first indication that herring are entering the nets, the men

(A) try not to frighten the fish away
(B) strain every muscle to haul in the catch
(C) glisten like silver
(D) collect the nets quickly
(E) row quickly along the edge of the nets

38. Which quality of the sea is not mentioned?

(A) Its sudden changes
(B) Its generosity
(C) Its beauty
(D) Its power
(E) Its destroying strength

39. The fishermen are described as

(A) patient, brave, and cautious
(B) angry, weary, and sickly
(C) strong, angry, and reckless
(D) skillful, impatient, and weary
(E) hardworking, surly, and excitable

40. Which is not mentioned as a problem to fishermen?

(A) Destruction of the nets
(B) Too large a catch
(C) Rough seas
(D) Unexpected storms
(E) Theft of the nets by other fishermen

STOP

END OF SECTION THREE. IF YOU HAVE ANY TIME LEFT, GO OVER YOUR WORK IN THIS SECTION ONLY. DO NOT WORK IN ANY OTHER SECTION OF THE EXAM.

SECTION FOUR: QUANTITATIVE

25 QUESTIONS • TIME—25 MINUTES

Directions: Each question below is followed by five possible answers. Select the one that is best, and mark the appropriate letter on your answer sheet.

1. In two days a point on the Earth's surface rotates through an angle of approximately

(A) 90°

(B) 180°

(C) 360°

(D) 480°

(E) 720°

2. Which of the following groups is arranged in order from smallest to largest?

(A) $\frac{3}{7}, \frac{11}{23}, \frac{15}{32}, \frac{1}{2}, \frac{9}{16}$

(B) $\frac{3}{7}, \frac{15}{32}, \frac{11}{23}, \frac{1}{2}, \frac{9}{16}$

(C) $\frac{17}{23}, \frac{3}{7}, \frac{15}{32}, \frac{1}{2}, \frac{9}{16}$

(D) $\frac{15}{32}, \frac{1}{2}, \frac{3}{7}, \frac{11}{23}, \frac{9}{16}$

(E) $\frac{1}{2}, \frac{5}{32}, \frac{3}{7}, \frac{11}{23}, \frac{9}{16}$

3. The rectangle below has a length twice as long as its width. If its width is x, its perimeter is

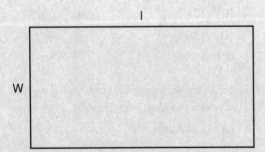

(A) 6

(B) $2x^2$

(C) $4x$

(D) $6x$

(E) $8x$

4. This square has a side of 1". The diagonal distance from one corner to another is

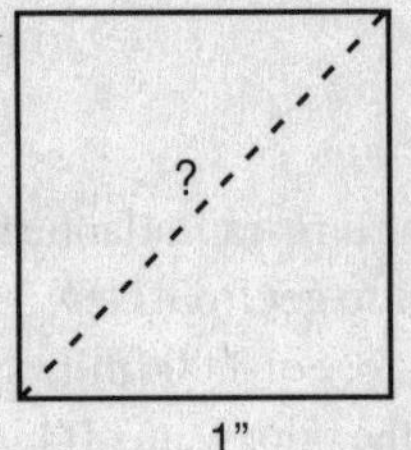

(A) 1 inch

(B) $\sqrt{2}$ inches

(C) $\sqrt{3}$ inches

(D) 2 inches

(E) 3 inches

5. A plumber needs eight sections of pipe, each 3'2" long. If pipe is sold only by the 10' section, how many sections must he buy?

(A) 1

(B) 2

(C) 3

(D) 4

(E) 5

GO ON TO THE NEXT PAGE

6. The ratio of the area of the shaded part to the unshaded part is

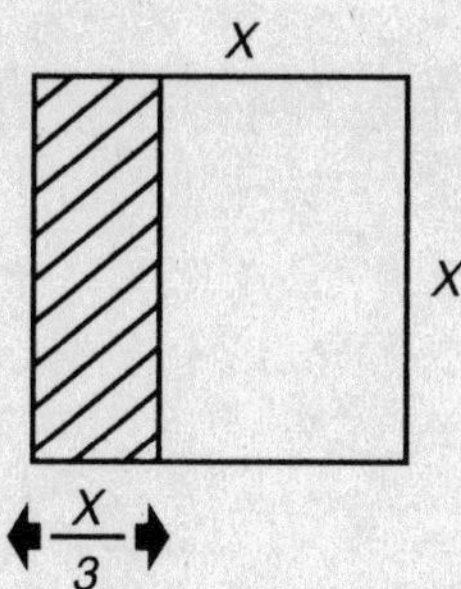

(A) $x:\frac{x}{3}$
(B) 2:1
(C) 1:3
(D) 1:2
(E) 3:1

7. An airplane on a transatlantic flight took 4 hours 20 minutes to get from New York to its destination, a distance of 3,000 miles. To avoid a storm, however, the pilot went off his course, adding a distance of 200 miles to the flight. How fast did the plane travel?

(A) 640 mph
(B) 710 mph
(C) 739 mph
(D) 750 mph
(E) 772 mph

8. A photograph measuring 5" wide × 7" long must be reduced in size to fit a space four inches long in an advertising brochure. How wide must the space be so that the picture remains in proportion?

(A) $1\frac{4}{7}$"
(B) $2\frac{6}{7}$"
(C) $4\frac{3}{5}$"
(D) $5\frac{3}{5}$"
(E) $8\frac{3}{4}$"

9. The total area of the shaded part of the figure is

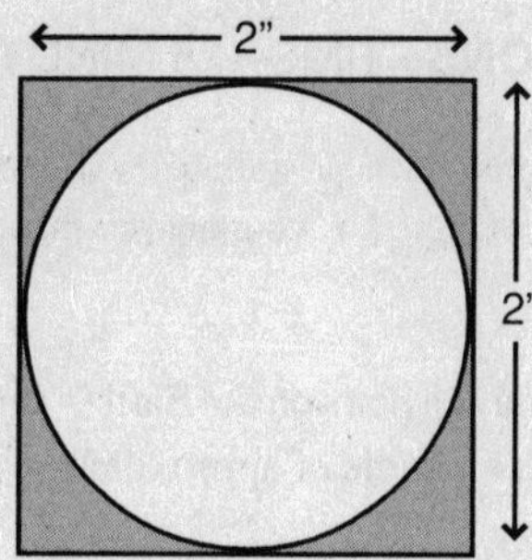

(A) $\frac{2}{7}$ in.^{2}
(B) $\frac{1}{2}$ in.^{2}
(C) $\frac{6}{7}$ in.^{2}
(D) $1\frac{3}{7}$ in.^{2}
(E) $2\frac{1}{3}$ in.^{2}

10. A certain population of microbes grows according to the formula $P = 2^n$, where P is the size of the population and n is the number of times the population reproduces itself. If each microbe reproduces itself every 20 minutes, how large would a population of only one microbe become after four hours?

(A) 16
(B) 64
(C) 128
(D) 1,028
(E) 4,096

11. If x is a positive number > 0 and $y = \frac{1}{x}$, as x increases in value, what happens to y?

(A) y increases
(B) y decreases
(C) y is unchanged
(D) y increases then decreases
(E) y decreases then increases

12. A box was made in the form of a cube. If a second cubical box has inside dimensions three times those of the first box, how many times as much does it contain?

(A) 3
(B) 9
(C) 12
(D) 27
(E) 33

13. Mr. Adams has a circular flower bed with a diameter of 4 feet. He wishes to increase the size of this bed so that it will have four times as much planting area. What must be the diameter of the new bed?

(A) 6 feet
(B) 8 feet
(C) 12 feet
(D) 16 feet
(E) 20 feet

14. A train left Albany for Buffalo, a distance of 290 miles, at 10:10 AM. The train was scheduled to reach Buffalo at 3:45 PM. If the average rate of the train on this trip was 50 mph, it arrived in Buffalo

(A) about 5 minutes early
(B) on time
(C) about 5 minutes late
(D) about 13 minutes late
(E) more than 15 minutes late

15. If $3x - 2 = 13$, the value of $12x + 20$ is

(A) 5
(B) 20
(C) 30
(D) 37
(E) 80

16. A bakery shop sold three kinds of cake. The prices of these were 25¢, 30¢, and 35¢ per pound. The income from these sales was $36. If the number of pounds of each kind of cake sold was the same, how many pounds were sold?

(A) 120 pounds
(B) 90 pounds
(C) 60 pounds
(D) 45 pounds
(E) 36 pounds

17. How many more 9" × 9" linoleum tiles than 1' × 1' tiles will it take to cover a 12' × 12' floor?

(A) 63
(B) 98
(C) 112
(D) 120
(E) 144

18. If p pencils cost c cents, n pencils at the same rate will cost

(A) $\frac{pc}{n}$ cents
(B) $\frac{cn}{p}$ cents
(C) npc cents
(D) $\frac{np}{c}$ cents
(E) $n + p + c$ cents

19. Which, if any, of the following statements is always true?

(A) If the numerator and denominator of a fraction are increased or decreased by the same amount, the value of the fraction is unchanged.
(B) If the numerator and denominator of a fraction are squared, the value of the fraction is unchanged.
(C) The square of any number is greater than that number.
(D) If unequal quantities are added to unequal quantities, the sums are unequal.
(E) none of these

GO ON TO THE NEXT PAGE

20. If the length and width of a rectangle are each doubled, by what percent is the area increased?

(A) 50%

(B) 75%

(C) 100%

(D) 300%

(E) 400%

21. If one pipe can fill a tank in $1\frac{1}{2}$ hours, and another can fill the same tank in 45 minutes, how long will it take for the two pipes to fill the tank together?

(A) $\frac{1}{3}$ hour

(B) $\frac{1}{2}$ hour

(C) $\frac{5}{6}$ hour

(D) 1 hour

(E) $1\frac{1}{2}$ hours

22. A baseball team has won 50 games out of 75 played. It has 45 games still to play. How many of these must the team win to make its record for the season 60%?

(A) 20

(B) 22

(C) 25

(D) 30

(E) 35

Question 23 pertains to the pie charts below, which show how much oil and electricity is consumed in the United States.

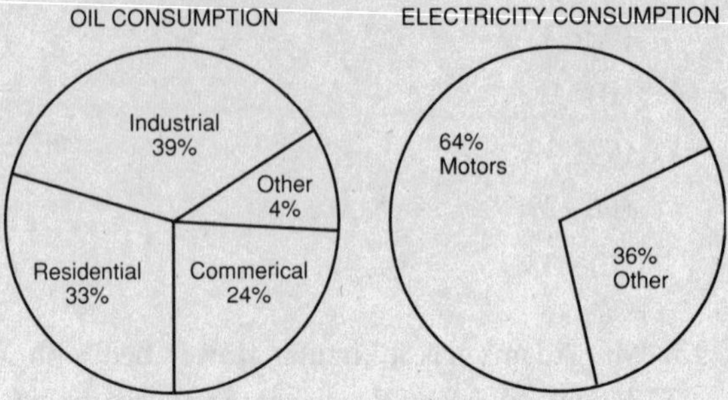

23. If nine million barrels of oil daily are required to produce electricity in the United States, how many barrels are required to meet commercial and industrial needs?

(A) 2,840,000

(B) 3,420,000

(C) 4,750,000

(D) 5,670,000

(E) 7,400,000

24. A real estate investor buys a house and lot for \$44,000. He pays \$1,250 to have it painted, \$1,750 to fix the plumbing, and \$1,000 for grading a driveway. At what price must he sell the property in order to make a 12% profit?

(A) \$53,760

(B) \$52,800

(C) \$52,000

(D) \$49,760

(E) \$44,480

25. The shadow of a man six feet tall is 12 feet long. How tall is a tree that casts a 50-foot shadow?

(A) 100'

(B) 50'

(C) 25'

(D) 15'

(E) 10'

STOP

END OF SECTION FOUR. IF YOU HAVE ANY TIME LEFT, GO OVER YOUR WORK IN THIS SECTION ONLY. DO NOT WORK IN ANY OTHER SECTION OF THE EXAM.

Secondary School Admission Test
Practice Exam 2

Answer Key

SECTION ONE: VERBAL

1. **E**	13. **C**	25. **E**	37. **A**	49. **E**
2. **A**	14. **A**	26. **A**	38. **B**	50. **A**
3. **B**	15. **C**	27. **B**	39. **D**	51. **D**
4. **C**	16. **D**	28. **D**	40. **C**	52. **A**
5. **E**	17. **C**	29. **A**	41. **A**	53. **B**
6. **E**	18. **B**	30. **B**	42. **E**	54. **E**
7. **B**	19. **A**	31. **B**	43. **A**	55. **D**
8. **A**	20. **C**	32. **C**	44. **B**	56. **A**
9. **A**	21. **D**	33. **E**	45. **A**	57. **C**
10. **B**	22. **B**	34. **A**	46. **C**	58. **B**
11. **D**	23. **E**	35. **B**	47. **C**	59. **A**
12. **E**	24. **D**	36. **C**	48. **D**	60. **A**

SECTION TWO: QUANTITATIVE

1. **B**	6. **C**	11. **E**	16. **A**	21. **A**
2. **C**	7. **A**	12. **E**	17. **A**	22. **D**
3. **D**	8. **B**	13. **A**	18. **A**	23. **B**
4. **D**	9. **C**	14. **B**	19. **C**	24. **C**
5. **B**	10. **C**	15. **D**	20. **E**	25. **D**

SECTION THREE: READING

1. **C**	9. **A**	17. **B**	25. **A**	33. **D**
2. **D**	10. **B**	18. **A**	26. **C**	34. **C**
3. **B**	11. **E**	19. **C**	27. **E**	35. **B**
4. **E**	12. **A**	20. **E**	28. **D**	36. **E**
5. **C**	13. **C**	21. **E**	29. **A**	37. **A**
6. **B**	14. **D**	22. **D**	30. **D**	38. **C**
7. **D**	15. **B**	23. **A**	31. **B**	39. **A**
8. **E**	16. **A**	24. **C**	32. **B**	40. **E**

SECTION FOUR: QUANTITATIVE

1. **E**	6. **D**	11. **B**	16. **A**	21. **B**
2. **B**	7. **C**	12. **D**	17. **C**	22. **B**
3. **D**	8. **B**	13. **B**	18. **B**	23. **D**
4. **B**	9. **C**	14. **D**	19. **E**	24. **A**
5. **C**	10. **E**	15. **E**	20. **D**	25. **C**

Secondary School Admission Test
Practice Exam 2

Explanatory Answers

Part I: WRITING SAMPLE

Example of a well-written essay.

I can understand why some schools require students to maintain their grades if they want to be in sports. Sports are time consuming and cut into study time. But, I think that less competent students should not be deprived of the benefits of sports participation.

The argument that students should keep up their grades if they want to be in sports is worth listening to. After all, the purpose of going to school is to get an education. And sports practice and games do take a lot of time. The grades of a few students might in fact suffer from sports participation, but I think that more students will work harder and will learn to manage time better if they are allowed to play on the team. Learning to organize time is also an important lesson to be gained from school. Happy people tend to reach to meet expectations, and less capable students may even do better in school to prove that being in sports did not do them any harm.

An equally good argument is that everyone must succeed at something. If a poor student can excel at sports, that student will develop self-esteem. Once that student feels good about himself or herself, the student may transfer that confidence to schoolwork and actually get better grades. The old adage that success breeds success applies here.

While the attitude that schoolwork comes first does make a good point, I think that permitting a student to participate in sports and to develop a good self-image is more important. The school should give extra help to the less competent student, especially help in learning time management. Then it should let that student contribute to school spirit on the playing fields as well as in the classroom.

Part II: EXPLANATORY ANSWERS

SECTION ONE: VERBAL

Synonyms

1. **(E)** The AGENDA is the *program of things to be done* or the *schedule*. Preparation of next year's budget was the top item on the agenda for the meeting.
2. **(A)** CREDIBLE means *plausible, reliable,* or *believable*. The presence of many squirrels in my yard is a credible explanation for the many holes.
3. **(B)** PLACID means *tranquil, calm,* or *peaceful*. Lake Placid in New York is so placid that its waters are seldom stormy.
4. **(C)** To INTERVENE is to *come between two persons or things* either to *interfere* or to influence positively. *Intervene* is a verb. An *intermediary* (noun) may intervene in a dispute.
5. **(E)** MUNDANE means commonplace, earthly, or ordinary. Every morning I perform the mundane tasks of brushing my teeth and making my bed.
6. **(E)** To dehydrate is to remove water, therefore DEHYDRATED means *waterless*. The root *hydr-* refers to water, and the prefix *de-* is a negative prefix. Dehydrated foods are lightweight and are easy to store for long periods of time.
7. **(B)** PREVALENT means *widely existing, prevailing,* or *generally accepted*. The prevalent mood among the Boy Scouts was one of eager anticipation. *Preeminent* means *excelling*.
8. **(A)** SUCCINCT means *brief* and *to the point*. The legislator gave a succinct background of the reasons for the proposed law.

9. **(A)** That which is NOCTURNAL *happens at night.* Bats do not fly about in the daytime because they are nocturnal creatures.

10. **(B)** EQUITABLE means *fair* and *just.* You should see the root *equal* in this word. The will provided for an equitable distribution of the property.

11. **(D)** To EXPEDITE is to *speed up the action* or to *send quickly.* The Latin derivation of this word is "to free one caught by the feet." You can expedite the delivery of mail by using ZIP Code plus four.

12. **(E)** TURBULENT means *unruly* or *agitated.* As the airplane passed through turbulent air we all felt rather queasy.

13. **(C)** TENACIOUS means *holding on tightly* or *persistent.* The tenacious salesman calls twice a week between 5 and 7 PM.

14. **(A)** PERTINENT means *relevant.* Testimony is admitted in court only if it is pertinent to the charges in the case.

15. **(C)** DOGMATIC means *dictatorial* or *opinionated.* The word has to do with doctrine or dogma, not with dogs. My uncle is so dogmatic that he refuses to even listen to my point of view.

16. **(D)** One who is UNSCRUPULOUS is *not restrained by ideas of right and wrong.* The unscrupulous stockbroker used inside information to sell before the stock price plummeted.

17. **(C)** WILY means *crafty* or *sly.* The wily wolf outwitted Red Riding Hood.

18. **(B)** BLATANT means *loud* and *obtrusive.* The misspelling in the address was a blatant error in an otherwise excellent letter.

19. **(A)** A PRETEXT is a *false reason* or an *excuse.* Illness was his pretext for absence from school; actually he went to the beach.

20. **(C)** ACUMEN is *keenness and quickness in understanding and dealing with a situation.* Acumen with respect to foreign cultures is a great asset in the diplomatic corps.

21. **(D)** EVASION is *subterfuge* or *avoidance.* His manner of evasion of embarrassing questions was to make a long speech on another topic.

22. **(B)** That which is INDISPENSABLE *cannot be dispensed with,* that is, it is absolutely *essential.* The president of the company refused to take a vacation because he had the mistaken notion that his presence was indispensable.

23. **(E)** To OBLITERATE is to *destroy without leaving a trace.* The washing waves obliterated our footsteps in the sand.

24. **(D)** AMIABLE means *pleasant, friendly,* and *good-natured.* The amiable shopkeeper allowed us to continue trying on shoes even though it was already past closing time.

25. **(E)** To WRITHE is to *twist, squirm,* or *contort,* usually in discomfort. The skier writhed in pain when she broke her ankle.

26. **(A)** To ABATE is to *diminish.* We will stay tied up in port until the winds abate.

27. **(B)** An ENDORSEMENT is a *statement of approval.* The governor gave his endorsement to the candidate for mayor of the city.

28. **(D)** To CONVERT is to change from one form to another. Use a transformer to convert DC current to AC current.

29. **(A)** ERUDITE means *learned* or *scholarly.* He has little information, but his beautiful command of the English language makes him appear to be erudite.

30. **(B)** To ENDEAVOR is to *attempt* or to *try.* The expedition endeavored to reach the mountaintop before the thunderstorm.

Analogies

31. **(B)** The relationship of the terms is one of degree. *None* is the ultimate, the empty set, of *little; never* bears the same relationship to *infrequently.*

32. **(C)** If you think in terms of a house, you can see that the terms on each side of the relationship are synonymous. You can *receive* a person into your home or *admit* the person. Once the person decides to *remain,* that person *settles* in.

33. **(E)** Here the cause-and-effect relationship is clear. Recognized *dishonesty* leads to *distrust; carelessness* leads to *accidents.*

34. **(A)** The relationship is that of actor to object. A *sociologist* studies *groups;* a *psychologist* studies *individuals.* The relationship of the children to the pediatrician is in reverse order.

35. **(B)** The terms are antonyms. *Generous* is the opposite of *frugal;* a *philanthropist* is truly the opposite of a *miser*. The terms in choices (C) and (E) are also antonyms. When faced with questions in which the same relationship is maintained by a number of the choices, you must look for a relationship among all four terms. In this case, the theme to be carried through among the choices of the correct analogy is "money."

36. **(C)** The relationship is one of degree. *Translucent* is denser than *transparent,* that is, one can actually see through something that is transparent whereas only light passes through a translucent medium. Carrying on to the next degree, *opaque* is denser than *translucent*. Not even light can pass through something that is opaque. Choice (A) is incorrect because it skips a degree and jumps from transparent to opaque. Choice (D) reverses the order. Glass and crystal (B) may both be transparent.

37. **(A)** This is a classic cause-and-effect relationship. *Discontent* leads to *rebellion; friction* creates a *spark*.

38. **(B)** The relationship is that of worker to tool. A *chemist* uses a *beaker* in the laboratory; a *geologist* uses a *hammer* to chip at rocks in the field or laboratory. Avoid the "trap" of choice (C). A hammer is certainly used in construction, but the relationship of the first two terms requires that a person be involved to complete the analogy.

39. **(D)** This one is easy. The basis of the analogy is antonyms.

40. **(C)** This is a part-to-whole analogy. A *state* is part of a *country;* a *country* is part of a *continent*.

41. **(A)** Cause and effect. An *accelerator* causes the *motion* of the car; a *catalyst* causes the chemical *change*.

42. **(E)** The relationship is one of degree. *Probable* is likely, but less likely than *certain; plausible* is possible, but less likely than *definite*.

43. **(A)** The relationship is one of true synonyms.

44. **(B)** This analogy involves true antonyms.

45. **(A)** The relationship is that of object to actor. The *nucleus* is the object that is orbited by an *electron;* the *Earth* is the object that is orbited by a *satellite*. Choice (B) reverses the order of the relationship.

46. **(C)** Here the relationship is that of actor to object. A *sculptor* creates a *statue;* a *composer* creates *music*. An actor performs in a play but does not create it. A programmer creates a program while working at a computer.

47. **(C)** The analogy is based on an antonym relationship.

48. **(D)** This analogy is also based on antonyms.

49. **(E)** It is hard to categorize this relationship. One *interrupts* by *speaking* out of turn; one *intrudes* by *entering* out of turn. The relationship in (B) might be that of opposites.

50. **(A)** The first two terms are true opposites. Only choice (A) offers true opposites. *Financial stability* is the opposite of *poverty,* but finance bears no relationship to poverty at all.

51. **(D)** This analogy is best understood as a negative cause and effect. *Adversity* leads to a lack of *happiness; vehemence* leads to a lack of *serenity*.

52. **(A)** The relationship is that of actor to action. An *extortionist blackmails;* a *kleptomaniac steals*.

53. **(B)** This is a whole-to-part relationship. A *monsoon* is a major storm of which *rain* is a crucial component; a *tornado* is a major storm of which *wind* is a crucial component.

54. **(E)** The first two terms are synonyms; the analogous relationship of the second two terms is that they are also synonyms. The terms on the two sides of the analogy are antonyms, but since these are the only two sets of synonyms, the relationship is complete and the analogy a correct one.

55. **(D)** You needn't categorize an analogy; you only need to understand it. The equator is the midline that circles the world; the waist is the midline that circles the man.

56. **(A)** On each side of the analogy, the first term is a characteristic of the second.

57. **(C)** This analogy is based on characteristics of bodies of water. A *pond* may be *stagnant;* a *stream* is likely to *flow*. Sheep may be noisy but since there are two choices that involve characteristics, you must choose the one that is closest in other aspects to the first set of terms, that is, the one involving water.

58. **(B)** This is a purposeful or functional relationship. A *fortress* gives *sanctuary;* a *house* gives *shelter*.

59. **(A)** The terms are synonyms.

60. **(A)** This analogy is also based on synonyms. Choice (E) is incorrect because pensive means thoughtful. If you made this choice, you were mistaking *pensive* for *pendant,* which does mean hanging.

SECTION TWO: QUANTITATIVE

1. **(B)** Change $\frac{3}{5}$ to a decimal: $\frac{3}{5} = .60$.

$.60 + 1.25 + .004 = 1.854$

2. **(C)** $\frac{10^6}{10^3} = 10^{6-3} = 1{,}000$

or $10^6 = 1{,}000{,}000$

$10^3 = 1{,}000$

$1{,}000{,}000 \div 1{,}000 = 1{,}000$

3. **(D)**

$$\begin{array}{r} 71.4 \\ \times 98.2 \\ \hline 1428 \\ 5712 \\ 6426 \\ \hline 7{,}011.48 \end{array}$$

4. **(D)** Simplify the numerator.

$$\frac{4\frac{2}{3} + \frac{1}{6}}{\frac{1}{3}} = \frac{4\frac{4}{6} + \frac{1}{6}}{\frac{1}{3}} = \frac{4\frac{5}{6}}{\frac{1}{3}}$$

Proceed as you would to divide any fraction.

$$4\frac{5}{6} \div \frac{1}{3} = \frac{29}{{}_2\not{6}} \bullet \frac{\not{3}^1}{1} = 14\frac{1}{2}$$

5. **(B)** $(.25)^2 = .25 \times .25 = .0625$

6. **(C)** Begin with the innermost group and work outward.

$(3 + 1) + [(2 - 3) - (4 - 1)]$

$= (3 + 1) + [(-1) - (3)]$

$= (3 + 1) + [-1 -3]$

$= (3 + 1) + [-4]$

$= 4 + -4 = 0$

7. **(A)** Try to estimate the answer rather than calculate.

$$\begin{array}{r} 10{,}001 \\ -\ 8{,}093 \\ \hline 1{,}908 \end{array}$$

8. **(B)** Three gallons contain 12 quarts. The ratio is 3 quarts: 12 quarts, or, in simplest form, 1:4.

9. **(C)** One fifth of $50.00 is $10.00. Ten percent, or $\frac{1}{10}$, of $10.00 is $1.00.

10. **(C)** Borrow one minute from the minutes column, and one hour from the hours column. Then subtract.

$$\begin{array}{r} 3 \text{ hr. } 71 \text{ min. } 70 \text{ sec.} \\ -\ 2 \text{ hr. } 48 \text{ min. } 35 \text{ sec.} \\ \hline 1 \text{ hr. } 23 \text{ min. } 35 \text{ sec.} \end{array}$$

11. **(E)** By doubling the size of one of the factors of the numerator and the size of the denominator, we do not change the value of the fraction. We are actually writing an equivalent fraction. Try this with fractions having numerical values for the numerator and denominator.

12. **(E)** This is a good problem for estimation. Note that 10% of 220 = 22. One percent of 220 = 2.2 and 24.2 = 22 (10 percent) + 2.2 (1 percent). Or, $\frac{24.2}{200} = .11$.

13. **(A)** Be careful. This problem asks you to reduce 98 by $\frac{5}{7}$. In other words, find $\frac{2}{7}$ of 98.

$$98 \bullet \frac{2}{7} = \frac{\overset{14}{\not{98}}}{1} \bullet \frac{2}{\not{7}_1} = 28$$

14. **(B)** Since one foot corresponds to $\frac{1}{4}$ inch in the drawing, the drawing should be $6\frac{1}{2} \bullet \frac{1}{4}$ inches long.

$$6\frac{1}{2} \bullet \frac{1}{4} =$$

$$= \frac{13}{2} \bullet \frac{1}{4}$$

$$= \frac{13}{8} = 1\frac{5}{8}''$$

15. **(D)** Bracket the multiplication and division operations from left to right. Then calculate.

$$\left[12\frac{1}{2} \div \frac{1}{2}\right] + \left[\frac{3}{2} \times 4\right] - 3$$

$= [25] + [6] - 3$

$= 28$

16. **(A)** Since $y + 2 > 10$, $y > 10 - 2$, or $y > 8$.

17. **(A)** This is a problem that must be done carefully.

$a = 1, b = 2, c = 3, d = 5$

$\sqrt{b(d + a) - b(c + a)}$

$= \sqrt{2(5 + 1) - 2(3 + 1)}$

$= \sqrt{2(6) - 2(4)}$

$= \sqrt{12 - 8}$

$= \sqrt{4} = 2$

18. **(A)** The denominator of a fraction can never be equivalent to zero. Division by zero has no meaning in mathematics.

19. **(C)** $.0515 \times 100 = 5.15$, and so does $.00515 \times 1{,}000$. You should be able to do this problem by moving decimal points and not by multiplying out. To *divide* by 10, move the decimal point one place to the *left*. Move it two places to the left to divide by 100, three places to divide by 1,000, and so forth. To *multiply* by 10, 100, 1,000 and so forth, move the decimal point the corresponding number of places to the *right*. This is an important skill to review.

20. **(E)** This is a tricky problem. Answers (B), (C), and (D) might be true in some cases, depending upon the exact measurements of $\angle 1$ and $\angle 3$. The only answer that is true no matter what the measures of $\angle 1$ and $\angle 3$ is the one in which their sum is equal to 120°.

21. **(A)** This can be set up as a proportion where x is the unknown number.

$$\frac{45}{x} = \frac{90}{.45}$$

This is a good problem for estimation. Study the numerators of the fractions and note that 45 is one half of 90. Therefore, the denominators of the fractions must have the same relationship. One half of .45 is .225.

22. **(D)** The square root of 20 is less than the square root of 25, which is 5, and greater than the square root of 16, which is 4. Therefore, n is between 4 and 5.

23. **(B)** To find the difference, we subtract –6 from 4 and move from –6 to 4, a distance of +10 units.

24. **(C)** Simply divide $\frac{4}{5}$ by $\frac{1}{6}$ to find the answer.

$$\frac{4}{5} \div \frac{1}{6} = \frac{4}{5} \bullet \frac{6}{1} = \frac{24}{5} = 4\frac{4}{5}$$

25. **(D)** Four games averaging 36,500 people per game total 146,000 attendance. The total for the first three games was 105,500. The fourth game attracted 40,500 people.

SECTION THREE: READING COMPREHENSION

1. **(C)** You will find the answer to this detail question in the last two sentences of the selection.
2. **(D)** This detail is given in the last sentence of the first paragraph. All the other answer choices were true of the history of Riker's Island but are not true at the present time.
3. **(B)** You can infer that the discards of city households included garbage. Decayed garbage is an excellent fertilizer.
4. **(E)** See the next-to-last sentence of the selection.
5. **(C)** This is the meaning of the second sentence of the first paragraph.
6. **(B)** Since the thrust of the selection is the threatened extinction of the bald eagle, you really do not need to search for the precise words that answer this question. However, you can find them in the second paragraph.
7. **(D)** This definition is given in the second sentence of the third paragraph: " . . . aeries, the eagles' mammoth nests."
8. **(E)** The selection tells us that the bald eagle appears on the Great Seal of the United States, our national emblem. An emblem is a symbol. "Emblematic" is the adjective form of the noun, "emblem."
9. **(A)** This detail may be found in the first sentence of the last paragraph.

10. **(B)** The author tells you his reason in the second sentence.
11. **(E)** See the third sentence.
12. **(A)** The fourth sentence gives this detail.
13. **(C)** The sixth sentence tells that the garden led to a forest. The selection says that the garden extended so far that the gardener did not know where it ended, but it does not say that he was unable to care for it because of its size.
14. **(D)** In the last sentence we learn that the forest went down to the sea, and in the trees of the forest at seaside lived a nightingale.
15. **(B)** This really is a vocabulary question. A *sojourn* is a visit or a temporary stay.
16. **(A)** The context of the second paragraph should help you to figure out the meaning of this word. In other contexts, *decipher* may mean to *decode.* Here it means to *make out the meaning of ancient, nearly illegible inscriptions or writings.*
17. **(B)** See the last sentence of the first paragraph. By enlarging on hitherto known tales of the named persons, the scroll is giving new details about persons already known of. The scroll is the last of the seven found in 1947, not the first. It tells of Abraham's stay in Egypt, but it was found in the Judean desert of Israel.
18. **(A)** The second paragraph opens by telling us that the scroll belongs to Hebrew University. If you were not certain that Hebrew University is an Israeli university, the statement that the work is being done under the supervision of Israeli scholars (last sentence) should confirm this.
19. **(C)** If this question gives you trouble, reread the middle of the second paragraph. The readable material included: four full pages, legible parts of five other pages, and some lines and words on additional pages.
20. **(E)** See the first sentence. A century ago was 100 years ago.
21. **(E)** The first sentence of the second paragraph says that the boats are equipped for various jobs, which means that they vary in function.
22. **(D)** By checking on the operation of the junk boats, the harbor police ensure that their activities are legal.
23. **(A)** The other choices all include some activity that is not mentioned as an activity of the harbor police.
24. **(C)** The 450 disabled boats that were towed and the thousands that needed some sort of help (next-to-last sentence) could not possibly have all been of the same kind.
25. **(A)** Context should help you here. "... veneration due to its sacred origin ..." implies something religious and related to worship.
26. **(C)** This is an inferential question. The speaker probably enjoys and celebrates Christmas (choice B) as well, but the primary reason for this speech is defending the holiday to his Uncle Scrooge by listing its advantages to mankind.
27. **(E)** This is the whole point of the first paragraph.
28. **(D)** Again, use of the word in context should lead you to its meaning. The paragraph speaks of good will among all men and women. This *one consent* therefore is *unanimous* good feeling.
29. **(A)** Read the last paragraph carefully. Scrooge is first reacting to the clerk who has just applauded the speech in defense of Christmas. Scrooge threatens the clerk with firing. He then turns and makes a sarcastic remark to his nephew. It can be assumed that he is angry with both characters.
30. **(D)** "Just stopped by ..." is quite a matter-of-fact way of speaking.
31. **(B)** The raised eyebrows of the first sentence of the second paragraph imply disbelief.
32. **(B)** Mr. Holter had a caravan of animals; was in New York on his way to Dayton, Ohio; and actually lived in Anaheim, California. You can infer that he made his living traveling and showing his animals.
33. **(D)** The article discusses high blood pressure as a familial disease, a disease that runs in families. It goes on to discuss the role of genetic makeup in determining reaction to dietary factors. Genetic makeup refers to hereditary factors.
34. **(C)** This is a main-idea question. The main point of the selection is that there is an interplay of genetic and environmental factors influencing the development of high blood pressure.

35. **(B)** The first paragraph speaks of the perils of fishing, the second about its rewards.

36. **(E)** The middle of the first paragraph discusses the problems created by rough seas. None of the other choices is a mentioned difficulty.

37. **(A)** In the middle of the second paragraph we learn that when the fishermen note that herring are entering the nets they sit in quiet excitement so as not to frighten the fish away. They row along the net (E) in order to find out if the net is filling, and haul in the nets (B) and (D) when the nets are full. It is the fish that glisten, not the fishermen.

38. **(C)** Everything is mentioned except the beauty of the sea.

39. **(A)** All other choices contain at least one trait that is not ascribed to the fishermen.

40. **(E)** One might add honesty to the traits of the fishermen. Theft is not mentioned as a problem.

SECTION FOUR: QUANTITATIVE

1. **(E)** Any point on the surface rotates once each day relative to a point in space. Each revolution is an angle of 360°. In two days, two revolutions take place, $360° \times 2 = 720°$.

2. **(B)** $\frac{3}{7}$, $\frac{15}{32}$, and $\frac{11}{23}$ are all less than $\frac{1}{2}$; $\frac{9}{16}$ is larger than $\frac{1}{2}$. Compare the size of fractions this way.

$$\frac{3}{7} \times \frac{15}{32}$$

Because the product of 7 and 15 is larger than the product of 32 and 3, $\frac{15}{32}$ will be found to be larger. Using the same method, $\frac{5}{32} < \frac{11}{23}$.

3. **(D)** If the width is x, the length, which is twice as long, is $2x$. The perimeter is equal to the sum of the four sides: $2x + 2x + x + x = 6x$.

4. **(B)** Use the Pythagorean Theorem $c^2 = a^2 + b^2$ to find the length of the diagonal.

$$c^2 = 1^2 + 1^2$$
$$c^2 = 2$$
$$c = \sqrt{2}$$

5. **(C)** Eight sections, each 3'2" long, is equivalent to $8 \times 38" = 304"$.

$304" = 25\frac{1}{3}$ feet, therefore three ten-foot sections are needed.

6. **(D)** The width of the shaded area is $\frac{1}{3}$ of the width of the square. Therefore, the area of the shaded part is $\frac{1}{3}$ the area of the whole square. The unshaded part is twice as large as the shaded part. The ratio of the shaded part to the unshaded, therefore, is 1:2.

7. **(C)** Since distance = rate × time, rate = distance ÷ time. Total distance traveled is 3,200 miles. Total time is 4 hours 20 minutes.

Rate = 3,200 miles ÷ 4 hours 20 minutes
= 3,200 miles ÷ $4\frac{1}{3}$ hours
= 739 mph, approximately

8. **(B)** This is a simple proportion: $\frac{7}{4} = \frac{5}{x}$. x is the unknown width. Cross-multiply:

$$7x = 20$$
$$x = \frac{20}{7}, \text{ or } 2\frac{6}{7}"$$

9. **(C)** Subtract the area of the circle from the area of the square to find the area of just the shaded part.

Note that the diameter of the circle equals the width of the square.

Area of square = $s^2 = 4$ sq. in.

Area of circle = $\pi r^2 = \pi(1)^2 = \pi$ sq. in.

Area of square – Area of circle

$= 4$ sq. in. $- \frac{22}{7}$ sq. in.

$= \frac{6}{7}$ sq. in., or $\frac{6}{7}$ in.^{2}

10. **(E)** The population would reproduce 12 times in four hours. The size then is $P = 2^{12}$
$= 2 \cdot 2 \cdot 2 \cdot 2 \cdot 2 \cdot 2 \cdot 2 \cdot 2 \cdot 2 \cdot 2 \cdot 2 \cdot 2$
$= 4{,}096$

11. **(B)** The larger the number of the denominator of a fraction, the smaller the quantity represented. For example, $\frac{1}{4}$ represents a lesser quantity than $\frac{1}{2}$. Therefore, as x becomes greater, y becomes smaller.

12. **(D)** If the second box has each dimension 3 times that of the first box, then its volume is $3 \times 3 \times 3 =$ 27 times as great.

13. **(B)** The area of the flower bed is 4 π sq. ft. (A = πr^2). The area of the new bed is to be four times as great, or 16π sq. ft. A bed with an area of 16π sq. ft. must have a diameter of 8', and a radius of 4', since A = r^2.

14. **(D)** Use the formula D = R × T to find the time it actually took to get to Buffalo: time = distance ÷ rate. Travel time of trip was equal to 290 miles ÷ 50 mph.

    Travel time = $5\frac{4}{5}$ hours, or 5 hours 48 minutes. Scheduled travel time was between 10:10 AM and 3:45 PM, an interval of 5 hours 35 minutes. Therefore, the train took about 13 minutes longer than scheduled.

15. **(E)** Solve the equation for x:

    $3x - 2 = 13$

    $3x = 15$

    $x = 5$

    If $x = 5$, then $12x + 20 = 12(5) + 20 = 80$.

16. **(A)** Since the number of pounds of each kind of cake sold was the same, we can say that a pound of cake sold for an average price of 30¢ per pound.

    25¢ + 30¢ + 35¢ = 90¢ ÷ 3 = 30¢ per lb.

    Divide the total sales income of $36 by 30¢ to find how many pounds were sold.

    $36 ÷ .30 = 120.

17. **(C)** A floor 12' × 12' is 144 sq. ft. in area, and would require 144 tiles that are each one foot by one foot. Twelve tiles would be placed along the width and length of the room. If 9" tiles are used, it requires 16 of them placed end to end to cover the length of the room. Therefore, it requires 16 × 16 tiles to cover the floor, or 256 tiles. It requires 112 more 9" tiles than 12" tiles to cover the floor.

18. **(B)** If p pencils cost c cents, the cost of each pencil is $\frac{c}{p}$ cents. To find the cost of n pencils, we multiply the cost of each times n.

    $$\frac{c}{p} \bullet n = \frac{cn}{p}$$

19. **(E)** If necessary, try each of the answers for yourself, to see that each is false. Answer (C) is untrue for the number 1.

20. **(D)** Think of a rectangle with the dimensions 1" by 2". Its area is 2 square inches. If we double each dimension, to 2" by 4", the area becomes 8 square inches, which is four times the area of the first rectangle. An increase of four times is equal to an increase of 300%.

21. **(B)** The first pipe can fill the tank in $1\frac{1}{2}$, or $\frac{3}{2}$, hours; that is, it can do $\frac{2}{3}$ of the job in 1 hour. The second pipe can fill the tank in 45 minutes, or $\frac{3}{4}$ of an hour, or it can do $\frac{4}{3}$ of the job in 1 hour. Together the pipes can complete $\frac{4}{3} + \frac{2}{3} = \frac{6}{3}$ of the job in one hour. $\frac{6}{3} = 2$, or twice the job in one hour. Therefore, together the two pipes could fill the tank in $\frac{1}{2}$ hour.

22. **(B)** The whole season consists of 120 games. For a season record of 60%, the team must win 72 games. Since it has already won 50, it must win 22 more games out of those left.

23. **(D)** Commercial and industrial needs total 63% of daily oil consumption. Since consumption is 9 million barrels, 63% of 9 million is 5,670,000 barrels.

24. **(A)** Add the cost of the house, driveway, painting and plumbing.

    $44,000 + $1,250 + $1,750 + 1,000 = $48,000

    If he wants to make a 12% profit when reselling the house, he should increase the total cost by 12% to find the new selling price.

    12% of $48,000 = $5,760

    $48,000 + $5,760 = $53,760

25. **(C)** This is a simple proportion. A man casts a shadow twice as long as his height. Therefore, so does the tree. Therefore, a tree that casts a shadow 50' long is 25' high.

SCORE YOURSELF

Check your answers against the correct answer key. Count up the number of answers you got right and the number you got wrong.

Section	No. Right	No. Wrong
Synonyms		
Verbal Analogies		
Total Verbal		
Reading Comprehension		
Quantitative		

Now, for each test subject divide the number of answers you got wrong by 4. Round down for fractions below .5; up from .5. Subtract this number from the number of correct answers in each section to find your raw score. Use this raw score to figure your percentage score on the score sheet below.

Section	Raw Score ÷ No. of questions	× 100 =	%
Synonyms	÷ 30	× 100 =	%
Verbal Analogies	÷ 30	× 100 =	%
Total Verbal	÷ 60	× 100 =	%
Reading Comprehension	÷ 40	× 100 =	%
Quantitative	÷ 50	× 100 =	%

High percentage scores should make you feel very good about yourself, but low percentages do not mean that you are a failure.

Remember:

- Scores are not reported as percentages. A low percentage may translate to a respectable scaled score.
- The same exam is given to students in grades 8 through 12. Unless you have finished high school, you have not been taught everything on the exam. You are not expected to know what you have not been taught.
- You will be compared only to students in your own grade.

Use your scores to plan further study if you have time.

TEAR HERE

Independent School Entrance Examination
Practice Exam 1

Answer Sheet

TEST ONE: VERBAL ABILITY

1. Ⓐ Ⓑ Ⓒ Ⓓ	9. Ⓐ Ⓑ Ⓒ Ⓓ	17. Ⓐ Ⓑ Ⓒ Ⓓ	25. Ⓐ Ⓑ Ⓒ Ⓓ	33. Ⓐ Ⓑ Ⓒ Ⓓ
2. Ⓐ Ⓑ Ⓒ Ⓓ	10. Ⓐ Ⓑ Ⓒ Ⓓ	18. Ⓐ Ⓑ Ⓒ Ⓓ	26. Ⓐ Ⓑ Ⓒ Ⓓ	34. Ⓐ Ⓑ Ⓒ Ⓓ
3. Ⓐ Ⓑ Ⓒ Ⓓ	11. Ⓐ Ⓑ Ⓒ Ⓓ	19. Ⓐ Ⓑ Ⓒ Ⓓ	27. Ⓐ Ⓑ Ⓒ Ⓓ	35. Ⓐ Ⓑ Ⓒ Ⓓ
4. Ⓐ Ⓑ Ⓒ Ⓓ	12. Ⓐ Ⓑ Ⓒ Ⓓ	20. Ⓐ Ⓑ Ⓒ Ⓓ	28. Ⓐ Ⓑ Ⓒ Ⓓ	36. Ⓐ Ⓑ Ⓒ Ⓓ
5. Ⓐ Ⓑ Ⓒ Ⓓ	13. Ⓐ Ⓑ Ⓒ Ⓓ	21. Ⓐ Ⓑ Ⓒ Ⓓ	29. Ⓐ Ⓑ Ⓒ Ⓓ	37. Ⓐ Ⓑ Ⓒ Ⓓ
6. Ⓐ Ⓑ Ⓒ Ⓓ	14. Ⓐ Ⓑ Ⓒ Ⓓ	22. Ⓐ Ⓑ Ⓒ Ⓓ	30. Ⓐ Ⓑ Ⓒ Ⓓ	38. Ⓐ Ⓑ Ⓒ Ⓓ
7. Ⓐ Ⓑ Ⓒ Ⓓ	15. Ⓐ Ⓑ Ⓒ Ⓓ	23. Ⓐ Ⓑ Ⓒ Ⓓ	31. Ⓐ Ⓑ Ⓒ Ⓓ	39. Ⓐ Ⓑ Ⓒ Ⓓ
8. Ⓐ Ⓑ Ⓒ Ⓓ	16. Ⓐ Ⓑ Ⓒ Ⓓ	24. Ⓐ Ⓑ Ⓒ Ⓓ	32. Ⓐ Ⓑ Ⓒ Ⓓ	40. Ⓐ Ⓑ Ⓒ Ⓓ

TEST TWO: QUANTITATIVE ABILITY

1. Ⓐ Ⓑ Ⓒ Ⓓ	9. Ⓐ Ⓑ Ⓒ Ⓓ	17. Ⓐ Ⓑ Ⓒ Ⓓ	25. Ⓐ Ⓑ Ⓒ Ⓓ	33. Ⓐ Ⓑ Ⓒ Ⓓ
2. Ⓐ Ⓑ Ⓒ Ⓓ	10. Ⓐ Ⓑ Ⓒ Ⓓ	18. Ⓐ Ⓑ Ⓒ Ⓓ	26. Ⓐ Ⓑ Ⓒ Ⓓ	34. Ⓐ Ⓑ Ⓒ Ⓓ
3. Ⓐ Ⓑ Ⓒ Ⓓ	11. Ⓐ Ⓑ Ⓒ Ⓓ	19. Ⓐ Ⓑ Ⓒ Ⓓ	27. Ⓐ Ⓑ Ⓒ Ⓓ	35. Ⓐ Ⓑ Ⓒ Ⓓ
4. Ⓐ Ⓑ Ⓒ Ⓓ	12. Ⓐ Ⓑ Ⓒ Ⓓ	20. Ⓐ Ⓑ Ⓒ Ⓓ	28. Ⓐ Ⓑ Ⓒ Ⓓ	36. Ⓐ Ⓑ Ⓒ Ⓓ
5. Ⓐ Ⓑ Ⓒ Ⓓ	13. Ⓐ Ⓑ Ⓒ Ⓓ	21. Ⓐ Ⓑ Ⓒ Ⓓ	29. Ⓐ Ⓑ Ⓒ Ⓓ	37. Ⓐ Ⓑ Ⓒ Ⓓ
6. Ⓐ Ⓑ Ⓒ Ⓓ	14. Ⓐ Ⓑ Ⓒ Ⓓ	22. Ⓐ Ⓑ Ⓒ Ⓓ	30. Ⓐ Ⓑ Ⓒ Ⓓ	38. Ⓐ Ⓑ Ⓒ Ⓓ
7. Ⓐ Ⓑ Ⓒ Ⓓ	15. Ⓐ Ⓑ Ⓒ Ⓓ	23. Ⓐ Ⓑ Ⓒ Ⓓ	31. Ⓐ Ⓑ Ⓒ Ⓓ	39. Ⓐ Ⓑ Ⓒ Ⓓ
8. Ⓐ Ⓑ Ⓒ Ⓓ	16. Ⓐ Ⓑ Ⓒ Ⓓ	24. Ⓐ Ⓑ Ⓒ Ⓓ	32. Ⓐ Ⓑ Ⓒ Ⓓ	40. Ⓐ Ⓑ Ⓒ Ⓓ

TEST THREE: READING COMPREHENSION

1. Ⓐ Ⓑ Ⓒ Ⓓ	9. Ⓐ Ⓑ Ⓒ Ⓓ	17. Ⓐ Ⓑ Ⓒ Ⓓ	25. Ⓐ Ⓑ Ⓒ Ⓓ	33. Ⓐ Ⓑ Ⓒ Ⓓ
2. Ⓐ Ⓑ Ⓒ Ⓓ	10. Ⓐ Ⓑ Ⓒ Ⓓ	18. Ⓐ Ⓑ Ⓒ Ⓓ	26. Ⓐ Ⓑ Ⓒ Ⓓ	34. Ⓐ Ⓑ Ⓒ Ⓓ
3. Ⓐ Ⓑ Ⓒ Ⓓ	11. Ⓐ Ⓑ Ⓒ Ⓓ	19. Ⓐ Ⓑ Ⓒ Ⓓ	27. Ⓐ Ⓑ Ⓒ Ⓓ	35. Ⓐ Ⓑ Ⓒ Ⓓ
4. Ⓐ Ⓑ Ⓒ Ⓓ	12. Ⓐ Ⓑ Ⓒ Ⓓ	20. Ⓐ Ⓑ Ⓒ Ⓓ	28. Ⓐ Ⓑ Ⓒ Ⓓ	36. Ⓐ Ⓑ Ⓒ Ⓓ
5. Ⓐ Ⓑ Ⓒ Ⓓ	13. Ⓐ Ⓑ Ⓒ Ⓓ	21. Ⓐ Ⓑ Ⓒ Ⓓ	29. Ⓐ Ⓑ Ⓒ Ⓓ	37. Ⓐ Ⓑ Ⓒ Ⓓ
6. Ⓐ Ⓑ Ⓒ Ⓓ	14. Ⓐ Ⓑ Ⓒ Ⓓ	22. Ⓐ Ⓑ Ⓒ Ⓓ	30. Ⓐ Ⓑ Ⓒ Ⓓ	38. Ⓐ Ⓑ Ⓒ Ⓓ
7. Ⓐ Ⓑ Ⓒ Ⓓ	15. Ⓐ Ⓑ Ⓒ Ⓓ	23. Ⓐ Ⓑ Ⓒ Ⓓ	31. Ⓐ Ⓑ Ⓒ Ⓓ	39. Ⓐ Ⓑ Ⓒ Ⓓ
8. Ⓐ Ⓑ Ⓒ Ⓓ	16. Ⓐ Ⓑ Ⓒ Ⓓ	24. Ⓐ Ⓑ Ⓒ Ⓓ	32. Ⓐ Ⓑ Ⓒ Ⓓ	40. Ⓐ Ⓑ Ⓒ Ⓓ

TEST FOUR: MATHEMATICS ACHIEVEMENT

1. Ⓐ Ⓑ Ⓒ Ⓓ	11. Ⓐ Ⓑ Ⓒ Ⓓ	21. Ⓐ Ⓑ Ⓒ Ⓓ	31. Ⓐ Ⓑ Ⓒ Ⓓ	41. Ⓐ Ⓑ Ⓒ Ⓓ
2. Ⓐ Ⓑ Ⓒ Ⓓ	12. Ⓐ Ⓑ Ⓒ Ⓓ	22. Ⓐ Ⓑ Ⓒ Ⓓ	32. Ⓐ Ⓑ Ⓒ Ⓓ	42. Ⓐ Ⓑ Ⓒ Ⓓ
3. Ⓐ Ⓑ Ⓒ Ⓓ	13. Ⓐ Ⓑ Ⓒ Ⓓ	23. Ⓐ Ⓑ Ⓒ Ⓓ	33. Ⓐ Ⓑ Ⓒ Ⓓ	43. Ⓐ Ⓑ Ⓒ Ⓓ
4. Ⓐ Ⓑ Ⓒ Ⓓ	14. Ⓐ Ⓑ Ⓒ Ⓓ	24. Ⓐ Ⓑ Ⓒ Ⓓ	34. Ⓐ Ⓑ Ⓒ Ⓓ	44. Ⓐ Ⓑ Ⓒ Ⓓ
5. Ⓐ Ⓑ Ⓒ Ⓓ	15. Ⓐ Ⓑ Ⓒ Ⓓ	25. Ⓐ Ⓑ Ⓒ Ⓓ	35. Ⓐ Ⓑ Ⓒ Ⓓ	45. Ⓐ Ⓑ Ⓒ Ⓓ
6. Ⓐ Ⓑ Ⓒ Ⓓ	16. Ⓐ Ⓑ Ⓒ Ⓓ	26. Ⓐ Ⓑ Ⓒ Ⓓ	36. Ⓐ Ⓑ Ⓒ Ⓓ	46. Ⓐ Ⓑ Ⓒ Ⓓ
7. Ⓐ Ⓑ Ⓒ Ⓓ	17. Ⓐ Ⓑ Ⓒ Ⓓ	27. Ⓐ Ⓑ Ⓒ Ⓓ	37. Ⓐ Ⓑ Ⓒ Ⓓ	47. Ⓐ Ⓑ Ⓒ Ⓓ
8. Ⓐ Ⓑ Ⓒ Ⓓ	18. Ⓐ Ⓑ Ⓒ Ⓓ	28. Ⓐ Ⓑ Ⓒ Ⓓ	38. Ⓐ Ⓑ Ⓒ Ⓓ	48. Ⓐ Ⓑ Ⓒ Ⓓ
9. Ⓐ Ⓑ Ⓒ Ⓓ	19. Ⓐ Ⓑ Ⓒ Ⓓ	29. Ⓐ Ⓑ Ⓒ Ⓓ	39. Ⓐ Ⓑ Ⓒ Ⓓ	49. Ⓐ Ⓑ Ⓒ Ⓓ
10. Ⓐ Ⓑ Ⓒ Ⓓ	20. Ⓐ Ⓑ Ⓒ Ⓓ	30. Ⓐ Ⓑ Ⓒ Ⓓ	40. Ⓐ Ⓑ Ⓒ Ⓓ	50. Ⓐ Ⓑ Ⓒ Ⓓ

TEAR HERE

ISEE Practice Exam 1

TEST ONE: VERBAL ABILITY

40 QUESTIONS • TIME—20 MINUTES

The Verbal Ability Section includes two types of questions. There are separate directions for each type of question.

Directions: Each question is made up of a word in CAPITAL letters followed by four choices. Choose the one word that is most nearly the same in meaning as the word in CAPITAL letters and mark its letter on your answer sheet.

1. EARN
(A) long for
(B) practice for
(C) work for
(D) wish for

2. CHEERFUL
(A) happy
(B) discontented
(C) lecturing
(D) soothing

3. GENTLE
(A) cruel
(B) kindly
(C) true
(D) intolerant

4. AMIABLE
(A) forgetful
(B) friendly
(C) strange
(D) great

5. DANGER
(A) hazard
(B) safety
(C) defy
(D) venture

6. COMPELLED
(A) calculated
(B) combined
(C) collected
(D) forced

7. ALLY
(A) opponent
(B) passage
(C) friend
(D) preference

8. INTERNATIONAL
(A) between countries
(B) within a state
(C) about the country
(D) between schools

9. ENCOUNTER
(A) avoid
(B) discuss
(C) review
(D) meet

10. EXPLICIT
(A) ambiguous
(B) clearly stated
(C) give information about
(D) to blow out

GO ON TO THE NEXT PAGE

11. RETAIN
(A) pay out
(B) play
(C) keep
(D) inquire

12. CORRESPONDENCE
(A) letters
(B) files
(C) testimony
(D) response

13. LEGITIMATE
(A) democratic
(B) legal
(C) genealogical
(D) underworld

14. DEDUCT
(A) conceal
(B) understand
(C) subtract
(D) terminate

15. EGRESS
(A) extreme
(B) extra supply
(C) exit
(D) high price

16. HORIZONTAL
(A) marginal
(B) in a circle
(C) left and right
(D) up and down

17. CONTROVERSY
(A) publicity
(B) debate
(C) revolution
(D) revocation

18. PREEMPT
(A) steal
(B) empty
(C) preview
(D) appropriate

19. PER CAPITA
(A) for an entire population
(B) by income
(C) for each person
(D) for every adult

20. OPTIONAL
(A) not required
(B) infrequent
(C) choosy
(D) for sale

Directions: Each of the following questions is made up of a sentence containing one or two blanks. The sentences with one blank indicate that one word is missing. Sentences with two blanks have two missing words. Each sentence is followed by four choices. Choose the one word or pair of words that will best complete the meaning of the sentence as a whole, and mark the letter of your choice on your answer sheet.

21. Custom has so _____ our language that we can _____ only what has been said before.
(A) improved . . . repeat
(B) changed . . . understand
(C) enslaved . . . say
(D) dominated . . . hear

22. A few of the critics _____ the play, but in general they either disregarded or ridiculed it.
(A) discredited
(B) criticized
(C) denounced
(D) appreciated

23. Politicians are not the only ones who have made _____; being human, we have all blundered at some time in our lives.

(A) explanations
(B) arguments
(C) errors
(D) excuses

24. Because of his _____ nature, he often acts purely on impulse.

(A) stoic
(B) reflective
(C) passionate
(D) wistful

25. A system of education should be _____ by the _____ of students it turns out, for quality is preferred to quantity.

(A) controlled . . . intelligence
(B) justified . . . number
(C) examined . . . wealth
(D) judged . . . caliber

26. We seldom feel _____ when we are allowed to speak freely, but any _____ of our free speech brings anger.

(A) angry . . . defense
(B) blessed . . . restriction
(C) scholarly . . . understanding
(D) enslaved . . . misuse

27. The worst team lost because it had many players who though not completely _____ were also not really _____.

(A) qualified . . . agile
(B) clumsy . . . incompetent
(C) inept . . . proficient
(D) ungraceful . . . amateurish

28. Although the _____ of the legislature become law, the exact _____ of the law is the result of judicial interpretation.

(A) ideas . . . enforcement
(B) bills . . . wording
(C) works . . . punishment
(D) words . . . meaning

29. Since movies have become more _____, many people believe television to be _____.

(A) helpful . . . utilitarian
(B) expensive . . . necessary
(C) common . . . inadequate
(D) costly . . . useless

30. Spores are a form of life that remain _____ until environmental conditions exist in which they can become _____.

(A) inactive . . . vibrant
(B) hidden . . . dangerous
(C) suppressed . . . visible
(D) controlled . . . rampant

31. The spirit of science is always trying to lead people to the study of _____ and away from the spinning of fanciful theories out of their own minds.

(A) tradition
(B) order
(C) legalities
(D) literature

32. Both good and bad tastes exist in the world of art, and arguments about taste are _____.

(A) necessary
(B) exciting
(C) extraneous
(D) meaningful

33. The fame of the author does not _____ the quality of his or her works. We must avoid equating success with infallibility.

(A) prejudice
(B) assure
(C) dignify
(D) extol

GO ON TO THE NEXT PAGE

34. The mechanisms that develop hatred in man are most potent, since there is more _____ than _____ in the world.

(A) tolerance . . . prejudice

(B) joy . . . rapture

(C) love . . . hatred

(D) strife . . . tranquility

35. Mining is often called the _____ industry, since it neither creates nor replenishes what it takes.

(A) robber

(B) ecology

(C) natural

(D) evil

36. The racial problem is of such _____ that it makes going to the moon seem _____.

(A) complexity . . . helpful

(B) certainty . . . problematic

(C) magnitude . . . child's play

(D) docility . . . effortless

37. To be _____ a theatrical setting must resemble _____.

(A) believable . . . home

(B) effective . . . reality

(C) reasonable . . . beauty

(D) respectable . . . ideas

38. The _____ mob roamed through the streets of the city, shouting their _____ of law and order.

(A) influential . . . fear

(B) indifferent . . . horror

(C) disciplined . . . disrespect

(D) hysterical . . . hatred

39. Errors in existing theories are discovered, and the theories are either _____ or _____.

(A) improved . . . obeyed

(B) removed . . . followed

(C) altered . . . discarded

(D) explained . . . excused

40. In observing the _____ society of the ant, the scientist can learn much about the more _____ society of man.

(A) hostile . . . evil

(B) elementary . . . complicated

(C) plain . . . homogeneous

(D) unadorned . . . unsophisticated

STOP

END OF TEST ONE. IF YOU HAVE ANY TIME LEFT, GO OVER YOUR WORK ON THIS SECTION ONLY. DO NOT WORK IN ANY OTHER TEST OF THE EXAM.

TEST TWO: QUANTITATIVE ABILITY

40 QUESTIONS • TIME—35 MINUTES

General Directions: You may assume that all figures accompanying Quantitative Ability questions have been drawn as accurately as possible EXCEPT when it is specifically stated that a particular figure is not drawn to scale. Letters such as x, y, and n stand for real numbers. The Quantitative Ability Test includes two types of questions. There are separate directions for each type of question.

Directions: For questions 1–20 work each problem in your head or in the margins of the test booklet. Mark the letter of your answer choice on the answer sheet.

1. Two hundred million one hundred seventy-three thousand sixty three =

(A) 2,173,063

(B) 20,173,063

(C) 200,173,063

(D) 200,173,630

2. Which pair of values for x and □ will make the following statement true? $2x$ □ 8

(A) (6, <)

(B) (4, >)

(C) (0, <)

(D) (–3, >)

3. Complete the following statement: $7(3 \times \_\_\_\_\_) + 4 = 2104$

(A) 10

(B) 10 + 2

(C) 10^2

(D) 10^3

4. .5% is equal to

(A) .005

(B) .05

(C) $\frac{1}{2}$

(D) .5

5. A scalene triangle has

(A) two equal sides

(B) two equal sides and one right angle

(C) no equal sides

(D) three equal sides

6. A millimeter is what part of a meter?

(A) $\frac{1}{10}$

(B) $\frac{1}{100}$

(C) $\frac{1}{1,000}$

(D) $\frac{1}{10,000}$

7. What is the least common denominator for $\frac{2}{3}$, $\frac{1}{2}$, $\frac{5}{6}$, and $\frac{7}{9}$?

(A) 36

(B) 32

(C) 24

(D) 18

8. Find the area of a triangle whose dimensions are: $b = 14$ inches, $h = 20$ inches

(A) 140 square inches

(B) 208 square inches

(C) 280 square inches

(D) 288 square inches

9. What is the difference between $(4 \times 10^3) + 6$ and $(2 \times 10^3) + (3 \times 10) + 8$?

(A) 168

(B) 1,968

(C) 3,765

(D) 55,968

GO ON TO THE NEXT PAGE

10. $(10 \div 2) + (20 \times 3) + (6 + 7) =$
   (A) $(20 \div 2) + (10 \times 3) + (6 + 7)$
   (B) $(20 \times 3) + (6 + 7)\ (10 \div 2)$
   (C) $(20 \times 3) - (6 + 7) + (10 \div 2)$
   (D) $(6 + 7) \times (10 \div 2) + (20 \times 3)$

11. The set of common factors for 30 and 24 is
   (A) {1, 2, 3, 6}
   (B) {1, 2, 3, 4, 6}
   (C) {1, 2, 4, 6}
   (D) {1, 2, 4, 6, 12}

12.

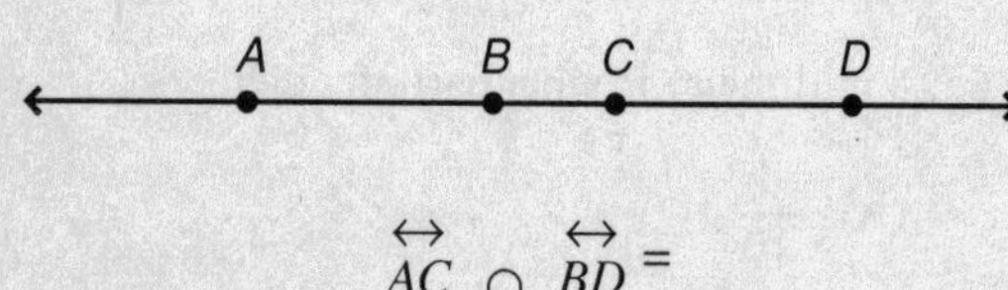

$\overleftrightarrow{AC} \cap \overleftrightarrow{BD} =$

   (A) $\overleftrightarrow{BC}$
   (B) $\overleftrightarrow{BD}$
   (C) $\overleftrightarrow{AC}$
   (D) $\overleftrightarrow{AD}$

13. The board shown below is six feet long, four inches wide, and two inches thick. One-third of it will be driven into the ground. How much surface area remains above ground?

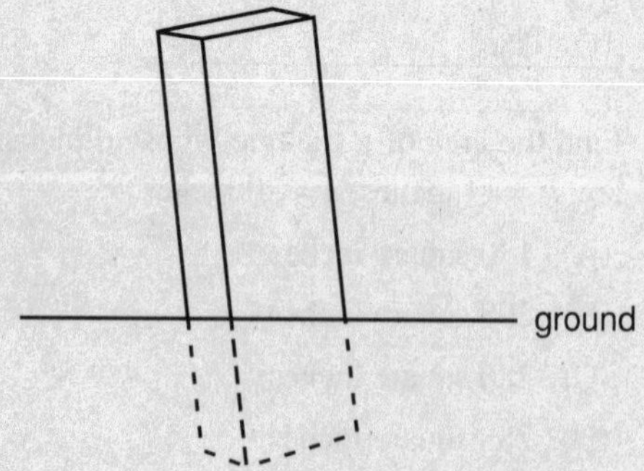

   (A) about 4 sq. ft.
   (B) slightly less than 5 sq. ft.
   (C) slightly more than 5 sq. ft.
   (D) about 8 sq. ft.

14. One runner can run M miles in H hours. Another faster runner can run N miles in L hours. The difference in their rates can be expressed as
   (A) $\dfrac{M - N}{H}$
   (B) $MH - HL$
   (C) $\dfrac{HN}{M - L}$
   (D) $\dfrac{N}{L} - \dfrac{M}{H}$

15. If Mary is x years old now and her sister is 3 years younger, then 5 years from now her sister will be what age?
   (A) $x + 5$ years
   (B) $x + 3$ years
   (C) $x + 2$ years
   (D) 8 years

16. In the figure below, the largest possible circle is cut out of a square piece of tin. The area of the remaining piece of tin is approximately (in square inches)

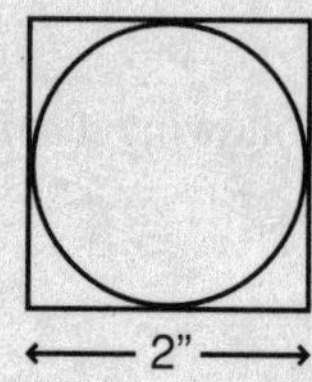

   (A) .14
   (B) .75
   (C) .86
   (D) 3.14

17. A square has an area of 49 sq. in. The number of inches in its perimeter is
   (A) 7
   (B) 14
   (C) 28
   (D) 98

18. If an engine pumps G gallons of water per minute, then the number of gallons pumped in half an hour may be found by

(A) taking one-half of G

(B) dividing 60 by G

(C) multiplying G by 30

(D) dividing 30 by G

19. $+1 - 1 + 1 - 1 + 1$ . . . and so on where the last number is + 1, has a sum of

(A) –1

(B) 0

(C) +1

(D) 2

20. Two cars start from the same point at the same time. One drives north at 20 miles an hour and the other drives south on the same straight road at 36 miles an hour. How many miles apart are they after 30 minutes?

(A) less than 10

(B) between 10 and 20

(C) between 20 and 30

(D) between 30 and 40

Directions: For questions 21–40, two quantities are given—one in Column A and the other in Column B. In some questions, further information concerning the quantities to be compared is centered above the entries in the two columns. Compare the quantities in the two columns and mark your answer sheet as follows:

(A) if the quantity in Column A is greater

(B) if the quantity in Column B is greater

(C) if the quantities are equal

(D) if the relationship cannot be determined from the information given

	Column A		Column B
21.	5% of 34		The number 34 is 5% of
22.		$s = 1$ $t = 3$ $a = -2$	
	$[5a(4t)]^3$		$[4a(5s)]^2$
23.		$4 > x > -3$	
	$\frac{x}{3}$		$\frac{3}{x}$

GO ON TO THE NEXT PAGE

COLUMN A		COLUMN B

24.

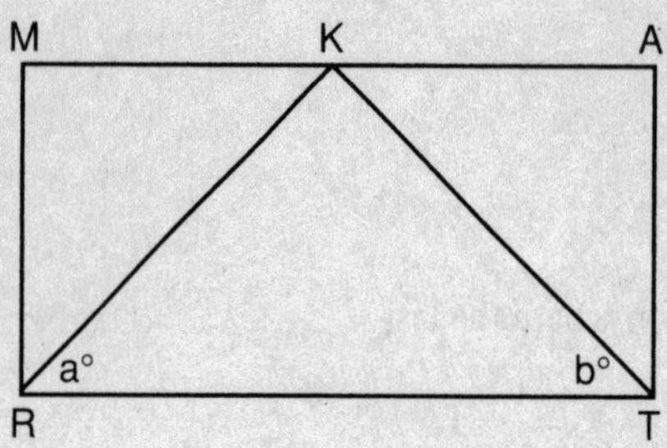

$a < b$

KR		*KT*
25. $\frac{2}{3} + \frac{3}{7}$		$\frac{16}{21} - \frac{3}{7}$

26.

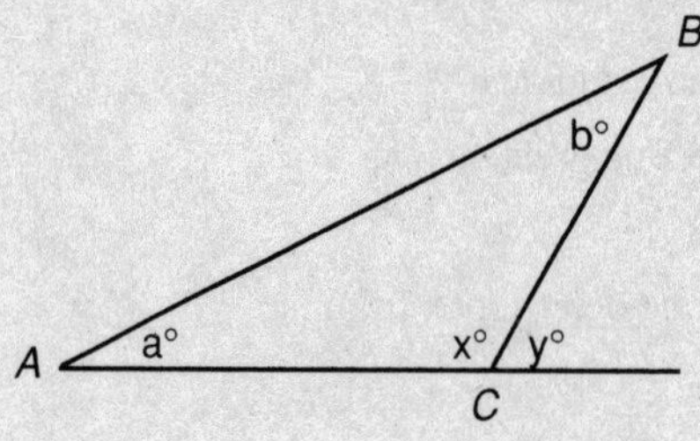

$a > b$

$x < a + b$

$a + b$		y

27. y = an odd integer

The numerical value of y^2		The numerical value of y^3
28. $(8 + 6) \div (3 - 7(2))$		$(6 + 8) \div (2 - 7(3))$
29. three-fourths of $\frac{9}{9}$		$\frac{9}{9} \bullet \frac{3}{4}$

	Column A		Column B

30.

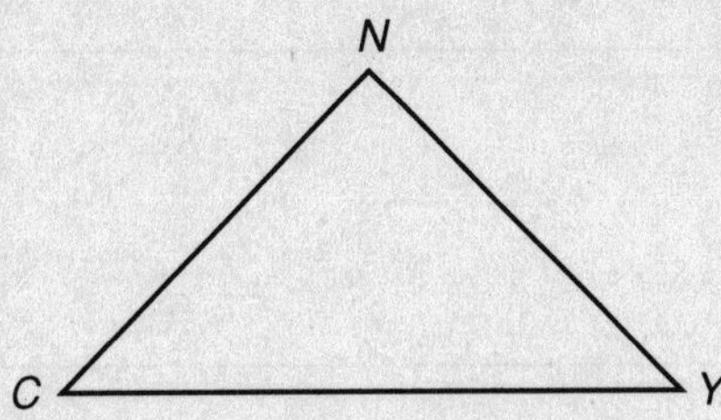

$NC = NY$

$\angle N > \angle C$

	Column A	Column B
30.	NC	CY
31.	$\frac{1}{\sqrt{9}}$	$\frac{1}{3}$
32.	$(5)\left(\frac{2}{3}\right)$	$\left(\frac{5}{3}\right)(2)$

33.

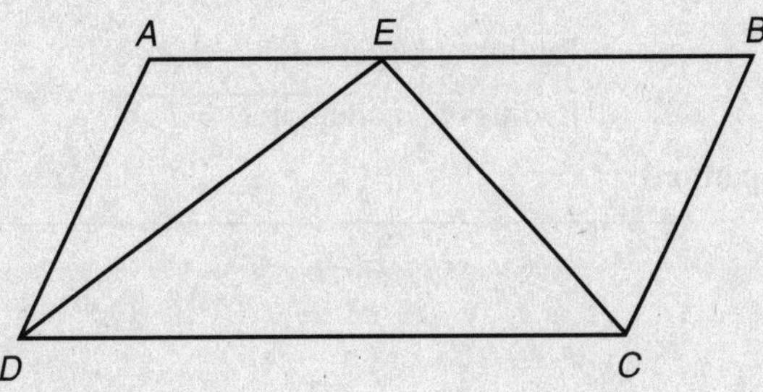

Parallelogram $ABCD$

E is a point on AB

	Column A	Column B
33.	Area of ΔDEC	Area of ΔAED + Area ΔEBC

34. $x = -1$

	Column A	Column B
34.	$x^3 + x^2 - x + 1$	$x^3 - x^2 + x - 1$

GO ON TO THE NEXT PAGE

	Column A	Column B
35.	The edge of a cube whose volume is 27	The edge of a cube whose total surface area is 54
36.	$\dfrac{\frac{1}{2}+\frac{1}{3}}{\frac{2}{3}}$	$\dfrac{\frac{2}{3}}{\frac{1}{2}+\frac{1}{3}}$
37.	Area of a circle whose radius is x^3	Area of a circle whose radius is $3x$
38.	Area of a circle with radius 7	Area of an equilateral triangle with side 14

39.

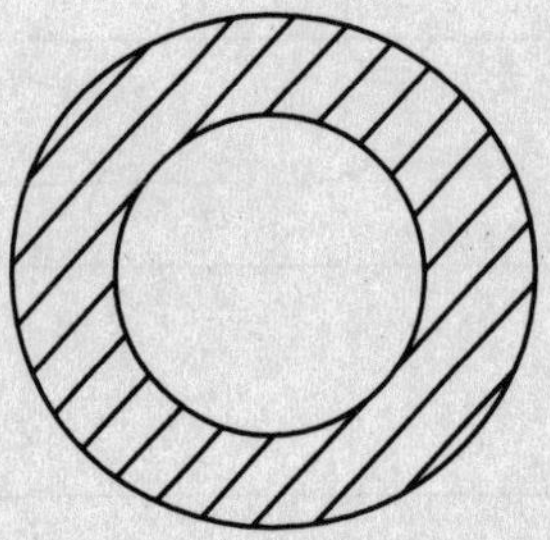

Radius of larger circle = 10

Radius of smaller circle = 7

Column A	Column B
Area of shaded portion	Area of smaller circle

40.

$a < 0 < b$

Column A	Column B
a^2	$\frac{b}{2}$

STOP

END OF TEST TWO. IF YOU HAVE ANY TIME LEFT, GO OVER YOUR WORK ON THIS SECTION ONLY. DO NOT WORK IN ANY OTHER TEST OF THE EXAM.

TEST THREE: READING COMPREHENSION

40 QUESTIONS • TIME—40 MINUTES

Directions: Each reading passage is followed by questions based on its content. Answer the questions on the basis of what is *stated* or *implied* in the passage. On your answer sheet, mark the letter of the answer you choose.

When we say a snake "glides," we have already persuaded ourselves to shiver a little. If we say that it "slithers," we are as good as undone. To avoid unsettling ourselves, we should state the simple fact—a snake walks.

A snake doesn't have any breastbone. The tips of its ribs are freemoving and amount, so to speak, to its feet. A snake walks along on its rib tips, pushing forward its ventral scutes at each "step," and it speeds up this mode of progress by undulating from side to side and by taking advantage of every rough "toehold" it can find in the terrain. Let's look at it this way: A human or other animal going forward on all fours is using a sort of locomotion that's familiar enough to all of us and isn't at all dismaying. Now: Suppose this walker is enclosed inside some sort of pliable encasement like a sacking. The front "feet" will still step forward, the "hind legs" still hitch along afterward. It will still be a standard enough sort of animal walking, only all we'll see now is a sort of wiggling of the sacking without visible feet. That's the snake way. A snake has its covering outside its feet, as an insect has its skeleton on its outside with no bones in the interior. There's nothing more "horrid" about the one arrangement than about the other.

1. The title below that expresses the main idea of this selection is
   - (A) Snake's "Legs"
   - (B) Comparing Snakes to People
   - (C) The Movement of a Snake
   - (D) A Slimy Animal

2. A snake's "feet" are its
   - (A) toes
   - (B) ribs
   - (C) side
   - (D) breastbone

3. The word *terrain* means
   - (A) terraced
   - (B) rocky ledge
   - (C) vertical hole
   - (D) ground areas

4. We may conclude that the author
   - (A) raises reptiles
   - (B) dislikes snakes
   - (C) is well informed about snakes
   - (D) thinks snakes move better than humans

When a luxury liner or a cargo ship nudges into her slip after an ocean crossing, her first physical contact with land is a heaving line. These streamers with a weight at the end called a "monkey fist" arch gracefully from deck to pier. On board the ship the heaving lines are tied to heavy, golden yellow manila mooring lines. Longshoremen quickly pull in the heaving lines until they can fasten the mooring lines to iron bollards (posts). Soon the ship is strung to her pier by four, eight, or as many as twenty-one nine-inch or ten-inch manila lines with perhaps a few wire ropes to stay motion fore and aft. The ship is secure against even the wrath of the storm or hurricane. A ship could dock without the aid of tugboats—and may have in New York in maritime strikes—but not without the lines to moor her to her berth.

GO ON TO THE NEXT PAGE

The maritime and the related fishing industry find perhaps 250 applications for rope and cordage. There are hundreds of different sizes, constructions, tensile strengths, and weights in rope and twine. Rope is sold by the pound but ordered by length, and is measured by circumference rather than by diameter. The maritime variety is made chiefly from fiber of the abaca, or manila plant, which is imported from the Philippines and Central America. Henequen from Mexico and Cuba, and sisal from Africa, the Netherlands East Indies, and other areas, are also used, but chiefly for twine. Nylon is coming into increasing use, particularly by towing companies. But it is six times more expensive than manila. However, nylon is much stronger, lighter in weight, and longer-wearing than manila. It is also more elastic and particularly adaptable for ocean towing.

5. In docking a ship, rope is

(A) only a little less important than a tugboat

(B) essential

(C) helpful but not necessary

(D) seldom used

6. A *monkey fist* is a

(A) device for weaving rope

(B) slang term for a longshoreman

(C) rope streamer

(D) weight at the end of a rope

7. Mooring ropes are

(A) ten inches in diameter

(B) twenty-one inches in circumference

(C) six times thicker than heaving ropes

(D) nine inches in circumference

8. Which of the following are not correctly paired?

(A) sisal from the Philippines

(B) henequen from Cuba

(C) abaca from Central America

(D) sisal from the Netherlands East Indies

In August of 1814, when news came that the British were advancing on Washington, three State Department clerks stuffed all records and valuable papers—including the Articles of Confederation, the Declaration of Independence, and the Constitution—into coarse linen sacks and smuggled them in carts to an unoccupied gristmill on the Virginia side of the Potomac. Later, fearing that a cannon factory nearby might attract a raiding party of the enemy, the clerks procured wagons from neighboring farmers, took the papers 35 miles away to Leesburg, and locked them in an empty house. It was not until the British fleet had left the waters of the Chesapeake that it was considered safe to return the papers to Washington.

On December 26, 1941, the five pages of the Constitution together with the single leaf of the Declaration of Independence were taken from the Library of Congress, where they had been kept for many years and were stored in the vaults of the United States Bullion Depository at Fort Knox, Kentucky. Here they "rode out the war" safely.

Since 1952, visitors to Washington may view these historic documents at the Exhibition Hall of the National Archives. Sealed in bronze and glass cases filled with helium, the documents are protected from touch, light, heat, dust, and moisture. At a moment's notice, they can be lowered into a large safe that is bombproof, shockproof, and fireproof.

9. Before the War of 1812, the Constitution and the Declaration of Independence were apparently kept in

(A) Independence Hall

(B) Fort Knox, Kentucky

(C) an office of the State Department

(D) a gristmill in Virginia

10. Nowadays, these documents are on view in the

(A) National Archives Exhibition Hall

(B) Library of Congress

(C) United States Bullion Depository

(D) United States Treasury Building

11. An important reason for the installation of a device to facilitate the quick removal of the documents is the

(A) possibility of a sudden disaster
(B) increasing number of tourists
(C) need for more storage space
(D) lack of respect for the documents

12. The documents have been removed from Washington at least twice in order to preserve them from

(A) dust, heat, and moisture
(B) careless handling
(C) possible war damage
(D) sale to foreign governments

On a population map of the world, deserts are shown as great blank spaces, but in fact, these areas contribute many things to our lives.

When you go to the market to buy a box of dates, you are buying a bit of sunshine and dry air from the oases of the Sahara Desert or the Coachella Valley. Fresh peas or a lettuce salad for your winter dinner might be the product of an irrigation farmer in the Salt River Valley or the Imperial Valley. That fine broadcloth shirt you received for your birthday was made from silky, long-fibered cotton grown in Egypt. A half-wool, half-cotton sweater might contain Australian wool and Peruvian cotton, which are steppe and desert products.

These are only a few of the contributions these desert areas make to the quality of our lives. They have also made important cultural contributions.

Our number system is derived from the system used by the ancient civilizations of Arabia. The use of irrigation to make farming of dry areas possible was developed by the inhabitants of desert regions. The necessity of measuring water levels and noting land boundaries following flooding by the Nile River led to the development of mathematics and the practice of surveying and engineering. The desert people were also our early astronomers. They studied the locations of the stars in order to find their way across the limitless expanse of the desert at night.

13. The population of the world's deserts is

(A) scattered
(B) starving
(C) large
(D) small

14. The Imperial Valley produces

(A) vegetables
(B) winter dinners
(C) shirts
(D) irrigation

15. According to this passage, broadcloth is made of

(A) wool
(B) cotton
(C) silk
(D) half wool, half cotton

16. Culturally, desert civilizations have

(A) made no contributions
(B) made important contributions
(C) not influenced western civilizations
(D) been blank spaces

17. Surveying was developed because people needed to

(A) study astronomy
(B) find their way across the deserts
(C) determine land boundaries after floods
(D) irrigate their crops

Residents of Montana laughingly refer to the small, windblown settlement of Ekalaka in the Eastern badlands as "Skeleton Flats," but as curious as it may sound, the name is appropriate. So many fossils have been dug up in this otherwise unremarkable town that it has become a paradise for paleontologists, scientists who use fossils to study prehistoric life forms. In fact,

GO ON TO THE NEXT PAGE

dinosaur bones are so plentiful in this area that ranchers have been known to use them as doorstops!

Ekalaka's fame began to grow more than 50 years ago when Walter H. Peck, whose hobby was geology, found the bones of a Stegosaurus, a huge, plant-eating dinosaur. The entire community soon became infected with Peck's enthusiasm for his find, and everyone began digging for dinosaur bones. Led by the local science teacher, groups of people would go out looking for new finds each weekend, and they rarely returned empty-handed. It would seem there is no end to the fossil riches to be found in Ekalaka.

Among the most prized finds were the remains of a Brontosaurus, an 80-foot-long monster that probably weighed 40 tons. The skeleton of a Triceratops was also found. The head of this prehistoric giant alone weighed more than 1,000 pounds. Careful searching also yielded small fossilized fishes, complete with stony scales, and the remains of a huge sea reptile.

The prize find was a Pachycephalosaurus, a dinosaur whose peculiar skull was several inches thick. When descriptions of it reached scientific circles in the east, there was great excitement because this particular prehistoric animal was then completely unknown to scientists.

18. In the first sentence, the author places "Skeleton Flats" in quotation marks to show that this phrase is

(A) a nickname given to the town by Montana residents, not the actual name of the town

(B) spelled incorrectly

(C) being spoken by someone other than the author

(D) a scientific term

19. This article is primarily about

(A) paleontology

(B) products of the state of Montana

(C) fossil finds in Ekalaka

(D) the Pachycephalosaurus

20. According to this passage, a paleontologist is

(A) someone whose hobby is geology

(B) a paradise

(C) a plant-eating dinosaur

(D) someone who studies fossils

21. In the third paragraph, the author is describing the

(A) bones of a Stegosaurus

(B) discovery of the first fossil finds in Ekalaka

(C) town of Ekalaka

(D) people of Ekalaka

22. Discovery of the Pachycephalosaurus caused excitement because

(A) its skull was several inches thick

(B) it was the first evidence of this creature ever found and reported to scientists

(C) news of it reached eastern scientific circles

(D) it received a prize

Powdered zirconium is more fiery and violent than the magnesium powder that went into wartime incendiary bombs. Under some conditions, it can be ignited with a kitchen match, and it cannot be extinguished with water. Munitions makers once tried to incorporate it into explosives, but turned it down as too dangerous for even them to handle.

But when this strange metal is transformed into a solid bar or sheet or tube, as lustrous as burnished silver, its temper changes. It is so docile that it can be used by surgeons as a safe covering plate for sensitive brain tissues. It is almost as strong as steel, and it can be exposed to hydrochloric acid or nitric acid without corroding.

Zirconium is also safe and stable when it is bound up with other elements to form mineral compounds which occur in abundant deposits in North and South America, India, and Australia. Although it is classified as a rare metal, it is more abundant in the earth's crust than nickel, copper,

tungsten, tin, or lead. Until a few years ago, scarcely a dozen people had ever seen zirconium in pure form, but today it is the wonder metal of a fantastic new industry, a vital component of television, radar, and radio sets, an exciting structural material for chemical equipment and for superrockets and jet engines, and a key metal for atomic piles.

23. The title that best expresses the main idea of this selection is

(A) A Vital Substance
(B) A Safe, Stable Substance
(C) Zirconium's Uses in Surgery
(D) Characteristics of Zirconium

24. The word *docile* in line 11 means

(A) calm
(B) pliable
(C) strong
(D) profuse

25. The selection emphasizes that

(A) zirconium rusts easily
(B) chemists are finding uses for zirconium
(C) keys are often made of zirconium nowadays
(D) zirconium is less abundant in the earth's crust than lead

26. Zirconium is *not* safe to handle when it is

(A) lustrous
(B) powdered
(C) in tubes
(D) in bar form

27. The selection tells us that zirconium

(A) is a metal
(B) is fireproof
(C) dissolves in water
(D) is stronger than steel

28. Zirconium is likely to be useful in all of these fields *except*

(A) surgery
(B) television
(C) atomic research
(D) the manufacture of fireworks

About the year 1812 two steam ferryboats were built under the direction of Robert Fulton for crossing the Hudson River, and one of the same description was built for service on the East River. These boats were what are known as twin boats, each of them having two complete hulls united by a deck or bridge. Because these boats were pointed at both ends and moved equally well with either end foremost, they crossed and recrossed the river without losing any time in turning about. Fulton also contrived, with great ingenuity, floating docks for the reception of the ferryboats and a means by which they were brought to the docks without a shock. These boats were the first of a fleet that has since carried hundreds of millions of passengers to and from New York.

29. The title that best expresses the main idea of this selection is

(A) Crossing the Hudson River by Boat
(B) Transportation of Passengers
(C) The Invention of Floating Docks
(D) The Beginning of Steam Ferryboat Service

30. The steam ferryboats were known as twin boats because

(A) they had two complete hulls united by a bridge
(B) they could move as easily forward as backward
(C) each ferryboat had two captains
(D) two boats were put into service at the same time

GO ON TO THE NEXT PAGE

31. Which statement is *true* according to the selection?

(A) Boats built under Fulton's direction are still in use.

(B) Fulton planned a reception to celebrate the first ferryboat.

(C) Fulton piloted the first steam ferryboats across the Hudson.

(D) Fulton developed a satisfactory way of docking the ferryboats.

32. Robert Fulton worked in the

(A) seventeenth century

(B) eighteenth century

(C) nineteenth century

(D) twentieth century

33. In line 14, the word *shock* is used to mean

(A) an unpleasant surprise

(B) an impact

(C) an illness following an accident

(D) an electrical impulse

Between 1780 and 1790, in piecemeal fashion, a trail was established between Catskill on the Hudson and the frontier outpost, Ithaca, in the Finger Lakes country. This path, by grace of following the valleys, managed to thread its way through the mountains by what are on the whole surprisingly easy grades. Ultimately, this route became the Susquehanna Turnpike, but in popular speech it was just the Ithaca Road. It was, along with the Mohawk Turnpike and the Great Western Turnpike, one of the three great east-west highways of the state. Eventually it was the route taken by thousands of Yankee farmers, more especially Connecticut Yankees, seeking new fortunes in southwestern New York. Along it, the tide of pioneer immigration flowed at flood crest for a full generation.

As the road left Catskill, there was no stream that might not be either forded or crossed on a crude bridge until the traveler reached the Susquehanna, which was a considerable river and a real obstacle to his progress. The road came down out of the Catskills via the valley of the Ouleout Creek and struck the Susquehanna just above the present village of Unadilla. Hither about the year 1784 came a Connecticut man, Nathaniel Wattles. He provided both a skiff and a large flat-bottomed scow so that the homeseeker, his family, team, and household baggage, and oftentimes a little caravan of livestock, might be set across the river dry-shod and in safety. Wattles here established an inn where one might find lodging and entertainment, and a general store where might be purchased such staples as were essential for the journey. So it was that Wattles' Ferry became the best known landmark on the Ithaca Road.

34. The author indicates that the Susquehanna Turnpike

(A) began as a narrow trail

(B) was the most important north-south highway in the state

(C) furnished travelers with surprising obstacles

(D) went out of use after a generation

35. The western end of the Susquehanna Turnpike was located at

(A) the Hudson River

(B) the Connecticut border

(C) Ithaca

(D) Catskill

36. The Susquehanna Turnpike was also known as

(A) the Ithaca Road

(B) Wattles' Ferry

(C) the Catskill Trail

(D) the Mohawk Turnpike

37. According to this selection, Nathaniel Wattles was prepared to offer travelers all of the following *except*

(A) guides

(B) a place to sleep

(C) entertainment

(D) groceries

As of December, 1983, there were 391 species listed as endangered. Today over 650 have been listed including 282 mammals, 214 birds, 59 reptiles, 49 fishes, 26 mollusks, 16 amphibians, and 8 insects. We hope to provide protection to another 600 species by the end of 1988. Although only four species of plants have been designated as endangered, with the establishment of five botanist positions in 1985, it is expected that 200 will be listed by the end of 1987.

Success should not be measured by the number of species listed; the goal is to return the species to the point where they are no longer endangered. This Department would be just as negligent in the performance of its duties under the Act for not delisting a species that has recovered as it would be for not listing a critical species. We have not had the staffing or funding to review all of the species listed at the time of the 1983 Act.

38. It can be inferred that very few plants had been listed by 1983 because

(A) very few are close to extinction

(B) the Department doesn't classify plants

(C) no botanists were on the staff at the time

(D) some endangered mammals eat plants

39. Which of the following is not stated in the passage?

(A) Eight insects have been listed as endangered.

(B) By the end of 1987, many plants will be added to the list.

(C) The Department considers listing species more important than de-listing them.

(D) The Department lacked staffing to review all listed species.

40. "Success should not be measured by the number . . . " What is a reasonable inference concerning the purpose of this statement?

(A) To avoid mentioning that the computer that kept count malfunctioned

(B) Because measurement is always statistically difficult

(C) Because the concept of success has been abused in recent years

(D) To counteract criticism that the Department was not listing enough species

STOP

END OF TEST THREE. IF YOU HAVE ANY TIME LEFT, GO OVER YOUR WORK ON THIS SECTION ONLY. DO NOT WORK IN ANY OTHER TEST OF THE EXAM.

TEST FOUR: MATHEMATICS ACHIEVEMENT

50 QUESTIONS • TIME—40 MINUTES

Directions: Each question is followed by four answer choices. Choose the correct answer to each question, and mark its letter on your answer sheet.

1. A square measures 8 inches on one side. By how much will the area be increased if its length is increased by 4 inches and its width decreased by 2 inches?

(A) 14 sq. in.

(B) 12 sq. in.

(C) 10 sq. in.

(D) 8 sq. in.

2. $r = 35 - (3 + 6)(-n)$

$n = 2$

$r =$

(A) 53

(B) 17

(C) –17

(D) –53

3. $(3 + 4)^3 =$

(A) 21

(B) 91

(C) 343

(D) 490

4. Aluminum bronze consists of copper and aluminum, usually in the ratio of 10:1 by weight. If an object made of this alloy weighs 77 pounds, how many pounds of aluminum does it contain?

(A) 7.0

(B) 7.7

(C) 10

(D) 70.0

5. How many boxes 2 inches × 3 inches × 4 inches can fit into a carton 2 feet × 3 feet × 4 feet?

(A) 100

(B) 144

(C) 1000

(D) 1728

6. An elderly couple took a prepaid bus tour from their home near Ft. Lauderdale to Disney World. The trip, which included transportation, motel, meals, and admissions, cost them $143 each. With their first restaurant dinner, they each ordered a cocktail and dessert, which was "extra" on the dinner. The charge was $7.00. The second evening, they had cocktails before dinner at a cost of $4.50. When they returned to Ft. Lauderdale, they tipped the bus driver $3.00. How much cash did they spend on the trip?

(A) $14.50

(B) $29.00

(C) $157.50

(D) $300.50

7. A clerk can add 40 columns of figures an hour by using an adding machine and 20 columns of figures an hour without using an adding machine. What is the total number of hours it will take the clerk to add 200 columns of figures if $\frac{3}{5}$ of the work is done by machine and the rest without the machine?

(A) 6 hours

(B) 7 hours

(C) 8 hours

(D) 9 hours

8. Mr. Lawson makes a weekly salary of $150 plus 7% commission on his sales. What will his income be for a week in which he makes sales totaling $945?

(A) $196.15

(B) $206.15

(C) $216.15

(D) $226.15

9. Solve for x: $x^2 + 5 = 41$

(A) 6

(B) 7

(C) 8

(D) 9

10. Two rectangular boards each measuring 5 feet by 3 feet are placed together to make one large board. How much shorter will the perimeter be if the two long sides are placed together than if the two short sides are placed together?

(A) 2 feet

(B) 4 feet

(C) 6 feet

(D) 8 feet

11. If a plane travels 1,000 miles in 5 hours 30 minutes, what is its average speed in miles per hour?

(A) $181\frac{9}{11}$

(B) $191\frac{1}{2}$

(C) 200

(D) 215

12. A jacket that normally sells for $35 can be purchased on sale for 2,975 pennies. What is the rate of discount represented by the sale price?

(A) 5%

(B) 10%

(C) 15%

(D) 20%

13. A stock clerk has on hand the following items:

500 pads worth four cents each

130 pencils worth three cents each

50 dozen rubber bands worth two cents per dozen

If, from this stock, he issues 125 pads, 45 pencils, and 48 rubber bands, the value of the remaining stock would be

(A) $6.43

(B) $8.95

(C) $17.63

(D) $18.47

14. Two years ago a company purchased 500 dozen pencils at 40 cents per dozen. This year only 75 percent as many pencils were purchased as were purchased two years ago, but the price was 20 percent higher than the old price. What was the total cost of pencils purchased by the company this year?

(A) $180

(B) $187.50

(C) $240

(D) $257.40

15. An adult's ski lift ticket costs twice as much as a child's. If a family of three children and two adults can ski for $49, what is the cost of an adult ticket?

(A) $7

(B) $10

(C) $12

(D) $14

16. Solve for x: $\frac{x}{2} + 36 = 37.25$

(A) 2.5

(B) 3.5

(C) 12.5

(D) 18.5

GO ON TO THE NEXT PAGE

17. A group of 6 people raised $690 for charity. One of the people raised 35% of the total. What was the amount raised by the other 5 people?

(A) $448.50

(B) $241.50

(C) $89.70

(D) $74.75

18. If the scale on a blueprint is $\frac{1}{4}$ inch = 1 foot, give the blueprint dimensions of a room that is actually 29 feet long and 23 feet wide.

(A) $6\frac{3}{4}" \times 6"$

(B) $7\frac{1}{4}" \times 5\frac{1}{2}"$

(C) $7\frac{1}{4}" \times 5\frac{3}{4}"$

(D) $7\frac{1}{2}" \times 5\frac{1}{4}"$

19. On a recent trip, the Smiths drove at an average speed of 55 miles per hour. If the trip took $5\frac{1}{2}$ hours, how many miles did they drive?

(A) 320.75

(B) 320.5

(C) 312.50

(D) 302.5

20. Find the area of a rectangle with a length of 176 feet and a width of 79 feet.

(A) 13,904 sq. ft.

(B) 13,854 sq. ft.

(C) 13,804 sq. ft.

(D) 13,304 sq. ft.

21. The scale used on a blueprint is $\frac{1}{4}" = 1$ foot. If a room is drawn as $10" \times 13"$, what are its actual dimensions?

(A) $40' \times 52'$

(B) $36' \times 40'$

(C) $20.5' \times 30.5'$

(D) $2\frac{3}{4}' \times 3\frac{1}{2}'$

22. $63 \div \frac{1}{9} = ?$

(A) 7

(B) 56

(C) 67

(D) 567

23. With an 18% discount, John was able to save $13.23 on a coat. What was the original price of the coat?

(A) $69.75

(B) $71.50

(C) $73.50

(D) $74.75

24. If it takes 3 men 56 minutes to fill a trench $4' \times 6' \times 5'$, and two of the men work twice as rapidly as the third, the number of minutes that it will take the two faster men alone to fill this trench is

(A) 70 minutes

(B) 60 minutes

(C) 50 minutes

(D) 40 minutes

25. Population figures for a certain area show there are $1\frac{1}{2}$ times as many single men as single women in the area. The total population is 18,000. There are 1,122 married couples, with 756 children. How many single men are there in the area?

(A) 3,000

(B) 6,000

(C) 9,000

(D) cannot be determined from the information given

26. If a vehicle is to complete a 20-mile trip at an average rate of 30 miles per hour, it must complete the trip in

(A) 20 minutes

(B) 30 minutes

(C) 40 minutes

(D) 50 minutes

27. Solve for x: $2x^2 + 3 = 21$

(A) 3

(B) 5

(C) 9

(D) 10

28. Find the area of a circle whose diameter is 6".

(A) 29.26

(B) 28.26

(C) 27.96

(D) 27.26

29. The scale on a map is $\frac{1}{8}$" = 25 miles. If two cities are $3\frac{7}{8}$" apart on the map, what is the actual distance between them?

(A) 31 miles

(B) 56 miles

(C) 675 miles

(D) 775 miles

30. A house was valued at $83,000 and insured for 80% of that amount. Find the yearly premium if it is figured at $.45 per hundred dollars of value.

(A) $83.80

(B) $252.63

(C) $298.80

(D) $664.00

31. If a certain job can be performed by 18 clerks in 26 days, the number of clerks needed to perform the job in 12 days is

(A) 24 clerks

(B) 30 clerks

(C) 39 clerks

(D) 52 clerks

32. $72.61 \div .05 = ?$

(A) 1.45220

(B) 14.522

(C) 145.220

(D) 1,452.20

33. A car dealer sold three different makes of cars. The price of the first make was $4,200, the second $4,800, and the third $5,400. The total sales were $360,000. If three times as many of the third car were sold as the first, and twice as many of the second make were sold than the first, how many cars of the third make were sold?

(A) 15

(B) 24

(C) 36

(D) insufficient information

34. One third of the number of people attending a football game were admitted at $\frac{1}{2}$ the normal price of admission. How many people paid full price, if the gate receipts were $42,000?

(A) 2,800

(B) 3,500

(C) 5,000

(D) insufficient information

35.
 7 days 3 hours 20 minutes
− 4 days 9 hours 31 minutes

(A) 2 days 17 hours 49 minutes

(B) 2 days 17 hours 69 minutes

(C) 3 days 10 hours 49 minutes

(D) 3 days 10 hours 69 minutes

36. Find the area of a triangle whose dimensions are b = 12', h = 14'.

(A) 168 sq. ft.

(B) 84 sq. ft.

(C) 42 sq. ft.

(D) 24 sq. ft.

37. Increased by 150%, the number 72 becomes

(A) 108

(B) 170

(C) 180

(D) 188

GO ON TO THE NEXT PAGE

38. Which equation represents the statement four times a certain number divided by three, minus six, equals two?

(A) $\frac{4n}{3} - 6 = 2$

(B) $4n^2 - 6 = 2$

(C) $4n^2 \div 3 - 6 = 2$

(D) $\left(\frac{1}{4}n \div 3\right) - 6 = 2$

39. If $14x - 2y = 32$ and $x + 2y = 13$, then $x = ?$

(A) 8

(B) 5

(C) 4

(D) 3

40. A die is thrown. What are the odds that it will come up 1?

(A) $\frac{1}{4}$

(B) $\frac{1}{6}$

(C) $\frac{1}{8}$

(D) $\frac{1}{12}$

41. Which is the longest time?

(A) 25 hours

(B) 1,440 minutes

(C) $\frac{1}{2}$ a day

(D) 3,600 seconds

42. Two cars are 550 miles apart, both traveling on the same road. If one travels at 50 miles per hour, the other at 60 miles per hour, and they both leave at 1:00 PM, what time will they meet?

(A) 4:00 PM

(B) 4:30 PM

(C) 5:45 PM

(D) 6:00 PM

43. Write 493 in expanded form, using exponents.

(A) $(4 \times 10^3) + (9 \times 10^2) + (3 \times 10)$

(B) $(4 \times 10^2) + (9 \times 10) + 3$

(C) $(4 \times 10^2) + (9 \times 10) - 7$

(D) $(4 \times 10^1) + (9 \times 10) + 3$

44. If 10 workers earn $5,400 in 12 days, how much will 6 workers earn in 15 days?

(A) $10,500

(B) $5,400

(C) $4,050

(D) $2,025

45. The scale of a particular map is $\frac{3}{8}$" = 5 miles. If the distance between points A and B is $4\frac{1}{2}$" on the map, what is the distance in actuality?

(A) 12 miles

(B) 36 miles

(C) 48 miles

(D) 60 miles

46. Find the diameter of a circle whose area is 78.5 sq. in.

(A) 25 feet

(B) 10 feet

(C) 25 inches

(D) 10 inches

47. If $ab + 4 = 52$, and $a = 6$, $b = ?$

(A) 4

(B) 8

(C) 21

(D) 42

48. If $\frac{2}{3}$ of a jar is filled with water in one minute, how many minutes longer will it take to fill the jar?

(A) $\frac{1}{4}$

(B) $\frac{1}{3}$

(C) $\frac{1}{2}$

(D) $\frac{2}{3}$

49. A group left on a trip at 8:50 AM and reached its destination at 3:30 PM. How long, in hours and minutes, did the trip take?

(A) 3 hours 10 minutes
(B) 4 hours 40 minutes
(C) 5 hours 10 minutes
(D) 6 hours 40 minutes

50. A square is changed into a rectangle by increasing its length 10% and decreasing its width 10%. Its area

(A) remains the same
(B) decreases by 10%
(C) increases by 1%
(D) decreases by 1%

STOP

END OF TEST FOUR. IF YOU HAVE ANY TIME LEFT, GO OVER YOUR WORK ON THIS SECTION ONLY. DO NOT WORK IN ANY OTHER TEST OF THE EXAM.

TEST FIVE: ESSAY

TIME—30 MINUTES

Directions: Write a legible, coherent, and correct essay on the following topic.

Topic: If you could spend an afternoon with any author, living or dead, with whom would you spend it? What would you talk about?

Independent School Entrance Examination Practice Exam 1

Answer Key

TEST ONE: VERBAL ABILITY

1. **C**	9. **D**	17. **B**	25. **D**	33. **B**
2. **A**	10. **B**	18. **D**	26. **B**	34. **D**
3. **B**	11. **C**	19. **C**	27. **C**	35. **A**
4. **B**	12. **A**	20. **A**	28. **D**	36. **C**
5. **A**	13. **B**	21. **C**	29. **B**	37. **B**
6. **D**	14. **C**	22. **D**	30. **A**	38. **D**
7. **C**	15. **C**	23. **C**	31. **B**	39. **C**
8. **A**	16. **C**	24. **C**	32. **C**	40. **B**

TEST TWO: QUANTITATIVE ABILITY

1. **C**	9. **B**	17. **C**	25. **A**	33. **C**
2. **C**	10. **B**	18. **C**	26. **C**	34. **A**
3. **C**	11. **A**	19. **C**	27. **D**	35. **C**
4. **A**	12. **A**	20. **C**	28. **B**	36. **A**
5. **C**	13. **A**	21. **B**	29. **C**	37. **D**
6. **C**	14. **D**	22. **B**	30. **B**	38. **A**
7. **D**	15. **C**	23. **D**	31. **C**	39. **A**
8. **A**	16. **C**	24. **A**	32. **C**	40. **D**

TEST THREE: READING COMPREHENSION

1. **C**	9. **C**	17. **C**	25. **B**	33. **B**
2. **B**	10. **A**	18. **A**	26. **B**	34. **A**
3. **D**	11. **A**	19. **C**	27. **A**	35. **C**
4. **C**	12. **C**	20. **D**	28. **D**	36. **A**
5. **B**	13. **D**	21. **D**	29. **D**	37. **A**
6. **D**	14. **A**	22. **B**	30. **A**	38. **C**
7. **D**	15. **B**	23. **D**	31. **D**	39. **C**
8. **A**	16. **B**	24. **A**	32. **C**	40. **D**

TEST FOUR: MATHEMATICS ACHIEVEMENT

1. **D**	11. **A**	21. **A**	31. **C**	41. **A**
2. **A**	12. **C**	22. **D**	32. **D**	42. **D**
3. **C**	13. **D**	23. **C**	33. **C**	43. **B**
4. **A**	14. **A**	24. **A**	34. **D**	44. **C**
5. **D**	15. **D**	25. **C**	35. **A**	45. **D**
6. **A**	16. **A**	26. **C**	36. **B**	46. **D**
7. **B**	17. **A**	27. **A**	37. **C**	47. **B**
8. **C**	18. **C**	28. **B**	38. **A**	48. **C**
9. **A**	19. **D**	29. **D**	39. **D**	49. **D**
10. **B**	20. **A**	30. **C**	40. **B**	50. **D**

Independent School Entrance Examination Practice Exam 1

Explanatory Answers

TEST ONE: VERBAL ABILITY

SYNONYMS

1. **(C)** To EARN is to *gain* or to *receive as a result of one's labors or services*. If you study hard, you may earn a high score on your ISEE.
2. **(A)** CHEERFUL, full of cheer, means *joyful* and *happy*. The cheerful child skipped into the kindergarten room each morning.
3. **(B)** GENTLE, from a root meaning "noble," means *courteous, soft,* and *kind*. The wise principal had a gentle manner even when correcting misbehavior.
4. **(B)** AMIABLE means *good-natured* and *loveable*. The amiable dog wagged its tail at the letter carrier.
5. **(A)** A DANGER is a liability to harm, a peril, a risk, or a hazard. Upstairs windows without safety guards present a danger to small children.
6. **(D)** To COMPEL is to *force*. Our government compels us to pay income taxes each year on April 15th.
7. **(C)** An ALLY is another with a common purpose, an associate, or a helper. Great Britain was our ally during World War II. The word meaning "passage" is "alley."
8. **(A)** INTERNATIONAL means *between or among nations*. Because each country has its own special interests, international relations require a great deal of tact and diplomacy.
9. **(D)** To ENCOUNTER is to *meet face-to-face*, either accidentally or in hostilities. The opposing attorneys had a brief encounter in the courthouse corridor.
10. **(B)** EXPLICIT means *distinct, observable,* or *clearly stated*. The explicit instructions on the package left no opportunity for misunderstanding or error.
11. **(C)** To RETAIN is to *hold on to* or *to keep*. Retain the receipt as proof of payment.
12. **(A)** CORRESPONDENCE is *an exchange of letters* or the *letters* themselves. I save all my correspondence with the schools to which I have applied in an envelope marked "High Schools."
    Note: "Correspondence" can also mean "agreement" or "conformity." Your exam will never offer you a choice of two correct meanings for the same word.
13. **(B)** LEGITIMATE means *conforming to the law* or *abiding by the rules*. Since his name is on the deed, he has a legitimate claim to ownership of the property.
14. **(C)** To DEDUCT is to *subtract*. Each week, my employer deducts social security taxes from my paycheck. The word with a meaning close to "understand" is "deduce."
15. **(C)** The EGRESS is the *way out*. The egress is marked with a red "EXIT" sign.
16. **(C)** HORIZONTAL, parallel to the horizon, means *flat* or *left-to-right* as opposed to "vertical." Place the large books horizontally on the shelf so that they do not topple over.
17. **(B)** CONTROVERSY is *exchange of opposing opinions* or *argument*. The choice of new wallpaper is a subject of controversy.
18. **(D)** To PREEMPT is to *seize before anyone else can* or to *appropriate*. No dishonesty is implied, just speed or privilege. The president's speech will preempt the time slot usually taken by my favorite game show.
19. **(C)** PER CAPITA literally means *for each head*, therefore *for each person*, one-by-one, with age irrelevant. The per capita consumption of red meat has dropped to two pounds per week.
20. **(A)** That which is OPTIONAL is *left to one's choice* and is therefore *not required*. You must study English and history, but study of a musical instrument is optional.

SENTENCE COMPLETIONS

21. **(C)** The sense of the sentence calls for a word with a negative connotation in the first blank; therefore, we need consider only (C) and (D). Of these choices, ENSLAVED . . . SAY, (C), is clearly the better completion.
22. **(D)** Since it is stated that most critics disregarded or ridiculed the play, the few critics remaining must have done the opposite, or APPRECIATED the work.
23. **(C)** The word that is needed must be a synonym for blunder (a stupid or gross mistake). That word is ERROR.
24. **(C)** One who acts purely on impulse is most likely to have a PASSIONATE (emotional or intense) nature.
25. **(D)** If "quality is preferred to quantity" in an educational system, then the measure by which that system should be JUDGED is the CALIBER (degree of ability or merit) of the students it produces.
26. **(B)** Freedom of speech is something we take for granted, so we do not feel BLESSED when allowed to exercise this freedom; however, we do become angry when any RESTRICTION (limit) is imposed on our right to speak freely.
27. **(C)** The qualities attributed to the players on the worst team must be opposites for comparison and adjectives for parallelism within the sentence. INEPT, which means awkward, and PROFICIENT, which means skilled, comprise the only choice that meets both requirements.
28. **(D)** It is the function of the legislature to write laws (their WORDS become law). It is the function of the judiciary to interpret the words of the law (to determine their MEANING).
29. **(B)** Movies and television are both media of entertainment. The sentence compares the two media in terms of their cost, stating that many people believe television (which is free after the initial investment in the set) is NECESSARY because movies have become so EXPENSIVE (and therefore out of reach for many people).
30. **(A)** The sense of the sentence calls for two words that are opposites and that can both be applied to life forms. Spores are the tiny particles in certain plants that act as seeds in the production of new plants. These spores remain dormant or INACTIVE until the proper conditions exist to render them vigorous or VIBRANT, thus creating a new generation of plants.
31. **(B)** The completion needed is a word that is opposite in meaning to "the spinning of fanciful theories." Of the choices given, the study of ORDER best fulfills this requirement.
32. **(C)** Taste is a matter of individual preference, and personal preference in the world of art is a private concern with no effect on the world at large. Therefore, arguments about taste are EXTRANEOUS (unnecessary).
33. **(B)** The second sentence provides the clue to the meaning of the first. If success does not mean infallibility (certainty), then the fame of an author does not ASSURE the quality of his or her work.
34. **(D)** The completion here demands words that are opposites. In addition, the first blank requires a word that would promote hatred. Only STRIFE, meaning conflict, and TRANQUILITY, meaning peace, fulfill these requirements and complete the meaning of the sentence.
35. **(A)** Since mining takes away without replacing what it takes, it may be called a ROBBER industry. With these characteristics, mining might also be considered to be evil, but ROBBER is the most specific completion. It is the adjective that best describes an industry that does not replenish what it takes.
36. **(C)** This sentence presents two problems that are being compared in terms of the ease of their solution. The only choices that fulfill the requirements of such a comparison are MAGNITUDE and CHILD'S PLAY.
37. **(B)** A theatrical setting serves to create a mood or a feeling of being in another time or place. If the setting is to be EFFECTIVE (to make the desired impression on the audience), it must have some semblance of REALITY.
38. **(D)** The word "mob" has a negative connotation and requires an adjective that is also negative. HYSTERICAL (emotional and unmanageable) best meets this requirement. The emotion that a shouting mob is most likely to show is HATRED of law and order.

39. **(C)** When errors are discovered in existing theories, those theories must either be ALTERED (changed) in the light of the new information or they must be DISCARDED altogether, if the new information renders the old theories false.

40. **(B)** The sentence compares two different societies and therefore requires completions that are both parallel and opposite. ELEMENTARY (simple) and COMPLICATED (intricate) best meet these requirements.

TEST TWO: QUANTITATIVE ABILITY

1. **(C)**

2. **(C)** If $x = 0$, then $2x < 8$ because $2(0) < 8$. None of the other pairs results in a true statement.

3. **(C)** Substitute n for the blank space.

$$7(3 \times n) + 4 = 2104$$
$$7(3n) + 4 = 2104$$
$$21n + 4 = 2104$$
$$21n = 2100$$
$$n = 100, \text{ or } 10^2$$

4. **(A)** Since 1% = .01, one half of one percent is written .005. Refer to the percentage review section for help if necessary.

5. **(C)** A scalene triangle has no equal sides.

6. **(C)** There are 1,000 millimeters in a meter.

7. **(D)** Answer (A) is also a common denominator, but it is not the least common denominator.

8. **(A)** The area of a triangle is found by using $A = \frac{1}{2}bh$.

$$A = \frac{1}{2} \bullet 14 \bullet 20$$
$$= 140 \text{ sq. in.}$$

9. **(B)** $(4 \times 10^3) + 6 = 4{,}006$

$(2 \times 10^3) + (3 \times 10) + 8 = 2{,}038$

The difference is 1,968.

10. **(B)** The order of the addends does not affect the value of the sum.

11. **(A)** The set of factors for 24 is:

{1,2,3,4,6,8,12,24}

The set of factors for 30 is:

{1,2,3,5,6,10,15,30}

The set of common factors is:

{1,2,3,6}

12. **(A)** The intersection of the two line segments is the place they overlap. Note that they overlap in the interval marked $\overline{BC}$.

13. **(A)** One third of the board will be driven into the ground, leaving 4 feet exposed. The exposed part of the board has 5 faces: two faces 4 feet long by 4 inches wide; two faces 4 feet long by 2 inches wide; and one face (the end) 2 inches by 4 inches. Because the answer choices are in units of square feet, we will calculate in square feet:

$$2 \bullet 4 \bullet \frac{1}{3} = \frac{8}{3} \text{ or } 2\frac{2}{3} \text{ sq. ft.}$$
$$2 \bullet 4 \bullet \frac{1}{6} = \frac{8}{6} \text{ or } 1\frac{1}{3} \text{ sq. ft.}$$
$$1 \bullet \frac{1}{3} \bullet \frac{1}{6} = \frac{1}{18} \text{ sq. ft.}$$

The sum is $4\frac{1}{18}$ sq. ft. of board remaining above ground.

14. **(D)** The rate of the first runner is $\frac{M}{H}$ miles per hour. The rate of the second is $\frac{N}{L}$ miles per hour. The second runner is faster, so the difference in their rates is written $\frac{N}{L} - \frac{M}{H}$.

15. **(C)** Mary's age now = x.

Her sister's age now = $x - 3$.

In five years her sister's age will be $x - 3 + 5 = x + 2$.

16. **(C)** The area of square = s^2.

The area of this square = $2^2 = 4$.

The area of a circle = $\pi \bullet r^2$

$$\left(r = \frac{1}{2}d\right)(\pi = 3.14)$$

The area of this circle = $\pi \bullet 1^2 = \pi \bullet 1 = \pi$

The difference between the area of this square and the area of this circle is

$4 - 3.14 = .86$.

17. **(C)** Area of a square = s^2

    $49 = 7^2$

    one side = 7 inches

    $P = 4s$

    $P = 4 \times 7" = 28$ inches

18. **(C)** One half hour = 30 minutes

    Amount = rate (G) × time (30 minutes)

19. **(C)** Each minus 1 cancels out the plus 1 before it. Since the final term is +1, which is not cancelled out by a –1, the sum is +1.

20. **(C)** One car went 20 mph for $\frac{1}{2}$ hour = 10 miles. The other car went 36 mph for $\frac{1}{2}$ hour = 18 miles. Since they went in opposite directions, add the two distances to find the total number of miles apart. 10 + 18 = 28

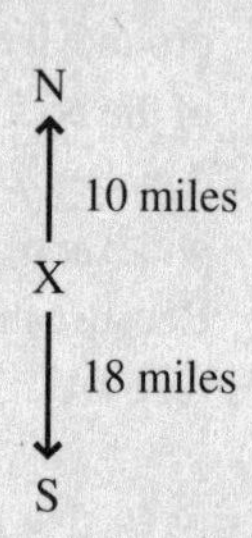

21. **(B)** You should not have to figure out this question. You should see the answer through inspection and common sense. If you want to work it out:

    $$\frac{5}{100} = \frac{x}{34} \qquad \frac{5}{100} = \frac{34}{x}$$

    $$100x = 170 \qquad 5x = 3400$$

    $$x = 1.7 \qquad x = 680$$

22. **(B)** $[5a(4t)]^3 = [-10(12)]^3$

    $= (-120)^3$

    = negative answer

    $[4a(5s)]^2 = [-8(1)]^2$

    $= (-8)^2$

    = positive answer

    A positive product is greater than a negative one.

23. **(D)** Since x could be any integer from –2 to 3, the values of the fractions are impossible to determine.

24. **(A)** $a < b \therefore b > a$ (given).

    $\therefore KR > KT$ (in a triangle the greater side lies opposite the greater angle)

25. **(A)**

    $$\frac{2}{3} + \frac{3}{7} = \frac{14}{21} + \frac{9}{21} = \frac{23}{21} \quad \Bigg| \quad \frac{16}{21} - \frac{3}{7} = \frac{16}{21} - \frac{9}{21} = \frac{7}{21}$$

26. **(C)**

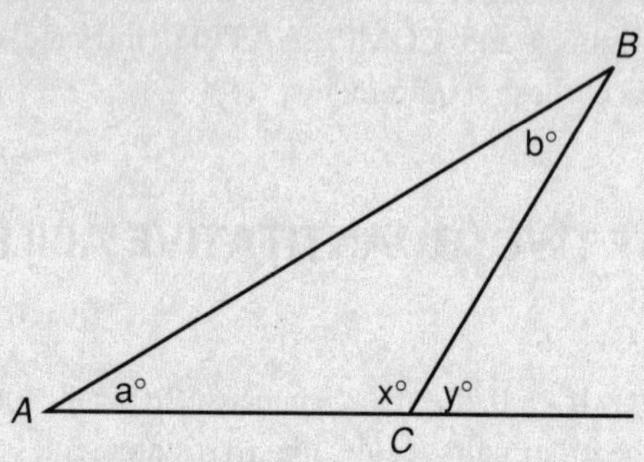

$y = a + b$ (an exterior angle of a triangle is equal to the sum of the two interior remote angles)

27. **(D)** There is not enough information, as y could equal 1, which would make both quantities equal; or y could be greater than 1, which would make y^3 greater than y^2. If y were a negative integer, then y^2 would be greater than y^3.

28. **(B)** $(8 + 6) \div (3 - 7(2))$

    $= (14) \div (-11) = \frac{14}{-11}$

    $(6 + 8) \div (2 - 7(3))$

    $= (14) \div (-19) = \frac{14}{-19}$

29. **(C)** $\frac{3}{4} \times \frac{9}{9} = \frac{3}{4} \qquad \frac{9}{9} \times \frac{3}{4} = \frac{3}{4}$

30. **(B)**

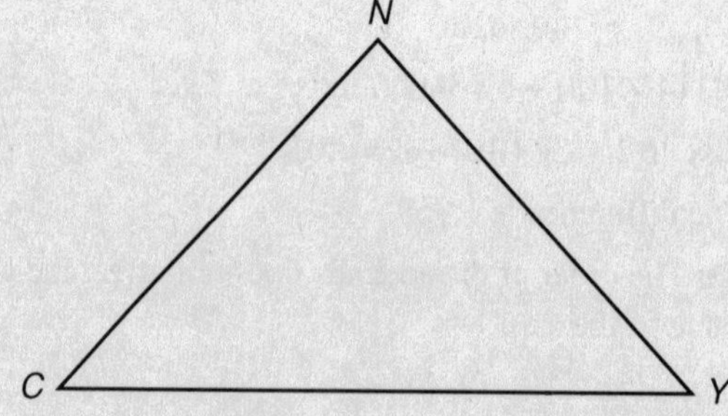

$NC = NY$ (given)

$\angle C = \angle Y$ (angles opposite equal sides are equal)

$\angle N > \angle C$ (given)

$\angle N > \angle Y$ (substitution)

$CY > NC$ (the greater side lies opposite the greater angle)

31. **(C)** $\frac{1}{\sqrt{9}} = \frac{1}{3}$

32. **(C)**

$5\left(\frac{2}{3}\right) = \frac{5}{1} \bullet \frac{2}{3} = \frac{10}{3} \qquad \left(\frac{5}{3}\right)2 = \frac{5}{3} \bullet \frac{2}{1} = \frac{10}{3}$

33. **(C)** A triangle inscribed in a parallelogram is equal in area to one-half the parallelogram. Therefore the area of ΔDEC equals the combined areas of ΔADE and ΔEBC.

34. **(A)**

$x^3 + x^2 - x + 1 =$

$(-1)^3 + (-1)^2 - (-1) + 1$

$= -1 + 1 + 1 + 1$

$= 2$

$x^3 - x^2 + x - 1 =$

$(-1)^3 - (-1)^2 + (-1) - 1$

$= -1 -1 -1 -1$

$= -4$

$\therefore$ Column A > Column B

35. **(C)** $e^3 = 27 \qquad 6e^2 = 54$

$e = 3 \qquad e^2 = 9$

$e = 3$

$\therefore$ Column A = Column B

36. **(A)**

$$\frac{\frac{1}{2} + \frac{1}{3}}{\frac{2}{3}} = \frac{\frac{3+2}{6}}{\frac{2}{3}} = \frac{\frac{5}{6}}{\frac{2}{3}}$$

(multiplying numerator and denominator by $\frac{3}{2}$)

$$= \frac{\frac{15}{12}}{1} = \frac{15}{12} = \frac{5}{4}$$

$$\frac{\frac{2}{3}}{\frac{1}{2} + \frac{1}{3}} = \frac{\frac{2}{3}}{\frac{3+2}{6}} = \frac{\frac{2}{3}}{\frac{5}{6}}$$

(multiplying numerator and denominator by $\frac{6}{5}$)

$$= \frac{\frac{12}{15}}{1} = \frac{12}{15} = \frac{4}{5}$$

$\frac{5}{4} > \frac{4}{5}$ $\therefore$ Column A > Column B

37. **(D)** We cannot determine the areas of the circles unless the value of x is known.

38. **(A)** Area of circle $= \pi r^2$

$= \pi(7)^2$

$= 49\pi$

Area of equilateral triangle $= \frac{8^2}{4}\sqrt{3}$

$= \frac{(14)^2}{4}\sqrt{3}$

$= \frac{196}{4}\sqrt{3}$

$= 49\sqrt{3}$

$49\pi > 49\sqrt{3}$

$\therefore$ Column A > Column B

39. **(A)**

(Area of shaded portion) = (Area of larger circle) − (Area of smaller circle)

$= \pi(10^2) - \pi(7^2)$

$= 100\pi - 49\pi$

$= 51\pi$

(Area of smaller circle) $= \pi r^2$

$= \pi(7^2)$

$= 49\pi$

$51\pi > 49\pi$

$\therefore$ Column A > Column B

40. **(D)** A number smaller than 0 is a negative number, so a is a negative number. A negative number squared becomes a positive number. Without knowing absolute values of a and b there is insufficient information to determine the answer to this question.

TEST THREE: READING COMPREHENSION

1. **(C)** The selection graphically details the movement of a snake. While much of the description is in terms of legs and feet, the point of the selection is to fully describe the means of locomotion.
2. **(B)** The second sentence of the second paragraph makes this statement. The remainder of the paragraph expands on the theme.
3. **(D)** This word appears in line 13. Read carefully and you can figure out the meaning from the context. *Terrain* means *earth,* with reference to its topographical features.
4. **(C)** The detail in this selection indicates that the author knows a good deal about snakes.
5. **(B)** The last sentence of the first paragraph tells us that rope is absolutely vital for docking.
6. **(D)** The second sentence serves by way of definition.
7. **(D)** In lines 11–12 we learn that the ship is secured by nine-inch or ten-inch mooring lines. Since rope is measured by circumference rather than by diameter (line 24), (D) is the correct answer.
8. **(A)** Check back and eliminate. Sisal does not come from the Philippines.
9. **(C)** Since State Department clerks took charge of getting the Constitution and Declaration of Independence out of Washington before the British burned the city, these important documents must have been housed in the State Department offices.
10. **(A)** See the first sentence of the last paragraph.
11. **(A)** The last sentence enumerates the disasters protected against.
12. **(C)** The documents were removed in 1814 to protect them from the War of 1812; in 1941, they were removed for protection from possible damage in World War II.
13. **(D)** Great blank spaces on a population map indicate very small population.
14. **(A)** (See line 7). You may eat the vegetables at a winter dinner, but the farm produces only the vegetables; it does not cook the dinner.
15. **(B)** In line 12 we learn that broadcloth is made from silky cotton grown in Egypt.
16. **(B)** The third paragraph makes the statement that desert civilizations have made important cultural contributions. The last paragraph tells what these contributions are.
17. **(C)** See lines 23–26.
18. **(A)** The name of the town is *Ekalaka,* but they call it "Skeleton Flats."
19. **(C)** The answer to this main-idea question should be clear. The article is about the various fossil finds.
20. **(D)** Lines 7–8 give the definition: "... paleontologists, scientists who use fossils to study prehistoric life forms." Walter Peck's hobby was geology, and in the course of pursuing his hobby he made the first find, but he was not a paleontologist.
21. **(D)** The third paragraph discusses the people of Ekalaka in terms of their enthusiasm for digging and fossil discovery.
22. **(B)** See the last sentence.
23. **(D)** The selection describes the properties of zirconium in its various forms.
24. **(A)** Consider the use of the word *docile* as applied to solid zirconium, in contrast to the use of the word *violent* as applied to powdered zirconium.
25. **(B)** An emphasis of the selection is that increasing uses are being found for zirconium.
26. **(B)** The first paragraph makes this point.
27. **(A)** In both the second and third paragraphs, zirconium is described as a metal.
28. **(D)** If zirconium is too dangerous to be used in ammunition, it is most certainly too dangerous to be used in fireworks.
29. **(D)** The selection is about the beginning of Hudson ferryboat service.

30. **(A)** See lines 5–7.

31. **(D)** The next-to-last sentence discusses Fulton's invention of floating docks for the ferryboats.

32. **(C)** 1812 was in the nineteenth century.

33. **(B)** In the context of the paragraph, *shock* must refer to the *impact* of the boat running into the dock.

34. **(A)** The first paragraph describes the original trail as a path. The road is also described as an east-west route. It presented travelers with surprisingly few obstacles.

35. **(C)** The frontier outpost, Ithaca, was at the western end of the highway.

36. **(A)** See line 9.

37. **(A)** Guides are not mentioned in the selection.

38. **(C)** We are told that five positions for botanists have been created. The implication is that these are new positions.

39. **(C)** See lines 14–17. The Department says that listing and delisting are equally important.

40. **(D)** This is a difficult question. You can instantly eliminate choices (A) and (B), but (C) appears possible. If you reread the selection carefully a few more times, you will realize that past concepts of success are not really spelled out. Therefore, (D) would seem the most likely correct answer. The writer is anticipating a criticism and answering it in advance.

TEST FOUR: MATHEMATICS ACHIEVEMENT

1. **(D)** Area = length × width

   Area of square = 8 × 8 = 64 sq. in.

   Area of rectangle = (8 + 4) (8 – 2) = 12 × 6 = 72 sq. in.

   72 – 64 = 8 sq. in.

2. **(A)** $r = 35 - (9)(-n)$

   $r = 35 - (9)(-2)$

   $r = 35 - (-18)$

   $r = 35 + 18 = 53$

   To subtract signed numbers, change the sign of the subtrahend and proceed as in algebraic addition.

3. **(C)** First perform the operation within the parentheses. To cube a number, multiply it by itself, two times.

   $(3 + 4)^3 = (7)^3 = 7 \times 7 \times 7 = 343$

4. **(A)** Copper and aluminum in the ratio of 10:1 means 10 parts copper to 1 part aluminum.

   Let x = weight of aluminum

   Then $10x$ = weight of copper

   $10x + x = 77$

   $11x = 77$

   $x = 7$

5. **(D)** Volume = L × W × H

   Volume of carton = 2' × 3' × 4'

   = 24 cubic feet

   Volume of one box = 2" × 3" × 4"

   = 24 cubic inches

   $\frac{1728 \times \cancel{24}^{1}}{\cancel{24}_{1}}$ = 1728 boxes will fit in carton

6. **(A)** On the trip, they spent \$7 + \$4.50 + \$3 = \$14.50. These figures are given as total costs in the problem, so should not be doubled. The major cost of the trip, \$143 each, totaling \$286, was prepaid.

7. **(B)** $\frac{3}{5}$ of 200 = 120 columns by machine @ 40 columns per hour = 3 hours

   200 – 120 = 80 columns without machine @ 20 columns per hour = 4 hours

   3 hours + 4 hours = 7 hours to complete the job.

8. **(C)** His total income is equal to 7% of his sales plus \$150; 7% of his sales is \$945 × .07 = \$66.15.

   \$66.15 + \$150 = \$216.15

9. **(A)** If

   $x^2 + 5 = 41$

   $x^2 = 41 - 5$

   $x^2 = 36$

   $x = 6$

10. **(B)** Perimeter = $2l + 2w$

If the two long sides are together, the perimeter will be

$$5 + 3 + 3 + 5 + 3 + 3 = 22$$

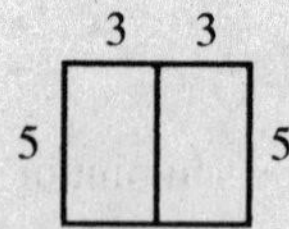

If the two short sides are together, the perimeter will be

$$3 + 5 + 5 + 3 + 5 + 5 = 26$$

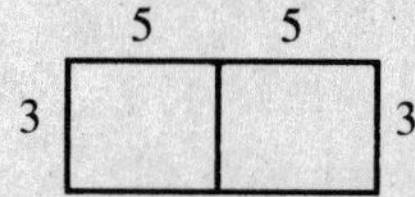

$26 - 22 = 4$ feet shorter

11. **(A)** 5 hours 30 minutes = $5\frac{1}{2}$ hours

1000 miles $\div 5\frac{1}{2}$ hours

$= 1000 \div \frac{11}{2} = 1000 \times \frac{2}{11} = 181\frac{9}{11}$ mph

12. **(C)** 2,975 pennies = \$29.75

\$35.00 – \$29.75 = \$5.25 saved

Rate of discount = $\frac{5.25}{35} \times 100 = .15 \times 100$

$= 15\%$

13. **(D)** 500 – 125 = 375 pads @ \$.04 = \$15.00

130 – 45 = 85 pencils @ \$.03 = \$2.55

50 dozen – 4 dozen = 46 dozen rubber bands @ \$.02 = \$.92

\$15 + \$2.55 + \$.92 = \$18.47

14. **(A)** 500 dozen @ \$.40 per dozen = purchase of two years ago

75% of 500 dozen = 375 dozen pencils purchased this year

20% of \$.40 = \$.08 increase in cost per dozen

375 × \$.48 = \$180 spent on pencils this year

15. **(D)** A child's ticket costs x dollars. Each adult ticket costs twice as much, or $2x$ dollars. $2(2x)$ = 2 adult tickets; $3x$ = 3 children's tickets. Write a simple equation, and solve for x.

$$2(2x) + 3x = \$49$$
$$4x + 3x = \$49$$
$$7x = \$49$$
$$x = \$7$$

\$7 is the cost of a child's ticket; \$14 is the cost of an adult's ticket.

16. **(A)** $\frac{x}{2} + 36 = 37.25$

$$\frac{x}{2} = 37.25 - 36$$
$$\frac{x}{2} = 1.25$$
$$x = 2.50$$

17. **(A)** One person raised 35% of \$690.

\$690 × .35 = \$241.50.

The remainder raised by the others was \$690 – 241.50 = \$448.50

18. **(C)** For the length, 29 feet would be represented by 29 units of $\frac{1}{4}$", resulting in $\frac{29}{4}$, or $7\frac{1}{4}$ inches. For the width, 23 feet would be represented by 23 units of $\frac{1}{4}$", resulting in $\frac{23}{4}$, or $5\frac{3}{4}$ inches.

19. **(D)** Distance = rate × time

$= 55$ mph $\times 5\frac{1}{2}$ hours

$= 302.5$ miles

20. **(A)** Area = length × width

= 176 ft. × 79 ft.

= 13,904 sq. ft.

21. **(A)** Since $\frac{1}{4}$" = 1 ft, 10" on the blueprint equals 40' in the room, because there are 40 $\frac{1}{4}$"-units in 10". Similarly, 13" contains 52 $\frac{1}{4}$"-units, each representing 1 foot. The dimensions are 40' × 52'.

22. **(D)** $63 \div \frac{1}{9} = 63 \times \frac{9}{1} = 567$

This is a good answer to estimate. By dividing a number by $\frac{1}{9}$, you are, in effect, multiplying it by 9. Only one of the suggested answers is close.

23. **(C)** The problem asks, "What number is $13.23 18% of?" $13.23 ÷ .18 = $73.50.

24. **(A)** Each fast worker is equivalent to two slow workers; therefore, the three men are the equivalent of five slow workers. The whole job, then, requires 5 × 56 = 280 minutes for one slow worker. It also requires half that time, or 140 minutes, for one fast worker, and half again as much, or 70 minutes, for two fast workers.

25. **(C)** Subtract from the total population of 18,000 the 756 children and the 2,244 married people. 18,000 – 756 – 2,244 = 15,000 single men and women.

    Because there are $1\frac{1}{2}$ times as many men as women, we know that 60% of the 15,000 single people are men, and 40% are women. 60% of 15,000 = 9,000.

26. **(C)** No calculations are needed here. Note that a 20-mile trip at 60 mph (which is 1 mile per minute), would take 20 minutes. Since the vehicle is traveling half as fast (30 mph), the 20-mile trip should take twice as long, or 40 minutes.

27. **(A)**

$$2x^2 + 3 = 21$$
$$2x^2 = 21 - 3$$
$$2x^2 = 18$$
$$x^2 = 9$$
$$x = 3$$

    You should have been able to predict that x would be a small number, since, according to the equation, twice its square is no longer than 21.

28. **(B)** The area of a circle is $A = \pi r^2$, when the radius equals $\frac{1}{2}$ the diameter. $r = 3$, and $\pi = \frac{22}{7}$, or 3.14.

$$A = \pi r^2$$
$$A = \pi(3)^2$$
$$A = 9\pi$$
$$A = 9(3.14) = 28.26 \text{ sq. in.}$$

29. **(D)** The scale is $\frac{1}{8}$" = 25 miles. In $3\frac{7}{8}$" there are 31 $\frac{1}{8}$" units. The distance is 31 • 25 = 775 miles.

30. **(C)** The amount the house was insured for is 80% of $83,000, or $66,400. The insurance is calculated at 45¢ per hundred, or $4.50 per thousand of value. Since there are 66.4 thousands of value, 66.4 × $4.50 per thousand equals the yearly premium of $298.80.

31. **(C)** The size of the job can be thought of this way: 18 clerks working for 26 days do 18 × 26 or 468 clerk-days of work. To do 468 clerk-days of work in only 12 days would require 468 ÷ 12 = 39 clerks.

32. **(D)** The digits are all alike, so you do not need to calculate. Move the decimal point of the divisor two places to the right; do the same for the dividend.

33. **(C)** Solve this problem as you would any mixture-value problem. The numbers of cars sold are all related to the number of those sold for $4,200. Call the number of $4,200 cars sold x. Then, the number of $5,400 cars sold is $3x$, and the number of $4,800 cars is $2x$.

    The value of $4,200 cars sold is $4,200 • x.

    The value of $4,800 cars sold is $4,800 • $2x$.

    The value of $5,400 cars sold is $5,400 • $3x$.

    The sum of these values equals the total sales.

$$(\$4{,}200 \bullet x) + (\$4{,}800 \bullet 2x) + (5{,}400 \bullet 3x) = \$360{,}000$$

$$\$4{,}200x + \$9{,}600x + \$16{,}200x = \$360{,}000$$

$$\$30{,}000x = \$360{,}000$$

$$x = \$360{,}000 \div \$30{,}000$$

$$x = 12$$

    Since x = 12 $4,200-cars, $3x$, or 36 of the $5,400-model, were sold.

34. **(D)** There is not enough information to answer this problem. We must know how many attended the game to determine how many paid full price.

35. **(A)** You must borrow one day's worth of hours and one hour's worth of minutes and rewrite the problem as:

	6 days	26 hr.	80 min.
–	4 days	9 hr.	31 min.
	2 days	17 hr.	49 min.

36. **(B)** The formula for the area of a triangle is A = $\frac{1}{2}$bh. Plug in the numbers:

$$A = \frac{1}{2} \bullet 12 \bullet 14$$

$$A = 84 \text{ sq. ft.}$$

37. **(C)** This is a tricky question. It doesn't ask for 150% of 72, but rather to increase 72 by 150%. Since 150% of 72 = 108, we add 72 and 108 for the correct answer, 180.

38. **(A)** Answer (B) is read, "Four times the square of a certain number minus 6 equals 2." Answer (C) is read, "Four times a number squared divided by 3 minus 6 equals 2." Answer (D) is read, "One-fourth a given number divided by 3 minus 6 equals 2."

39. **(D)** Write down both equations and add them together.

$$\begin{array}{r} 14x - 2y = 32 \\ + \;\; x + 2y = 13 \\ \hline 15x \qquad = 45 \\ x \qquad = 3 \end{array}$$

40. **(B)** A die has six sides, each having a different number of dots. The chance of any face coming up is the same—$\frac{1}{6}$.

41. **(A)** First, pick the two longest times, then compare them. 1,440 minutes and 25 hours are obviously the longest periods. 25 hours contains 1,500 minutes.

42. **(D)** The cars are traveling toward each other, so the distance between them is being reduced at 60 + 50 or 110 miles per hour. At a rate of 110 mph, 550 miles will be covered in 5 hours. If both cars left at 1:00 PM, they should meet at 6:00 PM.

43. **(B)** (A) is 4930; (C) is 483; (D) is 133.

44. **(C)** If 10 men earn $5,400 in 12 days, each man earns $540 in 12 days, or $45 per day. Therefore, 6 men working for 15 days at $45 per day will earn $4,050.

45. **(D)** The map distance is $4\frac{1}{2}$", or $\frac{9}{2}$" or $\frac{36}{8}$". Each $\frac{3}{8}$" = 5 miles, and we know there are 12 $\frac{3}{8}$"-units in $\frac{36}{8}$". Therefore, the 12 $\frac{3}{8}$"-units correspond to 60 miles in actuality.

46. **(D)** The area of a circle is found by $A = \pi r^2$. The radius is $\frac{1}{2}$ the diameter. To find the diameter when the area is known, divide the area by π to find the square of the radius.

$$78.5 \div 3.14 = 25$$

Since the square of the radius is 25, we know the radius is 5, and the diameter is twice the radius, or 10 inches.

47. **(B)** If $a = 6$, $ab + 4 = 52$ becomes $6b + 4 = 52$.

$$\text{If } 6b + 4 = 52$$

$$6b = 52 - 4$$

$$6b = 48$$

$$b = 8$$

48. **(C)** If $\frac{2}{3}$ of the jar is filled in 1 minute, then $\frac{1}{3}$ of the jar is filled in $\frac{1}{2}$ minute. Since the jar is $\frac{2}{3}$ full, $\frac{1}{3}$ remains to be filled. The jar will be full in another $\frac{1}{2}$ minute.

49. **(D)** First convert to a 24-hour clock.

3:30 PM	=	15:30 o'clock
15:30	=	14:90
–8:50	=	–8:50
		6:40 = 6 hours 40 minutes

To subtract a larger number of minutes from a smaller number of minutes, borrow 60 minutes from the hour to enlarge the smaller number.

50. **(D)** Assign arbitrary values to solve this problem:

A square 10 ft. × 10 ft. = 100 sq. ft.

A rectangle 9 ft. × 11 ft. = 99 sq. ft.

$100 - 99 = 1; \frac{1}{100} = 1\%$

TEST FIVE: ESSAY

Sample of a well-written essay.

If I could spend an afternoon with any author, I would have a wonderful conversation with Jules Verne. I think of Jules Verne as the father of science fiction. We would talk about his books and why they make such good reading. I would tell him how much of his fiction has become fact. Then we would probably talk about recent science fiction and about the latest scientific and technological advances. Perhaps we would predict future developments.

The first book I would mention is my favorite, Twenty Thousand Leagues under the Sea. I would ask Mr. Verne how he thought up the book and would tell him how much I admire his works and how I respect his imagination. Then I would tell him about submarines and submarine warfare and would describe all the deep sea explorations that I know about. It is hard to predict a conversation in advance, but Around the World in Eighty Days would certainly be a good next topic, and we might well consume the remainder of the afternoon with discussion of modern travel and of all the countries and cultures that can be visited today.

No conversation with Jules Verne could conclude without mention of modern science fiction and of how predictive it might be. I wonder what Jules Verne would think of Star Trek. Finally I would tell him about space exploration, moon landings, satellites, and all the exciting space work that is unfolding.

The prospect of a conversation with Jules Verne is very appealing. Even though I know it cannot happen, I am thinking of more and more things I would like to discuss with him. What a stimulating afternoon it would be.

SCORE YOURSELF

Check your answers against the correct answer key. Count up the number of answers you got right on each question type and enter these numbers on the score sheet. These numbers are your raw scores. Use your raw scores to figure your percentage scores on the score sheet below.

Test	Raw Score ÷ No. questions	× 100 =	%
Synonyms	÷ 20	× 100 =	%
Sentence Completions	÷ 20	× 100 =	%
Total Verbal Ability	÷ 40	× 100 =	%
Multiple-choice Quantitative	÷ 20	× 100 =	%
Quantitative Comparisons	÷ 20	× 100 =	%
Total Quantitative Ability	÷ 40	× 100 =	%
Reading Comprehension	÷ 40	× 100 =	%
Mathematics Achievement	÷ 50	× 100 =	%

High percentage scores should make you feel very good about yourself, but low percentages do not mean that you are a failure.
Remember:

- Scores are not reported as percentages. A low percentage may translate to a respectable scaled score.
- The same exam is given to students in grades 8 through 12. Unless you have finished high school, you have not been taught everything on the exam. You are not expected to know what you have not been taught.
- You will be compared only to students in your own grade.

Use your scores to plan further study if you have time.

TEAR HERE

Independent School Entrance Examination
Practice Exam 2

Answer Sheet

TEST ONE: VERBAL ABILITY

1. Ⓐ Ⓑ Ⓒ Ⓓ	9. Ⓐ Ⓑ Ⓒ Ⓓ	17. Ⓐ Ⓑ Ⓒ Ⓓ	25. Ⓐ Ⓑ Ⓒ Ⓓ	33. Ⓐ Ⓑ Ⓒ Ⓓ
2. Ⓐ Ⓑ Ⓒ Ⓓ	10. Ⓐ Ⓑ Ⓒ Ⓓ	18. Ⓐ Ⓑ Ⓒ Ⓓ	26. Ⓐ Ⓑ Ⓒ Ⓓ	34. Ⓐ Ⓑ Ⓒ Ⓓ
3. Ⓐ Ⓑ Ⓒ Ⓓ	11. Ⓐ Ⓑ Ⓒ Ⓓ	19. Ⓐ Ⓑ Ⓒ Ⓓ	27. Ⓐ Ⓑ Ⓒ Ⓓ	35. Ⓐ Ⓑ Ⓒ Ⓓ
4. Ⓐ Ⓑ Ⓒ Ⓓ	12. Ⓐ Ⓑ Ⓒ Ⓓ	20. Ⓐ Ⓑ Ⓒ Ⓓ	28. Ⓐ Ⓑ Ⓒ Ⓓ	36. Ⓐ Ⓑ Ⓒ Ⓓ
5. Ⓐ Ⓑ Ⓒ Ⓓ	13. Ⓐ Ⓑ Ⓒ Ⓓ	21. Ⓐ Ⓑ Ⓒ Ⓓ	29. Ⓐ Ⓑ Ⓒ Ⓓ	37. Ⓐ Ⓑ Ⓒ Ⓓ
6. Ⓐ Ⓑ Ⓒ Ⓓ	14. Ⓐ Ⓑ Ⓒ Ⓓ	22. Ⓐ Ⓑ Ⓒ Ⓓ	30. Ⓐ Ⓑ Ⓒ Ⓓ	38. Ⓐ Ⓑ Ⓒ Ⓓ
7. Ⓐ Ⓑ Ⓒ Ⓓ	15. Ⓐ Ⓑ Ⓒ Ⓓ	23. Ⓐ Ⓑ Ⓒ Ⓓ	31. Ⓐ Ⓑ Ⓒ Ⓓ	39. Ⓐ Ⓑ Ⓒ Ⓓ
8. Ⓐ Ⓑ Ⓒ Ⓓ	16. Ⓐ Ⓑ Ⓒ Ⓓ	24. Ⓐ Ⓑ Ⓒ Ⓓ	32. Ⓐ Ⓑ Ⓒ Ⓓ	40. Ⓐ Ⓑ Ⓒ Ⓓ

TEST TWO: QUANTITATIVE ABILITY

1. Ⓐ Ⓑ Ⓒ Ⓓ	9. Ⓐ Ⓑ Ⓒ Ⓓ	17. Ⓐ Ⓑ Ⓒ Ⓓ	25. Ⓐ Ⓑ Ⓒ Ⓓ	33. Ⓐ Ⓑ Ⓒ Ⓓ
2. Ⓐ Ⓑ Ⓒ Ⓓ	10. Ⓐ Ⓑ Ⓒ Ⓓ	18. Ⓐ Ⓑ Ⓒ Ⓓ	26. Ⓐ Ⓑ Ⓒ Ⓓ	34. Ⓐ Ⓑ Ⓒ Ⓓ
3. Ⓐ Ⓑ Ⓒ Ⓓ	11. Ⓐ Ⓑ Ⓒ Ⓓ	19. Ⓐ Ⓑ Ⓒ Ⓓ	27. Ⓐ Ⓑ Ⓒ Ⓓ	35. Ⓐ Ⓑ Ⓒ Ⓓ
4. Ⓐ Ⓑ Ⓒ Ⓓ	12. Ⓐ Ⓑ Ⓒ Ⓓ	20. Ⓐ Ⓑ Ⓒ Ⓓ	28. Ⓐ Ⓑ Ⓒ Ⓓ	36. Ⓐ Ⓑ Ⓒ Ⓓ
5. Ⓐ Ⓑ Ⓒ Ⓓ	13. Ⓐ Ⓑ Ⓒ Ⓓ	21. Ⓐ Ⓑ Ⓒ Ⓓ	29. Ⓐ Ⓑ Ⓒ Ⓓ	37. Ⓐ Ⓑ Ⓒ Ⓓ
6. Ⓐ Ⓑ Ⓒ Ⓓ	14. Ⓐ Ⓑ Ⓒ Ⓓ	22. Ⓐ Ⓑ Ⓒ Ⓓ	30. Ⓐ Ⓑ Ⓒ Ⓓ	38. Ⓐ Ⓑ Ⓒ Ⓓ
7. Ⓐ Ⓑ Ⓒ Ⓓ	15. Ⓐ Ⓑ Ⓒ Ⓓ	23. Ⓐ Ⓑ Ⓒ Ⓓ	31. Ⓐ Ⓑ Ⓒ Ⓓ	39. Ⓐ Ⓑ Ⓒ Ⓓ
8. Ⓐ Ⓑ Ⓒ Ⓓ	16. Ⓐ Ⓑ Ⓒ Ⓓ	24. Ⓐ Ⓑ Ⓒ Ⓓ	32. Ⓐ Ⓑ Ⓒ Ⓓ	40. Ⓐ Ⓑ Ⓒ Ⓓ

TEST THREE: READING COMPREHENSION

1. Ⓐ Ⓑ Ⓒ Ⓓ	9. Ⓐ Ⓑ Ⓒ Ⓓ	17. Ⓐ Ⓑ Ⓒ Ⓓ	25. Ⓐ Ⓑ Ⓒ Ⓓ	33. Ⓐ Ⓑ Ⓒ Ⓓ
2. Ⓐ Ⓑ Ⓒ Ⓓ	10. Ⓐ Ⓑ Ⓒ Ⓓ	18. Ⓐ Ⓑ Ⓒ Ⓓ	26. Ⓐ Ⓑ Ⓒ Ⓓ	34. Ⓐ Ⓑ Ⓒ Ⓓ
3. Ⓐ Ⓑ Ⓒ Ⓓ	11. Ⓐ Ⓑ Ⓒ Ⓓ	19. Ⓐ Ⓑ Ⓒ Ⓓ	27. Ⓐ Ⓑ Ⓒ Ⓓ	35. Ⓐ Ⓑ Ⓒ Ⓓ
4. Ⓐ Ⓑ Ⓒ Ⓓ	12. Ⓐ Ⓑ Ⓒ Ⓓ	20. Ⓐ Ⓑ Ⓒ Ⓓ	28. Ⓐ Ⓑ Ⓒ Ⓓ	36. Ⓐ Ⓑ Ⓒ Ⓓ
5. Ⓐ Ⓑ Ⓒ Ⓓ	13. Ⓐ Ⓑ Ⓒ Ⓓ	21. Ⓐ Ⓑ Ⓒ Ⓓ	29. Ⓐ Ⓑ Ⓒ Ⓓ	37. Ⓐ Ⓑ Ⓒ Ⓓ
6. Ⓐ Ⓑ Ⓒ Ⓓ	14. Ⓐ Ⓑ Ⓒ Ⓓ	22. Ⓐ Ⓑ Ⓒ Ⓓ	30. Ⓐ Ⓑ Ⓒ Ⓓ	38. Ⓐ Ⓑ Ⓒ Ⓓ
7. Ⓐ Ⓑ Ⓒ Ⓓ	15. Ⓐ Ⓑ Ⓒ Ⓓ	23. Ⓐ Ⓑ Ⓒ Ⓓ	31. Ⓐ Ⓑ Ⓒ Ⓓ	39. Ⓐ Ⓑ Ⓒ Ⓓ
8. Ⓐ Ⓑ Ⓒ Ⓓ	16. Ⓐ Ⓑ Ⓒ Ⓓ	24. Ⓐ Ⓑ Ⓒ Ⓓ	32. Ⓐ Ⓑ Ⓒ Ⓓ	40. Ⓐ Ⓑ Ⓒ Ⓓ

TEST FOUR: MATHEMATICS ACHIEVEMENT

1. Ⓐ Ⓑ Ⓒ Ⓓ	11. Ⓐ Ⓑ Ⓒ Ⓓ	21. Ⓐ Ⓑ Ⓒ Ⓓ	31. Ⓐ Ⓑ Ⓒ Ⓓ	41. Ⓐ Ⓑ Ⓒ Ⓓ
2. Ⓐ Ⓑ Ⓒ Ⓓ	12. Ⓐ Ⓑ Ⓒ Ⓓ	22. Ⓐ Ⓑ Ⓒ Ⓓ	32. Ⓐ Ⓑ Ⓒ Ⓓ	42. Ⓐ Ⓑ Ⓒ Ⓓ
3. Ⓐ Ⓑ Ⓒ Ⓓ	13. Ⓐ Ⓑ Ⓒ Ⓓ	23. Ⓐ Ⓑ Ⓒ Ⓓ	33. Ⓐ Ⓑ Ⓒ Ⓓ	43. Ⓐ Ⓑ Ⓒ Ⓓ
4. Ⓐ Ⓑ Ⓒ Ⓓ	14. Ⓐ Ⓑ Ⓒ Ⓓ	24. Ⓐ Ⓑ Ⓒ Ⓓ	34. Ⓐ Ⓑ Ⓒ Ⓓ	44. Ⓐ Ⓑ Ⓒ Ⓓ
5. Ⓐ Ⓑ Ⓒ Ⓓ	15. Ⓐ Ⓑ Ⓒ Ⓓ	25. Ⓐ Ⓑ Ⓒ Ⓓ	35. Ⓐ Ⓑ Ⓒ Ⓓ	45. Ⓐ Ⓑ Ⓒ Ⓓ
6. Ⓐ Ⓑ Ⓒ Ⓓ	16. Ⓐ Ⓑ Ⓒ Ⓓ	26. Ⓐ Ⓑ Ⓒ Ⓓ	36. Ⓐ Ⓑ Ⓒ Ⓓ	46. Ⓐ Ⓑ Ⓒ Ⓓ
7. Ⓐ Ⓑ Ⓒ Ⓓ	17. Ⓐ Ⓑ Ⓒ Ⓓ	27. Ⓐ Ⓑ Ⓒ Ⓓ	37. Ⓐ Ⓑ Ⓒ Ⓓ	47. Ⓐ Ⓑ Ⓒ Ⓓ
8. Ⓐ Ⓑ Ⓒ Ⓓ	18. Ⓐ Ⓑ Ⓒ Ⓓ	28. Ⓐ Ⓑ Ⓒ Ⓓ	38. Ⓐ Ⓑ Ⓒ Ⓓ	48. Ⓐ Ⓑ Ⓒ Ⓓ
9. Ⓐ Ⓑ Ⓒ Ⓓ	19. Ⓐ Ⓑ Ⓒ Ⓓ	29. Ⓐ Ⓑ Ⓒ Ⓓ	39. Ⓐ Ⓑ Ⓒ Ⓓ	49. Ⓐ Ⓑ Ⓒ Ⓓ
10. Ⓐ Ⓑ Ⓒ Ⓓ	20. Ⓐ Ⓑ Ⓒ Ⓓ	30. Ⓐ Ⓑ Ⓒ Ⓓ	40. Ⓐ Ⓑ Ⓒ Ⓓ	50. Ⓐ Ⓑ Ⓒ Ⓓ

TEAR HERE

ISEE Practice Exam 2

TEST ONE: VERBAL ABILITY

40 QUESTIONS • TIME—20 MINUTES

The Verbal Ability Section includes two types of questions. There are separate directions for each type of question.

Directions: Each question is made up of a word in CAPITAL letters followed by four choices. Choose the one word that is most nearly the same in meaning as the word in CAPITAL letters, and mark its letter on your answer sheet.

1. IMPLIED
(A) acknowledged
(B) stated
(C) predicted
(D) hinted

2. FISCAL
(A) critical
(B) basic
(C) personal
(D) financial

3. STRINGENT
(A) demanding
(B) loud
(C) flexible
(D) clear

4. PERMEABLE
(A) penetrable
(B) durable
(C) unending
(D) allowable

5. SCRUPULOUS
(A) conscientious
(B) unprincipled
(C) intricate
(D) neurotic

6. STALEMATE
(A) pillar
(B) deadlock
(C) maneuver
(D) work slowdown

7. REDUNDANT
(A) concise
(B) reappearing
(C) superfluous
(D) lying down

8. SUPPLANT
(A) prune
(B) conquer
(C) uproot
(D) replace

9. COMMENSURATE
(A) identical
(B) of the same age
(C) proportionate
(D) measurable

10. ZENITH
(A) depths
(B) astronomical system
(C) peak
(D) solar system

GO ON TO THE NEXT PAGE

11. SUCCOR
(A) assistance
(B) nurse
(C) vitality
(D) distress

12. DISPATCH
(A) omit mention of
(B) send out on an errand
(C) tear
(D) do without

13. PORTABLE
(A) drinkable
(B) convenient
(C) having wheels
(D) able to be carried

14. VERBOSE
(A) vague
(B) brief
(C) wordy
(D) verbal

15. SUBVERSIVE
(A) secret
(B) foreign
(C) evasive
(D) destructive

16. VACILLATING
(A) changeable
(B) equalizing
(C) decisive
(D) progressing

17. PETTY
(A) lengthy
(B) communal
(C) small
(D) miscellaneous

18. INTREPID
(A) willing
(B) fanciful
(C) cowardly
(D) fearless

19. NEGOTIATE
(A) argue
(B) think
(C) speak
(D) bargain

20. STERILE
(A) antique
(B) germ-free
(C) unclean
(D) perishable

Directions: Each of the following questions is made up of a sentence containing one or two blanks. The sentences with one blank indicate that one word is missing. Sentences with two blanks have two missing words. Each sentence is followed by four choices. Choose the one word or pair of words that will best complete the meaning of the sentence as a whole, and mark the letter of your choice on your answer sheet.

21. Undaunted by his many setbacks, Joshua _____.

(A) crumpled

(B) drew back

(C) canceled

(D) persevered

22. Nationwide, college arts and science departments are taking _____ measures to attract students.

(A) no

(B) puny

(C) innovative

(D) few

23. With less capital available and fewer deals being done, it has clearly become a (an) _____ market.

(A) heinous

(B) inflationary

(C) sellers'

(D) buyers'

24. The penalty for violating the law would _____ for multiple offenses.

(A) accede

(B) nullify

(C) diminish

(D) escalate

25. The hotel was a world-class _____ property and, thanks to recent refurbishing and clever marketing efforts, it is experiencing a _____.

(A) luxury … renaissance

(B) communal … withdrawal

(C) opulent … decline

(D) decadent … stalemate

26. Some colleges, rather than _____ students to take arts courses, simply force them.

(A) requiring

(B) enticing

(C) demanding

(D) allowing

27. Requiring _____ by the criminal to the victim would be a far better way of dealing with many lawbreakers than _____, she argued.

(A) punishment … freedom

(B) imprisonment … pardon

(C) restitution … imprisonment

(D) mea culpa … negligence

28. Knowledge gained from books without the benefit of practical experience is usually not as profitable in everyday work as the opposite, _____ without _____.

(A) culture … manners

(B) experiments … science

(C) experience … scholarship

(D) learning … knowing

29. To _____ some of its _____ over the huge increase in state insurance premiums for employees, the school district invited one insurance expert to speak at a recent board meeting.

(A) quell … anxiety

(B) dispel … myths

(C) aggravate … nervousness

(D) foment … trepidation

30. While many elderly indeed are _____, poverty is _____ among the millions of older Americans who rely solely on Social Security.

(A) penurious … rampant

(B) invalid … abolished

(C) absolute … widespread

(D) comfortable … pervasive

GO ON TO THE NEXT PAGE

31. A police officer's _____ job is to prevent crime.
(A) primary
(B) only
(C) ostentatious
(D) ostensible

32. In view of the extenuating circumstances and the defendant's youth, the judge recommended _____.
(A) conviction
(B) a defense
(C) a mistrial
(D) leniency

33. Despite religious differences, the family _____ clashes by respecting each other's values.
(A) denied
(B) averted
(C) condescended
(D) declined

34. While marketing to health-conscious consumers will _____ a restaurant change, it will also have an effect in supermarkets.
(A) denigrate
(B) cancel
(C) encourage
(D) emit

35. Despite the politician's overwhelming loss, he _____ his popularity with a small core of followers.
(A) revoked
(B) maintained
(C) restrained
(D) encouraged

36. The decision to seek therapeutic treatment is often provoked by a(n) _____, such as an arrest or a domestic dispute.
(A) dearth
(B) crisis
(C) enigma
(D) casualty

37. Knowing that any particular new business can _____, Joshua avoided investing in one even if the potential _____ was high.
(A) succeed ... down side
(B) reduce ... profit
(C) do well ... monies
(D) fail ... payoff

38. The writer's style showed both the _____ and _____ of those she imitated.
(A) talent ... wealth
(B) strengths ... flaws
(C) intelligence ... bravery
(D) humor ... experience

39. The management is providing all needed building facilities to help the scientists _____ their research project.
(A) magnify
(B) retard
(C) relinquish
(D) implement

40. We can easily forgo a _____ we have never had, but once obtained it often is looked upon as being _____.
(A) requirement ... unusual
(B) gift ... useless
(C) luxury ... essential
(D) bonus ... unearned

STOP

END OF TEST ONE. IF YOU HAVE ANY TIME LEFT, GO OVER YOUR WORK ON THIS TEST ONLY. DO NOT WORK ON ANY OTHER TEST OF THE EXAM.

TEST TWO: QUANTITATIVE ABILITY

40 QUESTIONS • TIME—35 MINUTES

General Directions: You may assume that all figures accompanying Quantitative Ability questions have been drawn as accurately as possible EXCEPT when it is specifically stated that a particular figure is not drawn to scale. Letters such as *x*, *y*, and *n* stand for real numbers. The Quantitative Ability Test includes two types of questions. There are separate directions for each type of question.

Directions: For questions 1–20, work each problem in your head or in the margins of the test booklet. Mark the letter of your answer choice on the answer sheet.

1. If the decimal point in a number is moved one place to the right, the number has been

(A) divided by 10

(B) multiplied by 10

(C) divided by 100

(D) multiplied by 100

2. What is the total number of degrees found in angles *A* and *C* in the triangle below?

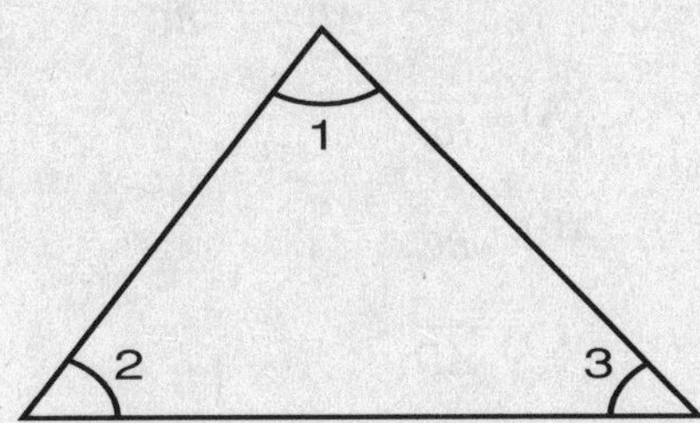

(A) 180°

(B) 100°

(C) 90°

(D) 75°

3. Using exponents, write 329 in expanded form.

(A) $(3^2 \times 10) + (2 \times 10) + 9$

(B) $(3 \times 10^2) + (2 \times 10) + 9$

(C) $(3 \times 10^2) + (2 \times 10^2) + 9$

(D) $(3 \times 10^3) + (2 \times 10) + 9$

4. Find the circumference of a circle whose radius is 21 feet.

(A) 65.94 feet

(B) 132 feet

(C) 153 feet

(D) 1,769.4 feet

5. If $x > -4$, and $y < 2$, then $\{x, y\}$ includes

(A) –4, 0, 1, 2

(B) –2, –1, 1, 2

(C) 1, 2, 3, 4

(D) –3, –2, 0, 1

6. Seventeen million sixty thousand thirty-four =

(A) 17,634

(B) 1,760,034

(C) 17,060,034

(D) 17,600,034

7. $(6 \times 2) + (7 \times 3) =$

(A) $(6 \times 7) + (2 \times 3)$

(B) $(7 - 6) + (3 - 2)$

(C) $(7 \times 3) + (6 \times 2)$

(D) $(7 \times 3) \times (6 \times 2)$

8. Which of the following will substitute for *x* and make the statement below true?

$$56 - (7 - x) = 53$$

(A) 4

(B) 3

(C) 2

(D) 1

GO ON TO THE NEXT PAGE

9. An angle that is greater than 90° and less than 180° is

(A) an acute angle

(B) a right angle

(C) a reflex angle

(D) an obtuse angle

10. Which of the following has the least value?

(A) 5.0

(B) 0.5

(C) 0.05

(D) 0.005

11. $\frac{17}{30}$ is greater than

(A) $\frac{7}{8}$

(B) $\frac{9}{20}$

(C) $\frac{8}{11}$

(D) $\frac{20}{25}$

12. 1 centimeter equals what part of a meter?

(A) $\frac{1}{10}$

(B) $\frac{1}{100}$

(C) $\frac{1}{1{,}000}$

(D) $\frac{1}{10{,}000}$

13. What is the lowest common denominator for the fractions $\frac{3}{4}$, $\frac{6}{9}$, $\frac{2}{6}$, and $\frac{5}{12}$?

(A) 24

(B) 32

(C) 36

(D) 48

14. The set of common factors of 36 and 64 is

(A) {1, 2, 4}

(B) {1, 2, 3, 4}

(C) {1, 2, 4, 6, 18}

(D) {1, 2, 3, 4, 6}

15. Which of the following statements is true?

(A) $7 \times 11 > 78$

(B) $6 + 4 < 10.5$

(C) $8 - 3 = 7 + 4$

(D) $16 \div 2 > 9$

16. If one angle of a triangle measures 115°, then the sum of the other two angles is

(A) 245°

(B) 195°

(C) 75°

(D) 65°

17.

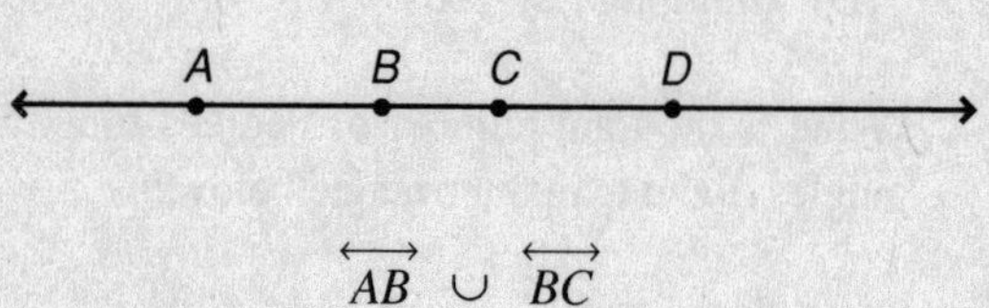

$\overleftrightarrow{AB} \cup \overleftrightarrow{BC}$

(A) $\overleftrightarrow{BD}$

(B) $\overleftrightarrow{BC}$

(C) $\overleftrightarrow{AD}$

(D) $\overleftrightarrow{AC}$

18. If a playing card is drawn from a standard deck, what are the chances it will be a six?

(A) $\frac{1}{4}$

(B) $\frac{4}{13}$

(C) $\frac{4}{52}$

(D) $\frac{6}{52}$

19. The scale on a map is $\frac{1}{2}$" = 8 miles. If 2 towns are 28 miles apart, how many inches will separate them on a map?

(A) $1\frac{3}{4}$

(B) $1\frac{5}{8}$

(C) $1\frac{1}{2}$

(D) $1\frac{3}{8}$

20. A certain highway intersection has had A accidents over a 10-year period, resulting in B deaths. What is the yearly average death rate for the intersection?

(A) $A + B - 10$

(B) $\frac{B}{10}$

(C) $10 - \frac{A}{B}$

(D) $\frac{A}{10}$

Directions: For questions 21–40, two quantities are given—one in Column A and the other in Column B. In some questions, additional information concerning the quantities to be compared is centered above the entries in the two columns. Compare the quantities in the two columns, and mark your answer sheet as follows:

(A) if the quantity in Column A is greater
(B) if the quantity in Column B is greater
(C) if the quantities are equal
(D) if the relationship cannot be determined from the information given.

	Column A		Column B
21.	6% of 42		7% of 36
22.		$x = -2$	
	$3x^2 + 2x - 1$		$x^3 + 2x^2 + 1$

23.

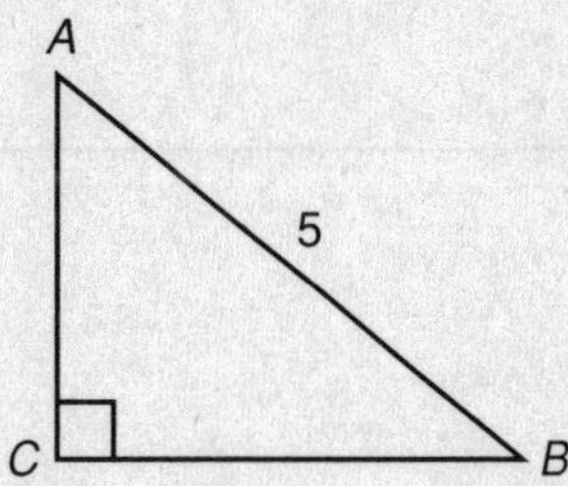

	Column A	Column B
23.	AC	BC
24.	$(16 \div 4) + (8 \times 2) - 8$	$(3 \times 4) + (10 \div 5) - 3$

GO ON TO THE NEXT PAGE

	Column A		Column B
25.		A radio priced at $47.25 includes a 5% profit (based on cost)	
	$44.89		The original cost before profit
26.		$a - b = -1$ $-b - a = -3$	
	b		a
27.		25% of the 300 girls in the school have blond hair	
	The ratio of girls with blond hair to those without blond hair		$\frac{1}{3}$
28.		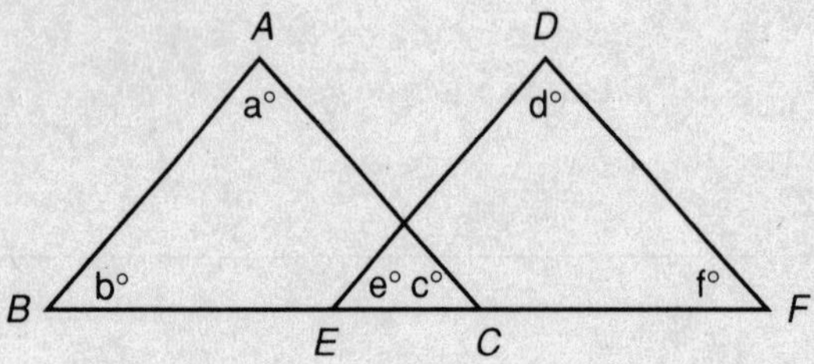 $e + c = 90$	
	$b + a + d + f$		270

	COLUMN A		COLUMN B
29.		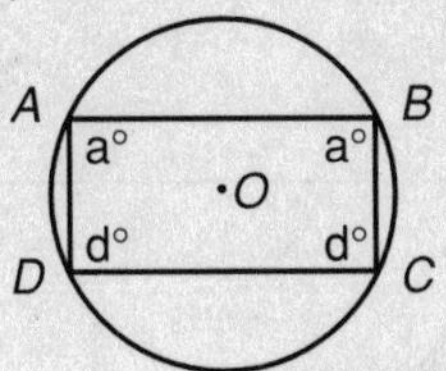 *ABCD* is a parallelogram inscribed in circle *O*	
	$a + c$		$b + d$
30.	Difference between $\frac{3}{5}$ and $\frac{9}{8}$		.5
31.	$\frac{3}{5}\%$		.06
32.		*A* can do a job alone in 4 days *B* can do a job alone in 3 days	
	The number of days it takes *A* and *B* working together to do the job		2 days
33.		In a certain college, the ratio of the number of freshmen to the number of seniors is 3:1	
	$\frac{1}{3}$		The ratio between the number of seniors and the total enrollment
34.		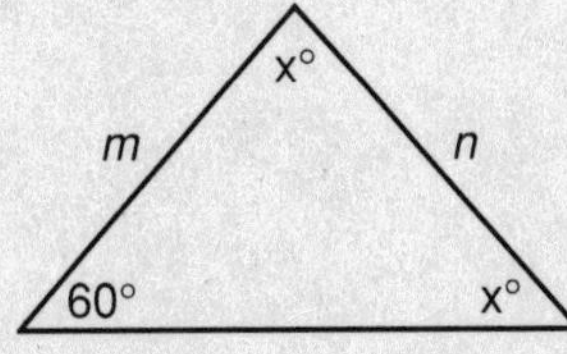	
	m		n

GO ON TO THE NEXT PAGE

	Column A		Column B
35.		$a + b = x$ $a - b = y$	
	x		y
36.		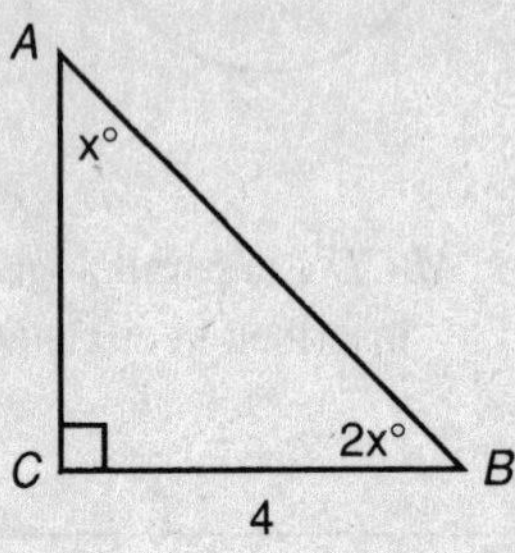	
	5		AB
37.	$\sqrt[3]{125}$		$\sqrt{25}$
38.		$x > 0$ $y < 0$	
	$x - y$		$x + y$
39.		During a store sale, a $43.50 radio can be purchased at a 15% discount	
	The selling price of the radio with the discount		$36
40.	75% of $\frac{1}{2}$		50% of $\frac{3}{4}$

STOP

END OF TEST TWO. IF YOU HAVE ANY TIME LEFT, GO OVER YOUR WORK ON THIS TEST ONLY. DO NOT WORK ON ANY OTHER TEST OF THE EXAM.

TEST THREE: READING COMPREHENSION

40 QUESTIONS • TIME—40 MINUTES

Directions: Each reading passage is followed by questions based on its content. Answer the questions on the basis of what is *stated* or *implied* in the passage. On your answer sheet, mark the letter of the answer you choose.

Coming into the relay station with a rush, the Pony Express rider swung down from his exhausted mount and up onto a fresh horse with his precious mochilla, the saddle bag containing the mail. He was off again without a moment's delay. He was expected to reach the next post station, and he did, or he died trying.

A rider might come into a station at dawn only to find that the station had been burned, the keepers killed, and the horses run off by attacking Indians. In that case he would continue to the next station without food or rest.

"Buffalo Bill," a boy of 18, made the longest continuous run in the history of the Pony Express, 384 miles. By riding 280 miles in just 22 hours, Jim Moore earned the distinction of having made the fastest run.

Ninety riders covered the trail at all times of the day and night, often risking their lives to get the mail through within the ten-day limit. Most made it in eight days.

On the average, the riders could travel 11 miles an hour, a quick pace over terrain that might require the horse to swim rivers or cat-foot its way along narrow cliff trails.

The Pony Express riders carried the mail between Missouri and California for less than two years. They stopped riding in 1861 when a telegraph line offered a swifter means of communication.

1. The Pony Express rider stopped at a station to
   (A) get a few hours sleep
   (B) get a fresh mount
   (C) sort the mail
   (D) escape Indian attacks

2. The *mochilla* refers to the
   (A) Pony Express rider's saddle bags
   (B) Pony Express horses
   (C) post stations
   (D) trails

3. This passage implies that most of the Pony Express riders were
   (A) sure-footed
   (B) faithful to their jobs
   (C) mountain-bred
   (D) killed

4. Those sending mail by Pony Express could expect that it would reach its destination within
   (A) ten days
   (B) five days
   (C) a month
   (D) before dawn

5. The longest continuous run was
   (A) completed within 22 hours
   (B) 280 miles
   (C) made by traveling 11 miles per hour
   (D) 384 miles

Hatting was one of the first industries to develop in the colonies. As early as 1640, American hats were one of the domestic products used for barter and exchange.

Wool was the principal raw material used by hatters, but large numbers of hats were also made of fur felt that came from native beaver pelts. The average price of a wool hat was between 40 and 80 cents, and beaver hats ranged from $2.50 to $3.50.

GO ON TO THE NEXT PAGE

By the beginning of the eighteenth century, hatting had become one of New England's most important industries, and in the 1730s, hats were being exported from the colonies in sufficient numbers to arouse uneasiness among hatters in England. Pressure was exerted, and Parliament passed a law prohibiting the export of hats from one colony to another, and from any colony to Great Britain.

6. The title that best expresses the main idea of this selection is

(A) Colonial Exports

(B) Kinds of American Hats

(C) An Early American Industry

(D) How Colonial Hats Were Made

7. A law restricting hat exports was enacted by Parliament in response to complaints by

(A) colonists

(B) English hatmakers

(C) English noblemen

(D) citizens of foreign countries

8. This law made it illegal for

(A) Great Britain to export hats

(B) the colonies to import hats

(C) the hatters to use beaver fur

(D) the colonies to export hats

9. American hats

(A) were made principally of wool

(B) did not suit customers in Great Britain

(C) were an unimportant part of New England's industry

(D) were not made until 1730

10. Beaver felt hats were

(A) unpopular

(B) cheaper than wool hats

(C) more expensive than wool hats

(D) not exported

The use of wood as a material from which to make paper was first suggested by Réne de Réaumer, a celebrated French naturalist, in 1719. Réaumer had observed wasps as they built their nests, and he concluded that the wood filaments used by these insects to construct their paperlike nests could also be used in the manufacture of paper.

Wasps look for dry wood which they saw or rasp in their jaws. This material is then mixed with a gluey substance secreted by the wasp's body to make a paste that, when spread, becomes the paper substance of the nest.

Wasp nests are exceptionally lightweight, dark in color, and bound repeatedly by bands of paper to the place where they are suspended. The nests are nearly waterproof because of their rounded tops and the fact that the paper strips overlap like the shingles on the roof of a house.

11. The word *filament* as used in line 5 of this passage probably means

(A) a large chunk

(B) a threadlike piece

(C) a file

(D) dust

12. The man who first suggested making paper from wood was a

(A) farmer

(B) industrialist

(C) lumberjack

(D) naturalist

13. According to the passage, a wasp nest is usually

(A) attached to a house

(B) exceptionally lightweight

(C) waterproofed with a gluey substance

(D) constructed with chunks of wood

14. The primary material used by wasps in nest building is

(A) dirt

(B) water

(C) paste

(D) wood

15. Wasp nests are waterproof because
   (A) they are constructed of heavy materials
   (B) they hang from the boughs of trees
   (C) the strips of paper overlap
   (D) bands are placed around them

About 86 percent of the total weight of a glass of milk is water. The remaining 14 percent is a combination of nutritious solids suspended in the water. The solids consist of milk sugar, fat, protein, minerals, and vitamins.

Milk is a unique food because it meets most of the body's requirements for growth and health. It is especially rich in vitamins A and B and the minerals calcium and phosphorus, none of which can be easily obtained from other foods. These substances are essential for normal development and maintenance of healthy bones and teeth.

In spite of this, it is fortunate for us that we do not have to live on milk alone, as it does not supply us with the iron we need to prevent anemia. In its natural state, milk also lacks vitamin D, whose production within the body can be stimulated by sunshine, and the commercial preparation of milk eliminates its vitamin C. It is therefore necessary to get these essential vitamins and minerals from other food sources.

16. The largest part of milk is
   (A) water
   (B) sugar
   (C) vitamins
   (D) minerals

17. Milk is an especially important food because
   (A) it is cheap
   (B) it is easily available
   (C) it contains so much protein
   (D) a number of its nutrients are not easily obtained from other food sources

18. Milk does not contain
   (A) phosphorus
   (B) iron
   (C) fat
   (D) vitamin A

19. According to the article, sunshine is important in the production of
   (A) vitamin A
   (B) vitamin C
   (C) vitamin D
   (D) calcium

For generations, historians and boat lovers have been trying to learn more about the brave ship that brought the Pilgrims to America. The task is a difficult one because *Mayflower* was such a common name for ships back in early seventeenth-century England that there were at least twenty of them when the Pilgrims left for the New World.

An exact duplicate of the *Mayflower* has been built in England and given to the people of the United States as a symbol of good will and common ancestry linking Britons and Americans. The Pilgrims' *Mayflower* apparently was built originally as a fishing vessel. It seems to have been 90 feet long by 22 feet wide, displacing 180 tons of water. The duplicate measures 90 feet by 26 feet, displaces 183 tons, and has a crew of 21, as did the original vessel. The new *Mayflower* has no motor but travels faster than the old boat.

What happened to the historic boat? So far as can be told, the *Mayflower* went back to less colorful jobs and, not too many years later, was scrapped. What happened to the beams, masts, and planking is questionable. In the English city of Abingdon, there is a Congregational church that contains two heavy wooden pillars. Some say these pillars are masts from the *Mayflower*. A barn in the English town of Jordans seemed to be built of old ship timbers. Marine experts said these timbers were impregnated with salt and, if put together, would form a vessel 90 feet by 22 feet. The man who owned the farm when the peculiar barn was built was a relative of the man who appraised the *Mayflower* when it was scrapped.

GO ON TO THE NEXT PAGE

So the original *Mayflower* may still be doing service ashore while her duplicate sails the seas again.

20. A long search was made for the Pilgrims' boat because it

(A) contained valuable materials

(B) might still do sea service

(C) has historical importance

(D) would link Great Britain and America

21. It has been difficult to discover what happened to the original *Mayflower* because

(A) many ships bore the same name

(B) it was such a small vessel

(C) the search was begun too late

(D) it has become impregnated with salt

22. The British recently had a duplicate of the *Mayflower* built because

(A) the original could not be located

(B) they wanted to make a gesture of friendship

(C) parts of the original could be used

(D) historians recommended such a step

23. Compared with the original *Mayflower*, the modern duplicate

(A) is longer

(B) is identical

(C) carries a larger crew

(D) is somewhat wider

24. When the author says that the original boat may still be doing service ashore, he means that

(A) it may be whole and intact somewhere

(B) present-day buildings may include parts of it

(C) it may be in a boat lover's private collection

(D) it may be in the service of pirates

Few animals are as descriptively named as the varying hare *(Lepus americanus)*, also commonly known as the snowshoe hare, white rabbit, or snowshoe rabbit. The species derives its various names from its interesting adaptations to the seasonal changes affecting its habitat.

The color changes are effected by means of a molt, and are timed (although the hares have no voluntary control over them) to coincide with the changing appearances of the background. The periods of transition—from white to brown in the spring, and from brown to white in the fall—require more than two months from start to completion, during which time the hares are a mottled brown and white. In addition to the changes in color, in the fall the soles of the feet develop a very heavy growth of hair that functions as snowshoes.

In New York State, hares are most abundant in and around the Adirondack and Catskill Mountains. Thriving populations, with less extensive ranges, are found in Allegany, Cattaraugus, Rensselaer, and Chenango counties. Smaller colonies of limited range are found in scattered islands.

25. The title that best expresses the main idea of this selection is

(A) Seasonal Changes in Birds

(B) The Varying Hare

(C) An American Animal

(D) The Abundance of Hares

26. Terms used to name these rabbits are related to their

(A) abundance in many parts of New York State

(B) sensitivity to weather conditions throughout the state

(C) ability to adapt to the change of seasons

(D) thick white coats

27. These rabbits have both brown and white markings in

(A) summer and winter

(B) spring and fall

(C) spring and summer

(D) fall and winter

28. The parts of New York State where rabbit populations are most plentiful are

(A) Allegany, Cattaraugus, Rensselaer, and Chenango counties
(B) Adirondack and Catskill Mountain regions
(C) islands within the state
(D) snowy areas in the hills

29. Which statement about these rabbits is *true* according to the selection?

(A) They are becoming fewer in number.
(B) They are capable of leaping great distances.
(C) They are more plentiful in winter.
(D) They have no control over their color changes

Like the United States today, Athens had courts where a wrong might be righted. Since any citizen might accuse another of a crime, the Athenian courts of law were very busy. In fact, unless a citizen was unusually peaceful or very unimportant, he would be sure to find himself in the courts at least once every few years.

At a trial, both the accuser and the person accused were allowed a certain time to speak. The length of time was marked by a water clock. Free men testified under oath as they do today, but the oath of a slave was counted as worthless.

To judge a trial, a jury was chosen from the members of the assembly who had reached 30 years of age. The Athenian juries were very large, often consisting of 201, 401, 501, 1,001, or more men, depending upon the importance of the case being tried. The juryman swore by the gods to listen carefully to both sides of the question and to give his honest opinion of the case. Each juryman gave his decision by depositing a white or black stone in a box. To keep citizens from being too careless in accusing each other, there was a rule that if the person accused did not receive a certain number of negative votes, the accuser was condemned instead.

30. The title that best expresses the main idea of this selection is

(A) Athens and the United States
(B) Justice in Ancient Athens
(C) Testifying Under Oath
(D) The Duties of Juries

31. People in Athens were frequently on trial in a law court because

(A) they liked to serve on juries
(B) a juryman agreed to listen to both sides
(C) any person might accuse another of a crime
(D) the slaves were troublesome

32. An Athenian was likely to avoid accusing another without a good reason because

(A) the jury might condemn the accuser instead of the accused
(B) the jury might be very large
(C) cases were judged by men over 30 years old
(D) there was a limit on the time a trial could take

33. Which statement is *true* according to the selection?

(A) An accused person was denied the privilege of telling his side of the case.
(B) The importance of the case determined the number of jurors.
(C) A jury's decision was handed down in writing.
(D) A citizen had to appear in court every few years.

The temperature of the Earth's upper atmosphere is one of the most revealing properties of the Earth's near environment. Not only does it vary widely with time and location but it also reacts strongly to changes in solar activity. The variation of temperature with altitude and with time reflects directly the different energy sources that in large measure govern the dynamic behavior of

GO ON TO THE NEXT PAGE

the upper atmosphere. The temperature also controls the rate of change of density with altitude through the requirement of hydrostatic balance. In hydrostatic balance the atmospheric pressure at any height equals the total weight of the overlying gas, a condition that requires that the pressure and density of the gas decrease exponentially at a rate inversely proportional to the temperature.

Thus, if the altitude profile of the temperature is known, one can calculate the altitude profiles of pressure and density provided the mean molecular weight of the gas is also known. This proviso is necessary because the rate of decrease of pressure and density is proportional to the mean molecular weight. Since heavy gases, such as argon and carbon dioxide, are more tightly bound by the earth's gravitational field, they tend to concentrate at low altitudes, while the density of light constituents, such as hydrogen and helium, decreases very slowly with height. At altitudes below about 110 kilometers, however, this tendency toward gravitational separation of the constituents is fully counteracted by turbulent mixing processes so the mean molecular weight of the atmosphere varies very little from its sea-level value of 29 atomic mass units (amu). At higher altitudes there is little mixing. The heavy constituents become progressively more rare, and the dominant atmospheric constituent changes, with increasing altitude, from molecular nitrogen (28 amu), to atomic oxygen (16 amu), to helium (4 amu), and, at very high altitudes, to atomic hydrogen (1 amu).

34. All of the following affect the temperature of the Earth's upper atmosphere EXCEPT

(A) Sun
(B) altitude
(C) time
(D) weather

35. Which of the following most strongly affects the upper atmosphere?

(A) lack of oxygen
(B) seasonal changes
(C) air pressure
(D) heat of the Sun

36. At the highest altitude one would find

(A) helium
(B) oxygen
(C) hydrogen
(D) nitrogen

37. Which statement best reflects the main idea of this article?

(A) There is a great variability in the temperature of the Earth from place to place and from time to time.
(B) Control of the Earth's upper atmosphere depends upon control of its temperature.
(C) Our environment is controlled by the Earth's temperature.
(D) High altitude temperature tells much about the Earth's atmosphere.

On May 8, 1939, folk song collector and scholar Herbert Halpert arrived in Mississippi to document folklore and folk music during a recording tour of the South sponsored by the Joint Committee on the Arts of the Works Progress Administration (WPA). He drove into the state in an old ambulance outfitted with cabinets, a small cot, food, and clothes. The ambulance also had specially built shelves for the latest in recording equipment—an acetate disc recorder lent by the Archive of American Folk Song at the Library of Congress.

To take full advantage of Halpert's short visit, local WPA workers acted as intermediaries, preceding the recording truck to make arrangements with the folk musicians he would visit and grouping artists in convenient places to minimize travel and maximize recording time. Following their schedule, with a few side trips to pursue a couple of leads of his own, Halpert cut 168 records between May 8 and June 11, 1939. Abbott Ferriss, a Mississippi native, assisted him.

In addition to helping with the actual recording, Ferriss kept field notes on the trip and took photographs of the musicians, their families, homes, and surroundings. At the project's conclusion the recordings became part of the folk-music collections at the Library of Congress. The photographs and much of the manuscript material related to the project remained in Mississippi.

38. According to the passage, the purpose of Halpert's journey to Mississippi was

(A) to make arrangements for the writing of folk songs

(B) to consult with a local native

(C) to record the folk music of Mississippi performers

(D) to photograph the Mississippi landscape

39. Which of the following is *not* stated in the passage?

(A) The WPA sponsored a recording project in the South.

(B) Local workers helped Halpert by searching for musicians.

(C) The local workers sought to minimize Halpert's travel time.

(D) The photographs were sent to the Library of Congress.

40. Which of the following can be reasonably inferred about the WPA?

(A) It was only interested in folk music.

(B) It took full advantage of short visits to the Library of Congress.

(C) It was a national organization with local offices.

(D) It was sponsored by the Joint Committee on the Arts.

STOP

END OF TEST THREE. IF YOU HAVE ANY TIME LEFT, GO OVER YOUR WORK ON THIS TEST ONLY. DO NOT WORK ON ANY OTHER TEST OF THE EXAM.

TEST FOUR: MATHEMATICS ACHIEVEMENT

50 QUESTIONS • TIME—40 MINUTES

Directions: Each question is followed by four answer choices. Choose the correct answer to each question, and mark its letter on your answer sheet.

1. A recipe for 6 quarts of punch calls for $\frac{3}{4}$ cup of sugar. How much sugar is needed for 9 quarts of punch?

(A) five-eighths of a cup

(B) seven-eighths of a cup

(C) $1\frac{1}{8}$ cups

(D) $2\frac{1}{4}$ cups

2. How many yards of ribbon will it take to make 45 badges if each badge uses 4 inches of ribbon?

(A) 5

(B) 9

(C) 11

(D) 15

3. In making a bracelet a girl uses three 10-inch strips of cord. How many bracelets can she make from a 5-yard roll of cord?

(A) 2

(B) 5

(C) 6

(D) 15

4. As an employee at a clothing store, you are entitled to a 10% discount on all purchases. When the store has a sale, employees are also entitled to the 20% discount offered to all customers. What would you have to pay for a $60 jacket bought on a sale day?

(A) $6

(B) $10.80

(C) $36

(D) $43.20

5. A section of pavement that is 10 feet long and 8 feet wide contains how many square feet?

(A) 18 sq. ft.

(B) 80 sq. ft.

(C) 92 sq. ft.

(D) 800 sq. ft.

6. In 1972, approximately 19,000 fatal accidents were sustained in industry. There were approximately 130 nonfatal injuries to each fatal injury. The number of nonfatal accidents during 1972 was approximately

(A) 146,000

(B) 190,000

(C) 1,150,000

(D) 2,500,000

7. What is the value of x when $5x = 5 \times 4 \times 2 \times 0$?

(A) 6

(B) 8

(C) 1

(D) 0

8. Mr. Jones has agreed to borrow $3,500 for one year at 10% simple interest. What is the total amount he will pay back to the bank?

(A) $350

(B) $3,675

(C) $3,700

(D) $3,850

9. A particular store has a 100% mark-up from wholesale to retail prices. A dress that costs $130 retail will cost how much wholesale?

(A) $260

(B) $100

(C) $90

(D) $65

10. The scale used on a blueprint is $\frac{1}{8}$" = 1 foot. If a room is actually 17' × 22', how large will it be on the drawing?

(A) $1\frac{1}{8}$" × $2\frac{1}{4}$"

(B) $2\frac{1}{8}$" × $2\frac{3}{4}$"

(C) $2\frac{1}{2}$" × 3"

(D) $2\frac{3}{4}$" × $3\frac{1}{8}$"

11. A roll of carpeting contains 90 square feet of carpet. How many rolls will be required to carpet a room 28' × 20'?

(A) $6\frac{2}{9}$

(B) 6

(C) $5\frac{8}{9}$

(D) $5\frac{3}{8}$

12. $100 - x = 5^2$. What is the value of x?

(A) 75

(B) 50

(C) 25

(D) 5

13. Two trains are 500 miles apart. One is traveling 70 miles per hour and the second 30 miles per hour. If they both leave at 6:00 AM, when will they meet?

(A) 9:00 AM

(B) 10:00 AM

(C) 11:00 AM

(D) 12:00 AM

14. If $72x = 6y$, and $y = 2$, $x = ?$

(A) $\frac{1}{2}$

(B) $\frac{1}{6}$

(C) 6

(D) 12

15. 60 hr. 21 min.
<u>–5 hr. 37 min.</u>

(A) 54 hr. 44 min.

(B) 54 hr. 84 min.

(C) 55 hr. 44 min.

(D) 55 hr. 84 min.

16. Which of the following represents one half of a certain number squared, minus 6?

(A) $6 = \frac{1}{2}x^2$

(B) $\frac{1}{2}x - 6$

(C) $\frac{x^2}{\frac{1}{2}} - 6$

(D) $\frac{1}{2}x^2 - 6$

17. A mixture contains 20 gallons of water and 5 gallons of nitric acid. If 10 more gallons of water are added, the part that is water is

(A) $\frac{1}{7}$

(B) $\frac{2}{9}$

(C) $\frac{1}{4}$

(D) $\frac{6}{7}$

GO ON TO THE NEXT PAGE

18. Which is the longest time?

(A) $\frac{1}{24}$ of a day

(B) $1\frac{1}{2}$ hours

(C) 100 minutes

(D) $\frac{1}{30}$ of a month

19. What percentage of a circle graph would be represented by a portion having a right angle?

(A) 90%

(B) 45%

(C) 25%

(D) 20%

20. Find the perimeter of a rectangle with the dimensions 115' × 63'.

(A) 7,245'

(B) 356'

(C) 187'

(D) 178'

21. 6.28 × 1.003 = ?

(A) .629884

(B) 6.29884

(C) 62.9442

(D) 629.884

22. Solve for x: $\frac{x^2}{2.5} = 10$

(A) 5

(B) 10

(C) 20

(D) 25

23. If $2,000 were borrowed at 12% simple interest for 2 years, what would the total interest charge be?

(A) $240

(B) $360

(C) $420

(D) $480

24. The pup tent shown is 3 feet wide and 2 feet high. Find its volume if it is 6 feet long.

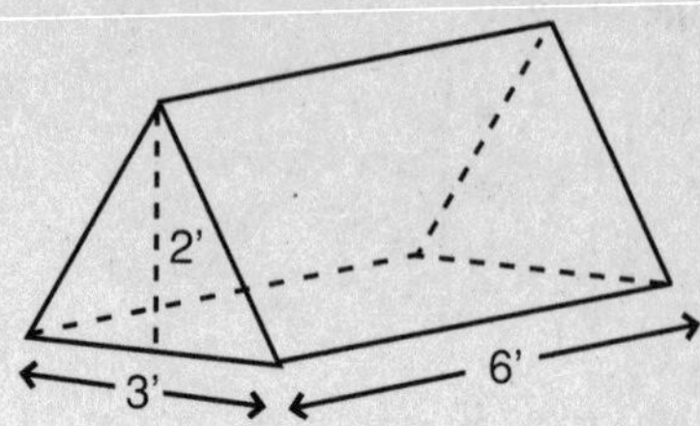

(A) 36 sq. ft.

(B) 18 cu. ft.

(C) 24 cu. ft.

(D) 36 cu. ft.

25. A board 30' long is cut into three unequal parts. The first is three times as long as the second. The third is twice as long as the first. How long is the longest piece?

(A) 6'

(B) 9'

(C) 12'

(D) 18'

26. A wine merchant has 32 gallons of wine worth $1.50 a gallon. If he wishes to reduce the price to $1.20 a gallon, how many gallons of water must he add?

(A) 10

(B) 9

(C) 8

(D) 7

27. Six is four more than $\frac{2}{3}$ of what number?

(A) 1

(B) 3

(C) 4

(D) 6

28. The winner of a race received $\frac{1}{3}$ of the total purse. The third-place finisher received one-third of the winner's share. If the winner's share was $2,700, what was the total purse?

(A) $8,100

(B) $2,700

(C) $1,800

(D) $ 900

29. A police officer found his 42-hour work week was divided as follows: $\frac{1}{6}$ of his time in investigating incidents on his patrol post; $\frac{1}{2}$ of his time patrolling his post; and $\frac{1}{8}$ of his time in special traffic duty. The rest of his time was devoted to assignments at precinct headquarters. The percentage of his work spent at precinct headquarters is most nearly

(A) 10%

(B) 15%

(C) 20%

(D) 25%

30. Two men working together can build a cabinet in $2\frac{1}{2}$ days. The first man, working alone, can build the cabinet in 6 days. How long would it take the second man to build the cabinet working alone?

(A) $5\frac{1}{7}$ days

(B) $4\frac{7}{8}$ days

(C) $4\frac{2}{7}$ days

(D) $3\frac{7}{8}$ days

31. Two cars start toward each other along a road between two cities that are 450 miles apart. The speed of the first car is 35 mph, and that of the second is 48 mph. How much time will elapse before they meet?

(A) 6.01 hours

(B) 5.42 hours

(C) 5.25 hours

(D) 4.98 hours

32. A stock clerk had 600 pads on hand. He then issued $\frac{3}{8}$ of his supply of pads to Division *X*, $\frac{1}{4}$ to Division *Y*, and $\frac{1}{6}$ to Division *Z*. The number of pads remaining in stock is

(A) 48

(B) 125

(C) 240

(D) 475

33. One man can load a truck in 25 minutes, a second can load it in 50 minutes, and a third can load it in 10 minutes. How long would it take the three together to load the truck?

(A) $5\frac{3}{11}$ minutes

(B) $6\frac{1}{4}$ minutes

(C) $8\frac{1}{3}$ minutes

(D) 10 minutes

34. If $4x - y = 20$, and $2x + y = 28$, then $x = ?$

(A) 24

(B) 16

(C) 8

(D) 6

35. If $6 + x + y = 20$, and $x + y = k$, then $20 - k =$

(A) 0

(B) 6

(C) 14

(D) 20

36.

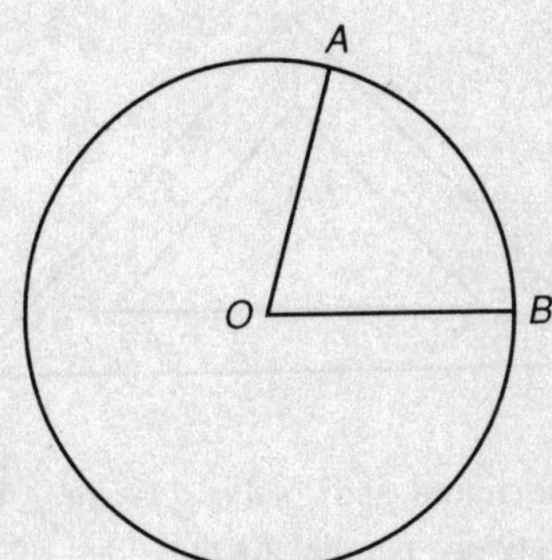

In the figure above, $\angle AOB = 60°$. If *O* is the center of the circle, then minor arc *AB* is what part of the circumference of the circle?

(A) $\frac{1}{2}$

(B) $\frac{1}{3}$

(C) $\frac{1}{6}$

(D) $\frac{1}{8}$

GO ON TO THE NEXT PAGE

37. If all P are S and no S are Q, it necessarily follows that

(A) all Q are S

(B) all Q are P

(C) no P are Q

(D) no S are P

38. A is older than B. With the passage of time

(A) the ratio of the ages of A and B remains unchanged

(B) the ratio of the ages of A and B increases

(C) the ratio of the ages of A and B decreases

(D) the difference in their ages varies

39. From a temperature of 15°, a drop of 21° would result in a temperature of

(A) 36

(B) –6

(C) –30

(D) –36

40.

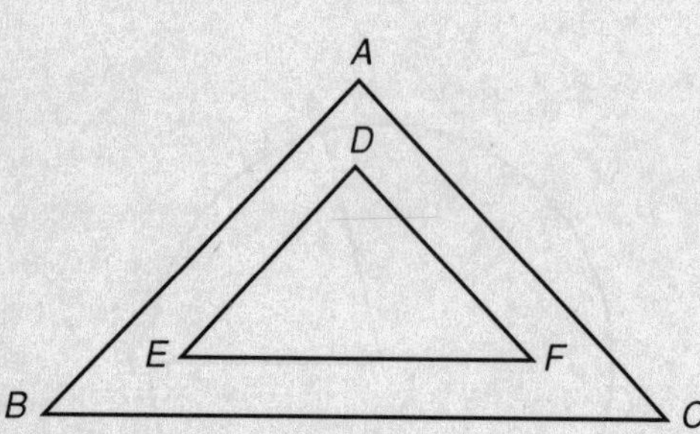

In the figure above, the sides of ΔABC are respectively parallel to the sides of triangle DEF. If the complement of A is 40°, then the complement of D is

(A) 20°

(B) 40°

(C) 50°

(D) 60°

41. A line of print in a magazine article contains an average of 6 words. There are 5 lines to the inch. If 8 inches are available for an article that contains 270 words, how must the article be changed?

(A) Add 30 words.

(B) Delete 30 words.

(C) Delete 40 words.

(D) Add 60 words.

42.

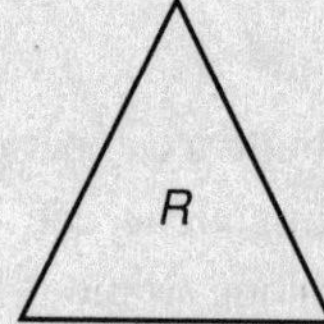

Triangle R is 3 times triangle S. Triangle S is 3 times triangle T. If triangle $S = 1$, what is the sum of the three triangles?

(A) $2\frac{1}{3}$

(B) $3\frac{1}{3}$

(C) $4\frac{1}{3}$

(D) 6

43. If 5 pints of water are needed to water each square foot of lawn, the minimum gallons of water needed for a lawn 8' by 12' is

(A) 5

(B) 20

(C) 40

(D) 60

44. In the formula $l = p + prt$, what does l equal when $p = 500$, $r = 20\%$, $t = 2$?

(A) 700

(B) 8,000

(C) 10,000

(D) 12,000

45. A car owner finds he needs 12 gallons of gas for each 120 miles he drives. If he has his carburetor adjusted, he will need only 80% as much gas. How many miles will 12 gallons of gas then last him?

(A) 90

(B) 96

(C) 150

(D) 160

46. What is the maximum number of books each $\frac{1}{4}$ inch thick that can be placed standing on a shelf 4 feet long?

(A) 16

(B) 48

(C) 96

(D) 192

47. In a bag there are red, green, black, and white marbles. If there are 6 red, 8 green, 4 black, and 12 white, and one marble is to be selected at random, what is the probability it will be white?

(A) $\frac{1}{5}$

(B) $\frac{2}{5}$

(C) $\frac{2}{15}$

(D) $\frac{4}{15}$

48.

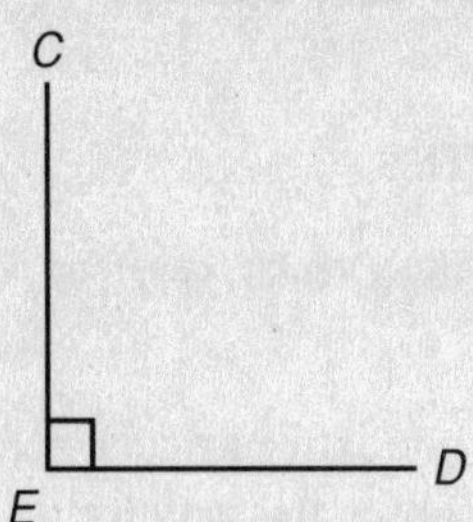

In the diagram above, $CE \perp ED$. If $CE = 7$ and $ED = 6$, what is the shortest distance from C to D?

(A) 6

(B) 7

(C) $\sqrt{85}$

(D) $4\sqrt{12}$

49. If $a = 3$, then $a^a \cdot a =$

(A) 9

(B) 18

(C) 51

(D) 81

50. $(3 + 2)(6 - 2)(7 + 1) = (4 + 4)(x)$. What is the value of x?

(A) 13 + 2

(B) 14 + 4

(C) 4 + 15

(D) 8 + 12

STOP

END OF TEST FOUR. IF YOU HAVE ANY TIME LEFT, GO OVER YOUR WORK ON THIS TEST ONLY. DO NOT WORK ON ANY OTHER TEST OF THE EXAM.

TEST FIVE: ESSAY

TIME—30 MINUTES

Directions: Write a legible, coherent, and correct essay on the following topic.

Topic: Tell about one extracurricular activity in which you hope to participate in high school. Give reasons why you have chosen this activity.

Independent School Entrance Examination Practice Exam 2

Answer Key

TEST ONE: VERBAL ABILITY

1. **D**	9. **C**	17. **C**	25. **A**	33. **B**
2. **D**	10. **C**	18. **D**	26. **B**	34. **C**
3. **A**	11. **A**	19. **D**	27. **C**	35. **B**
4. **A**	12. **B**	20. **B**	28. **C**	36. **B**
5. **A**	13. **D**	21. **D**	29. **A**	37. **D**
6. **B**	14. **C**	22. **C**	30. **D**	38. **B**
7. **C**	15. **D**	23. **D**	31. **A**	39. **D**
8. **D**	16. **A**	24. **D**	32. **D**	40. **C**

TEST TWO: QUANTITATIVE ABILITY

1. **B**	9. **D**	17. **D**	25. **B**	33. **A**
2. **C**	10. **D**	18. **C**	26. **A**	34. **C**
3. **B**	11. **B**	19. **A**	27. **C**	35. **D**
4. **B**	12. **B**	20. **B**	28. **C**	36. **B**
5. **D**	13. **C**	21. **C**	29. **C**	37. **C**
6. **C**	14. **A**	22. **A**	30. **A**	38. **A**
7. **C**	15. **B**	23. **D**	31. **B**	39. **A**
8. **A**	16. **D**	24. **A**	32. **B**	40. **C**

TEST THREE: READING COMPREHENSION

1. **B**	9. **A**	17. **D**	25. **B**	33. **B**
2. **A**	10. **C**	18. **B**	26. **C**	34. **D**
3. **B**	11. **B**	19. **C**	27. **B**	35. **D**
4. **A**	12. **D**	20. **C**	28. **B**	36. **C**
5. **D**	13. **B**	21. **A**	29. **D**	37. **D**
6. **C**	14. **D**	22. **B**	30. **B**	38. **C**
7. **B**	15. **C**	23. **D**	31. **C**	39. **D**
8. **D**	16. **A**	24. **B**	32. **A**	40. **C**

TEST FOUR: MATHEMATICS ACHIEVEMENT

1. **C**	11. **A**	21. **B**	31. **B**	41. **B**
2. **A**	12. **A**	22. **A**	32. **B**	42. **C**
3. **C**	13. **C**	23. **D**	33. **B**	43. **D**
4. **D**	14. **B**	24. **B**	34. **C**	44. **A**
5. **B**	15. **A**	25. **D**	35. **B**	45. **C**
6. **D**	16. **D**	26. **C**	36. **C**	46. **D**
7. **D**	17. **D**	27. **B**	37. **C**	47. **B**
8. **D**	18. **D**	28. **A**	38. **C**	48. **C**
9. **D**	19. **C**	29. **C**	39. **B**	49. **D**
10. **B**	20. **B**	30. **C**	40. **B**	50. **D**

Independent School Entrance Examination Practice Exam 2

Explanatory Answers

TEST ONE: VERBAL ABILITY

SYNONYMS

1. **(D)** To IMPLY is to *indicate indirectly,* to *suggest,* or to *hint.* By her strange smile, the Mona Lisa implies that she knows a secret.
2. **(D)** That which is FISCAL has to *do with money.* A fiscal year is the 12-month period between settlement of accounts.
3. **(A)** STRINGENT means *rigidly controlled, strict,* or *severe.* Prospective firefighters must pass a stringent physical exam to prove that they can meet the demands of the job.
4. **(A)** That which is PERMEABLE can be *penetrated,* especially by *fluids.* The rain barrel was covered with a permeable cloth that strained out solid particles. The word meaning "allowable" is "permissible"; that meaning "durable" or "unending" is "permanent."
5. **(A)** SCRUPULOUS means *careful to do the right, proper, or correct thing in every detail.* The legislator took scrupulous care to fill out the ethics form accurately.
6. **(B)** A STALEMATE is a *deadlock* or *impasse.* Neither the union nor management would concede a point, so the negotiations were at a stalemate.
7. **(C)** REDUNDANT means *more than necessary* or *superfluous.* The word "join" indicates that units are put together, therefore, in the expression "join together" the word "together" is redundant.
8. **(D)** To SUPPLANT is to *supersede* or to *replace.* The Constitution supplanted the Articles of Confederation.
9. **(C)** COMMENSURATE means *proportionate.* The two-year-old's vocabulary was commensurate with her age.
10. **(C)** The ZENITH is the *point directly overhead* or the *highest point.* The sun reaches its zenith at noon.
11. **(A)** SUCCOR is *aid, help,* or *relief.* It is treason to give succor to the enemy by distributing false propaganda.
12. **(B)** To DISPATCH is to *send out quickly.* Do not rely on the mails; dispatch a messenger to deliver the package.
13. **(D)** PORTABLE means *easily moved or carried.* A television set with a three-inch screen is a portable set. The word meaning "drinkable" is "potable."
14. **(C)** VERBOSE means *containing too many words* or *long-winded.* The speaker was so verbose that we thought the evening would never end.
15. **(D)** SUBVERSIVE means *seeking to overthrow* or *to destroy something established.* Subversive elements in the government are extremely dangerous to stability.
16. **(A)** That which is VACILLATING tends to *wave to and fro* or to *be indecisive.* The student had a hard time making up his mind; he kept vacillating between two schools that had accepted him.
17. **(C)** PETTY means *trivial, narrow,* or *small.* The crotchety old man was full of petty complaints.
18. **(D)** INTREPID means *bold, brave,* and *fearless.* The intrepid astronauts went on their mission as if there had never been an accident.
19. **(D)** To NEGOTIATE is to *make arrangements* or to *bargain.* The buyer and seller of a property must negotiate to reach a fair price.
20. **(B)** STERILE means *extremely clean, barren,* or *germ-free.* For the safety of the patient, the surgeon must work in a sterile environment.

SENTENCE COMPLETIONS

21. **(D)** Since Joshua was undaunted (not discouraged) by his failures, a positive word is necessary. PERSEVERED is the only positive word.
22. **(C)** In order to attract students, INNOVATIVE (new, novel) methods are necessary.
23. **(D)** Since there is less money available and fewer business transactions are being conducted, BUYERS have the upper hand in how they spend their money.
24. **(D)** Multiple offenses would require an *increased* penalty; therefore, ESCALATE is the only correct choice.
25. **(A)** All the adjectives describing the hotel are positive; therefore, a positive description is necessary.
26. **(B)** The opposite of forcing students to take courses is ENTICING them to do so.
27. **(C)** An innovative method of dealing with criminals is being suggested in contrast to the usual method, which is IMPRISONMENT.
28. **(C)** The sentence mentions "knowledge gained without experience" and then asks for the opposite condition, which must be EXPERIENCE without SCHOLARSHIP.
29. **(A)** By having an insurance expert discuss the changes, the school system was attempting to reduce, or QUELL, ANXIETY over those increased fees.
30. **(D)** The first half of the sentence requires a word that contrasts with poverty (COMFORTABLE). The second word must show that poverty is widespread among older Americans.
31. **(A)** A little common sense should give you this answer immediately. Choice (C) makes no sense at all. A police officer's job is to prevent crime, but that is not the officer's only job, just the PRIMARY job.
32. **(D)** Extenuating circumstances mitigate the seriousness of a crime. A young defendant also tends to be offered a "second chance." It is therefore most plausible that the judge would have recommended LENIENCY.
33. **(B)** The fact that the family respected one another means that they AVERTED clashes.
34. **(C)** Health-conscious consumers will ENCOURAGE change.
35. **(B)** Although the politician lost the election, he MAINTAINED his popularity with some followers.
36. **(B)** An arrest or domestic dispute is considered a serious CRISIS.
37. **(D)** A negative word (FAIL) must be followed by a positive word (PAYOFF).
38. **(B)** Since the sentence is about one writer's style, "those he imitated" must also be writers. The words needed to complete the thought therefore must be opposites that apply to even the best writers. STRENGTHS and FLAWS (weaknesses) best satisfy this requirement.
39. **(D)** The word "help" indicates the need for a positive word to complete this sentence. Therefore, you need consider only choices (A) and (D). Of these two, IMPLEMENT (meaning put into action) is a better choice than magnify (meaning to make larger).
40. **(C)** The words required to complete the thought must be opposites. A LUXURY is something we can easily do without, but once we have had that luxury for awhile we can no longer do without it and it becomes a necessity (an ESSENTIAL).

TEST TWO: QUANTITATIVE ABILITY

1. **(B)** It is useful to know how to multiply and divide by 10, 100, 1,000, and so on by moving the decimal point.
2. **(C)** The sum of the angles of a triangle is 180°. Angle B is 90°. Angles A and C, therefore, must total 180° – 90°, or 90°.
3. **(B)**
4. **(B)** Circumference = $\pi \cdot$ diameter

   Diameter = $2 \cdot$ radius

   $$\pi = \frac{22}{7}$$

   $$C = \pi \cdot 21 \cdot 2$$

   $$C = 42 \cdot \pi = 42 \cdot \frac{22}{7} = 132'$$

You can also estimate this problem and choose the closest answer.

5. **(D)** The set $\{x, y\}$ includes all those numbers larger than –4 and smaller than 2. Considering only whole numbers, this set includes –3, –2, –1, 0, 1.
6. **(C)**
7. **(C)** The order in which numbers are added does not affect the sum.
8. **(A)** We want the amount in the parentheses to be equal to 3. The value of x that will make the amount in parentheses equal to 3 is 4.
9. **(D)** Refer to the Geometry Review section if necessary.
10. **(D)** The number is read "five thousandths."
11. **(B)** Note that $\frac{17}{30}$ is slightly larger than $\frac{15}{30}$ or $\frac{1}{2}$. Answers (A), (C), and (D) are closer in value to 1 than to $\frac{1}{2}$.
12. **(B)** 100 centimeters = 1 meter. Each centimeter is $\frac{1}{100}$ of a meter.
13. **(C)** Find the LCM (least common multiple) of 4, 9, 6, and 12, and this becomes the least common denominator.
14. **(A)** The set of factors of 36 is

    {1, 2, 3, 4, 6, 9, 12, 18, 36}.

    The set of factors of 64 is

    {1, 2, 4, 8, 16, 32, 64}.

    The set of common factors is

    {1, 2, 4}.
15. **(B)** $10 < 10.5$
16. **(D)** The sum of the angles of a triangle is 180°.

    $180° - 115° = 65°$.
17. **(D)** The union of the two adjacent line segments creates one continuous line segment.
18. **(C)** The 52 playing cards in a deck consist of 4 suits of 13 cards each. There is one 6 in each of the four suits, making the probability of drawing a 6 $\frac{4}{52}$ or $\frac{1}{13}$.
19. **(A)** Every 8 miles is represented on the map by $\frac{1}{2}$ inch. $28 \div 8 = 3\frac{1}{2}$, so $3\frac{1}{2}$ $\frac{1}{2}$-inch units are needed to represent 28 miles. $3\frac{1}{2} \times \frac{1}{2} = \frac{7}{2} \times \frac{1}{2} = \frac{7}{4} = 1\frac{3}{4}$. You may solve the problem another way: If $\frac{1}{2}" = 8$ miles, $1" = 16$ miles. $28 \div 16 = 1\frac{3}{4}$, so $1\frac{3}{4}"$ are required to represent 28 miles.
20. **(B)** The number of accidents is irrelevant to the question, so A has no place in the equation.

    B (total deaths) ÷ 10 years = $\frac{B}{10}$ average deaths per year.
21. **(C)** $6\% = .06$ $\quad$ $7\% = .07$

    $.06(42) = 2.52$ $\quad$ $.07(36) = 2.52$

    ∴Column A = Column B
22. **(A)**

$3x^2 + 2x - 1$	$x^3 + 2x^2 + 1$
$3(-2)^2 + 2(-2) - 1$	$(-2)^3 + 2(-2)^2 + 1$
$3(4) - 4 - 1$	$-8 + 8 + 1$
$12 - 4 - 1$	$+1$
7	

∴Column A > Column B

23. **(D)** The relationship between column A and column B cannot be determined from the information given.
24. **(A)**

    $(16 \div 4) + (8 \times 2) - 8$

    $4 + 16 - 8$

    $20 - 8$

    12

    $(3 \times 4) + (10 \div 5) - 3$

    $12 + 2 - 3$

    $14 - 3$

    11

    ∴Column A > Column B
25. **(B)** Original Cost + Profit = Selling Price

    Let x = original cost

    then $x + .05(x) = \$47.25$

    $1.05x = \$47.25$

    $x = \$45$

    $\$45 > \$44.89$

    ∴Column B > Column A
26. **(A)** $a - b = -1$ $\quad$ $a - b = -1$ $\quad$ $a - d = -1$

    $-a - b = -3$ $\quad$ $a - (2) = -1$

    $-b = -4$ $\quad$ $a = 1$

    $b = 2$

    ∴Column A > Column B

27. **(C)** $.25(300) = 75$ (girls with blond hair)

$300 - 75 = 225$ (girls without blond hair)

$$\frac{75}{225} = \frac{1}{3}$$

∴Column A = Column B

28. **(C)** The sum of the angles of a triangle equal 180°

$$a + b + c = 180$$

$$\text{and } d + e + f = 180$$

$$\therefore a + b + c + d + e + f = 360$$

also $e + c = 90$. Therefore,

$b + a + d + f = 270$ (subtraction)

∴Column A = Column B

29. **(C)** A parallelogram inscribed in a circle is a rectangle. Therefore, all angles equal 90°.

Hence, $a + c = b + d$

∴Column A = Column B

30. **(A)** $\frac{9}{8} = 1.125$

$\frac{3}{5} = .60$

$1.125 - .60 = .525$

$.525 > .5$

∴Column A > Column B

31. **(B)** $\frac{3}{5}\% = .6\% = .0060$

$.06 > .006$

∴Column B > Column A

32. **(B)** Let x = the no. of days *A* & *B* take working together.

A can do the job in 4 days or *A*'s rate is $\frac{1}{4}$.

B can do the job in 3 days or *B*'s rate is $\frac{1}{3}$.

$$\frac{x}{4} + \frac{x}{3} = 1$$

$$\frac{7}{x} = 1$$

$$x = 1\frac{5}{7} \text{ days}$$

$2 \text{ days} > 1\frac{5}{7}\text{days}$

∴Column B > Column A

33. **(A)** The ratio between seniors and the total of seniors and freshmen is 1:4. The ratio between seniors and the total enrollment (including sophomores and juniors) would actually decrease.

∴Column A > Column B

34. **(C)** Since the sum of the three angles of a triangle equals 180°

then, $x + x + 60° = 180°$

$$2x = 120°$$

$$x = 60°$$

Therefore, the triangle is equilateral.

Hence, side m = side n

∴Column A = Column B

35. **(D)** The relationship cannot be determined from the information given.

36. **(B)** Since the sum of the angles of a triangle equals 180° then,

$$x + 2x + 90° = 180°$$

$$3x = 90°$$

$$x = 30°$$

Therefore ABC is a 30-60-90 right triangle. In a 30-60-90 right triangle the hypotenuse is equal to twice the side opposite the 30° angle.

∴AB = 8

$8 > 5$

∴Column B > Column A

37. **(C)** $\sqrt[3]{125} = 5$ $\sqrt{25} = 5$

∴Column A = Column B

38. **(A)** $x > 0$, x is positive

$y < 0$, y is negative

Substitute some arbitrary figures of your choosing,

for example: $x = 10$; $y = -2$

$x - y =$	$x + y =$
$10 - (-2) = 12$	$10 + (-2) = 8$

Column A > Column B

39. **(A)** $15\% = .15$

$.15\ (43.50) = 6.525$

$\$43.50 - 6.53 = 36.97$

$\$36.97 > \$36$

∴Column A > Column B

40. **(C)** $75\% = \frac{3}{4}$ $\quad 50\% = \frac{1}{2}$

$$\frac{3}{4}\left(\frac{1}{2}\right) = \frac{3}{8} \qquad \frac{1}{2}\left(\frac{3}{4}\right) = \frac{3}{8}$$

$\therefore$Column A = Column B

TEST THREE: READING COMPREHENSION

1. **(B)** See the first sentence.
2. **(A)** This definition is given in the explanatory statement at the end of the first sentence.
3. **(B)** The entire selection extols the dedication of the Pony Express riders in the face of the hazards they met.
4. **(A)** The fourth paragraph tells us that there was a ten-day limit in which the route must be covered.
5. **(D)** See paragraph 3. Buffalo Bill made the longest continuous run of 384 miles; Jim Moore made the fastest run, 280 miles in 22 hours.
6. **(C)** The selection discusses hatmaking as an early American industry, touching on materials, costs, and markets.
7. **(B)** See lines 15–16.
8. **(D)** Prohibition of export of hats from one colony to another and from any colony to Great Britain was an effective ban on export of hats altogether.
9. **(A)** See the second paragraph.
10. **(C)** Price comparisons are in the second paragraph.
11. **(B)** The dictionary definition of *filament* is "a very slender thread or fiber." You do not need to know the dictionary definition to answer this question. Wasps could not possibly be handling large chunks or files. The word *filaments* in the selection appears in the plural. If the meaning were "dust," the word would be in the singular.
12. **(D)** The first sentence describes Réne de Réaumer as a French naturalist.
13. **(B)** See the beginning of the third paragraph.
14. **(D)** The entire selection describes the manner in which wasps use wood to make the paper from which they construct nests.
15. **(C)** See the last sentence.
16. **(A)** See the first sentence.
17. **(D)** See lines 8–10.
18. **(B)** See lines 14–15.
19. **(C)** See lines 17–18.
20. **(C)** Clues may be found in the first sentence, which states that historians are trying to learn more about the *Mayflower,* and in the first sentence of the third paragraph, which describes the boat as historic.
21. **(A)** If you got this wrong, reread the second sentence of the first paragraph.
22. **(B)** See the first sentence of the second paragraph.
23. **(D)** The original *Mayflower* was 22 feet wide; the duplicate is 26 feet wide. The lengths are both 90 feet.
24. **(B)** You can infer this meaning from the fact that the author describes two buildings in England that may contain parts of the *Mayflower*.
25. **(B)** The selection describes the varying hare.
26. **(C)** As the names imply, the rabbits vary their appearance with the seasons.
27. **(B)** The rabbits are mottled brown and white while in the middle of the molting process during spring and fall.
28. **(B)** See the first sentence of the last paragraph.
29. **(D)** A parenthetical statement in the second paragraph states that the hares have no voluntary control over the changes in their appearance.
30. **(B)** The entire selection is about court practices in ancient Athens.
31. **(C)** The answer is in the second sentence.
32. **(A)** See the last sentence.
33. **(B)** See lines 15–17. The accused was allowed a certain time to speak; the jury voted by depositing black or white stones in a box.
34. **(D)** The second sentence tells us that the temperature of the Earth's upper atmosphere varies with time, location (altitude), and solar activity (the Sun). No mention is made of the weather.
35. **(D)** The first paragraph makes clear that the temperature (the heat of the Sun) directly affects many other measures and dimensions in the upper atmosphere.

36. **(C)** See the last sentence.
37. **(D)** See the first sentence.
38. **(C)** See the first sentence.
39. **(D)** The last sentence tells us that the photographs remained in Mississippi. The recordings themselves were sent to the Library of Congress.
40. **(C)** The second paragraph tells of local WPA workers and the assistance they gave.

TEST FOUR: MATHEMATICS ACHIEVEMENT

1. **(C)** First find out how much sugar is needed for one quart of punch.

   $\frac{3}{4}$ cup $\div 6 = \frac{3}{4} \times \frac{1}{6} = \frac{\cancel{3}^1}{4} \times \frac{1}{\cancel{6}_2} = \frac{1}{8}$

   For 9 quarts of punch: $9 \times \frac{1}{8} = \frac{9}{8} = 1\frac{1}{8}$
2. **(A)** 45 badges × 4 inches each = 180 inches needed

   There are 36 inches in one yard.

   180 inches ÷ 36 = 5 yards of ribbon needed
3. **(C)** 10 inches × 3 strips = 30 inches per bracelet; 36 inches per yard × 5 yards of cord = 180 inches in the roll; 180 ÷ 30 = 6 bracelets can be made from the roll.
4. **(D)** $60 × .10 = $6 (employee discount)

   $60 – $6 = $54

   $54 × .20 = $10.80 (sale discount)

   $54 – $10.80 = $43.20
5. **(B)** Area equals Length times Width.

   $A = L \times W$

   $A = 10$ ft. $\times 8$ ft.

   $A = 80$ sq. ft.
6. **(D)** For each of the 19,000 fatal accidents there were 130 nonfatal injuries. To find the total number of nonfatal accidents we multiply 19,000 × 130 = 2,470,000. There were approximately 2,500,000 nonfatal accidents in 1972.
7. **(D)** Any number multiplied by 0 equals 0. Since one multiplier on one side of the = sign is 0, the product on that side of the sign must be 0. The value on the other side of the = sign must also be 0.

   $5x = 5 \times 4 \times 2 \times 0$

   $5x = 40 \times 0$

   $5x = 0$

   $x = 0$
8. **(D)** He will pay back $3,500 plus 10% interest. Ten percent of $3,500 is $350. $3,500 + $350 = $3,850
9. **(D)** An item marked up 100% has a retail price twice the wholesale price. The coat now costs $130, which is twice $65.
10. **(B)** The width of the room will be $17 \times \frac{1}{8}$", or $2\frac{1}{8}$". The length of the room will be $22 \times \frac{1}{8}$", or $2\frac{3}{4}$".
11. **(A)** The room has an area of 28' × 20' = 560 sq. ft. Each roll of carpet can cover 90 sq. ft. The number of rolls required is $560 \div 90 = 6\frac{2}{9}$ rolls.
12. **(A)** To square a number multiply it by itself.

   $100 - x = 5^2$

   $100 - x = 5 \times 5$

   $100 - x = 25$

   $100 - 25 = x$

   $x = 75$
13. **(C)** Because they are traveling toward each other, the trains will cover the distance between them at a rate equal to the sum of their speeds, or 70 + 30 = 100 mph. They begin 500 miles apart, and thus will cover the distance between them in 5 hours. If they leave at 6:00 AM, they should meet at 11:00 AM.
14. **(B)** If $y = 2$,

   then $72x = 6(2)$

   $72x = 12$

   $x = \frac{1}{6}$
15. **(A)** Borrow 60 minutes and rewrite as:

   59 hr. 81 min.
   <u>–5 hr. 37 min.</u>
   54 hr. 44 min.
16. **(D)**

17. **(D)** Ten more gallons of water would bring the volume of the mixture to 30 gallons of water + 5 gallons of acid = 35 gallons. The part that is water is $\frac{30}{35}$, or $\frac{6}{7}$.

18. **(D)** $\frac{1}{30}$ of a month is about one day.

19. **(C)** A circle graph contains 360°, while a right angle contains 90°. A right angle, therefore, contains $\frac{1}{4}$, or 25%, of the circle.

20. **(B)** The perimeter is the sum of the lengths of the four sides. A rectangle has two pairs of sides of equal length. The perimeter then is (2 × 115) + (2 × 63) = 356 feet.

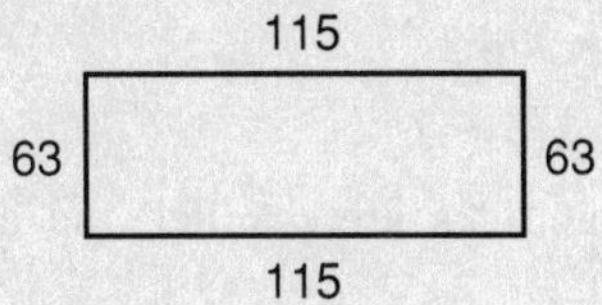

$$115 + 63 + 115 + 63 = 356$$

This is a good problem to solve by estimation. You can readily discard three of the possible answers without doing any calculation.

21. **(B)** Don't bother to calculate here! Notice that your answer will be very close to 6 × 1. There is only one answer anywhere near that estimate.

22. **(A)** The square of a number divided by 2.5 equals 10. The square of the number, then, equals 10 multiplied by 2.5.

$$x^2 = 10 \times 2.5$$

$$x^2 = 25$$

$$x = 5$$

23. **(D)** Each year, 12% is charged as interest. On $2,000, 12% interest is $2,000 × .12 = $240. For two years, the amount is $240 × 2 = $480.

24. **(B)** Find the volume by finding the area of the triangular end, and multiplying by the length. A = $\frac{1}{2}$ *bh*. The area of the triangular end is A = $\frac{1}{2}$(3)(2) = 3 sq. ft. Multiply 3 sq. ft. by the length to find the volume: 3 sq. ft. × 6 ft. = 18 cu. ft.

25. **(D)** Note that the second piece is the shortest. We don't know its exact length, so call it x feet long. The first piece is three times as long as the second, or $3x$ feet long. The third is twice as long as the first, or $6x$ feet long. All the pieces total $x + 3x + 6x$, or $10x$ feet long. The board is 30 feet long, and the pieces are $10x$ feet long. $10x = 30$, so $x = 3$, which is the length of the shortest piece. The largest piece is six times the shortest, or 18 feet long.

26. **(C)** We assume that the merchant wants to have the same total value of wine after reducing the price. He now has (32 • $1.50) or $48.00 worth of wine. At $1.20 per gallon, he would need 40 gallons to have $48.00 worth. Therefore, he must add 8 gallons of water.

27. **(B)** If six is four more than $\frac{2}{3}$ of a number, then 6 – 4 equals $\frac{2}{3}$ of the number. Since 6 – 4 = 2, we know that 2 is $\frac{2}{3}$ of the number, so the number is 3. If you are good at algebra, write an equation, and solve for x.

$$\frac{2}{3}x + 4 = 6$$

28. **(A)** You have to read only the first and third sentences of the problem. The information in the second sentence contains information not relevant to the problem. The winner received $\frac{1}{3}$ of the total, or $2,700. Thus, the total purse was $2,700 × 3 = $8,100.

29. **(C)** Add $\frac{1}{6}$, $\frac{1}{2}$, and $\frac{1}{8}$. The sum is $\frac{19}{24}$, which represents the fraction of the officer's job away from the precinct. This leaves $\frac{5}{24}$ of the job to be spent at the precinct. $\frac{5}{24}$ is slightly larger than $\frac{4}{24}$, or $\frac{1}{6}$, which is $16\frac{2}{3}$%, and slightly smaller than $\frac{6}{24}$, or $\frac{1}{4}$, which is 25%. The best answer of those given is 20%, which represents the approximate percentage of time spent at the precinct.

$$\frac{5}{24} = 5 \div 24 = .208 = \text{approx. } 20\%$$

Note that you didn't need to figure in hours how much time he spent in the headquarters.

30. **(C)** The total job requires $2\frac{1}{2}$, or $\frac{5}{2}$, days for both men. In one day, $\frac{2}{5}$ of the job is done. Working alone, the first man requires 6 days. He can do $\frac{1}{6}$ of the job in 1 day. Since both men can do $\frac{2}{5}$ of the job in one day, and the first man can do $\frac{1}{6}$ of the job in one day, $\frac{2}{5} - \frac{1}{6}$ represents how much the second man can do alone in one day.

$$\frac{2}{5} - \frac{1}{6} = \frac{12}{30} - \frac{5}{30} = \frac{7}{30}$$

If he can do $\frac{7}{30}$ of the job in one day, the whole job requires $\frac{30}{7}$, or $4\frac{2}{7}$, days. Reread the section on work problems if necessary.

31. **(B)** The distance between the cars is being reduced at a rate equal to the sum of their speeds. They are coming closer together at 35 + 48 = 81 miles per hour. Since the distance between them was 450 miles, the time required for traveling is 450 ÷ 83 = 5.42 hours. Remember that distance is the product of rate and time, or d = rt.

32. **(B)** Of his total, he issued $\frac{3}{8} + \frac{1}{4} + \frac{1}{6} = \frac{19}{24}$, so he had $\frac{5}{24}$ pads remaining. His total in stock was 600. $600 \bullet \frac{5}{24} = 125$ pads remaining.

33. **(B)** The first man can load $\frac{1}{25}$ of the truck in 1 minute. The second man can load $\frac{1}{50}$ of the truck in 1 minute. The third man can load $\frac{1}{10}$ of the truck in 1 minute. Together they can load $\frac{1}{25} + \frac{1}{50} + \frac{1}{10}$ of the truck each minute.

$$\frac{1}{25} + \frac{1}{50} + \frac{1}{10} =$$

$$\frac{2}{50} + \frac{1}{50} + \frac{5}{50} =$$

$$\frac{8}{50} = \frac{4}{25} \text{ of the truck loaded per minute}$$

The whole job then requires $\frac{25}{4}$ minutes, or $6\frac{1}{4}$ minutes.

34. **(C)** This is a difficult question unless you have had some algebra. The equations are "added." The y term drops out, leaving x only.

$$\begin{array}{r} 4x - y = 20 \\ +\ 2x + y = 28 \\ \hline 6x = 48 \\ x = 8 \end{array}$$

35. **(B)** $6 + x + y = 20$

$x + y = 14 = k$; now substitute

$20 - 14 = 6$

36. **(C)** A circle is 360°; 60° is $\frac{1}{6}$ of 360°.

37. **(C)** Diagram this problem:

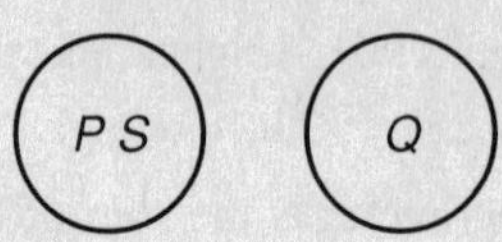

38. **(C)** Pick a pair of ages and try for yourself. A is 2; B is 4; the ratio of their ages is 2 to 4 or 1 to 2. In two years, A is 4 and B is 6. The ratio of their ages is 4 to 6 or 2 to 3.

39. **(B)** 15° – 21° = –6°

40. **(B)** If the sides are parallel, the angles are congruent.

41. **(B)** 6 words per line × 5 lines per inch = 30 words per inch.

30 words per inch × 8 inches = 240 words.

If the article has 270 words and there is space for only 240 words, then 30 words must be deleted.

42. **(C)** $S = 1$; $R = 3 \times 1$; $T = \frac{1}{3}$

$$1 + (3 \times 1) + \left(\frac{1}{3}\right) = 4\frac{1}{3}$$

43. **(D)** The lawn is 8' × 12' = 96 sq. ft.

96 × 5 = 480 pints of water needed

8 pts. in 1 gal.; 480 ÷ 8 = 60 gallons needed

44. **(A)** $I = 500 + (500 \times .20 \times 2)$

$I = 500 + 200$

$I = 700$

45. **(C)** Right now he gets 120 mi. ÷ 12 gal. = 10 mpg. With 80% more efficiency, he will need 80% of 12 or 9.6 gal. to go 120 miles. He will then get 120 mi. ÷ 9.6 gal. = 12.5 mpg.

12 gal. × 12.5 mpg = 150 miles on 12 gal.

46. **(D)** 4 feet = 48 inches

$48 \div \frac{1}{4} = 48 \times 4 = 192$ books

47. **(B)** There are 6 + 8 + 4 + 12 = 30 marbles.

$12 \div 30 = .40 = \frac{2}{5}$

48. **(C)** $\overline{CD}$ is a hypotenuse, so use the Pythagorean Theorem:

$$CD = \sqrt{CE^2 + ED^2}$$

$$CD = \sqrt{7^2 + 6^2} = \sqrt{49 + 36} = \sqrt{85}$$

49. **(D)** $3^3 \times 3 = 27 \times 3 = 81$

50. **(D)** $(3 + 2)(6 - 2)(7 + 1) = (4 + 4)(x)$

$$(5)(4)(8) = 8x$$

$$8x = 160$$

$$x = 20 = 8 + 12$$

TEST FIVE: ESSAY

Example of a well-written essay.

When I enter high school, I plan to become an active member of the drama club. The drama club offers a variety of activities within one organization. In the course of a single year, a member of the drama club can get involved in acting, set building, lighting design, publicity, ticket sales, and much more. And because of the variety of activities, I expect to make friends with classmates with varied interests and abilities.

People involved with theater appear to be having a lot of fun. While there may be some competition among stars, a production is generally a cooperative effort. Teamwork is key to making an amateur production appear to be professional. Even in kindergarten I got high marks from my teachers in "works and plays well with others," and I would like to carry this aspect of my personality into joining a cast and crew that creates theater.

Another reason for joining the drama club is that it will give me a chance to perform. I have always been a bit of a show-off. Being on stage will allow me to strut about without being criticized. I hope that my acting will contribute to successful productions along with my work as part of the behind-the-scenes crew.

Finally, any cooperative effort must be a social activity. There should be lots of give and take and conversation during preparations and rehearsals. And I do look forward to cast parties when the show closes. Drama club seems like the perfect extracurricular activity; I will have a good time while doing something worthwhile.

SCORE YOURSELF

Check your answers against the correct answer key. Count up the number of answers you got right on each question type and enter these numbers on the score sheet. These numbers are your raw scores. Use your raw scores to figure your percentage scores on the score sheet below.

Test	Raw Score ÷ No. of questions	× 100 =	%
Synonyms	÷ 20	× 100 =	%
Sentence Completions	÷ 20	× 100 =	%
Total Verbal Ability	÷ 40	× 100 =	%
Multiple-choice Quantitative	÷ 20	× 100 =	%
Quantitative Comparisons	÷ 20	× 100 =	%
Total Quantitative Ability	÷ 40	× 100 =	%
Reading Comprehension	÷ 40	× 100 =	%
Mathematics Achievement	÷ 50	× 100 =	%

High percentage scores should make you feel very good about yourself, but low percentages do not mean that you are a failure.

Remember:

- Scores are not reported as percentages. A low percentage may translate to a respectable scaled score.
- Scores are not reported as percentages. A low percentage may translate to a respectable scaled score.
- The same exam is given to students in grades 8 through 12. Unless you have finished high school, you have not been taught everything on the exam. You are not expected to know what you have not been taught.
- You will be compared only to students in your own grade.

Use your scores to plan further study if you have time.

PART

NINE

EVERYTHING YOU NEED!

Other Exams

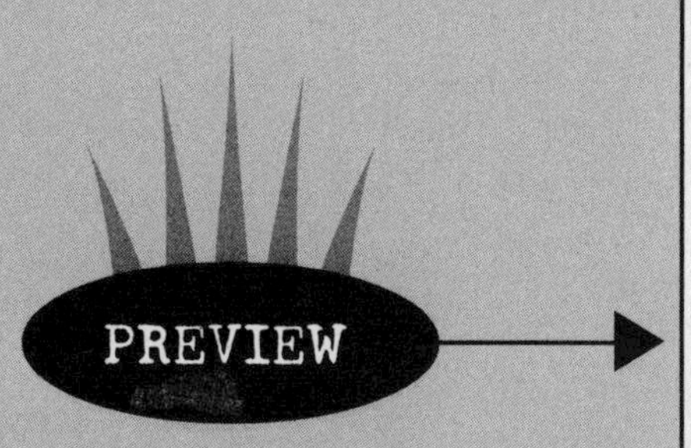

CHAPTER 16

High School Placement Test (HSPT): An Overview

PLAN A: ACCELERATED

- *Skim* this chapter.

PLAN B: TOP SPEED

- *Skip* this chapter.

You'll Find Answers to These Questions

Who takes the HSPT?
What does the HSPT test?
How is the exam structured?
What do the questions look like?
How is the HSPT scored?
Where can I get more information?

WHO TAKES THE HSPT?

About 120,000 eighth graders in the United States take the HSPT each year. Most of these eighth graders are applying for admission to Catholic High Schools. Others are applicants to independent Lutheran schools or to unaffiliated independent secondary schools. A smaller group hopes to enter specialized public academic high schools.

HERE'S THE ANSWER

What's Catholic about the Catholic high school entrance exams?

Nothing at all. The exams are used by Catholic high schools because they are designed for school systems with the typical Catholic school 8/4 split. There are no religion questions.

WHAT DOES THE HSPT TEST?

The HSPT measures aptitude and preparation for entrance to a four-year high school program. It is a five-part multiple-choice test of verbal, quantitative, reading, mathematics, and language skills. The exam consists of 298 questions and takes about $2\frac{1}{2}$ hours to complete.

HOW IS THE EXAM STRUCTURED?

The HSPT is divided into five separately-timed sections. The questions are numbered consecutively from 1 through 298 so that students do not need to worry about marking answers in the wrong section of the answer sheet. Here is a timetable and analysis of a typical HSPT:

VERBAL SKILLS—16 minutes, 60 questions

Verbal Analogies—10 questions

Synonyms—15 questions

Logic—10 questions

Verbal Classifications—16 questions

Antonyms—9 questions

QUANTITATIVE SKILLS—30 minutes, 52 questions

Number Series—18 questions

Geometric Comparison—9 questions

Nongeometric Comparison—8 questions

Number Manipulation—17 questions

READING—25 minutes, 62 questions

Comprehension—40 questions

Vocabulary—22 questions

MATHEMATICS—45 minutes, 64 questions

Concepts—24 questions

Problem Solving—40 questions

LANGUAGE SKILLS—25 minutes, 60 questions

Punctuation and Capitalization—12 questions

Usage—28 questions

Spelling—10 questions

Composition—10 questions

WHAT DO THE QUESTIONS LOOK LIKE?

Here are some typical HSPT questions. An explanation of the kind of thinking involved follows each question.

VERBAL SKILLS

Verbal Analogies

1. Throw is to ball as shoot is to
   (a) policeman
   (b) kill
   (c) arrow
   (d) hunting 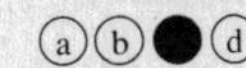

Choice (**c**) is correct. This is an action-to-object relationship. You *throw* a ball, and you *shoot* an arrow.

Synonyms

2. Meager most nearly means
   (a) well received
   (b) long overdue
   (c) valuable
   (d) scanty 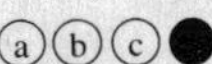

Choice (**d**) is correct. *Meager* means "lacking in quality or quantity." *Sparse* and *scanty* are synonyms for *meager*.

Logic

3. Bill runs faster than Mike. Jeff runs faster than Bill. Jeff is not as fast as Mike. If the first two statements are true, the third statement is
   (a) true
   (b) false
   (c) uncertain 

Choice (**b**) is correct. If the first two statements are true, Jeff runs faster than both Bill and Mike.

Verbal Classification

4. Which word does *not* belong with the others?
   (a) car
   (b) plane
   (c) van
   (d) truck 

Choice (**b**) is correct. A plane is the only vehicle that flies; all others are modes of ground transportation.

Antonyms

5. Loyal means the opposite of
   (a) lovely
   (b) unfaithful
   (c) unlucky
   (d) usual

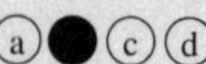

Choice (**b**) is correct. *Loyal* means "faithful." The best opposite is *unfaithful*.

QUANTITATIVE SKILLS

Number Series

6. Look at this series: 10, 14, 18, 22, 26, . . . What number should come next?
   (a) 28
   (b) 29
   (c) 30
   (d) 32

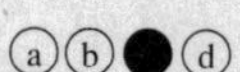

Choice (**c**) is correct. The pattern in this series is to add 4 to each number. 26 + 4 = 30.

Geometric Comparison

7. Examine hourglasses (A), (B), and (C) and find the best answer.

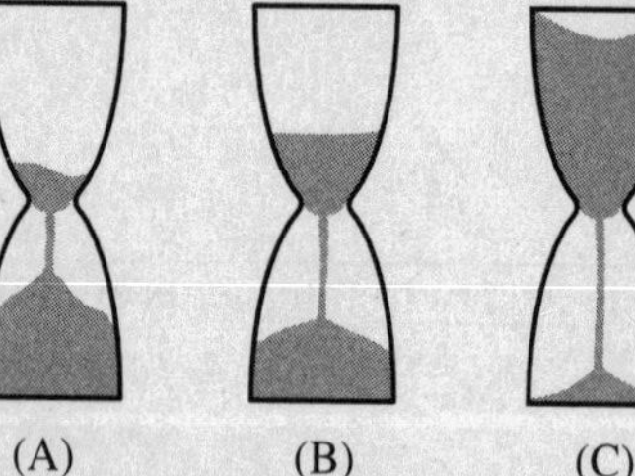

   (a) (B) shows the most time passed.
   (b) (A) shows the most time passed.
   (c) (C) shows the most time passed.
   (d) (A), (B), and (C) show the same time passed.

Choice (**b**) is correct. Be especially careful to avoid response errors when answering these questions. The correct answer is hourglass (A), but you must mark the letter of the correct statement, which, of course, is (**B**).

Nongeometric Comparisons

8. Examine (A), (B), and (C) and find the best answer.

(A) $(4 \times 2) - 3$

(B) $(4 \times 3) - 2$

(C) $(4 + 3) - 2$

(a) (A) is greater than (C)
(b) (A), (B), and (C) are equal
(c) (C) is greater than (B)
(d) (A) and (C) are equal 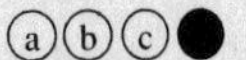

Choice (**d**) is correct. Determine the numerical value of (A), (B), and (C). Then test each answer choice to see which one is true.

(A) $(4 \times 2) - 3 = 8 - 3 = 5$
(B) $(4 \times 3) - 2 = 12 - 2 = 10$
(C) $(4 + 3) - 2 = 7 - 2 = 5$

Number Manipulation

9. What number is 5 more than $\frac{2}{3}$ of 27?

(a) 14
(b) 32
(c) 9
(d) 23 

Choice (**d**) is correct: First find $\frac{2}{3}$ of 27. $\frac{2}{3} \times 27 = 18$. Then add: $18 + 5 = 23$.

READING

Comprehension

The impressions that an individual gets from his environment are greatly influenced by his emotional state. When he is happy, objects and people present themselves to him in a favorable aspect; when he is depressed, he views the same things in an entirely different light. It has been said that a person's moods are the lenses that color life with many different hues. Not only does mood affect impression; impression also affects mood. The beauty of a spring morning may dissipate the gloom of a great sorrow, the good-natured chuckle of a fat man may turn anger into a smile, or a telegram may transform a house of mirth into a house of mourning.

10. According to the passage, an individual's perception of his environment

(a) depends on the amount of light available

(b) is greatly influenced by his emotional state

(c) is affected by color

(d) is usually favorable

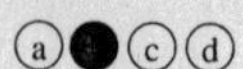

Choice (**b**) is correct. The first sentence of the passage makes the point that one's perceptions are influenced by one's emotional state.

Vocabulary

11. As used in the passage above, the word dissipate probably means

(a) condense

(b) draw out

(c) melt away

(d) inflate

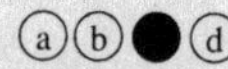

Choice (**c**) is correct. Other synonyms for dissipate are "scatter," "dissolve," and "evaporate."

MATHEMATICS

Concepts

12. To the nearest tenth, 52.693 is written

(a) 52.7

(b) 53

(c) 52.69

(d) 52.6

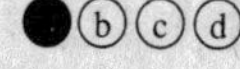

The correct choice is (**a**). To "round off" to the nearest tenth means to "round off" to one digit to the right of the decimal point. The digit to the right of the decimal point is 6. However, the next digit is 9, which means you must round up to 52.7.

Problem Solving

13. On a map, 1 inch represents 500 miles. How many miles apart are two cities that are $1\frac{1}{2}$ inches apart on the map?

(a) 750

(b) 1,000

(c) 1,250

(d) 1,500

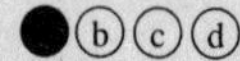

Choice (**a**) is correct. If 1 inch = 500 miles, then $\frac{1}{2}$ inch = 250 miles. Therefore, $1\frac{1}{2}$ inches = 500 + 250 = 750 miles.

LANGUAGE SKILLS

Punctuation and Capitalization

14. Find the sentence that has an error in capitalization or punctuation. If you find no mistake, mark (D) as your answer.

(a) Sally asked, "What time will you be home?"

(b) Doug hopes to enter John F. Kennedy High School next Fall.

(c) The letter arrived on Saturday, January 15.

(d) No mistakes.

Choice (**b**) has an error in capitalization. The word *fall* should not be capitalized.

Usage

15. Find the sentence that has an error in usage. If you find no mistake, mark (d) as your answer.

(a) Many children adopt the beliefs of their parents.

(b) "Is he always so amusing?" she asked.

(c) All the officers declined except she.

(d) No mistakes.

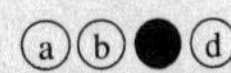

Choice (**c**) has an error in usage. The word *she* should be *her*, since it acts as the object of the preposition "except."

Spelling

16. Find the sentence that has an error in spelling. If you find no mistake, mark (d) as your answer.

(a) We recieved a letter from the principal.

(b) The library closes at 5 o'clock tomorrow.

(c) I have an appointment with the doctor on Wednesday.

(d) No mistakes.

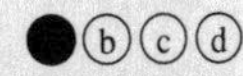

There is an error in choice (**a**) The word *received* is incorrectly spelled.

Composition

17. Choose the best word or words to join the thoughts together.

I left my key at school; _____ I had to ring the bell to get in the house.

(a) however

(b) nevertheless

(c) therefore

(d) None of these 

Choice **(c)** is correct. *Nevertheless* and *however* are used to express a contrast. *Therefore* is used to express a result. The second half of this sentence is clearly a result of the first half.

HOW IS THE HSPT SCORED?

Your score on the HSPT is based on the number of questions you answer correctly. No points are subtracted for wrong answers. Scholastic Testing Service, creator and administrator of the HSPT, converts raw scores to standard scores that are reported on a scale of 200 to 800. Your HSPT score report includes your standard scores and your percentile ranking compared with local and national test takers.

WHERE CAN I GET MORE INFORMATION?

Your first resource is the school to which you are applying. If the school requires the HSPT, it will supply the necessary information and forms. Scholastic Testing Service may be reached at:

Scholastic Testing Service, Inc.
480 Meyer Road
Bensenville, IL 60106-1617
(708) 766-7150

If you will be taking the HSPT, study from ARCO's *Catholic High School Entrance Examinations*. This book prepares for the unique questions on the HSPT and contains two full-length practice exams.

CHAPTER 17

Cooperative Entrance Exam (COOP): An Overview

PLAN A: ACCELERATED

- ***Skim*** this chapter.

PLAN B: TOP SPEED

- ***Skip*** this chapter.

You'll Find Answers to These Questions

Who takes the COOP?
What does the COOP test?
How is the exam structured?
What do the questions look like?
How is the COOP scored?
Where can I get more information?

WHO TAKES THE COOP?

Students planning to enter the ninth grade of competitive Catholic high schools in the Archdiocese of New York City, Diocese of Brooklyn and Rockland County (NY), Diocese of Rockville Center, NY, and the Archdiocese of Newark, NJ, all must take the COOP. Students applying to ninth grade in some other Catholic school systems or in some independent schools may be required to take the COOP or may be offered it as an option.

WHAT DOES THE COOP TEST?

The COOP measures academic aptitude and skills achievement of eighth graders. It is a seven-part multiple-choice test of memory, reasoning, reading comprehension, mathematics, and language skills. The COOP is used mainly by Catholic high schools, but there are no religion questions. The exam consists of 200 questions and takes about three hours to complete.

HERE'S THE ANSWER

What's Catholic about the Catholic high school entrance exams?

Nothing at all. The exams are used by Catholic high schools because they are designed for school systems with the typical Catholic school 8/4 split. There are no religion questions.

HOW IS THE EXAM STRUCTURED?

The COOP is divided into a designated time period for memorizing and seven separately-timed test sections. Answer choices on the COOP alternate between (A), (B), (C), (D), and sometimes (E) and (F), (G), (H), (J), and sometimes (K). This arrangement helps students keep their place as they move back and forth between test booklet and answer sheet.

Here is a timetable and analysis of a typical COOP:

Presentation of 20 definitions for memorization.

Test 1. Sequences—15 minutes, 20 questions

Test 2. Analogies—7 minutes, 20 questions

Test 3. Memory—5 minutes, 20 questions

Test 4. Verbal Reasoning—15 minutes, 20 questions

15-minute break

Test 5. Reading Comprehension—40 minutes, 40 questions

Test 6. Mathematics Concepts and Applications—35 minutes, 40 questions

Test 7. Language Expression—30 minutes, 40 questions

WHAT DO THE QUESTIONS LOOK LIKE?

Here are some typical COOP questions. An explanation of the kind of thinking involved follows each question.

Test 1. Sequences

Directions: There are three forms of question designed to measure sequential reasoning ability. In each case, you must choose the answer that would best continue the pattern or sequence.

1.

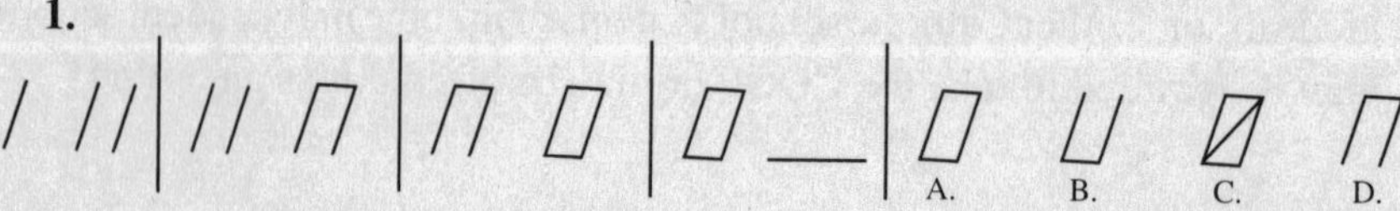

Ⓐ Ⓑ ● Ⓓ

Choice **(C)** is correct. Each frame contains two figures. The second figure within each frame has one more line than the first figure. In the final frame, the first figure has four lines; the second must have five, as in (C).

2. 2 4 6 | 3 5 7 | 15 17 _____

18 16 19 15

F. G. H. J. ⒻⒼ●Ⓙ

Choice **(H)** is correct. Within each frame, the pattern is simply the number plus 2, plus 2. 17 plus 2 equals 19.

3. Abcde aBcde abCde _____ abcdE

AbcdE abCDe aBcDe abcDe

A. B. C. D. ⒶⒷⒸ●

Choice **(D)** is correct. In each group of letters, the single capitalized letter moves progressively one space to the right.

Test 2. Analogies

Directions: Analogy questions test the ability to recognize and understand relationships. In these questions you must choose the picture that would go in the empty box so that the bottom two pictures are related in the same way that the top two are related.

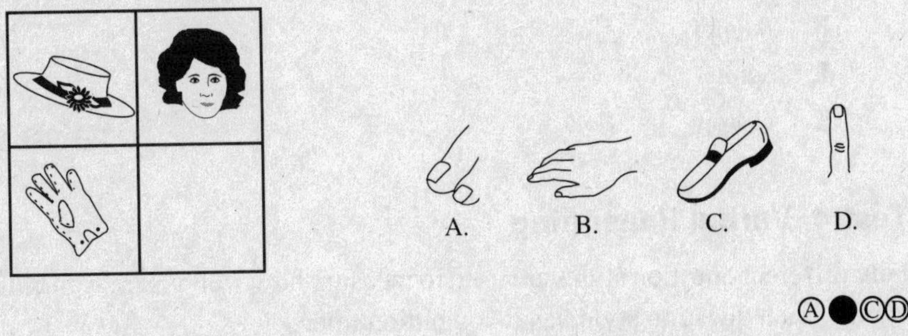

Ⓐ●ⒸⒹ

Choice **(B)** is correct. The relationship of hat to head is that a hat is a head covering; therefore, the best answer is hand because a glove is a hand covering.

Test 3. Memory

At the very beginning of the testing session, after you fill out forms and receive general directions, but before Test 1, question 1, you will learn 20 nonsense words and their definitions. The proctor will read the words aloud slowly while you follow along reading the printed list before you. You will then have 10 additional minutes to commit the words and their definitions to memory. Here are some typical nonsense words and their definitions.

1. A *polat* is a kind of reptile.
2. *Adrole* means to fall.
3. *Charop* is a poisonous gas.
4. *Rhumpf* means very high.
5. An *injing* is a fruit.

After you learn the words and their definitions, you will be told to begin Test 1, Sequences. You will follow directions for answering questions in Tests 1 and 2, observing the start and stop signals as instructed. When you turn to Test 3, you will have to answer questions that measure your memory—not your reasoning ability or your reading comprehension, just your power of memorization.

Directions: Choose the word that means the same as the underlined phrase.

1. Which word means very high?

A. charop
B. rhumpf
C. polat
D. injing
E. adrole

2. Which word means to fall?

F. injing
G. polat
H. thumpf
J. adrole
K. charop

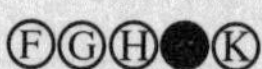

Test 4. Verbal Reasoning

Four different question styles are used to measure how well you reason with words. Each question style has its own directions.

Directions: Find the word that names a necessary part of the underlined word.

1. claustrophobia

A. closet
B. fear
C. door
D. space

Choice (**B**) is correct. Claustrophobia is fear of being in small, enclosed places. While the person who suffers from claustrophobia would surely be uncomfortable in a closet or behind a closed door, the *necessary* ingredient of claustrophobia is *fear*.

Directions: The words in the top row are related in some way. The words in the bottom row are related in the same way. Find the word that completes the bottom row of words.

2.

best	better	good
worst	worse	____

F. bad

G. worser

H. okay

J. good 

Choice **(F)** is correct. The words in the top row are in a comparative series, with the superlative on the left. Likewise, the words in the bottom row must be a similar comparative series. The comparison descends from *worst* to *worse* to just *bad*.

Directions: Find the statement that must be true according to the given information.

3. Julie is in second grade. Laura is in third grade. Julie's sister Anne rides a tricycle.

A. Laura is smarter than Julie.

B. Anne is physically handicapped.

C. Julie is behind Laura in school.

D. Julie and Laura are sisters. 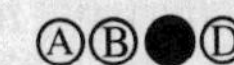

Choice **(C)** is correct. The only certainty is that Julie is behind Laura in school. The fact that Laura is ahead in school does not necessarily mean that she is smarter, possibly only older. Anne may well be a normal, healthy two-year-old. Julie and Anne are sisters, but Laura's relationship to them is not given.

Directions: Here are some words translated from an artificial, imaginary language. Read the words and answer the question.

4. ababawayla means somewhere

parimoodu means nobody

pariwayla means somebody

Which word means nowhere?

F. waylapari

G. pariababa

H. mooduababa

J. ababamoodu 

Choice **(J)** is correct. You will notice that elements of words are repeated among the English words as well as among the artificial words. By noticing the pattern of repetition, you can define and isolate word elements. In this sample wayla means some; pari means body; ababa means where; moodu means no. The order of the elements of words in this artificial language is the reverse of the order in English but is consistent within the language. Your answer choice must reflect that order, which is the reason that choice H is not correct.

Test 5. Reading Comprehension

Directions: Read the passage and the questions following it. Answer each question based upon what you have read.

The man is in utter darkness. Only the wavering beam of light from his flashlight pierces the blackness. The air, damp and cold, smells of dank, unseen decaying material.

The man stumbles over stones, splashes into a hidden puddle. He bangs into a cold rocky wall. The flashlight cocks upward, and suddenly the air is filled with the flutter of thousands of wings and the piping of tiny animal wails. He ducks, startled, then grins. He's found what he's looking for—bats!

For this man is a "spelunker," another name for someone who explores caves for the fun of it. Spelunkers actually enjoy crawling on their stomachs in narrow, rocky tunnels far below the surface of the earth.

Spelunkers have discovered new caves. Some have formed clubs, sharing safety knowledge, developing new techniques, and teaching novices, for spelunkers believe that earth's inner spaces are as exciting as the universe's outer spaces.

1. The first two paragraphs of this passage describe a cave's

A. rocks

B. depth

C. atmosphere

D. streams

Choice **(C)** is correct. The utter darkness, dampness and cold, smells of decay, and puddles are all part of the cave's atmosphere.

2. The man ducked when the bats flew because he was

F. angry

G. afraid

H. surprised

J. hurt

Choice **(H)** is correct. The man ducked because he was startled. *Startled* means surprised. Then he grinned, so clearly he was not angry, afraid, or hurt.

3. According to this passage, spelunkers ignore

A. safety rules

B. light

C. discomfort

D. other spelunkers 

Choice **(C)** is correct. The passage describes many discomforts, then tells us that spelunkers enjoy crawling on their stomachs.

4. According to this passage, which word would most nearly describe spelunkers?

F. Experimental

G. Cautious

H. Antisocial

J. Adventurous 

Choice **(J)** is correct. The underground exploration described represents high adventure and excitement.

Test 6. Mathematics Concepts and Applications

The computations in this test are not complicated, but you must have a firm grasp of the meaning of mathematics and a little bit of common sense in order to answer the questions.

1. 350 students are taking this examination in this school today; $\frac{4}{7}$ of these students are girls. How many boys are taking the exam in this school?

A. 150

B. 200

C. 500

D. 550 

Choice **(A)** is correct. If $\frac{4}{7}$ are girls, $\frac{3}{7}$ are boys.

$$\frac{3}{7} \text{ of } 350 = \frac{3}{7} \times \frac{350}{1} = 150$$

2. Which number sentence is true?

F. $-12 > 9$

G. $-5 > -8$

H. $-3 = 3$

J. $2 < -6$ 

Choice **(G)** is correct. Draw a number line to prove this to yourself, if necessary.

3. Mrs. Breen came home from the store and put two half-gallon containers of milk into the refrigerator. Jim came home from school with a few friends, and they all had milk and cookies. When they had finished, only $\frac{1}{2}$ of one container of milk remained. How much milk did the boys drink?

A. $1\frac{1}{2}$ pints

B. $1\frac{1}{2}$ quarts

C. 3 quarts

D. $1\frac{1}{2}$ gallons

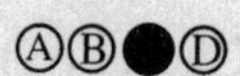

Choice (C) is correct. There are four quarts in a gallon; so there are two quarts in each half-gallon container.

4. Look at the figure below. Then choose the statement that is true.

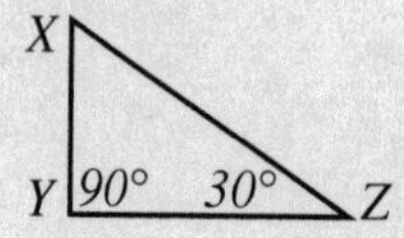

F. $\angle X > \angle Y > \angle Z$

G. $\angle X < \angle Y < \angle Z$

H. $\angle X = \angle Z < \angle Y$

J. $\angle X > \angle Z < \angle Y$

Choice (J) is correct. Since the sum of the angles of a triangle is 180°, angle X must be 60°. 60 is greater than 30, which is smaller than 90.

5. Look at the graph below. Then read the question and choose the correct answer.

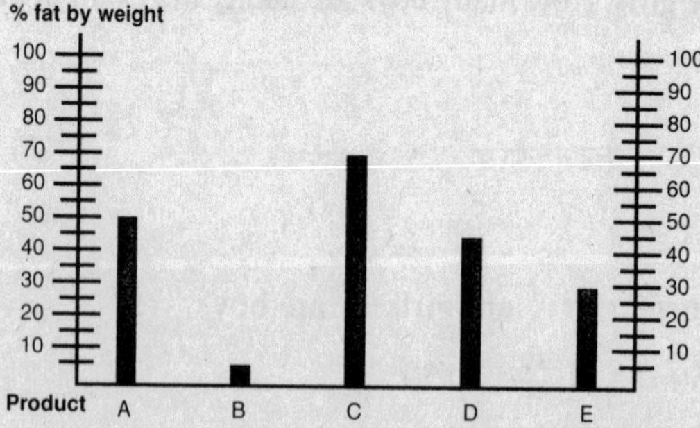

According to FDA regulations, in order to print the designation "light" on its labels, a product must contain no more than 45% fat by weight. Which of these products may be labeled "light"?

A. D only

B. B and E only

C. B, D, and E only

D. A and C only

Choice **(C)** is correct. The regulations state that a "light" product contains *no more than 45% fat*. Product D, which contains exactly 45% fat, may be labeled "light" along with B and E.

6. The piece of property shown below is to be divided into uniform building lots of 100 × 100 sq. ft. Twenty percent of the property must be left undeveloped. How many houses may be built on this property?

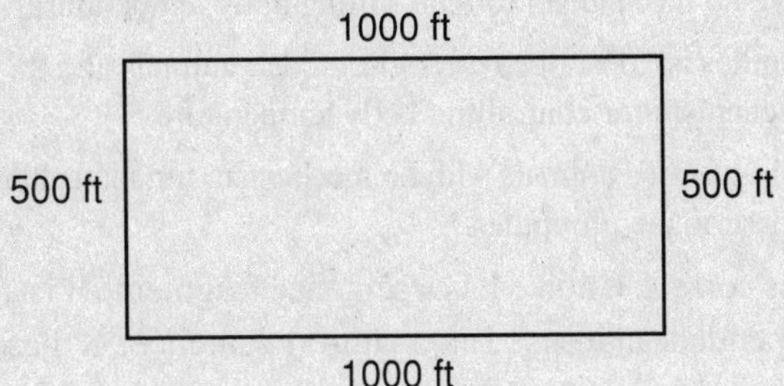

F. 20
G. 40
H. 50
J. 100

Choice **(G)** is correct. The entire property is 1000 ft. × 500 ft. = 500,000 sq. ft. Twenty percent must be left undeveloped. 500,000 × 20% = 100,000. 500,000 – 100,000 = 400,000 sq. ft. to be developed. Each building lot is 100 × 100 = 10,000 sq. ft. 400,000 divided by 10,000 = 40 houses.

Test 7. Language Expression

The COOP uses ten different question styles to test your knowledge of English usage and structure. In this portion of the exam, you will have to answer only a few questions of each style, but you will have to draw on your organizational skills, your common sense, and your knowledge of grammar. We will give you a sample of each question.

Directions: Choose the word that best completes the sentence.

1. I would bring grandma to visit you, _____ I have no car.

A. while
B. because
C. but
D. moreover
E. therefore

Choice **(C)** is correct. The conjunction *but* is the only choice that makes any sense in the context of the sentence.

Directions: Choose the sentence that is complete and correctly written.

2. **F.** Cold blooded reptiles with no mechanism for controlling body temperature.
   G. Reptiles, which have no mechanism for controlling body temperature, are described as cold-blooded animals.
   H. Reptiles are described as cold blooded animals, this means that they have no mechanism for controlling body temperature.
   J. Reptiles are described as cold-blooded animals and they have no mechanism for controlling body temperature.
   K. Cold-blooded animals with no mechanism for controlling temperature, a description of reptiles. Ⓕ●ⒽⒿⓀ

Choice **(G)** is correct. Choice F is a sentence fragment: H is a comma splice of two independent clauses: J is a run-on sentence: K has no verb so is nothing more than a sentence fragment.

Directions: Choose the sentence that uses verbs correctly.

3. **A.** While we were waiting for the local, the express roared past.
   B. The sky darkens ominously and rain began to fall.
   C. The woman will apply for a new job because she wanted to earn more money.
   D. I wish I knew who will be backing into my car.
   E. The wind blows, the thunder clapped, lightning will fill the sky, and it rains. ●ⒷⒸⒹⒺ

Choice **(A)** is correct. All other choices mix tenses in illogical order.

Directions: Choose the underlined word that is the simple subject of the sentence.

4. The first step in improving your writing is to know what makes a good
   F. step **G.** improving **H.** writing **J.** what
   sentence.
   K. sentence ●ⒼⒽⒿⓀ

Choice **(F)** is correct.

Directions: Choose the underlined word or group of words that is the simple predicate (verb) of the sentence.

5. A decrease in the incidence of contagious diseases proves that sanitation
   A. decrease **B.** incidence **C.** proves
   is worthwhile.
   D. is **E.** worthwhile ⒶⒷ●ⒹⒺ

Choice **(C)** is correct. The subject of the sentence is *decrease,* and the decrease *proves* the value of sanitation.

Directions: Choose the sentence that best combines the two underlined sentences into one.

6. Fish in tropical waters are colorful.
They swim among coral reefs.

   F. In tropical waters there are coral reefs swimming with colorful fish.

   G. Fish swim among coral reefs in tropical waters, and they are colorful.

   H. When fish swim among coral reefs, they are colorful in tropical waters.

   J. Colorful fish swim among coral reefs in tropical waters.

   K. Colorful tropical waters are home to swimming fish and coral reefs. Ⓕ Ⓖ Ⓗ ● Ⓚ

Choice **(J)** is correct.

Directions: Choose the topic sentence that best fits the paragraph.

7. ______________________________

However, in reality, they are adaptable, intelligent, and often beautiful. A squid's body appears to be all head and feet. These feet, commonly referred to as arms, have little suction cups on them.

   A. Because the squid is shy, it is often misunderstood.

   B. Scientists consider squid the most intelligent mollusks.

   C. Squid are considered a tasty treat by the other inhabitants of the sea.

   D. The body of the squid is uniquely adapted for locomotion and for grabbing in its liquid environment.

   E. Squid are considered by many to be ugly, unpleasant creatures. Ⓐ Ⓑ Ⓒ Ⓓ ●

Choice **(E)** is correct. The second sentence contradicts the topic statement about the squid's appearance.

Directions: Choose the pair of sentences that best develops the topic sentence.

8. Children's tastes in literature tend to change with age.

   F. Picture books should be lavishly illustrated. Artists should depend heavily on primary colors.

   G. Young girls often enjoy adventure stories. Teenage girls prefer romantic novels.

   H. Some boys like to read science fiction. Other boys read only animal stories.

J. Historical fiction is an excellent teaching medium. It holds one's interest while introducing historical facts.

K. Fairy tales and science fiction represent two manifestations of the same interest. We never outgrow our delight with fantasy. Ⓕ●ⒽⒿⓀ

Choice **(G)** is correct. This is the choice that carries through with an illustration of how girls' reading tastes tend to change with age. Choice K is almost a contradiction of the topic sentence in that it suggests that tastes do not really change; they only mature.

Directions: Choose the sentence that does not belong in the paragraph.

9. 1) Modern computers are no longer the size of a large room. 2) These contain no wires. 3) Some are so small that they can be held in one hand. 4) The large vacuum tubes of the early computers were replaced by tiny transistors. 5) These, in turn, have given way to infinitesimal microchips.

A. Sentence 1

B. Sentence 2

C. Sentence 3

D. Sentence 4

E. Sentence 5 Ⓐ●ⒸⒹⒺ

Choice **(B)** is correct. The paragraph is about the size of computers, not about their wiring.

Directions: Read the paragraph and choose the sentence that best fills the blank.

10. A glass case in the British Museum houses the mummified remains of two Egyptian kings who lived beside the Nile. The exhibit includes a broken plow, a rusted sickle, and two sticks tied together with a leather strap. ____. They are not unlike the tools used by 18th century American farmers, and, in fact, similar sickles may be viewed at Mount Vernon, George Washington's Virginia home.

F. The two kings were the most important kings of ancient Egypt.

G. The farm implements were preserved by the same methods as were the remains of the kings.

H. English farmers have spent hours at the British Museum studying these tools in hopes of improving the yields of their farms.

J. It is interesting to note that no farm animals were found buried in the kings' tombs.

K. These were the "bread tools" of Egyptians who lived 4,000 years ago during the reigns of the two kings. ⒻⒼⒽⒿ●

Choice **(K)** is correct. This sentence explains the use of the tools described in the previous sentence and is followed by a sentence explaining the continued usefulness of tools of this type.

HOW IS THE COOP SCORED?

Your score on the COOP is based on the number of questions you answer correctly. No points are subtracted for wrong answers. Your raw score for each part is converted to a scaled score and your scores are compared to scores of all other students taking the exam. Your percentile rank shows where you stand compared to others who took the test at the same time. A percentile rank is reported for each part of the test as well as for the test as a whole.

WHERE CAN I GET MORE INFORMATION?

All parochial elementary schools in COOP regions have application materials and information. If you are not in parochial school now, you can go to the office at your nearest parochial school to pick up booklets and forms. For other information, contact:

CTB/McGraw-Hill
20 Ryan Ranch Road
Monterey, CA 93940-5703
(800) 569-COOP

If you will be taking the COOP, study from ARCO's *Catholic High School Entrance Examinations*. This book prepares for the unique questions on the COOP and contains two full-length practice exams.